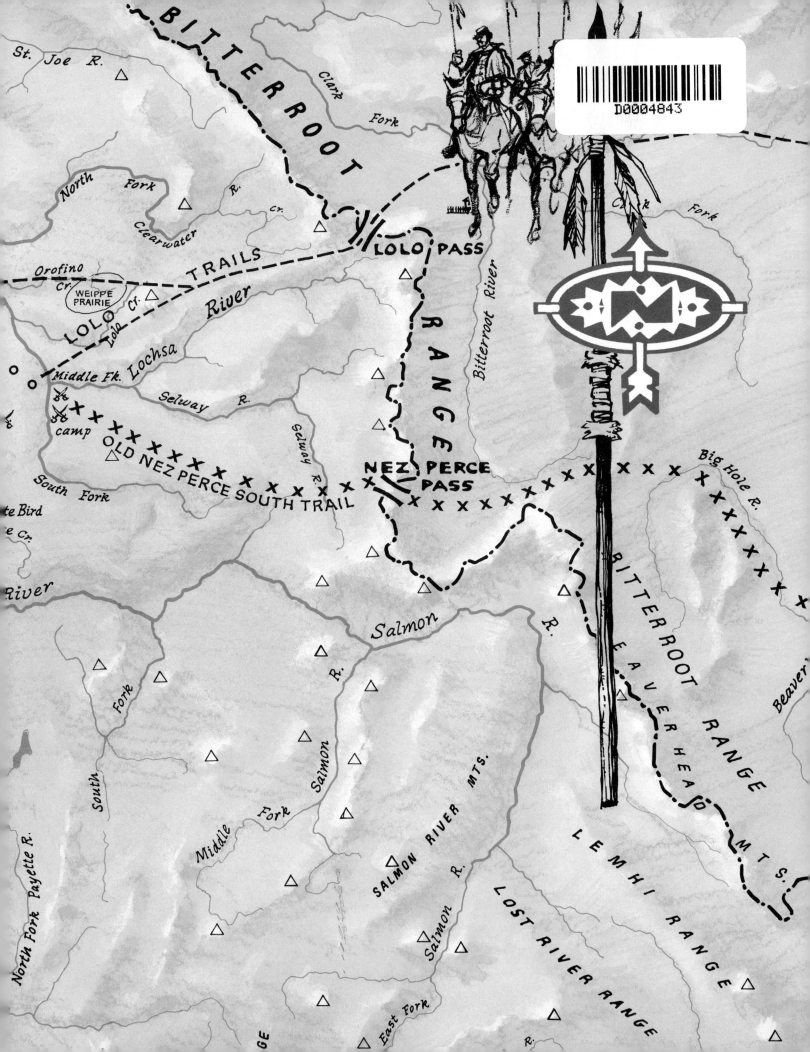

BITTERROOT

St. Joe R.

Clark Fork

North Fork

Clearwater R.

Cr.

LOLO PASS

Orofino Cr.

WEIPPE PRAIRIE

LOLO TRAILS

Lolo Cr.

River

Bitterroot River

RANGE

Middle Fk. Lochsa

Selway R.

Selway R.

Selway R.

camp

OLD NEZ PERCE SOUTH TRAIL

NEZ PERCE PASS

Clark Fork

Big Hole R.

BITTERROOT RANGE

South Fork

te Bird e Cr.

River

Salmon

R.

R.

BEAVERHEAD

South Fork

Salmon Fork

Middle Fork Salmon

SALMON RIVER MTS.

Salmon R.

LOST RIVER RANGE

LEMHI RANGE

Beaver

MTS.

North Fork Payette R.

East Fork

R.

D0004843

Chief Joseph Country

CHIEF JOSEPH COUNTRY

Land of the Nez Perce

by

Bill Gulick

For Bill Barr,
with Best Regards,
— Bill Gulick

To Bill Barr,
Best Wishes
Dave Manuel

The CAXTON PRINTERS, Ltd.
Caldwell, Idaho 83605
1981

Gulick, Bill, 1916-
    Chief Joseph Country.

    Bibliography: p.
    Includes index.
    1. Nez Perce Indians—History. 2. Nez
Perce Indians—Government relations.
3. Indians of North America—Government
relations. I. Title.
E99.N5G84   970.004′97   79-51577
ISBN 0-87004-275-0   AACR2

Printed and bound in the United States of America by
The Caxton Printers, Ltd.
Caldwell, Idaho 83605
138911

DEDICATION

Dedicated to my wife, Jeanne, who for thirty-five years has shared the trials and triumphs of my life without complaint or adequate credit, and who, as a careful research librarian, has checked the accuracy of every statement in the book — except this one.

CONTENTS

Page

Acknowledgments ix
Introduction xiii
Chapter
  1. The Land 1
  2. The People 6
  3. The Horse 13
  4. Lewis and Clark: 1805–1806 20
  5. Beaver and Empire: 1806–1830 33
  6. Book of Heaven: 1831–1832 47
  7. The Fur Traders: 1832–1835 51
  8. The Missionaries: 1835–1839 62
  9. The Tewat's Son-in-Law: 1840–1843 79
 10. Disillusionment: 1843–1847 85
 11. The Nez Perces Choose Peace: 1847–1851 90
 12. The First Treaty Council: 1855 96
 13. To the Buffalo Country: June 16–October 25, 1855 112
 14. The Six Million Dollar Indian War: 1855–1858 118
 15. Whose Side Is the Army On?: 1856–1858 122
 16. The Second Walla Walla Council: September 1856 129
 17. The Steptoe Disaster: May 1858 135
 18. Colonel Wright Takes Over: August 1858 138
 19. Gold and New Treaties: 1860–1863 145
 20. The "Steal" Treaty: 1863–1868 151
 21. Henry Spalding Comes Home: 1869–1874 161
 22. The Religious Agent, John B. Monteith: 1871–1876 167
 23. A Commission of Reasonable Men: November 1876–May 1877 . 185
 24. Toward the Promised Land 195
 25. The Battle of White Bird Canyon 203
 26. Hide and Seek 211
 27. Battle of the Clearwater: July 11–12, 1877 217
 28. Flight across Lolo Trail: July 16–27, 1877 222
 29. Fort Fizzle 228
 30. Battle of the Big Hole: August 9, 1877 232
 31. Lean Elk Takes Over 242
 32. Through Yellowstone National Park: August 23–
         September 6, 1877 250
 33. Canyon Creek to Cow Island Landing: September 13–23, 1877 . 255
 34. Battle of Bear's Paw Mountains: September 30–October 5, 1877 260
 35. Flight to Canada: October 1877 271
 36. *Eeikish Pah* — the Hot Country: 1878–1885 274

CONTENTS

Page

37. Return of the Exiles: May 21–28, 1885 279
38. Land Allotment: 1889–1892 286
39. Twilight Years at Colville: 1885–1904 295
40. The Nez Perces Today: 1905–1980 303
Bibliography 311
Index 314

ACKNOWLEDGMENTS

SINCE ACCESS to a good library is essential to any writer dealing with historical material, I am fortunate that one of the best, Penrose Library, Whitman College, in Walla Walla, has graciously permitted me free use of its facilities for more than thirty years. In turn I have let Penrose use the services of my wife, Jeanne, as a librarian for thirteen of those years — but I made them pay for that. Whatever mutual gain has been garnered, we thank Head Librarian Arley Jonish, Reference Librarian Marilyn Sparks, and Curator of Manuscripts and Special Materials Lawrence Dodd for the great amount of assistance given us during the research and writing of this book. Larry Dodd, in particular, has given freely of his time and knowledge when help was needed to locate obscure material.

To Dr. Robert Skotheim, President of Whitman College, and to former President Chester Maxey, both of whom are personal friends who have endured hearing a portion of the book read when it was still in manuscript form, my thanks for many favors.

Since Presbyterian missionaries played such important roles in the lives of the Nez Perces, special credit must be given to Dr. Clifford Merrill Drury, whose first book, *Henry Harmon Spalding,* was published in 1936 and whose most recent book, *Chief Lawyer of the Nez Perces,* was published in 1979. During the intervening forty-three years he has devoted his life to researching and writing the most accurate and complete record in existence of the missionary movement in the Pacific Northwest.

For the Indian side of the Nez Perce War, present-day writers must depend heavily upon two books written by Lucullus Virgil McWhorter, who, between 1908 and 1946 interviewed one hundred survivors of that struggle and recorded their first-person accounts as told to him through interpreters. *Yellow Wolf, His Own Story,* was published by Caxton in 1940, while *Hear Me, My Chiefs,* which McWhorter had not completed at the time of his death in 1946, was edited and completed by Ruth Bordin, with the cooperation of Washington State University, and published by Caxton in 1952. At the time I reviewed the book for the Walla Walla *Union-Bulletin,* I wrote that it "is a book that comes as close to telling the real story as any book ever will."

That statement is still valid today.

All of the McWhorter research notes and materials have been catalogued and deposited at the Washington State University Library in Pullman. Terry Abraham, Manuscript-Archives Librarian, not only helped me go through this material in search of photographs that might be used in this book, he also pointed me in the right direction to acquire photographs from other sources, such as the National Archives Center in Seattle. For this help, I am most grateful.

At the Idaho Historical Society, Dr. Merle Wells kept me from stubbing my toe on a number of historical rocks, as he has done on other books for the past twenty years, while James H. Davis, photographic expert, lent much valuable assistance. Merle also was kind enough to browse through the book while it was in manuscript form but is in no way responsible for any errors that may have crept in during the cutting and editing process.

In the process of selecting photographs to be used in the book I examined a thousand or so pictures in twenty collections held by historical societies, libraries, and individuals. When known I have given proper credit to the photographer and to the owner of the picture, as well as listing the names and tribes of the Indians shown. But in some cases I have found the identical photograph credited to different photographers and "owned" by two or more institutions. Further confusing the issue I have seen the same photograph in collections owned by five different institutions, with the Indian subjects identified as belonging to five different tribes. In such cases all I can do is credit the historical society or library which made the print available to me and leave the detective work to the experts.

At the University of Washington Library, Robert D. Monroe, Head, Special Collections Division, has been most helpful. At the Washington State Historical Society and Museum, Director Bruce LeRoy, the board of directors, and staff were most generous. For the Yakima Nation, Robert Pace, Director of Media Services, and Gary Young, Director of the newly completed Museum and Library Center, have done me a number of favors.

Alfred W. Schulmeyer, Superintendent of the Big Hole National Battlefield, gave valued assistance. In Oklahoma during two summer visits, Mary Lee Ervin, in the Indian Archives Center of the Oklahoma Historical Society, and Manon T. Atkins, Photographic Curator, kindly provided me with microfilm copies of the Agency Letterpress-books and helped me look for photographs taken of the Nez Perces during their exile in Indian Territory between 1878 and 1885. Unfortunately, we found none. Later, I asked a longtime friend, Donald E. Worcester, a writer and professor of history at Texas Christian University in Fort Worth, whether he had ever run across such photographs. He said he had not, then referred me to George C. Younkin, formerly Chief Archivist for the National Archives Regional Office in Fort Worth, who, in answer to my query, wrote that during all the years he had been in the area he had seen only one or two photographs and these had been in very poor condition.

Bill Burchardt, on the eve of his retirement as editor of the *Oklahoma Today* magazine, pursued the matter further, with no luck, but I appreciate his efforts. In the Western History Collection at the University of Oklahoma, Dr. John S. Ezell, Curator, Shelly Arlen, June Witt, and Jack Haley did help my wife and me find information related to the stay of the Nez Perces in Indian Territory and several excellent photographs of Plains Indian tribes who were in contact with the Nez Perces in the buffalo country. They had been collected, I noted nostalgically, by the late Walter S. Campbell, in whose Professional Writing class I enrolled in 1940 and who wrote a number of books about the Sioux.

In Lewiston, Idaho, George Anderjack, Executive Director, and Lora A. Dillon, Curator, of the Luna House Historical Society, kindly let me select

a number of photographs from their collection. At the Visitor Center of the nearby Nez Perce National Historical Park, Superintendent Steve Shawley and Assistant Kenneth L. Adkisson provided a number of photographs and an excellent guide to the many points of historical interest in the surrounding region. The new Visitor Center, now under construction should be open by the time this book is published.

At the Oregon Historical Society, Executive Editor Priscilla Knuth and Assistant Susan Seyl were prompt in answering queries and providing photographs. The same can be said of Dale Johnson, University of Montana Library; Lory Morrow and Diana Wilkison, at the Montana Historical Society; the photographic staff at the Museum of the American Indian, New York City; and the National Archives Center, Seattle.

In Spokane, at the Museum of North American Culture, Father Wilfred P. Schoenberg, Ann Myers, John Turney, and Bertin Arsenault went out of their way to be helpful. So did Edward Kemp, Phillip J. Zorich, and Deirdre Malarkey at the University of Oregon Library and Paula Fleming at the Smithsonian Institution in Washington, D.C.

A number of present-day residents of Chief Joseph's homeland, the Wallowa Valley, have taken a keen interest in the book and have been of assistance in many ways. These include librarians Jane Williams, Mary Lee Farnsworth, and Mary Pillar. Steve Kickert and Mona Wright deserve thanks for setting up a two-evening program, "Talks With the Nez Perce," during late August 1979, which was sponsored by the Wallowa County Historical Society and partially funded by a grant made by the Oregon Committee for the Humanities, of which Carolyn M. Baun, Portland, is Associate Director. One evening, Alvin M. Josephy, Jr., the author of the most comprehensive and to my mind the best history of the tribe, *The Nez Perce Indians and the Opening of the Northwest,* talked on events leading up to the War of 1877, following which I screened slides of some of the photographs I had gathered. The next evening Josephy talked on the Treaty of 1855, following which Nez Perce representative Clifford Allen discussed what the treaty means to the Nez Perce today.

Before leaving the area I must give special credit to Grace Bartlett, local historian and author from whose book, *The Wallowa Country, 1867–1877,* I excerpted most of the material used in my account of events leading up to the Nez

Perce War. The day Jeanne and I talked to her, she had just returned from a twenty-four-mile hike that would have incapacitated a person half her age for a week. But she cheerfully agreed to read the chapter, promptly did so, and by letter pointed out several errors I had made, which I hope I have corrected to her satisfaction. I greatly appreciate her kindness.

Waible Patton, for many years a professional photographer in Pendleton, Oregon, helped in a number of ways. Erwin N. Thompson, a longtime friend now retired from the National Park Service, gave generously of his notes on Fort Lapwai and the Spalding Mission while we enjoyed his food and hospitality in Golden, Colorado. Marcus Ware, in Lewiston, did us several favors. At Whitman College, Dr. Robert L. Whitner, Professor of History, and Dr. George Castile, Professor of Cultural Anthropology, shared their considerable knowledge with us.

Thanks to Dr. E. G. Chuinard, a retired orthopedic surgeon living in Portland who had just completed a book on the medical aspects of the Lewis and Clark Expedition, we were able to arrange an interview with Erskine Wood, who, as a boy, spent the summers of 1892 and 1893 living with Chief Joseph at Nespelem as a member of his family. When we taped the fifty-minute interview, Erskine Wood lacked five months of being one hundred years old, but his memory still was keen.

LeRoy Allen, legal representative for the Corps of Engineers in the Walla Walla District, provided photographs and information regarding the relocation of Indian graves made necessary by the building of dams on the Snake River. George Hatley, former Executive Secretary of the Appaloosa Horse Club, Moscow, Idaho, helped search for an elusive letter related to the history of the breed. Mike Morris, U.S. Forest Service, helped identify flora and fauna. Laura Woolschlager, Omak, Washington, artist, put us on the track of an elusive photograph. Gregory Zuck, Pendleton librarian, helped us find some dusty eighty-year-old glass plates from which prints as sharp as those reproduced from yesterday's negatives could be made.

Dick Frost, at the Whitney Museum of Western Art in Cody, Wyoming, and John Tyers, National Park Service Archivist at Mammoth Hot Springs, Yellowstone Park, guided us to fruitful sources of information — as did the friendly ranger naturalists at the Fishing Bridge Visitor Center, Jean Merriman and Lisa Eckert. For their knowledgeable copyediting, I appreciate the work of Ruth and Joe Wilson.

Last, but by no means least, I must thank Gordon Gipson, of Caxton Printers. Ten years ago he and the publishing company he represents took a sizable gamble that a book entitled *Snake River Country* would sell enough copies to warrant its publication. He won that wager — earning my eternal gratitude in the process. Now, at his suggestion and with his encouragement, we are trying again. We hope for another winner.

Bill Gulick
Walla Walla, Washington

INTRODUCTION

My dear Michelet, admit that historians are better the more their works read like novels, while novels are best the more they read like history.
— Alexandre Dumas

MOST OF MY years as a writer have been spent in the world of historical fiction — short stories, novels, and dramas for the outdoor stage. In this world, character, conflict, meaningful dialog, and a concise development of scenes toward a significant climax are all-important, for the attention of the audience can be held only so long and the story must be kept within the budget whether in print or onstage.

For example, in 1955 I was commissioned to write and stage a re-enactment of the Stevens Treaties, which had been negotiated one hundred years earlier in the Walla Walla Valley, under whose terms five tribes of Native Americans ceded 30,000 square miles of ancestral lands. Five thousand Indians took part in the negotiations, which were spread over nineteen days. The secretarial transcript of the talks, which I obtained from the National Archives, would have been as lengthy as a novel if published in book form — a full day's work for the average person to read.

Unfortunately for the cause of historical accuracy, the sponsors of the re-enactment would not let me hire five thousand Indians (half of whom must be superb riders mounted on superior horses, as the Nez Perces were) or permit me to write a drama containing nineteen acts that would run for as many days. Instead, I was asked to make do with sixteen Indian principles, a dozen whites in similar roles, and fifty mixed Indians and whites playing minor parts. Including a twenty-minute intermission, during which it was hoped that enough hot dogs and Cokes could be sold to recoup a portion of the cost of the production, its time frame was set at two and a half hours.

Like most such productions, staying within the time frame proved to be less of a problem than keeping within the budget. But once the sponsor's grumblings at the cost overrun had subsided and the deficit had been taken care of, all parties concerned agreed that we had accomplished our aim — bringing alive to a layman audience an important event in regional history in a dramatic way.

That is what I have attempted to do in this book.

To me the history of the Nez Perces is epic drama. Certainly no setting could be more spectacular than the rugged, beautiful homeland of this tribe. No story can equal in historic scope the seventy-five-year relationship between the Nez Perces and the white newcomers whom they greeted as friends. And no event is more poignant, bitter, and tragic than the Nez Perce War.

"Too many trained professionals consider narrative history, history rendered as story, to be something faintly disreputable," Wallace Stegner once wrote. "Speaking as an amateur, I should guess that the trick is to make the twin cutting tools of sound research and a sense of the dramatic, work together like scissor blades. . . . Dramatic narrative is simply one means by which a historian can make a point vividly."[1]

Though I don't accept Stegner's statement that he is an amateur historian — few writers are more professional than he — I have gladly appropriated the twin cutting tools he recommends as the ones best suited to shape the work that follows. From the most reliable sources available I have selected, excerpted, and edited; then I have supplied the

1. Wallace Stegner, *The Sound of Mountain Water* (New York: Doubleday & Co., 1969), chapter 4, "On the Writing of History," pp. 202–204.

connective narrative needed to link one historic scene with another. Inevitably, in the need for dramatic unity and impact, I have simplified. But in no case have I invented happenings or put words into mouths that did not say them.

If there is a bias in this book, it is that I have given more credence to statements made by Indians than to words written by white men. Time and again in my research I have come across references to the importance that the Indian placed on telling the plain, simple truth when relating any event in which he was involved. To the contrary, time and again I have found statements made by white leaders such as Governor Isaac Stevens and General O. O. Howard so contradictory and at variance with the truth that I began to question everything they wrote.

Many years ago at the University of Oklahoma I studied with Dr. Walter S. Campbell, a former Rhodes Scholar, who, under the pen name Stanley Vestal, wrote such books as *Sitting Bull, Kit Carson,* and *The Missouri River.* The son of an Indian agent, Walter Campbell had been raised on a reservation, knew sign language and the Sioux tongue, and was so respected by the Sioux that when he died in 1958 he was buried in the Custer National Battlefield Monument Cemetery with full tribal ceremonial honors. Regarding the reliability of Indian testimony, he wrote:

"Any one who is familiar with old-time Indians will prefer their version of a fight to that of any other witness. For the Indian was not only a better and less imaginative observer than the white man. He was also a more interested observer, because war was his greatest and most absorbing sport. More than that, his rating in the tribe depended upon his proven *coups,* and he took great care to claim all he was entitled to, and to demolish any false claims advanced by his comrades. Therefore, in any kind of fracas he had all the keen, clear-eyed alertness of a professional sportsman. And he had the advantage of steady nerves; he was less likely to get excited than most men. He saw just what happened. And as long as he lived, whenever he counted *coups* in public, he had to rehearse just what he had seen."[2]

Since they had no written language until white missionaries devised one for them in 1839, the Nez Perces put great importance on the spoken word. In his book *Adventures of Captain Bonneville,* Washington Irving describes a feast Bonneville and his men attended when they visited the Lower Nez Perces in the Grande Ronde area in 1834:

"When the repast was over, a long talk ensued. . . . The chief, and all present, listened with profound attention, and evidently with great interest; nor were the important facts thus set forth confined to the audience in the lodge; for sentence after sentence was loudly repeated by a crier for the benefit of the whole village.

"This custom of promulgating everything by criers is not confined to the Nez Perces, but prevails among many other tribes. It has its advantage where there are no gazettes to publish the news of the day, or to report the proceedings of important meetings. And in fact, reports of this kind, *viva voce,* made in the hearing of all parties, and liable to be contradicted or corrected on the spot, are more likely to convey accurate information to the public mind than those circulated through the press.

"The office of crier," Irving concludes, "is generally filled by some old man, who is good for little else."[3]

As in all epic dramas, forces beyond the understanding or control of the people involved were at work as the Nez Perces and the whites confronted one another, driving them toward a fate neither could foresee.

Here, I have recorded that confrontation from the Indian point of view.

2. Stanley Vestal, *Kit Carson, the Happy Warrior of the Old West* (Boston: Houghton Mifflin Co., 1928), p. 67.
3. Washington Irving, *The Adventures of Captain Bonneville, U.S.A., in the Rocky Mountains and the Far West* (1837); reprint ed., Norman: University of Oklahoma Press, 1961, Edgeley W. Todd, ed.), pp. 247–248.

Chief Joseph Country

CHAPTER ONE

THE LAND

This whole vast region has been built up by basaltic lava flows — scores of them — which in some places have an aggregate thickness of nearly a mile . . . a spread in time of more than 30,000,000 years.
— Edward F. Rhodenbaugh, 1961

SINCE CHARACTER is strongly influenced by environment, it is not surprising that the Nez Perces were a unique tribe of Indians. Theirs was a unique land. Containing towering mountain ranges, deep

Photo by Dave Jensen

The High Wallowa Country

canyons, big rivers, and widely varied types of climate and terrain, it was an invigorating land in which to live. Although five hundred miles inland from the Pacific Ocean and as far north as the state of Maine, its climate was moderated by warm, moist air pushed into the region by the Japan current, while the white gravel stream beds of the area served as the finest natural hatchery in North America for anadromous fish such as salmon, steelhead, and sturgeon.[1]

Sheltered sandbars provided ideal locations for winter villages. Vast open areas at higher altitudes grew fine stands of grass for wild game, while the wet areas adjacent to these prairies offered perennial supplies of edible roots such as camas and kouse. In the high country, slow-melting snowbanks kept the streams flowing all summer long with cold, clean water, and the numerous mountain lakes teemed with fish.

Photo by Bill Gulick
Redfish Lake

Through the land of the Nez Perces flowed one of the major rivers of the West, the Snake.[2] With its principal tributaries, the Salmon, Clearwater, Imnaha, and the Grande Ronde, the Snake River not only carried tremendous volumes of water down from the western slope of the Continental Divide to the Columbia and the sea but had carved eons ago a fantastic maze of canyons, cliffs, slides, and rapids that defied travel by foot, horse, or boat to outsiders unfamiliar with the age-old trails.

To the north of the Nez Perce country rose the Clearwater Mountains, covered with some of the finest stands of timber in the West. Eastward rose the rugged crests of the Bitter Root Mountains;[3] southeast loomed the Sawtooths; to the south the Salmon River range overlooked an area still as primitive and roadless today as it was then; southwest, on the Idaho side of the Snake, the Seven Devils Mountains thrust their jagged spires toward the sky; while westerly across the awesome depths of Hell's Canyon the high Wallowas guarded the Oregon side of the river.

The lowest point in the region was the spot where the Palouse River joined the Snake fifty miles above its junction with the Columbia, 440

From a painting by John Mix Stanley   Courtesy Penrose Library, Whitman College
The Mouth of the Palouse River

Before the white man came, the land occupied by the Nez Perces covered what is now north-central Idaho, a substantial corner of northeastern Oregon, and a somewhat smaller segment of southeastern Washington. Roughly measuring one hundred fifty miles from north to south and one hundred eighty miles from east to west, the domain of the various bands of the tribe covered approximately twenty-seven thousand square miles.

1. From the Greek word meaning "up-running." These fish spawn in fresh water, go to sea to mature for two or three more years, then return to the stream beds of their birth to lay their eggs and propagate their species.
2. In length, land area drained, and amount of water carried, the Snake ranks sixth among the nation's rivers. It is 1,036 miles long, drains 109,000 square miles, and carries 36 million acre-feet of water to the Columbia each year.
3. Until recent years brought on the abominable practice of jamming words together and eliminating apostrophes this rugged range was written Bitter Root Mountains, not Bitterroot. Hell's Canyon had not yet been shortened into the meaningless term Hells Canyon. I prefer the old-fashioned spellings.

feet above sea level. The highest point, on the southeastern edge of the land claimed by the Nez Perces, was Mount Borah, 12,662 feet.[4]

The Salmon River, which flows through the heart of Nez Perce country, is the longest American river contained solely within a single state; from its source to its junction with the Snake just below Hell's Canyon, it is 390 miles in length. Most of those miles are filled with white water rapids and waterfalls far too violent to be navigated in primitive Indian dugout canoes. Through the Hell's Canyon sector the Snake is even more powerful and dangerous, though the Nez Perces did manage to cross it when the need arose.

Geologically, special character has been given to the land of the Nez Perces by two major features: the numerous lava flows that have spread

once were hot and viscous, before being crystallized, is assumed."[5]

Still another unique physical feature of the region is the wide distribution of a type of soil called *loess*. This is a fine-grained, yellowish brown, extremely fertile loam deposited by the wind. Blowing from west to east up the Columbia River Gorge and over the vast lava flows of the interior plateau through eons of time, millions of dust storms have lost their force and deposited their burden in places like Camas Prairie in central Idaho and the Palouse Hills in southeastern Washington. Blessed with sufficient rainfall and abundant sunshine, these grew tremendous stands of stirrup-high bunchgrass, offering ideal food for the tens of thousands of horses which the Nez Perces owned when they first met the white man.

Photo by Bill Gulick

Sawtooth Mountains

across the region during the past thirty million years and the massive batholith which covers much of central and northern Idaho.

" 'Batholith' comes from two Greek words: *bathos* (deep) and *lithos* (stone)," writes geologist Edward F. Rhodenbaugh. "This takes on significance when we recall that granites are the universal basement rocks beneath the continents. . . . That such intruded masses

With the coming of the horse to their part of the world around 1730, the Nez Perces became avid travelers. Of the three main routes out of their country, one led west down the Snake and Col-

4. See topographic map of the Nez Perce country.
5. Edward F. Rhodenbaugh, *Sketches of Idaho Geology*, 2d ed. (Caxton Printers, 1961), p. 31.

From a painting by John Mix Stanley   *Courtesy Penrose Library, Whitman College*
Source of the Palouse River

umbia rivers to the great regional fishing and trading center, Celilo Falls. The other two trails led east across the Bitter Root Mountains to the buffalo country.

In all probability it was on a trip to Celilo Falls that a young Nez Perce brave picked up a piece of personal adornment that gave his tribe its name. Observing some nameless coastal Indian wearing a polished skewer of seashell pushed through a hole in the septum of his nose, this equally nameless Nez Perce traded for a piece of dentalium, pierced his septum, inserted the skewer of seashell, then rode home and showed off the latest fad he had brought back from a distant land.

But a fad it proved to be. The custom of punching a hole in one's nose and wearing a piece of seashell in it never really caught on among the young blades of the tribe. However, the first white man to visit the tribe did see at least one brave so adorned. Being French he named the tribe *"Nez Percé"* or *"Pierced Nose."* So long as the French-Canadian influence remained strong in the region, the French pronunciation *"Nay Pair-say"* was used. But when the Americans took over, the purity of the French words gradually was diluted, then finally forgotten entirely, with the Indians themselves settling for the Americanized *"Nezz Purses."*

Unlike the relatively easy route to Celilo Falls, the two trails east to the buffalo country were extremely difficult to traverse. One was called the Old Nez Perce Trail; the other, the Lolo Trail.

Sometimes called the South Trail, the Old Nez

Perce Trail began at what is now Harpster, Idaho, about eighty miles up the South Fork of the Clearwater from Lewiston.

"After leaving Harpster, the trail climbed to the ridge between the South and Middle forks [of the Clearwater] and followed the highest country until a descent was made into Newsome Creek; then the way led over the Elk Summit and down into the Elk City Valley, or basin. Here it was joined from the north by the Tahoe branch, swung directly south to American River, up this to its junction with Red River, and thence to the head of this stream. From there it ascended to and followed the main divide between the Clearwater and Salmon rivers to the Nez Perce Pass where it left Idaho and dropped down into the head of the Bitter Root Valley."[6]

The longer, more northerly route to the buffalo country was called the Lolo Trail. The origin of the name Lolo or "Lou Lou," as it is spelled on all the earlier maps, is obscure, writes Elers Koch.[7] One local historian says that an old-time trapper named Laurence once lived in the area and that the Indians, who found it difficult to articulate an "r," called him Lolo instead. Another theory is that Lolo was a corruption of the French name *Le Louis,* which was given to the stream and pass in honor of Meriwether Lewis.

Still another possibility has been pointed out by Lewiston attorney and regional historian Marcus J. Ware, who says: "In Chinook Jargon — the universal trade language which all Northwest Indians knew — *lolo* meant to pack or to carry. Even before they acquired horses, the Nez Perces crossed the mountains to the buffalo country. Every man, woman, and child — even the dogs — carried a pack of some sort as they climbed and descended the steep, twisting trail. Its weight must have been the dominant factor of the journey. So whenever they spoke of the trail, the first word that came to mind was *Lolo.*"

However it got its name, the Lolo Trail had been in use for many years when the Lewis and Clark party was led across it in 1805. The trail proper

"has its beginnings on the western or Idaho side at the junction of the North Fork of the Clearwater with the main stream (near present-day Orofino). Its eastern end is where the Lolo Creek empties its waters into the Bitter Root River, about ten miles south of Missoula [Montana]. This section of the trail is about one hundred

6. Robert G. Bailey, *River of No Return,* rev. ed. (Lewiston, Idaho: R. G. Bailey Printing Co., 1935, 1947), pp. 88–91.
7. Ibid., p. 74.

miles long. . . . The trail reaches its highest altitude near what is called the Indian Postoffice. Here the trail pierces the sky at an altitude of 7,035 feet . . .

"In later years when the writer visited the place, this large pile of stones was still to be seen as were many of lesser size. Indians yet living on the Nez Perce Reservation claim to be able to read the messages conveyed by these stone heaps."[8]

Since "going to the buffalo country" was such an important part of Nez Perce life, the reader may ask: "Why did they have to cross the Bitter Root Mountains to hunt buffalo? Did none of these animals graze on the grass-covered hills and valleys of their own country?

Why there were no buffalo in the land of the Nez Perces when the white men came is something of a puzzle. On the plains of southwestern Idaho and in the upper Salmon River Valley of eastern Idaho remains of "bison jumps" have been found, which indicate that for a period of seven to eight thousand years Indians living in these areas drove buffalo over cliffs to supply themselves with meat.[9] This would have been long before the coming of

the horse, of course, and the amount of manual labor required to pile up the long rows of rocks used to guide the animals to their doom is awesome to consider. Some experts think the mobility given the Indians by the acquistion of the horse, perhaps aided by drought, fire, or disease, led to the extinction of the animal in a region to which it was never as well adapted as it was to the great plains east of the Continental Divide.

At any rate, once they got the means to travel extensively, the Nez Perces — like tourists today — needed little excuse to get up and go. But before taking to the trail with them, perhaps we should examine the way they lived in olden times.

8. Ibid., pp. 62–63.

9. L. D. Agenbroad, "The Five Fingers Buffalo Jump" (Paper delivered at the Thirty-Third Annual Meeting of the Society of American Archaeology, Santa Fe, N. Mex., May 1968); Agenbroad, "The 'Y' Buffalo Jump, Owyhee County, Idaho" (Paper delivered at the annual meeting of the same society in Mexico City, May 1970); "A Bison Jump in the Upper Salmon River Valley of Eastern Idaho," Tebiwa 14, no. 1, pp. 4–32, Idaho State University Museum.

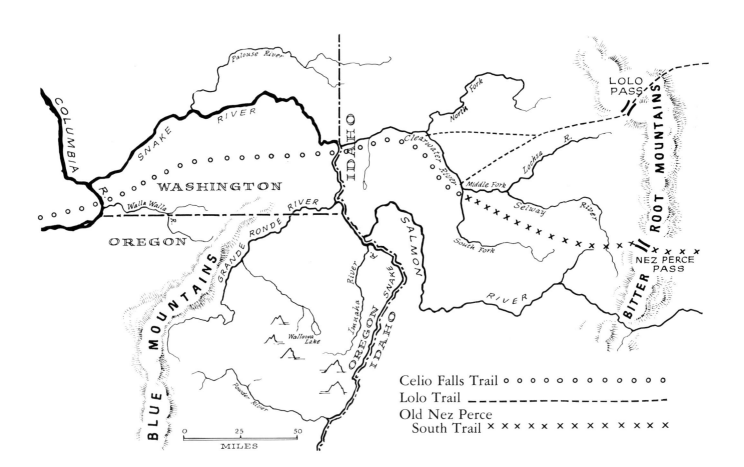

Celio Falls Trail o o o o o o o o o o o o

Lolo Trail _ _ _ _ _ _ _ _ _ _ _ _ _ _ _ _ _

Old Nez Perce
South Trail × × × × × × × × × × × × ×

CHAPTER TWO

THE PEOPLE

*"My people, my country." Who in white
America can say these words with as much fervor
and conviction as the Indian?*
— John Greenway, 1970

THE NEZ PERCES have no tradition of their ancestors migrating into the region from some distant land far back in the mists of time. They were created here, the Indians say, by the Coyote Spirit, *Speelyi,* who fought an epic battle with a monster, slew it, and cut its body into little pieces which he threw in all directions. Each piece then came to life and became an Indian tribe.

Site of the battle was the Kamiah Valley on the Middle Fork of the Clearwater. According to legend, Coyote's friend, Fox, stood by and watched in admiration while the monster was being

Photo by Jane Gay

Courtesy Idaho Historical Society

Forks of the Clearwater River at Kooskia

butchered. When the work was finished Fox said: "Well done! But now you have nothing left for this beautiful valley, which deserves a tribe of its own."

"Ah, I *do* have something left!" Coyote answered with a smile. Shaking his fingers, still red with the fresh, warm blood of the monster's heart, he sprinkled the drops over the region, creating the last and best tribe of all — the Nez Perces — saying: "Let this be their homeland forever."[1]

Regarding when the Indians first came to America, one native Nez Perce historian writes: "Archaeologists now tell us that we have been living in America upwards of twenty to thirty thousand years."[2]

In an equally vague generalization, a white anthropologist writes that the American Indians "came to this land from the vast mountains and open plains of Siberia about fifteen thousand years ago following great herds of ice-age mammals such as mammoths, giant bison, camels, three-toed horses, giant bear, and deer. . . . Mammoth is from the Yakut word *mamma* showing Siberian influence or origin . . ."[3]

It is in the rock-shelters of the Nez Perce country that the most credible evidence of the prehistory of the tribe has been found. Located deep in sheltered canyons along the Snake, Salmon, and Clearwater rivers, these are natural cavelike formations protected from wind and weather. While a number of these sites have been identified by archaeologists, the painstaking labor of investigating them and classifying their contents has barely begun.

Excavations made at the Weis rock-shelter near the town of Cottonwood in northern Idaho show that people lived there continuously from about 5,000 B.C. to about 1,400 A.D.[4] Investigations done at the Marmes Site on the lower Snake indicate that its occupancy by man dates back at least 8,000 years. More recently an important find has been made on the Clearwater six miles upstream from Lewiston.

"This is a new chapter in Northwest archaeology because it proves human populations in central Idaho were much larger than believed previously," says a Boise State University scientist, Kenneth Ames. "Remains of ten dwellings have been found, and another 20 or 30 still are buried."[5]

It is not definitely known when the cavemen ancestors of the Nez Perces moved from rock-shelters into dwellings they had constructed themselves. But the transition was a natural one, com-

From a painting by John Mix Stanley   Courtesy: Penrose Library, Whitman College
Palouse Falls

bining the protection of canyon walls from weather with ready access to food supplied by the river. Digging down five feet or so in the soft white sand deposited by the rise and fall of rushing waters, the Indians created circular pits up to seventy-five feet

1. Francis Haines, *Red Eagles of the Northwest: The Story of Chief Joseph and His People* (Portland, Oreg.: Scholastic Press, 1939), p. 7.

2. Allen P. Slickpoo, Sr., Project Director, Nez Perce Tribe, and Deward F. Walker, Jr., Technical Advisor, *Noon Nee-me-poo (We the Nez Perces); Culture and History of the Nez Perces,* vol. 1 (Boulder: University of Colorado Press, 1973), p. 5. Published for the Nez Perce Tribal Council, Lapwai, Idaho.

3. Joseph J. S. Feathers, ed., and guest authors, *These Are the Nez Perce Nation* (Lewiston, Idaho: Lewis-Clark Normal Press, 1970), Introduction (pages unnumbered). Dr. Feathers is a professor of anthropology.

4. B. Robert Butler, "Contributions to the Prehistory of the Columbia Plateau," *Occasional Papers,* no. 9, Idaho State College Museum, 1962, pp. 54, 56.

5. *Union-Bulletin* (Walla Walla), Nov. 27, 1978.

in diameter or rectangular excavations measuring eighteen by one hundred feet. Using driftwood brought downriver by spring floods, they erected slanting frameworks and ridgepoles, which they covered with grass mats. An opening through which smoke could escape was left along the center of the roof of the longhouse; on its floor a cooking fire was built every ten or twelve feet. While these dwelling places looked cramped and primitive from the outside, they were surprisingly roomy, comfortable, and clean on the inside, for the Nez Perces were noted for their love of a daily bath, no matter how cold the weather.

Nearby, two smaller structures completed the village — a sleeping chamber for older boys and young men, and an underground lodge in which women spent their menstrual period and gave birth. If space on the sandbar were limited, its occupants might be little more than an extended family of fifteen or twenty people. If the area were larger, the village might contain thirty or forty families under the roof of a single longhouse and be capable of furnishing one hundred warriors for its defense.[6]

Even before they acquired the horse, the Nez Perces were a seminomadic tribe, since the distances they had to travel to reach a radically different environment were relatively short. From their winter homes on the low-lying sandbars where grass turned green and wildflowers blossomed early in March, to the higher slopes where *keh-kheet* (an edible root) became ready to dig in April, to the mountain meadows where camas bloomed in early July and matured for harvest in August, to the still higher mountainsides where huckleberries ripened in September, required only a few days of leisurely travel between each food-gathering place. Once there, camp was made for a week or more, with the women doing most of the work while the men hunted, fished, gambled, ran footraces, smoked, told stories, and enjoyed themselves.

Since they accepted the environment as they found it and did not try to alter it, food-gathering was the principal occupation of the Nez Perces nine months out of the year. Although migrating fish of one kind or another came upriver to spawn from early spring until late fall, most of the salmon the Nez Perces depended upon for food were caught in July, August, and September. When properly dried in the sun or smoked over a slow-burning fire of willow or alder in a lodge, this

Courtesy Lewiston Morning Tribune
Nez Perce National Historic Park

Staged scene — digging kouse roots. Left to Right: Kay Bohnee, Else Maynard, Helene Youngman.

protein-rich meat would keep well through the winter. Crushed into powder, packed into salmon skins or tightly woven grass baskets, and sealed with hot grease, it would keep for years.

Edible roots were an important part of the Nez Perce diet. One of these was the biscuitroot, called kouse by the Indians.

"Biscuitroots are perennial herbs and constitute a large rather variable genus of the carrot or parsnip family (*Umbelliferae*)," according to plant experts. "The plants are also known locally as hogfennel, prairiefennel, whiskbroom-parsley, wildcarrot, wildparsley, and by the generic name, Cogswellia . . .

"These herbs are among the first plants to bloom in the spring. . . . The fresh roots have a parsnip-like flavor, but, on drying, become brittle and white, with a somewhat celery-like taste."[7]

Because of the importance of kouse as a nourishing, easily gathered food that became avail-

6. Haines, *Red Eagles,* pp. 8–10.
7. U.S., Department of Agriculture, Forest Service, *Range Plant Handbook,* 1937, p. W55.

able at a time when hunger often stalked the land, the Nez Perces called the month of May *Ah-pah-ahl,* which means "season of making of *Up-pa* [baked loaf] from ground kouse." April was called *Ke-khee-tahl,* which means "first harvest of a root known as *Keh-kheet.*"[8] Sometimes called wild potato *(Lomatium canbyi),* this was the first plant of the season. It was boiled with the skin on, then peeled and eaten fresh. Unlike kouse, it was never ground or dried by the Nez Perces.[9]

First in importance as a wild vegetable food was the camas, which grew in abundance in wet mountain meadow areas.

Photo by Jane Gay   *Courtesy Idaho Historical Society*
Frame for an Indian Sweat Lodge

"This small North American genus of the lily family (*Quama sia* spp., syn. *Camas sia* spp.) is composed of about six species, which with a single exception are confined to the far West. . . . The plants are often called blue camas, to distinguish them from the poisonous, greenish- or whitish-flowered deathcamases (*Zygadenus* spp.)."[10]

The early-day Catholic missionary, Pierre Jean De Smet, who traveled through the Nez Perce country in 1845–46, wrote:

"I cannot pass over in silence the camash root, and the peculiar manner in which it is prepared. It is abundant, and, I may say, is the queen root of this clime. It is a small, white, vapid onion, when removed from the earth, but becomes black and sweet when prepared for food. The women arm themselves with long, crooked sticks, to go in search of the camash. After having procured a certain quantity of these roots, by dint of long

and painful labor, they make an excavation in the earth from 12 to 15 inches deep, and of proportional diameter, to contain the roots. They cover the bottom with closely cemented pavement [rocks], which they make red hot by means of fire. After having carefully withdrawn all the coals, they cover the stones with grass or wet hay; then place a layer of camash, another of wet hay, a third of bark overlaid with mold, whereon is kept a glowing fire for 50, 60, and sometimes 70 hours. The camash thus acquires a consistency equal to that of the jujube [a sweet, datelike, tropical fruit]. It is sometimes made into loaves of various dimensions. It is excellent, especially when boiled with meat; if kept dry, it can be preserved a long time."[11]

When the normal foods were in short supply, the Nez Perces eked out a meager diet on what they called "starvation foods" — rose haws, tree moss, lichens, inner bark peeled from Ponderosa pine trees. They would not eat grizzly bear meat because that animal had a reputation for digging up and devouring people who had died. No matter how hungry, the Nez Perces would not eat dogs or kill horses for food, though they appear to have eaten horsemeat readily enough after a horse was killed and cooked by the Lewis and Clark party.

Before acquiring guns, the Nez Perces were renowned among western Indian tribes for the superior quality and power of bows made from the horns of mountain sheep. Boiling the horns until they were soft and pliable, the craftsman shaped them into a three-foot-long bow backed with carefully wrapped and glued sinew, giving it great strength. But by the early 1800s mountain sheep became scarce and difficult to kill. Wooden bows made of yew, syringa, wild cherry, or the thornbush became popular, firearms came into use, and the horn bows were seen no more.[12]

Numbering five or six thousand people residing in three hundred separate villages, the Indians were divided into two groups, the Upper and Lower Nez Perce. The line of division roughly followed the Snake River. The Nez Perce living in the region drained by the Salmon and Clearwater in

8. Lucy Jane Harbinger, "The Importance of Food Plants in the Maintenance of Nez Perce Cultural Identity," (Master's thesis, Washington State University, 1964), p. 14; Slickpoo, *Noon Nee-me-poo,* p. 30.

9. Harbinger, "Importance of Food Plants," p. 15.

10. *Range Plants,* p. W160.

11. Pierre Jean De Smet, *Oregon Missions and Travels over the Rocky Mountains in 1845–46* (New York, 1847).

12. Alvin M. Josephy, Jr., *The Nez Perce Indians and the Opening of the Northwest* (New Haven: Yale University Press, 1971), p. 18; Slickpoo, *Noon Nee-me-poo,* p. 42.

Courtesy Nez Perce National Historic Park

John Miller (White Hawk)

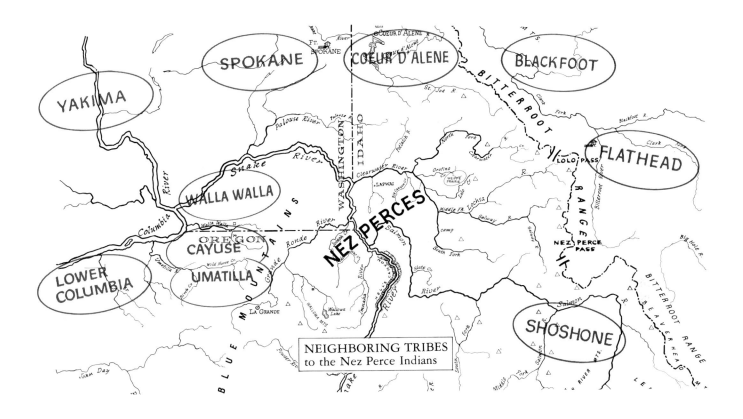

NEIGHBORING TRIBES
to the Nez Perce Indians

what is now Idaho were called Upper Nez Perces, while those in the watersheds of the Imnaha and Grande Ronde in present-day northeastern Oregon and southeastern Washington were called Lower.

Since the Lower Nez Perces were closer to Columbia River and coastal Indian tribes, their culture tended to adapt from that group, while the Upper Nez Perces, whose territory adjoined that of the Plains tribes east of the Bitter Root Mountains, tended to borrow from the Indians living in that area.

And the Nez Perces were great borrowers. Possessed of a lively curiosity and a quick intelligence, they loved to trade and acquire new things: seashells from the coast with which to adorn their persons; feathered warbonnets and buffalo-horn headdresses from the Plains; or whatever else struck their fancy.

Among Western Indians, the Nez Perces were one of the few tribes that understood both the sign language of the Plains and the Chinook Jargon of the coast.

East of the Continental Divide, the Blackfeet, Sioux, Crow, and many other tribes long ago had learned to communicate with one another by means of hand gestures, even though they could not understand the spoken word. Along the lower Columbia and the Northwest coast. Indians such as the Wishrams, Celilos, Klickitats, and others long since had devised a simple trade language comprised of French, English, and Indian words, which in their area was universally understood.

West of the Nez Perce country few Indians could speak sign language. East of the Nez Perce country, few Indians could speak Chinook Jargon. In touch with both cultures, the Nez Perces were multilingual.

As noted earlier, the lands occupied by the tribe during the years when they were known as

Courtesy Penrose Library, Whitman College
Mother and Child

Tssop-nit-palu, "The Walking People,"[13] covered approximately twenty-seven thousand square miles. Given the means to roam over still more territory, the travel-loving Nez Perces soon would expand the range of mountains, valleys, and plains over which they felt it their right to make seasonal migrations tenfold.

They found that means in the horse.

13. Slickpoo, *Noon nee-me-poo,* p. iii.

CHAPTER THREE

THE HORSE

Said the little Eohippus:
"I'm going to be a horse,
And on my middle fingernails
To run my earthly course."
— Eugene Manlove Rhodes, 1912

WHEN COLUMBUS discovered the New World in 1492, no horses existed in North or South America. Since the horse family appears to have originated in America some sixty million years ago and to have endured here in one form or another until it became extinct ten thousand years ago, its sudden disappearance long has been a baffling puzzle to naturalists.

The earliest ancestor to the horse was a small, rabbitlike beast called *Hyracotherium* by the discover of its fossil remains, paleontologist Richard Owen, who did not recognize it as even related to the horse family until later stages of its evolutional development were found.

"With the exception of the *Hyracotherium*, the *Eohippus* is the oldest known horse," writes historian Robert Moorman Denhardt. "It was a tiny being no larger than a fox terrier, and it had a skull so small that it could be concealed in a man's hand. . . . The tips of his toes were tiny hoofs very much like those of later horses."[1]

Popularly called "the dawn horse" because it occurred in the Eocene ("dawn of the recent") epoch, the *Eohippus* developed into several different species, varying in size from ten to twenty inches at the shoulders.[2] From it over a long period of time evolved the *Mesohippus, Parahippus, Merychippus, Pliohippus,* and finally *Equus,* the horse of the Glacial Age..

"During these long ages the early horse was extremely abundant," writes Denhardt, "and at least four migrations took place from the New World to the Old. Of these migrations, only the last group of wanderers survived. In the Americas the original stock died out completely."[3]

Gradually, during the course of its development, the horse had grown in size, developed an undivided hoof, and evolved from an animal that browsed on low-growing plants to one that grazed on grass.

Archaeologists now believe that man began populating the Western Hemisphere thirty to forty thousand years ago, though definite evidence of human habitation in the Pacific Northwest so far found and radiocarbon dated goes back to only 10,000 B.P.[4] Why have so few traces of the migration from Siberia to Alaska been found? Because the likely route of those migrations — which then was high and dry — is now buried underwater.

"Overall, world ocean level fell four hundred feet during the last glacial maximum," says Dr. Richard Daugherty, Washington State University archaeologist. "Sixteen thousand years ago the western border of Washington stretched five or six miles west of where it is today. Crossing from Siberia to Alasaka was made over a broad plain of land called Beringia. It was as much as eight hundred miles wide and looked no different than the Asian steppes, presenting no unfamiliar ecological challenges to wandering bands of hunters and foragers.

"With this route now underwater, evidence of man's

1. Robert Moorman Denhardt, *The Horse of the Americas* (Norman: University of Oklahoma Press, 1947), p. 6.
2. George Gaylord Simpson, *Horses* (New York: Doubleday Anchor Books, 1961), p. 151. Published in cooperation with the American Museum of Natural History.
3. Denhardt, *Horse*, pp. 7–9.
4. "Before Present." Instead of using the terms B.C. or A.D., which require a bit of subtraction or addition, author Ruth Kirk and archaeologist Richard D. Daugherty simplify dating with the letters B.P. If an event happened in 8,820 B.C., this would date it at 10,000 B.P.

passage can be assessed only by sea floor scouring and scuba diving, both activities costly and difficult."[5]

As glaciers advanced and receded and as ocean levels fell and rose, Berengia was available as a bridge several times before 35,000 B.P., Daugherty says, to both horses and man. But after living successfully in America for sixty million years and evolving from a ten-inch-high, rodentlike creature to a full-sized horse, *Equus* in the New World suddenly became extinct.

Why?

Since there is ample evidence that the horse existed in America when the first Indians arrived — and that the Indians killed horses for food — it may be that man was a contributing factor in wiping out the species. But since the Indian also hunted buffalo, elk, deer, and other animals without seriously depleting their numbers, scientists do not find this a satisfactory explanation.

"The extinction of horses over the whole of North and South America, where they had roamed in vast herds during the Pleistocene, is one of the most mysterious episodes of animal history," writes George Gaylord Simpson. "There is no doubt about the fact, but the reason for it is doubtful, to say the least. . . . It was not the glaciation of the great Ice Age; not the disappearance of prairie grasses; not competition of other grazers; not an environmental enemy . . .

"These suggestions eliminated, few possible explanations remain. . . . This seems at present one of the situations in which we must be humble and honest and admit that we simply do not know the answer."[6]

In any case, there were no horses in America when Columbus discovered the New World in 1492. Spanish soldiers always rode stallions; so, for breeding purposes, the Crown insisted that *every* ship sailing to the New World must contain some brood mares.

When Cortes landed at Vera Cruz in February 1519, bringing the horse back to its ancestral home on the American continent, his ship carried eleven stallions, five mares, and a newly born colt. The terror induced in the natives by sight of this fierce, awesome beast and its armored rider has been amply recorded by contemporary historians. Later, Indians farther north would be awed by exploring parties led from Florida to the Mississippi by de Soto and across the American Southwest by Coronado, each party mounted on a number of strong Spanish horses.

Romantic writers have perpetuated the myth that the progenitors of the wild horses of the American West were mares that escaped from de Soto's party in the swamps of the lower Mississippi and a freedom-loving stallion that ran away from the Coronado expedition in the high deserts of New Mexico. Seeking their own kind in this new continent, the mares roamed west, the stallion east, keen eyes seeking, sensitive nostrils testing the wind, until at last on the high plains of West Texas they met — and a new breed of horse was born.

In a prefatory note to a poem titled "The Distant Runners," Mark Van Doren writes that it is based on a legend that "six great horses of Spain, set free after his death by de Soto's men, ran west and restored to America the wild race there lost some thousands of years ago."

But Texas historian J. Frank Dobie, in his book *The Mustangs,* demolishes "the pretty legend" by pointing out that all of de Soto's horses were stallions (as were almost all of Coronado's) and that no wild horses ever have been reported in the lower Mississippi region. He concludes caustically: "If another fable had placed Adam in Asia and Eve in Africa, the chances of mating would be about as high."[7]

Well aware of the power over the natives which horses gave them, the conquerors of New Spain prohibited any Indian from riding a horse for any purpose at any time. In this country of great distances, a man afoot was no man at all. In fact, as missions were established among the Indians of northern Mexico, the American Southwest, and southern California, Christianized Indians were contemptuously called *reducidos* — that is, people reduced to living as pedestrians.

"No tribe *reducido*," Dobie says sadly, "ever became riders of freedom."[8]

Because beef on the hoof was a dependable and portable food supply, cattle accompanied the *conquistadores* on all their quests for God, glory, and gold. But once the God part had been taken over by priests at permanent mission sites, such mundane chores as raising gardens and tending cattle were left to the good fathers and their newly made native converts. Cattle could not be herded

5. Ruth Kirk with Richard D. Daugherty, *Exploring Washington Archaeology* (Seattle: University of Washington Press, 1978), p. 16.
6. Simpson, *Horses,* pp. 198–200.
7. J. Frank Dobie, *The Mustangs* (Boston: Little, Brown & Co., Bantam Books 1954), p. 26.
8. Ibid., p. 11.

Prehistoric forms of the horse

Bronze by Dave Manuel

Marksman of the Plains

on foot. So even though horses officially were forbidden to the Indians, a few natives were permitted to ride in order to look after the growing herds of the missions. Inevitably, an occasional young man sent out to bring in the cows failed to return. With a strong horse between his legs, the *reducido* suddenly realized he could become a rider of freedom

Sedentary Indians like the Pueblos, who long had lived in fixed villages and raised irrigated gardens, cared nothing for horses as a means of transportation. But they did recognize the value of the horse as an article of trade. Mountain and desert Indians like the Apaches, whose country was so rugged that it could be covered more easily afoot than mounted, killed and ate the first horses they encountered, liked the taste, and began raiding the mission horse herds for a supply of meat.

"In order to discourage runaway slaves, the Spaniards offered to buy them back from any tribe managing to capture them," Haines says. "Sometimes the Indians refused to surrender them except for horses. Since the missionaries could not bear to lose their converts to the Indians, they induced the civil authorities to suspend the law in such special cases. The early records show that some Spanish settlers, captured in raids, were also ransomed for horses."[9]

A breed of men called *Comancheros* — many of them half-white and half-Indian, possessing the worst traits of both races — became the used-car dealers of their day, swapping horses they bought

or stole from the missions to transportation-hungry Indians for buffalo meat, hides, or anything else of value, with no questions asked by either party as to the legitimacy of the title.

Thus, in thin trickles, horses were distributed to the Indians.

In 1680 the Pueblo Indians near Santa Fe staged a successful revolt against their conquerors, driving the Spaniards down the Rio Grande to El Paso and below. Now the spread of horses expanded from a trickle to several widening streams. On the plains of West Texas the Comanches became the finest horseman on the North American continent. In northern Mexico, the fiercely independent Indian tribes living there rivaled the Comanches in the quality of their horsemanship. Together with the Comanches (boasting that the only reason they did not completely wipe out the white settlements on the lower Rio Grande was that "we want the whites to raise horses for us") they raided the ranches with such success and regularity that the expression "Comanche Moon" would send shivers of terror up the spines of whites living in the area for generations to come.

By the early 1700s a northward-flowing branch of the horse-distributing streams reached the Shoshones, who inhabited the Snake River country directly to the south and southeast of the land of the Nez Perce. Though usually hostile toward one another, these two tribes now and again "declared peace" in order to make mutually advantageous trades. According to Nez Perce tradition, such a truce was arranged now. The Nez Perces had heard about the "big medicine" animals recently acquired by their neighbors and were determined to acquire some horses for themselves. When asked, the Shoshones indicated a willingness to deal if articles of sufficient value were offered in return.

"A party of Nez Perces, made up of men from several villages, went across the old war trail to the Boise Basin, taking with them a supply of Indian money — dentalia — which they had obtained in trade from the tribes at The Dalles. [Dentalia was a Pacific Coast seashell greatly prized by inland tribes of the Northwest.] After much dickering, they were able to secure several animals which they led back across the mountains to be distributed one by one among the various villages participating in the venture.

9. Francis Haines, *Appaloosa: The Spotted Horse in Art and History* (Austin: University of Texas Press, 1963), p. 68. Published for the Amon Carter Museum of Western Art, Fort Worth.

"To a little village near the mouth of Asotin Creek went the prize of the lot, a white mare. Throngs of people came to observe her. From this one white mare and the colt born to her a few months after her purchase are supposed to have descended all the Nez Perce herds of later times."[10]

Probable date of the acquistion, Haines says, was between 1710 and 1720.

Within a generation, by 1750, the Nez Perce had become horse Indians. In all probability they took to the horse as people of this century took to the car and the plane — the elders skeptically and with many reservations, letting the beast carry their burdens but not their own fragile bodies; the mature men cautiously, riding only the quieter animals; the young men gleefully, climbing aboard whichever horse appeared to have the most dashing looks, spirit, and speed — broken limbs and heads be damned.

Indian tradition of the Columbia Basin has preserved two accounts of early attempts to learn to ride:

"The Sanpoil, living to the north of the Spokanes, had been neighbors of mounted Indians for about a hundred years before they secured their first horses in 1840. When they started learning to ride, one man would walk slowly along (leading the horse) while the rider balanced himself with two long sticks, one in either hand, reaching to the ground . . .

"One band of Coeur d'Alenes had their first lesson from a visiting Flathead warrior. They were much bolder than the Sanpoil, having no one to lead the horse and using no sticks for support. Only one of them was able to keep from falling off when the horse trotted, and one can imagine his glory from such success."[11]

By whatever method the Nez Perces learned to ride, they soon became expert horsemen, renowned for both the quantity and the quality of the horses they owned and bred. Since the country in which they lived was well watered and grassed, contained few natural enemies, and had a climate perfectly suited to the horse, it is not surprising that horses flourished in it. Nor should it be surprising that the horses raised by the Nez Perces were sound of wind and limb, hard-hoofed, sure-footed, and incredibly durable. The Indians did not coddle their animals with hay, grain, and stables; they let them run free in the narrow canyons, broad prairies, and high meadows of an extremely rugged terrain. Thus, only the fittest survived.

In time to come, white settlers from the East — most of whom were farmers — would contemptuously call the Indian horses raised in the Nez Perce country "cayuses," shooting stray stallions on sight least they breed with their big, sturdy mares and sire offspring incapable of pulling a plough. But as Haines, Dobie, and other writers have pointed out, the horses raised by the Nez Perces and their Cayuse "cousins" were not scrubs; they were highly valued as mountain, buffalo, and war horses, and possessed great endurance.

How many of them were of the distinctly spotted coloring that later would be called Appaloosa and whether the Nez Perces deliberately bred this type of horse for hunting buffalo and waging war are controversial questions still being argued by historians. The point we wish to make here is that the Nez Perce system of letting horse herds breed with little or no supervision was not haphazard.

"The common idea that wild horses gradually degenerated through uncontrolled breeding is contrary to the fact," says Dobie. "Only the fittest stallions had a chance to breed. The defect of their natural system lay in the non-selection of mares. The stallions were as lacking in discrimination as the old cowman who declared he never had tasted bad whiskey or seen an ugly woman."[12]

"The high quality of the horses raised by the Nez Perces is quite significant," Haines points out, "since they obtained their better stock by the application of two elementary principles of selective breeding. The poorer stallions were castrated, and all the lower grade animals were traded in large numbers to the neighboring tribes to the east, north, and west. Also, choice breeding stock was imported from the Southwest, via the Shoshones, Utes, and Navajos and from California by trade in the early 1800's."[13]

When and from whom the Nez Perces learned the gelding process is not known; in all likelihood, they learned it soon after they acquired the horse from an Indian familiar with the practice as he had observed it at the Spanish mission near Santa Fe. In addition to using the knife with consummate skill, they developed a method of tying off the organ sac with a thong of wet rawhide, which, when it dried and shrank, caused the testicles to atrophy and drop off without loss of blood or risk of infection. Among Indian tribes the Nez Perces were one of the few that consistently practiced

10. Haines, *Red Eagles*, p. 18.
11. Ibid., p. 20.
12. Dobie, *Mustangs*, p. 111.
13. Haines, *Red Eagles*, p. 23.

Photo by Bill Gulick

A typical Indian Horse

selective breeding; thus, the horses they raised were superior.[14]

Acquisition of horses drastically changed the life-style of the Nez Perces. The horse became a form of personal wealth, an item of trade, a means of transportation, an ally on the hunt or the warpath, a treasure to be stolen or protected, and a way of expanding limited horizons to distances formerly undreamed of.

Before the horse, Nez Perce domain covered country drained by the Salmon, Clearwater, and lower Snake rivers — roughly twenty-seven thousand square miles. After the Indians became a mounted tribe, they began making seasonal journies westward across the vast Columbia plain to The Dalles and the land of the Yakimas and eastward across the Continental Divide to the buffalo country along the headwaters of the Missouri, Yellowstone, and Colorado rivers — an area roughly two hundred thousand square miles in extent.

Since the entire family of husband, wife, children, grandparents, horses, dogs, shelters, and all portable possessions went along, these were leisurely trips, taking weeks, months, or even years according to the distance traveled, the food supply acquired, or the trade goods exchanged.

"The enterprising red men carried a surprising variety of articles to their customers," Haines writes in reference to the Nez Perces and their trade with tribes in the buffalo country. "From their own country they brought cakes of camas and of dried berries; horns of the mountain sheep and the bowls, ladles, and spoons manufactured from them; coiled basket ware, flat wallets of woven work, eagle feathers, arrows, and the famous Nez Perce bows, each valued at the price of a good horse. In addition they carried salmon oil and dried sal-

14. Dr. Franklin F. Cline, for many years a veterinarian in the Walla Walla area, says that on the Umatilla Reservation during modern times he has seen the Indians use a bloodless method of castrating their horses. They tie two sticks together, forcepslike, on the organ sac, which cuts off circulation and causes the testicles to atrophy and drop off. Pain to the animal is brief, Dr. Cline says, for numbness soon sets in.

mon, pounded to powder, both packed in salmon skins; Indian hemp and twine; dentalia and other sea shells, all obtained at The Dalles. On the Plains they traded all these for buffalo products — bone beads, horns, horn spoons, pemmican, wallets and parfleches of rawhide, and buffalo robes, particularly the finely tanned robes ornamented with bead work which were the pride of the Crow women. Another Plains product in great demand was the Sioux war bonnet with its long double tail of eagle feathers, an article useless except to a horseman, and entirely unknown west of the mountains in the earlier times."[15]

Even as the horse vastly expanded the horizons of the Nez Perces for travel and trade, so did it enlarge the opportunities for conflict and war. The Shoshones were a mounted nation now. So were the Blackfeet, Crow, and Sioux. Between them, smaller tribes such as the Flatheads, Coeur d'Alene, and Spokanes acted as buffers to keep the larger nations from abrasive direct contact, joining them when brief periods of peace were declared for purposes of trade. But since all the Indians felt themselves entitled to a share of the vast herds of buffalo that roamed the plains of the Bitter Root, Yellowstone, and Missouri rivers, these areas became a perpetual battleground on which frequent engagements were fought.

So long as the weapons used were the bow and arrow, war club, and spear, no major casualties were inflicted upon any of the participants. As in all long-standing feuds, alliances changed frequently. The Crows joined the Sioux to fight the Blackfeet. The Nez Perces sided with the Crows against the Sioux. The Blackfeet fought the Flatheads, who called upon the Shoshones for help. The Shoshones appealed to the Nez Perces for aid. But no great damage was done.

Shortly after the Nez Perces acquired the horse, a new factor was introduced into the conflict. Firearms. From the Hudson's Bay Company, whose trapping brigades were moving west across Canada, the Blackfeet were being supplied with guns, powder, and lead. With their superior weapons, the Blackfeet decided they now were capable of taking all the buffalo country for themselves.

"They ravaged all of Montana east of the divide," Haines writes, "driving back the Shoshones and Flatheads. Then their war parties penetrated into the Snake, Salmon, and Bitter Root valleys, a serious threat to the western tribes."[16]

So serious was the threat to the Nez Perces that in the early 1800s they refrained from making their annual hunting trips across the Lolo Trail into the Bitter Root Valley. Instead, they traveled the Old Nez Perce Trail southeast to the Lemhi Valley, then to the plains of the upper Snake, and did their buffalo hunting there. This brought them into direct conflict with their ancient enemy-neighbors, the Shoshones.

15. Haines, *Red Eagles*, p. 25.
16. Ibid., p. 27.

CHAPTER FOUR

LEWIS AND CLARK: 1805–1806

*Chief Broken Arm pulled off his leather shirt
and gave it to me. In return I gave him a shirt.*
— Captain William Clark, May 12, 1806

BECAUSE THEY had no written language to preserve their history for posterity, the great men of the Nez Perce tribe prior to the coming of the white man can be known only by traditions handed down through the generations. Usually it was the grandfather who told tales of his people's past to the grandson, for the father was far too busy hunting, fishing, tending horses, and protecting his family from enemies to tell stories. But however dimly remembered by oral history and a few lines recorded in the Lewis and Clark *Journals,* it is certain that Chief Tun-nach-e-mul-tolt, "the Broken Arm," was a great man.

The band of Nez Perces which he headed lived in the Kamiah area on the Middle Fork of the Clearwater. Because of its central location this was often used as a meeting place when councils were called to discuss matters affecting the tribe as a whole. Faced with the loss of an important food supply because of the takeover of the buffalo country by the well-armed Blackfeet, leaders from a number of Nez Perce villages met at Kamiah in the spring of 1805, tribal tradition tells us, and, after long discussion, decided upon a bold course of action.

As fire is fought with fire, so guns must be fought with guns. The nearest point of supply, so far as the Nez Perces knew, was in the land of the *Hidatsa,* the Dakota country, over a thousand miles to the east. Between here and there loomed snow-choked Lolo Pass and the open plains of the Bitter Root, Yellowstone, and Missouri rivers, where the only protection from hostile Blackfeet, not-to-be-trusted Crows, and probably unfriendly Sioux would be a shrewd choice of route, a lot of night riding, and a string of fast horses.

Three young men from Chief Broken Arm's band were chosen to make the dangerous journey. Soon after they set out, Chief Broken Arm sent another delegation of three men southward to the Shoshones, carrying a peace pipe and a proposal that a meeting be arranged so that joint measures could be taken by the two tribes to curb the growing aggression by the Blackfeet.

The Shoshones murdered the envoys.

Now there must be war.

Miraculously enough, the three young men returned from the land of the *Hidatsa* in late summer with six guns, a supply of powder and lead, and an interesting piece of news. A large party of white men had spent the winter in the Mandan villages, they had heard, and now were heading this way. No, they had not seen them, the young men said. All they had heard was that the party of whites was traveling in this direction.

While this was an intriguing bit of information, Chief Broken Arm and his band of warriors were far more concerned with their expedition against the Shoshones. On September 17, 1805, the Nez Perce war party rode south, taking along all the experienced fighting men and young braves eager to distinguish themselves in battle. They left behind the women, the children, the old people, and a few minor chiefs, who, because of infirmity or age, now tended such stay-at-home jobs as looking after the horse herds and supervising the gathering of roots and the catching of fish.

Weippe Prairie, an extensive, well-watered meadow lying at the western base of the Lolo Trail, was covered each summer with vast stands of blue-flowered camas, which, when dried, ground, and baked into loaves, provided the Nez Perces with a substantial part of their winter's food supply. Under the leadership of Chief Twisted Hair, who was too old to fight, and Chief Tetoharsky, who was a peace chief rather than a war chief, several bands of Nez Perces now moved into Weippe Prairie and began their fall harvest of camas.

On September 20, just three days after the departure of the war party, news reached camp that a group of white men had been sighted only a few miles away.

The confrontation between Indians and whites could have been a deadly one, for it came at a time when both were weak and vulnerable. Among the Nez Perces, most of the able-bodied warriors and the leading chiefs were gone. Among the whites, hunger, cold, and exhaustion had sapped the strength and impaired the judgment of the members of the expedition to such a degree that the slightest hostile gesture on the part of the Indians might have triggered a violent reaction that would have poisoned the relationship between the two races for years to come.

Certainly, by their own admission, the whites were in a bad way. The Lewis and Clark party had relied on the best cartographers of the day, who assured them that the easiest way to cross the continent was to ascend the Missouri to its source, cross "a ridge of hills half a day by horse or foot," and then float tranquilly down the "River of the West" to the Pacific Ocean. Clinging to this theory of ascending one river to its source, then crossing "a low divide" to the headwaters of another, the party had followed a roundabout way up the Jefferson and Beaverhead and then north to the Bitter Root. For the past month and a half it had found itself hopelessly entangled in the most rugged terrain it had encountered during its entire journey.

In the days when the Nez Perces were still making their annual trips to the buffalo country, before the Blackfeet acquired firearms, it took them only four days of easy travel to go from the crest of Lolo Pass to the Gates of the Mountains on the Missouri River. It had taken the Lewis and Clark party fifty-two days of punishing effort to traverse the same distance.

Even though September was only half gone, bad weather already had come to the high country, and the party's hunters could find no game. On September 14 the exhausted explorers crested Lolo Pass.

"Here we were compelled to kill a colt for our men and selves to eat," Clark wrote. "We named the South Fork 'Colt Killed Creek.' The Flathead name is *Koos-koos-ke.*"

"Several horses slipped and rolled down steep hills," he wrote next day, "which hurt them very much. . . . From this mountain I could observe high, rugged mountains in every direction as far as I could see . . .

"I have been wet and as cold in every part as I ever was in my life. Indeed, I was at one time fearful my feet would freeze in the thin moccasions which I wore . . ."[1]

This, then, was the physical condition in which the members of the Lewis and Clark party found themselves on the fateful day when they met the Nez Perce Indians, September 20, 1805.

If the grandfather tales which make up tribal tradition are true, an elderly Nez Perce woman called Wet-khoo-weis — meaning "to wander back or return home" — should hold a high place of honor so far as Indian-white relationships are concerned. Captured by Blackfeet as a young woman when her family was sojourning in the buffalo country, she had been taken to Canada and sold from tribe to tribe until finally she became the possession of a French-Canadian in the Red River settlements, far to the east. Living with the whites for some years, she came to know them well, calling them *so-ya-po* or "crowned ones" because of the hats they wore.

Though they treated her kindly, she ran away after giving birth to a child, and at last returned to her own land and people. Somewhere along the way the child died but she never forgot the good treatment she had received while living among the *so-ya-po.*

By now she had grown old. When news of the approach of the party of whites reached the camp on Weippe Prairie and the chiefs called a council to decide whether the whites should be greeted with hostility or friendship, she insisted on making herself heard, even though women normally did not take part in important debates.

Do not harm the whites, Wet-khoo-weis pleaded. They were kind to me. If we treat them well, they will be true friends.

Whether her appeal or the innate good sense of the peacefully inclined Nez Perce leaders was the deciding factor in the course of action finally chosen by the council, no one can definitely say. But instead of ambushing the straggling, weary, hungry members of the Lewis and Clark party —

1. Reuben Golden Thwaites, ed., *Original Journals of the Lewis and Clark Expedition* (New York: Dodd, Mead & Co., 1904), vol. 3, pp. 67–69.

Photo by H. W. Steward   *Courtesy Idaho Historical Society*

Lewis and Clark Trail

who already had killed and butchered a Nez Perce horse without permission — the Nez Perces greeted the strangers with open-hearted hospitality.

The elderly chief, Twisted Hair (Wa-lam-mot-ti-nin) and the somewhat younger chief, Tetoharsky — whose name is not translated in the *Journals* — needed no interpreter to tell them that the whites were hungry.

"Though we could talk to them only in sign language, they proved friendly and hospitable," Clark wrote. "They supplied us with their two staples, dried salmon and flour made from the camas root."[2]

Well-intentioned though this gift of nutritious food was, the drastic change in diet did not agree with the half-starved white men.

"Capt. Lewis very sick . . . I am a little unwell . . . our men nearly all complaining of their bowells," Clark wrote.

As unofficial doctor for the party, Clark attacked the illness forthrightly, dosing himself and the others with "Rushes Pills," which consisted of

ten grains of calomel and ten grains of jalap, both of which were powerful laxatives, supplementing them with large doses of Glauber's salts and emetics.[3] It is a tribute to the ruggedness of their constitutions that the patients survived both the complaint and the cure.

Readily understanding the desire of the whites to reach the Pacific by the quickest, easiest way possible, the well-traveled Nez Perces drew them a map on buckskin of the country to the west. From the point where the Chopunnish (North Fork) joined the *Koos-koos-kee* (Clearwater), the river was navigable by dugout canoe. A day's travel

2. Ibid., pp. 87–88.

3. Ibid., p. 89. For an excellent account of the medical knowledge of the day and the training received by Lewis and Clark before setting out on the expedition, see *Only One Man Died: The Medical Aspects of the Lewis and Clark Expedition,* by E. G. Chuinard, M.D. (Glendale, Calif.: Arthur H. Clark Co., 1979). Lewis was instructed in Philadelphia by the country's leading physician, Dr. Benjamin Rush, but after Lewis had passed on what he learned to Clark, it was Clark who did most of the doctoring.

below the forks, the *Koos-koos-kee* joined a much bigger river called the *Ki-moo-e-nim* (Snake).[4]

A week's travel down the *Ki-moo-e-nim* would take the party to its long-sought goal, the Columbia, down which, with a few portages around dangerous falls and rapids, the party of whites could make its way to the Great Stinking Water (the Pacific Ocean) which the Nez Perces had heard of but never seen.

Yes, they would permit the whites to cut down trees and make dugout canoes, said Twisted Hair and Tetoharsky. For two rifles and one hundred rounds of ammunition they would care for the horses of the party until it returned next spring. In addition they would accompany the whites down the Clearwater and the Snake at least as far as the Columbia, in order to make sure that the tribes living there — who were closely related to the Nez Perces — gave them a friendly reception. Perhaps they would even go to the great trading station of the Pacific Northwest, Celilo Falls, where the coastal Indian culture met that of the Columbia Plateau.

The two chiefs kept their word. Sometimes riding in one of the canoes, sometimes going ashore and riding ahead, and all the way accompanied by bands of friendly Indians who helped right canoes and salvage goods spilled during upsets in rapids, Twisted Hair and Tetoharsky took great pleasure in their roles as guides. When the Lewis and Clark party reached the junction of the Snake with the Columbia on October 16, 1805,

"We halted above the point on the river *Ki-moo-e-nim* to smoke with the Indians who had collected there in great numbers," Clark wrote. "Here we met our two Chiefs who had left us two days ago and proceeded on to this place to inform those bands of our approach and friendly intentions towards all nations."[5]

So far as future relations between white Americans and Columbia Plateau Indians were concerned, the "smokes" held at this point would be important for many years to come. This was a traditional meeting place for tribes allied by blood, tongue, and tradition, later to be classified as belonging to the Sahaptian group of Northwest Indians: Nez Perce, Palouse, Walla Walla, Cayuse, Umatilla, and Yakima — a loose alliance of mounted, far-roaming Indians whose access to the fish resources of the great Columbia River system and the game resources of the buffalo country gave them a strength and knowledge of the interior region found in few other groups.

Photo by H. W. Steward   *Courtesy Idaho Historical Society*

White Sands and Kooskoosie forming the Lochsa River on the Lewis and Clark Trail.

4. Mistaking the upper Salmon for the Snake, Clark wrote on August 21, 1805: "I shall in justice to Captain Lewis, who was the first white man ever on this fork of the Columbia, call this 'Lewis's River.'" In justice, the name should have stuck, for if ever an explorer earned his river, Meriwether Lewis did. But the truth was, this was not the main tributary to the Columbia, and when, in later years, the Snake itself was discovered and mapped in its middle and upper reaches, the name "Lewis's River" fell into gradual disuse.

5. Thwaites, *Original Journals*, p. 120.

Photo by Bill Gulick

Lochsa River

Courtesy Nez Perce National Historic Park
National Park Service

A Nez Perce dugout canoe formerly displayed at Sacajawea Museum, Spalding, Idaho.

Apparently enjoying themselves immensely, Twisted Hair and Tetoharsky continued downriver with the Lewis and Clark party. On October 18, Clark wrote:

"At 4 o'clock, we set out down the Great Columbia,

Photo by Bill Gulick

Wallula Gap on the Columbia River where it makes its western bend toward the Pacific Ocean.

accompanied by our two old Chiefs. One young man wished to accompany us, but we had no room for more and he would be of no service to us . . ."[6]

Nearing Celilo Falls, three hundred miles west of the heart of the Nez Perce country, Clark testified to the widespread influence of the tribe when he wrote that the Indians here

"appear to be the same nation; speak the same language with a little corruption of many words; dress and fish in the same way. All have pierced noses and the men, when dressed, wear a long tapered piece of shell or bead through the nose."[7]

As the greatest fishing and trading center in the interior Pacific Northwest, Celilo Falls attracted many tribes of Indians, not all of them as friendly and hospitable as the Nez Perces. On October 23, Clark wrote:

"One of the old chiefs informed us that he had heard the Indians say that the nation below intended to kill us. We examined all the arms. . . . The natives leave us earlier this evening than usual, which gives a shadow of confirmation to the information of our old chief . . ."[8]

Next day:

"Our two old chiefs expressed a desire to return to their band from this place, saying that they could be of no further service to us, as their nation extended no further down the river than those falls, and as the nation below had expressed hostile intentions against us, would certainly kill them, particularly as they had been at war with each other.
"We requested them to stay with us two nights longer . . . that they might inform is of any designs of the natives, and, if possible, to bring about a peace between them and the tribes below."

The two chiefs did stay the requested two more nights and apparently managed to make peace with the hostile tribe living downriver from Celilo Falls, for on October 25, Clark wrote:

"Here we met with our two old chiefs, who had been to the village below to smoke a friendly pipe . . . we had a parting smoke with our two faithful friends, who accompanied us from the head of the river. They had purchased a horse each with two robes and intended to return on horseback."[9]

So while the Lewis and Clark party proceeded on down the Columbia, Twisted Hair and Tetoharsky made the long ride home. There they

6. Ibid., p. 128.
7. Ibid., p. 144.
8. Ibid., p. 150.
9. Ibid., pp. 152–158.

From a painting by John Mix Stanley   Courtesy Penrose Library, Whitman College
The Dalles of the Columbia River, with Mount St. Helens in the background.

found Chief Broken Arm and his band of warriors basking in glory, for their mission against the Shoshones had resulted in a tremendous victory. Forty-two Shoshones had been killed, with the loss of only three Nez Perce braves. Chief Broken Arm now was recognized as a great leader of his people.

He was pleased with the flag left for him by the two white captains, whom he looked forward to meeting next spring. He approved of the way they had been treated by Twisted Hair and Tetoharsky. But he sternly disapproved of the way some of the young men in Twisted Hair's band had ridden and abused the horses left in the care of the chief. From now on, he said, *he* would look after the horses of the whites.

There is ample evidence that Chief Broken Arm, in addition to being a great war leader, was also a skilled diplomat. Instead of waiting for the Lewis and Clark party to return to the Nez Perce country the next spring, he appears to have sent a representative to meet them at The Dalles and act as their guide upriver, for on April 18, 1806, Clark wrote:

"Early this morning I was awoke by an Indian man of the Chopunnish [Nez Perce] Nation who informed me that he lived in the neighborhood of our horses. This man delivered me a bag of powder and ball which he had picked up this morning at the place the goods were exposed yesterday."[10]

By the end of April the party had reached the domain of the Walla Walla tribe of Indians, whose powerful, friendly Chief Yel-lept invited the explorers "to remain at his village three or four days and assured us that we should be furnished with plenty

of such food as they had themselves, and some horses to assist us on our journey."

After informing the whites of an overland route that would save them eighty miles, the head man of the Walla Wallas gave Clark a present.

"This morning early the Great Chief Yel-lept brought a very elegant white horse to our camp and presented him to me, signifying his wish to get a kettle, but being informed that we had already disposed of every kettle we could possibly spare, he said he was content with whatever I thought proper to give him. I gave him my sword, 100 balls and powder and some small articles of which he appeared perfectly satisfied."[11]

Meanwhile, the Nez Perces were making sure the party of Americans received every possible assistance on the return trip. Chief Broken Arm earlier had sent four Indians with food and horses to meet the explorers, but they had missed connections — probably because the whites were returning overland instead of following the Snake as they has done on their journey downriver. Then, on May 3, Clark wrote:

"This morning we set out at 7 A.M. We met with We-ark-koomt, whom we have usually distinguished by the name of the Big Horn Chief from the circumstance of his always wearing a horn of the animal suspended by a cord to his left arm. He is a first chief of a large band of the Chopunnish Nation. He had ten of his young men with him. This man went down Lewis's river [The Snake] by land as we descended it by water last fall quite to the Columbia, and I believe was very instrumental in procuring us a hospitable and friendly reception among the natives. He had now come a considerable distance to meet us."[12]

Next day near the mouth of Alpowa Creek, a few miles west of the junction of the Clearwater with the Snake:

"Here we met with Tetoharsky, the youngest of the two chiefs who accompanied us last fall to the great falls of the Columbia," Lewis wrote. "We also met with our pilot who descended the river with us as far as the Columbia. These Indians recommended our passing the river [crossing the Snake] at this place and ascending the *Koos-koos-kee* [Clearwater] on the N.E. side. They said it was nearer and a better route to the forks of that river where the Twisted Hair resides, in whose charge we had left our horses; thither they promised to conduct us . . ."

Lewis also noted a custom strictly observed in

10. Ibid., vol. 4, p. 296.
11. Ibid., pp. 332–333.
12. Ibid., pp. 352–353.

An Indian village

all Nez Perce villages and camps, whether permanent or temporary, the confinement of women to a separate menstrual lodge.

"At all these lodges of the Chopunnish I observe an appendage of a small lodge with one fire which seems to be the retreat of their women in a certain situation. The men are not permitted to approach this lodge within a certain distance and if they have anything to convey to the occupants of this little hospital they stand at the distance of 50 or 60 paces and throw it towards them as far as they can and retire." [13]

Frequently called upon to treat the Indians for aches and pains and eye trouble, Clark exchanged his services for horses and food, expressing a philosophy still a cardinal rule with doctors today: "We take care to give them no article which can possibly injure them."

Sometimes the food acquired as medical fees came in the form of dogs, which all members of the party except Captain Clark had learned to relish, though the Nez Perces themselves disdained to eat their canine pets. Clark wrote:

"While at dinner an Indian fellow very impertinently threw a half-starved puppy nearly into the plate of Capt. Lewis by way of derision for our eating dogs and laughed very heartily at his own impertinence. Captain Lewis was so provoked at the insolence that he caught the puppy and threw it with great violence at him and struck him in the breast and face, seized his tomahawk, and showed him by sign that if he repeated his insolence that he would tomahawk him. The fellow withdrew apparently much mortified and we continued our dinner without further molestation." [14]

Before heading downriver the party had buried saddles, powder, and canisters of lead in caches near the river, taking care to make the deposits only when no Indians were around to observe them. This proved to be a needless precaution, for, as Clark wrote May 7:

"A man of this lodge produced two canisters of powder, which he informed us he had found by means of his dog where they had been buried in the bottom of the river a few miles above. . . . As he had kept them safe and had honesty enough to return them, we gave him a fire steel by way of compensation." [15]

For the Nez Perces, this was the hungriest time of the year, for by now most of their stored food supply was gone, and salmon had not yet returned to the river. Even so, Clark records the generosity of a Nez Perce man who offered to give him "twelve small fish, which I declined accepting as I found from his signs that his house was a short distance above and that those fisheries afforded the principal part of the food for his children." [16]

After so many of the Indians had gone out of their way to be friendly, Lewis and Clark were greatly surprised at their first meeting with Chief Twisted Hair, whom they thought to be their warmest friend.

"The Twisted Hair received us very coolly," Lewis wrote, "an occurrence as unexpected as it was unaccountable to us. He shortly began to speak with a loud voice and in an angry manner. When he had ceased to speak, he was answered by the Cutnose Chief, or Neesh-ne-park-kee-ook. We readily discovered that a violent quarrel had taken place between these Chiefs but at that instant knew not the cause; we afterward learned that it was on the subject of our horses." [17]

Having heard earlier that "the natives had discovered the deposit of our saddles and taken them away and that our horses were much scattered, we were very anxious to learn the particulars or truth of these reports," Lewis wrote.

Getting at the truth proved difficult.

Somewhere along the way the Americans had picked up a Shoshone boy who could speak the Nez Perce tongue and translate it to the Shoshone woman, Sacajawea, who passed it on to her husband, Charbonneau, who then put it in English.

13. Ibid., p. 355.
14. Ibid., p. 361.
15. Ibid., p. 370.
16. Ibid., vol. 5, p. 8.
17. Ibid., p. 5.

This team of interpreters was called in now. But its most important link clammed up.

"The Shoshone boy refused to speak," Lewis wrote in exasperation. "He alleged it was a quarrel between two Chiefs and that he had no business with it. It was in vain that we urged that his interpreting what we said on this subject was not taking the responsibility of the interference on himself — he remained obstinately silent."

George Drewyer, a party member skilled both as a hunter and a sign language expert, returned to camp in an hour or so and was appealed to for help.

"We sent him to the Twisted Hair to make some enquiries relative to our horses and saddles and to ask him to come and smoke with us. The Twisted Hair accepted the invitation and came to our fire. The Twisted Hair informed us that according to the promise he had made us when he separated from us at the falls of the Columbia he collected our horses on his return and took charge of them; that about this time the Cutnose or Nessh-ne-park-kee-ook and Tun-nach-e-moo-toolt or the Broken Arm returned from a war excursion against the Shoshones on the South branch of Lewis's river, which had caused their absence when we were in this neighborhood; that these men had become dissatisfied with him in consequence of our having confided the horses to his care; and that they were eternally quarreling with him insomuch that he thought it best, as he was an old man, to relinquish any further attention to the horses; that they had consequently become scattered; that most of the horses were near this place, a part were in the forks between the Chopunnish and *Koos-kooskee* rivers, and three or four others were at the lodge of the Broken Arm about half a days march higher up the river.

"He informed us with respect to our saddles that on the rise of the water this spring the earth had fallen from the door of the cache and exposed the saddles. He being informed of their situation, had taken them up and placed them in another cache, where they were at this time. He said it was probable that a part of them had fallen into the water but of this he was not certain. The Twisted Hair said if we would spend the day tomorrow at his lodge, which was only a few miles from hence and on the road leading to the Broken Arm's lodge, he would collect such of our horses as were near this place and our saddles, that he would also send some young men over the *Koos-koos-kee* to collect those in the forks and bring them to the lodge of the Broken Arm to meet us.

"He advised us to go to the lodge of the Broken Arm, as he said he was a Chief of great eminence among them, and promised to accompany us thither if we wished him. We told him that we would take his advice in every particular, that we had confided the horses to his care and expected that he would collect them and deliver them to us, which, when he performed, we should pay him the two guns and ammuni-

tion we had promised him for that service. He seemed much pleased and promised his utmost exertions.

"We sent Drewyer to the Cut Nose, who also came to our fire and smoked with ourselves and the Twisted Hair. We took occasion in the course of the evening to express our regret that there should be a misunderstanding between these Chiefs. The Cut Nose told us in the presence of the Twisted Hair that he, the Twisted Hair, was a bad old man, that he wore two faces, that instead of taking care of our horses as he had promised us that he had suffered his young men to ride them hunting and had injured them very much; that this was the cause why himself and the Broken Arm had forbid his using them. The other made no reply."[18]

If George Drewyer obtained all this information by using sign language and the few Nez Perce words he had learned, it is a tribute to his skill and to the fluency of the "hand-talk" medium. At any rate, late in the evening, next day

"the Twisted Hair and Willard returned; they brought about half of our saddles, and some powder and lead which had been buried at that place. My saddle was among the number of those which were lost. About the same time the young men arrived with 21 of our horses. The greater part were in fine order. Five of them appeared to have been so much injured by the Indians riding them last fall that they had not yet recovered and were in low order. Three others had sore backs . . .

"The Cut Nose lodged with the Twisted Hair. I believe they have become good friends again."[19]

Located in the Kamiah valley some sixteen miles upriver, the village of Chief Broken Arm had

18. Ibid., pp. 5–7.
19. Ibid., pp. 12–13.

Mat Tepee Indian Village

made elaborate preparations to honor the explorers. When their party arrived, the American flag left there the previous fall

"was now displayed on a staff placed at no great distance from the lodge. Underneath the flag the Chief met my friend, Captain Clark, and conducted him about 80 yards to a place on the bank of the creek where he requested we should camp. I came up in a few minutes and we collected the Chiefs and men of consideration, smoked with them, and stated our situation with respect to provisions.

"The Chief spoke to his people and they produced us about two bushels of the quamas [camas] roots, dryed, four cakes of the bread of cows [kouse], and a dried salmon trout [steelhead]. We thanked them for this store of provision but informed them that our men not being accustomed to live on roots alone we feared it would make them sick, to obviate which we proposed exchanging a good horse in rather low order for a young horse in tolerable order, with a view to kill.

"The hospitality of the chief revolted at the idea of an exchange. He told us that his young men had a great abundance of young horses, and if we wished to eat them we should be furnished with as many as we wanted, Accordingly, they soon produced us two fat young horses . . .

"This is a much greater act of hospitality than any we have witnessed from any nation or tribe since we have passed the Rocky Mountains."[20]

In addition to providing the party with food, Chief Broken Arm "had a large conic lodge of leather erected for our reception and a parcel of wood collected and laid at the door, after which he invited Captain Clark and myself to make that lodge our home while we remained with him . . ."

Lewis wrote that Chief Broken Arm's village consisted of

"one house only, which is 150 feet in length, built in the usual form of sticks, mats, and dry grass. It contains twenty-four fires and about double that number families. From appearances, I presume they could raise 100 fighting men. The noise of their women pounding roots reminds me of a nail factory."[21]

With living arrangements settled and representatives present from most of the outlying bands, the time had come to have a serious talk.

"We now pretty well informed ourselves that Tunnach-e-moo-toolt, Neesh-ne-park-kee-ook, Yoompark-kar-tim, and Ho-has-till-pilp were the principal Chiefs of the Chopunnish nation and rank in the order here mentioned," Lewis wrote. "As all those chiefs were present in our lodge, we thought it a favorable time to repeat what had been said yesterday and to enter more minutely into the views of our government with respect to the inhabitants of this western part of the continent."[22]

What the government wished to do, Lewis and Clark told the Nez Perces, was establish trading posts "for their relief" and "restore peace and harmony among the natives." In order to show the Indians how big, powerful, and wealthy the United States was, the two captains drew a map of the country "with a coal on a mat" and spent nearly half a day relaying information through English, French, Minataree, Shoshone, and the Nez Perce language.

The process, wrote Clark, was "tegious."

After the council was over:

"We amused ourselves with shewing them the power of magnetism, the spye glass, compass, watch, airgun, and sundry other items," Lewis wrote. "They informed us that after we had left the Minatarees last spring three of their people had visited that nation and that they had informed them of us and told them we had such things in our possession but that they could not place confidence in the information until they had now witnessed it themselves."[23]

After exchanging shirts with Captain Clark as a token of lasting friendship, Chief Broken Arm told him:

"They had listened to our advice and the whole nation were determined to follow it; that they had only one heart and one tongue on this subject; that they wished to be at peace with all nations. Some of their men would accompany us to the Missouri."[24]

While Captain Clark was willing to prescribe simple medicines for ordinary ailments, he was reluctant to attempt to cure a Nez Perce chief who had been totally paralyzed for several years, even though the Indian's relatives implored him to do something. Making a wild guess that the paralysis might have been brought on by a root diet, Clark finally recommended

"a diet of fish and flesh for this man and a cold bath every morning. We had also given him a few doses of cream of tartar and flour of sulphur, to be repeated every third day. This poor wretch thinks that he feels himself somewhat better, but to me there appears to be no visible alteration . . ."

Still, the relatives persisted in bringing the chief back for further treatment, so in desperation Clark told them that he should be given daily sweat

20. Ibid., pp. 14–15. Italics mine.
21. p. 16.
22. Ibid., p. 19.
23. Ibid.
24. Ibid., p. 27.

baths, followed by doses of laudanum to relieve his great pain.

"They all appear extremely attentive to this sick man, notwithstanding he had been sick and helpless upwards of three years," Lewis wrote. "The Chopunnish appear to be very attentive and kind to their aged people and treat their woman with more respect than the nations of the Missouri."[25]

Much to the surprise of Captain Clark, the treatment proved effective, for, after it had been continued for several weeks, he wrote:

"The Sick Chief is much mended. He can bear his weight on his legs and recovers his strength."[26]

While waiting for the snow to melt in the high country to the east, the whites were given a demonstration of Nez Perce skill with horses. Clark already had observed:

"These people have immense herds of horses, 50 or 60 or a hundred head is not unusual for an individual to possess."[27]

But when it came to trading, the Nez Perces were shrewd bargainers.

"We made several attempts to exchange our stallions for geldings or mares, without success," Clark wrote. "We even offered two for one. These horses [stallions] are troublesome and cut each other very much. As we can't exchange them, we think it best to castrate them and begin the operation this evening. One of the Indians present offered his services on this occasion. He cut them without tying the string of the stone, as is usual. He scraped it very clean and separated it before he cut it."[28]

Later, Clark reported:

"Our horses are all recovering. I have no hestiation in declaring that I believe that the Indian method of gelding is preferable to that practiced by ourselves."[29]

After giving the headmen time to think over and discuss the matters presented to them by the whites, Chief Broken Arm prepared a feast of roots and kouse-flour-thickened soup, then proposed that they vote in a unique way.

"He concluded by inviting all such men as had resolved to abide by the decree of the council to come and eat, and requested such as would not be bound to show themselves by not partaking of the feast," Clark wrote. "There was not one dissenting vote on this great national question, but all swallowed their objections, if any they had, very cheerfully with their mush."[30]

During the harangue by Chief Broken Arm, Captain Clark noted that the women "cried, wrung their hands, tore their hair, and appeared to be in the utmost distress," an apparently ritual protest against a major change in tribal policy toward its enemy neighbors.

In a final speech the great war chief said that the Nez Perces would welcome trade with the whites, that it would give them much pleasure to be at peace with other tribes, that they were poor but their hearts were good, and that "on the subject of one of their chiefs accompanying us to the land of the white men, they could not yet determine, but that they would let us know before we left them."

Clark was concerned about getting across Lolo Pass, where snowdrifts still lay deep on the rugged trail. On June 3, 1806, the Nez Perces told him that he should be able to cross Lolo "in twelve or fourteen days."

Though Chief Cut Nose had informed them that two young chiefs "would overtake us with a view to accompany us to the Falls of the Missouri and probably to the Seat of our Government,"[31] the party impatiently set out for the mountains without waiting for its guides — and soon regretted it. On June 16 Clark wrote:

"A great quantity of snow . . . in many places the banks are four feet deep . . . our route this evening was over the snow which has become sufficiently firm to bear our horses, otherwise it would have been impossible for us to proceed, as it lay in immense masses in some places eight or ten feet deep. We found much difficulty in finding the road . . ."

Next day:

"We found ourselves enveloped in snow from eight to twelve feet deep even on the south side of the mountain. I was in front and could only pursue the direction of the road by the trees which had been peeled by the natives for the inner bark, of which they scraped and ate . . . one mile further to the top of the mountain where I found the snow from twelve to fifteen feet deep . . . here was winter with all its rigors . . . we knew it would require four days to reach the point where we would find food for our horses . . .

"Under these circumstances, we conceived it madness to proceed without a guide . . . we therefore came to the resolution to return . . . we began our retrogade

25. Ibid., p. 69.
26. Ibid., p. 118.
27. Ibid., p. 31.
28. Ibid., p. 36.
29. Ibid., p. 100.
30. Ibid., p. 79.
31. Ibid., p. 132.

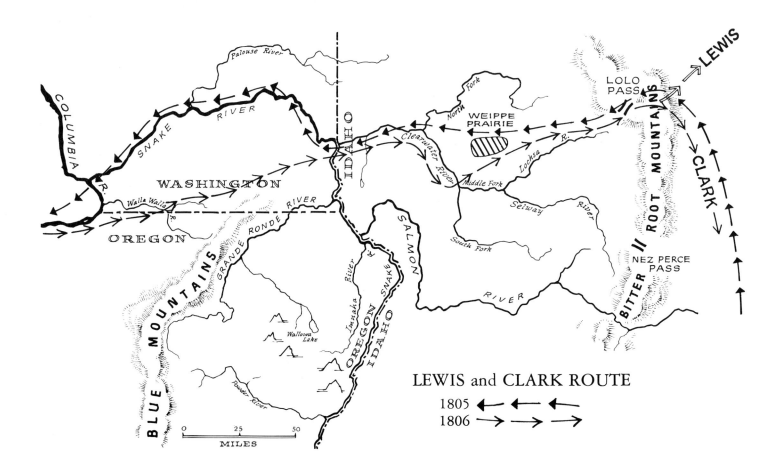

LEWIS and CLARK ROUTE
1805 ← ← ←
1806 → → →

march at 1 P.M. . . . *this is the first time since we have been on this tour that we have ever been compelled to retreat.*"[32]

But the Nez Perces had not forgotten their promise to supply the party with guides. On June 23,

"Shannon and Drewyer brought with them three Indians who had consented to accompany us to the falls of the Missouri [Great Falls] for the compensation of two guns. One of these is the brother of the Cut Nose; the other two are the same who presented Captain Lewis and myself with a horse on a former occasion at the lodge of the Broken Arm, and who promised to pursue us in nine days after we left the river. These are all young men of good character and much respected by their nation."[33]

That evening the Indians entertained the explorers by setting the branches of a fir tree afire "to bring fair weather for our journey." One of them "complained of being unwell . . . generally the prelude to his abandoning any enterprise with which

he is not well pleased," but next morning he felt fine and continued with the party.

On June 27 the party neared the crest of Lolo Pass, and at Indian Post Office:

"By the request of the guides we halted a few minutes on an elevated point and smoked a pipe. On this eminence the natives have raised a conic mound of stones six or eight feet high and erected a pine pole fifteen feet long. From this place we had an extensive view of these stupendous mountains . . . without the assistance of our guides, I doubt much whether we who had once passed this way could find our way to Travelers Rest . . .

"These Indians are most admirable pilots."[34]

Reaching Travelers Rest Creek at the eastern foot of the Lolo Trail June 29, the explorers in-

32. Ibid., p. 144. Italics mine.
33. Ibid., p. 166.
34. Ibid., p. 180.

From a painting by Gustavus Sohon   *Courtesy Penrose Library, Whitman College*
Entrance to the Bitter Root Mountains by the Lo Lo Fork

Photo by H. W. Steward   *Courtesy Idaho Historical Society*
Nez Perce Indian post office on Lolo Trail

dulged themselves in the luxury of baths in the hot springs, while their weary horses grazed on the new grass.

"In the course of the day, we had much conversation with the Indians by signs, our only mode of communicating our ideas," Lewis wrote on July 2. "They informed us that they wished to go in search of the *Cotlashoots,* their friends, and intended leaving us tomorrow morning. I prevailed on them to go with me as far as the east branch of Clark's river and put me on the road to the Missouri. I gave the Chief a medal of the small size; he insisted on exchanging names with me according to their customs, which was accordingly done. I was called Yo-me-kol-lick, which interpreted as 'the white bearskin folded.'"[35]

Exactly who "their friends, the *Cotlashoots,*" were is not clear. After learning that the Lewis and Clark party planned to split up here, with Clark and the majority of the men heading east toward the Yellowstone River while Lewis and the rest traveled northeast toward the Marias River and the heart of the Blackfoot country, the Nez Perce guides probably decided that the venture was too risky for them. Not wishing to offend the whites by flatly declining to accompany them further, they simply found pressing business that called them elsewhere.

What is clear is the high regard Meriwether Lewis and his Nez Perce namesake held for each other. The grizzly bear was respected above all animals, and for as long as he might live the young Indian chief could bear his white name with honor.

On July 4, 1806, Captain Lewis wrote:

"I now ordered the horses saddled, smoked a pipe with these friendly people, and at noon bade them adieu. . . . These affectionate people, our guides, betrayed every emotion of unfeigned regret at separating from us."[36]

Captain William Clark, in summing up the hardships of crossing and recrossing Lolo Pass, said he had "experienced cold and hunger of which I shall ever remember."

He noted that on the westward trip, from September 14 to 19, 1805, snow fell on the party most of the time and that on the eastward journey, be-

35. Ibid., p. 187.
36. Ibid., p. 175n.

From a painting by John Mix Stanley   *Courtesy Penrose Library, Whitman College*
Hot Springs at the source of Lou Lou Fork, Bitter Root Mountains, looking West.

tween June 24 and 28, 1806, the snowdrifts had been "six to eight feet deep all the way."

Passable only three months out of the year, the road into the land of the Nez Perces from the buffalo country was not an easy one. But over it and other difficult trails, in time to come, would travel a number of white men from the East — not all of whom would be as friendly and understanding as Captain Meriwether Lewis and Captain William Clark.

CHAPTER FIVE

BEAVER AND EMPIRE: 1806–1830

But the Indians, free and independent as the air they breathed or the wind that blew, could not brook the restraint which the whites were always affecting to exercise over them.
— Alexander Ross, 1812

THE APPREHENSION OF the Nez Perce guides that Captain Lewis would run into trouble in the Marias River country proved to be well founded. Encountering a group of eight Piegans — one of three Blackfoot tribes — Lewis smoked with them and exchanged information by means of sign language.

Though the Indians appeared to welcome the prospect of making peace with the Flatheads and Nez Perces and trading with the Americans, whom Lewis said soon would establish a post in their country, they waited only until the whites relaxed their guard, then made a bold attempt to steal the party's rifles and horses. During the ensuing fight one Piegan was stabbed to death and another was shot in the belly. After a brief fracas on a branch of the Marias which Lewis named Battle River, the two parties fled in opposite directions as fast as their horses could run.

Minor as the encounter was in terms of casualties, its results were extremely serious. First, it created a bitter enmity between Americans and the Blackfeet, which would last for fifty years. Second, it gave British traders a firm claim to the support of the Blackfeet in the decades-long struggle over the then not-so-manifest destiny of the Pacific Northwest.

On the surface, British and American fur companies were merely competing for the pelt of a timid, hard-working, family-oriented rodent — the beaver. But the real prize was the immensely valuable empire-sized country drained by the Columbia River and its tributaries.

The land of the Nez Perces lay in the exact center of this area, which for many years would be claimed by two great nations and fought over by three powerful, greedy, monopolistic companies with only one common goal — profit.

Trapping beaver in the wilderness was cold, fatiguing, dangerous work. Since the most productive ponds and streams lay in high country fed by melting snowbanks, the temperature of the water that must be waded to make sets was only a few degrees above freezing. Since late autumn, winter, and early spring were the seasons when fur was prime, the temperature of the air ranged from uncomfortably cool to unbearably frigid. Whether white, Indian, or a mixture of both, trappers got their best results when they worked in groups of no more than three — two of the men making sets and lifts while the third person, ideally an Indian wife of one of the partners, tended camp, cooked meals, and dressed out the pelts.

Such a small party was highly vulnerable to attack, and with buyers of plews indifferent as to how they had been obtained, so long as they could be purchased cheaply, the woods usually were full of hostiles. Perpetually wet and half frozen, weighed down with traps and pelts, perfumed to high heaven by the pungent castoreum with which beaver were lured to their doom, eternally on the move through difficult, dangerous country, often on the verge of starvation, and eternally in debt to the fur company that had outfitted him, the trapper led a miserable life.

Aware of this, the Nez Perces refused to become trappers.

As Meriwether Lewis made his way down the Missouri River August 12, 1806, he met two white men from Illinois, Joseph Dixon and Forrest Hancock.

"They informed me that they had left the Illinois in the summer of 1804," Lewis wrote, "since which time they had been searching the Missouri, hunting and trapping beaver . . . they as yet had caught little beaver, but were still determined to proceed . . ."[1]

They were the vanguard of a legion of adventurous men who, during the next thirty years, would trap and explore every stream, valley, mountain, and plain in the American West.

In Canada the monolithic Hudson's Bay Company and its rambunctious new rival, the North West Company, were moving westward, too, fighting each other every step of the way but never losing sight of the goal they both coveted, the furs of the Columbia River system. In St. Louis the Missouri Fur Company was being organized, with William Clark as one of the partners. In New York a German immigrant named John Jacob Astor conceived a grandiose scheme that would give him control of the Pacific fur trade from California to Alaska — if it worked. By sea he would send a well-supplied ship to the mouth of the Columbia, where a trading post would be built. By land he would send a party of men up the Missouri and through the land of the Nez Perces over the route taken by Lewis and Clark. Along the way small groups of trappers would drop off when they reached good beaver country, trap for a season, then send or bring their furs to the new post at the mouth of the Columbia.

In concept, the plan was sound; in execution, it went awry.

Problems arose at once. Captain Jonathan Thorn, commander of the supply ship, *Tonquin,* proved to be a thick-headed martinet totally lacking in understanding and judgment. After a near-mutiny at sea and the loss of eight men by drowning at the mouth of the Columbia, Thorn got himself and his crew attacked and killed by Indians in Nootka Sound, with a briefly surviving crew member managing to complete the destruction by creeping to the powder magazine, lighting a match, and blowing himself, the ship, and a number of Indians into oblivion. Later, two other Astor supply ships sent around Cape Horn were lost with all their goods and a number of lives.

The overland effort also met disaster. Unable to hire a sufficient number of experienced Americans, Astor employed as trappers and took in as partners a number of French-Canadians, Scotchmen, Irishmen, and Britishers, whose loyalties inclined more toward the North West Company than toward his own fledgling enterprise. One of the men he took in as a partner was the former North Wester, Donald MacKenzie, whom Alexander Ross describes as a big, powerful man, weighing 312 pounds. Another was an American named Wilson Price Hunt, a man whose loyalty to Astor was complete but whose decisions as a leader often were vacillating and weak.

The Hunt party contained sixty-four people and a large quantity of trade goods, traps, ammunition, and baggage. Most of its members were seasoned frontiersmen. Though the original plan had been to take the water route west, as Lewis and Clark had done, Hunt became concerned over the threatened hostility of the Blackfeet. He abandoned the Missouri in the land of the Aricaras and decided to make the rest of the journey by a more southerly route. Taking a leisurely month to trade his boats and extra supplies for horses, he traveled west through the Big Horn Mountains and the Wind River country and came into Jackson Hole by way of the Hoback River. There he detached a trapping party of four men, who would remain for the winter.

Because of the dawdling pace he had set, it was now September 26.

Crossing the Tetons, the party reached an abandoned trading post on Henry's Fork October 8, 1811. Here Hunt "committed the great mistake of the expedition."[2]

One hundred miles to the west over relatively easy terrain lay Lemhi Pass and the known trail blazed six years earlier by Lewis and Clark. With one hundred and eighteen horses, the party was well mounted. In four days it could easily have reached the land of the Shoshones, who were friendly and who would have been glad to supply the whites with a guide across the Nez Perce Pass or Lolo Trail. Once the party reached the Clearwater in the land of the even more hospitable Nez Perces, the rest of the journey would have been easy.

But to the waterway-oriented French-Canadians, Henry's Fork looked very inviting.

1. Bernard DeVoto, ed., *The Journals of Lewis and Clark* (Boston: Houghton Mifflin Co., 1953), p. 436.
2. Hiram Martin Chittenden, *American Fur Trade of the Far West* (1902; reprint ed., Stanford, Calif.: Academic Reprints, 1954), vol. 1, p. 191.

Hunt knew nothing about the country other than the fact that this southward-flowing river joined the Snake southwest of Jackson Hole and that the Snake flowed west, then north, and then west again, finally to meld its waters with those of the mighty Columbia. Local Indians he talked to by means of sign language warned him that the Snake was unnavigable. But the *voyageurs* in the party were the finest rivermen in North America. What did western Indians know about navigating white water, compared to what they knew? Furthermore, one of the partners was suffering "with an ailment that made riding a horse torture."

So Hunt made a bad decision.

"He yielded to the desires of the party, abandoned the horses, and decided to trust to the river the rest of the way. He at once set about manufacturing canoes, and this work was completed and the flotilla loaded within ten days."[3]

Detaching four more trappers to winter in the vicinity — plus the partner, Joseph Miller, who had grown so disgusted with the enterprise that he decided to give up his share — the party left its horses in the care of two Snake Indians and on October 19 embarked in fifteen canoes on the strong, dark, rapid stream.

"It was a delightful change, and the swift progress of the first day was for the time being a complete confirmation of the wisdom of having adopted it. But the satisfaction was of short duration. The river soon began to show its true character."[4]

As the true character of the river revealed itself, the *voyageurs* changed its name from Mad River, which they had first called it, to *La Maudite Rivière Enragée,* "The Accursed Mad River." In rock-strewn gorges and white water rapids expressively named the Devils Scuttle Hole and Caldron Linn, a boat was wrecked and one of the men, Antoine Clappine, drowned. Belatedly, Hunt suspended further attempts at navigation until the downstream hazards could be appraised.

His own inspection of a forty-mile stretch convinced him that the rapids could not be negotiated. Other members of the party thought differently, made the attempt with four boats, and lost them all. Faced with the grim prospect of being set afoot in the midst of the bleak Snake River desert (probably in the vicinity of Twin Falls) Hunt called "a bewildered counsel," out of which came the desperation-inspired decision to fragment the party into four smaller groups.

One would dig caves in which to cache excess supplies; one would head northwest toward the Nez Perce country; one would return to Henry's Fork for the horses left there; one would proceed downriver. Where and when the groups would reunite in the bleak, unknown terrain ahead was left mostly to chance.

After three days the group which had been sent back for the horses declared their mission too risky, turned around, and rejoined the men digging caches. Five days later the group sent downriver came back, reporting the Snake's waters absolutely unnavigable. The final decision was made to travel afoot. Dividing the party into two groups, one to follow the right and the other the left bank of the Snake, Hunt gave the order to march. It was November 9, and winter had come.

The wanderings, retrograde marches, and sufferings from cold, starvation, and illness were too prolonged and involved to be detailed here. Donald MacKenzie, Robert McClellan, and John Reed, leader of the most fortunate group, made their way across the mountains to the Clearwater in twenty-one days, and, with the help of the friendly Nez Perces, floated down the Snake and Columbia without serious incident, reaching Astoria January 18, 1812.[5]

Finding it impossible to follow the Snake through Hell's Canyon, the right and left bank parties reunited, made a midwinter crossing of the Blue Mountains over what would become the Oregon Trail, and reached the mouth of the Columbia on February 15. Behind, near Farewell Bend on Snake River, they had left half a dozen party members too weak or ill to travel, two men who had gotten lost, and the body of Baptise Prevost, who had become so frenzied at the sight of food he had "danced in a delirium of joy" in a canoe, upset it, and drowned.

In May 1812 the two lost men, Ramsey Crooks and John Day, were found wandering, naked, starving, and destitute, on the banks of the Columbia. One band of Indians, the Umatillas, had treated them kindly, fed them, and sent them on their way. Another, the Wishrams, had robbed them, stripped them, and turned them loose to die.

---

3. Ibid.

4. Ibid.

5. E. E. Rich, ed., *Peter Skene Ogden's Snake Country Journals, 1824–25 and 1825–26* (London: Hudson's Bay Record Society, 1950), vol. 13, p. xxxiv.

From a painting by John Mix Stanley   *Courtesy Penrose Library, Whitman College*
Falls of the Spokane River

Eventually found by white friends and taken to Astoria, Crooks recovered, but John Day became mentally deranged and did not regain his health until months later.

In order to forestall competetion with the British, the Astorians sent parties upriver to establish trading posts in three key locations: (1) Fort Okanogon, on the upper Columbia, with partner Ross Cox in charge; (2) Fort Spokane, on that river, with partner John Clarke in charge; and (3) Fort Nez Perces, near the juncture of the Clearwater and the Snake, with partner Donald MacKenzie in charge.

In view of the fact that the Nez Perces had been most receptive to the idea of having a trading post established in their territory, it is a curious irony of history that of the three American posts establihed at this time the one built by Donald MacKenzie was the least successful, the shortest lived, and the first to be abandoned.

Blame lay on three disparate happenings: a missing silver goblet, war between Great Britain and the United States, and the utter disdain of the proud Nez Perces for any work that could not be done while mounted on a galloping horse.

John Clarke, the Pacific Fur Company partner in charge of building the post in the Spokane country, appears to have been something of a dandy, accustomed to having his fine wines, well-set table, and purebred hunting dogs even when traveling in the most remote wilderness.

Going to and from the Spokane post, the trip up the Columbia and Snake to the mouth of the Palouse River was made by canoe. Here, arrangements were made with an accommodating Palouse chief to care for the boats in exchange for a modest amount of goods until they were needed again. Ethnically the Palouse Indians were a branch of the Nez Perce tribe, though the country in which they lived was far more arid and less appealing than that along the Clearwater and Salmon.

After a successful season at Fort Spokane, John Clarke loaded thirty-two horses with the furs he had gathered, departed the post May 25, 1813, and headed for the mouth of the Palouse River, which then was called Pavilion River. Reaching it in six days, he was pleased to find that the accommodating chief had taken good care of the company's canoes. He made him a present of some ammunition and tobacco and then set about transferring the contents of the horses' packs into the canoes for transport downriver to Fort Astoria.

"They set about packing up the different articles in order to embark," writes Alexander Ross, "and among others two silver goblets belonging to Mr. Clarke himself, who took this opportunity of showing them to the chief, and expatiated on their high value; then pouring a little wine into one of them made the chief drink out of it, telling him when done that he was a greater man now than ever he was before.

"The chief was delighted, and turning the goblet over and over in his hands, and looking at it with intense interest, handed it over to the next great man, and he to another, and so on till, like the pipe of peace, it had gone round the whole circle. The precious curiosity was then laid by, and the Indians retired.

"Next morning, however, the pearl of great price was gone! Everything in and about the camp was turned topsy-turvy in search of the silver goblet, but to no purpose. All business was now suspended — the goblet must be found. At last it was conjectured the Indians must have stolen it; and Mr. Clarke, with fury in his countenance, assembled the whole *Catatouch* [Palouse Indian] camp, and made known his loss — the loss of his silver goblet!

"He coaxed, he flattered, he threatened to bring down vengeance upon the whole tribe for the loss of his goblet, and, in his wrath and vexation, denounced death upon the offender should he be discovered. The poor Indians stood gazing in amazement; they sympathized with him, pitied him, and deplored his loss, and promised to do their utmost to find the goblet.

"With this solemn declaration they went off, the whole tribe was called together, the council sat, and soon afterwards they returned in a body, like messengers of peace, bringing the glad tidings to Mr. Clarke that the silver goblet was found. At the same time, the chief, stepping forward and spreading out his robe, laid the precious vessel before him.

" 'Where is the thief?' vociferated Mr. Clarke.

"The chief then pointed to a fellow sitting in the ring as the criminal.

" 'I swore,' said Mr. Clarke, 'that the thief should die, and white men never break their word.'

"The fellow was told of his fate; but he kept smiling, thinking himself, according to Indian custom, perfectly safe, for the moment the stolen article is returned to the rightful owner, according to the maxims of Indian law, the culprit is exonerated. Mr. Clarke, however, thought otherwise, and, like Herod of old, for the sake of his oath considered himself bound to put his threat into execution, and therefore instantly commanded the poor, unsuspecting wretch to be hung up; and hung he was accordingly; and the unhallowed deed was aggravated by the circumstance of their taking the poles of his own lodge to make the gallows.

"The Indians all the time could not believe that the whites were in earnest, till they beheld the lifeless body. The deed was, however, no sooner committed than Mr. Clarke grew alarmed. The chief, throwing down his robe on the ground, a sign of displeasure, harangued his people, who immediately mounted their fleetest horses, and scampered off in all directions to circulate the news and assemble the surrounding tribes, to take vengeance on the whites. In the meantime, leaving the enraged Indians to follow their inclinations, the canoes were thrown into the water, loaded, and down the current Mr. Clarke and his men pushed their way day and night till they reached the Walla Walla, where they arrived safe on the 4th of June."[6]

Earlier, Donald MacKenzie had led a party of men up the Snake to the mouth of the Clearwater, in whose vicinity he had built a post with the aim of trading with the Nez Perces. Unable to persuade the Nez Perces to trap for him, MacKenzie equipped a party of seven men and sent them out on a hunt for beaver.

"But they had to go to the mountains, and on their way thither the Indians annoyed them, stole their traps, and frightened them back to the post. M'Kenzie then resolved to abandon that post, and proceed further up the river . . ."[7]

Before taking this step, MacKenzie went to Fort Spokane to confer with John Clarke. While he was there, a partner in the North West Company, George McTavish, arrived with a strong reinforcement of men and goods from eastern Canada. McTavish bore a startling piece of news.

War had broken out between Great Britain and the United States.

Convinced that the struggling, so far unsuccessful, Pacific Fur Company could not possibly survive in the face of cutthroat competition and a major war, MacKenzie hurried back to his post near the mouth of the Clearwater, put his goods in cache, and set off with all his men for Astoria, where he arrived January 15, 1813. There he urged the other partners that the enterprise be abandoned. Partner McDougall agreed with MacKenzie that the sensible thing to do was sell out to the North West Company at the best price they could get. Partners Stuart and Clarke "viewed things in a different light, and condemned the proposed step as premature."[8]

Deciding to be prepared for any eventuality, Donald MacKenzie, headed back upriver to close down the post near the mouth of the Clearwater, recover the goods placed in cache, and bring them back to Astoria.

"He was mortified," Ross writes, "to find his cache robbed. The Indians indicated their guilt by their shyness, for scarcely one of them came to visit the trader. M'Kenzie therefore summoned the chiefs, and they appeared, expecting no doubt to receive something. When they were all seated, he opened the business of the cache, and demanded the goods; adding, that if they were given up, friendship would again be restored."[9]

After denying that they, personally, had had anything to do with the theft, the chiefs finally admitted and deplored the misconduct of their young men, then philosophically pointed out that the goods were gone now and there was nothing they could do about it. On that note, the conference ended.

"M'Kenzie at once resolved on a bold and hazardous step; namely, to dash into the heart of the Indian camp, and recover what he could. . . . [He] ordered Mr. Seaton, who commanded the men, to surround the first wigwam or lodge reached with charged bayonets, while he and Mr. Reed entered the lodge, ransacked it, turning everything topsy-turvy, and with their drawn daggers cutting and ripping open everything that might be supposed to conceal the stolen property. In this manner they went from one lodge to another till they had searched five or six with various success, when the chiefs demanded a parley, and gave M'Kenzie to understand that if he desisted they would do the business themselves, and more effectually."[10]

6. Alexander Ross, *Adventures of the First Settlers on the Oregon or Columbia River, 1810–13*, ed. Reuben Golden Thwaites (London, 1849; reprint ed., Glendale, Calif.: Arthur H. Clark Co., 1904), vol. 7, pp. 212–214.

7. Ibid., p. 216.

8. Ibid., p. 217.

9. Ibid.

10. Ibid., p. 218.

Agreeing to a truce, MacKenzie and Reed desisted in their destructive search. Within three hours the chiefs recovered most of the pilfered goods. Though the whites were "well pleased with their hairbreadth adventure, the Indians were determined to be even with them in another way."

That way was soon found.

In order to eat and to transport their goods when they started overland to the Columbia, the whites needed horses. But not a single horse would the Nez Perces sell them.

"All intercourse between the parties was at an end; not an Indian was to be seen about M'Kenzie's camp . . ."

Not by daylight, that is. For MacKenzie, resourceful man that he was, managed to employ five Nez Perces, who reported to him every night, as spies "to watch the motions of the Indians, and through them he knew every move in the hostile camp."[11]

The first Indian move was an attempt to starve the whites by refusing to sell them horses. MacKenzie countered by sending ten or twelve well-armed men to the grazing grounds of the Nez Perce herds every few days, carrying with them the quantity of trade articles customarily paid for a horse. While the Indians watched in consternation, the whites shot the fattest horse they could find, butchered it, carried the flesh back to camp, and left the bundle of trade goods stuck up on a pole alongside the head of the dead horse.

"This manoeuver succeeded several times, and annoyed the Indians very much; some of them lost their best horses by it."[12]

The next move of the Nez Perces, Ross says, was a decision to attack the camp of the whites. However, they had a problem — a shortage of powder and ball for their rifles. The solution? An offer to sell horses to the whites, taking only powder and ball in payment, until enough ammunition had been acquired to mount a successful attack.

Uncharitably, MacKenzie refused to trade on these terms. So the attack was indefinitely postponed.

Moving his camp to an island in the middle of the river where his party could not be taken by surprise, MacKenzie continued to send a well-armed butchering party into the Nez Perce horse herd every few days, always leaving a bundle of trade goods near the horse's head so that its owner

could not say he had not been paid. Finally growing tired of these predatory excursions, the Nez Perces offered a deal: They would sell horses to the whites at the usual price if the whites would give up their marauding practices.

MacKenzie accepted.

"The trade in horses went on briskly, and without interruption," Ross writes, "M'Kenzie getting all his wants supplied. He bought, besides, an extra reserve of eight horses for contingencies, which he sent off to Spokane; and on the return of his men he left the island, apparently on good terms with the Indians."[13]

Apparently the Nez Perces respected a trader who paid a fair price for what he bought, even though he took what he wanted without the seller's consent.

Or it may be they had a sense of humor.

Leaving the now-defunct post in late May, MacKenzie and his men traveled overland to the Columbia, reaching the mouth of the Walla Walla June 1.

"We were at a loss to account for the unusual movement and stir among the Indians, who seemed to be assembling from all quarters in great haste," Ross writes. "The mystery was, however, soon cleared up when Mr. Clarke joined us, and related the affair of the silver goblet . . .

"What could any man say? The reckless deed had been committed, and Clarke's countenance fell when the general voice of disapprobation was raised against him."[14]

Ross relates that Tum-me-a-ta-pam, a Walla Walla chief who long had been friendly to the whites, came riding up to their camp at full speed.

"What have you done, my friends?" called out the old and agitated chief. "You have spilt blood on our lands!" Pointing to a cloud of dust raised by a group of Indians riding angrily back and forth, the chief cried, "There, my friends, do you see them? What can I do?"

Understanding the meaning of his rhetorical question — that he could and would do nothing — Ross writes:

"Taking the hint, we lost no time. Tents were struck . . . kettles and dishes were all huddled together into the

11. Ibid., p. 219.
12. Ibid., p. 220.
13. Ibid., p. 221.
14. Ibid., p. 222.

canoe, and, embarking pell-mell, we pushed with all haste from the inauspicious shore . . ."[15]

After a great deal of bickering among themselves and some vociferous bargaining with representatives of the North West Company, the partners of the Pacific Fur Company currently in residence at Fort Astoria sold the post, its trade goods, and furs to the British-owned company. For the time being at least, the ill-fated Astor venture was finished.

And ill-fated it certainly had been. In contrast to the Lewis and Clark expedition, which had lost only one man, the Astor by-sea and by-land parties over a similar period of time had registered sixty-five fatalities.[16]

By a fluke of fate the enterprise ended on a happy, if slightly cockeyed, note.

Shortly after the North West Company took over the post, renaming it Fort George, a British man-of-war, the *Raccoon,* dropped anchor, and its captain came ashore. A state of war now existed between Great Britain and the United States, he told the traders, and he had orders to seize the post. It's already British property, you say? No matter. He would seize it anyway.[17]

When the war ended, one of the peace treaty terms required that all property seized by Great Britain must be returned to the United States.[18] The question arose: did sale or seizure take precedence? It was decided that seizure did. In a comic-opera scene, Fort Astoria — that is, Fort George — was solemnly given back to representatives of its former American owners, who then, having gone to work for the North West Company, reaffirmed its sale and solemnly turned it over to the British company.

Thus, on a technicality, Astor managed to sell out and withdraw from the fur business in the Pacific Northwest without compromising his country's political claims to sovereignty in the region. Now the American government took steps to solidify those claims.

The area in dispute lay between the forty-second and forty-ninth parallels and extended from the Continental Divide westward to the Pacific Ocean. In a treaty made with Spain, the United States persuaded that nation to set its northern limits at the forty-second parallel.[19] But Great Britain, a more stubborn bargainer, refused to give up its claims to the Snake and Columbia rivers. The result was the Joint Occupancy Treaty of 1818,

which granted access to the area to citizens of both English-speaking countries for ten years. Given this period of grace, future diplomats might be able to settle the question peacefully. If not, there was always war.

Following the sale of the Pacific Fur Company November 12, 1813, Donald MacKenzie went East, delivered the proceeds, and "endeavoured to associate himself again with Astor but was unable to do so because Astor was unhappy over the sale of his company."

So MacKenzie went to work for the North West Company and returned to Fort George in October 1816.[20]

He found things going badly. James Keith, head trader at the fort, was doing very little business in the upriver country. He was accustomed to staying in a fixed post to which Indian and mixed-blood trappers brought their furs. He used natural waterways and canoes, rather than horses, to transport supplies and plews. Donald MacKenzie, with his usual show of energy, proposed substituting horses for canoes, traveling with well-equipped parties of trappers over the country where beaver were to be found, and aggressively harvesting the pelts.

"His primary object was to conclude an arrangement with the Nez Perces, and in the Snake country to conciliate the Indians, with a view to open the way for extending the trade."[21]

For a year and a half Keith strongly opposed this idea, but at length the directors of the company

"grew tired of the obstructionist tactics of Keith, and in their 1818 meeting gave him direct and peremptory orders to furnish MacKenzie with 100 men and allow him to establish a fort among the Nez Perces Indians. Men and materials were furnished, and on July 11, 1818, the brigade arrived at the new fort site on the east bank of

15. Ibid. Versions of this incident as told by Ross Cox and Washington Irving vary in details but agree on the main points — that the Indian was hanged, that John Clarke's contemporaries condemned him for a lack of judgment, and that the act had dire consequences insofar as future relations with the Indians of the area were concerned.
16. Chittenden, *Fur Trade,* Vol. 2, p.905.
17. Hubert Howe Bancroft, *History of the Northwest Coast. Works,* vol. 28 (San Francisco, 1884), p. 331.
18. Treaty of Ghent, 1814.
19. February 22, 1819.
20. *Ogden's Journals,* vol. 12, p. xxx.
21. Ibid., p. xxi.

From a painting by John Mix Stanley   Courtesy Penrose Library, Whitman College
Old Fort Walla Walla

the Columbia River, about a half mile from the mouth of the Walla Walla River."[22]

MacKenzie had several good reasons for establishing the new post here instead of at the juncture of the Clearwater and the Snake, 130 miles to the east, where his earlier trading post had been located. For all practical purposes the mouth of the Walla Walla was the head of upriver canoe travel on the Columbia; from here on, horses supplied both convenient transport and necessary food. Indian tribes living in the area — Walla Walla, Cayuse, amd Umatilla — owned vast herds of horses and were so closely related, intermarried, and associated by customs and language with the Nez Perces that they commonly were grouped under that name.

"After days of negotiation trade was established with the Nez Perces," Alexander Ross writes, "and about 280 horses were secured. The party left the fort at the end of September, 1818. It consisted of 55 men, 195 horses, 300 beaver traps, and a considerable stock of merchandise under command of MacKenzie."[23]

Ross was left behind to finish and man the fort. Built of sawn timbers twenty feet long, two and a half feet broad, and six inches thick, Fort Nez Perces was designed as an unusually strong station, Ross writes, "on account of the many war-like tribes that infest the country."

A system of double doors and walls, an outer gate that opened and shut by a pulley, and an eighteen-inch-square aperture secured with an iron door, through which all trade with the Indians was conducted, gave security to the clerks. Neither MacKenzie nor the Indians liked the arrangement, but Ross did. In fact, he thought it worked so well "that it ought to be adopted wherever the natives are either hostile or troublesome."[24]

A strong gallery, five feet broad, ran all around the enclosure below the top of the palisades; at each angle a 200-gallon water reservoir was placed as protection against fire, a danger to be dreaded in this extremely dry, hot, windy climate.

"Our weapons of defence were composed of four pieces of ordnance from one to three pounds, besides ten wall pieces or swivels, sixty stand of muskets and bayonets, twenty boarding pikes, and a box of hand grenades. The fort was defended by two strong wooden bastions and a culverin above the gate. It was therefore at once the strongest and most complete fort west of the Rocky Mountains and might be called the Gibralter of the Columbia."[25]

Meanwhile, MacKenzie crossed the Blue Mountains and continued on into the Snake River country. Along the Boise River and further to the east on Bear River and Green River he found streams rich in beaver. Returning to Fort Nez Perces with a good catch of furs in midwinter, he set out again early next spring with a small party, this time going up the Snake from the mouth of the Clearwater by barge in order to determine the navigability of the river in the Hell's Canyon sector.

Incredibly, he made it, reaching the vicinity of Farewell Bend before sending the barge and four of his men back downriver. Since the round trip had required two months of superhuman effort, it was not repeated. In fact, fifty years would pass before a boat of any kind ventured into the treacherous rapids of Hell's Canyon again.

For four successive years MacKenzie led parties of trappers out of Fort Nez Perces to work the streams of the Snake River watershed. Each trip he brought back more plews than the year before. On June 22, 1820, for example, he came in with 154 horses loaded with beaver, nearly double the catch of earlier years. Taking just twelve days to rest his horses and men, he

"headed back to the Snake Country on July 4, 1820, with a party of seventy men. He returned on July 10, 1821, with returns even better than the preceding year and without the loss of a single man."[26]

Though Donald MacKenzie had worked out a successful system for trapping the upriver country,

22. Ibid., p. xxxii.
23. Ibid.
24. Alexander Ross, *The Fur Hunters of the Far West*, ed. Kenneth Spaulding (London: Smith Elder, 1855; reprint ed. Norman: University of Oklahoma Press, 1956), pp. 144–145.
25. Ibid., p. 146.
26. *Ogden's Journals*, vol. 13, p. xxxiv.

his efforts to make peace between the Nez Perces and the Snakes (Shoshones) were a dismal failure.

Equally unproductive were MacKenzie's attempts to teach the Iroquois members of his trapping party the value of the horses, traps, and supplies with which he outfitted them at the beginning of each trip. Though presumably civilized and educated by their long contact with the whites in eastern Canada, they were as improvident as children, invariably getting the short end of the trade when dickering with the shrewd Nez Perces.

In spite of his failures in these areas MacKenzie brought in so many plews that the North West Company made him a chief factor when he returned to the East. Of him, Alexander Ross wrote admiringly:

"Capable of enduring fatigue and privations, no labour appeared too great, no hardship too severe . . . but [he] had a great aversion to writing, preferring to leave the details of his adventures to the pen of others.

"To travel a day's journey on snowshoes was his delight; but he detested spending five minutes scribbling in a journal. His traveling notes were often kept on a beaver skin written hieroglyphically with a pencil or a piece of coal, and he would often complain of the drudgery of keeping accounts. When asked why he did not like to write his answer was, 'We must have something for others to do.'

"Few men could fathom his mind, yet his inquisitiveness to know the minds and opinions of others had no bounds. Every man he met was his companion; and when not asleep, he was always upon foot strolling backward and forward full of plans and projects, and so peculiar was this pedestrian habit that he went by the name of 'Perpetual Motion.' "[27]

After years of fierce, bloody competition, the North West Company and the Hudson's Bay Company made peace by merging March 20, 1821. MacKenzie left the country and went East. In 1824 the Hudson's Bay Company completed the take over by acquiring all rights to the stock of its formal rival. Now the competition was not between two companies for beaver but between two nations for ownership of an empire.

With Astoria sold, the American trading posts in the interior abandoned, and only an occasional trapper venturing across the Rockies during the years between 1813 and 1823, the chances that this vast region would fall into American hands on a "squatters' rights" basis seemed remote. But to make absolutely sure the area became British, George Simpson, head of the Hudson's Bay Company in North America, took ruthless measures.

As a conservation policy, it was usual company practice to trap a fur-bearing district only once every five years, so as not to wipe out its beaver population. But Simpson decided the surest way to keep Americans out of the Snake River watershed was to eradicate its only attraction — beaver. With that goal in mind, he ordered yearly parties to go out and "strip the country bare."

Between 1821 and 1828, they did exactly that.

From Fort Nez Perces, from Spokane House, or from Flathead Post, expeditions were sent out each year as soon as the beaver plews turned

Courtesy Oregon Historical Society

Old Fort Walla Walla

prime in the fall and were kept in the field until summer made then valueless.

To anyone familiar with the ruggedness, deep snows, and frigid high-country winters of the Snake River watershed, it is difficult to believe that a large body of men and horses, laden with traps and baggage, could traverse it from November until June and survive by living off the land, let alone wading icy ponds and creeks and making a substantial catch of beaver. Add the fact that hostile Blackfeet, thieving Crows, and Snakes made treacherous by hunger were an ever-present danger, and the feats accomplished by the trapping parties become incredible.

It took a special kind of man to lead such a party, and for some of these men once was

27. Ross, *Fur Hunters,* pp. 208–209.

enough. For example, in 1823 a dour Scot named Finan McDonald spent several months leading a party through the country. Upon his return he reported four thousand skins collected, six white men and sixty-eight Indians killed, than added this bitter comment:

"I got Safe home from the Snake Cuntre, thank God, and when that Cuntre will see me agane the Beaver will have Goulde Skin."[28]

Alexander Ross, who stayed on in service with the Hudson's Bay Company, gives an interesting description of a trapping expedition which he headed. Though authorized to hire eighty men, he could muster only forty at Spokane House "many of them questionable." Leaving there on November 12 he preceeded to Flathead Post, where he picked up fourteen more, making his party

"in all, 55 persons, each of which had to be fitted out according to his capacity as a hunter with a gun, from two to four horses, and from six to ten steel traps besides clothing and ammunitions, and generally on credit. With this number I made preparations for setting out on my expedition.

"On assembling my people I smiled at the medley, the variety of dresses, habits, and ideas; but above all, at the confusion of languages in our camp, in which were two Americans, seventeen Canadians, five half-breeds from the east side of the mountains, twelve Iroquois, two Abanakee Indians from Lower Canada, two natives from Lake Nepissing, one Saultman from Lake Huron, two Crees from Athabaska, one Chinook, two Spokanes, two Kouttanois [Kootenai], three Flatheads, two Callispellums [Kalispell], one Palooche [Palouse], and one Snake slave. Five of the Candians were above sixty years of age, and two were on the wrong side of seventy . . .

"In summing up however, we must not forget that twenty-five of the party were married and several of the youngsters carried guns; so that in our camp there were exclusive of the men twenty-five women and sixty-four children. The rest of the equipment consisted of seventy-five guns, a brass three pounder, two hundred and twelve beaver traps, and three hundred ninety and two horses, together with a good stock of powder and ball and some trading articles."[29]

In view of the fact that, in the American system of trapping, a party of three persons was considered most efficient, this was not an expedition but an armed invasion. Considering that horses and people had to live off the country late fall, winter, and early spring, consuming every sprig of vegetation available, killing every edible game animal that could be shot, and trapping everything that wore

fur, such an expedition must have left a wide wake of devastation wherever it traveled, literally obeying the Simpson edict, to "strip the country bare."

Going east from Flathead Post to the vicinity of present-day Missoula, Montana, the Ross party turned south and moved up the Bitter Root Valley, trapping as it went. One day a nervous party member suddenly cried: "Enemies!" But they turned out to be friends, Ross says, though of a dubious sort. They were

"six Nez Perces whom we supposed to be horses thieves; none of them had saddles and yet they were driving horses before them."

A Spokane Indian named Pallade, who Ross says was a good fellow in his way but not accustomed to long journeys, got fainthearted. He wanted to quit the party and accompany the Nez Perces, so Ross gave him his discharge and let him go.

"As we left the Indians, however," Ross writes in exasperation, "four of the Iroquois kept in the rear and exchanged with the Nez Perces two of their guns for horses! If they had not guns to defend themselves, they had a relay of horses to carry then out of danger! Such improvident and thoughtless beings as Iroquois should always be restricted to their hunting implements; all the rest goes in traffic among the natives to no purpose."[30]

This was strictly a matter of viewpoint, of course. To the six Nez Perce "natives," skinning Iroquois was a lot easier than trapping and skinning beaver.

And a "skinning" the trade proved to be, for a few days later in the upper Bitter Root Valley, two of the hunters came running into camp almost breathless, calling out; "A war party! A war party!"

"They however proved to be a mixture of Nez Perces and Shaw-ha-ap-tens [both names for the same tribe], eighty-four in number, headed by two of their principal chiefs. We then all joined the camp . . .

"They [the horses] belonged to our visitors, and the chiefs claimed them as soon as they arrived, mentioning the six Nez Perces and the place where they had stolen the horses. The Iroquois had therefore to deliver them up and I was not displeased at it. When the Indians were going off however, I interposed in their behalf and the chiefs consented to give them two old guns in lieu of the new ones they had given for the horses!

"At the expiration of two days," Ross concludes in disgust, "all the Indians left us but not before they had

28. *Ogden's Journals*, vol. 13, p. xxxvi.
29. Ross, *Fur Hunters*, pp. 208–209.
30. Ibid., p. 221.

rifled the unprincipled Iroquois of almost every article they possessed, in exchange for Indian toys.''[31]

In an oblique way the Iroquois and Alexander Ross played roles in an incident that may have influenced the Nez Perce and their Flathead cousins to seek closer ties with the Americans. While trapping in the southeastern part of the Snake River country, a dozen or so Iroquois were attacked by hostiles. They saved their scalps but in their wanderings got themselves hopelessly lost. Encountering an American trapping party led by Jedediah Smith, a man who combined the instincts of a Yankee trader with the principles of a new England preacher, they asked if he would do them the favor of guiding them to Pierre's Hole, where they were supposed to rendezvous with their employer, Alexander Ross.

Good Christian that he was, Jed Smith agreed. However, since they had managed to save a hundred beaver plews, he would charge a slight fee for his services. Say, a hundred beaver plews?

The lost Iroquois paid the fee gladly enough; Smith cached the pelts and then led the Indians north to Ross, who was not pleased with the bargain. He uncharitably called Smith and his party of American trappers ''spies.'' In a sense they were, for after traveling with the Ross party to Flathead Post, where he observed and listened intently, Smith made a report to General Henry Atkinson in St. Louis of such interest and importance that the army officer wasted no time forwarding it to the War Department, noting in the letter of transmittal that Smith was ''an intelligent young man who was employed by General Ashley beyond the Rocky Mountains.''[32]

One of the most remarkable men ever to engage in the American fur trade, Jedediah S. Smith became a trapper at the age of eighteen, proved his courage in dangerous circumstances at nineteen, and became a trusted leader of men at twenty. But it was neither his youth nor his enterprise that made him stand out from the crowd.

It was his religion.

''Smith was a bold, outspoken, professing, and consistent Christian,'' William Waldo wrote, ''the first and only one known among the early Rocky Mountain trappers and hunters. No one who knew him doubted his piety.''[33]

Smith liked the Flatheads, and, since he customarily carried a Bible and hymn book on his person, he may have told them something about his religion. He was a Wesleyan Methodist, a breed new to the Flatheads, though from the Iroquois and the Canadians they had heard of Catholic priests, whom they called ''Black Robes.'' That both Methodists and Catholics believed a person should not steal, lie, or speak ill of his fellowman did not surprise these western Indians, for they held the same beliefs themselves.

But could only Christians possess the secret of gunpowder? This was a thought to brood on.

While the British-owned fur companies in the Pacific Northwest were establishing trading posts and sending out large expeditions to gather plews, American based in St. Louis were developing a radically different system. As might be expected of a country that in 1776 had rebelled against, and in 1812 again had fought, the monarchy that had founded it, the American system was based on freedom.

Key figure in it was the mountain man, the physical and philosophical descendant of men like Daniel Boone, the type of man who required only a knife, an axe, and a long rifle to conquer the wilderness. Now his name was John Colter, Kit Carson, Jim Bridger, Thomas Fitzpatrick, Joe Meek, Robert Newell, or William Craig. In contrast to the rigidly controlled employees of the British companies, he was known as a ''free trapper.''

Well, yes, he did owe a certain sum of money to the St. Louis-based fur company that supplied him with traps, arms, ammunition, and ''possibles'' for a year's stay in the high country of the West. The *bourgeois* (boss-man) of that company would deduct the sum owed from the free trapper's catch of beaver when the brigade brought out fresh supplies to some convenient spot of rendezvous next summer. But other than that, the mountain man was free.

Free to roam and trap where he pleased. Free to starve, freeze, or die of thirst. Free to lose or take a scalp. Free to make a fortune or remain eternally in debt. But *free,* by God, *free!*

Beginning in 1824, small American fur companies like that established by William Ashley held a rendezvous each summer at some central place on the western side of the Continental Divide —

31. Ibid.
32. Maurice S. Sullivan, *Jedediah Smith, Trader and Trailbreaker* (New York: Press of the Pioneers, 1936), p. 59.
33. Chittenden, *Fur Trade,* vol. 1, p. 272.

Green River, Pierre's Hole, Jackson Hole, Brown's Hole. Here the free trappers would exchange their plews for next year's supplies, meanwhile doing their best to drink up whatever profit they had on the company books during the two or three weeks of high carnival that obtained while the rendezvous lasted. Usually their best was good enough, and they ended up in debt. But as free men they cared little.

Since the surest way to survive in the wilderness was to adapt to it, as the Indians had done, American mountain men soon learned to live like Indians. Many of them dressed like Indians, took Indian wives, and for all practical purposes became members of the tribe. Particularly close relationships were established between the freedom-loving American trappers and the independent-minded Nez Perces.

Try though they would, the Britishers had little success in persuading the Nez Perces to become trappers, though now and then the Indians did give the trade a try. On one Hudson's Bay Company expedition led by Peter Skene Ogden in 1825, he recorded in his diary:

"*Friday 23rd* [December]. Very cold. We remained in camp. Mid-day two Fort Nez Perces Indians arrived, having each two traps for the purpose of accompanying us in quest of beaver."[34]

But after two weeks, on Monday, January 9, 1826:

"The two Nez Perces Indians who joined us on the 22nd ultimo intimated to me their intentions of leaving us tomorrow . . . starving does not agree with them — only two beavers this day."[35]

That sentiment pretty well typified the Nez Perce attitude toward trapping. Though they were friendly enough toward the Britishers, often traveled with them for brief periods of time, obliged Ogden as carriers of letters back to the posts, and always had horses to trade for guns and ammunition, they would not take up trapping as an occupation.

Even so, Ogden liked the Nez Perces more than any other Indian tribe, with the possible exception of their "cousins" the Flatheads, one of whose young women he married and lived with the rest of his life.[36] On one occasion he reported:

"One of the Nez Perces shot off two of his fingers from his gun going off accidentally. He certainly had a most narrow escape. We had the wound washed and dressed. . . . He suffers greatly and no doubt will do so for some time."[37]

By 1826 a truce of sorts seems to have been declared between the Nez Perces and the Shoshones, for Ogden wrote:

"We are now encamped on the same spot where the Fort Nez Perces Tribes and Snake Indians assembled last summer and made peace. We are informed [they] are again to meet this season for the purpose of trade."[38]

William Kittson, second in command to Ogden, recorded a domestic tragedy, January 13, 1825:

"During the night a dispute took place between a Nez Perce and his wife. He struck her a blow with the butt of his gun on the head. She fell, and he, thinking that she was dead, shot himself through the breast. He died soon after and the woman came to life. Traded a horse on that account in order to sacrifice something to his memory."[39]

Following the Hudson's Bay Company takeover, George Simpson insisted that Spokane House or Flathead Post should be the starting

34. *Ogden's Journals,* vol. 13, p. 107.

35. Ibid., p. 112.

36. In a biography of Peter Skene Ogden (Portland, Oreg.: Binfords & Mort, 1968), Archie Binns states that as a young man Ogden lived with a Cree woman who bore him two half-blood sons. Sarah, Peter's mother in England, knew about the union, accepted the need of a wilderness man for a woman, but would not bear the thought of her son's giving an Indian woman the Ogden name. She asked Peter to vow never to legalize the relationshop. He gave her his promise.

The Cree woman died in 1823. Leaving the two children with their mother's family, Peter journeyed west to Spokane House. This was a pleasant post among the most enlightened and reasonable of western Indians, the Salish — or Flatheads. There he met Julia, a Salish woman a few years older and somewhat taller than he, beautiful, intelligent, once married to an Indian man but now a widow, and was attracted to her.

After a courtship during which she made him adhere to every rule — including the gift of fifty horses to her father — Julia and Peter were married according to Flathead custom. He sent for the children born to his dead Cree wife; Julia raised them as her own and they came to love her as their own mother.

Of this remarkable woman Binns notes: "Peter Odgen loved her increasingly and never considered having any other wife; in time, he even learned to be faithful to her."

Within a year of their marriage Julia bore Peter a son, the first of some eight or ten children she produced (the record is hazy as to the exact number) despite the fact that she was in her thirties when they met. She accompanied him on five of the six expeditions he led, usually carrying a newly born child and taking care of the rest of her brood, which she always took along.

When urged by his old friend, Dr. John McLoughlin, to marry Julia in a Christian ceremony, Peter Ogden refused, saying: "What more, in God's name, could make it a marriage than a lifetime of living together?"

Ogden died after a brief illness September 27, 1854. Moving to Lake la Hache, British Columbia, Julia lived out her years with her son-in-law, daughters, and grandchildren, where many Ogdens still reside. She died in 1886 at the age of ninety-eight.

37. *Ogden's Journals,* vol. 13, p. 152.

38. Ibid., p. 194.

39. Ibid., p. 213.

point for the annual expeditions, despite the protests of first Ross, then Ogden, that it was difficult to transport to those posts and bring pelts back from them. Fort Nez Perces was a far better base, they felt, because large numbers of good horses were always available there, excellent beaver country could be reached with only eight days of traveling, and upon the return of the expeditions to that post, the packs of furs could be shipped down the Columbia to Fort George or Fort Vancouver by canoe.

Eventually Simpson came around to their way of thinking. In their correspondence on the subject, which was discussed over a period of several years, the post was referred to more and more by the name of the river near which it was located rather than by the tribe of Indians for whom it originally had been named. By 1828 the name Fort Nez Perces had fallen into disuse, replaced by what would be its name for the rest of its existence, Fort Walla Walla. Since no official changing of names appears to have been recorded, we can only assume that they found it more convenient to identify the post by a place name rather than that of a widely scattered Indian tribe.

Between 1824 and 1830, American trappers in ever-increasing numbers traveled across the region jointly occupied by Great Britain and the United States, though it still nominally belonged to the natives who had lived there for thousands of years. While working in the Weiser River area, Odgen reported finding evidence of what he suspected was a party of American trappers, writing:

"*Wednesday, 25th* [September 1827]. We were not long left in doubt, for shortly after an American by name Johnson made his appearance and informed us he and five others were on this stream a short distance from this.[40] Their party consists of forty men; six are in the direction Mr. McKay has taken; six have gone with goods accompanied by a band of Nez Perces to trade on the Columbia; and the remainder are dispersed in this quarter, so my hopes of returns for beaver, which was yesterday rather sanguine, are now blasted."

Two days later Ogden wrote:

"From all accounts the Nez Perce Indians have taken a number of beaver. The Americans inform me they would not part with one. I hope this may be true."[41]

Whether the Nez Perces had taken the beaver from traps they themselves had set, Ogden does not say, but two months later, in the southeastern part of the Snake River country, he wrote:

"*Thursday, 22nd* [November 1827]. The great Snake [Shoshone Indian] camp is not more than a mile from us. About fifty paid us a visit, also seven Nez Perce Indians, who from their own accounts have lately separated from an American party who had been to their country and had traded thirty-five horses and some beaver."[42]

This is a good example of how far the travel-loving Nez Perces had extended their range. Ogden records on December 3 that eight Nez Perces accompanied his party to its base in the Salt Lake region, which, as the crow flew, was 350 miles southeast of Kamiah, heartland of Nez Perce country. In his diary Ogden made some shrewd comments on the economics of the fur trade.

"*Monday, 3rd.* [December 1827]. Three-fourths of the horses I received last fall from Mr. Black were young, two years old and ill suited to undergo the severe privations they met with in the Snake Country, and which unfortunately from the numerous horse thieves we have to contend with, cannot be avoided . . .

"I again repeat that no trapper can do justice to his traps without he has four good horses. My party at present average this number, but unfortunately they are most indifferent. It would be far more to the interest of the concern [the Hudson's Bay Company] to pay an increase to the natives and select good horses. It is said by doing so it would prove detrimental to the returns, but from my knowledge of that quarter I am of a contrary opinion . . .

"The Upper Nez Perce tribe are those from whom good horses can be obtained and very few beaver. For the last two years the Americans have traded with them; this year they procured thirty-five prime ones from them. No doubt they paid double [over what] we do, but they will in due season fully pay their value, whereas those we obtain never can.

"When the American party left us, eight Nez Perce Indians accompanied them to request their traders to return the ensuing season to their country to trade with their tribe."[43]

In response to Ogden's warning that most of his men would desert him and go to work for the Americans if they were not paid better, Simpson let him double the going price for beaver. Simpson also authorized him to pay the Nez Perces whatever necessary to obtain good horses. But it was a matter of too little, too late. By now the far-roaming, trade-loving Nez Perces had gotten acquainted with a number of Americans, such as

40. *Ogden's Journals, 1827–28 and 1828–29*, p. 10. The American was John Johnson, killed by Blackfeet on Bear River in 1828.
41. Ibid., p. 11.
42. Ibid., p. 28.
43. Ibid., p. 31.

Jedediah Smith, who again had visited his favorite Indians, the Flatheads, while on his way to rendezvous with his partner, David Jackson, in Jackson Hole. And again he may have told them something about the white man's religion.

By 1830 the region jointly occupied by Great Britain and the United States had been stripped so bare of beaver that even small parties of trappers found no profit in working its streams. It would seem that George Simpson's plan to impoverish the country so that Americans would have no incentive to come West had worked beautifully.

But the forces that move men are not always measured in dollars and cents. Even now, the Flatheads and the Nez Perces were holding a council to discuss several important questions. Was the technology of the white man related to his religion? Were his secrets in the Book Jedediah Smith carried? If so, should they not send a delegation of chiefs to their old friend, William Clark, in St. Louis and get a copy of that Book?

Who would volunteer to go?

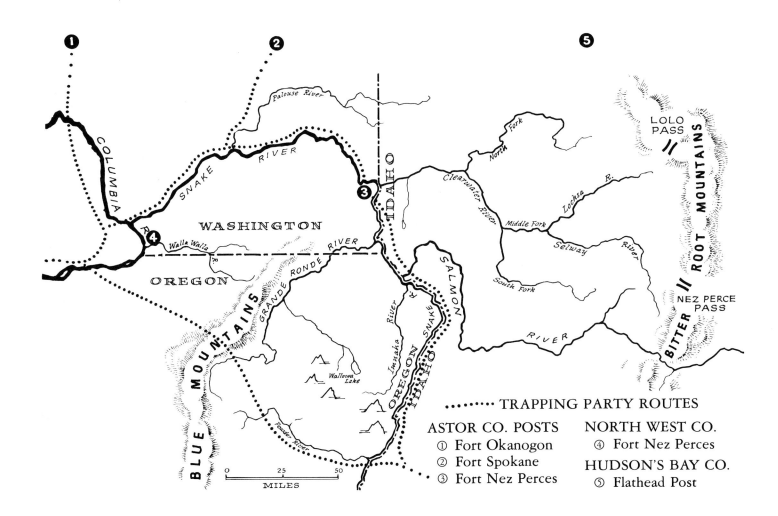

•••••••••• TRAPPING PARTY ROUTES

ASTOR CO. POSTS
① Fort Okanogon
② Fort Spokane
③ Fort Nez Perces

NORTH WEST CO.
④ Fort Nez Perces

HUDSON'S BAY CO.
⑤ Flathead Post

CHAPTER SIX

BOOK OF HEAVEN: 1831–1832

*It appeared that some white man had pene-
trated into their country, and happened to be a
spectator at one of their religious ceremonies . . .
he informed them that their mode of worshipping
the Supreme Being was radically wrong.*
— William Walker, January 19, 1833

IT IS KNOWN beyond question that in the autumn of 1831 three Nez Perces and a Flathead reached St. Louis and sought out General William Clark, who had become superintendent of Indian Affairs for the far-flung Missouri River country and the Pacific Northwest. Why they made the trip, what they were seeking, and whether they expected spiritual or material rewards, must forever remain in the realm of speculation, for the only answers to these queries have come from white historians, thus cannot be relied upon.

Exposure to the white man's ideas of religion could have come from four sources, Dr. Clifford M. Drury points out: Lewis and Clark, the Iroquois, white trappers, or neighboring Indians whom the Hudson's Bay Company had sent to eastern Canada as boys to be schooled and grounded in religion.

One of these neighbor boys was Spokane Garry, who at the age of fourteen was sent by George Simpson to a Church of England mission school near present-day Winnepeg, Manitoba, where he remained from 1825 to 1830. By the time he returned home he could read and write English.

"He brought back with him from the Red River school his Bible. All reports show that he earnestly sought to give his people a conception of the Christian religion."[1]

Curious Indians from nearby tribes came to listen to Garry and look at his Bible. One of these was the son of Chief Twisted Hair, now a leader of the Kamiah band, named Ish-hol-hoats-toats. Because of his persuasive abilities and talents as a shrewd bargainer he was called "The Lawyer" by the whites. Another was Timothy, chief of a Nez Perce band living opposite the juncture of the Clearwater with the Snake.[2]

Impressed with what they heard and saw during their visit with Spokane Garry, Timothy and Lawyer came home and reported to their people. Soon afterwards, six Indians set out for St. Louis "in search," Lawyer later said, of Christian teachers."[3]

It is likely that they journeyed to fur rendezvous grounds on the headwaters of Green River, there joined a party of Americans returning to St. Louis, and made the rest of the eastbound trip in its company. At Council Bluffs two of the Indians turned back, while the remaining four went on to St. Louis: a Flathead chief named Man-of-the-Morning, a Nez Perce chief named Black Eagle, and two young Nez Perce braves named No-Horns-on-His-Head and Rabbit-Skin-Leggings.

During the autumn the two older Indians sickened, died, and were buried in St. Louis. Given

1. Clifford M. Drury, *Henry Harmon Spalding* (Caldwell: Caxton Printers, 1936), p. 76–78.

2. Ibid., p. 79. Drury says that Lawyer first learned about the Sabbath from Spokane Garry. In the Nez Perce tongue, *Ha-lah-pa-wit* meant "Sabbath rest" or "Sabbath." One of the first Christian converts in the tribe, Timothy, named his village *Al-po-wa,* a derivative of *Ha-lah-pa-wit.* In *Historic Glimpses of Asotin Country, Washington* by Judge Elgin V. Kuykendall (Clarkston Herald Press, 1954), p. 3, the author quotes Timothy's recollections of having hidden and watched Lewis and Clark.

3. Drury, *Spalding,* p. 79. Some accounts say seven Indians started out.

Rabbit-Skin-Leggings and No-Horns-On-His-Head, Nez Perces, sketched by George Catlin aboard the steamboat Yellowstone the summer of 1832.

the Christian name Narcisse, the first was buried October 31, 1831; the other, given the Christian name Paul, was interred on November 17, 1831. Before they died both chiefs were given the final rites of the Catholic church. They were buried in the Catholic cemetery.

The two younger Indians, No-Horns-on-His-Head and Rabbit-Skin-Leggings, remained in St. Louis all winter. In late spring, 1832, they were put aboard the steamer *Yellowstone,* were seen and sketched by the wandering artist, George Catlin —

George Catlin sketches of what he calls a "normal" Chinook boy of fifteen and a Chinook woman whose head has been flattened and who is putting her baby through the same process. Published with the Nez Perce sketches in 1841.

who did not learn of their mission until later — and were given new clothes by friendly Sioux in the upper Missouri River country. One of them died near the mouth of the Yellowstone, leaving the other to return home alone. He is said to have been killed in the buffalo country a year or so later.

In a letter dated December 31, 1831, the Rt. Rev. Joseph Rosati, bishop of St. Louis, wrote the editor of a Catholic publication in Lyons, France:

"Some three months ago four Indians, who live at the other side of the Rocky Mountains, near the Columbia River, arrived in St. Louis. After visiting General Clark who, in his celebrated travels, had seen the nation to which they belong, and had been well received by them, they came to see our church, and appeared to be exceedingly well pleased with it. Unfortunately there was no one who understood their language. Sometime afterward two of them fell dangerously ill. I was then absent from St. Louis. Two of our priests visited them, and the poor Indians seemed delighted with their visit. They made signs of the Cross and other signs which appeared to have some relation to baptism. This sacrament was administered to them; they gave expression of their satisfaction. A little cross was presented to them; they took it with eagerness, kissed it repeatedly, and it could be taken from them only after their death. It was truly distressing that they could not be spoken to. Their remains were carried to the church for the funeral, which was conducted with all the Catholic ceremonies. The other two [the younger Nez Perces] attended and acted with great propriety. They have returned to their country.

"We have since learned from a Canadian, who has crossed the country which they inhabit, that they belong to the nation of Tetes-Plates (Flatheads), which, as with another called the Pieds-Noirs (or Blackfeet) have received some notions of the Catholic religion from two Indians who had been to Canada . . .

"These nations have not yet been corrupted by intercourse with others; their manners and customs are simple and they are very numerous. We have conceived the liveliest desire to not let pass such a good occasion. Mr. Condamine has offered himself to go to them next spring with another. In the meantime, we shall obtain information on what we have been told, and on the means of travel."[4]

4. C.T. Johnson, "The Evolution of a Lament," *Washington Historical Quarterly* 2, no. 2 (April 1908), pp. 198–199. Actually, "C. T. Johnson" was a pseudonym for the highly respected Pacific Northwest historian, T. C. Elliott. At the time he wrote, a heated controversy was raging over whether or not the martyred missionary, Marcus Whitman, had "saved Oregon for the United States" by going East in 1842, leading the Great Migration of 1843 to Oregon, and thus persuading the American government to take over the area on a permanent basis rather than let Daniel Webster "trade it to Great Britain for a Newfoundland codfish bank."

Since Elliott's article proved that the early-day missionaries were not above bending the truth a bit, if it served their purpose, he was treading on dangerous ground — thus, his use of the assumed name.

For the Christian Advocate and Journal.

THE FLAT-HEAD INDIANS.

The plans to civilize the savage tribes of our country are among the most remarkable signs of the times. To meliorate the condition of the Indians, and to preserve them from gradual decline and extinction, the government of the U. States have proposed and already commenced removing them to the region westward of the Mississippi.— Here it is intended to establish them in a permanent residence. Some powerful nations of these aborigines, having accepted the proposal, have already emigrated to their new lands, and others are now preparing to follow them. Among those who still remain are the Wyandots, a tribe long distinguished as standing at the head of the great Indian family.

The earliest travellers in Canada first discovered this tribe while ascending the St. Lawrence, at Montreal. They were subsequently driven by the Iroquois, in one of those fierce internal wars that characterize the Indians of North America, to the northern shores of lake Huron. From this resting place also their relentless enemy literally hunted them until the remnant of this once powerful and proud tribe found a safe abode among the Sioux, who resided west of lake Superior. When the power of the Iroquois was weakened by the French the Wyandots returned from the Sioux country, and settled near Michilimackinac. They finally took up their abode on the plains of Sandusky, in Ohio, where they continue to this day.

The Wyandots, amounting to *five hundred*, are the only Indians in Ohio who have determined to remain upon their lands. The Senecas, Shawnees, and Ottawas have all sold their Ohio possessions, and have either removed, or are on their way to the west of the Mississippi. A small band of about seventy Wyandots from the Big Spring have disposed of their reservation of 16,000 acres, but have not accepted the offered lands of the government in exchange. They will retire into Michigan, or Canada, after leaving some of their number at the main reservation of Upper Sandusky.

The wonderful effects of the Gospel among the Wyandots are well known. Providence has blessed

From the point of the nose to the apex of the head, there is a perfect straight line, the protuberance of the forehead is flattened or levelled. You may form some idea of the shape of their heads from the rough sketch I have made with the pen, though I confess I have drawn most too long a proboscis for a flat-head. This is produced by a pressure upon the cranium while in infancy. The distance they had travelled on foot was nearly three thousand miles to see Gen. Clarke, their great father, as they called him, he being the first American officer† they ever became acquainted with, and having much confidence in him, they had come to consult him as they said, upon very important matters. Gen. C. related to me the object of their mission, and, my dear friend, it is impossible for me to describe to you my feelings while listening to his narrative. I will here relate it as briefly as I well can. It appeared that some white man had penetrated into their country, and happened to be a spectator at one of their religious ceremonies, which they scrupulously perform at stated periods. He informed them that their mode of worshipping the supreme Being was radically wrong, and instead of being acceptable and pleasing, it was displeasing to him ; he also informed them that the white people *away* toward the rising of the sun had been put in possession of the true mode of worshipping the great Spirit. They had a book containing directions how to conduct themselves in order to enjoy his favor and hold converse with him ; and with this guide, no one need go astray, but every

William Walker's Flathead — It was this article, published in 1833, that inspired the religious world to send missionaries to the Far Western Indians.

Titled "The Catholic Account" by the historian who discovered it many years later, this appears to have been the earliest contemporary piece of correspondence on the 1831 Indian delegation.

Now let us examine "The Methodist Account."

In 1831 a proposal was made to move the Wyandotte Indian tribe from its reservation near Sandusky, Ohio, to a larger tract farther west. A number of the tribe were sent out to explore that country before a decision was made. William Walker, a well-educated, intelligent man who was either a full or part-blood Wyandotte, acted as interpreter and correspondent for the party.

Early in November 1831 the group passed through St. Louis on its way west. This would have been after the death of the first chief but before the death of the second. In a letter to a friend, G. P. Disosway, William Walker wrote:

"Immediately after we landed in St. Louis, on our way to the West, I proceeded to Gen. Clark's, superintendent of Indian affairs . . . he informed me that three chiefs from the Flathead nation were in his house and were quite sick, and that one (the fourth) had died a few days ago. They were from the west of the Rocky Mountains. Curiosity prompted me to step into the adjoining room to see them. . . . I was struck by their appearance . . . small in size, delicately formed, except the heads. . . . The head is flattened thus:

"From the point of the nose to the apex of the head, there is a perfect straight line, the protrubance of the forehead is flattened or leveled. You may form some idea of the shape of their heads from the rough sketch I have made with the pen, though I confess I have drawn most too long a probiscus for a flat-head. This is produced by a pressure upon the cranium while in infancy . . .

"Gen. Clark related to me the object of their mission, and, my dear friend, it is impossible for me to describe to you my feelings, while listening to his narrative. . . . It appeared that some white man had penetrated into their country, and happened to be a spectator at one of their religious services. . . . He informed them that their mode of worshipping the supreme Being was radically wrong . . . that the white people away toward the rising sun had been put in possession of a book containing directions how to conduct themselves . . .

"They called a national council to take this subject into consideration . . . some said if this be true it is certainly high time we put in possession of this mode. . . . They accordingly deputed four chiefs to proceed to St. Louis to see their great father, Gen. Clark."[5]

Historians doubt that William Walker even saw the delegation of Indians, let alone described them accurately. Though head-flattening still was practiced to some extent among the Indians of the lower Columbia, it was a custom in which neither the Nez Perces or the Flatheads ever indulged. For that matter, the deformed head sketched by Walker was pointed, rather than flat, and it is certain he never saw *that* kind of Indian.

But the religious zeal and missionary fervor of the day did not permit questioning such small details of an appealing story. In passing the letter along to the *Christian Advocate and Journal and Zion's Herald,* which published it with his added comments, March 1, 1833, G. P. Disosway wrote:

"How deeply touching is the circumstances of the four natives traveling on foot 3,000 miles through thick forests and extensive prairies, sincere searchers after truth. The story has scarcely a parallel in history. . . . May we not indulge the hope that the day is not far distant when the missionaries will penetrate into these wilds where the Sabbath bell has never yet tolled since the world began!"[6]

In the eastern United States the religious world caught fire. Until now Americans had been led to believe that the only thing of value in the Pacific Northwest was the pelt of a fur-bearing animal which was rapidly being exterminated. Now they learned that this distant wilderness contained a far more precious commodity — poor benighted heathens, with flattened heads and souls to be saved, eager to be converted.

"We will not cease," proclaimed one evangelist, "until we shall have planted the standard of Christianity high on the summit of the Stony Mountains!"[7]

All over the East, church bells began to ring.[8]

5. Chittenden, *Fur Trade,* vol. 2, pp. 915–917. He and a number of other writers use the spelling "Disoway," but Drury spells the name "Disosway." Drury is correct.
6. Ibid., p. 919.
7. Ibid., p. 925. In a letter dated April 17, 1833, signed by A. M'Allister, this quote is attributed to "Bishop Soule, when preaching at a camp in this country."
8. A legend erroneously repeated by many writers even in recent times says that before the two surviving Indians left St. Lewis one of them made a touching speech, which was copied by a listener who happened to be in an adjacent room. As T. C. Elliott conclusively proves in his *"Evolution of a Lament,"* it did not happen — nor was the speech printed in religious publications of the day, as several latter-day writers have carelessly claimed.
    Instead, as Elliott points out, the supposed speech did not see the light of print until February 1866, in the Walla Walla *Statesman,* and then it came from the not very accurate pen of Henry Spalding. But it made such a big hit it was later refined, revised, and finally accepted as authentic by some partisan historians. The 1883 version, composed in pure *McGuffey Reader* style, has been the most widely quoted, so we'll give it to you here:
    "I came to you over the trail of many moons from the setting sun. You were the friends of my fathers, who have all gone the long way. I came with one eye partly opened, for more light for my people, who sit in darkness. I go back with both eyes closed. How can I go back blind to my blind people? I made my way to you with strong arms, through many enemies and strange lands, that I might carry back much to them. I go back with both arms broken and empty. The two fathers who came with me — the braves of many winters and wars — we leave asleep by your great water. They were tired in many moons and their moccasins wore out.
    "My people sent me to get the white man's Book from Heaven. You took me where you allow your women to dance as we do not ours, and the Book was not there. You took me where they worship the Great Spirit with candles, and the book was not there. You showed me the images of good spirits and pictures of the Good Land beyond, but the book was not among them. I am going back the long, sad trail to my people in the dark land. You make my feet heavy with burdens of gifts, but the Book is not among them. When I tell my poor, blind people, after one more snow, in the big council, that I did not bring the Book, no word will be spoken by our old men or by our young braves. One by one they will rise up and go out in silence. My people will die in darkness, and they will go on the long path to other hunting grounds. No white man will go with them and no white man's Book to make the way plain. I have no more words."

CHAPTER SEVEN

THE FUR TRADERS: 1832–1835

I have again to repeat to you the advice which I before gave you — not to come with a small party to the American Rendezvous. There are here a great collection of scoundrels.
— Nathaniel J. Wyeth, June 1834

APPARENTLY THE INDIANS expected quick results, for at rendezvous the summer of 1832 one hundred and twenty lodges of Nez Perces and eighty lodges of Flatheads were pitched in the lush-green, well-watered, high-mountain valley called Pierre's Hole. Though they may have been

Photo by Bill Gulick

Redfish Lake

told by fur company people that the two older chiefs had died in St. Louis and that the two young braves were returning home by the Missouri River route, the Indians could not have known that their appeal for religious instructions — if indeed such an appeal had been intended — would not be publicized in eastern church circles until the following spring.

Whatever disappointment they may have felt in not receiving an early answer to their plea soon was forgotten in the excitement of the biggest get-together of whites, Indians, horses, pack animals, wagons, tepees, tents and trade goods ever assembled west of the Continental Divide. In addition to the Nez Perces and Flatheads, the Shoshones, Crows, and Utes were there in large numbers. At least two hundred white trappers representing the American Fur Company, the Rocky Mountain Fur Company, and an independent company owned by Nathaniel J. Wyeth also were present.

Though they did not reach Pierre's Hole in time to take part in the trading, two other groups of Americans were in the area, planning to trap beaver on their own during the coming season or acquire it by purchase from the Indians. One was a seasoned band of mountain men led by Lucien Fontenelle, with whom the four Indians seeking religious enlightenment had journeyed part of the way to St. Louis the previous summer. The other was a large, well-equipped, paramilitary body of men under the command of Captain Benjamin Louis Eulalie de Bonneville, an army officer temporarily on leave.

Since both Wyeth and Bonneville became closely involved with the Nez Perces during the next few years, a brief account of the background of each is in order here.

An energetic, ambitious man of thirty, Nathaniel Wyeth had managed a farm and ice-selling business in Cambridge, Massachusetts. Becoming convinced that there would be great opportunities for profit in the Oregon Country once the Joint Occupancy Treaty expired in 1838 (it had been renewed for another ten years in 1828), he had put together an Astor-type enterprise on a somewhat smaller scale, outfitting a ship filled with ice, barrels, salt, and trade goods, and sending it around Cape Horn to the lower Columbia, while he led a party of twenty-three men overland. Following a few months' stay in the Pacific Northwest, the ship would sail back to Boston with a highly

Photo by Bill Gulick

Main Salmon River near the mouth of the North Fork. This is where Captain Bonneville wintered with the Nez Perces.

profitable cargo of salted salmon caught in the great River of the West and valuable packs of beaver pelts trapped inland. Or so Wyeth planned.

At Independence Wyeth and his band of greenhorns fell in with the veteran trader, William Sublette, who, with sixty-two men of the Rocky Mountain Fur Company, was headed for the mountains. Crossing the Continental Divide, Jackson Hole, and Teton Pass, the combined parties reached rendezvous grounds in Pierre's Hole on July 8, 1832.

Here they found large numbers of friendly, curious Indians waiting for them. Here, also, was assembled formidable competition — ninety men employed by the Astor-backed American Fur Company, which soon would demand nothing less than total monopoly of the western fur trade.

Leading the Kamiah band of Nez Perces was Ish-hol-hoats-toats — called Lawyer by the whites. He and Wyeth soon became friends. It was agreed that when rendezvous broke up, a group of Nez Perces would guide Wyeth west down Snake River and across the Blue Mountains to Fort Walla Walla.

After making demands which Wyeth refused to meet, half of his men quit, some to return East, others to work for the rival companies.[1] Down to

1. John Ball, *Autobiography*, Kate Ball Powers, Flora Ball Hopkins, and Lucy Ball, comps. (Grand Rapids: Dean-Hicks Company, 1925), p. 60. An autobiography of Ball compiled by his daughters.

eleven men, Wyeth broke camp on July 17. Traveling with Milton Sublette's party of trappers and Chief Lawyer's band of Nez Perces, the Cambridge entrepeneur got a baptism in blood next morning in a conflict typical of the upper Snake River country.

In addition to being a convenient meeting place for Indians and white traders, Pierre's Hole was a major crossroads for north-south, east-west traffic. From time immemorial, Shoshones, Flatheads, Nez Perces, Bannocks, and other tribes passed through the area, sometimes keeping an uneasy peace when they encountered one another, sometimes engaging in bitter conflict. When the Blackfeet appeared, as they did now and then, there was always serious trouble.

That happened now. Apparently unaware that large numbers of red and white enemies were in the vicinity, a band of Blackfeet, with women and children, blundered into the breakup of rendezvous. Too encumbered to flee and too outnumbered to fight, the normally hostile Indians responded favorably to overtures of peace, prudently moving women, children, and horses into a marsh covered with brush and scrub timber, while the Blackfoot chief came forward to parley and stall for time.

One of Sublette's men, Antoine Godin, was a half blood whose father not long before had been killed by Blackfeet. One of Godin's friends (prob-

ably a relative) was a Flathead Indian who also had old scores to settle. By their code, they acted as men owing a blood debt could be expected to act. By Wyeth's civilized standards, their behavior was shocking.

"The Blackfoot chief was advancing singly and unarmed, bearing the pipe of peace. When Antoine grasped the extended hand of the Indian, he ordered the Flathead to fire. The Blackfoot fell to the ground. Instantly, the valley was alive with warriors."[2]

The ensuing Battle of Pierre's Hole was one of the bloodiest ever fought in the area. Wyeth describes it:

"The Indians, finding they were caught, fortified themselves in a masterly manner in the woods. We attacked them and continued the attack all day. They decamped during the night, leaving most of their utensils, lodges, etc., and many dead. Probably 20 of them were killed, and 32 horses were found dead. We had lost three whites killed, eight badly wounded, among them William Sublette, who was extremely active in the battle. About ten of the Nez Perces and Flatheads were killed or mortally wounded. In the morning we visited their deserted fort; they had dug into the ground to reach water and to secure themselves from our shot. It was a sickening scene of confusion and bloodshed."[3]

Struck in the left hip by a bullet which lodged in the bone and was never removed, Chief Lawyer was among the Nez Perces seriously wounded. For the rest of his life he would walk with a pronounced limp and use a cane.

No longer a greenhorn, the Cambridge farm manager and ice seller hurried on west across the lava deserts of the Snake River country and crossed the Blue Mountains by what soon would become the route of the Oregon Trail. He paused briefly at Fort Walla Walla, where Factor Pambrun provided him with a suit of clothes and boat passage downriver, and arrived at Fort Vancouver October 29, exhausted and destitute.

Bad news awaited him. His supply ship, the *Sultana,* had been wrecked on a South American reef. Most of his men quit. Though he found Dr. McLoughlin "a fine old gentlemen, truly philanthropic in his ideas," he was told politely but firmly that the Hudson's Bay Company and the Indians

Photo by Bill Gulick

Salmon River near Clayton, Idaho

2. Jennie Broughton Brown, *Fort Hall on the Oregon Trail* (Caldwell: Caxton Printers, 1932), p. 93. Pierre's Hole got its name from Pierre Tevanitagon, leader of a group of Iroquois Indians who trapped for Donald MacKenzie and the North West Company. This was the group rescued by Jedediah Smith in 1824. Reference Series, Idaho Historical Society, No. 241.

3. Brown, *Fort Hall,* pp. 94–95.

under its control would not trade with him on any terms. However, if he wished ship passage back to Boston or an escort overland, that could be arranged.

Accompanied by two still-loyal men, Wyeth headed east on February 3, 1833, going up the Columbia and the Snake, then across the Spokane country, making the usual stop with the Nez Perces and Flatheads, whom he called "the best of western Indians . . . devout, honest, brave."

A less determined man would have gone back to farm managing and ice selling. Not Wyeth. Meeting Milton Sublette, who mentioned the fact that the Rocky Mountain Fur Company would be needing trade goods next year, Wyeth drew up a contract for $3,000 worth of supplies, promised delivery at rendezvous midsummer of 1834, and returned to the East.

He was not beaten yet. In fact, he was just beginning to fight.

Exactly what Captain Bonneville was up to in the West is unclear. A career army officer of French descent, he was granted a leave of absence to extend from August 1831 to October 1833. The letter from the War Department granting him this leave stated that it was

"for the purpose of carrying into execution your design of exploring the country to the Rocky mountains and beyond, with a view to ascertaining the nature and character of the several tribes inhabiting those regions; the trade which might be profitably carried on with them; the quality of the soil, the productions, the minerals, the natural history, the climate, the geography and topography, as well as the geology of the various parts of the country."[4]

Bonneville took such a liking to the Nez Perces that he decided to winter with them on the upper Salmon River, leaving the duller task of trapping beaver along the Snake River Plain to a detachment sent in that direction. Camping with his Indian friends near the present-day town of Salmon, Idaho, he found them generous hosts. So did raiding parties of Blackfeet, who repeatedly stole horses which the Nez Perces indifferently guarded.

Observing the perpetual state of war that existed between his hosts and the Blackfeet, Captain Bonneville put forward a suggestion: Why not make peace? This thought struck the Nez Perces as so novel that the head men called a council, debated the idea for two days, then rejected it on these grounds:

Photo by Bill Gulick

Little Salmon

"War is a bloody business and full of evil; but it keeps the eyes of the chiefs always open, and makes the limbs of the young men strong and supple. In war, everyone is on the alert. If we see a trail, we know it must be an enemy. If the Blackfeet come to us, we know it is for war, and we are ready.

"Peace, on the other hand, sounds no alarm; the eyes of the chiefs are closed in sleep, and the young men are sleek and lazy. The horses stray into the mountains; the women and their little babes go about alone.

"But the heart of a Blackfoot is a lie, and his tongue is a trap. If he says peace, it is to deceive. He comes to us as a brother; he smokes the pipe with us; but when he sees us weak and off our guard, he will slay and steal. We will have no such peace; let there be war!"[5]

Because of the mild winter, raiding Blackfeet, and vanishing game, the village was moved into the steep, narrow canyon of the North Fork of the Salmon. Here game was plentiful, and horses and people could be protected with a minimum of effort. Captain Bonneville settled down to enjoy life, which was the thing he did best. Described as "a compact, muscular man, with a merry eye and a prematurely bald head," he was well liked by the Indians and was dubbed the "Bald-Headed Chief."

Next summer Bonneville took the furs he had gathered to rendezvous, shipped them East, then,

4. Chittenden, *Fur Trade*, vol. 1, p. 398.

5. Washington Irving, *Adventures of Captain Bonneville*, p. 102.

after some months of wandering, established winter quarters on the Portneuf. Ere long he became restless. What he should do, he decided, was go down the Snake and Columbia and look into the possibility of establishing a post in direct competition with the British.

No sooner decided than done. On Christmas Day, 1833, with three companions, he rode away from the Portneuf camp, blithely telling the detachment left behind that he would return in early March.

"They were obliged to travel slowly," Irving wrote, "to spare the horses; for the snow had increased in depth to eighteen inches; and though somewhat packed and frozen, was not sufficiently so as to yield firm footing."[6]

Thus began one of the most incredible journeys ever taken through the most rugged part of the Nez Perce country. Because Irving, who wrote the narrative, never saw the region, he misplaces streams and landmarks, but since he is specific on dates we can trace Bonneville's route with reasonable accuracy. Moving along the south and west bank of the Snake, he reached the vicinity of Farewell Bend January 12, 1834. There, instead of crossing the Blues by the route taken by Robert Stuart, Wyeth, and many Hudson's Bay Company brigades, Bonneville hired an Indian guide, who gave him a bad piece of advice.

"Stick to the river; there will be less snow."

This was true. But the guide neglected to add that the river route led into Hell's Canyon — impassable in any season. After a few days the guide deserted, and Captain Bonneville found himself and his three companions in serious trouble.

"The river forced its way into the heart of the mountains, winding between tremendous walls of basaltic rock . . . the snow was from two to three feet deep, but soft and yielding, so that the horses had no foothold . . . sometimes the crags and promontories forced them onto the narrow ribbon of ice that bordered the shore . . . to scramble over vast masses of rock that had tumbled from the impending precipices . . . to cross streams on bridges of ice and snow . . . to pass along narrow cornices . . . two of their horses fell into the river, one saved, the other lost."[7]

In desperation the four men considered killing and skinning their horses, making bullboats of the hides, and committing themselves to the mercies of the river. If they had done so, Washington Irving would not have written his book. For in Hell's Canyon the Snake is a merciless river.

Photo by Bill Gulick

West of Stanley, Idaho

Deserting the water's edge, the freezing, exhausted, starving men climbed out of the canyon and crossed a six-thousand-foot spur of the Wallowa Mountains to the headwaters of the Imnaha. They descended that river to its lower valley, climbed again until the towering ridge dividing the watersheds of the Imnaha and Grande Ronde rivers had been crested, and at last descended into gentler country near the present-day border between Oregon and Washington.

This was the land of the Lower Nez Perces, several bands of whom lived in substantial villages along the left bank of the Snake.[8] By the Indian grapevine they had heard about the Bald-Headed Captain and his sojourn with their cousins, the

6. Ibid., p. 220.
7. Ibid., p. 231–232.
8. In military terminology the words "left" or "right" bank of a river always are written as if facing downstream, no matter which direction a person is traveling. The usage stems from Roman days, military experts tell me. Irving and Bonneville call this particular stream the *Way-lee-way,* which apparently was what the Nez Perces called the lower Grande Ronde before the white man came. See Kuykendall, *Historic Glimpses,* pp. 6–7.

Hell's Canyon

Upper Nez Perces, in the Salmon River country and were determined not to be outdone in the quality of their hospitality.

They also were shrewd traders. After seeing to it that Bonneville was fed and given comfortable quarters, the "venerable old chief" who was acting as his host made him a "present" of a beautiful young horse, of a brown color, solely as "a mark of friendship." Having lived with the Upper Nez Perces, Bonneville knew, of course, that such an expression of friendship must be reciprocated.

"He accordingly placed a handsome rifle in the hands of the venerable chief, whose benevolent heart was evidently touched and gratified by this outward and visible sign of amity."

Having balanced the account, Captain Bonneville started to shift his saddle to the new mount,

but, as he did so, the chief plucked him by the sleeve and introduced him to an elderly, sad-faced woman, saying: "This is my wife . . . she loves him a great deal . . . I do not know how I shall comfort her."

Fortunately the Bald-Headed Captain knew. Producing a pair of glittering earbobs, he presented them to the wife, who "eagerly placed the precious baubles in her ears . . . and went off with a coquettish air."

By now the captain had saddled the horse and was putting his foot in the stirrup when the chief stepped forward again. "This is my son," he said, "who always took care of this very fine horse . . . he loves him like a brother."

From his slender stores, Captain Bonneville produced a hatchet, presented it to the youth, and sent him away "rejoicing."

Mounting, the Bald-Headed Chief was about to ride away when his venerable Nez Perce friend laid one hand gently on the mane of the horse and held up the rifle in the other.

"This rifle," said he, "shall be my great medicine. . . . But a rifle, by itself, is dumb — I cannot make it speak. If I had a little powder and ball, I would take it out with me, and would now and then shoot a deer; and when I brought the meat home to my hungry family, I would say — This was killed by the rifle of my friend, the Bald-Headed Chief, to whom I gave that very fine horse."

Who could resist such an appeal? Not Captain Bonneville, certainly, who

"forthwith furnished the coveted supply of powder and ball; but at the same time, put spurs to his very fine gift horse."[9]

While visiting in one village, a Nez Perce brave became interested in a horse that Bonneville had purchased earlier from a band of Indians living some distance to the south. It looked very much like a horse that had been stolen from him, he said. Invited to make a closer inspection, he did. Yes, it was the same horse.

"However," said the considerate savage, "you got him in fair trade — you are more in want of horses than I am; keep him; he is yours — he is a good horse; use him well."[10]

A few days later an incident similar to that of the purloined silver goblet of earlier years occurred

9. Irving, *Bonneville*, pp. 240–241.
10. Ibid., p. 249.

Photo by Bill Gulick
Farewell Bend — this is where the Snake River enters Hell's Canyon and where Captain Bonneville and his party undertook to navigate in the late winter of 1835.

when a unique fur pelt owned by one of Bonneville's men disappeared. Probably an ermine skin, it had been shown to the residents of the village and to a band of Upper Nez Perces who were visiting them, passing from hand to hand as the silver goblet had done, then, after being admired by all who viewed it, suddenly was not to be found.

Indignantly the chief of the Lower Nez Perce village accused his cousins of besmirching the honor of his lodge by stealing the precious pelt. Just as indignantly the Upper Nez Perces denied the accusation. As the argument grew heated, Captain Bonneville tried to cool it down by saying the skin may have been mislaid. In any case, its loss was a matter of no great importance. But the squabble had gone beyond the point of being resolved by soothing words.

"All were at a loss on whom to fix the crime of abstracting the invaluable skin, when by chance the eyes of the worthies from beyond the water [the Upper Nez Perces who lived on the east side of Snake River] fell upon an unhappy cur, belonging to the owner of the hut . . . he was instantly accused of having devoured the skin in question . . . his thievish looks substantiated his guilt, and he was condemned by his judges from across the river to be hanged.

In vain the Indians of the hut, with whom he was a great favorite, interceded in his behalf. In vain Captain Bonneville and his comrades petitioned that his life

might be spared. His judges were inexorable. He was doubly guilty; first, in having robbed their good friends, the Big Hearts of the East; secondly, in having brought a doubt on the honor of the Nez Perce tribe. He was, accordingly, swung aloft, and pelted with stones to make his death more certain.

"The sentence of the judges being thoroughly executed, a post mortem examination of the body of the dog was held, to establish his delinquency beyond all doubt, and to leave the Nez Perces without a shadow of suspicion. Great interest, of course, was manifested by all present, during this operation. The body of the dog was opened, the intestines rigorously scrutinized, but, to the horror of all concerned, not a particle of the skin was to be found — the dog had been unjustly executed!

"A great clamor now ensued."[11]

Like Meriwether Lewis and William Clark, Captain Bonneville often was asked to provide medical services to the Indians. But in contrast to Lewis, who had been given several weeks of intensive training by one of the best doctors of his day, and Clark, who was supplied with calomel, laudunum, eyewash ingredients, and Dr. Rush's Bilious Pills,[12] Bonneville's medical science, by his own admission, "was of a most haphazard kind."[13] Still that did not prevent him from prescribing what might have been a dangerous course of treatment for the daughter of Chief O-push-y-e-cut, who for three days had been wracked with pains that the Nez Perce *tewats* (medicine men) could find no means to allay.

"His kind heart was already touched by the sufferings of the poor girl," Irving writes, "for she was but about sixteen years of age, and uncommonly beautiful in form and feature. . . . After considering and cogitating for some time . . . he made a desperate dash at a remedy. By his directions, the girl was placed in a sort of rude vapor bath, much used by the Nez Perces, where she was kept until near fainting. He then gave her a dose of gunpowder dissolved in cold water, and ordered her to be wrapped in buffalo robes and put to sleep under a load of furs and blankets.

"The remedy succeeded; the next morning she was free from pain, though extremely languid; whereupon, the captain prescribed for her a bowl of colt's head broth, and that she should be kept for a time on simple diet.

"The great chief was unbounded in his expressions of gratitude."[14]

Accepting the gift of a horses and the services

11. Ibid., p. 253–254.
12. Chuinard, *Only One Man Died.*
13. Irving, *Bonneville,* p. 256.
14. Ibid., p. 257.

of a young Nez Perce man who would accompany him to the next village and help him "to carry the talk," Captain Bonneville left the elevated table-land of the foothills and turned as the Snake River did from a northerly to a westerly course.

"They now traversed a gently undulating country, of such fertility that it excited the rapturous admiration of two of the captain's followers, a Kentuckian and a native of Ohio. They declared that it surpassed any land that they had ever seen, and often exclaimed what a delight it would be just to run a plough through such a rich and teeming soil, and see it open its bountiful promise before the share."[15]

Reaching Fort Walla Walla, Captain Bonneville and his men were greeted courteously by the Hudson's Bay Company factor, Pierre C. Pambrun, who then proceeded to stuff the captain full of an awesome amount of nonsense regarding the Nez Perces. According to Irving, Pambrun

"had been at some pains to introduce the Christian religion, in the Roman Catholic form, among them, where it had evidently taken root . . . had given them a code of laws, to which they conformed with scrupulous fidelity. Polygamy, which once prevailed among them to a great extent, was now rarely indulged. All the crimes denounced by the Christian faith met with severe punishment among them. Even theft . . . had recently been punished with hanging, by sentence of a chief . . . they would seem to be one of the very, very few [tribes] that have benefited in morals and manners by inter-course with white men.

"The parties which visited them about twenty years ago, in the expedition fitted out by Mr. Astor, com-plained of their selfishness, their extortion, and their thievish propensities," Irving wrote. "The very reverse of those qualities prevailed among them during the pro-longed sojourns of Captain Bonneville."[16]

According to all the contemporary sources we have examined, there is not a shred of truth in any of the statements attributed to Pambrun.

After attempting to buy supplies for his return journey and being curtly turned down, Captain Bonneville began to mistrust the Hudson's Bay Company factor's motives and refused to travel with François Payette, who was leading a party eastward by an easier, though longer, route, be-cause he doubted "the sincerity of his [Pambrun's] advice."

Instead, Bonneville decided to go back the way he had come, with minor modifications of route across the Wallowa Mountains suggested by his Nez Perce guides. Leaving Fort Walla Walla March 6, 1834, the party reached the most difficult part of the trip a week or so later. Ahead lay a steep,

snow-packed, nine-mile pass through the most rugged part of the mountains.

"The horses could not possibly cross the snows," the Nez Perces guides said. "They advised, therefore that the party should proceed on foot, and they should take the horses back to the village, where they would be well taken care of until Captain Bonneville should send for them. They urged this advice with great earnestness; declaring that their chief would be extremely angry, and treat them severely, should any of the horses of his good friends, the white men, be lost in crossing under their guidance."

But even after one of his men went ahead, sur-veyed the pass, and brought back the information that the snow was at least a hundred feet deep, Bonneville was determined to attempt the crossing with the horses.

"About dark there was a slight drizzling rain. An ex-pedient now suggested itself. This was to make two light sleds, place the packs on them, and drag them to the other side of the mountain, thus forming a road in the wet snow, which should it afterward freeze, would be sufficiently hard to bear the horses."

This was done. The night turned out clear and cold, and the next morning:

"they set out on their icy turnpike, and got on well enough, expecting that now and then a horse would sidle out of the track, and immediately sink up to the neck. Then came on toil and difficulty, and they would be obliged to haul up the floundering animal with ropes. One, more unlucky than the rest, after repeated falls, had to be abandoned in the snow. Notwithstanding these repeated delays, they succeeded, before the sun had acquired sufficient power to thaw the snow, in get-ting all the rest of their horses safely to the other side of the mountain.

"Their difficulties and danger, however, were not yet at an end. They had now to descend, and the whole surface of the snow was glazed with ice. It was neces-sary, therefore, to wait until the warmth of the sun should melt the glassy crust of sleet, and give them a foothold in the yielding snow. They had a frightful warn-ing of the danger of any movement while the sleet re-mained. A wild young mare, in her restlessness, strayed to the edge of a declivity. One slip was fatal to her; she lost her balance, careened with headlong velocity down the slippery side of the mountain for more than two thousand feet, and was dashed to pieces at the bottom. When the travellers afterward sought the carcass to cut it up for food, they found it torn and mangled in the most horrible manner."[17]

15. Ibid. Known as the Palouse Hills Country, this region today produces tremendous amounts of wheat and peas.
16. Ibid., p. 259.
17. Ibid., p. 272–273.

Photo by Bill Gulick

The Wallowa River

an irreclaimable wilderness, intervening between the abodes of civilization, and affording a last refuge to the Indians. . . . Here, in time, the Indians and white men of every nation will produce hybrid races like the mountain Tartars of the Caucases, who will become a scourge to the civilized frontier."[19]

Like George Simpson, Irving labored under the delusion that beaver was the only thing of value in the Pacific Northwest. But the appeal to save heathen souls, which had been broadcast to the religious world little more than a year earlier, now had been answered.

White missionaries had come.

With the $3,000 worth of trade goods he had contracted to the Rocky Mountain Fur Company, Nathaniel Wyeth and a well-equipped party of men reached Green River rendezvous grounds in early July 1834. He had chartered another ship, the *May Dacre,* which he planned to meet on the lower Columbia. Accompanying him were two scientists, Thomas Nuttall, a Harvard botanist, and John K. Townsend, a Philadelphia physician and ornithologist, who rapturously classified flora, fauna, and birds, filled journals with copious notes, and behaved with such reckless disregard for their scalps while passing through dangerous Indian country that the hostiles, thinking them mad, left them strictly alone.

Also included in the party were the first men of the cloth to respond to the Indians' plea for missionaries: the Methodist minister, Jason Lee; his nephew, Daniel; and three lay brethren. Observing the stars, shooting the sun, and making accurate recordings of longitude and latitude, with his feet set firmly upon the ground rather than on the heaving deck of a ship, was Wyeth's second in command, an old sea dog, Captain Joseph Thing.

Rendezvous was bigger and more riotous than ever that summer, for, in addition to many lodges of Flatheads, Nez Perces, and Snakes, Bonneville's men, Wyeth's men, Rocky Mountain Fur Company trappers, men employed by the American Fur Company, deserters from the Hudson's Bay Company, and free trappers owing allegiance to no one but themselves — all were there.

Seeing the missionaries, the Flatheads and Nez Perces were first delighted then disappointed. Sorry, Jason Lee said, we do not plan to establish

Having seen the party across the pass, the Nez Perce guides took a long farewell smoke with their white friends, exchanged good wishes and good-byes, mounted their horses, and returned home. At river level next day, Bonneville found the weather mild and warm. There was new grass in great abundance eight inches high. Without serious incident he reached on May 12, 1834, the Portneuf campsite which he had left the previous Christmas Day. After a two-week search of the area he found the party he had left behind. Like his, it had barely managed to stay alive during the winter and spring months, let alone make much of a catch of beaver.

No matter. Opening a nearby cache, the captain threw a party.

"Being thus reunited, a general treat from Captain Bonneville to his men was a matter of course. Two days, therefore, were given up to such feasting and merriment as their means and situation afforded. What was wanting in good cheer was made up in good will."[18]

After one more winter in the West, Captain Bonneville would forsake trading, return to the East, and meet Washington Irving. The writer would praise him as a leader and for the information he had turned over to the federal government. But it is to be doubted that Irving's summation of the Snake River country came from Bonneville's lips:

"An immense belt of rocky mountains and volcanic plains, several hundred miles in width, must ever remain

18. Ibid., p. 275.
19. Ibid., p. 372.

a mission in your country, which we hear is uncivilized. We're going on west to the Willamette Valley, near Fort Vancouver. Perhaps later . . .

Now it was Wyeth's turn to be disappointed. Locked in a dog-eat-dog conflict with the American Fur Company, the Rocky Mountain Fur Company was being driven to the wall. Milton Sublette, who had signed the contract with Wyeth, had turned back short of Green River because of an increasingly painful leg injury. William Sublette, his brother, refused to honor the contract, taking only a small part of the trade goods at bargain-basement prices.

Wyeth was furious. In retaliation for the breach of contract, he would "roll a stone into the garden of the Rocky Mountain Fur Company that they could never dislodge."[20]

Leaving rendezvous and crossing over into the Snake River watershed, he chose a site "in the low, rich bottom of a valley formed by the confluence of Portneuf River with the Snake, which it enters about nine miles below"[21] and commenced building a trading post July 15, 1834. Among the interested observers was Thomas McKay, leader of a Hudson's Bay Company brigade which happened to be in the neighborhood. It was McKay who had convinced Jason Lee that the Willamette Valley would be a more logical place to establish a mission than the country of the Flatheads and Nez

Perces. After all, he no doubt told Lee, when the Joint Occupancy matter is settled, the Snake River country will become British while the Willamette Valley will become American.

Lee did consent to preach a sermon Sunday afternoon, July 27, to the Indians, whites, half bloods, Americans, British, and combinations thereof assembled near Wyeth's still-building fort. The listeners were most attentive. Afterwards the Sabbath was broken by a series of horse races, in the last of which a French-Canadian named Kanseau was tragically thrown and killed.

Next day Jason Lee participated in a three-denominational burial service, reading the Ninth Psalm, which begins: "I will praise thee, O Lord, with my whole heart."

Wyeth wrote:

"Services for him were performed by the Canadians in the Catholic form, by Mr. Lee in the Protestant form, and by the Indians in their form, as he had an Indian family. He at least was well buried."[22]

Accompanied by the Hudson's Bay Company brigade, which had offered to see it through to the lower Columbia, the Lee party set out shortly thereafter. Building of the post, which Wyeth named after his principal backer, Henry Hall, went on. The morning of August 5, 1834, a homemade American flag was raised over Fort Hall. One of the three barrels of alcohol Wyeth had brought along was tapped, and the day was spent in celebration.

Townsend, the physician and naturalist, viewed it with disapproving eyes:

"At sunrise this morning the *Star Spangled Banner* was raised on the flagstaff of the fort, and a salute fired by the men. . . . All in camp were then allowed the free and uncontrolled use of liquor, and, as usual, the consequence was a scene of rioting, noise, and fighting during the whole day. . . . We had gouging, biting, fisticuffs, and stamping in the most scientific perfection."[23]

Leaving eleven men to take care of the post and initiate trading with the Indians, Wyeth and the remainder of his party moved northwest by way of Godin's River and Malade River, detaching small groups to trap these streams. Appropriately, Antoine Godin, whose father had been killed by Blackfeet near the river bearing his name, was one of them.

Dr. John McLoughlin

20. Ibid., p. 153.
21. Ibid., p. 139.
22. Ibid., p. 146.
23. Ibid., p. 148.

On September 2 Wyeth caught up with the Jason Lee party, which had traveled more slowly, at Fort Walla Walla. He noted with puzzlement that the leader and several men of the Hudson's Bay Company brigade were missing.

"Mr. McKay for some reason had remained in the mountains."

The reason soon became apparent. After seeing Wyeth start to build Fort Hall, Thomas McKay decided that the Hudson's Bay Company should have a post in the area, too. Divulging his plans to no one, he and a few men lingered behind the brigade, chose a site on the Boise River ten miles upstream from its juncture with the Snake, and began building a fort whose flagstaff would bear the British banner.

It would be called Fort Boise.

As the crow flew, it was located some two hundred and fifty miles west of Fort Hall — just good "neighboring" distance in this country. But exchanging neighborly visits was not its intended function. In the game of rolling stones into gardens, any number could play, and the Hudson's Bay Company was adept at bowling on the green.

Meantime Wyeth reached the lower Columbia, and his supply ship, the *May Dacre,* soon was anchored in the stream. The British still were polite, but they still would not trade. The Indians had furs, but not for him. The river was full of fat, gleaming salmon which the Indians caught, cured, stored, and sold to the British in great numbers, but would not catch for him. Work though they would, his own men lacked the equipment and know-how to obtain a substantial number of fish themselves. They grew disgusted and quit him to seek their fortunes in other fields, for other employers.

Hearing that trade was going badly at Fort Hall, Wyeth hired thirteen Sandwich Islanders, whom he called "Kanakas," and sent them inland with Captain Joseph Thing and a load of fresh supplies. But the Hawaiians disliked the looks of the interior country. Deserting their landlocked commander west of the Blue Mountains, they returned to the lower Columbia. Captain Thing continued inland

to Fort Hall. He spent a brutal, frustrating winter there, competing with the Hudson's Bay Company and fighting Blackfeet, then came back to his employer's fishery just across the river from Fort Vancouver in July, 1835, "emaciated, pale, and apparently seven years older than the season before."[24]

Reluctantly, Wyeth sent the *May Dacre* back to Boston with half a cargo of salmon and furs. Recognizing the fact that he was facing financial ruin, he headed overland to Fort Hall to do what he could there. Again his best efforts failed, and he returned to Boston to consult with his backers, They could give him no more help, they said; he must carry on alone.

In a final attempt to salvage what little could be saved, Wyeth made one more trip west to Green River rendezvous in July 1836. He arranged to sell Fort Hall to the only interested buyer, the Hudson's Bay Company. He learned that the Rocky Mountain Fur Company was now in its death throes; it would be succeeded by Astor's American Fur Company.

Well and good. Now the game would be played to its bitter end by two giant monopolies, one American, the other British, and the most ruthless would win. He would go back to farm managing and ice selling.

By now he should have been immune to surprises, but one sight he observed at the 1836 rendezvous moved him deeply. White women were there, traveling west. Lord in Heaven! Did they really mean to settle and make homes for their husbands in this wild, remote country?

They certainly did. For these were missionary couples drawn west by the pealing of a distant bell, responding to the New Testament's Great Command:

"Go ye therefore . . ."

Unlike Jason Lee and his party, this band of missionaries intended to live among, and minister to, the uncivilized Nez Perces.

24. Ibid., p. 163.

CHAPTER EIGHT

THE MISSIONARIES: 1835–1839

The first chief of the Nez Perces, Tai-quin-watish, rose and said he had heard from white men a little about God, which had only gone into his ears; he wished to know enough to have it go down into his heart.
— Samuel Parker, August 15, 1835

GROUNDWORK FOR the first crossing of the continent by white women had been laid a year earlier, during the summer of 1835, when the Presbyterian minister, Samuel Parker, and the doctor-missionary, Marcus Whitman, had journeyed to fur rendezvous with Lucien Fontenelle and consulted with Nez Perce tribal leaders regarding their desire to have a Protestant mission established in their country.

Fontenelle was not happy with the escort chore. Like the rough-hewn men in his employ, he equated men of the cloth with a loss of freedom and sensed that a cherished way of life was coming to an end. While in St. Louis he dared not violate company policy of friendship to the missionaries, but once the brigade left Liberty (near present-day Kansas City) and headed out across the open plains he did his best to discourage Parker and Whitman from tagging along.

First he refused to carry their baggage in his wagons, forcing Whitman, a rank greenhorn at packing, to tie and attempt to keep all their provisions and gear on the bony back of one "poor old mule." When the two missionaries declined to travel on the Sabbath, Fontenelle and the brigade continued without them. At river fords, members of the brigade attempted to destroy a raft, constructed to float their own gear across the stream, so that Parker and Whitman could not use it. On one occasion some of the more boisterous members of the party threw rotten eggs at Marcus Whitman; others attempted to force Samuel Parker to break his temperance vows and take a drink of whiskey.

Fifty-six years of age, overweight, bookish, and pompous of manner, Samuel Parker was far more at home in an upstate New York pulpit than aboard a horse in the western wilderness. Marcus Whitman, thirty-three, big-boned, and muscular, could carry his share of the work load when it came to bridging streams, prying wagons out of mudholes, or other tasks of camp and trail. Because the Reverend Parker's official title was "Missionary," While Whitman's was "Assistant Missionary," it was Whitman's lot to saddle and unsaddle, pack and upack, pitch and strike the tent, cook the meals, wash the dishes, and do everything else that had to be done, while Parker observed the scenery, enjoyed the ride, and made entries in his journal.

How long the hostility between the trapping brigade and the missionaries might have lasted became a moot question when the caravan reached Bellevue, two weeks out from Liberty, and an epidemic of Asian cholera struck the bridgade.

"At this place the Lord had a great change for us," Marcus Whitman wrote, "for the Cholera appearing in camp, my aid was greatly sought. Mr. Fontenelle himself being one of the subjects of the disease and recovering (as also most of his men), he showed his gratitude, as well as all other persons in the company, by bestowing upon us *every* favor in his power."[1]

Since it was not unusual for a cholera epidemic to kill half the community through which it raged, the fact that they lost only three members of the

1. Clifford M. Drury, *Marcus and Narcissa Whitman and the Opening of Old Oregon* (Glendale, Calif.: Arthur H. Clark Co., 1973), vol. 1, p. 124. Whitman Letter No. 62.

Indian woman with children in front of hide tepee

brigade — which numbered more than fifty — says a great deal for the skill with which Dr. Whitman treated the sick men.

At rendezvous, which the caravan reached August 12, 1835, word of Dr. Whitman's skills had preceeded him. His first patient was Jim Bridger, who three years earlier had caught a Blackfoot arrow in his back. The three-inch head, which still was imbedded there, was "bothering him some," and he would be obliged if the doctor would cut it out.

"It was a difficult operation," Samuel Parker wrote, "because the arrow was hooked at the point by striking a large bone and a cartilagenous substance had grown around it. The Doctor pursued the operation with great self-possession and perserverance; and his patient manifested equal firmness."[2]

Because of the warm, friendly reception given them by Insala, the most influential chief among the Flatheads, and by Tai-quin-watish, an important Nez Perce chief, Parker and Whitman came to the conclusion that a mission station should be established in their country as soon as possible.

"So desirable did this object appear," Parker wrote, "that Doctor Whitman proposed to return with the caravan and to obtain associates to come out with him the next year. . . . I readily consented to the proposal, and to go alone with the Indians the remainder of my exploring tour. Dr. Whitman on further consideration felt some misgivings about leaving me to go alone with the Indians, lest, if any calamity should befall me, he should be blamed by the Christian public. I told him to give himself no uneasiness upon this subject; for we could not go safely together without divine protection, and with it, I could go alone."[3]

While Samuel Parker's faith in divine protection no doubt was sincere, the conduct and character of the Nez Perces and Flatheads during the few days he had known them must have impressed him very favorably, else he would not have entrusted his aging, not very rugged, body to their care. Upon telling the chiefs of the contemplated return of Whitman, Parker found the Indians

"much pleased. They selected one of their principal young men for my personal assistant, as long as I should have need of him, who was called Kentuc; and I engaged a *voyageur,* who understood English, and also Nez Perce sufficiently well to interpret in common business . . . while I should continue with these tribes."[4]

At that time it was the policy of the American Board for Foreign Missions, headquartered in Boston, to send only married couples into distant

Samuel Parker

lands. The reception given Parker and Whitman by the Nez Perces and Flatheads, coupled with the aid given them by the fur brigade after the cholera epidemic struck, answered the two most important questions in the minds of the missionaries: first, that the Indians truly desired religious instructions; second, that wagons could cross the country, as Fontenelle's had done, with no great difficulty, thus making it possible to bring women and household goods along.

A bachelor now, Marcus Whitman had made a tacit agreement with an attactive, strong-minded young lady back in Angelica, New York, that if a mission were established among the Indians in the Oregon Country he would return, they would marry, and she would join him as a helpmate in his work. A full year's time would be saved by having Parker go on to the Nez Perce country to select a

2. Samuel Parker, *Journal of an Exploring Tour Beyond the Rocky Mountains* (Ithaca, N.Y., 1838), p. 72.

3. Ibid., p. 78.

4. Ibid. Kentuc was a good-humored Nez Perce who had been taught to sing one American song, "The Hunters of Kentucky," which he sang quite badly and with amusing results, thus his name. Josephy, *Nez Perce Indians,* p. 126.

site for the mission while Whitman went East to wed Narcissa Prentiss, enlist another couple to join them, and assemble the vast array of supplies they would need for a permanent station in the distant land to which they were journeying.

It appears to have been Whitman's idea that a young Nez Perce boy return to New York with him, as, years earlier, Spokane Garry had gone to eastern Canada under the aupices of the Hudson's Bay Company. After some discussion with the boy's father (who is not named) a young Nez Perce lad called Tack-i-too-tis or Tack-i-ton-i-tis was selected to make the trip.

"My reason for taking him," Whitman said, "is that he can speak the English language a little and by being with white people he will soon speak so as to interpret or assist in learning his language."[5]

Three days later another Nez Perce chief begged Whitman to take *his* son along too. Whitman wrote:

"The father said he had but one more son, but he was willing to part with this one that he might be taught the religion of the whites."[6]

The first boy was renamed Richard; the second, whose Indian name was Ais, was called John.

Parker and Whitman exchanged farewells August 22, the young doctor heading east with the returning fur brigade, while Samuel Parker and his Indian escort set out for the Nez Perce country. Accompanied by Jim Bridger and a party of fifty men bound for the beaver-rich streams rising in the ruggedly beautiful range of mountains called the Grand Tetons, the band crossed the Continental Divide and entered Jackson Hole by way of the Hoback River. When Parker learned that the Snake River was an upper branch of the Columbia, he wrote:

"It was interesting to find myself, for the first time, upon the waters of this noble river. The Indians were very attentive to all my wants — took the entire care of my packed animals, cooking, etc. They preserve particular order in their movements. The first chief leads the way, the next chiefs follow them, then the common men, and after these the women and children. The place assigned me was with the first chief."[7]

Certainly Parker received first-class treatment from the Nez Perces.

"Two little girls brought me a quart of strawberries, a rare dish for the season of the year. And an Indian brought me some service berries, which are pleasantly sweet, and somewhat resemble whortleberries."[8]

A day or so later:

"Kentuc, my Indian, brought me today some very good currants which were a feast in this land. There are several species, yellow, pale red, and black. The yellow and pale red were the best flavored."[9]

Leaving Jackson Hole by way of Teton Pass, the party turned north and rode across the wide, well-watered plain called Pierre's Hole. In his *Journal,* published three years later, Parker gives his account of the Battle of Pierre's Hole, scolds the Americans for having been the agressors, and accuses a writer with "a graphic hand" (obviously Washington Irving) of having grossly exaggerated the engagement. Perhaps Irving did. But had he been able to express himself, the Nez Perce chief, Tai-quin-watish — or, more correctly spelled, Tack-en-su-a-tis, which translated meant "Rotten Belly" — could have given Parker a personal account of the battle, for he had been there.

Fighting on the side of the Americans as Lawyer had done, Tack-en-su-a-tis had caught a Blackfoot bullet in his stomach. The festering wound was healed now, but the name lingered on — as did his friendship for the Americans. Yet even if the Nez Perce chief had been able to express himself fluently, the story would have been incomplete, for tribal warrior code required that a man tell only what he himself had done in a battle, without presuming to relate what men fighting beside him had done. Call it modesty or a special regard for personalized truth. This was the Nez Perce way.

Near the spot where in 1811 the Wilson Price Hunt party had decided to abandon their horses and descend Snake River by boat, the Reverend Samuel Parker made his first attempt to instruct the Nez Perces in religious matters by teaching them the ten Commandments.

"My method of instructing them was to give to the first chief the first commandment, by repeating it until he could repeat it; and the second commandment to another chief in the same way, and so on through the ten, with directions for them to retain what was given to each, and to teach them to their people . . . on examination in no case did I find more than one material mistake."[10]

5. Drury, *Whitman,* p. 138. Whitman Letter No. 11.
6. Ibid.
7. Parker, *Journal,* pp. 82–83.
8. Ibid., p. 85.
9. Ibid., p. 86.
10. Ibid., pp. 90–91.

Shortly thereafter, the Jim Bridger party and some of the Flatheads headed northeast toward trapping grounds in country claimed by the ever-dangerous Blackfeet, while Parker's escort of Nez Perces and the rest of the Flatheads turned northwest toward the Salmon River. The social conduct of the Nez Perces impressed Parker.

"The Indians are very kind to each other, and if one meets with any disaster, the others will wait and assist him. Their horses often turn their pack and run, plunge, and kick until they free themselves from their burdens. Yesterday a horse turned his saddle under him upon which a child was fastened, and started to run, but those near hovered at once around with their horses so as to enclose the one to which the child was attached, and it was extricated without hurt . . .

"They are so well supplied with horses that every man, woman, and child are mounted on horseback, and all they have is packed on horses. Small children, not more than three years old, are mounted alone, and generally upon colts. They are lashed upon the saddle to keep them from falling, and especially when they go asleep, which they often do when they become fatigued. Then they recline upon the horses's shoulders; and when they awake, they lay hold of their whip, which is fastened to the wrist of their right hand, and apply it smartly to their horses; and it is astonishing to see how these little creatures will guide and run them. Children which are still younger are put into an encasement made with a board at the back and a wicker work around the other parts, covered with cloth inside and without, or more generally with dressed skins; and they are carried upon their mother's back, or suspended from a high knob upon the fore part of their saddles."[11]

The morning of September 5, Parker noted, was very cold, and the party remained in camp in order for a large band of Salmon River Nez Perces, which they learned was nearby, to join them.

"About the middle of the day they came; the principal chief marching in front with his aide, carrying an American flag by his side. They all sung a march, while a few beat a sort of drum."[12]

The leader of this band was named Charle. Although Parker called him "first chief of the Nez Perce nation," he could not have been, for they had no such office. Nevertheless, he was an important individual, described by Parker as

"a good-looking man, his countenance rather stern, intelligent, and expressive of much decision of character. I never saw joy expressed in a more dignified manner than when he took me firmly by the hand and welcomed me . . .

" 'I have been like a little child,' Charle said, 'feeling about in the dark after something; but not knowing what; but now I hope to learn something which will be substantial, and which will help me to teach my people to do right.' "[13]

Next day being the Sabbath and a "good interpreter" having arrived from Fort Hall, the Reverend Mr. Parker agreed to preach a formal sermon to the combined bands. When Parker asked if the large crowd could be accommodated in the willows along the creek, the chiefs said they could do better than that — and did.

"I found them all assembled, men, women, and children, between four and five hundred, in what I would call a sanctuary of God, constructed with their lodges, nearly one hundred feet long and about twenty feet wide; and all were arranged in rows, through the length of the building, upon their knees, with a narrow space in the middle, lengthwise, resembling an aisle. The whole area within was carpeted with their dressed skins, and they were all attired in their best . . .

"I never spoke to a more interesting assembly, and I would not have changed my audience for any other upon earth."[14]

Since Parker's sermon began with a description of man's creation and carried on through his fall, the birth, life, and death of the Savior, and then "endeavored to show them the necessity of renovation of heart by the power and grace of the Holy Spirit," all of which passed through a probably not very well educated interpreter, it is questionable how much of it the Nez Perces understood. But

"they gave the utmost attention, and entire stillness prevailed, excepting when some truth arrested their mind forcibly, a little humming sound was made through the whole assembly, occupying two or three seconds."

Though Parker's health had been good until now, he caught a cold September 8 as they pursued their journey, causing a pain in his chest that grew steadily worse. A few days ahead lay the most fatiguing portion of the trip, a crossing of the mountains from the Salmon to the Clearwater by way of the Old Nez Perce Trail. Food was in short supply, but, as Parker noted:

"They are not very anxious about the future. When they have a plenty, they are not sparing; and when they are in want, they do not complain."[15]

Fortunately, a large herd of buffalo was encountered September 9, a rather unusual occurr-

11. Ibid., pp. 92–93.
12. Ibid., p. 95.
13. Ibid., pp. 97–98.
14. Ibid., p. 98.
15. Ibid., p. 100.

Courtesy Luna House Historical Society
Lewiston, Idaho

Two Nez Perce women

ence for that part of the country, and for several days the Indians were engaged in killing and drying meat. Between fifty and sixty beasts were slain, giving the band a plentiful supply of food for the mountain passage, which would take twelve to fifteen days.

Parker continued unwell, the pain in his chest moving to the right side of his head and becoming so severe that "I was obliged to resort to medicine." What sort of medicine, he does not say. Probably calomel, jalap, or some other strong purgative, possibly combined with a pain-killer such as laudanum, which was an opium derivative.

On September 11, three hundred Nez Perces and Flatheads left the one hundred and fifty Indians in the Tack-en-su-a-tis band, heading north for the Bitter Root Valley and the buffalo country. Before leaving they presented Parker with a token of their regard, "a very valuable present of twenty

very fine buffalo tongues, which are a great delicacy, together with a large quantity of dried meat."[16]

Two days later, Parker noted:

"The inflamation in my head still continued with throbbing, pain, and fever — my pulse one hundred a minute. Bled myself again and took medicine . . .

"*Sabbath, 13th.* My health no better, and my strength was failing. I felt that all was right, and I needed this trial to lead me to an examination of my spiritual condition, my motives in engaging in this mission, and whether I could give up all for Christ to promote his kingdom in the world."[17]

With Charle as a guide and ten Indians as an escort, Parker left the slow-traveling band behind and climbed a six-thousand-foot ridge. He found the way much encumbered by fallen trees and began to fear that he would not live to complete his journey.

"The inflamation in my head continuing, I bled myself copiously, which reduced my pulse for a while, but increased my weakness, so that I could walk but a few rods without much fatigue.

"Sometimes, amidst all the evidences of God's mercy to me, I found my heart sinking into despondency, and was ready to say, I shall perish in these wild, cold mountains. It seemed that such was my failure of strength, and I was become so emaciated, that I could not endure the fatigue of traveling eight days more over these mountains."[18]

But the crisis passed. Somehow he did endure and began to make a recovery, for he does not mention his ailment again, except to say on September 28, "In better health. Make a long day's march and emerged from the mountains."

The day before, Charle had told him:

"We are now near our country, and when we come into it, I wish you to look over it, and see if it is good for missionaries to live in."[19]

The rigors of the trip, the aftereffects of his illness, and the realization that age was taking its toll, had greatly diminished Parker's zeal for missionary work. Moving through the heart of the Nez Perce country as rapidly as he could travel, he reached the confluence of the Clearwater with the Snake (at present-day Lewiston, Idaho) October 1, where

16. Ibid., p. 102.
17. Ibid., p. 104.
18. Ibid., p. 111.
19. Ibid., p. 116.

he wrote the casual comment: "This place combines many advantages for a mission station."[20] At the Hudson's Bay Company post, Fort Walla Walla, where he was welcomed by the British factor, Pierre Pambrun, he wrote:

"I never felt more joy in entering a habitation of civilized people, and whose language was not strange. I felt that I had a great cause of thankfulness."[21]

Though the original plan had been for Samuel Parker to inspect the country of the Flatheads and the Nez Perces, select the best site for a mission, and return to rendezvous to meet and advise the Whitman party the next summer, he did not carry it through. Instead, he spent the fall and winter as a guest of the Hudson's Bay Company at Fort Vancouver. In the spring of 1836 he did journey up the Columbia as far as Fort Colville, on the northwest edge of Nez Perce country. He later wrote that he would have returned to the States via the overland route if he had found a brigade heading east along the way he wanted to go.

But his "way was hedged up," he wrote Whitman May 10, 1836; hence, he would return to the East Coast by ship, his passage courtesy of the Hudson's Bay Company.

"We cannot say how much good Mr. Parker's tour will do others," Whitman later wrote with some bitterness. "It has done us none, for instead of meeting us at rendezvous as he agreed, he neglected even to write a single letter containing any information concerning the country, Indians, prospects, or advice of any kind whatever."[20]

Undoubtedly Parker had reached the age where weakness of the flesh overwhelmed willingness of the spirit. Going home by sea offered a much more comfortable prospect than subjecting his stiffening joints to the jolting a horse would give them. But even an ocean voyage was no luxury trip in that day. Sailing from Fort Vancouver to Hawaii on June 12, he was obliged to lay over there until November 14 before he could take passage on a ship bound for New London, Connecticut. The trip around Cape Horn proved to be tiring, dull, and at times dangerous. The food and water were bad, and it took five long months.

He reached New London May 18, 1837, after an absence from the United States of two years and two months and after having traveled 28,000 miles. Not a bad achievement for a man of his age and physical condition. When published the following year, his *Journal of an Exploring Tour Beyond the Rocky Mountains* became a best seller among people interested in the Oregon Country, going through five American and three European editions. Though his role may not have turned out as originally planned, he had done his bit toward taking the course of empire westward on its way.

Meanwhile, Marcus and Narcissa Whitman, Henry and Eliza Spalding, the two Nez Perce boys, Richard and John, Joe Meek, Tack-en-su-a-tis, Lawyer, and Kentuc had a joyous meeting at rendezvous on Green River July 6, 1836. Present were a hundred or so American trappers, two hundred Nez Perces and Flatheads, a few Cayuse Indians, and several hundred Indians from other tribes, such as Utahs and Shoshones. As might be expected, the two white women immediately became the center of attention for both the trappers and the Indians.

"It was truly pleasing," Narcissa wrote, "to see the meeting of Richard and John with their friends. Richard was affected to tears. His father is not here but several of his band and brothers are. When they met, each took off his hat and shook hands as respectful as in civilized life."[23]

It is probable that Samuel Parker had told the Cayuses of the coming of the missionaries, for a rivalry quickly developed between them and their Nez Perce "cousins" as to where the first mission station should be established. Narcissa wrote:

"The Nez Perce women said we were going to live with them, and the Cayuses said we were going to live with them. The contradiction was so sharp they nearly came to blows."[24]

As matters turned out, both groups of Indians were satisfied when it was decided to establish two missions rather than one. The reason for this decision lay in a strong conflict between personalities.

As noted earlier, Marcus Whitman was a doctor-missionary, though not an ordained minister. His wife, Narcissa, was blonde, lovely, cheerful, outgoing, and in the best of health, enjoying every new experience that came her way.

The other missionary couple, Henry and Eliza Spalding, were more somber, less worldly people

20. Ibid., p. 119.
21. Ibid., p. 121.
22. Drury, *Whitman*, p. 192.
23. Ibid., p. 194.
24. Ibid., p. 196. Letter No. 34.

— the husband (who *was* an ordained minister) a stern, straitlaced man whom Narcissa once had rejected as a suitor, the wife feeble and often ill, though somehow she always managed to find strength enough to do what must be done. Though both the Whitmans and the Spaldings tried their best to conceal it, friction existed between them, a rift so deep that they could not possibly work together in the same mission.

The site chosen by Dr. Whitman for his mission was in Cayuse country south and east of the mouth of the Snake, in the fertile Walla Walla Valley. He chose well, for here the climate was mild, the soil "a delight to run a plough through," and the trail from East to West nearby. In the Cayuse tongue the spot was called Waiilatpu, the "Place of the Rye Grass."

Spalding chose a site 120 miles east, in the heart of the Nez Perce country, twelve miles above the juncture of the Clearwater and the Snake. This sheltered valley was called Lapwai by the Nez Perce, which meant "Place of the Butterflies."

Because of the hot, dry summers and the steep, bare hills, the Clearwater Valley offers a bleak visual prospect in early October, which was when Henry Spalding first saw the region. His spirits fell to dismal depths. He wrote:

"The appearance of the country for the last half day greatly discouraged us. It was very mountainous and broken; the vallies were narrow and without good soil. As we drew near the place we were still more discouraged. . . . I was riding far behind, almost disheartened. I thought it was all over with the poor Nez Perces. To take them from their country would prove ruinous to the nation, and to commence an establishment without soil or timber would prove equally ruinous to the mission."[25]

His escort, Tack-en-su-a-tis, sensed Spalding's feelings. After dropping back and riding beside him for some time, the Nez Perce chief said:

"We are now near the place where there is good land, if anywhere in the Nez Perce country. Perhaps it will not answer, but if it does I am happy. This is all my country, and where you settle, I shall settle. And you need not think you will work by yourself; only let us know what you want done, and it shall be done."[26]

Ten miles above the juncture of the Clearwater with the Snake, Tack-en-su-a-tis and the band of Nez Perces turned south up the valley of Lapwai Creek. Here Spalding's spirits lifted, for this valley contained good soil, was over half a mile wide, and supported a growth of small trees. Two and a half miles up the creek, the missionary halted and told

Courtesy Penrose Library, Whitman College
Old woman with firewood

his Nez Perce guide that this site met all his requirements.

"The Indians could scarcely contain themselves for joy when they heard us pronounce the word good," Spalding wrote. "They had watched every motion with trembling anxiety, as though life and death were at stake. We rode late and camped, thankful that the Lord had been better to us than our fears."[27]

Until dwelling places could be built for them, Eliza Spalding and Narcissa Whitman were to live as guests of the Hudson's Bay Company at Fort Vancouver. Dr. John McLoughlin, the factor there, had anticipated that the two ladies would be with him all winter, but their energetic husbands had other plans. Spalding selected a building site at the foot of Thunder Mountain near a good spring, and on October 12, 1836, he told the Nez Perces he

25. Drury, *Spaulding,* p. 159.
26. Ibid.
27. Ibid., p. 160. Spaulding Letter No. 11.

intended to leave at once for Fort Vancouver. He asked the Indians to meet him at Fort Walla Walla in five weeks. Assuring him that they would be there, they offered to go up the Clearwater into more heavily timbered country during his absence, where they would cut down trees and obtain the logs he would need for his buildings. Afraid that he could not adequately communicate his needs without being present, Spalding instructed them to wait until his return.

Meanwhile, Marcus Whitman and William H. Gray, an outspoken, contentious carpenter with ambitions to be a missionary, had been hard at work building a house at Waiilatpu. Arriving at Fort Vancouver on October 18, Spalding told a surprised Dr. McLoughlin his plans, assembled baggage and supplies, and with his wife and Mrs. Whitman headed back upriver November 3. Reaching Fort Walla Walla ten days later, he shared Sunday worship with Gray and the Whitmans. Then, accompanied by Gray, and an escort of 125 Nez Perces, he set out for Lapwai on November 22. The Indians, Spalding wrote, were most helpful.

"They took entire direction of everything, pitched and struck our tent, saddled our horses, and gladly would have put victuals to our mouths, had we wished it. So eager were they to do all they could to make us comfortable, I was astonished at the ease with which they handled and packed our heavy bags and cases, the latter sixteen inches square, thirty inches long, and weighing usually 125 pounds. Our effects loaded twenty horses."[28]

In addition to the five thousand pounds of farming tools, provisions, clothing, books, and building materials the horses were carrying, Spalding took five cows, one bull, and two calves out of the herd of cattle that the missionary party had driven out from the states. On November 22 the packtrain left Fort Walla Walla. After saying a sympathetic goodbye, Narcissa Whitman wrote of Eliza:

"This dear sister goes very cheerfully to her location, expecting to live in a skin lodge until her house is built; and this, too, in the dead of winter; but she prefers it to remaining here, and so should I."[29]

Because of the inevitable comparison with blonde, lovely, cheerful, healthy Narcissa Whitman, dark homely, serious, and often ill Eliza Spalding has been pictured by many writers as being a weak, whining, spineless woman, sadly lacking in the strength of character required in a female missionary. Such a picture is false. The daughter of a prosperous merchant in Cincinnati when she married Henry Spalding, she helped him work his way through Western Reserve College by running a boardinghouse. She was more intelligent and far better educated than Marcus and Narcissa Whitman. She was an accomplished linguist, having mastered Hebrew and Greek. During the two months it took the missionary party to travel from the fur company rendezvous on Green River to Fort Walla Walla, she learned the Nez Perce language well enough to converse with the Indians in their own tongue. Later she worked with her husband inventing a Nez Perce alphabet and translating hymns and the Gospel of Matthew into Nez Perce.

Her health *was* frail, but she certainly did not complain about it excessively or let it keep her from doing what had to be done. Her first child had been stillborn before she left the East. When the opportunity arose for the Spaldings to go to the Oregon Country instead of to the nearer Osage Mission to which they had been assigned, her father threatened to disinherit her if she went to Oregon. She defied him — and he did disinherit her. When the state of her health was brought up as an objection to her making the long overland journey, she said; "I like the Command just as it stands — 'Go ye therefore into all nations' — and no exceptions for poor health."

Her husband, Henry Spalding, was not an easy man to live with. He had been born out of wedlock November 6, 1803, in the small village of Wheeler, New York. Being publicly branded a bastard was no small handicap in those days. Emotionally, it scarred him for life.

"What memories!" he wrote upon revisiting his birthplace in the twilight of his life thirty-five years after leaving home. "The place where I was born, and the place where my unfeeling mother gave me, but fourteen months old, to a stranger and saw her child no more, and the place where I was brought up by an adopted mother, and where I was kicked out, and the brook and the willow and the hill where I fished and played and tumbled with other children . . . and the hills and the bottom where I gathered chestnuts and butternuts and the road I took when he kicked me out after whipping my mother and me, to a neighbor, sad, destitute, crying,

28. Ibid., p. 161. Spaulding Letter No. 14.

29. Ibid., p. 162; *Transactions of the Oregon Pioneer Association, 1891,* p. 89.

a cast off bastard, wishing myself dead! What memories!"

Unacknowledged by his real father, deserted by his real mother, whipped and kicked out of the house of his foster parents at the age of seventeen, Spalding went to Prattsburg, New York, where he found shelter in the home of a schoolteacher, Ezra Rice. He remained there four years, working for his board and room, going to school, and being treated decently for the first time in his life.

Until then his opportunities for education had been extremely limited. When he was twenty-one years old, he later noted in his diary, he could read only with difficulty and could laboriously "write after copy." He enrolled in newly opened Franklin Academy when he was twenty-two and had a difficult time. He was five years older than most of his classmates, dressed in the plainest of clothes, was extremely bashful when called upon to speak, and, as he later described himself was "worse than an orphan."

But he was tenacious in his struggle. Though he often had to interrupt his studies to work or teach in country schools, he managed to transform himself from a virtual illiterate at the age of seventeen to a graduate of Western Reserve College at Hudson, Ohio, with an A.B. degree at the age of thirty.

Tact was not one of Spalding's virtues. When asked by a visitor why two separate missions had been established he replied bluntly: "Do you suppose I would have come off here all alone a hundred and twenty miles if I could have lived with him [Marcus] or Mrs. Whitman?"

At first, relationships between the Spaldings and the Nez Perces at Lapwai were extremely good. Spalding and Gray designed a house eighteen feet wide by forty-two feet long that could be used both as living quarters and as a meeting place. With considerable help from the Indians, they completed the principal work on the structure in three and a half weeks. Logs for the building, which had been cut some distance upriver and then floated down the Clearwater, were carried more than two miles from the river to the site on the shoulders of the Indians. Boards were whipsawed for the floor. The roof was made of timbers covered with a layer of grass and then a layer of clay — a not very satisfactory covering, for when it rained mud oozed through cracks between the timbers into the rooms below.

Anxious "to do good on his own hook" by going back to the states, obtaining reinforcements, and establishing a mission station of his own, William Gray left for Waiilatpu December 28, 1836, to seek Whitman's support of his plans. Even though the building lacked two doors, two windows, and a part of the floor, the Spaldings moved in. During the next two months Henry dug a cellar for storage purposes, made a rough sled, and with the help of the Nez Perces moved stones to the site and laid a chimney and two fireplaces. By February 20, 1837, he wrote Greene, his house had "three windows, four doors, buttery, closet, recess for bed, cedar bedstead, and table." He had made everything himself, using the materials at hand and the skills taught him at Franklin Academy and Western Reserve.

"Bless the day," he wrote, "that shone upon the first manual labor college."

In noting the abundance of fish supplied them by the Indians, Henry Spalding emphasized the importance of this food resource to the Nez Perces. "For two months past," he wrote on May 1, 1837, "we have had a plenty of fresh trout, usually weighing from eight to ten pounds."[30]

In September, at one of the Indian fisheries, he saw the Nez Perces catch

"202 large salmon, weighing from ten to twenty-five pounds. There were probably as many taken at fifty other stations in the Nez Perce country. This fishery will always be of great importance to this mission."[31]

Whatever his faults as a missionary, Henry Spalding clearly saw that a stable food supply was vital to the Nez Perces if they were to be civilized

30. Drury, *Spalding,* pp. 166–167, Spalding Letter No. 18. The eight-to-ten-pound fish described by Spalding no doubt were what we now call steelhead, or steelhead-trout, classified as *Salmo gairdnerii* by the Washington State Game and Fish Department. This is a rainbow trout that spawns in the gravel streambeds of the Nez Perce country, goes to sea, remains in salt water for two to four years where it makes a tremendous growth, then returns to the streambeds of its birth to spawn and renew its kind. Unlike the salmon it does not die after spawning but drifts downstream to the Pacific, then may return to fresh water and spawn again. Eight to ten pounds is its average weight, though an occasional steelhead may go as high as twenty-five pounds.

The ten-to-twenty-five-pound fish mentioned by Spalding were true salmon, which do die after spawning. Several species were native to the region. The largest was the Chinook, some of which weighed sixty pounds or more.

Of recent years this extremely important food and sportsfishing source has been endangered to the point of extinction by the building of dams on the Snake and Columbia river systems. The watersheds of these two rivers now contain a total of 161 dams.

31. Ibid., p. 167.

and taught religion. Already the buffalo herds of the Great Plains were being decimated, he knew. From rendezvous he had written Secretary Greene:

"What is done for the poor Indians of this western world must be done soon. The only thing that can save them from annihilation is the introduction of civilization. Their only means of support, which is buffalo, is fast diminishing. It is observed by those acquainted that in ten years there will probably not be a buffalo in the country."[32]

It was Spalding's conviction that before the Indians could be saved they must be settled — that is, persuaded to cease their roving life and reside in permanent abodes as herders of domestic livestock and tillers of the soil. With that purpose in mind he went with William Gray to the country of the Spokanes in late March 1837, where he conducted services with Spokane Garry acting as interpreter. Horses were cheap in the Pacific Northwest, running from $8 to $14 a head. The Indians wanted cattle, but the Hudson's Bay Company would not sell cows to them. Spalding, Gray, and Spokane Garry, discussed the problem and devised a plan by which William Gray would go East with a herd of Nez Perce horses, trade them for cattle and sheep, obtain reinforcements from the white religious community, and return to start a new mission among the Flatheads or Spokanes.

The Nez Perces agreed to the horse-trading plan, offering to send four or five men with ten or twelve of their best horses East with William Gray that summer.

As a farmer, teacher, doctor, and preacher, Spalding had more than enough work to do. Richard and John, the two Nez Perce boys whom Whitman had taken East, had split up on their return. Richard went to live with the Whitmans at Waiilatpu, while John dwelt with the Spaldings at Lapwai. Eliza handled most of the teaching, instructing a hundred or so Indians of all ages.

"Having no books, Mrs. Spalding, with her numerous other cares, is obliged to supply the deficiency with her pen, and print her own books; consequently, she can spend but a short time each day in school. But her absence does not close the school. From morning till night they are assembled in clusters, with one teaching a number of others."[33]

Spalding frequently was called upon to doctor the Indians, though as he himself admitted:

"I am no physician, but have more or less sickness to look after, sometimes eight or ten cases on my hands at once, usually bowell complaints caused by eating bad food or too much of it, or in other words, gluttony, requiring, as I suppose, cathartics. These I issue at order sometimes five or six before I am dressed in the morning, not often finding time to go near the patients, especially if they are any distance off; besides, by my ignorance, I can do as well by ear as by the eye.

"In the winter, however, there are many cases of lung complaint occasioned by bare feet in the wet and snow, which often terminates in consumption and death after a lapse of a few years. Blood letting is a favorite remedy among them, and I often go by the lot, opening five or six at a time and go about more pressing business, leaving them to stop the blood when they please. If they cannot get me to open their veins for them, they do it themselves with an arrow, digging away until they find the blood from the veins or artery, which they usually dig for, occasioning swelled arms, legs, and sometimes, I believe, death."[34]

Here Spalding was treading on dangerous ground, for being a medicine man — or *tewat,* as the Nez Perces called such a practitioner — was a high-risk profession. If the patient recovered, the *tewat* was well paid with horses, food, or goods. But if the patient died, the *tewat* must be clever enough to put blame for the death upon some person or force other than himself — or risk being killed by the agggrieved relatives.

As a minister with a limited command of the Nez Perce tongue, Henry Spalding made good use of Eliza's talent for painting, getting her to draw representations of various Biblical scenes, which fascinated the Indians.

"My manner of teaching is as follows," Spalding wrote. "We have represented in paintings several events recorded in the Scriptures, such as the passage through the Red Sea, the crucifixion of Christ, etc. These I explain to my crier. I then go over the subject to the people, the crier correcting my language and carrying out my history."[35]

While it is difficult to pinpoint *every* specific event that contributed to a deterioration of the feelings of goodwill between the Nez Perces and the white missionaries, William Gray's trip East the summer of 1837 certainly was one.

Spalding had approved Gray's proposed trip; Whitman had not. Gray went anyway. Traveling with fourteen horses and four or more Indian companions, Gray reached rendezvous grounds several

32. Ibid., p. 168. Spalding Letter No. 10.
33. Ibid., p. 172. Spalding Letter No. 17.
34. Ibid., p. 173. Spalding Letter No. 44.
35. Ibid., p. 174n. Spalding Letter No. 14.

weeks before the caravan from St. Louis was due to arrive. Though he originally had planned to cross the plains under the protection of the returning fur brigade, he impatiently decided to proceed without it. Jim Bridger advised him against such a rash act, warning that the Sioux would attack such a small party, kill the Indians in it, and steal the horses.

William Gray ignored the advice.

Near Ash Hollow, in Sioux country, Bridger's prediction came true. The Indians who were with Gray were killed and the horses stolen, Gray himself barely managing to escape with his life. Despite his later self-justification for his behavior, the verdict among Indians and mountain men was that he cravenly deserted his Indian friends in a pinch, trading their horses and lives to the Sioux for his own.

Though the American Board was displeased with Gray's unauthorized trip East and horrified by his account of the killing of his Indian friends, they did come up with the funds and personnel to supply a substantial reinforcement to the missions in the Oregon Country.

Since he wanted to build a gristmill and needed Gray's assistance as a carpenter, Spalding reluctantly accepted him at Lapwai upon his return in late summer, 1838. But after hearing what had happened on the way east, Spalding was deeply concerned about the reaction of the Nez Perces to the killings.

"It is said," he wrote Greene, "they will demand my head or all my property."

This did not happen, but he was obliged to give cows to the Indians who had lost horses.[36] From that time on, the mountain men living near Lapwai, several of whom had taken Nez Perce wives, had little use for the missionaries.

Following a visit to Lapwai by U.S. Navy Lieutenant Slacum and Methodist missionary Jason Lee in 1838, both Spalding and Whitman caught "expansionist fever." Lee was requesting $40,000 and fifty-one more workers from the Methodist Board (he got both the money and the workers), while Slacum was optimistic that all the Oregon Country soon would become part of the United States. Surely the American Board of Foreign Missions could do as well or better than the Methodists for such a worthy cause!

With Whitman's approval, Spalding urgently asked the board to send out "thirty ordained minis-

ters, thirty farmers, thirty-nine schoolteachers, and ten mechanics, with their wives," a total of two hundred and twenty adults!

"You have only to make the request known and the men and money are at your command at once," Spalding wrote.

Since a depression gripped the East and the American Board faced a $40,000 deficit, Spalding did not get the aid he requested. In fact, the board consistently misunderstood the needs for supplies of the Indian missions. In listing Lapwai's requirements, Spalding once asked for ten tons of iron, from which he meant to make hoes, spades, and other agricultural tools. He also asked for 7,200 awls, 2,000 gunflints, 100 dozen scalping knives, and a quantity of powder and lead. Though all these items were to be used for subsistence meat-hunting and garment-making, Secretary Greene reacted with horror.

"What would be said of you and the Cause?" he wrote indignantly, "should it be known that you traded with the Indians in such articles as these?"[37]

Spalding should have pointed out that "scalping knives" were used for everything from skinning game to paring toenails. They might just as well have been called butcher knives.

By December 1838 the white population of Lapwai had increased from two to nine. In residence were Henry and Eliza Spalding, William and Mary Gray, a twenty-three-year old bachelor teacher named Cornelius Rogers, the French-Canadian Charles Compo and three ex-mountain men, James Conner, Richard Williams, and George Ebberts. Employing these men to help with the physical work around the mission, Spalding now could devote more time to religious matters.

Truth was, Spalding found it more difficult to Christianize ex-trappers than to convert Indians. Compo soon grew dissatisfied with Lapwai and went west to Waiilatpu. Following a sermon on the parable of the prodigal son, Ebbert's heart was so visibly touched that Spalding wrote in his diary: "Oh, Lord, in great mercy, bring into thy kingdom all these mountain men."

Shortly thereafter it appeared that his prayer had been answered when James Conner and

36. Ibid., p. 201. Spalding Letter No. 39. Tack-en-su-a-tis lost horses, relatives, or friends in this incident and turned cool toward the Spaldings.
37. Drury, Whitman, vol. 1, p. 290.

MRS. ELIZA WARREN
NEE MISS SPALDING

MRS. HARRIET JEWETT.
NEE MRS. KIMBALL

MRS. E. L. CHAPMAN
NEE MISS BEWLEY

MRS. S. M. WIRT.
NEE MISS KIMBALL

MRS. O. N. DENNY.
NEE MISS HALL

Missionary Wives

Richard Williams joined the church. But before long Williams got drunk and beat his Nez Perce wife so badly she deserted him. Ebberts lost interest in Spalding's sermons. And James Conner backslid to such a degree that he was publicly suspended from the church for "Sabbath-breaking, neglect of duties, fighting, polygamy, sending a challenge to fight a duel, and vending liquor."

Among the Nez Perces, Spalding was more successful in converting several influential chiefs. His first was Tu-e-ka-kas, leader of the Wallowa band, who was given the Christian name Joseph. On December 2 Spalding mentions him for the first time in his diary, writing:

"Joseph speaks most affectingly, urging all present to give their hearts to Jesus Christ without delay."[38]

The second important convert was Ta-moot-sin, renamed Timothy, leader of the Alpowa band, who as a boy had hidden in the bushes to observe the members of the Lewis and Clark party and had been a staunch friend of the whites ever since.

Curiously enough, neither Lawyer nor Tack-en-su-a-tis joined the church at this time. Their reasons for not doing so are implied, rather than stated, but they appear to have had something to do with territoriality. Though Tack-en-su-a-tis had told Spalding that the Lapwai Valley was his country, he could have meant only that this was where he lived, not that he owned and controlled it white-man fashion. That control was strongly disputed by Hin-mah-tute-ke-kaikt ("Thunder Strikes"), a politically powerful medicine man called Old James by the whites. Reinforced by his white son-in-law, William Craig, who had married his daughter, Isabel, Old James had no use for missionaries and felt that Tack-en-su-a-tis had no right to give the Spaldings land in the Lapwai Valley without making them pay him, Old James, for it.

Lawyer, whose home territory lay in the Kamiah Valley sixty-five miles upriver, supported the Americans in general but was wise enough to stay aloof from the dispute he saw arising between the newcomers at Lapwai and the Nez Perces who long had lived there. Until now it had been a common practice for bands of Upper Nez Perces to visit bands of Lower Nez Perces, or the reverse, for a few weeks each year. But since the Spalding Mission had been established, Joseph and Timothy both had moved to Lapwai to be near the Spaldings and had stayed there for months at a time. Both had become favorites of the missionaries, while local leadeers like Old James were ignored. It was only natural that Joseph and Timothy should be resented by many members of the local band.

For a time the relationship between Spalding and Joseph was that of blood brothers. On one occasion after Joseph had returned to his village in the Wallowa Valley for the summer, the chief became ill. A messenger was sent to Lapwai bearing the disturbing news that he was not expected to live. In following these excerpts from Spalding's diary, it should be borne in mind that the distance

38. Drury, *Spalding*, p. 213.

between Lapwai and the Wallowa Valley was over one hundred miles, twenty hours of the hardest kind of riding over very rough terrain. On August 26, 1840, Spalding wrote:

"About 4 P.M. I jump onto one of the horses the Indians rode up and start to see my dear brother Joseph . . . find the horse very hard. Reach the river [the Snake] and cross, dark. My guides are soon far behind and asleep. Stop 11:30 P.M.

"*August 27th.* Start early, eat a bit of dry buffalo, my horse is too weak to ride easy. Suffer much from riding. Reach the spruce plain about 5 P.M. Am in great pain. Find two young men with a spare horse waiting . . . find it extremely easy. Ride fifteen miles and arrive about sundown. Find Joseph weak with high fever, pulse ninety, no passage for several days. I give dose of calomel and jalap and bleed . . .

"*August 28th.* Give Joseph another dose of calomel and jalap. Soon copious passage. Pulse at eve down to seventy. Thank the Lord for his goodness.

"*August 31st.* Joseph speaks again of giving me a horse. I refuse again and tell him I came not for horses but because I loved him. Finding Joseph grieved, I consented. The horse is large, stout, and tame."[39]

A few month's later Joseph returned the favor by saving the missionary from a cold-water ducking that could have been fatal. In late December 1840, Spalding reported going up the Clearwater a few miles with three white men and thirty-two Indians. While one group cut white pine on the south bank, the other crossed to the north bank and cut cedar. Once the trees were down, they were slid into the river and compacted into rafts:

"*Dec. 26th.* Three rafts completed, including twenty-eight beautiful logs and six or seven timbers for the sills, plates and beams for the school house. I take the heavy raft with Timothy and Luke. Strike a bar at the foot of the island and wreck most of our couplings but save our timber. After some lifting in the wet, get off."

As they neared home, the rafts hung up again:

"Timothy goes off on two logs, which start the whole raft rolling, and with great difficulty, by jumping square up and down, keeps from being drawn between two logs. Joseph sends in a horse on which I reach the shore in safety."[40]

Early in January 1839, Spalding conducted a series of religious meetings at Lapwai to which about two thousand Nez Perces from outlying bands came. During the twice-daily services, temperance and fidelity in marriage were stressed in his sermons. Many Indians signed the abstinence pledge and vowed to give up polygamy and be faithful to one — and only one — spouse. With so many Indians on hand, William Gray took advantage of the labor supply to supervise the digging of a ditch that would bring water to the new gristmill.

Using no other tools than two shovels, a few hoes, and axes, a millrace half a mile long, four feet wide, and in places fifteen feet deep was dug. The Indians worked in the morning until a bell called them to worship at noon. After that service was over they were given a few potatoes for their labor. A second service was held following the afternoon work session, with more potatoes given them as compensation.

"In this way," Spalding wrote, "multitudes were enabled to remain through the meeting, which continued eight days, who otherwise would have been under the necessity of returning home soon for want of provisions."[41]

A verbal tradition persists among the Nez Perces that Henry Spading supervised the digging of the millrace with a whip in his hand, which he used freely upon the backs of shirkers, whether male or female, young or old. It is hard to believe that the proud, independent Nez Perces would tolerate such punishment, let alone work for weeks to complete such a big project while under the lash. Several pieces of evidence exist that individual Nez Perces were whipped now and then, possibly at

39. Clifford M. Drury, ed., *The Diaries and Letters of Henry H. Spalding* (Glendale, Calif.: Arthur H. Clark Co., 1958), pp. 297–298 (hereafter called *Spalding Diaries*).
40. Ibid., p. 305.
41. Drury, *Spalding*, p. 215.

The Spalding Mission at Lapwai

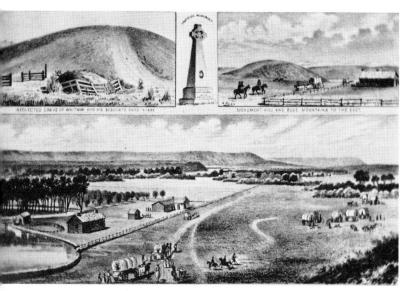

The Whitman Mission prior to 1847, from an artist's sketch.

the direction and with the approval of the chiefs. Spalding wrote in his diary:

"*Jan. 9 (1839).* Williams wife left him last night. Joseph and others go after her.
"*Jan. 12.* Williams wife is whipped 70 lashes. Indians come nigh whipping him."

Later, Missionary A. B. Smith, an extremely capable linguist but a chronic critic of Spalding, wrote of this same incident, which he had heard about but had not witnessed:

"He has been much in the habit of using the whip or causing it to be used upon the people. He has however failed not infrequently in getting individuals whipped when he had attempted . . .

"In another instance after we arrived here, Mr. Spalding caused a woman to be whipped seventy lashes. He had married her to Williams, the blacksmith. He abused her so that she ran away. She was brought back and whipped. After she had been whipped the people were determined to whip Williams, and it was with great difficulty that Mr. Spalding could prevent it. He deserved it probably more than the woman and the Indians knew it."[42]

In the spring of 1839, a printing press that was no longer needed at the American Board Mission in Honolulu was shipped to Lapwai. Accompanying it was Missionary E. O. Hall and his wife, a sickly woman whom it was thought the trip would help. Spalding valued the "press, type, paper, binding materials, sugar, molasses, and salt" sent from Hawaii at $400. The press was set up shortly after it arrived, and five days later, May 18, 1839, a proof sheet was struck off.

This was the first press used in the Oregon Country.

On May 24, four hundred copies of an eight-page book designed for children and beginners were printed. Spalding used an alphabet he had devised, in which some of the consonants used in the English language but not in the Nez Perce were given vowel sounds. The alphabet proved to be too clumsy and awkward and soon was given up.

A few months after the arrival of the printing press, Spalding, Whitman, and the missionary-linguist, Asa Smith, who quickly mastered the Nez Perce tongue under the tutelage of Chief Lawyer at Kamiah, agreed on a system of letters that would greatly simplify the written language. Based on the alphabet used in the Sandwich Islands, known as the Pickering alphabet, it included the twelve letters used in Hawaii — a, e, i, o, u, h, k, l, m, n, p, and w — plus the additional letters s and t. The letters b, d, f, g, r, v, and z were used only in foreign words.[43]

Tragedy struck at Waiilatpu that summer when Alice Clarissa Whitman, the first white child born in the Oregon Country, wandered away from the house, fell into the Walla Walla River, and drowned. An Indian bearing the sad news galloped the 120 miles to Lapwai in twenty-five hours. Since Spalding and Hall were the only ordained ministers in the country, Marcus and Narcissa requested that they come to Waiilatpu and conduct the burial services for Alice Clarissa, who had been only two years, three months, and nine days old when she died.

Starting at once, Hall made the gruelling horseback trip in twenty-four hours. Still suffering from a fall that had injured his side severely a few weeks earlier, Spalding was unable to ride a horse, but with the help of the Indians, he, his wife, and their little daughter went by canoe down the Clearwater, Snake, and Columbia to Fort Walla Walla, then overland by horse to the Whitman Mission twenty-three miles to the east.

The funeral service was held Thursday afternoon, June 26, 1839. Spalding took for his text the verse from II Kings, 4:26:

"Is it well with thee? Is it well with thy husband? Is it well with the child?"

42. Ibid., p. 216.
43. Ibid., p. 225.

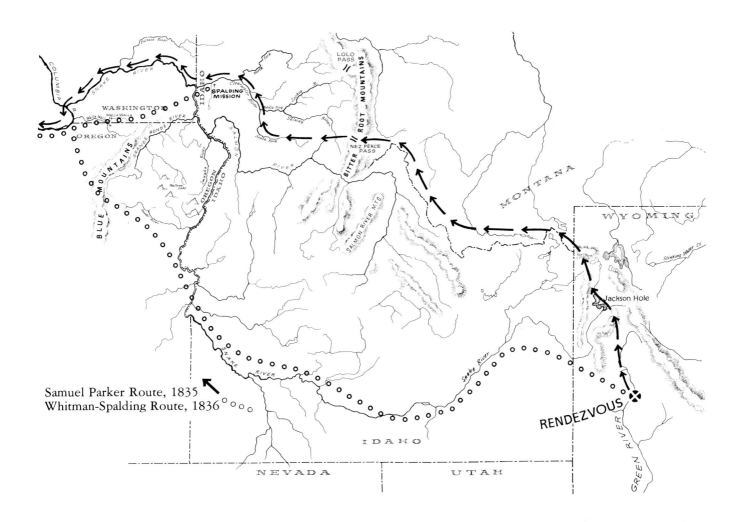

Samuel Parker Route, 1835
Whitman-Spalding Route, 1836 ° ° ° °

It was a sad time for all concerned. Spalding wrote sorrowfully in his diary:

"Who is to be second? Oh, my soul, who is to be second?"[44]

If given time and left alone, it is possible that the missionaries and the Indians could have learned to understand one another, work together, and bridge the ages-long cultural gulf separating white and red races. But neither time nor isolation was granted them.

In the world of fashion, beaver was now out, silk in. The day of the trapper was done. Though the two giant monopolies had the field all to themselves, there was nothing left to fight over. Two months before Spalding made his ride to dose Joseph with calomel and jalap, the American Fur Company held its final big rendezvous, and free trappers like Robert Newell, Joe Meek, and William Craig said their farewells to a way of life they would live no more.

"Come," said Newell to Meek, "we are done with this life in the mountains — done with wading in beaver dams and freezing or starving alternately — done with Indian trading and Indian fighting. The fur trade is dead in the Rocky Mountains, and it is no place for us, now, if ever it was. We are young yet and have life before us. We cannot waste it here."[45]

At this same rendezvous, the patient Flatheads, who for years had sought missionaries, seen them come, then go on to other localities, received an answer to their prayers. The Black Robes had sent out a Jesuit priest, Pierre Jean De Smet, who promised to establish a mission in their country.

Learning this, the Flatheads wept with emotion. Father De Smet wrote: "It was like children running to meet their father after a long absence."[46]

44. Ibid., p. 223.

45. Frances Fuller Victor, The River of the West (Hartford, Conn., 1870), p. 264.

46. John Upton Terrell, Black Robe: The Life of Pierre-Jean De Smet, Missionary, Explorer and Pioneer (New York: Doubleday & Co., 1964), p. 94.

Father Desmet

William Craig, unemployed trapper, was red-headed, fiercely independent, and had been a dropout from civilized society ever since he left his western Virginia home as a young man twenty-two years earlier. In the Clearwater country a few years ago he had married a Nez Perce woman, Isabel, who was a member of the Lapwai band. Her father, a medicine man and chief of some importance, was called Old James by the whites.

When Joe Meek and Robert Newell told Craig they intended to seek their fortunes in the Willamette Valley and invited him to come along, Isabel countered with the suggestion that he go home with her and settle down in the Lapwai Valley.

Well, she *was* his wife. In the Willamette Valley, it rained nine months out of the year. The Nez Perces were friendly people who enjoyed life, and he'd never cared much for civilized places.

Sure, he'd heard that a bunch of self-righteous missionaries had established a station in the Lapwai Valley and were giving his father-in-law all kinds of trouble.

But *he* knew how to deal with them.

CHAPTER NINE

THE TEWAT'S SON-IN-LAW: 1840–1843

*Craig and Larison, two mountain men, have
arrived, probably to spend the winter. I have seen
enough of mountain men.*
— Henry Spalding, November 20, 1840

LIKE MOST OF his kind, William Craig kept no journal, wrote few letters, and left very little written record of his life other than his acts as reported by other men. From an affidavit he filed as a settler on unsurveyed lands in Washington Territory in 1855, we learn three facts: he was born in Greenbrier County (now West Virginia) in 1807; he arrived in Old Oregon Country on July 25, 1829; and he was legally married to his wife, Isabel, in Missouri Territory on July 6, 1838.

A man of medium stature at maturity, he had a ruddy complexion, steel blue eyes, and reddish hair.

"All evidence indicates that he was a kind, generous, resourceful, and reticent man," writes Frederick A. Mark. "Only one picture of him is known to exist. It is very likely due to his reticent nature that so little is known of him. A principal reason for the Indians' great respect for him was his devotion to his wife."[1]

During his trapping days, between 1829 and 1840, Craig explored most of the streams of the West and associated with such men as Kit Carson, Osborne Russell, and James Clyman, though his closest friends were Robert ("Doc") Newell and Joe Meek. He was in the area, if not in the fight, of the encounter with Blackfeet in 1831 which was called the Battle of Pierre's Hole. He was a member of one of Bonneville's trapping brigades working northeast of Salt Lake. And he was in the party Bonneville sent to California under the leadership of Joseph Reddeford Walker.[2]

In his own eyes, in those of his wife, and in the eyes of his father-in-law, Craig had been married to Isabel for many years, by Indian custom, before he had an opportunity to legalize the union with a white minister. Mrs. Elkanah Walker, who came out with William Gray and the reinforcement party in 1838, noted in her diary that she "made a dress' for Craig's Indian wife at rendezvous on the Popo Agie. Since Craig later recorded that year as the one in which he "legally married," it is highly probable that the ceremony was performed there by the Reverend Elkanah Walker, who soon would establish a mission at Tshimakain in the Spokane country.

It is also probable that, having satisfied his wife's desire to have their union sanctified by a white preacher, Craig felt he had "seen enough of ministers" for a long time to come. But such a happy state of freedom from the restrictions of civilized society, from which he had fled in his youth, was not to be.

In the summer of 1840 a small missionary party led by Harvey Clark appeared at the final American Fur Company rendezvous with three farm wagons. Employing Robert Newell as a guide, the group managed to drive the wagons on to Fort Hall. By then their horses were exhausted, the wagons were badly battered, and the missionaries were ready to accept the advice of the Hudson's Bay Company employees that it would be folly to take the wagons any farther. Giving Newell the vehicles in payment for his services, the Clark party traded their jaded horses for fat ones and pro-

1. LeRoy R. Hafen, ed., *The Mountain Men and the Fur Trade of the Far West* (Glendale, Calif.: Arthur H. Clark Co., 1965), vol. 2, pp. 103–104, chapter on William Craig by Frederick A. Mark; *Lewiston Tribune,* March 3, 1918, article by Thomas J. Beall.
2. Hafen, *Mountain Men,* p. 107.

Courtesy Oregon Historical Society

William Craig. This photo probably was taken around 1865. Said to be the only Craig photo in existence.

ceeded to the Columbia via packtrain, while Newell remained at Fort Hall for a month or so.

"At the time I took the wagons, I had no idea of undertaking to bring them into this country," Newell later wrote. "But the American Fur Company had abandoned the country for good, so I concluded to hitch up and try the much dreaded job of bringing a wagon to Oregon."[3]

Traveling with him were his longtime friends, Joe Meek and William Craig, who also were quitting the trapping game. Details of this first wagon-train journey across the Snake River Country are sketchy, but we know that the party reached Fort Boise without incident. And we know that during its brief stay there, Hudson's Bay Company factor Francis Payette made three mistakes.

First, he invited Robert Newell to be his guest

in quarters within the fort, while Meek and Craig were left to camp outside the walls. Second, he sent out a company servant with filets of sturgeon for the two ex-trappers, who, feeling insulted, rejected them with pungent comments. Third, he told the three mountain men that taking wagons across the Blue Mountains was impossible; his considered advice was to leave them behind.

Robert Newell was level-headed; Joe Meek was bullheaded; and William Craig was redheaded. Being Americans; none would take a dare. A man could swallow an insult from a Britisher. But accept considered advice? Never!

Those wagons would cross the Blues if they had to be carried on three broad backs.

Floated across the Snake, tugged and pushed up brushy, rocky Burnt River Canyon, skidded, jolted, and careened across the dividing ridge to the Powder, driven across the lovely, fertile valley of the upper Grande Ronde, then again tugged and pushed, sweated and bullied, cajoled and cursed up steep grades and through thick trees that must be felled to make a road, until the 3,700-foot height to be called Deadman's Pass was crested, and then down through still bigger timber on the slopes of Emigrant Hill until the westward-flowing Umatilla was reached — the wagons moved.

Somewhere along the way they lost their beds, but when they pulled to a stop in the yard at the Whitman Mission their wheels and running gear were intact. For the first time it could be said that wheeled vehicles had crossed the continent to the Columbia River watershed.

Others soon would follow.

While Robert Newell and Joe Meek traveled on downriver to the Willamette Valley, William Craig and his friend Joe Larison rode east to Lapwai. There he saw, with dismay, that Spalding certainly was doing his best to spoil the Nez Perce way of life. Craig wasted no time in trying to undo the "good" Spalding had done these past four years.

"Old James and others say they have been stopped from going after timber by Craig, who tells them I am making dogs and slaves of them," Spalding wrote in his diary, December 1, 1840. "I ought to pay them for going after timber [Craig says]."[4]

3. Newell to Elwood Evans, quoted by Evans in his "Annual Address," Fifth Annual Reunion, Transactions of the Oregon Pioneer Association, 1877, p. 23.
4. Drury, Spalding, p. 261.

Photo by Major Lee Moorhouse   *Courtesy Smithsonian Institution*

Joe Craig — William Craig's son

Mrs. Joe Craig, Mrs. Ya-tina-ya-wits and Josephine

At Craig's instigation, Spalding claimed, the Indians destroyed his milldam.

"How is it possible," he wrote, "for a man born of Christian parents (his parents are members of the Presbyterian church) to be guilty of such deeds of darkness! We spend this day in fasting and prayer."

Turning the other cheek, Spalding rebuilt the milldam, this time using rocks to make it more durable. The Indians destroyed it again.

In an attempt to win William Craig's friendship, Spalding gave the ex-mountain man employment at his mill and sawed a number of logs for him so that he could build a house a short distance up the valley. This gesture appears to have helped relationships some, for Craig did not violently oppose Spalding again. But for a long while he evinced hostility toward the missionary's objectives and lent his influence to what Spalding called the "heathen" party.[5]

Still another problem faced by Spalding was the coming of rival missionaries to the area. On September 19, 1839, he wrote:

"Dr. Whitman speaks of some difficulty from the Catholic priest. He is now at Walla Walla, calling the Indians and telling the Indians that we are false teachers because we do not feed and clothe the people, that we have wives as other men, and wear pantaloons as common men, and not frocks as he does."[6]

Spalding's response to the threat of competition was to redouble his efforts to settle and educate the Nez Perces. Following the completion of a new schoolhouse during the summer of 1841, he proudly reported that the attendance averaged "about eighty-five, including a class of ten adults, six of whom are chiefs and principal men."

The latter included "Joseph, Timothy, Luke, Lawyer, Stephen, Jason, Five Crows [Joseph's brother], Hezikiah, Lot [Conners' father-in-law], and Mary [Jacob's wife]."[7]

The intriguing thing about this list of principal men is that at least four of them were far removed from their home villages; in fact, they appear to have been living at Lapwai the major portion of the time for at least four years. Joseph's home was the Wallowa Valley in summer, the lower Grande Ronde in winter; Timothy's, the Alpowa Valley opposite the junction of the Clearwater and the Snake; Lawyer's, the Kamiah Valley sixty-five miles up the Clearwater; and Five Crows's, who was part Cayuse, the Walla Walla Valley one hundred and twenty miles to the west.

Also of interest is the fact that neither Tack-en-su-a-tis, who formerly had been such a staunch friend of the Spaldings, or Old James, who for a time had attended church services, is mentioned in reference to the school.

Yet this was *their* valley.

In October 1841 Spalding held another series of religious meetings at Lapwai, attended by two thousand Nez Perces, with Timothy and Joseph assisting him. He felt that many of the Indians were ready to be taken into the church. Marcus Whitman, with whom he had been having difficulties, sharply disagreed, so for the time being the ripe new converts were not accepted.

Meanwhile, the tide of emigration to the Oregon Country was swelling. In 1841 twenty-four emigrants, including two families with small children, made the long overland journey. In 1842 a large party under the leadership of Dr. Elijah White, who had first come out as a Methodist medical missionary and had lived in the Willamette Valley from 1838 to 1840, made the trip. Armed with an appointment as Indian Agent for all of Oregon

5. Drury, *Spalding*, p. 263. Drury notes that as late as 1936 the Nez Perces still were using the title "heathen" without apology to designate the non-Christian party.

6. Ibid., p. 230.

7. Ibid., p. 273.

(even though the region was still under the Joint Occupancy Treaty with Great Britain), White had one hundred and twelve people and eighteen wagons in his party. The wagons were left at Fort Hall, and the rest of the trip was made on horseback — the last overland group that would make this transfer. White reached Waiilatpu September 14, 1842, bearing letters from the East. The one he gave Marcus Whitman from the American Board contained bad news. Because of the dissension of the past few years among the missionaries, as expressed in their many complaining letters sent East:

The Spaldings were being recalled . . .

Waiilatpu must be closed and sold . . .

The Whitmans must move to the Spokane country . . .

Since the seeds of dissension among the missionaries had been sown long before and had been nurtured by adversity, frustration, jealousy, unrequited love, conceit, and a zeal that at times lapsed into madness, we shall not consider anything here but the bitter harvest. Dr. Whitman called for an assembly of all parties concerned. After they had arrived, argued, confessed their errors, and devoutly expressed wishes for another chance, he made an astounding proposal.

He would leave for Boston at once, confront the board, and persuade it to change its collective mind.

His lone traveling companion would be Asa Lovejoy, a Massachusetts lawyer then visiting Waiilatpu and unaccustomed to the wilderness. The other missionaries felt the trip would be far too dangerous. Narcissa, concerned for her husband's health, felt a winter journey would be too much for him.

Impatiently he brushed the objections aside. On October 3 Whitman, Lovejoy, and a dog named Trapper, the family pet of the drowned little girl, Alice Clarissa Whitman, left Waiilatpu and headed East.

Ten days later the trio reached Fort Hall, a distance of five hundred miles. Already the early mountain winter was closing in on the high country; it promised to be a bitter one. They were warned by Hudson's Bay company factor Peter Grant that the Sioux and Pawnees were at war, making a crossing of the plains ahead an extremely risky business. Better go back to Waiilatpu and wait for spring.

No, Whitman said, they must go on now. In-

Photo by Major Lee Moorhouse   Courtesy Idaho Historical Society
Extended Indian tepees

stead of taking the direct route, they would swing south to Taos and Santa Fe, then back north to Bent's Fort. True, this detour would add a thousand miles to the trip, but he could not wait for spring.

Minus a mule and the family pet, Trapper, both of which had been eaten, Whitman and Lovejoy reached Taos in mid-December. Both men were suffering from exhaustion, frostbite, and starvation. After resting two weeks they moved on to Bent's Fort, where Whitman impatiently left Lovejoy behind in his haste to join a party heading for St. Louis.

Still wearing his disreputable, shaggy, smelly buffalo coat that had kept him from freezing to death in the high country, Whitman reached Washington, D.C. in early March 1843. Congress had just adjourned. After a brief stay there he went to New York, where a cabman, taking him for a hick from the sticks, fleeced him out of $2 of his almost exhausted funds. He had a session with Horace Greeley, who admired him for his courage and principles but thought anybody fool enough to go to Oregon was out of his mind. During a visit to the Methodist Board for Foreign Missions he learned that it was considering recalling Jason Lee, who seemed to be more concerned with real estate and politics that with saving heathen souls.

Broke and shaggy, he reached Boston in early May and presented himself to Secretary David Greene of the American Board for Foreign Missions. Greene was so shocked at Whitman's appearance and smell that he hastily gave him some money and told him to get a bath and some decent clothes.

There is ample evidence that the board did not approve of Whitman's fantastic journey. But the drama of what he had done overpowered the committee's conservatism. After due consideration, it granted his two most important requests:

Waiilatpu would be continued . . .

Spalding would be retained "on trial . . ."[8]

With his twelve-year-old nephew, Perrin, Dr. Marcus Whitman reached Westport May 31, 1843, homeward bound. During previous years, annual migrations to the Far West had been very small, consisting mostly of reinforcements for the missions: fourteen people in 1839, the Clark party of three wagons and six people in 1849, fifty-four people in 1841, one hundred and twelve in 1842 — and some of these were bound for California.[9] But this year there was astonishing evidence that a movement unparalleled in the nation's history was under way.

One hundred and twenty wagons; over a thousand men, women, and children; and five thousand oxen, horses, and cattle were preparing to move west, the surprised Dr. Whitman found. To the leaders of the migration, his name and feats were well known, and his appearance at this time and place was regarded as the greatest of good fortune. Eager questions peppered him from every quarter.

Was he returning to his mission station? Could wagons get through to the Columbia? Would he travel with them and give them the benefit of his medical services and advice?

To all questions, he answered yes.

Thus the legend that "Marcus Whitman saved Oregon for the United States" began. During the few years of life left him, Dr. Whitman made no such claim himself. In a memorial to Congress, sent through influential friends, he did stress the importance of the Oregon Country and proposed that the military establish a chain of forts along the Oregon Trail to supply and protect emigrants. But he was not the savior of Oregon that fanciful writers later painted him.

Though he neither claimed nor should be given credit for directly inspiring the Great Migration of 1843, his services to it were invaluable.

"His constant advice, which we knew was based upon a knowlege of the road before us," Jesse Applegate wrote, "was *travel, Travel,* TRAVEL — nothing else will take you to the end of your journey; nothing is wise that does not help you along; nothing is good for you that causes a moment's delay."[10]

Like air currents vagrantly stirring on the edges of a gigantic weather front, the winds of change had begun with the journey of the Flatheads and Nez Perces to St. Louis in 1831. Until that time there appeared to be nothing of value in the Pacific Northwest but beaver. Wyeth and Bonneville went to the West to establish commercial ventures, failed, and left the region. Fur companies of two great nations fought bitterly for thirty years over the peltries of the region, then gave up the struggle because of a change in fashion brought on by the lowly silkworm. But the missionaries, drawn West by a more altruistic purpose, not only came and stayed but proved two vital facts to the restless, land-hungry masses living in the East:

There was a vast amount of fertile land in Oregon, free for the taking . . .

Wagons could cross the continent carrying women, children, household goods, and farming equipment . . .

Time to get rolling.

Photo by Jane Gay   *Courtesy Idaho Historical Society*

An Indian fish trap near Lapwai

8. Nard Jones, *The Great Command,* (Little Brown, 1959) This is a dramatic, readable, yet accurate account of the missionary efforts in the Oregon Country. For Whitman's ride east, see pp. 151–162.

9. Miles Cannon, *Toward the Setting Sun,* (Columbian Press, Portland, Oregon, 1953) p. 89.

10. Jesse Applegate, *A Day With the Cow Column,* (Caxton Club, Chicago, 1934) p. 18.

CHAPTER TEN

DISILLUSIONMENT: 1843–1847

I have had a gun cocked and presented at my head for fifteen or twenty minutes, while four of the principal men stood and looked on with as much indifference as if a dog were to be shot down.

— Henry Spalding, January 25, 1846

THE OREGON COUNTRY really had no government, since it still was jointly occupied by Great Britain and the United States. However, Dr. Elijah White, though his appointment as Superintendent of Indian Affairs bore no legal validity whatsoever, managed to persuade Thomas McKay of the Hudson's Bay Company to go with him on a trip from the Willamette Valley to the interior to put legal restraints on the Indians. They were accompanied by Cornelius Rogers and Baptiste Dorion as interpreters and six civilian soldiers "to command respect."

At Lapwai they were cordially received. Through the interpreters White explained the urgent need for a set of laws under which all the people of the region could live in peace. A ninety-year-old man who had welcomed Lewis and Clark long ago spoke for the Nez Perces. He was called Bloody Chief.

"Clark pointed to this day, to you, and this occasion; we have long waited in expectation; sent three of our sons to Red River to prepare for it; two of them sleep with their fathers; the other is here, and can be ears, mouth, and pen for us."[1]

The son referred to by Bloody Chief was called Ellis by the whites. As a youth he had been sent to the Red River settlements, where he learned to speak English. Now thirty-two years old and ranked as a minor chief in the Lapwai band, he was appointed head chief of all the Nez Perces by Dr. White — for no other reason than that he could communicate effectively and would agree to whatever was proposed.

What *was* proposed by Dr. White was a set of eleven laws, which he says were "unanimously adopted." These were called:

LAWS OF THE NEZ PERCES

1. Whoever willfully takes life shall be hung.
2. Whoever burns a dwelling house shall be hung.
3. Whoever burns an outbuilding shall be imprisoned six months, receive fifty lashes, and pay all damages.
4. Whoever carelessly burns a house, or any property, shall pay all damages.
5. If anyone enters a dwelling without permission of the occupant, the chiefs shall punish him as they think proper. Public rooms are excepted.
6. If anyone steal, he shall pay back twofold; and if it be the value of a beaver skin or less, he shall receive twenty-five lashes, and if the value is over a beaver skin he shall pay back twofold and receive fifty lashes.
7. If anyone take a horse and ride it without permission, or take any article and use it without liberty, he shall pay for the use of it and receive from twenty to fifty lashes, as the chief shall direct.
8. If anyone enter a field, and injure the crops, or throw down the fence so that cattle or horses go in and do damage, he shall pay all damages, and receive twenty-five lashes for *every* offense.
9. Those only may keep dogs who travel or live

---

1. Miss A. J. Allen, *Ten Years in Oregon: Being the Record of Dr. Elijah White* (Ithaca, N.Y., 1848), p. 185.

among the game; if a dog kill a lamb, calf, or any domestic animal, the owner shall pay the damage and kill the dog.

10. If an Indian raise a gun or other weapon against a white man, it shall be reported to the chiefs, and they shall punish him. If a white person do the same to an Indian, it shall be reported to Dr. White, and he shall redress it.

11. If an Indian break these laws, he shall be punished by his chiefs; if a white man break them, he shall be reported to the agent and be punished at his instance.[2]

Obviously the laws had been devised to protect the property, garden, and livestock of the Spalding Mission and those "settled" Indians who were trying to follow the white man's way. Just as obviously, enforcement of the laws would prove as impossible for the chiefs as for the so-called "agent," Dr. Elijah White, who had no civil, military, or governmental authority to back him up.

As matters turned out, the code of laws caused more difficulties than it cured. The first of these stemmed from the killing of a Walla Walla Indian by white men in California.

Led by Chief Peo-peo-mox-mox ("Yellow Bird"), the Walla Wallas lived near the juncture of the river of that name with the Columbia. Trading first with Lewis and Clark, then with British representatives of the North West and Hudson's Bay Company, and now with American missionaries and emigrants bound for Oregon, the Walla Wallas long had been friendly with the whites. Peo-peo-mox-mox, in particular, had welcomed the Americans and had built up large herds of horses and cattle. His son, a Christianized Indian, had been baptized Elijah Hedding, which was the name of a Methodist bishop.

Traveling down to Sutter's Fort in California to buy some cattle, the young Indian chief was accused of stealing livestock by a gang of white ruffians — unjustly so, by all reliable accounts — and in the ensuing fight was killed. His grief-stricken father demanded that his murderers be punished under Dr. White's code of laws. When nothing was done, Ellis was appealed to. The "head chief" of the Nez Perces went down to the Willamette Valley and talked to Dr. White, who appeased him by making promises he could not and did not keep.

So the murderers of Chief Peo-peo-mox-mox's son never were brought to justice, showing the code of laws to be a sham. Shortly thereafter — in

August 1845 — Dr. White returned to the states, leaving the white missionaries in a state of uneasiness and the Indians in a sullen mood.

About the time William Craig returned to Lapwai, an educated Delaware Indian named Tom Hill came into the valley and began to oppose the teachings of the missionaries with every argument he could set forth.

"Tom Hill, a most blasphemous, debased infidel half breed Delaware, who has been some years in the mountains spreading his poison, returned this fall with this people from the buffalo country," Spalding wrote. "He pretended to know all about the origin of the white men's religion and the design of the missionary. . . . Perhaps one thousand have joined his party, including eight or nine chiefs. They have abandoned all forms of worship."[3]

With Tom Hill, Old James, and William Craig actively opposing Spalding at Lapwai, the influence of the Christianized chiefs began to wane. Joseph went back to his village in the Wallowa Valley and the lower Grande Ronde. Five Crows returned to the Cayuse country. Timothy, the most loyal convert of all, appears to have been evicted with un-

---

2. Ibid., pp. 189–190; Drury, *Spalding,* p. 296; William H. Gray, *History of Oregon, 1792–1849* (Portland, Oreg.: Harris & Holman; New York: American News Co.; San Francisco: H. H. Bancroft Co., 1870), p. 228.
3. Drury, *Spalding,* p. 322.

Sketch by Gustavus Sohon   *Courtesy Washington State Historical Society*
Ina-me-to-om-shi-la, called Old James

wonted rudeness from the vicinity of the Spalding Mission. In a letter to Greene, Whitman wrote:

"Mr. Spalding has had severe trials with regard to the action of the Indians in taking away the cultivated lands from Timothy, one of the church members. He [Spalding] is a fearless man to rebuke sin, and this gives him many enemies. But probably this is not all. His industry in cultivating has enabled him to have a surplus of grain to sell, which probably is a source of jealousy."[4]

In truth, this desire of the white man to accumulate surplus food in the form of vegetables stored in root cellars, grain ground into flour, meat cured and put away, along with growing herds of cattle, sheep, and swine, impressed a majority of the Nez Perces as greed rather than foresightedness. Accustomed to sharing freely with one another when food was in plentiful supply and to going hungry together when food was scarce, the Nez Perces could not understand the philosophy of looking ahead for more than a short period of time.

Because of increased rowdiness in the school, which Eliza could not handle, Henry Spalding took it over himself and ran it for a couple of years. But gambling, rebellion, and anti-Christian sentiment grew to such a degree that he was forced to close the school in early 1847. One cold winter night, he related to Greene, a party of Indians gathered near his house and began gambling. For warmth, they built a fire, feeding it with portions of his cedar rail fence.

Sketch by Gustavus Sohon   *Courtesy Washington State Historical Society*

William Craig

"The whole valley rang with their gambling songs and hideous yells, rendering it almost impossible to sleep and dangerous to go out of doors."

In an attempt to save his fence, Spalding donned a heavy buffalo-hide coat, went outside, and asked them to stop. Instead, they seized him and threw him "violently upon the ground six or seven times, and finally upon the fire."

Though he remained there for several moments, his thick coat saved him from injury. Getting up, he took the burning fence rails off the fire. Unable to cope with such stubbornness, the gamblers picked up their belongings and left.

"I returned to my room to weep with deep regret that such a flood of iniquity had been opened upon this defenseless tribe of babes by the hand of a single white man. His house is a resort for gamblers."[5]

The winter of 1846–47 was the worst ever known in the Lapwai Valley, with snow covering the ground for weeks and the temperature dropping to thirty degrees below zero. At least half the Nez Perce horses and cattle died of starvation and cold. Spalding, too, lost much of his livestock. Wild game perished, which meant a diminished food supply for the Indians of the region when spring came. This in turn meant lowered vitality and lessened resistance to the new diseases which the increasing tide of white emigrants was bringing in each summer.

In blind anger a group of militant Nez Perces seized Spalding's gristmill late in the spring of 1847, holding it through the period when high water would turn the wheel and then grudgingly giving it up when August came and the water ran too low for milling. Perversely, the Indians then blamed Spalding for not being able to grind their grain. He was informed of this blame-placing in a typically Indian way — not to his face but by means of a speech made by a Nez Perce to the wind and dark after the camp had gone to sleep.

"In June, have proceeded one day on a journey to visit a large collection [of Nez Perces] at a root ground and preach to them," Spalding wrote. "The speech was made after the camp had retired to rest. I was laying near, but not asleep. This is a common practice among this people. If anyone has anything of importance to communicate to the people, he waits till night, when all are at rest, then steps out and delivers his speech seemingly to the winds, not a person in sight, but all in hearing.

4. Ibid., p. 324.
5. Ibid., p. 325.

"His whole discourse was directed to me. Much was said about my sending the people away with their grain unground; not a word said, however, about their own savage conduct which had prevented me from grinding not only the grain of the people but my own. Much was said about the violence I might expect to meet at the root ground, etc."[6]

Next morning Spalding packed his horses and turned back to Lapwai. "I took this step not to save my life," he wrote, "for I do not think they will ever proceed so far as to kill me."

So far as the Nez Perces were concerned, Spalding was right. But 120 miles to the west, the Cayuses were brooding on desperate measures.

The warning Tom Hill had given the Nez Perces, *"Kill the whites or they will destroy you,"* had been heard for months now by the Indians living near the Whitman Mission. And events seemed to be proving him right. When Indian youngsters persisted in swiping melons out of the mission garden patch, an exasperated Dr. Whitman tried to teach them a lesson by inserting purgative powders into temptingly convenient melons. The boys stole and ate them and got sick as poisoned pups. In scolding a Cayuse brave for a minor offense, Whitman inadvertently laid a hand on his shoulder; that night the Indian got a bite of meat stuck in this throat and choked to death.

If the Cayuses failed to see ominous significance in these occurrences, Joe Lewis, who had become Tom Hill's disciple, was quick to point it out to them. Half French-Canadian and half Indian, Lewis came from Maine and knew what the white man had done to the Iroquois there. Though not as well educated and eloquent as Hill, he was his equal in bitterness and advocacy of violence.

Since the Whitman station lay directly on the Oregon Trail and was the only place emigrants could get supplies and medical services from a fellow American between Fort Laramie and the Willamette Valley, the demands on its resources were becoming increasingly burdensome. Jim Bridger had sent his half-blood daughter, Mary Ann, now twelve years old, to the Whitman Mission to be schooled and raised. Joe Meek, on his way to the Willamette, had done the same thing with his half-blood daughter, ten-year-old Helen Mar.

A bachelor too sick to travel with his train had been housed, nursed, and fed at the mission until he regained his health. Other indigents had been taken in for short or long periods of time. And what, in God's name, could you do with seven young brothers and sisters, ranging from five months to thirteen years of age, whose parents had died along the way? Well, you could say, as Narcissa Whitman did, that you would take only the girls. Then when you saw the looks in the eyes of the parentless children about to be parted, you could change your mind, as Marcus Whitman did, and, in God's name, say gruffly: "We'll take them all." [7]

In November 1847 there were sixty-nine more or less permanent residents with white blood in their veins living at Waiilatpu. The chief concern of the mission now was not saving Indian souls but feeding the hungry, clothing the naked, and nursing the ill Americans dropped off by wagon trains moving west. Understandably, the Cayuses resented the ever-growing white community occupying their lands. But resentment changed to horror when one of the ill Americans, sick with black measles, inadvertently passed on his disease to the Cayuses, who possessed no natural immunity to measles.

On November 28, 1847, Henry Spalding, who had ridden down from Lapwai, went with Dr. Whitman to a Umatilla Indian village some twenty-five miles south of Waiilatpu. Spalding knew that the epidemic of measles — now locally raging like an out-of-control prairie fire — had made several white children at the mission ill. He was deeply concerned, for his own daughter, Eliza, was attending school there.

He knew that the fatality rate among the Indians was extremely high. If the disease failed to kill them, their home remedy of a sweat bath followed by a plunge into an icy stream did.[8] He knew that Dr. Whitman, who was doing everything within his power to cope with the epidemic, was running a great risk in ministering to the Indians. By their savage code, when the *tewat* (medicine man) failed to effect a cure, his own life could become forfeit. But as a Christian and a doctor, Whitman could not neglect a person who was ill.

That afternoon Dr. Whitman said he must re-

6. Ibid., pp. 327–328.

7. For the poignant story of the seven Sager children, see *Shallow Grave at Waiilatpu* by Erwin N. Thompson (Portland: Oregon Historical Society, 1969). An extremely well written, as well as authentic, account.

8. Drury estimates that of four hundred members of the Cayuse tribe living in the vicinity, half of them died during this epidemic; the exact figure he states is 197. *Spalding Diaries*, p. 342.

turn to Waiilatpu, where his services were sorely needed. Was Spalding ready to go? Since he was very tired and suffering from a recent injury that made riding painful, Spalding told Whitman to go on without him — he would rest in the Indian village and come to Waiilatpu in a day or two.

So Whitman rode home alone.

At noon, next day, the Cayuses took the course of action Tom Hill, Joe Lewis, and grief for their dead long had urged them to take. By the time they finished their bloody work, Marcus Whitman, his wife Narcissa, and twelve more white people were dead, fifty-one whites were being held captive, and terror stalked the land.

By a freak of fate Spalding remained alive and free. But the Cayuses knew where he was — and had sworn to kill him.

CHAPTER ELEVEN

THE NEZ PERCES CHOOSE PEACE: 1847–1851

*Our only hope is the Nez Perces. The quicker
we throw ourselves upon them, the better.*
— Eliza Spalding, December 5, 1847

DURING HER eleven years at Lapwai Mrs. Spalding had borne four children, though her health remained fragile. With her in her husband's absence were Henry, eight; Martha, two; and the baby, Amelia, whose first birthday would be celebrated in just a week. As already noted, ten-year-old Eliza was in school at Waiilatpu.

The Whitman Massacre took place on Monday, November 29. In garbled form, word of it reached Mrs. Spalding at Lapwai through a loyal Nez Perce the following Sunday morning, December 5. The Indian did not know what had happened to her husband and daughter, but he had heard that a band of dissident Nez Perces was planning to attack tha Lapwai Mission and kill all the white people there, just as the Cayuses had done at Waiilatpu. William Craig and a few friendly Nez Perces would do what they could to protect her family, he said, but unless she and her children went quickly to Craig's house a few miles up the valley, their lives were in danger.

Very well, she replied. She would take the children to Craig's house tomorrow morning. Tomorrow? Why not today? Because this was the Sabbath, she said. Even at the risk of death, she would not violate the Lord's day.

How she passed that long Sunday, how every argument used by Craig and the loyal Nez Perces shattered on the rock of her obstinancy, and whether, when she prayed — as she surely did — she again voiced the phrase written in her diary eleven years earlier, *"Surely the Lord is my shepherd, and I shall have nothing to fear, if I will but repose my whole trust in Him,"* must remain in the realm of speculation, for no written record has survived. But the Nez Perces never forgot her courage. In memory they would hold this frail woman's spirit in awe long after her flesh had left their presence.

Monday morning Mrs. Spalding and her children moved to the safety of Craig's cabin. Shortly thereafter, a band of "heathen" Nez Perces vandalized the vacant mission buildings. They were led, one writer says, by a "renegade" who had participated in the Whitman killings.[1] But under Craig's protective wing, Mrs. Spalding and her children were safe.

She could only wait and wonder whether her husband and eldest daughter still lived.

Father J. B. A. Brouillet, a Catholic priest, who, with his associates, recently had established a mission near the Umatilla village, chanced to visit Waiilatpu the day after the massacre. As a Black Robe and a King George man, he was for the moment immune to Cayuse wrath, a neutral who would not be harmed so long as he minded his own business. He was horrified by what he saw, but he was in no position to chastise the Indians, who still were in a murderous mood. After baptizing several Cayuse children who were dying of black measles, he helped bury the whites who had been killed. Knowing that Spalding was in the Umatilla area and hearing the Cayuses say they intended to kill him, Father Brouillet jeopordized his neutrality and his life by hastening south to warn him. He intercepted Spalding, who was on his way to the mission, and told him what had occurred.

Spalding was stunned. "The Indians have killed

---

1. Alvin Josephy points out that the often-repeated story that the Nez Perces never shed white blood before 1877 is a myth. In view of the frequent intermarriages among Nez Perces, Cayuses, Walla Wallas, and Umatillas, all one can do is generalize and say that as a tribe the Nez Perces did not make war on the whites until 1877.

Catholic Priests

the Doctor!'' he cried. ''Is it possible! Is it possible! They will certainly kill me if I go to the camp. What shall I do?''[2]

According to Father Brouilllet's account, he told Spalding that the Cayuses had sent out war parties to kill all the Americans in the country. The priest gave Spalding what food he had with him and advised him to take the trail west to The Dalles as his only hope for safety.

Within twenty minutes after Spalding had left Brouillet and taken the trail west toward The Dalles, three armed Cayuses rode up and demanded the whereabouts of Spalding. They became very angry when they learned Spalding had fled and blamed Brouillet for aiding him in his escape. Off they set in pursuit.

Spalding, meanwhile, had recovered from the initial shock of the tragic news, conquered his impulse to think only of his own safety, and changed his plans. After riding a few miles in a westerly direction, his concern for his family at Lapwai (coupled with a firm belief that the Christianized Nez Perces there would not turn against the whites) induced him to ride north, then east, up the valley of the Touchet River, until he was traveling in the opposite direction from that his pursuers thought he had taken.

Riding all night Wednesday, hiding during the daylight hours on Thursday, then riding after dark that night, Spalding covered some forty miles before weariness forced him to lie down and rest. Since he neglected to hobble his horse, it got away, leaving him afoot in freezing December weather, still ninety miles from home. For food he had ''a small piece of bread and meat, perhaps half a pound'' that Father Brouillet had given him. His ill-fitting shoes, which Drury says probably were a gift from some missionary barrel, pinched so badly that he was forced to discard them and wrap his leggins around his feet. Still lame from a recent leg injury, he limped painfully. His blankets were too heavy to carry, so he dumped them. On Friday night he walked thirty miles. After resting the next day,

''Saturday night I made thirty miles more. My feet suffered from the frozen ground. I avoided the places of encampment and forded the streams far from the trail, lest the Cayuse might be waylaying. I secreted myself on the Sabbath — and hunger, pain in my feet, and weakness were very great; I wanted sleep, but could get none, for the cold. From the moment I stopped traveling in the morning till I started at night, I shook to the center of every bone with cold.''[3]

Feeling that Timothy, leader of the Alpowa band of Nez Perces, could be trusted if any Indian could, he headed for the village located on the south side of Snake River, reaching it after dark Sunday evening. A heavy rain was falling as he cautiously sought Timothy's lodge.

Because of the rain and cold, most of the dogs that usually roamed about an Indian village at night had sought shelter inside the tepees, so Spalding was able to creep close to what he thought was Timothy's lodge. The Indians inside were holding religious services; he could hear them singing and praying.

''In the prayer, I heard the speaker name Doctor and Mrs. Whiman as killed, and myself as probably. But he named no one as killed at my place. Oh, what an angel of mercy to the human family is hope!''

Though encouraged that the Nez Perces in this village still clung to the Christian faith, Spalding was afraid to reveal himself to anyone but Timothy. Not finding him, and being discovered and snarled at by dogs, he made a hasty retreat from the village and limped down to the sandy beach of the dark, wide, rapids-filled river.

By good chance he found a canoe. He rowed across to the north shore and made his way east over an extremely rocky trail. Going up the Clearwater he found another canoe, crossed to the south bank, and by dawn was just five miles from home. There he was discovered by a Nez Perce woman. She failed to recognize him at first because of his haggard appearance, but she finally did and notified her husband. Soon the half-frozen, exhausted, starving man was given dry clothes, hot food, and a warm bed.[4]

Spalding had not found Timothy in the Alpowa village because he was not there. As soon as Mrs. Spalding heard of the killings at Waiilatpu, she had asked Timothy to go there and see if he could procure the release of young Eliza. The Indian had left for Waiilatpu at once. Arriving at the mission he was horrified by what he saw.

''When Eliza saw him, she wept for joy,'' Drury writes, ''and Timothy picked up the little girl in his arms and mingled his tears with hers, 'Poor Eliza,' he said, 'don't cry, you shall see your mother.' ''[5]

2. J. B. A. Brouillet, ''Authentic Account of the Murder of Dr. Whitman,'' U.S., Congress, House Executive Document No. 38, 35th Cong., 1st ses., 1858.
3. Drury, Spalding, p. 339.
4. Ibid., p. 340.
5. Ibid., p. 344.

Despite the respect the Cayuses had for Timothy and much as they desired his services as a spokesman for peace, no argument would induce them to release the ten-year-old girl. In a sense she was the most valuable hostage. Of all the captives she was the most fluent in the Indian tongue, having heard and spoken it all her life. She thus was extremely useful as an interpreter who could be trusted to tell the truth in their negotiations with the whites.

Reunited at last with his wife and three of their children at Lapwai, Spalding concentrated on doing what he could to preserve the lives of young Eliza and the other captives. His immediate fear was that Americans living in the Willamette Valley would raise a force of volunteers and send it upriver to punish the Indians. In a letter to a Catholic missionary, Bishop Blanchet, he wrote:

"My daughter is yet a captive, I fear, but in the hands of our merciful Heavenly Father. Two Indians have gone for her [Timothy and Eagle]. . . . We do not wish the Americans to come from below to avenge the wrong. . . . The Nez Perces held a meeting yesterday. They pledged themselves to protect us from the Cayuses, if we would prevent the Americans from coming up to avenge the murders. This we have pledged to do, and for this we beg for the sake of our lives at this place and at Mr. Walker's. By all means keep quiet, and send no war reports; send nothing but proposals for peace."[6]

Ever since the Joint Occupancy Treaty had been terminated and the country south of the forty-ninth parallel ceded to the United States, Hudson's Bay Company factors in the area had devoted their energies to winding up business affairs. Conflict between Indians and Americans in the region was not their concern. But to their eternal credit the British reacted to the tragedy with the cool-headedness that long had marked their dealings with the Indians.

Soon after word of the massacre reached Fort Walla Walla, twenty-three miles west of Waiilatpu, Factor William McBean dispatched a courier downriver with a secret, urgent message to be delivered to the only man who, in McBean's judgment, was capable of handling such a ticklish situation — the factor now in charge at Fort Vancouver, Peter Skene Ogden.

Two decades had passed since the former "Prince of Good Fellows and Terror of All Indians" had made his gruelling treks across the Snake River country, and the years had taken their toll.

White-haired, pudgy, and full of an old man's aches and pains, Ogden could have said this was not his problem, sent Oregon Governor Abernethy a sympathetic note, and gone back to his paperwork.

Being Peter Skene Ogden, he did no such thing.

Instead, he ordered two bateaux filled with trade goods drawn from company stores. He sent a brief note to the governor requesting that he make no move that might jeopardize ransom negotiations. Then he stepped into the lead bateau and headed upriver.

His protective force, if such it could be called, consisted of sixteen French-Canadians — men notorious for their lack of enthusiasm when it came to fighting Indians — and his well-earned reputation for never making a promise he did not keep.

His mission was successful. He told the Indians that, although he could not guarantee they would

6. Drury, *Spalding Diaries*, p. 346. Bishop Blanchet passed on the letter to an Oregon newspaper, which published it, embarrassing Spalding and sowing the seed of a lifelong feud between Spalding and the Catholics, whom he later came to blame for the massacre itself.

George Abernethy
First Governor of Oregon Territory

not be punished for what they had done, he would urge the Americans not to go to war against them. The price agreed upon for ransom of the captives was sixty-two blankets, sixty-three cotton shirts, twelve guns, six hundred loads of ammunition, and thirty-seven pounds of tobacco. On December 29, 1847, fifty-one captives from Waiilatpu were brought to Fort Walla Walla. On January 1, 1848, the Spalding family arrived, having been escorted from Lapwai by a party of fifty armed Nez Perces. Spalding found his daughter badly shaken by the experience she had gone through "too weak to stand, a mere skeleton, and her mind as much impaired as her health."[7]

In parting with Mrs. Spalding, for whom he had a special reverence, Timothy said sadly:

"Now, my beloved teacher, you are passing over my country for the last time. You are leaving us forever, and my people, Oh, my people, will see no more light. We shall meet no more in the schoolroom, and my children, Oh, my children, will live only in a night that will have no morning. When we reach Walla Walla, I shall look on your face for the last time in this world. But this book [holding it in his hand] in which your hands have written and caused me to write the words of God I shall carry in my bosom till I lie down in the grave."[8]

On January 2, Peter Skene Ogden supervised the loading into boats of fifty-seven men, women, and children with white blood in their veins and started them on their way down the Columbia. Sad to relate, one part-white child that nobody wanted was left behind.

As noted earlier, the Whitman Mission long had been a dropping-off place for homeless children such as the seven Sager orphans and the mixed-blood offspring of men such as Jim Bridger and Joe Meek. But this child had neither known parents nor a recorded name. On March 2, 1842, Mrs. Whitman wrote, she had found a little "miserable looking child, a boy between three and four years old."

Nothing appears to have been known about the child, other than the fact that his father was a Spaniard, his mother an Indian, and that he had been terribly treated and abused. Childless Narcissa — who soon would be caring for eleven motherless children — took the little boy in, cleaned him up, fed him, and raised him as one of her own. In a nostalgic moment she named him David Malin, after a former schoolmate back home in Prattsburg, New York, who had become a minister.

Now nine years old, the half-Spanish, half-Indian boy was twice cursed so far as his chances of being taken into the home of a white "Christian" family in the Willamette Valley were concerned. So he was left behind. One of the orphan Sager girls, who had become fond of him, later wrote:

"The last look I had of him was when we moved away from Fort Walla Walla, leaving him standing on the bank of the river crying as though his heart were breaking."[9]

Shortly after the boats pulled away from the landing, a band of angry Cayuses rode up, looking for Spalding. They had heard that a volunteer army of Americans was heading upriver to make war on them, and they thought Spalding had reneged on his promise to send out only peace messages. Actually, Spalding had made a plea for peace in his letter to Bishop Blanchet. But the impatient white settlers in the Willamette Valley, eager for blood vengeance, had gone ahead and raised an expeditionary force of three hundred men. Meeting these amateur soldiers at The Dalles, Spalding changed his tune, demanding

"for the barbarian murders and violators . . . eternal remembrance; let them be pursued with unrelenting hatred and hostility, until life-blood has atoned for their infamous deeds."[10]

For two years a series of desultory, indecisive skirmishes called the Cayuse War spread misery over the land. Deciding at last that the only way to end it was to give up the "murderers," five Cayuse braves were surrendered by their tribal leaders. Taken to Oregon City, they were tried May 22, 1850, found guilty, and sentenced to death. When asked why he and the others had surrendered, Tiloukaikt replied:

"Did not your missionaries teach us that Christ died to save his people? So die we to save our people."[11]

The multiple hangings took place June 3, 1850. The officiating officer was U.S. Marshal Joe

7. Drury, *Spalding*, p. 345.
8. Ibid., pp. 349–350. In prefacing this quote Drury writes: "One of the faithful Christians, perhaps Timothy, is reported to have said this to Mrs. Spalding."
9. Matilda Sager Delaney, *The Whitman Massacre* (Spokane, 1920), p. 17; Drury, *Spalding*, p. 346.
10. Hubert Howe Bancroft, *History of Oregon. Works*, vol. 29 (San Francisco, 1886), p. 701.
11. Ibid., p. 95.

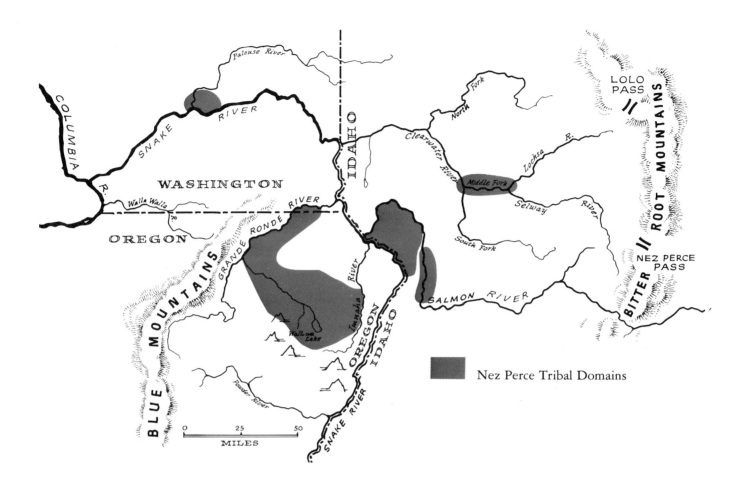

Nez Perce Tribal Domains

Meek. In happier days a trapper friend had loaned Meek the only romantic novel he ever struggled through. Its heroine was a lovely, ethereal girl named Helen Mar. He was so entranced by the fictional character that when his Shoshone woman, Mountain Lamb, bore him a daughter, he had a name all ready for her.

Joe and Mountain Lamb long since had parted, and the dirty, vermin-infested, frightened child he had given Narcissa Whitman to raise bore no resemblance to the heroine of a romantic novel. When the Cayuses struck, the child, now ten years old, had been ill. Though the Indians did not harm her, without a doctor and proper care she died ten days later.

It may be that Meek was remembering Helen

Mar when he gave the execution order. Certainly if the doomed Cayuses knew he had lost a daughter because of their acts — as they probably did — it helped them die with dignity, for they well understood the justice of blood vengeance taken by a father for the loss of a child.[12]

12. In one of a series of sketches based on historical happenings, Robert Ormond Case has the five doomed Indians trembling in anticipation of hanging — a kind of death they particularly abhorred — with Joe Meek bolstering their courage and pride by whispering to them just before the traps were sprung that they had killed his daughter. "Once to Every Warrior," by Robert Ormond Case, Peabody Award Winning Radio Drama, Station KOIN, Portland, Oregon, 1944; published as a short story in the collection *The Empire Builders* (New York: Doubleday & Co., 1947), pp. 233–242.

CHAPTER TWELVE

THE FIRST TREATY COUNCIL: 1855

*My people, what have you done? While I was
gone you have sold my country. I have come
home and there is not left me a place on which to
pitch my lodge.*
— Chief Looking Glass, June 9, 1855

GIVEN NEITHER POWER nor pay by the Americans and neither support nor obedience by the Nez Perces, Ellis soon lost interest in being "head chief." He quit trying to live as a "settled" Indian and resumed his nomadic ways. While on a meat-hunting expedition to the buffalo country during the summer of 1847, he and sixty members of his band died, succumbing not to their traditional enemies, the Blackfeet, but falling victim to the dealiest killer of all, an epidemic of white man's disease to which they had no immunity.[1]

With the Spaldings gone, the Code of Laws no longer enforced, and few white men in their country, the natural thing for the Nez Perces to do was to slip back into their old style of free and easy communal living. But fifty years of association with Americans had so deeply altered their way of life that they found it impossible to return to their earlier customs.

"Although abandoned by Mr. Spalding, they by no means discarded the good he had taught them. They maintained, unaided, their simple religious worship, and held services every Sabbath, with preaching, singing of hymns, and reading of the Bible, all in their own language, with the books translated and printed for them by the devoted missionary. They prided themselves upon their superior intelligence, upon having young men who could read and write."

Though removed from the main route of the Oregon Trail, the Nez Perces were well aware of the large numbers of emigrants coming west during the years between 1843 and 1855.

"The Nez Perces used to go down to the emigrant road on the Grande Ronde or Umatilla, with bands of fat, sleek, handsome ponies, and exchanged them with the emigrants for their worn-out horses, oxen, and sometimes a cow, clothing, groceries, ammunition, etc. The Pikes, as the Missourians who comprised the majority of the emigrants were called, 'allowed that the Nez Perces could beat a Yankee on a trade.' "[2]

Meanwhile, the winds of change were swirling with ever-increasing velocity over the Nez Perce country. In 1846 the Joint Occupancy Treaty with Great Britain was abrogated, and the entire watershed of the Snake River and the Columbia south of the forty-ninth parallel was declared American property. In 1847 the Whitman Massacre focused the attention of the nation on the Pacific Northwest as no other event could have done. Color was added to the story when Joe Meek, ex-mountain man and now a U.S. marshal, carried word of the killings to Washington, D.C. and, in buckskins, was feted and interviewed at the White House with his cousin, President James Knox Polk, a rabid expansionist.

As early as 1843, when a provisional government had been established jointly by American and British citizens in the Willamette Valley on the slim majority of a single vote, any white or half-white male over the age of eighteen was invited to file on, claim, and hold 640 acres of land, with no regard for Indian rights. In 1849 Oregon Territory was organized, and on September 27, 1850, only a few months after the multiple hangings officially

1. Josephy, *Nez Perces,* p. 257n. Other writers say Ellis died of smallpox or was killed by Blackfeet, but Josephy says the chief and the Nez Perces with him were taken off by measles, the same disease that decimated the Cayuses in the fall of 1847.
2. *The Life of Isaac Ingalls Stevens* by his son, Hazard Stevens, (Boston: Houghton Mifflin Co., 1901), vol. 2, p. 19.

ended the Cayuse War, the Donations Claims Act validating the action of the provisional government was made the law of the land.

In 1853 the land lying north of the Columbia River was separated from Oregon Territory. Its boundaries were redrawn, and it was given a name honoring the country's first president — Washington Territory. Appointed as its first governor by newly elected President Franklin Pierce was a thirty-four-year-old army officer, Isaac Ingalls Stevens.

Born in Andover, Massachussetts, a West Point graduate in the Corps of Engineers, and a veteran of the Mexican War, Stevens was aggressive, energetic, and politically ambitious. An ordinary man would have had more than enough to do by becoming the top executive of a newly organized territory whose borders stretched from the forty-sixth parallel on the south to the forty-ninth parallel on the north and from the Pacific Ocean on the west to the Continental Divide on the east — an area that later would contain not only the State of Washington but most of Idaho and half of Montana and Wyoming as well.

But not Isaac Stevens.

On his way out to his new office in the capitol being established at the southern end of Puget Sound, he might as well survey a northern route for a transcontinental railroad, he told President Pierce. While doing this he also could make contacts with Indians encountered along the way, with the aim in mind to come back later, treat with them, and "extinguish title to their lands."

Within two years he had accomplished all those objectives.

In his whirlwind tour west of the Cascades he had little trouble getting the small though numerous tribes to agree to accept reservations in or near where they had lived for generations. They were already "settled" Indians to a degree. Their homes were the forests, the streams, and the saltwater beaches on the rainy side of the mountains, where they need not roam far to find sustenance or nieghbors with whom to trade. Furthermore, they were intimidated by the large numbers of white people who had moved into their country, built cabins, cleared fields, and established farms. Most important of all, they had been tamed and their numbers drastically thinned by the greatest civilizing force of all — smallpox and other white man's diseases.

The tribes east of the Cascades — the horse

Courtesy Penrose Library, Whitman College

Isaac Ingalls Stevens. After serving as governor of Washington Territory from 1853 to 1857 he was elected to the national Congress and resigned as governor August 11, 1857. Serving in the Civil War he was killed at the Battle of Chantilly, September 1, 1862.

Indians — were quite another matter. In order to deal with them, Stevens knew, he would have to convene large numbers of well-armed warriors belonging to the most powerful tribes in the Pacific Northwest, impress them with the strength of the American government, shower their leaders with substantial gifts, and negotiate treaties that would put them in their place forever and open the rest of their lands to settlement by the whites.

The spot chosen for the meeting was an ancient, traditional Indian council grounds in the heart of the Walla Walla Valley, six miles east of the abandoned Whitman Mission. Invited to the treaty talks were members of five tribes: Nez Perce, Cayuse, Umatilla, Walla Walla, and Yakima. The

Sketch by Gustavus Sohon   *Courtesy Washington State Historical Society*

Arrival of the Nez Perce Indians at the Walla Walla Treaty Council grounds late May, 1855

time set for the talks was late May 1855. Joining Governor Stevens in the negotiations were Joel Palmer, Superintendent of Indian Affairs for Oregon Territory.

Between five and six thousand Indians came to the council grounds. The whites numbered one hundred, only forty of whom were soldiers. Lieutenant Lawrence Kip, who was there as a military observer, describes the arrival of the Nez Perces:

"*Thursday, May 24th.* This has been an exceedingly interesting day, as about 2,400 of the Nez Perce tribe have arrived. It was our first specimen of this Prairie chivalry, and it certainly realized all our conceptions of these wild warriors of the plains.

"When about a mile distant they halted, and half a dozen chiefs rode forward and were introduced to Governor Stevens and General Palmer[3], in order of their rank. Then came the rest of the wild horsemen in single file, clashing their shields, singing and beating their drums as they marched past us. Then they formed a circle and danced around us, while our little group stood

there, the center of their wild evolutions. They would gallop up as if about to make a charge, then wheel round and round, sounding their loud whoops until they had apparently worked themselves up into an intense excitement. Then some score or two dismounted, and, forming a ring, danced for about twenty minutes, while those surrounding them beat time on their drums. After these performances, more than twenty of the chiefs went over to the tent of Governor Stevens, where they sat for some time, smoking the 'pipe of peace,' in token of good fellowship, and then returned to their camping ground."[4]

Lieutenant Kip visited the lodge "of an old chief of the Nez Perces named Lawyer. He showed us a wound in his side from which he was yet suffering."

3. Palmer's exalted military title came from service with the Oregon Volunteers in earlier Indian skirmishes. In the years following such service all rank and file soldiers seem to have been promoted to "colonel," all officers to "general."

4. Lawrence Kip, *Indian Council at Walla Walla* (1897; facsimile reproduction, Seattle: Shorey Publications, 1971), pp. 10–11.

No doubt this was the hip wound Lawyer had received fighting on the side of the whites at the Battle of Pierre's Hole in 1831, twenty-four years earlier. It caused him to limp and walk with a cane for the rest of his life.

Visiting Chief Lawyer again the next day, Lieutenant Kip found him surrounded by his family, reading a portion of the New Testament. A German soldier, Gustavus Sohon, who had been employed by Governor Stevens in the railroad survey party and retained because of his talent as an artist, sketched Lawyer's portrait in crayons. "He afterwards presented me with a copy," Kip says, "which I keep as a memento of these pleasant days in the wilderness."[5]

After having lunch with Governor Stevens on Sunday, May 27, Lieutenant Kip again went to the Nez Perce camp,

"where we found they were holding services in one of the largest lodges; two of the chiefs were officiating, one of them delivering an address (taking the Ten Commandments for his text), and at the end of each sentence the other chief would repeat it in a louder tone of voice. This is their invariable custom with all their speeches. Everything was conducted with the greatest propriety, and the singing, in which they all joined, had an exceedingly musical effect."[6]

Since this was to be the most important council held east of the Cascades, elaborate preparations for it had been made. In a biography of his father, Hazard Stevens writes:

"A wall tent, with a large arbor of poles and boughs in front, stood on level, open ground a short distance from the creek and facing the Blue Mountains, all ready for the governor. This was also to serve as the council chamber, and ample clear space was left for the Indians to assemble and seat themselves on the ground in front of the arbor. A little further in front, and nearer the creek, were ranged the tents of the rest of the party, a stout log-house to safely hold the supplies and Indian goods, and a large arbor to serve as a banqueting-hall for distinguished chiefs, so that, as in civilized lands, gastronomy might aid diplomacy. A large herd of beef cattle and a pile of potatoes, purchased of Messrs. Lloyd Brooke, Bumford & Noble, who were occupying the site of the Whitman Mission, and ample stores of sugar, coffee, bacon, and flour furnished the materials for the feasts."[7]

In order to make sure that everyone understood what was said during the talks, six interpreters were appointed, one of whom was William Craig, Spalding's bitter enemy, Old James, also was there, as were his first converts and friends,

Sketch by Gustavus Sohon   Courtesy Washington State Historical Society
Feasting the chiefs

Joseph, and Timothy. According to the official transcript:

"Timothy, a Nez Perce chief, acted as crier for his nation, and he will also record in their language the full proceedings each day of the council and this will be preserved among the archives and handed down to future generations."[8]

Unfortunately for historians, this priceless document has not survived.

Provisions were issued to the Nez Perces at the rate of one and a half pounds of beef, two pounds of potatoes, and one half pound of corn per person. But the Cayuses, Walla Wallas, and Umatillas, who arrived and went into camp without a

5. Ibid., p. 12.

6. Ibid., p. 13.

7. Life of Stevens, pp. 31–32.

8. A true copy of the Record of the official proceedings at the Council in the Walla Walla Valley, held jointly by Isaac I. Stevens Gov. and Supt. W. T. and Joel Palmer Supt. Indian Affairs O.T. on the part of the United States with the tribes of Indians named in the Treaties made at that Council, June 9th and 11th, 1955, p.7 (hereafter called Transcript).

Regarding the fate of Timothy's record, the superintendent of Nez Perce National Historical Park, Jack R. Williams, wrote Lawrence Dodd, Curator of Manuscripts and Special Materials at Penrose Library, Whitman College, on February 11, 1975, as follows:

"According to Mylie Lawyer, a granddaughter of Chief Lawyer, Timothy worked very closely with Chief Lawyer. Both were students of the Rev. H. H. Spalding, and though Timothy could write for some unknown reason he always signed papers with an X — his mark!

"Chief Lawyer's wife, Mylie's grandmother, told Mylie that Timothy was a crier (which is not well known) and he did record the 1855 council proceedings. When Timothy died and was buried at Alpowa in 1890 the family followed the custom of disposing of the deceased's property by giving away and burning. Unfortunately, all of his papers were burned and the document you seek was among them."

salutation of any sort, refused to accept provisions from the whites. Pitching their lodges a mile distant, where they were screened from the camp of the whites and the Nez Perces by a growth of trees, they sent a messenger who, after rudely refusing to accept even a gift of tobacco, was overheard by an interpreter muttering as he rode off: "You will find out by and by why we won't take provisions."9

Two Caltholic priests, Father Chirouse with the Walla Wallas and Father Pandosy with the Yakimas, were there. They reported that most of the Indians they had talked to were well disposed toward the whites, with the exception of the leader of the Yakimas, Chief Kamiakin. Well aware that the Yakimas were a loosely knit association of fourteen bands that never had recognized a single person as "head chief," Kamiakin had been extremely reluctant to come to the council, let alone speak for a tribe second only in numbers and power to the Nez Perces. But he and a few other Yakima leaders finally did come, though they were the last to arrive.

Rumors began flying around the camp of the whites that a plot had been agreed upon by Kamiakin, Peo-peo-mox-mox, Young Chief, and other Indian leaders to oppose making a treaty in the most violent way possible — by murdering the commissioners and their military escort.

Upon arriving at the council grounds, the Yakima leader gave credence to these rumors by curtly refusing to accept presents or provisions from the whites, saying that he "had never accepted anything from the whites, not even to the value of a grain of wheat, without paying for it, and that he did not wish to purchase the presents."10

How real the conspiracy was, how much of it was self-serving to Indian leaders who professed friendship toward the commissioners in hopes of personal gain, or how much was concocted by writers long after the council ended will never be known. It seems probable that some of the Indians did talk violence, others magnified their roles as peacemakers, and participants in the happenings of the council interpolated later events as part of a plot that never really existed.

After getting all the Indian leaders to agree to begin the talks at noon, May 29, Governor Stevens and Secretary Doty visited Lawyer in his lodge, "as his wound had broken out afresh [and] he was unable to walk without pain and difficulty."

He showed them a map he had drawn of his country at Governor Steven's request. A Nez Perce

Sketch by Gustavus Sohon   *Courtesy Washington State Historical Society*
Peo-Peo Mox-Mox. Head chief of the Walla Walla Indians

chief called Spotted Eagle came in and told Stevens the Cayuses had sent a messenger who had urged them to come to the Cayuse camp for a council before the treaty talks began, but the Nez Perces refused.

"Our chiefs will not go. We have our own people to take care of; they give us trouble enough, and we will not have the Cayuse troubles on our hands."

To Stevens this was further evidence that a plot against the whites was brewing, but he was reassured when Lawyer opened a book and read the advice left him by the former "head chief," Ellis:

"Whenever the great chiefs of the Americans shall come into your country to give you laws, accept them. Ellis's advice is to accept the white law. I have read it to you to show you my heart."11

In return, Governor Stevens showed the Indian *his* heart by giving Lawyer a paper certifying him as "head chief" of the Nez Perces. This curious document, which has survived, specifically states that the "head chief" will retain his office only as long as he carries out his duties in a satisfactory manner; if and when he fails to perform them to the satisfaction of the agent, he will be replaced.

9. *Life of Stevens,* p. 32.
10. Ibid., p. 38.
11. *Transcript,* p.3.

Designated as chiefs and delegates representing their respective bands and tribes were the following:

For the Nez Perces: Lawyer, Joseph, James, Timothy, Red Wolf, and others.

For the Cayuses: Young Chief, Stickus, and Co-mos-pilo.

For the Walla Wallas: Peo-peo-mox-mox.

For the Yakimas: Kamiakin, Ow-hi, and Skloom.

Other tribes, such as the Palouses, Spokanes, Pisquose, Methows, and Okanogans, had sent observers, though few members of these tribes were present.

Because it was rainy and cool, the council was adjourned on the first day, after the interpreters had been sworn in, but the next afternoon, May 30, was sunny and clear. Governor Stevens made the opening speech, during which he told the Indians of the sincere concern for their welfare in the heart of the President of the United States.

"I went back to the Great Father last year to say that you had been good, you had been kind, he *must do something for you.* [Italics are in copy of the transcript.] My brother [Palmer] wrote to the Great Father in like manner.

"He told the Great Father, these men have farms; the Great Father said, I want them to have more and larger farms; I told him you had cattle and horses; he answered, he wanted your cattle and horses to increase; I told him, some of your grown people could read and write; he answered, I want all the grown people and all

the children to learn to read and write; I told him that some of you are handy at trades; he answered, that he desired to give all who choose the means to learn these trades."[12]

The Great Father loved his red children fully as much as he did his white children, Steven went on, and wanted to protect them. Twenty years ago in the East, Great Father Andrew Jackson had cared for his red children by escorting them west across a great river into a fine country, where they now had their own government and laws. No white man could go into that tract of land without the consent of the Indians, Stevens said; thus, they were protected and had become prosperous there.

What Governor Stevens referred to, of course, was the forcible removal of the Cherokees and other eastern tribes to Indian Territory (later Oklahoma) during the 1830s, an event so tragic and costly in human lives that the removal came to be called the Trail of Tears.

But the picture Stevens drew of reservation life was a pleasant one.

"We want you and ourselves to agree upon tracts of land where you will live . . . we must pay you for the land which you give to the Great Father . . . these payments are something you will have to think much about. Whatever is done, is done with your free consent."[13]

Because of the need to pause after each phrase so that it could be translated into the various Indian dialects, with criers repeating the words so that those sitting in distant ranks could hear, Steven's opening remarks took over three hours to deliver.

Next day, May 31, Governor Stevens became more specific as to what the Indians would gain by ceding the lands they did not need and agreeing to live on reservations.

"Besides clothing, we would wish to furnish you with tools and implements for the shops; for the blacksmith; for the wheelwright; for the tinsmith and such other tools as you might need . . ."

He reminded the Indians of the great blessings that the white man's civilization had brought them during the last hundred years:

"The horse carries you whither you wish to go, yourself, your wife, your children, and your packs, and he works in your fields. Your cattle now furnish you with a portion of your food; your cows furnish you with milk

Sketch by Gustavus Sohon   *Courtesy Washington State Historical Society*
Ow-Hi. Chief of the Yakimas

12. Ibid., p. 8.
13. Ibid., pp. 9–10.

and you already know how to make butter. . . . Formerly you raised no wheat, no potatoes. Now you have both grain and vegetables.

"Is not this a great change? A change which you have all seen? Has it not been for your good?"[14]

While the Indians were reflecting upon all the good that had been done them by the whites, Governor Stevens issued a special appeal to the bands of Nez Perces that were accustomed to making annual trips to the high meadows and buffalo plains for roots and meat.

"We want you if you wish to mount your horses and go to the Buffalo Plains. And we want more. We want you to have peace there. What has disturbed you on those plains? The Blackfeet."[15]

The Blackfeet were not all bad people, Stevens continued, and they had begun to notice that buffalo were not as plentiful as they used to be. They had begun to be envious of the Nez Perces.

"If we can agree here," he concluded, "you will be able to say to the Blackfeet: 'We will be friends, we will chase the buffalo together on the plains, we will be friends forever.' "[16]

Leaving that pleasant prospect in the minds of the Nez Perces, Stevens turned the council over to Superintendent Palmer, who gave a long, tedious review of three hundred and sixty years of conflict between the American Indians and the European settlers in the New World. They clearly showed "that the white man and red man cannot live happily together . . . there should be a line of distinction drawn so that the Indian may know where his land is and the white man where his land is."[17]

Taking June 1 off to recuperate from two days of speeches and to confer among themselves, the Indians returned to the council at noon Saturday, June 2. With the preliminary groundwork laid, Joel Palmer now got down to cases.

"I have said that the white man and the Indians could not live together in peace . . . it is but fifty years since the first white man came among you . . . now we have a good many settlers in the country below you . . .

"You may ask, why do they come? Can you stop the waters of the Columbia River from flowing on its course? Can you prevent the wind from blowing? Can you prevent the rain from falling? Can you prevent the whites from coming? You are answered: No . . . !

"This land was not made for you alone. . . . The fish that come up the rivers, the beasts that roam through the forests and plains, and the fowls of the air, were made alike for the white man and the red man . . .

"Now while there is room to select for you a home where there are no white men living, let us do so."[18]

Following the conclusion of Palmer's lengthy speech, Governor Stevens said:

"My children, my brother and myself have opened our hearts to you. We want you to open your hearts to us."

Five Crows then made the first Indian statement of the three days since the opening council, saying "We are tired."

Peo-peo-mox-mox, whose son had been killed by whites and his murderers never punished as promised under the Code of Laws, was more voluble and caustic:

"I know the value of your speech from having experienced it in California, having seen treaties made there. . . . From what you have said, I think you intend to win our country, or how is it to be? Suppose you show me goods. Shall I run up and take them . . . ? Goods and the Earth are not equal; goods are for using on the Earth. I do not know where they have given lands for goods."[19]

Some of the more boisterous Indian boys created a distubance at this time by their laughing, talking and horseplay. Co-mos-pilo, a Cayuse chief, scolded them sharply in his tongue, with an interpreter translating for the benefit of the secretaries:

"He said they consider him of no account any longer. They had knocked off his horns and his teeth were worn out. But once he had horns and he could hook; teeth and they were sharp and he could bite. You young men think yourselves very smart, but by and by you will learn. Now I am tired of your conduct. I am not speaking to Governor Stevens or General Palmer; I am speaking to you young men, as my children, to listen and behave yourselves."[20]

The council then adjoured for the day. Aware of the hostility of Peo-peo-mox-mox, Young Chief, and Kamiakin, Lawyer had had little to say, for he knew that he was treading upon shaky ground. But late that evening, according to Hazard Stevens, he

"came unattended to see Governor Stevens. He disclosed a conspiracy on the part of the Cayuses to suddenly rise upon and massacre all the whites on the council grounds . . .

" 'I will come with my family and pitch my lodge in

14. Ibid., p. 11.
15. Ibid., p. 12.
16. Ibid.
17. Ibid., p. 15.
18. Ibid., p. 16.
19. Ibid., pps. 18, 19.
20. Ibid., p. 19.

Sketch by Gustavus Sohon   *Courtesy Washington State Historical Society*

Hol-Lol-Sote-Tote, known as Lawyer, called head chief of
the Nez Perce Tribe by the whites.

his own status with Governor Stevens, or whether, as some Nez Perces have claimed, Lawyer had so angered the chiefs opposed to making a treaty that he feared for his life and moved his lodge into the heart of the white camp for *his* protection rather than Stevens' are questions that will never be answered to the satisfaction of historians.

But Governor Stevens certainly believed that the Nez Perce chief had saved the lives of the negotiators, for after reporting to the other Indians that the commissioners were under the protection of the Nez Perces, the governor

"imparted his knowledge of the conspiracy to Secretary Doty and Packmaster Higgins, and to them alone, for he feared that, should the party generally learn of it, a stampede would ensue. Having through these efficient officers quietly caused the men to put their arms in readiness and posting night guards, he determined to continue the council as usual, hoping that the Cayuses, foiled in their design, would finally conclude to treat."[22]

the midst of your camp,' Lawyer said, 'so that those Cayuses may see that you and your party are under the protection of the head chief of the Nez Perces.' "[21]

Whether the plot really existed, whether Lawyer exaggerated its threat in order to enhance

The next day's session, June 4, opened peacefully enough, considering the fact half the Indians present were said to have been prepared to massacre the whites the night before. Governor Ste-

21. *Life of Stevens*, p. 47.
22. Ibid., p. 48.

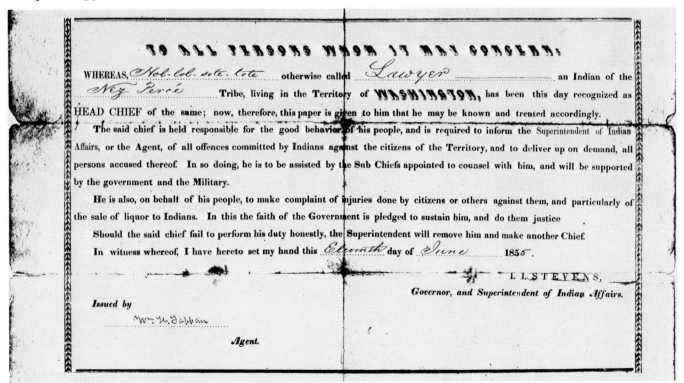

Courtesy Penrose Library, Whitman College

Certificate given Lawyer by Governor Stevens certifying that he is head chief of the Nez Perce Tribe

vens asked the chiefs to show the commissioners their hearts. Lawyer's speech was brief and vague:

"My country is poor. It is a trifling country. You see on the map the marks of our country. One stream runs one way, one another. It is all rock. The Big Chief said to you, go talk to these people, and you have done it. He says, go there to take care of your white people and your red people, and you have done it. As long as the Earth stands, take care of the people."[23]

Peo-peo-mox-mox expressed what was really bothering the Indians:

"You have spoken for lands generally. You have not spoken of any particular ones. . . . If you spoke as the watch goes, then we would say yes; the manner in which you have addressed the whole of us has made my heart heavy."[24]

The expression "as the watch goes" appears to have been a courteous way of saying that the talk of the commissioners had been unsteady and erratic; the Indians were saying as politely as they knew how: "Cut out the hokum and tell us what you want and how much you will pay for it."

Eagle-from-the-Light, an extremely articulate Nez Perce chief, made a long speech in which he disclosed some interesting pieces of history from the Indian viewpoint:

"I have been talked to by the French and by the Americans, and one says to me, go this way, and the other says, go another way; and that is the reason I am lost between them.

"A long time ago they hung my brother for no offence, and this I say to my brother here that he may think about it.[25]

"Afterwards came Spalding and Whitman. They advised us well and taught us well, very well. . . . They had pity on us and we were pitied. And Spalding sent my father to the East — the States — and he went. His body was never returned.[26] He was sent to learn a good counsel and friendship and many things. That is another thing to think of.

"At the time in this place here when there was blood spilled upon the earth, we were friendly to the whites and they to us.[27] My chief said, I will try to settle all the bad matters with the whites and he started to look for counsel; and there his body lies, beyond here. He has never returned.[28]

"At the time the Indians held a grand Council at Fort Laramie, I was with the Flatheads.[29] We were asked to go and find counsel, friendship and good advice. Many of my people started and died in the country. Died hunting what was right.

"A preacher came to us, Mr. Spalding. He talked to us to learn, and from that he turned to be a trader, as though there was two in one, one a preacher and the other a trader. He made a farm and raised grain and bought our stock, as though there was two in one; one a preacher, the other a trader . . .

"We will come straight here — slowly, perhaps — but we will come straight."[30]

Governor Stevens invited any other Indians who wished to talk to do so. No one spoke. He then answered the question on everybody's mind. Two reservations were planned: one in the Nez Perce country, another in the Yakima country. Placed on the Nez Perce Reservation would be the Spokanes, the Cayuses, the Walla Wallas, and the Umatillas, as well as the Nez Perces. Gathered on the Yakima Reservation would be the Colvilles, Okanogans, Palouse, Pisquose, Klickitats, and other bands, as well as the Yakimas. Ceded to the federal government by the Indians would be approximately thirty thousand square miles of territory, a piece of land roughly half the size of the present-day state of Washington.

Why only two reservations for a dozen or more tribes of Indians? Governor Stevens explained:

"We want as many tribes together as can be taken care of by one agent. We can do more with the same means. . . . Think over what I have said and hear the rest tomorrow."[31]

As explained by Governor Stevens next day, June 5, the rest consisted of thousands of dollars worth of tools, clothes, supplies, and equipment needed to make them "settled" Indians, houses and annuities for the head chiefs, schools and teachers for their children. Would the Indians be confined strictly to the reservations? Of course not! In proof of that, Stevens pointed to what eventually would be a far more important clause in the proposed treaty than was dreamed of at the time:

"You will be allowed to pasture your animals on land not claimed or occupied by the settlers, white men. You will be allowed to go on the roads, to take your

23. *Transcript*, p. 20.

24. Ibid., p. 21.

25. He may have been referring to the hanging of the Palouse Indian by John Clarke after the theft of his silver goblet in 1813. The term "brother" in Nez Perce usage did not necessarily mean a blood relationship.

26. This was a Nez Perce called The Hat, one of the Indians killed by Sioux during the journey east with William Gray during the summer of 1837.

27. The Whitman Massacre in 1847.

28. He is probably referring to the death of Ellis in the buffalo country the summer of 1847.

29. This council was held in 1851.

30. *Transcript*, p. 22.

31. Ibid., p. 24.

things to market, your horses and cattle. *You will be allowed to go to the usual fishing places and fish in common with the whites, and to get roots and berries and to kill game on land not occupied by the whites; all this outside the Reservation.*"[32]

A payment of $100,000 would be made the first year that the tribes went on the reservation, a further payment of $250,000 would be spread over a period of twenty years. After that it apparently was assumed that a people who had lived as Indians in the New World for thirty thousand years would have mastered the art of living like white men and would be self-sufficient. However, these sums of money would not be given in cash. Governor Stevens asked his "friend," Peo-peo-mox-mox, and the other chiefs to listen while he gave his reason for this.

"We can furnish you with nearly twice as many goods as you can get from the traders. We shall buy things you want in New York and San Francisco at cheap rates and good articles. The expense of getting them to you will not come out of your money; it will cost you nothing. At Fort Walla Walla, a flannel shirt costs you three dollars, we will give you three shirts for three dollars. You pay for a calico shirt at Walla Walla one and a half and two dollars; we can furnish you calico shirts for fifty cents apiece."[33]

And so on . . .

But it was not the method of distributing the money for their lands that disturbed the Indians now. It was the simple fact that they had been asked to sell those lands.

"My friends, I wish to show you my mind, interpret right for me," Stickus said. "How is it that I have been troubled in mind? If your mother were here in this country who gave you birth, and suckled you, and while you were sucking some person came and took away your mother and left you alone and sold your mother, how would you feel then? This is our mother, this country, as if we drew our living from her . . .

"I name three places for myself, the Grande Ronde, the Touchet towards the mountains, and the Tucannon."[34]

Since the lands lying along these streams had not been included in either reservation, thus forcing him to leave the land of his birth, Stickus was saying that he would resist removal to the Nez Perce Reservation with every fiber of his being.

On that note, the meeting adjourned.

At the council next day, June 7, Lawyer made a long, rambling speech in which he reviewed the discovery of America by Columbus, the way Co-

Sketch by Gustavus Sohon   *Courtesy Washington State Historical Society*
Stickus, Cayuse Chief

lumbus made an egg stand on end to make a point during an argument in the royal court in Spain, and the good relations between the Nez Perces and the Americans since the time of Lewis and Clark. In conclusion he said:

"I want the President to see what I, a poor man, have said. I have got your talk here [pointing to his notebook], and although a poor man, I can look at it from time to time . . .

"I think on the stream just below where Mr. Craig lives will be a good place for one mechanic or on one of the ranches you have shown me. I also think that perhaps in the country where I live may be a good place for some more of them, in case they were crowded below."[35]

Like the Timothy record of the council, the Lawyer notebook has not survived. Though he later would be criticized by some members of his tribe for having "sold" their country, he was realistic enough to see that the reservation, as its boundaries now were drawn, adequately covered the lands traditionally occupied by the Nez Perces. Since the treaty terms stipulated that no white man could come onto the reservation without Indian permission, since the Indians were to be permitted to go to the buffalo country, pick berries, dig roots,

32. Ibid., p. 25. Italics mine.
33. Ibid., p. 28.
34. Ibid.
35. Ibid., p. 30.

and pasture their horses upon "unoccupied lands," and, since, most important of all, the Indians could fish in their "usual and accustomed places," he judged it wise to accede to the treaty, accept the white man's payments in goods and annuities, and lead his people toward the goal of becoming "settled" Indians.

Certainly no white leader faced with deciding the future of so many people and such a large extent of land could have made a better compromise, given the same circumstances.

But the leaders of the three tribes being uprooted from the lands of their birth expressed their resentment with bitter eloquence. Young Chief said:

"I wonder if this ground has anything to say? I wonder if the ground is listening to what is said? I hear what this earth says . . .

"The earth says, God has placed me here to produce all that grows upon me, the trees, fruit, roots, and grass. It was from her that man was made. God on placing men on earth desired them to take good care of the earth and do each other no harm. God said: 'You Indians who take care of a certain portion of the country should not trade it off unless you get a fair price.' "[36]

Five Crows, when asked to speak, merely said that his heart was the same as that of Young Chief. Peo-peo-mox-mox asked for more time to consider the offer, though he made it clear he did not like the prospect of leaving his country. Kamiakin refused to speak for the Yakimas. But Ow-hi, also a Yakima, set forth a new argument for the commissioners to consider: "God named this land to us

and that is the reason I am afraid to say anything. I am afraid of the laws of the Almighty."[37]

Growing impatient, General Palmer scolded the Indians sharply.

"Young Chief says he does not see what we propose to give them. Peo-peo-mox-mox says the same. Can we bring these sawmills and these gristmills here on our backs . . . ? Can we build these schoolhouses and these dwellings in a day . . . ? It takes time to do these things . . .

"We don't come to steal your lands. We pay you more than it is worth. Here in this little valley and the Umatilla valley there is a little good land, but between these two streams and all around it is a parched up plain. What is it worth to you or to us? Not one-half of what we have offered for it. Why do we offer you so much? It is because our Chief has told us to take care of his red people. We come to you with his messages to try and do you good."[38]

The Indians still refused to give in. Co-mos-pilo protested moving from the fertile valley where he had established a productive garden to the land of the Nez Perces, much of which was heavily timbered. He said:

"How do you show your pity by sending me and my children to a land where there is nothing to eat but wood? That is the kind of land up there; that is the reason I cry. Look at my hands! An old man. I have them by hard work. Then I ask myself have I labored in vain? What have I to be glad for?"[39]

Realizing that the talks had reached a dead end, the commissioners saved face by saying that since the Nez Perces were satisfied and anxious to go home, the treaty would be signed tomorrow. Following this ceremony Stevens said optimistically: "We shall meet as friends, I hope."

With that, the council adjourned.

Like all treaty negotiations, the vital compromises that unsnarled the most knotty problems were made during talks held after council hours between leaders of both factions — talks not recorded for posterity by the official secretaries. Hazard Stevens sums up what no doubt was a long evening of off-the-record bargaining:

Sketch by Gustavus Sohon   *Courtesy Washington State Historical Society*

Young Chief, Cayuse

36. Ibid., p. 32.
37. Ibid.
38. Ibid., p. 33. The Indians were being offered about a cent and a half an acre for the land they were being asked to cede. Palmer's choice of words "to try to do you good" is a curious one, inviting the reply "and you sure did."
39. Ibid., p. 34.

"The feature of the treaties which met with the greatest opposition was the provision that the Cayuses, Walla Wallas, and Umatillas should relinquish the whole of their own lands and remove to a reservation in the Nez Perce country. The commissioners therefore decided to establish a separate reservation for these three tribes on the headwaters of the Umatilla, at the base of the Blue Mountains. Conferences were had with the recusant chiefs separately."[40]

When the council met next day, Young Chief put it quite well when he said:

"The reason why we could not understand you was that you selected this country for us to live in without our having any voice in the matter. . . . You embraced [took away] all my country. Where was I to go? Was I to be a wanderer like a wolf? Without a home, without a house, I would be compelled to steal, consequently I would die. I will show you the lands that I will give you. We will then take good care of each other."[41]

Palmer then officially set forth the proposal to create a third reservation, with the same provision for improvements, clothing, and annuities to the chiefs. In addition, it was agreed that a house would be built for Peo-peo-mox-mox on the Columbia River, where he had been accustomed to grazing his cattle and horses and trading with emigrants. Getting word that Looking Glass, an important Nez Perce chief who had been on a prolonged hunt in the buffalo country, was nearby, Governor Stevens was pleased.

"My friends, I am glad Looking Glass is coming," he said. "When he is close by, two or three of us will go and take him by the hand and set him down by his chief in the presence of his friend, Kamiakin. Let us now have Kamiakin's heart."

Kamiakin replied:

"The forest knows me; he knows my heart. He knows I do not desire a great many goods. All that I wish for is an Agent, a good Agent, who will pity the good and bad of us and take care of us. I have nothing to talk long about. I am tired. I am anxious to get back to my garden. That is all I have to say."[42]

Chief Joseph the Elder, who had been present from the beginning of the council, now spoke for the first time. His words have a prophetic ring to them:

"These are my children [looking around]. I see them all sitting here. Talking slowly is good. It is good for old men to talk straight; talk straight on both sides and take care of one another. It is not us we talk for, it is for our children who come after us. It is good for the old people to talk together good and straight on account of our

Sketch by Gustavus Sohon   *Courtesy Washington State Historical Society*
Kamiakin, head chief of the Yakimas

children on both sides to take care of each other till the last day."[43]

Skloom, a Yakima, tried to do some bargaining by relating that he once had seen a white man who

"took an axe and cut a tree, and marked it, as if he had made a watch; he went to that tree and looked up and saw a star. He took a line and measured the land from that tree. All the land he had measured, he ploughed. . . . For this country that he had ploughed up, he got eight hundred dollars for each mile . . .
"My friends, I have understood what you have said. When you give me what is just for my land, you shall have it."

In reply, Stevens said: "We do sell good lands for eight hundred dollars a mile, but not in this country. We do not expect to sell any of this land. Looking Glass is coming. We shall meet tomorrow morning."[44]

The description of the arrival of Looking Glass by Hazard Stevens cannot be improved upon, so we quote it verbatim here:

"Some commotion was now observed among the Indians, and suddenly a small party of warriors were

40. *Life of Stevens*, p. 53.
41. *Transcript*, p. 36.
42. Ibid., p. 38.
43. Ibid., p. 39.
44. Ibid.

Taowi-Tak-Hes, Joseph the Elder

seen approaching, painted and armed, singing a war-song, and flourishing on the top of a pole a freshly taken scalp. It proved to be a party of Nez Perces, headed by Looking Glass, the war chief, just from the Blackfoot country, where they had been for three years hunting the buffalo.

"Looking Glass was old, irascible, and treacherous, yet second only to Lawyer in influence. While hunting the buffalo he had several fights with the Blackfeet. At one time seventy of his horses were stolen by them; but the vigorous old chief hotly pursued the depredators, killed two, put the rest to flight, and recovered his horses.

"He had reached the Bitter Root Valley on his return home, when he heard that the Nez Perces were at a great council, and concluding a treaty without his presence. Leaving his party to follow more slowly, he pushed on with a few chosen braves, crossed the Bitter Root Mountains, where for some distance the snow was shoulder-deep on their horses, and, having ridden three hundred miles in seven days at the age of seventy, reached the council grounds while Governor Stevens was urging Kamiakin to give his assent to the treaty, for the governor, hearing the arrival of Looking Glass announced, seized the occasion to call upon the Yakima chief to sign the treaty in the name of Looking Glass, there being great friendship between them."

Kamiakin bluntly refused. And friendship was not what Looking Glass was feeling as he rode into the midst of his fellow tribesmen, who were conferring with the commissioners.

"My people, what have you done? While I was gone, you have sold my country. I have come home,

and there is not left me a place on which to pitch my lodge. Go home to your lodges. I will talk to you."

Turning then to Governor Stevens and General Palmer, the tough old chief said angrily: "I am head chief of the Nez Perces, not Lawyer. The boys talked yesterday. Now I will talk."[45]

To the stunned commissioners it appeared that two and a half weeks of patient negotiating and bargaining had been blown into irreparable pieces. The Cayuses retracted their assent to the treaty. Young Chief, Peo-peo-mox-mox, and Kamiakin appeared to be ready to support Looking Glass and back off from tentative commitments they had made. Lawyer, who had lowered his head and walked away when Looking Glass harangued his people and the whites, as if acknowledging the old chief's supremacy, came late in the evening to Governor Stevens' tent. He asked why the governor had not told Looking Glass that he, Lawyer, was recognized as head chief of the Nez Perces.

"I told the Lawyer that we considered all the talks of Looking Glass as the outpourings of an angry and excited old man, whose heart would become all right if left to himself for a while," Stevens said. He also told Lawyer: "Your authority will be sustained. . . . Looking Glass will not be allowed to speak as head chief. You, and you alone, will be recognized. Should Looking Glass persist, the appeal will be made to your people. They must sign the treaty agreed to by them through you as head chief, or the council will be broken up and

45. *Life of Stevens*, pp. 53–57.

Five Crows — Cayuse Chief. He was a half brother to Joseph the Elder.

you will return home, your faith broken, your hopes of a future gone."[46]

According to Stevens, the Nez Perces held a "stormy" meeting lasting all night, with the leaders at last agreeing that Lawyer was head chief and that the treaty must be signed. In the camps of the Cayuses, Walla Wallas, Umatillas, and Yakimas, pressure was also brought to bear in favor of signing the treaties.

Sunday, June 10, no talks were held. Instead, Timothy "preached a sermon for the times, and held up to the indignation of the tribe, and the retribution of the Almighty, those who would coalesce with the Cayuses, and break the faith of the Nez Perces."[47]

Even God, it appeared, was on the white man's side.

Early Monday morning, June 11, 1855, Governor Stevens summoned Lawyer to his tent.

"We are now ready to go into council," Stevens said. "I shall call upon your people to keep their word, and upon you as head chief to sign first. We want no speeches. This will be the last day of the council."[48]

And the last day it proved to be. One by one, as Governor Stevens called out their names, each chief stepped forward and touched the end of the pen as his name was written by a secretary, with an "X" inscribed after it. Even those Indians who were able to read and write signed the document — if such an act may be called signing — with nothing more than a mark. In order of importance they were:

Aleiva, or Lawyer,
Head Chief, of the Nez Perces, his X mark
Appushwa-hite, or Looking Glass, his X mark
Joseph, his X mark
James, his X mark
Timothy, his X mark

. . . and so on, until fifty-eight Nez Perce chiefs had signed the treaty. Led by Peo-peo-mox-mox, thirty-six chiefs of what later would be known as the Umatilla Confederated Tribes (Cayuse, Walla Walla, and Umatilla) stepped forward and let their hands be guided as a pen made their mark. Finally Kamiakin and thirteen other chiefs signed a third treaty for the Yakima Nation.

Stevens had said "no speeches," but closing nineteen days of talks without a few words would have been, to paraphrase General Palmer's earlier simile, like commanding the Columbia River to

Sketch by Gustavus Sohon   *Courtesy Washington State Historical Society*
Chief Looking Glass, Nez Perce, and a rival to Lawyer

stop flowing, the wind to stop blowing, and the grass to stop growing. Farewell speeches were made by both the commissioners and the Indians.

Tin-tin-meet-see, a Nez Perce, spoke with thinly veiled sarcasm when he said:

"I understand you well. We are never the beginners in doing wrong to the whites. All Indians here understood well what has been said. When your white children come into this country, they do things at random [to do injury to the Indians]. You have heard all that has been said and now let us go home and do right."

Eagle-from-the-Light, also a Nez Perce, gave a speech that reads like a prayer of benediction:

"My forefathers are all dead. I only am left. There is but the encampment remaining. It is good to hear and think of each other. . . . I do not want our hearts to come together wrong, but right, and remain so as long as we are people, and we will stop the bad people on both sides. The Lord will reward us both when our hearts are good that we will look and care for each other."[49]

In their joint report to George W. Manypenny, Commissioner of Indian Affairs in Washington, D.C., Governor Stevens and General Palmer gave tentative estimates of Indian population as supplied to them by the chiefs of the various bands. The Nez Perces numbered 2,500, according to figures

46. Ibid., p. 56.
47. Ibid., p. 57.
48. Ibid.
49. *Transcript*, p. 47.

given them; the Walla Wallas, 800; the Cayuses, 500; and the Umatillas, 200.

Lands ceded by the tribes were estimated as follows:

Nez Perces . . . . 24,138 square miles
Umatilla Confederation . . . . 6,270 square miles

    Total . . . . 30,508 square miles

Payments to the Nez Perces were to total $200,000, spread over twenty years; the salary of the head chief was to be $500 a year, also for twenty years, plus a house and ten acres of plowed and fenced land.

Payments to the confederation of Walla Walla, Cayuse, and Umatilla Indians were to total $150,000, spread over twenty years, with the head chief of each tribe to receive a salary of $500 a year for twenty years, plus a house and a plot of land.

As for the Yakimas, in his biography of his father Hazard Stevens says that their treaty

"contained the same general provisions. A large reservation on the Simcoe, a southern branch of the Yakima, and a smaller one on the Wenatchee, including the fishery there, were set apart for them. The payments include $200,000 in annuities, $60,000 for improving the reservations, house for the chief, etc. In all the treaties provision is made for finally dividing the land among the Indians in severalty.

"Kamiakin, Ow-hi, Skloom and eleven other chiefs signed the treaty."[50]

In his report to the Commissioner of Indian Affairs, Stevens noted that he "deemed it best to commence the negotiations with the Yakimas in open Council with the tribes common to the two

50. *Life of Stevens*, pp. 63–64.

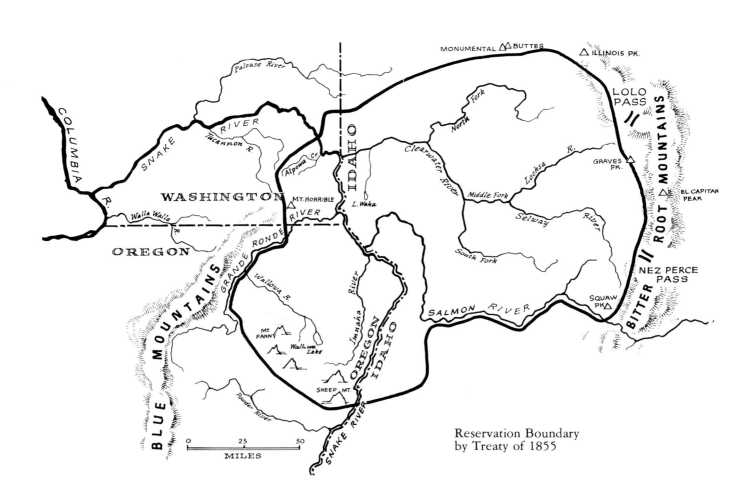

Reservation Boundary
by Treaty of 1855

Territories. . . . They were consumated in a separate and special council."[51]

Indeed they were. According to a tradition of long standing among the Yakimas today, Stevens held a private session late at night with Kamiakin and threatened to unleash a war on his tribe if he did not sign the treaty. The story is given credence by Andrew Dominique Pambrun, who was there as an interpreter and who must be considered a reliable witness. Like his father, Pierre Chrysologue Pambrun, he had been a Hudson's Bay Company factor at Fort Walla Walla and had the confidence of both Indians and whites. In an autobiography written in the 1890s, but only recently published in book form, Pambrun says:

"The Indians were called in council, including the Nez Perces, Yakimas, Cayouses [sic], Palouses, and Walla Wallas. Several days were occupied in feasting and talking, but apparently making no progress in the aim of the meeting, finally the Governor, getting out of patience, recapitulated all that had been said and offered and concluded by saying, If you do not accept the terms offered and sign this paper [holding up the paper] you will walk in blood knee deep. The Priest [either Father Chirouse or Pandosy] remarked that this is an error, he should not make such a threat. There were several interpreters. I was one of them and know whereof I speak. All the chiefs signed, Kamiakin was the last, and as he turned to take his seat the Priest hunched me and whispered, look at Kamiakin, we will all get killed, he was in such a rage that he bit his lips that they bled profusely."[52]

Governor Stevens then told the Indians that he planned to go north and east into the country of the Spokanes, Coeur d'Alenes, Flatheads, and Blackfeet to hold councils and make treaties. He invited them to send delegations, led by a chief, along with him to impress the distant tribes with the generosity of the whites, the advantages of moving onto reservations, and the great benefits that peace would bring them. He suggested that the Nez Perces supply a hundred braves, led by Lawyer or Looking Glass.

The two chiefs said they would give the matter some thought.

"Thus ended in the most satisfactory manner this great council," Stevens wrote in his journal, "a council which in the number of Indians assembled and the absolute necessity of opening this land by treaty to occupation by the whites, that bloodshed and the enormous expense of Indian wars might be avoided, and its general influence and difficulty — has never been equalled by any council held with the Indian tribes of the United States."[53]

Peace in our time. The usual self-laudatory praise of the negotiator with a signed treaty in hand.

He could not have been more wrong.

51. *Transcript,* Covering Letter, p. 2.
52. Andrew Dominique Pambrun, *Sixty Years on the Frontier in the Pacific Northwest,* ed. Glen C. Adams (Fairfield, Wash.: Ye Galleon Press, 1978), p. 95.
53. *Life of Stevens,* pp. 58–59.

CHAPTER THIRTEEN

TO THE BUFFALO COUNTRY: JUNE 16—OCTOBER 25, 1855

The heriditary enemies were visiting and hunting together on most friendly terms, their minds all attuned to peace and friendship, and all anxious for the council.
— Isaac Stevens, August 25, 1855

ALTHOUGH THE CAPITALS of Washington Territory and Nebraska Territory were two thousand miles apart, they shared a common boundary. The vaguely defined line separating the two newly created territories followed the crest of the Continental Divide along its convoluted windings from southeast to northwest between the headwaters of the Columbia and Missouri River systems. This vast grass-covered land of wide valleys and rugged mountains supported immense herds of buffalo. It was claimed, but never completely controlled, by the Blackfeet, who were constantly at war not only with the Americans but also with the meat-hungry Indians surrounding them, the Sioux, Crow, Shoshone, Nez Perce, Flathead, Kootenay, Pend Oreille, Couer d'Alene, and other tribes.

From a painting by John Mix Stanley   *Courtesy Penrose Library, Whitman College*
Governor Stevens meeting with the Nez Perces

Stevens, while exploring a route west for a railroad from St. Paul to Puget Sound two years earlier, had been told by the Blackfeet that they were willing to talk about making peace with the Americans and the neighboring tribes. As a result, Stevens, now governor of Washington Territory, and Colonel Alfred Cumming, commissioner of Indian Affairs for Nebraska Territory, were appointed to meet with the Blackfeet at Fort Benton, head of navigation on the upper Missouri.

Since the military escort of forty soldiers had returned to its post at The Dalles with Joel Palmer, the Stevens party now comprised a Coeur d'Alene Indian guide named Joseph, a small staff, eleven packers, two cooks, forty-one laden pack mules, and the governor's thirteen-year-old son, Hazard, who was a good rider, loved the outdoors, and was eager for adventure. Leaving the deserted council ground in the Walla Walla Valley on a beautiful sunny morning, June 16, the party headed northeast toward the upper Missouri River country six hundred miles away. Even though Hazard Steven's book about his father was not published until many years later, the events he experienced and the colorful people he met were vividly remembered and described.

Two particular men stood out, Hazard said: Delaware Jim, an interpreter for the Nez Perces, and W. H. Pearson, an express rider employed by Governor Stevens.

"By all odds the most skillful and picturesque of these mountain men, and having the most varied and romantic history, was Delaware Jim, whose father was a Delaware chief and his mother a white woman, and who had spent a lifetime — for he was now past middle age — in hunting and traveling over all parts of the country,

Sketch by Gustavus Sohon   *Courtesy Washington State Historical Society*

James Delaware

from the Mississippi to the Pacific, meeting with many thrilling adventures and hairbreadth escapes. He had a tall, slender form, a keen eye, an intelligent face, and reserved manners. He was reticent in speech, although he spoke English well; but when he was induced to relate his varied experiences and adventures, his simple and modest narrative impressed every auditor with the truth.

"One of the most remarkable men connected with the expedition was the express rider, W. H. Pearson," Hazard continues. "A native of Philadelphia, of small but well-knit frame, with muscles of steel, and spirit and endurance that no exertion apparently could break down, waving, chestnut hair, a fair, high forehead, a refined, intelligent, and pleasant face, the manners and bearing of a gentlemen — such was Pearson. He was destined that year to render services invaluable in character and incredible in extent."[1]

Reaching Timothy's village at the confluence of Alpowa Creek with the Snake River a few days later, Governor Stevens conferred with Lawyer, Red Wolf, and Timothy. In addition to agreeing to send a delegation of Nez Perces to the Blackfoot country, Lawyer also gave Stevens a great deal of information about his people and country.

"Climbing out of the deep canyon of the river next morning by an easy grade up a lateral creek, the party took a general N.N.E course across the high, rolling plains stretching away to the mountains, for five days traversing a fine, fertile, and diversified country, clothed with waving grass and bright flowers, well wooded with groves of pine, and abundantly watered.

"They passed on the second day six hundred Nez Perces gathering the camas roots, and having with them two thousand horses, and crossed the Palouse River, with its broad valley extending far eastward into the heart of the mountains. Says the governor:

" 'We have been astonished at the luxuriance of the grass and the fertility of the soil.' "[2]

In a council with the Flatheads, Pend Oreilles, and Kootenays, Governor Stevens obtained their reluctant approval of a treaty in which they ceded some twenty-five thousand square miles of land in exchange for a reservation one-tenth that size and payments in goods, buildings, and annuities for the head chiefs similar to those made at the Walla Walla council. Before the council ended

"agents Tappan and Craig arrived with the proposed delegation of Nez Perces under Looking Glass, Spotted Eagle, Eagle-from-the-Light, and other chiefs. It was agreed that they and the Flatheads and Pend Oreilles should cross the mountains to the buffalo country, and hunt on the plains south of the Missouri, until the time came for holding the great peace council at Fort Benton . . .

"These arrangements completed, on Wednesday, July 18, the second day after the close of the council, the governor dispatched Pearson, who had just returned to the party after his rapid trip to Olympia from the Walla Walla council, with full reports of the council just held."[3]

The essence of these reports was: that treaties had been made with most of the tribes east of the Cascades; that all of the land not included within the reservations had been ceded to the federal government; and that a vast area formerly claimed by the Indians now was open to mining exploitation and settlement by the whites. Though he had told the Indians and did say in the reports that the treaties would not become effective until ratified by the U.S. Senate and signed by the President, that minor clause — if mentioned at all by newspapers and word-of-mouth publicity — was totally ignored by miners and setters.

Unaware of what was happening behind him to the west, Governor Stevens found himself faced with an exasperating problem ahead of him to the east. This was the dilatory attitude of his fellow

1. *Life of Stevens*, p. 69.
2. Ibid., p. 71. It is interesting to compare this comment with Joel Palmer's statement to the Indians that there was little good land outside the Walla Walla Valley.
3. Ibid., p. 92.

commissioner, Colonel Alfred Cumming, Superintendent of Indian Affairs for Nebraska Territory, whose sense of timing was proving to be deplorably bad.

Though Fort Benton was considered to be the head of navigation on the Missouri River, the qualification must be made "only with the best of luck." Given a good winter snowfall and a slow, even runoff in spring and early summer to maintain a reasonably level river flow; given an early start upriver from St. Louis by a steamboat; given not too many rains that would cause a crest that a boat could not overcome or too few rains that would drop the river to an unnavigable level; given a hull in good shape and an engine that functioned well; given no serious trouble with hostile Indians, incompetent crew members, or outbreaks of disease along the way — given all these things, plus a sense of urgency and a determined captain, *then* Fort Benton could be reached by a moderately loaded boat.

All of which should have been known by Commissioner Cumming, whose duty it was to assemble and ship upriver the large quantity of supplies and trade goods that would be needed for the treaty talks. But if he knew, he did not appear to care. To Governor Stevens, who was always in a hurry and always on time, Alfred Cumming was proving to be an incompetent bungler, who seemed determined to wreck the most important Indian council ever held in this part of the country before it even began.

Reaching Fort Benton July 26, about the time he expected his fellow commissioner to join him, Stevens was disappointed in neither finding nor hearing from Colonel Cumming.

"The governor was seriously concerned to learn that the treaty goods and supplies were greatly delayed. Commissioner Cumming had been specially charged with the duty of transporting them to Fort Benton; but under his dilatory management the steamboat which carried them with himself up the Missouri, did not reach Fort Union until late in the season, and, instead of continuing up the river as far as possible, discharged her cargo and returned to St. Louis. The goods were then loaded into boats, which were now slowly proceeding up the river by cordeling, or towing by a force of men walking along the bank and pulling on a long tow-rope. This unexpected and inexcusable delay seriously imperiled the holding of the council."[4]

At the governor's insistence, messengers were sent downriver to ascertain how long it would be before the boats arrived and to the different bands

Sketch by Gustavus Sohon   *Courtesy Washington State Historical Society*
Col. Alfred Cumming — Governor of Nebraska Territory

of Indians to advise them that they must wait longer than expected for the council to begin. Meantime, Stevens suggested that they hunt buffalo, in order to feed themselves, and keep him informed of their whereabouts so that he could let them know when the long-overdue supplies arrived.

Running low on provisions for his own party, Stevens attempted to buy food at Fort Benton. Since their supplies were being shipped upriver on the same boat, they could furnish nothing "but a few hundred pounds of old jerked buffalo meat, exactly like worn-out boot leather in appearance — so black, dry, tough, and dirty was it."

However, two parfleches of pemmican of one hundred pounds each was found, Hazard writes, which turned out to be sweet and good even though two years old. It had become so hardened by age that it had to be chopped out of the containers with an axe. Consisting of jerked buffalo meat pounded fine and mixed with fat and dried berries and then packed in large bags of rawhide, pemmican kept indefinitely and, when softened in

4. Ibid., pp. 95–96.

From a painting by John Mix Stanley   *Courtesy Penrose Library, Whitman College*
Crossing the Bitter Root River

boiling water into a hash, was both palatable and nourishing.

Like the Indians, Stevens sent out a hunting party to make meat for his own camp. So complete was his confidence in the formerly hostile Blackfeet that he let his son accompany a band of Gros Ventres and a few whites with the packtrain eighty miles south to the Judith River country. In a few days of hunting they killed hundreds of buffalo and large numbers of deer, antelope, and bighorn sheep — enough meat, Hazard says, to supply the whole party for two months.

While awaiting the arrival of the supply boats, most of the Blackfeet stayed north of the Missouri River, while the western tribes hunted and camped south of the river. An impressive number of Indians were in the area. According to reports received in the camp of the commissioners from William Craig and other agents, the figures were:

"The Nez Perces, 108 lodges; Flatheads and Pend Oreilles, 68 lodges; and 40 lodges of the Snakes, numbering all told 216 lodges — or over 2,000 souls — were in one camp on the Muscle Shell [Musselshell] River, awaiting the call to the council. The whole camp of the Gros Ventres and Low Horn's band of the Piegans of 54 lodges were in the vicinity."[5]

On August 27 express rider Pearson arrived with letters from Olympia, the capitol of Washington Territory. He reported that everything was quiet west of the mountains and that many miners and settlers were going into the interior country. As described by Hazard Stevens, his riding feats are incredible.

"Pearson rode seventeen hundred and fifty miles by the route he took from the Bitter Root Valley to Olympia, and back to Benton, in twenty-eight days, during some of which he did not travel. He was less than three days going from Fort Owen to Fort Benton, a distance, by the route he pursued, of some two hundred and sixty miles, which he traveled without a change of animals, having no food but the berries of the country, except a little fish, which he killed on Travelers' Rest Creek of Lewis and Clark on the morning of starting from Fort Owen, which served him for a single meal."[6]

Pearson usually drove two extra horses ahead of him on his trips, Hazard writes, and when the one he was riding became tired he changed his saddle to a fresh one. He could "ride anything that wore hair" and was equally expert with the lariat which he carried at the horn of his saddle, in case he needed a horse in a hurry and could not spare the time to find or dicker with its owner.

Giving the express rider messages to be taken back to Olympia, Governor Stevens sent him on his way, then turned his own efforts toward speeding up the opening of the council. But Commissioner Cumming refused to be hurried.

"He was a large, portly man," Hazard writes, "pompous and full of his own importance, and having been named first as commissioner, and charged with bringing up the goods and the disbursements for the council, now attempted to arrogate to himself practically sole and exclusive authority."[7]

So while the supply boats made their slow way upriver, the two white commissioners bickered over such picayune matters as who was the senior official, whether $50,000 or $35,000 should be allowed the Blackfeet over a period of twenty years in exchange for ceding the major portion of their lands to the federal government, and whether or

5. Ibid., p. 99.
6. Ibid., pp. 101–102.
7. Ibid., p. 102.

From a painting by John Mix Stanley   *Courtesy Penrose Library, Whitman College*
Fort Benton

From a painting by John Mix Stanley   *Courtesy Penrose Library, Whitman College*

Distribution of goods to the Gros Ventres during the Stevens rail-route surveys, 1853-55.

not the Blackfeet would waste whatever monies were given them purchasing rum from British traders and then lifting the scalps of all Americans they encountered.

According to Governor Stevens, who admittedly held a biased opinion, Colonel Alfred Cumming had adopted *con amore* the theory currently being promulgated by Secretary of War Jefferson Davis, who, being a Southerner, was passionately opposed to the selection of a northern railroad route across the continent. In fact, Davis had asserted that this part of the country "is a vast and sterile region, which cannot sustain the animals required for even a limited emigration, and altogether unfitted for cultivation."[8]

In contrast to this pessimistic appraisal by a man who had never seen the region, Governor Stevens gave some interesting figures. Estimating the Blackfeet to number ten thousand souls, who, for their lodges, wearing apparel, and food, required one hundred and fifty thousand buffalo a year, he came to the conclusion that

"one million and a half buffalo of all ages must be roaming on these plains to enable the Indians to live. Yet, on a large portion of this region the grass is hardly touched from one year's end to another."[9]

In order to keep the widely scattered bands of Indians informed, Stevens kept Delaware Jim, William Craig, and other riders constantly in the saddle carrying messages back and forth. When the decision was finally made to change the site of the

council from Fort Benton to the mouth of the Judith, he even pressed his own son into service.

"At ten o'clock on Sunday morning, I started my little son as a messenger to the Gros Ventres," Governor Stevens writes with obvious pride. "Accompanied by the interpreter, Legare, he made that Gros Ventre camp before dark, a distance of seventy-five miles, and gave his message the same evening to the chiefs, and without changing horses they were in the saddle early in the morning, and reached my camp at half past three o'clock. Thus a youth of thirteen traveled one hundred and fifty measured miles from ten o'clock of one day to half past three o'clock in the afternoon of the next."[10]

Of the effort required to keep all parties informed of what was going on, Hazard writes:

"To realize the remarkable extent and efficiency of this express service, bear in mind Doty's trip to Bow River, three hundred miles north of Fort Benton; Tappan's and Adams' and Higgins' to the Yellowstone, two hundred miles southeast; and the expresses down the river to the boats, one hundred and fifty miles; not to speak of Pearson's trip to Olympia, one thousand miles. It was as though one in New York, without telegraphs, railroads, or mails, had to regulate by pony express the movements of bands of Indians at Boston, Portland, Montreal, Buffalo, and Washington."[11]

Though the council started six weeks late, it took only three days for the assembled parties to approve the treaty terms. Commissioner Cumming finally agreed that if the Senate and the President felt that $35,000 in annuities spread over a period of ten years was not enough, they could raise the amount another $15,000. The region north of the

8. Ibid., p. 104.
9. Ibid., p. 105.
10. Ibid., p. 111.
11. Ibid.

From a painting by Gustavus Sohon   *Courtesy Penrose Library, Whitman College*

Crossing the Hellgate River

Missouri River was reserved to the Blackfeet; the country south of the Missouri was to be a common hunting ground for all the tribes; and peace was to reign from now on among the Indians and whites in this part of the country.

"The tribes actually parties to this treaty numberd by the commissioners' calculation: Blackfeet, 11,500; Nez Perces, 2,500; Flathead Nation, 2,000; total, 16,000. Nearly all of their chiefs and principal men attended the council and signed the treaty."[12]

With the treaty signed, the presents distributed, and an unregretful farewell said to Commissioner Alfred Cumming, Governor Stevens packed up and began the thousand-mile journey home. Since it was now late October he was anxious to cross the Bitter Root Mountains before a heavy snowfall closed the passes. By October 29 the party was camped on the Teton River, thirty-five miles west of Fort Benton. There, Governor Stevens received a stunning piece of news.

"Supper was just over and the men were gathering around the campfires, for the evening was frosty, when a lone horseman was discerned in the twilight slowly making his way over the plains toward the camp, and soon Pearson rode in, or rather staggered in, for his horse was utterly exhausted, and tottered as it walked. The eager men crowded around, and helped the wiry expressman from the saddle and supported him to a seat, for he was unable to stand, and his emaciated, wild, and haggard appearance bore witness to the hardships he had undergone. He delivered his dispatches."[13]

Behind him, all the country was aflame with a major Indian war.

12. Ibid., p. 115.
13. Ibid., p. 120.

CHAPTER FOURTEEN

THE SIX MILLION DOLLAR INDIAN WAR: 1855–1858

> *The great tribes of the upper Columbia country, the Cayuses, Yakimas, Walla Wallas, Umatillas, Palouses, had all broken out in open war. They had swept the upper country clean of whites, killing all the settlers and miners found there, and murdered agent Bolon under circumstances of peculiar atrocity.*
>
> — Isaac Stevens, October 29, 1855

IN WHAT APPEARED to be a concerted uprising, most of the Indians east of the Cascades had attacked the whites. Agent Andrew J. Bolon had been killed. Major Granville O. Haller, sent into the Yakima country with a hundred regulars and a howitzer, had been defeated and forced to retreat by Kamiakin's warriors with the loss of a third of his force and his cannon.

If the stories Pearson had heard were true, a thousand well-armed hostiles under Kamiakin, Peo-peo-mox-mox, Young Chief, and Five Crows were gathered in the Walla Walla Valley waiting to wipe out the Stevens party on its return. Squads of young braves were visiting the Nez Perces, Spokanes, and Couer d'Alenes, vaunting their victories, displaying fresh, gory scalps, and using every effort to cajole or force them into hostility against the whites.[1]

The express rider's hazardous journey with the dispatches, as related by Hazard Stevens, is an epic of endurance.

"He left The Dalles on his return trip, fresh and well mounted, and, riding all day and night, reached Billy McKay's ranch on the Umatilla River at daylight, and stopped to get breakfast. The place was deserted. After eating he lassoed a fine powerful horse among a large band grazing nearby, and after a hard struggle managed to saddle, bridle, and mount it. The steed was wild, and started off jumping stiff-legged. As Pearson rode from under the trees surrounding the house and into the road, he saw a party of Indians racing down the hill into the valley, evidently on his trail, and heard their yells as they caught sight of him — 'Whup si-ah si-ah-poo!

Whup si-ah! Kill the white man! Kill the white!' — and redoubled their speed in pursuit.

"His new mount proved of speed and bottom, and under whip and spur gave over his jumping for swift running. As he climbed the hill leading out of the valley and on to the high plains and looked back, he again saw the red devils and heard their yells; and for mile after mile, from the top of every ridge and roll of the plains crossed by the trail, he would look back and see his pursuers, or the dust rising under the hoofs of their horses. But they could not lessen the distance between them; gradually they fell behind farther and farther, and at length were lost to sight.

"Pearson pushed his horse all day as rapidly as it could stand without breaking down, and, when night fell, turned off the trail at right angles for several miles, then struck a course parallel to it, traveled all night, crossed the Walla Walla River and valley above the usual ford and crossings, and, having found a secluded depression in the plains beyond, stopped to rest and let his horse feed a couple of hours. Pushing on without further adventure, and exchanging his worn-out steed for a fresh one at Red Wolf's ground, he reached Lapwai the next day. Here he obtained a day's rest.

"Thus refreshed and securing fresh horses and a young Nez Perce brave as a guide, he started across the Bitter Root Mountains by the direct Nez Perce trail, the shortest but also the most rugged and elevated route, and at dark made camp high in the mountains. That night a furious snowstorm set in. A tree fell and crushed his Indian companion. Pearson dragged his insensible body from beneath the tree, and said to himself, 'Now the Nez Perces, too, will break out. They will never believe this buck's death was accidental. They will deem me his murderer, and always hunt my scalp after this.'

1. *Life of Steves*, vol. 2, pp. 120–121.

"But to his great joy the young Indian came to his senses, and proved not to be seriously hurt. The storm raged for three days; several feet of snow fell, too deep for horses to travel. When it ceased, Pearson sent the Indian back with the horses, and, packing his dispatches, blankets, and some dried meat on his back, continued across on snowshoes, which he had made during the storm, cutting the bows with his knife, and unraveling his lariat for the webs.

"The trail was hidden under the snow, but he guided his course largely by the marks of packs against the trees made by Indians who had crossed in winter. Struggling on in this manner for four days, he emerged upon the Bitter Root Valley near Fort Owen, almost dead with fatigue and privation. Stopping only a few hours for rest, and procuring a good horse and equipments, from the ever friendly Flatheads, he again took the saddle, and on the third day staggered into the governor's camp on the Teton."[2]

Included with the dispatches were letters from Acting Governor Mason, Colonel Simmons, Major Tilton, and others warning the governor not to attempt to return home by the direct route across the mountains. That country was swarming with hostiles, they said; there were few troops in the area, and there was no way aid could be sent to him. They urged him to go down the Missouri River to St. Louis, thence to New York or New Orleans, then to Panama by ship, across the Isthmus to the Pacific, and then back to Puget Sound.

Impatiently, Governor Stevens rejected what he considered to be a craven retreat, deciding "to force his way back to his Territory by the direct route through all opposition and obstacles."[3]

Sending Secretary Doty and part of the pack-train back to Fort Benton for more arms and ammunition, Stevens headed southwest toward the Bitter Root Valley. He reached Fort Owen, a small trading post at the eastern portal of the Lolo Trail, four and a half days later. En route he met a band of Nez Perces returning from the Blackfoot council and conferred with them regarding the difficulties that lay ahead. "In response to the governor's request that some of their number would accompany him, the whole delegation, fourteen in number, offered to do so."[4]

Since it now was mid-November the Indians and the mountain men told him the mountains were impassable because of recent heavy snows. Stevens refused to believe them.

"Pushing on by forced marches, the Bitter Root River was crossed on the ice November 17th, and the summit of the mountains on the 20th. . . . The snow was from three to six feet deep for a long distance, and

From a painting by John Mix Stanley   Courtesy Penrose Library, Whitman College

Bitter Root River near Fort Owen

would have proved a serious obstacle, had not a large party of Coeur d'Alene Indians crossed a fortnight before and beaten down a passable trail; but ten dead horses lying stiff and stark within a distance of eight miles showed how severely their animals had suffered in the passage."[5]

Nearing the village of the Coeur d'Alene, Stevens decided that his best chance for peace depended upon his taking the Indians by surprise.

"At daylight the next morning, with Craig, Pearson, and the four Nez Perce chiefs, Looking Glass, Spotted Eagle, Three Feathers, and Captain John, the governor pushed on, leaving directions for the train to follow and come in the next day. The evening sun was just sinking behind the mountains when the seven well-armed horsemen dashed up in front of the Coeur d'Alene village, rifles in hand and presented to fire, and in peremptory tones demanded of the astonished Indians, as they poured out of their lodges, 'Are you friends or enemies? Do you want peace or war?' "

Certainly the most persuasive argument for peace was the presence of the four Nez Perce chiefs, whose death at the hands of the Coeur d'Alenes surely would have brought down upon that tribe the wrath and blood vengeance of the entire Nez Perce Nation.

The Coeur d'Alenes prudently opted for peace.

Next day Stevens dispatched Craig with all but three of the Nez Perces south to Lapwai, there to

2. Ibid., pp. 121–123.
3. Ibid., p. 124.
4. Ibid., p. 125.
5. Ibid., p. 127.

Crossing the Hellgate River in winter

confer with Lawyer, assemble the Nez Perces, and decide what must be done. Then, having heard that a group of white miners was in trouble in the Spokane country, Stevens, Looking Glass, Spotted Eagle, Three Feathers, and the rest of the party headed west. Making nineteen miles the first day and forty the next, the

"last four miles across the prairie was made at a round trot, and within thirty minutes after sighting the rapidly approaching column, the astonished Indians beheld thirty well-armed men gallop boldly up, range themselves in front of their lodges ready to open fire, and heard the peremptory summons to decide instantly for peace or war. Needless to say that they, too, were friendly and for peace."[6]

While in council with the Spokanes, Stevens claimed he discovered a plot between Chief Looking Glass and Spokane Garry by which they would entrap the governor and compel him to enlarge their reservation — a plot which he nipped in the bud by secretly sending a message to Lapwai "informing Craig of the plot, and instructing him how best to forestall and frustrate it by advising with Lawyer, and committing the other chiefs to a firm adherence to the treaty and active support of the governor."[7]

In light of their subsequent behavior, there is no evidence that such a plot existed, though it is probable that the two Indian leaders did discuss ways and means of getting more acceptable treaty terms.

With the council concluded, Governor Stevens

reduced his supplies to twelve days' rations, lightened the packs to eighty pounds, and set out for the Nez Perce country on December 6, "in condition that if the Nez Perce were really hostile and I was not strong enough to fight, I could make a good run!"[8]

Reaching Lapwai on December 11 after a cold, uncomfortable ride, Stevens was pleased to find that Lawyer had assembled 208 lodges, containing two thousand Indians, eight hundred of whom were warriors. Looking Glass was friendly, offering to lead the governor and his party through the country of the hostiles with an escort of two hundred and fifty Nez Perce warriors.

"I told the governor that the Walla Walla country was blocked up by bad Indians," Looking Glass said to his fellow tribesmen, "and that I would go ahead and he behind, and that is my heart now."

Before the party of whites and their Indian escorts could begin their journey, an Indian messenger arrived with important news. A force of five hundred Oregon Volunteers under Colonel Kelly had fought a four-day battle in the Walla Walla Valley, had defeated the hostiles, and driven them from the area.

"The way being thus opened, Governor Stevens was enabled to dispense with the proffered aid of the Nez Perces; but in order to confirm their fidelity and good feeling, he invited a hundred warriors to accompany his party as a guard of honor as far as the Walla Walla Valley."[9]

As Hazard Stevens remembers the mixed cavalcade of whites and Indians that left Lapwai on a clear, bright, frosty December morning, all concerned were in a happy, festive mood.

"Rarely has the Clearwater reflected a more picturesque or jovial crew. . . . Each of the warriors had three fine, spirited horses, which he rode in turn as the fancy moved him. . . . The bridle was a simple line of buffalo hair tied around the lower jaw of the steed, which yield implicit obedience to this scanty headgear. At a halt, the long end of the line is flung loosely on the ground, and the horse is trained to stand without other fastening.

"The demeanor of the young braves on this march was in marked contrast to the traditional gravity and stoicism of their race. They shouted, laughed, told stories, cracked jokes, and gave free vent to their native

6. Ibid., p. 131.
7. Ibid., p. 136.
8. Ibid., p. 141.
9. Ibid., p. 144.

gayety and high spirits. Craig, who accompanied the party, translated these good things as they occurred, to the great amusement of the whites.

"Crossing a wide, flat plain, covered with tall rye grass, he related an anedote of Lawyer, with the reminiscence of which the young braves seemed particularly tickled. When yet an obscure young warrior, Lawyer was traveling over this ground with a party of the tribe, including several of the principal chiefs. It was a cold winter day, and a biting gale swept up the river, penetrating their clothing and chilling them to the bone. The chiefs sat down in the shelter of the tall rye grass, and were indulging in a cosy smoke, when Lawyer fired the prairie far to windward, and in an instant the fiery element, in a long, crackling, blazing line, came sweeping down on the wings of the wind upon the comfort-taking chiefs, and drove them to rush helter-skelter into the river for safety, dropping robes, pipes, and everything that might impede their flight. For this audacious prank Lawyer barely escaped a public whipping."[10]

Stevens reached the Walla Walla Valley on December 20, thanked his Nez Perce escort, and complimented the Oregon Volunteers for their "gallantry in engaging and routing a superior force of the enemy." He then turned his attention to straightening out the mess that he felt had been made by the military commander of the Pacific Coast District in failing to conduct a counteroffensive against the hostile Indians.

Animosity between Governor Stevens and General John E. Wool, whose headquarters were in San Francisco, had originated in December 1854 during a discussion of the Mexican War. When the talk turned to the Battle of Buena Vista, General Wool "loudly claimed for himself all the credit for that battle, disparaging in an offensive manner General Taylor and the part he took in it."

Stevens had been only a lowly lieutenant and had served in a different area of the Mexican War. He was now out of military service and the governor of Washington Territory and felt it his right to speak as an equal. According to his own account, his sense of justice was so outraged by the boastful and unfair tirade, that he spoke up and said:

"General Wool, we all know the brilliant part you bore in the battle, but we all know and history will record that General Taylor fought and won the Battle of Buena Vista."[11]

Satisfying though the statement may have been to Steven's sense of justice and outrage, it was not a diplomatic thing to say under the circumstances, for a wounded general — like a wounded elephant

From a painting by John Mix Stanley   *Courtesy Penrose Library, Whitman College*
Coeur d'Alene Mission, St. Ignatius River

— never forgets his attacker. When word reached Wool that an Indian war had broken out in the Pacific Northwest, he made a quick trip north to Fort Vancouver. During his visit,

"he censured everybody, not omitting Raines and Haller [officers of federal troops], but was particularly severe upon territorial officers and volunteers. He ordered disbanded the company raised by Mason to go to the relief of Governor Stevens returning from the Blackfoot country, although Raines put forth every argument to induce him to send it forward."[12]

Furthermore, General Wool declared that the war had been deliberately provoked by white businessmen eager to sell goods to the military. Claiming that the Indians were victims rather than aggressors, he closed the entire region east of the Cascades to settlement by the whites, ordering those who were there to move to the west side of the mountains. He then used whatever political power he had in Washington, D.C., to persuade the Senate not to ratify the treaties Governor Stevens had made.

Chaos reigned supreme.

10. Ibid., pp. 145–146.
11. *Life of Stevens,* vol. 1, p. 437; Hubert Howe Bancroft, *History of Washington, Idaho, and Montana. Works,* vol. 31 (San Francisco, 1890), p. 117n. This was Zachary Taylor, who later was elected president but served only sixteen months, dying in office of typhus July 8, 1850.
12. Bancroft, *History of Washington, Idaho, and Montana,* p. 117.

CHAPTER FIFTEEN

WHOSE SIDE IS THE ARMY ON?: 1856–1858

*General Wool had arrived at Vancouver but
had refused to take active measures against the
enemy, assuming that the Indians were not at fault.*
— Isaac Stevens, January 1856

KNOWN TO BE a good friend to Kamiakin and the Yakimas, Andrew J. Bolon had been present as an interpreter at the Walla Walla council and, at its close, was appointed agent for the tribe. He was a tall, athletic man, with red hair and full beard, very fleet afoot. On one occasion in the spring of 1853 he challenged a mounted Klickitat Indian to a fifty-yard man-horse race at Fort Vancouver — and beat horse and rider by a margin of twelve feet.

Following the signing of the Walla Walla treaties, Governor Stevens ordered Bolon to purchase supplies west of the Cascades and transport them up the Columbia to the Spokane country in time for the talks to take place there. Traveling with these goods just east of The Dalles in mid-September, the agent was met by Spokane Garry, who informed him that several white prospectors going from Puget Sound to the Colville area had been killed by Indians in the Yakima Valley. Bolon felt he must investigate. Such was his confidence in the Yakimas that he left his party behind and rode north from The Dalles alone.

His intention was to seek out Chief Kamiakin at his village on Ahtanum Creek, near the Catholic Mission of St. Joseph. Before reaching that spot, he came upon the lodge of Show-a-wai Ko-to-a-kin, also known as Ice, a younger brother of Kamiakin. Bolon and Ice were good friends. Ice warned him that many of the Yakimas were in an ugly temper and urged him to return immediately to The Dalles if he valued his life. Bolon heeded the advice and turned back.

Ironically, the timing and course of his retrograde journey caused him to overtake a moody, rebellious young Yakima brave named Mo-sheel, who was Ice's son. As a boy, Mo-sheel had at-

tended the Methodist mission school conducted by Jason Lee in the Willamette Valley near Oregon City. Described as "spare, spinewy, quick in movement, and a wild young man," Mo-sheel had run away from the school in 1852 and had never gone back. Apparently the only lasting thing he learned from the missionaries had been to hate all white men.

At the moment Bolon caught up with the small party of Yakimas, Mo-sheel had fresh reason to hate the whites. Via the Indian grapevine he recently had received word of the hanging of four Indians by federal troops along the Oregon Trail to the east. Just as frightened white people in this part of the country never bothered to inquire into the details or possible justification when whites were killed by Indians, neither did Mo-sheel bother to get straight the whys and wherefores of the execution of the Indians.

Actually, both provocation and retribution had taken place in the Fort Boise area, 350 miles away. During the summer of 1854 a band of Bannock Indians attacked a party of emigrants and killed nineteen people in what was known as the Ward Party Massacre. Sent out to find and punish the perpetrators of this bloody deed, Major Granville O. Haller and his command of federal troops caught up with a group of Bannocks, gave four warriors a trial before a jury of three white officers, found them guilty, erected a gallows, and hanged them on the spot "as examples to other hostiles."[1]

Unfortunately, instead of intimidating the Bannocks it made them so mad that for years thereafter they took vengeance against all travelers in their

1. *Weekly Oregonian,* Aug. 25, 1855.

land. Word of the hangings spread rapidly to far-flung, unrelated tribes.

With Mo-sheel's party when Bolon overtook them were six men, several women, and a fourteen-year-old Yakima boy named Suel-el-lil. It is his eyewitness account of the event that is given here:

"Chief Mo-sheel was at the head of our party. He knew the white man, and he told the other Indians who he was.

"The white man said, 'Hello, Mo-sheel.'

"Then Chief Mo-sheel shook hands with the stranger, and, while the women kept on the trail, all the other men shook hands with him.

"Chief Mo-sheel spoke to his people: 'This is the man who hanged my uncles and cousins at Wallula.' Mo-sheel knew him and was mad."

As they rode on, Mo-sheel told the Indians riding with him that he was going to kill the white man. Two of the Yakima braves agreed that the deed should be done, but Nou-yah-nan, objected saying:

" 'No! We will all get into trouble. Let him alone. All at headquarters [Fort Walla Walla] know of this white man. Do not kill him; all will be trouble.'

" 'You are not chief,' Mo-sheel said. 'I am chief. I will kill this man, as he killed my brothers. I thought to meet him some time, and now I have met him this day. I will kill him.' "

Because the day was rainy and cold, the Indians halted toward noon near a sheltered spring called *Wahk-shum* and built a big fire to warm themselves. Agent Bolon unbridled his horse so that it could graze, took a package of food off the saddle, hung his canteen and a holstered six-shooter on the saddle horn, took off his overcoat, then brought his lunch to the fire, sharing it with the Indians while he ate and warmed himself.

"The white man stood, holding his hands up to the fire," Suel-al-lil relates. "Wah-pi-wah-pi-lah stood by him, on the left. Chief Mo-sheel stood on his right.

" 'We better hurry,' somebody said.

"I did not know what was up. I was eating hard-tack, which the white man had given me.

"Chief Mo-sheel again spoke to Wah-pi-wah-pi-lah, 'We better hurry!'

"Then Wah-pi-wah-pi-lah, the strong man, dropped quickly and caught the white man by the legs and jerked him to the ground. So-qiekt and Mo-sheel jumped on him, each catching an arm, Mo-sheel, on the right. The white man cried out in Chinook:

" 'Do not kill me! I did not come to fight you!'

"Stah-kin grabbed his beard, pulled back his head and called: 'Hurry!'

"So-qiekt threw him a knife, and Stan-kin cut the white man's throat. He struggled a short time and then lay still — the blood running from the big knife wound. He was dead.

"I ran around, squealing."

After debating what to do with Agent Bolon's horse, saddle, gun, and clothes, they decided to kill and conceal the horse and Bolon's body as best they could, keeping the rest of his possessions. Leading the horse to the brink of a canyon a quarter mile from camp, they shot it and dumped its body down the slope. They then buried the corpse of the agent in the cavity below a fallen pine tree.

Wah-tah-kon, father of the young Yakima boy who had witnessed the killing, had been absent on a hunt when the murder took place. When he rejoined the party and learned what had been done, he upbraided the warriors and told them they had done a bad thing.

"There will be trouble," he said.[2]

Trouble there certainly was. The response of the whites when they learned of the killing was to send Major Haller, fresh from his glorious victory over four hapless Bannocks in the Boise Valley area, north from The Dalles with a force of eighty-four federal troops, a mountain howitzer, and the firm resolve to teach the Indians a lesson.

It was not a brilliant campaign. Marching into a country they did not know; following streams and trails that left them exposed while the Indians made use of heavy timber, bushes, and rocks for cover; running short of water, food, and forage for their animals after only two days in the field — Major Haller and his command spiked and buried their little cannon, made stretchers for their wounded, interred their dead, and began their retreat before the campaign had really gotten under way.

In all, Major Haller lost five men killed and seventeen wounded in the aborted Yakima campaign, plus a large amount of government property destroyed, lost, or abandoned.

A major Indian war had begun.

Just as Kamiakin did not take part in the act of violence that resulted in Yakima involvement in the war, neither was Peo-peo-mox-mox present when

2. Lucullus Virgil McWhorter, *Tragedy of the Wahk-Shum: The Death of Andrew J. Bolon, Indian Agent to the Yakima Nation, in mid-September, 1855* (reprint ed., Fairfield, Wash.: Ye Galleon Press, 1968).

hostilities against the Walla Wallas were initiated by the whites. As stipulated by the recently signed treaty, he was to be permitted to live for a period of five years on the west side of the Columbia just below the mouth of the Yakima River, where he could carry on his prosperous business of trading horses and cattle with white emigrants. This was some twenty-two miles northwest of Fort Walla Walla, and on the opposite side of the Columbia. Here early in October, he received a visit from Nathan Olney, the Eastern Oregon Indian Agent. Despite the fact that Peo extended a warm welcome to the agent and had every right to be camped where he was, Olney decided that the situation looked ominous.

"Nathan found Chief PeuPeuMoxMox [sic] with a sizable band of warriors camped on the banks of the Columbia opposite the fort at Walla Walla. The sight convinced Nathan . . . the encampment of Old Peu and his warriors surely had the odor of an alliance with other tribes, already gathering for a war council at the least and most likely the attack that Nathan now knew was a definite threat."[3]

Based on what appears to have been only rumor and his own unproven suspicions, Olney wrote a hysterical letter to Governor George Curry, of Oregon Territory. Dated October 12, 1855, it literally created a state of war:

"All the Indians north and south of the Columbia, this side of the Nez Perces and Spokanes, have either commenced open hostilities upon the whites, or are concentrating their forces for that purpose . . .

"One thousand volunteers should be raised immediately and sent into this part of Oregon and Washington Territories. . . . These Indians must be taught our power. The winter is the very time to do it."

In a second letter addressed "To all Settlers in the Walla Walla and Umatilla Valleys" Agent Olney said:

"I am of the opinion that the Indians in this vicinity are about to join in the war commenced upon the whites on the north side of the Columbia by the Yakimas and others. In view of such an event, I have written to the Commanding Officer at Fort Dalles for a Military Force to escort you out of the country. . . . I do not deem it advisable to make a rush all at once to get out of the country, as it would cause an alarm among the Indians that might cause an immediate outbreak."[4]

Short of issuing permits to the white settlers giving them the right to shoot any Indian who looked suspicious, a more inflamatory statement could not have been made. It was like having the stage manager stop the show and shout to the audience:

"The theatre is on fire, folks, but please stay in your seats till the ushers come to show you to the exits."

Now that he had set into motion the forces sure to lead to a local Indian-white war,

"Nathan set about making the preparations he considered advisable when the outbreak his letters indicated he thought inevitable broke in earnest. He knew that the forces he could muster couldn't possibly hold Fort Walla Walla. . . . The Hudson's Bay Company had some $37,000 in stores, besides stocks of guns and ammunition belonging to the Army. Nathan dumped the entire stock and stores into the rolling Columbia rather than chance having such valuable loot fall into enemy hands.

"With the dumping task finished, Nathan ordered the Fort evacuated, for there was nothing left to guard."[5]

Following the departure of Agent Olney and the exodus of most of the whites residing in the Walla Walla Valley — who left without waiting for a military escort — only three white men remained in the region lying between the Columbia River and the juncture of the Clearwater with the Snake, a distance of 130 miles. These were a French-Canadian, P. M. Lafontain, and an American, H. M. Chase, who had ranches not far from Fort Walla Walla, plus another French-Canadian, Louis Raboin, who lived on the Tucannon River fifty miles to the east.

Chase and Lafontain

"though not being able by themselves to put up a stockade, determined to remain at all hazards, and continued defensive preparations as best they could. Bullets were run till a pail was nearly full; holes were cut through the log walls, just far enough so that a vigorous push with a gun-barrel from the inside would make an opening through which to fire upon an attacking party; meat was dried; potatoes were placed in the tunnel; flour was stored away in the building; a tunnel was run from the house to within a few feet of the creek, through which water could be obtained in case of siege, or to serve in the event of disaster, or as a possible avenue of escape or last resort for defense."

Considering the prodigious amount of work done by the two men and the great courage shown by them in the face of the predicted attack by Peo-peo-mox-mox and the one thousand blood-thirsty warriors now rumored to be under his

3. Roscoe Sheller, The Name was Olney (Yakima, Wash.: Franklin Press, 1965), pp. 78–79.
4. Ibid., p. 80.
5. Ibid., pp. 80–81.

command, it seems a shame that nothing happened. But nothing did.

"Not an Indian made his appearance, but the ceaseless watching for a foe that never came produced at last a depressing effect that finally caused them to abandon their stronghold and seek, with their stock, the protection of the Nez Perces, the long-tried friends of the Americans. On their way, one night was passed at the cabin of Raboin, who joined them, and there remained no longer an American in the hostile country."[6]

With no white enemies to fight, Peo-peo-mox-mox and whatever warriors he had at his command must have been at loose ends for something to do. According to Governor Stevens, who was not above recording rumor as fact, they finally did find some mischief to get into; they

"seized and plundered old Fort Walla Walla, which had no garrison, and distributed the goods found there, including a considerable supply of Indian goods, among his [Peo's] followers, who danced the war dance in front of his lodge around a fresh white scalp. These Indians, with the Cayuses and Umatillas, then drove the settlers out of the Walla Walla Valley, destroyed their houses and improvements, and killed or ran off the stock."[7]

Quite obviously Stevens and Olney had not gotten together on their story entitled "The Looting of Fort Walla Walla," an event that eventually must be explained to the Commissioner of Indian Affairs and the War Department in Washington, D.C. Since $37,000 worth of goods supplied by the federal government or owned by the Hudson's Bay Company had been destroyed, stolen, or done away with in some manner, "looted by Indians" sounded much better than "deep-sixed in the river by agent." So in the final draft, an official report by Governor Stevens to Congress, the Indians got the blame.

In mid-November, Colonel James K. Kelly, in charge of a force of 475 Oregon Volunteers moving up the Columbia, received an ominous dispatch from advance couriers:

"Their report was that Peu-peu-mox-mox had sent a large force of his warriors to watch the movements of the volunteers; and that Fort Walla Walla was already in possession of the Indians, about 1,000 of whom were occupying it and the adjacent advantageous positions."[8]

Colonel Kelly did not record whether he was bothered by being watched or by knowing that the Indians had taken over an empty fort. He apparently regarded both as hostile acts, for he determined to march against the Indians at once.

"His command moved with this purpose on the evening of December 2. . . . It was hoped that the enemy might be surprised at daybreak the next morning, but incidental delays of the night march prevented their reaching the locality until late in the following forenoon. The fort was found pillaged, defaced, deserted, and with its furniture destroyed."[9]

Accompanying Colonel Kelly's force of volunteers was Agent Nathan Olney, who may at this point have admitted pillaging and deserting the fort himself, though he certainly had *not* defaced it or destroyed its furniture.

While riding well in advance of the main body of troops a few days later, Captain Narcisse A. Cornoyer saw several Indians appear on the summit of a hill just ahead of him.

"In an instant the captain's gun was leveled upon the one in advance, but, before he could fire, a flag of truce was discovered in the hand of the savage; and the Captain's companions cried out: 'Don't shoot! Don't shoot! It's Peu-peu-mox-mox!' "

A parley then followed. Before it had gone on very long, a band of one hundred and fifty Indians crested the hill in the direction from which the chief had come. "In a twinkling" Captain Cornoyer's gun again covered Peo, who was told that if his followers advanced any nearer he would be shot. At a hand sign and shouted command from the chief, the warriors halted, dismounted, and stood silently beside their horses.

"The Chief asked if Nathan Olney, the Indian agent, was with the soldiers; and on being told that he was, expressed a desire to see him. He stated that he wanted no fighting . . . that he was willing to make all amends that lay in his power for what his tribe had done; and was anxious to secure a permanent peace."[10]

Since at that point about the only thing that his tribe could be convicted of having done was defacing and destroying the furniture of a deserted fort, the "war" could have been brought to an end then and there, if cool-headed judgment had prevailed. Unfortunately, only the weather remained cool.

6. Frank T. Gilbert, *Historic Sketches of Walla Walla, Whitman, Columbia, and Garfield Counties, Washington Territory, 1882* (Portland, Oreg., 1882), pp. 167–168.
7. *Life of Stevens*, vol. 2, p. 158.
8. Gilbert, *Historic Sketches*, p. 175.
9. Ibid., p. 177.
10. Ibid., p. 178.

Finally deciding that everybody concerned would be more comfortable if they would move on to the nearby Indian village, the entire body began traveling in that direction.

Then a threatening situation arose.

The trail entered a canyon.

What happened then baffled the historian who later tried to piece eyewitness accounts together into a credible narrative:

"It was discovered that the trail they were following passed through a dangerous canyon, when another halt was made. A portion of the troops had already entered the canyon, among whom was Captain Cornoyer, who, on turning back to learn what caused the delay, found that fears were entertained by some of the officers that treachery was intended by Peu-peu-mox-mox. Their only reason for thinking so was that the *opportunity* for treachery *was favorable, therefore contemplated*. [Italics

N. A. Cornoyer

by historian Gilbert] Captains Cornoyer, Bennett, and others were of a different opinion; they said treachery on his part would cost him his life, and he knew it.

" 'Put him in my charge,' said Captain Cornoyer. 'He will then know that the first gun fired into our ranks will be the signal of his own death, and there will be no danger. Let us go to their village tonight and the peace he promises will be a certainty, for we will have them in our power.' "

But this sensible advice was not taken. Both Colonel Kelly and Agent Olney insisted that if the offer by the Indians to take the troops to the village and give them food and shelter this evening had been made in good faith, it could be carried out just as well the next day. So the volunteers made a retrograde march out of the canyon, taking the six flag-of-truce Indians with them, and went into a cold, shelterless, supperless camp for the night on the open plain.

"On consultation with Hon. Nathan Olney, Indian agent," Colonel Kelly reported later, "we concluded that this [Peo's offer to make peace and feed the volunteers] was simply a ruse to gain time for removing his village and preparing for battle."

Captain Cornoyer thought otherwise. Pointing out that the chief and his followers had had plenty of time in which to get their noncombatants out of the way and prepare for battle, if that were what they had in mind, the captain later told Gilbert:

"I was thoroughly convinced then, and remain so still, that Peu-peu-mox-mox came with that flag of truce in good faith, and believe that if we had gone ahead that night, the war would have ended then and there."[11]

But the amateur soldiers did not go on. Instead:

"That night the camp and its vicinity was a scene of stormy councils and of stormy elements. The volunteers were tired, hungry and dissatisfied, while the inhospitable elements shedding their fleecy carpet of snow upon the ground for the soldiers to lie upon made them angry and almost mutinous, in their belief that it was the prisoners' fault that had placed them in their disagreeable position.

" 'Shoot the damned Indians!' was a cry frequently heard from different parts of the camp."

Growing uneasy because of the hostility being expressed toward him, Peo-peo-mox-mox asked that he and the other hostages be released and permitted to return to their camp, where they would feed the soldiers in the morning. Some of the officers favored letting the Indians go; some did

11. Ibid., pp. 178–179.

not. Since Colonel Kelly took the negative side, the hostages stayed where they were.

During the night Indians appeared on the hill-top and shouted questions down to Peo, though they were careful to stay some distance away. Since none of the Indians in the white camp was a "loud-mouth" (a man with a big voice), a strong-voiced Cayuse was brought into the camp of the volunteers to act as a communications aide. After much shouting back and forth, the interpreter, John McBean, said that the Indians on the hilltop were concerned for their safety and for the well-being of the hostages. But since some of the shouted exchanges were being made in the Cayuse tongue, a language few Indians and almost no whites understood, it was possible that secret messages were being exchanged that boded no good to the whites.

The next morning Peo-peo-mox-mox tried to delay the volunteers, saying that for such a large number of breakfast guests his people needed more time to prepare the meal. It was nearly noon when the march was resumed.

"The dangerous canyon was passed and the village was reached, but no signs of a prepared breakfast or friendly reception greeted them. The hungry, disgusted, disappointed command halted around the smoldering fires of this deserted village, and knew that the time had passed for parleying."[12]

Indeed it had. Captain Cornoyer did manage to persuade Peo's son to come into camp and talk to his father, who told him that he wished the Walla Wallas to make peace. It soon became obvious however, that control of the Indians had passed out of the old man's hands. They were waiting for the arrival of Five Crows, Peo's son said, before deciding what to do. With that he left the volunteer camp — to be heard from no more.

Aware that nothing had been accomplished and that a winter cantonment must be erected, Colonel Kelly ordered his troops to proceed to the mouth of the Touchet. From there they would march to the vicinity of the former Whitman Mission, where they would build permanent quarters out of whatever materials were at hand and settle in for the cold, bleak, dreary months ahead. The prospect was far from pleasant to men with families and farms in the Willamette Valley, volunteers who had thought the campaign would last no more than a month or two.

Ahead, a group of half-frozen foot soldiers was driving a herd of cattle. Scouts rode on either flank of the straggling column, while teamsters in supply wagons brought up the rear. On the nearby hills, well out of rifle range, sullen Indians watched and wondered what the white men were going to do with the hostages.

Someone fired a shot.

Someone responded.

The long-awaited battle had begun.

In the running fight that ensued, men were wounded and killed on both sides in bush-to-bush, hollow-to-hollow, and hill-to-hill exchanges of gunfire, with little sense of order or discipline. Captain A. V. Wilson, who had found a howitzer in the ruins of Fort Walla Walla, managed to get it into action, firing four rounds in the general direction of the Indians, which created great panic among them. But for years the piece probably had fired only lightly charged salutes, and on the next round it burst, wounding the captain.

By nightfall the volunteers had fallen back on a cabin owned by a former employee of the Hudson's Bay Company, a French-Canadian named LaRocque. To it were brought the dead and wounded, the latter being treated by the surgeon and his assistants. The flag-of-truce Indian hostages also were there, held under guard by a detail of soldiers.

"Everyone seemed electrified with suppressed excitement," Gilbert writes. "A wounded man came in with his shattered arm dangling at his side, and reported Captain Bennett killed at the front. This added to the excitement, and the attention of all of us was more or less attracted to the wounded man, when some one said, 'Look out, or the Indians will get away!' At this, seemingly everyone yelled, 'Shoot 'em! Shoot 'em!' and on the instant there was a rattle of musketry on all sides."[13]

Though accounts of supposed eyewitnesses vary in some detail and do not name the soldiers who acted as executioners, it appears that of the five or six hostages being held in the LaRocque cabin all were killed except one. The survivor was a fifteen-year-old Nez Perce boy who had come to the Cayuse country a short time before to pick up some horses and for some reason had not been

12. Ibid., p. 181.
13. Ibid., p. 182. In a footnote to this account Gilbert says that statements made by eyewitnesses he interviewed convinced him that Colonel Kelly said, in regard to the prisoners as he rode away from the cabin to the front: "Tie them or kill them, I don't care a damn which," and that the refusal of the big Indian and the chief to be tied caused the volunteers to kill them.

permitted to return to his people. Upon identifying himself — and perhaps because of his youth — he was spared and released.

Nathan Olney himself is said to have personally contributed to the death of Chief Peo-peo-mox-mox. In an eyewitness account, Amos Underwood, who claims that he was in charge of the detail guarding the Indian hostages, writes:

"Nathan Olney had gotten about a hundred yards away when he heard the shots. He came back and as he rode up, pulled his revolver and shot old PeuPeuMox-Mox."

Nathan Olney's biographer, Roscoe Sheller, adds a footnote to that statement, saying:

"In addition to the claimed 'eye-witness' account by Amos Underwood here quoted in part, Nathan's own grandson, the late Ben Olney, confirms it.

"A study of Nathan's life and family background would force the conclusion that he was acting in the line of duty as he saw it. He was Indian Agent for Oregon Territory, Captain in the Army, Sheriff of Wasco County, and Justice of the Peace — and he was an Olney."[14]

He was indeed. And the Indian war he had predicted in the Walla Walla Valley now was under way.

Except in the amount of misery spread over the land, it was not much of a war. For four days the Oregon Volunteers chased, and were chased by, groups of Indians through head-high clumps of sagebrush, up and down sandy hills and bluffs, and across the bunchgrass-covered floor of the wide valley and the foothills of the nearby Blue Mountains. Finally growing weary of the conflict, the hostiles simply "disappeared," leaving the cold, weary, disgruntled volunteers to care for their wounded, bury their dead, and go into quarters for the winter, which now in mid-December had come with its bitter-cold weather.

Casualties for the volunteers were seven dead and thirteen wounded. Scattered over the hills and plains, thirty-nine Indian bodies were found, and it was estimated that at least that many more warriors had been killed and their bodies taken away by friends. Against the volunteer force of 475 men, the hostiles were estimated to have numbered 600 — a figure set high enough that it could accurately be said to Governor Stevens when he arrived with his Nez Perce escort that the brave Oregon Volunteers had faced and defeated "a superior force."[15]

Though not identified by tribe, a hundred and fifty Indians in the valley remained friendly to the whites and were placed under the protection of Captain Cornoyer, whose company camped with them during the winter for that purpose. Certainly they needed protection — if not from the war-minded members of their own race then from some of the ghoulish white soldiers whose acts of dismemberment and desecration of Peo-peo-mox-mox's corpse had been savage beyond belief.

With the coming of spring the volunteers made a half-hearted attempt to stir up some action by leaving their winter quarters on March 10, 1856, and riding north across the Walla Walla Valley toward the mouth of the Palouse River, where they had heard some Indians could be found. A small village was discovered. An Indian defiantly waving a red blanket was shot off his horse at long range, but when the volunteers found boats and began crossing the Snake, the Indians took to their horses and rode away.

Since no rations had been received from the The Dalles and no beef cattle had been brought along on this campaign, the volunteers were reduced to eating whatever stray horses they could catch and shoot. After a bitter winter on the open range, these animals were invariably poor in flesh. On such a diet, many of the Oregon Vounteers declared. "The only thing it seemed to nourish was a disposition to buck and stampede for home."[16]

In early April the campaign against the Walla Walla Valley Indians was declared over, so far as the Oregon Volunteers were concerned. It had ended in a victory of sorts, for

"unaided, they had held the country east of the Cascades for four months; had met and vanquished the hostiles in battle; had humiliated their pride, and left them disorganized."[17]

All of which was true. But now that their country had been given back to them, it did not take the Indians long to regroup and prepare for the battles soon to come.

14. Sheller, *Olney*, pp. 92–93.
15. Gilbert, *Historic Sketches*, p. 188.
16. Ibid., p. 191.
17. Ibid., p. 203.

CHAPTER SIXTEEN

THE SECOND WALLA WALLA COUNCIL: SEPTEMBER 1856

The Cascades Range forms, if not an impass-
able barrier, an excellent line of defense, a most
valuable wall of separation between two races al-
ways at war when in contact. To permit settlers to
pass The Dalles and occupy the natural reserve is
to give up this advantage, throw down this wall,
and advance the frontier hundreds of miles to the
east, and add to the protective labors of the Army.
— General John E. Wool, November 1856

ON MARCH 26, 1856, the Yakimas and related tribes made a concerted surprise attack on the white settlements at the Lower Cascades, on the north bank of the Columbia fifty miles east of Fort Vancouver. Fourteen whites were killed, eleven wounded. Federal troops under Colonel George Wright, Lieutenant Phil Sheridan, and other officers responded to this outbreak of hostilities by coming to the aid of the settlers and engaging the Indians, but under the policy laid down by General Wool they had neither the manpower nor the inclination to fill the military vacuum created by the departure of the Oregon Volunteers from the interior country. That task was left to Governor Stevens.

Declaring a state of martial law in Washington Territory and asking citizens to enlist as soldiers for a period of six months, Stevens organized a regiment of mounted volunteers under the command of Colonel B. F. Shaw. By July 8 the six companies in this force had marched upriver from The Dalles and gone into camp on Mill Creek, eight miles east of the site of the Whitman Mission. Here the volunteers were joined by Lieutenant Colonel William Craig, Spotted Eagle, Captain John, and sixty Nez Perce Indians. In all, the force numbered three hundred and fifty fighting men.

Guided by Captain John over trails no white man knew, the volunteers crossed a steep spur of the Blue Mountains to the Grande Ronde Valley, seventy miles to the southeast, where they had heard a band of three hundred hostiles was encamped. They were there, all right. As the command halted half a mile from the Indian village,

"a large body of warriors came forward, singing and whooping, and one of them waving a white man's scalp on a pole. One of them signified a desire to speak, whereupon I [Colonel Shaw] sent Captain John to meet him and formed the command in line of battle. When Captain John came up to the Indians, they cried out to one another to shoot him, when he retreated to the command, and I ordered the four companies to charge."

For the next several days a series of running fights raged up and down Grande Ronde Valley and across an intervening ridge to the upper reaches of Burnt River. When the "battle" ended, Colonel Shaw claimed a great victory, for he had lost only five killed and half a dozen wounded, while his count of the Indian casualties was "at least forty slain, and many went off wounded."

In addition

"the command captured and afterwards destroyed about 150 horse-loads of camas, dried beef, tents, some flour, coffee, sugar, and a great quantity of tools and kitchen furniture. We also took about two hundred horses, most of which were shot, there being but about one hundred serviceable animals."

Returning with his victorious troops to the Walla Walla Valley, Colonel Shaw received a piece of bad news. A. H. Robie, the agent he had sent to Lapwai to distribute 100 mule packs of goods due the Nez Perces under terms of the treaty signed a year ago, had been greeted with hostility. The Indians had refused to accept the goods and had ordered Robie out of their country. They also had sent word that they did not wish William Craig to return. They appeared to be on the verge of joining forces with the still peaceable Spokanes and Coeur d'Alenes, aligning all three tribes with Kamiakin in a general war against the whites.

Appreciating the gravity of the situation, Colonel Shaw dispatched Captain John, the friendly Nez Perce chief who had participated in the recent battle, with a message to his people:

"I am your friend. I have not come to fight you, but the hostiles. But if you beat your drums for war, I will parade my men for battle."[1]

In the face of this threat, which no doubt was reinforced by Captain John's account of the successful Grande Ronde campaign, the hostile element among the Nez Perces lost its majority, the peace leaders regained ascendancy, and a friendly reply was returned to Colonel Shaw. Hearing the good news, Governor Stevens was delighted. On his way to the Walla Walla Valley to convene a second council and end the war east of the Cascades, he wrote on August 14:

"In an interview held yesterday with Colonel Wright at Fort Vancouver, I heard that he designs sending forward a force of four companies to occupy the Walla Walla Valley under the command of Lieutenant Colonel Steptoe. I shall accordingly raise no more troops . . .

"I push forward in person to Walla Walla tomorrow to meet the Indians, and establish relations of friendship with the tribes generally, and especially those struck by Colonel Shaw."[2]

Leaving The Dalles August 19 and pushing forward in advance of Colonel E. J. Steptoe, Governor Stevens took a train of thirty wagons, eighty oxen, and two hundred loose horses to Colonel Shaw's camp in the Walla Walla Valley. A few evenings later the hostile Indians gave evidence they were still around by capturing and driving off a portion of a packtrain belonging to the Washington Volunteers, who had carelessly dropped their guard. Chagrined at this first and only loss of supplies and animals during the campaign, Governor Stevens scolded the soldiers for their laxness, admonishing them that when fighting Indians

"bold and repeated charges upon the enemy, even when the disparity of numbers is great, will alone lead to results. In this way only can the superiority of our race be established."[3]

That such bold and repeated charges could also lead to disaster seems not to have entered his mind, even with Major Haller's recent defeat by the Yakimas as an example.

On August 30 William Craig arrived with some of the Nez Perce chiefs. Shortly thereafter Colonel Steptoe and his four companies of regulars showed up. For some reason they held themselves aloof from the Steven's party, setting up their camp four miles to the west. Lawyer came in with another group of chiefs and three hundred Nez Perces, half of whom were known to be friendly while the other half were rumored to be disaffected.

Father A. Ravalli, of the Coeur d'Alene Mission, brought word that the Coeur d'Alenes and Spokanes, though expressing friendliness, had declined to come. Kamiakin and the other Yakima chiefs would not attend, he said; neither would Looking Glass, "who was not well disposed."

Since the term of enlistment of the Washington Volunteers expired September 8 and four companies of regulars were on hand to protect his party, Governor Stevens dismissed the volunteers with thanks for a job well done. As they prepared to leave he requested Colonel Steptoe to send a company of dragoons to the council grounds as soon as practicable.

Instead of complying with the request, Colonel Steptoe moved his men from four miles west of Steven's camp to eight miles east. Well aware of the fact that the Indians regarded regular army troops and territorial volunteers as different breeds of people, with the former favorable to their cause and the latter their enemies, Stevens thought his recent conference with Colonel Wright had solved the problem and that the federal troops would support him. Puzzled by Steptoe's move, he again asked him to send a force to the council grounds.

Colonel Steptoe bluntly refused, giving several lame excuses and finally his real reason: ". . . and permit me to say that my instructions from General Wool do not authorize me to make any arrangements whatever of the kind you wish."[4]

Stevens was baffled and enraged that, as Governor of Washington Territory, Superintendent of Indian Affairs for the area, and a commissioner empowered by the President to negotiate treaties

1. Gilbert, *Historic Sketches*, pp. 204–206.
2. Ibid., p. 207.
3. *Life of Stevens*, vol. 2, p. 209.
4. Ibid., p. 212.

now being considered for ratification by the U.S. Senate, he was being given no protection by the federal government. He hastily sent word to Colonel Shaw and his volunteers, a day on their way west toward The Dalles, requesting their assistance. Obligingly Colonel Shaw, Captain Goff, and a company of sixty-nine men turned back and were on hand as a military guard when the council opened the next day, September 11.

A number of chiefs formerly friendly toward Stevens now were bitterly hostile, he discovered. Co-mos-pilo said he was willing to bet his country in a fight with the whites, with the winner to take it. Eagle-from-the-Light complained because a Nez Perce brave had been hanged in the valley last winter by the Oregon Volunteers, without cause. At night, half of the Nez Perces danced war dances and threatened physical harm to those of their chiefs who advocated peace. Many of the Indians appeared at the council with guns, tomahawks, and knives under their blankets. Word came that Kamiakin had changed his mind and decided to attend the council after all, bringing with him a strong force of Yakima warriors.

In desperation Governor Stevens wrote Colonel Steptoe a communication "marked confidential," though he warned the army officer it would go into his files:

"The want of a military force on the ground seriously embarrasses me . . . but having called the council in good faith as the Indian Superintendent, and also as the commissioner to treat with the Indian tribes by the appointment of the President, I shall go through with the duty I have undertaken . . .
"I particularly desire you to be present today, if your duties will permit, and I will also state that I think a company of your troops is essential to the security of my camp . . .
"I shall, as I said, go through with this business whatever be the consequences as regards my own personal safety."[5]

While giving Colonel Steptoe a few hours to brood on the consequences of having a massacred commissioner-governor and his party to explain to the press and public, Stevens tried to deal with the complaints of the Indians. A thorough investigation of the case of the Nez Perce who had been hanged by the Oregon Volunteers, he told Eagle-from-the-Light, had convinced him that the man had come into the white camp as a spy. Caught in the act, tried, and found guilty by a military court, he had been executed according to the white man's rules of war.

Speaking Owl, representing Chief Looking Glass, demanded:

"Will you give us back our lands? That is what we all want to hear about; that is what troubles us. I ask plainly to have a plain answer."

Instead of giving him one, Stevens called on Chief Lawyer to speak for him. Producing his commission as head chief and a copy of the treaty, Lawyer pointed out the boundaries of the lands that had been ceded, spoke of the other provisions of the treaty, and said that fifty-eight Nez Perce chiefs had fully understood it and signed it, and therefore the Nez Perces must abide by its terms.

Timothy and James backed him up. But Joseph, Speaking Owl, Eagle-from-the-Light, and Red Wolf denied they had understood the treaty terms or ever had intended to give away their lands. Lawyer had sold their country unfairly, they said, and they demanded that the treaty be annulled.

Thus, the rift between the treaty and nontreaty Nez Perces, which later would tear the tribe apart, first appeared.

That afternoon, in response to Governor Steven's urgent dispatch, a company of dragoons rode into camp. The letter handed Stevens indicated that Steptoe was badly upset:

"If the Indians are really meditating an outbreak," he wrote, "it will be difficult for me to provide for the safety of my own camp, impossible to defend both camps. Under these circumstances, if you are resolved to go on with your council, does it not seem more reasonable that you should move you camp to the vicinity of mine? I send down the company of dragoons to bring you up to this place, if you desire to come. My force is so small that to be efficient against the large number of savages in the neighborhood it must be concentrated; nor can I detach any portion of it, in execution of certain instructions received from General Wool, while the Indian host remains so near to me."[6]

Stevens accepted the compromise. Next day he moved his whole party and headquarters for the council eight miles east up Mill Creek to within a quarter mile of Colonel Steptoe's camp. It was well he did, Stevens says for on the way they were met by Kamiakin, Ow-hi, Qualchen, and a hundred Yakima warriors, who had just arrived and "clearly meant mischief." Seeing the strength of the whites being concentrated, the Yakimas "made no distur-

5. Ibid., pp. 215–216.
6. Ibid., pp. 217–218.

bance save attempting to provoke a quarrel with the friendly Nez Perce in the rear of the train."

As the council continued September 16 and 17 it became apparent that the Indians present were divided into three groups: (1) the Lawyer, Timothy, James, Craig faction, which was satisfied with the treaty, friendly toward the whites, and prepared to fight on their side against all adversaries, if it should come to that; (2) the Joseph, Speaking Owl, Looking Glass, Eagle-from-the-Light, Red Wolf faction, who claimed they had not meant to cede their lands, wanted the treaty annulled, but were not ready to commit themselves to a violent course of action; and (3) Kamiakin's faction of Yakimas, Walla Wallas, Cayuses, Umatillas and other bands who, having already gone to war, were prepared to fight to the bitter end.

In this delicate balance, a speech by Spotted Eagle, a great war chief of the Nez Perces and a strong supporter of Lawyer, appears to have carried substantial weight on the side of peace. He had no expectation of changing the hearts of those who were bent on fighing, he said, however, "I will not follow you into the war."[7]

Reluctantly accepting the fact that nothing could be accomplished at this time, Governor Stevens concluded the council. On the advice of the friendly chiefs, he decided to withdraw William Craig from the Lapwai area; he had heard rumors that the Yakimas and dissident Nez Perces were plotting to kill him as a means of creating an incident that would embroil the Nez Perces in a war against the whites. Though Craig still would remain agent for the Nez Perces, his headquarters would be moved west to the Walla Walla Valley — perhaps even to The Dalles — until the present crisis passed.

Hearing this, Spotted Eagle spoke sadly:

"If you [Craig] do not return with me, we shall go back as if our eyes were shut. I think my people will not go straight if Craig gets up from that place. But, my friend Craig, on account of the talking I have heard at this place, I am afraid for you."[8]

Though Governor Stevens had admitted the failure of his mission and was ready to pack up and go home, Colonel Steptoe could not resist trying his own hand at diplomacy.

"My mission is pacific," he told the Indians. "I have not come to fight you, but to live among you. Come into my camp when you please. I trust we shall live together as friends."

In Steven's view this was a deliberate attempt by the military arm of the government to contradict and subvert everything he had been commissioned to do as the civilian arm of the government.

"The Indians, sharp-sighted and constantly on the alert from the merest trifles to draw conclusions as to character and policy, saw there did not exist between the Indian Department and the military the proper cooperation."[9]

Nonetheless, as Governor Stevens packed and prepared to leave, Colonel Steptoe called for a conference with the Indian chiefs the next afternoon, during which they would work out terms of living amicably together. What happened next is graphically related by the governor in his report to Secretary of War Jefferson Davis:

"I was occupied the remainder of the day and the next morning in establishing Craig's agency in the neighborhood of Steptoe's camp, and a little before noon, with some fifty friendly Nez Perces in charge of sub-agent Craig, I started with the train and Goff's company [of Washington Volunteers] for The Dalles.

"The Indians did not, however, come to see Steptoe at the time appointed. They previously set fire to his grass, and, following me as I set out about eleven o'clock on my way to The Dalles, they attacked me within three miles of Steptoe's camp at about one o'clock in the afternoon.

"So satisfied was I that the Indians would carry into effect the determination avowed in their councils in their own camps for several nights previously to attack me, that in starting I formed my whole party, and moved forward in order of battle.

"I moved on under fire one mile to water, when, forming a corral of the wagons, and holding the adjacent hills and the brush on the stream by pickets, I made my arrangements to defend my position and fight the Indians. Our position in a low, open basin some five hundred or six hundred yards across was good, and with the aid of our corral we could defend ourselves against a vastly superior force of the enemy.

"The fight continued till late in the night. Two charges were made to disperse the Indians, the last led by Lieutenant-Colonel Shaw in person with twenty-four men, but whilst driving before him some one hundred and fifty Indians an equal number pushed into his rear, and he was compelled to cut his way through them towards camp, when, drawing up his men, and aided by the teamsters and pickets, who gallantly sprang forward, he drove the Indians back when in full charge upon the corral.

"Just before the charge, the friendly Nez Perces, fifty in number, who had been assigned to holding the side

7. Ibid., p. 219.
8. Ibid., p. 220.
9. Ibid.

on the south side of the corral, were told by the enemy, 'We came not to fight the Nez Perces, but the whites; go to your camp, or we will wipe it out.' Their camp, with their women and children, was on a stream about a mile distant, upon which I directed the Nez Perces to retire, as I did not require their assistance, and I was fearful that my men might not be able to distinguish them from the hostiles, and thus friendly Indians might be killed.

"Towards night I notified Lieutenant-Colonel Steptoe that I was fighting the Indians, and that I should move the next morning, and expressed the opinion that a company of his troops would be of service. In reply he stated that the Indians had burnt up his grass, and suggested that I should return to his camp, and place at this disposal my wagons, in order that he might move his whole command to the Umatilla, or some other point, where sustenance could be found for his animals. To this arrangement I assented."

So once again the more mobile force under Governor Stevens moved to the camp of the federal troops, whose concept of fighting Indians seems to have been to dig in and wait for the hostiles to attack. The move, made in the middle of the night, with time to dig rifle pits and set up a mountain howitzer, placed the combined force of regular and volunteer soldiers in a strong position when discovered by the Indians next morning.

"Soon after sunrise the enemy attacked, but were soon dislodged by the howitzer and a charge from Steptoe's command. . . . The Indians were greatly surprised at Steptoe's sending a force to my assistance."[10]

Now that it had been proved to the astonished Indians that Stevens and Steptoe were on the same side, the hostiles withdrew and dispersed. Taking advantage of the aura of goodwill, Governor Stevens urged Colonel Steptoe to build a blockhouse in the area, to leave one company to defend it and the supplies, then to march downriver to Fort Dalles or Fort Vancouver. After obtaining additional forces and supplies, Stevens said, Steptoe should return to the Walla Walla Valley, mount a vigorous winter campaign, and whip the Indians into submission. As a token of cooperation, the governor offered to place his teams and his Indian employees at Steptoe's disposal to build a blockhouse.

Still stunned by the fact that the Indians had set fire to his grass instead of coming to his conference, Steptoe acquiesced. In two days a blockhouse and stockade were built, the first of several such posts in the same general location six miles east of the site of the Whitman Mission. These would bear the same name as the now defunct

Hudson's Bay Company post thirty miles to the west, Fort Walla Walla.

A great change had come over Colonel Steptoe, Stevens wrote with a satisfaction he made no attempt to conceal, for the burning of his grass and the attack on his camp "were too strong even for the orders of Wool and his own prejudices." From his camp on the Umatilla, September 27, Steptoe wrote his immediate superior, Colonel George Wright:

"In general terms I may say that in my judgment we are reduced to the necessity of waging a vigorous war, striking the Cayuses at the Grande Ronde, and Kamiakin wherever he may be found."[11]

Though the skirmishes following the close of the council had involved four companies of regulars, one company of volunteers, and fifty Nez Perces, on one side, against an estimated four hundred and fifty Indians on the other, most of the fighting had been done at long range, thus casualties were light. The whites lost one killed, one dangerously wounded. Stevens estimated that thirteen Indians were killed or wounded.

Accompanied by William Craig and the fifty Nez Perce auxiliaries, the combined force — less a company left behind to man the newly built stockade — left for The Dalles on September 23, arriving there October 2.

Governor Stevens wrote:

"Circumstances had brought about the cooperation between the military and the Indian service which had not previously existed, and the words of Steptoe to the hostiles and mine to the friendly Indians corresponded."[12]

Perhaps they did. But neither Colonel Wright nor General George Wool yet saw the need for the white authorities in this part of the country to speak with one voice. Returning with Steptoe and an additional company of men to the Walla Walla Valley in early October, Colonel Wright held a council with the hostile chiefs, at which he assured them that "the bloody cloth should be washed, past differences thrown behind us, and perpetual friendship must exist between us."

After listening to the complaints of the Indians, Colonel Wright adopted their views in regard to the Walla Walla treaties, Stevens later complained, ac-

10. Ibid., pp. 221–23.
11. Ibid., p. 223.
12. Ibid.

tually recommending to the War Department that they not be confirmed. By order of General Wool, Steptoe issued a proclamation forbidding all white settlers to return to the country or reside there, except for missionaries, Hudson's Bay Company people, and miners in the Colville area.

"Warned by what has happened," General Wool wrote Colonel Wright, October 19, "you will be on your guard against the whites and prevent further trouble by keeping the whites out of the Indian country."[13]

As might be expected, Governor Stevens was incensed at the stand taken by the military. It was a curious one. As the governor pointed out, it made favored citizens out of aliens who really had no right to be in the area, while it excluded American citizens to whom a substantial portion of the region had been officially ceded by the British government and the Indian tribes that until recently had owned it.

Since all the Protestant American missionaries had been withdrawn from the interior country following the Whitman killings, the only missionaries now residing there were Catholic priests — either citizens of France or French-Canadians. Theirs was a strange position, and Governor Stevens called attention to this fact in his reports to the Indian Department.

"In times of peace, the influence of the Catholic missionaries is good in that quarter, and their good offices are desirable till some outrage is committed, or war breaks out. But since the war has broken out, whilst they have made every exertion to protect individuals, and to prevent other tribes joining in the war, they have occupied a position which cannot be filled on earth — a position between the hostiles and the Americans.

"So great has been their desire for peace that they have overlooked all right, propriety, justice, necessity, siding with the Indians, siding with the Americans, but advising the latter particularly to agree to all the demands of the former — murderers to go free, treaties to be abrogated, whites to retire to the settlements. And the Indians, seeing that the missionaries are on their side, are fortified in the belief that they are fighting in a holy cause. I state on my official responsibility that the influence of the Catholic missionaries in the upper country has latterly been most baneful and pernicious."[14]

Regarding the motives and influence of the Hudson's Bay Company, Stevens was equally caustic.

"I ask again, what is the interest of the Hudson's Bay Company? Most unquestionably to develop the British interior and its mines of gold, and to keep the Americans out, which will be most effectually accomplished by yielding to the demands of the Indians east of the Cascades, and making peace by an abandonment of the country.

"I charge no man of that company with collusion with the Indians, but I know what human nature is; it will look out sharply for its own interests, and the interest of the Hudson Bay Company is the same as the Indian conceives to be his interest in that quarter."[15]

13. Ibid., p. 226.
14. Ibid., pp. 228–229.
15. Ibid., p. 229.

CHAPTER SEVENTEEN

THE STEPTOE DISASTER: MAY 1858

*When the expedition started, one hundred
mules were required to pack the camping outfit. As
the last one was loaded, it was found that no room
remained for the ammunition.*
— F. T. Gilbert, Historian

DESPITE STRONG ARGUMENTS by Governor
Stevens, the philosophy set forward by General
Wool prevailed. In the spring of 1856 the U.S.
Senate ratified the Blackfoot Treaty. But the
treaties negotiated with the Nez Perces, Cayuses,
Walla Wallas, Umatillas, and Yakimas stayed
locked up in committee, nullifying them and leaving in effect the arbitrary Army edict closing the interior country to access by American settlers.

All through 1857 a peace of sorts lay over the
land. Hearing that two white miners had been
killed by Indians in the Colville area, Colonel Steptoe decided early in May 1858 that the time had
come "to show the flag" and demonstrate to the
Indians of the interior country that the army was
present not to make war but to keep peace. With
159 men and a large pack train, the colonel set out
May 8 intending to make a leisurely march north
through the country of the Palouses, Spokanes,
and Coeur d'Alenes.

Though historian Gilbert obtained his material
firsthand from soldiers who participated in the expedition, his statement that all the ammunition was
left behind is a exaggeration. In actuality the three
companies of dragoons and the partial company of
infantry carried forty rounds per man, along with
two mountain howitzers. But their arms were very
poor.

"Two of the dragoon companies were armed with
musketoons — short muskets with a very limited range,
useless beyond fifty yards. . . . The other dragoon company had Mississippi Yager rifles, which carried well but
could not be loaded on horseback. There were ten good
carbines in the infantry company. Some of the men had
revolvers, and others had only old-fashioned muzzle-
loading pistols. The cavalry did not have sabers."[1]

Reaching Snake River at the mouth of Alpowa
Creek, the command was joined by Chief Timothy
and three Nez Perce warriors, who agreed to go
along and act as guides and interpreters. By May
16 the troops were ninety miles north of the
Snake, deep in the heart of the Coeur d'Alene
country and surrounded by increasing numbers of
Indians who were strenuously objecting to what
they regarded as a trespass on their lands. If the
solders went any farther, the Indians said, they
would attack. Since they greatly outnumbered his
force, Colonel Steptoe told them that he would
turn back the next morning.

Monday, May 17, the command broke camp
and started the return march south.

"Daylight found the enemy hovering upon their rear
and flanks. A parley followed, in which a priest called
Father Joseph was interpreter for a chief of the Coeur
d'Alenes, with whom Steptoe was talking. This Indian,
whose name is given as Soltees, said to this officer that
no attack would be made upon this force, and then
shouted something to his followers, whereupon a
friendly Nez Perce named Levi, struck him over the
head with a whip, saying: 'What for you tell Steptoe no
fight and then say to your people wait a while? You talk
with two tongues.' "[2]

At first the retreat was orderly. Then, as the
soldiers reached the vicinity of present-day Rosalia,
Washington,

"Indians fired upon them from the timber on the south
side and from various elevated points along the line.

1. George W. Fuller, *A History of the Pacific Northwest*, 2d ed.,
rev. (New York: Alfred A. Knopf, 1938), p. 243; *Lewiston Tribune*,
July 18, 1916, article by chief packer, Thomas Beall.
2. Gilbert, *Historic Sketches*, p. 215.

Lieutenant Gaston, without waiting for orders, charged with his men and cleared an opening in front to the high lands on the south, and was followed by the entire force . . .

"Colonel Steptoe was in advance with 'H' troop and the pack animals."

As the morning passed and Indians continued to attack the column from all directions, the pace of the retreat quickened. Captain Taylor and Lieutenant Gaston with their troops fought a desperate rearguard action.

"Wearied, exhausted, and with their ammunition all gone, they still maintained their moving position. At last Lieutenant Gaston sent a courier named Tickey Highland, asking Colonel Steptoe to halt the command and give his men an opportunity to reload their guns. His request was not granted."

Out of ammunition, badly outnumbered, and deserted by the rest of the command, Captain Taylor, Lieutenant Gaston, and members of the rear guard were reduced to fighting the Indians hand to hand, using clubbed pistols and empty muskets against the knives, lances, bows and arrows, and guns of the Indians. It was in this battle that Private Victor C. DeMoy, a former French army officer who had served in both the Crimean and Algerian wars, began a legend when he cried as he swung his clubbed musket at the Indians: *"My God, my God, for a saber!"*

Wounded so badly that he could not ride or bear to be carried by a comrade on a horse, DeMoy asked that he be placed in a sitting position on the ground, with a loaded revolver in his hand.

After killing or wounding several Indians he used the last bullet on himself.

For many of the new recruits this was their first test under fire. So demoralized did they become that on one occasion, when Lieutenant Gregg called for volunteers to follow him in a counter-charge, only ten men answered the call.

"When he led off in the charge with these, he chanced to look over his shoulder and found that not one of them, even, were following him; and turning back he rode silently among the frightened mob without a word of censure."[3]

Hearing that Captain Taylor, Lieutenant Gaston, and a substantial portion of the rear guard had been killed, Colonel Steptoe finally halted the command on the slope of a hill, where the weary soldiers dug in and made a stand.

"At a council of war if was decided to bury their howitzers, and leave the balance of their stores and pack train for the Indians. . . . The abandoned property might give the soldiers an opportunity to steal through their lines."

Sure that they had the troops surrounded, the Indians broke off the seige as darkness fell. They went into camp and spent the night dancing, chanting, and celebrating. Checking on the supply of ammunition, Colonel Steptoe learned that the soldiers averaged only four rounds to the man. There was nothing to do but run for it.

According to some accounts it was at this point that Timothy led the command by a narrow, difficult trail known to few Indians and no whites, through the lines of the hostiles, with such stealth that the escape was not discovered until daylight. Other accounts, including official army reports, do not even mention Timothy's presence. Some Indian sources say that Kamiakin, who had masterminded the attack and supervised the strategy of the hostiles, even though not seen by the whites, urged the Indians to keep close watch lest their victims escape. But the exuberant Coeur d'Alenes, Spokanes, and Yakimas were so sure they had the soldiers bottled up that they did not heed his good advice. Still other accounts hint that there was a bit of bribery.

Whatever act of heroism, carelessness, or chicanery was involved, the escape attempt was successful. Leaving behind the dead and badly wounded, muffling spurs, bridle chains, and any-

Fort Walla Walla, from a sketch

3. Ibid., pp. 216–217.

thing metal that would clink, covering light-colored horses with dark blankets, and moving through the darkness with the silence of ghosts, the soldiers filtered one by one through the loosely manned lines of the hostiles until they were out of earshot, then mounted and rode for safety as fast as their horses would run.

Twenty-four hours and seventy miles later, what was left of the command reached the north bank of the Snake, opposite Timothy's village. Whether or not he had acted as guide and savior, a number of the Nez Perces in his band crossed and stood guard between the weary survivors and possible attack, while the women cared for the wounded and ferried them across the river to safety. Earlier, a lone Nez Perce brave had been dispatched as a messenger to Fort Walla Walla, 150 miles away. He returned to Timothy's village with Captain F. T. Dent and the company of soldiers that had been left behind at the garrison.

Riding in from the east a day later was a contingent of Nez Perces led by Chief Lawyer, carrying a large American flag. Informed of what had happened by the incredibly swift Indian system of passing signals from point to point, he had assembled a strong force of warriors, had brought them here, and was prepared to fight the enemies of his white friends.

But Colonel Steptoe and his weary soldiers had had enough. Seventeen officers and men had been killed, fifty had been wounded, and large quantities of arms, supplies, equipment, and pack animals had been deserted or lost. Coupled with Major Haller's defeat by the Yakimas, the Steptoe Disaster (as it came to be called) made the fighting ability of regular army troops look very bad indeed.

This was a state of affairs not to be tolerated by the War Department. Corrective measures must be taken at once.

Courtesy Idaho Historical Society

Lieutenant Colonel Edward J. Steptoe

CHAPTER EIGHTEEN

COLONEL WRIGHT TAKES OVER: AUGUST 1858

What the programme of the campaign is, none of us know. An Indian war is a chapter of accidents.
— Lieutenant Lawrence Kip, August 28, 1858

GENERAL JOHN E. WOOL had been removed as army commander of the Department of the Pacific in May 1857, with General Newman S. Clarke named as his successor. Since a state of peace existed east of the Cascades, Clarke had seen no reason to change the Wool policy of exclusion of American settlers from the interior country.

The Steptoe Disaster drastically altered his attitude.

Moving his headquarters from San Francisco to Fort Vancouver, Clarke ordered the Hudson's Bay Company agents at Fort Colville to stop selling arms and ammunition to the Indians and to turn over all horses and mules taken by the hostiles from the Steptoe command and later sold to the company. If the Indians wanted peace, they must return all property stolen or captured. Furthermore, they must identify and surrender for punishment any of their people who had committed acts of violence against the whites.

Failure to comply completely with these terms would result in only one thing — a war of extermination.

Made confident by their recent victories, the Indians disdainfully turned down the proffered peace terms.

Lieutenant Lawrence Kip, a young army officer who had been present as an interested observer at the Stevens Treaty Council in June 1855, returned to the Walla Walla Valley in July 1858 as one of the seven hundred officers and men who would participate in a campaign designed to make a critical public forget how inept regular army troops had been.

Stationed at Fort Walla Walla when he arrived July 19 were four companies of the First Dragoons and two of the Ninth Infantry. Built near the site of the council, the post was well supplied with water, grass, and nearby timber.

On this expedition Colonel George Wright would be in command of the seven-hundred-man force, while Lieutenant Colonel Steptoe with a hundred men would be left behind to garrison Fort Walla Walla. In his inspections, reviews, and twice-a-day drills, Colonel Wright soon revealed himself to be a cold-blooded martinet who meant business.

General George Wright

"A few days ago sixty Nez Perces arrived," Kip writes, "under an old chief, named Lawyer, whom I knew at the council in 1855. . . . Colonel Wright has had a talk with the deputation of the tribe, and made arrangements by which they have become our allies."[1]

On August 5 Kip's unit, Company M of the Third Artillery, received orders to march to the juncture of the Tucannon with the Snake sixty miles to the northeast, where the soldiers would spend a week erecting a fort. This was planned as an advance base on the edge of hostile country, where troops could fall back if strongly pressed by the Indians. It would be called Fort Taylor, in honor of one of the fallen officers of the rear guard that had saved Steptoe's command from annihilation.

The force left Fort Walla Walla on August 7. It was a formidable one, consisting of one company of dragoons, six companies of artillery, two twelve-pound howitzers, and two six-pound guns. Instead of short-ranged musketoons, the soldiers carried "rifle-muskets" shooting a minie ball that could kill at six hundred yards. This time, the dragoons wore sabers. Thirty thousand rations were transported on pack mules and in wagons.

Since it now was late summer, in a semiarid land where little rain fell during June and July, the Indians had made the route to their country difficult by burning off a wide expanse of grass, forcing the column to march for miles through choking clouds of dust.

With the fort nearly complete and Colonel Wright and the rest of the command due the next day, Lieutenant Kip saw the glow of grass fires burning north of the river.

"The Nez Perces tell us that the Indians are collected in large numbers at the Lakes, about five days' march from here, where they are going to meet us. We trust it is so, as it will give us an opportunity of finishing the war."[2]

Once the Snake had been crossed, Kip wrote, the campaign would begin in earnest. This time, the soldiers were well prepared.

"Our transportation consists of six mules to a company, and a mule to each officer, besides the three hundred and twenty-five mules which the quartermaster has in his train. Our entire train, therefore, consists of about four hundred mules. Baggage wagons cannot go beyond Snake River. We shall attempt to take only one light vehicle, which Lieutenant Mullan needs for his instruments.

"Now as to our fighting force. The dragoons number

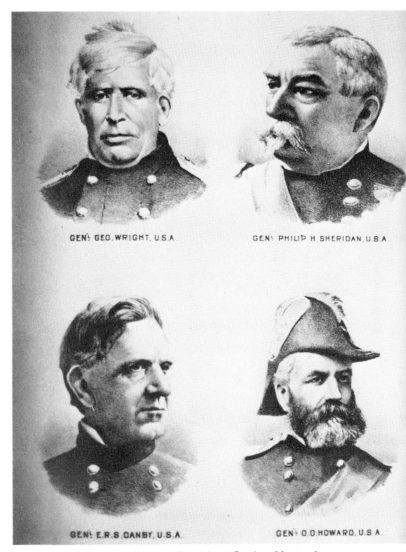

GEN. GEO. WRIGHT, U.S.A.   GEN. PHILIP H SHERIDAN, U.S.A.

GEN. E.R.S. CANBY, U.S.A.   GEN. O.O.HOWARD, U.S.A.

Army generals Wright, Sheridan, Canby, Howard

one hundred and ninety; the artillery, four hundred; the infantry (as Rifle Brigade), ninety. Total, about six hundred and eighty soldiers, besides about two hundred *attachés,* packers, wagon-masters, headers, etc.

"Then we have thirty Nez Perces, and three chiefs to act as scouts and guides. They are placed under the command of Lieutenant John Mullan. These, our allies, have been dressed in uniforms, to distinguish them, during a fight, from the hostiles. Like all Indians, they are particularly delighted with their clothes, and no young officer, just commissioned, thinks as much of his uniform as they do. They insist, indeed, upon having every minute portion, even to the glazed cap covers."[3]

1. Lawrence Kip, *Army Life on the Pacific: A Journal of the Expedition Against the Northern Indians . . .* (Redfield, N.Y., 1859), pp. 33–35.
2. Ibid., p. 44.
3. Ibid., pp. 44–45.

Though the command planned to cross the Snake at daybreak, August 23, a violent wind and rain storm delayed them for two days. First, the sand and dust blew so thick, Kip says, "that we could with difficulty see two feet ahead." Then the rain fell in torrents, turning the sand and dust to mud, while at the same time extinguishing the grass fires on the far side of the river.

With the horses and mules swimming and the men and packs ferrying across the swift, dangerous river in flatboats, the command was transferred to the north shore in two days' time.

Some sixty miles north of the Snake, two of the Nez Perce scouts rode into camp the evening of August 30 with the news that a large body of Indians had been sighted ahead. The dragoons saddled their horses and rode out to investigate, while the artillery and infantry prepared for battle. But after a long-distance exchange of fire between the dragoons and what apparently was a contingent of scouts for the hostiles, both groups fell back with no damage done on either side.

On this day Lieutenant Kip recorded two casualties among his comrades: "This afternoon two men of the artillery died from eating poisonous roots."[4]

The roots probably were deathcamases, which were misidentified and eaten by two white soldiers curious to sample what they thought to be staple Indian fare. Earlier in the summer when the plants were in bloom, it would have been easy to distinguish between the edible and the poisonous variety, for the flower of the former is bluish purple while that of the latter is greenish white. But by late August the blooms would have withered and fallen, and only an expert — an Indian woman used to gathering and preparing them — could tell the difference. Since no such expert was present, the two soldiers paid for their curiosity with their lives.[5]

The next day, August 31, as the column marched north over fairly level country sprinkled with clumps of cedar, fir, and pine trees, groups of hostiles exhanged fire with the Nez Perces, who were acting as scouts. Though nominally under the command of Lieutenant Mullan, who found them bold and fearless,

"their individuality developed so strongly that it was difficult for him to induce them to obey orders. Each one was fighting on his own responsibility."[6]

Since men and animals were tired, Colonel Wright decided to remain in camp at a spot some twenty miles south of the Spokane River for a few days. Reading this as a sign of indecision on the part of the soldiers, the hostiles grew more aggressive, swarming over the nearby hills, shouting taunts, inviting an attack. After placing the four hundred mules and the extensive stores under a strong guard in a secure location, Colonel Wright prepared for battle.

"After advancing about a mile and a half," Kip writes, "we reached the hill and prepared to dislodge the enemy from it. Major Grier, with the dragoons, march to the left, while the party of Nez Perces, under the direction of Lieutenant Mullan, wound round the hill and ascended it at the right. The main column came next, with Colonel Wright and staff at its head, followed by Captain Keyes, commanding the artillery, the third artillery, the rifles, and the howitzer battery.

"As soon as the dragoons reached the top of the hill, they dismounted — one half holding the horses and the others acting as skirmishers. After exchanging a volley with the Indians, they drove them off the hill and held it until the foot soldiers arrived. On our way up, Colonel Wright received a message from Major Grier, stating that the Indians were collected in large numbers [about five hundred, he thought] at the foot of the hill, apparently prepared to fight. Colonel Wright immediately advanced the battalion rapidly forward, ordering Captain Ord's company to the left to be deployed as skirmishers.

"My place, as adjutant of the artillery battalion, was, of course, with Captain Keyes. We rode to the top of the hill, where the whole scene lay before us like a splendid panorama. Below us lay 'four lakes' — a large one at the foot of the barren hill on which we were, and just beyond it three smaller ones, surrounded by rugged rocks, and almost entirely fringed with pines . . .

"On the plain below we saw the enemy. Every spot seemed alive with the wild warriors we had come so far to meet. . . . Mounted on their fleet, hardy horses, the crowd swayed back and forth, brandishing their weapons, shouting their war cries, and keeping up a song of defiance. Most of them were armed with Hudson Bay muskets, while others had bows and arrows and long lances."[7]

Thus the Battle of Four Lakes, as it would be called, began.

"Orders were at once issued for the artillery and infantry to be deplored as skirmishers and advance down the hill, driving the Indians before them from their coverts, until they reached the plain where the dragoons

4. Ibid., p. 72.
5. *Range Plant Handbook*, p. W209, says that several varieties of death camases are to be found in all the western states, the grassy and meadow death camases being the most deadly. Grazing sheep sometimes are victims in early spring and summer, when these plants are green and succulent far in advance of other plants.
6. Kip, *Army Life*, p. 45.
7. Ibid., pp. 54–55.

could act against them. At the same time, Lieutenant White, with the howitzer battery, supported by Company 'A', under Lieutenant Tyler, and the rifles, was sent to the right to drive them out of the woods. The latter met with a vigorous resistence, but a few discharges of the howitzer, with their spirited attack, soon dislodged the enemy, and compelled them to take refuge on the hills.

"In the meanwhile the companies moved down the hill with all the precision of a parade. . . . As soon as they were within six hundred yards, they opened their fire and delivered it steadily as they advanced. Our soldiers aimed regularly, though it was no easy task to hit their shifting marks . . .

"But minie balls and long range rifles were things with which now for the first time they were to be made acquainted. As the line advanced, first we saw one Indian reel in his saddle and fall — then, two or three — then, half a dozen. . . . The instant, however, that the 'braves' fell, they were seized by their companions and dragged to the rear, to be borne off. We saw one Indian leading off a horse with two of his dead companions tied on it.

"But in a few minutes, as the line drew nearer, the fire became too heavy, and the whole array broke and fled toward the plain. This was the chance for which the dragoons had been impatiently waiting. As the line advanced they had followed behind it, leading their horses. Now the order was given to mount, and they rode through the company intervals to the front. . . . Taylor's and Gaston's companies were there, burning for revenge, and soon they were on them. We saw the flash of their sabers as they cut them down. Lieutenant Davidson shot one warrior from his saddle as they charged up, and Lieutenant Gregg clove the skull of another. . . . It was a race for life, as the flying warriors streamed out of the glens and ravines and over the open plain, and took refuge in the clumps of woods or on the rising ground."[8]

If the horses of the dragoons had been fresh, the troopers would have made a terrible slaughter of the hostiles, Kip felt, but after twenty-eight days on the march, the mounts were exhausted. Entirely blown, the horses halted, their riders dismounted, and the foot soldiers passed through their ranks, pursuing the Indians across the rolling, broken country for two miles — then they, too, ran out of strength and had to stop and rest.

Thus the battle ended for that day with the Indians routed and the soldiers victorious.

"What the Indian loss was, we cannot exactly say, as they carry off their dead. Some seventeen however, were seen to be killed, while there must have been between forty and fifty wounded . . .

"Strange to say, not one of our men was injured. One dragoon horse alone was wounded. This was owing to the long range rifles now first used by our

troops, and the discipline which enabled them so admirably to use them."[9]

For three days the command rested, with the Nez Perce scouts sent out to reconnoitre. During this time the weather changed, growing damp and cold. On September 5 the soldiers broke camp and, after marching north about five miles, saw Indians collecting in large bodies to their right. As the command emerged from rough, broken country and entered a broad prairie fringed by trees, the Indians attacked. This time the hostiles tried a new strategy.

"We had nearly reached the woods when they advanced in great force, and set fire to the dry grass of the prairie. . . . Under cover of the smoke, they formed round us in one-third of a circle, and poured in their fire upon us, apparently each one on his own account. The pack train immediately closed up . . .

"It was curious to witness the scene — the dust and smoke, and the noise and shouting of the Mexican muleteers driving forward to the centre four hundred overloaded animals, while the troops were formed about them with as much order and far greater rapidity than if no danger threatened. Then on the hills to our right, if we could have had time to have witnessed them, were feats of horsemanship which we have never seen equalled. The Indians would dash down a hill five hundred feet high and with a slope of forty-five degrees, at the most headlong speed, apparently with all the rapidity they could have used on level ground."[10]

Again, the long-range rifle-muskets, the howitzers, and alternate charges of horse and foot soldiers did deadly work. All day long the running fight continued, with the column advancing until it reached the banks of the Spokane River, where it camped for the night.

"We had marched during the day twenty miles," Kip writes, "the last fourteen miles fighting all the way. No water could be procured for the whole distance, and the men by the time they reached the river were entirely exhausted. Nothing kept them up but the excitement of the contest."[11]

Incredibly, considering the number of hostiles involved and the length of the engagement, only one soldier was slightly wounded. Estimating that some five hundred Indians had been in the battle, Kip made no attempt to guess at their casualties.

After camping near Spokane Falls the evening

8. Ibid., pp. 56–57.
9. Ibid., p. 59.
10. Ibid., pp. 63–64.
11. Ibid., p. 65.

of September 7, Colonel Wright soon began to see signs that the will of the Indians to resist further had been broken. Chief Garry expressed a wish to have a "talk" with the colonel. When it was granted, he said that he had always been opposed to fighting, but that the young men and many of the chiefs were against him, and he could not control them. Now all he wanted was peace.

"I have met you in two battles," Colonel Wright said coldly. "You have been badly whipped. You have had several chiefs and many warriors killed or wounded. I have not lost a man or animal. . . . I did not come into the country to ask you to make peace; I came here to fight. Now, when you are tired of war and ask for peace, I will tell you what you must do.

"You must come to me with your arms, with your women and children, and everything you have, and lay them at my feet. You must put your faith in me and trust to my mercy. If you do this, I shall then tell you the terms upon which I will give you peace. If you do not do this, war will be made on you this year and the next, until your nations shall be exterminated."[12]

While Chief Garry spread Colonel Wright's stark ultimatum among the Spokane and Yakima leaders, the command marched east toward the land of the Coeur d'Alenes. After advancing ten miles, the Nez Perce scouts rode in to say they had discovered a band of Indians on the right. Halting the pack train and placing it under a strong guard, the dragoons under Major Grier moved on at a trot, with the foot soldiers trailing behind.

"We found it difficult to advance as fast as we wished, there being a very steep hill to climb," Kip writes. "The dragoons and Nez Perces, therefore, outstripped us, and we soon saw them passing over the hills. They had discovered that the Indians were driving off their stock to the mountains, which they had nearly reached. Our horsemen were obliged to dismount on account of the nature of the ground, and, after a sharp skirmish, succeeded in capturing the whole band, consisting of nine hundred horses."[13]

If the Indians of the interior country formerly had feared volunteer soldiers because of their brutality, while holding regulars in contempt, they now got a lesson in how regular army troops could behave when commanded by a cold-blooded martinet. Receiving a report from the Nez Perces that they had found a herd of Indian cattle and a number of lodges filled with wheat, Colonel Wright dispatched two companies of artillery and one of dragoons to the village with orders to burn the lodges and grain and drive in the cattle. Too wild to be rounded up, the cattle took to the hills. But the lodges and the grain were burned.

That evening,

"The case of our Palouse prisoner was investigated, and it having been proved beyond doubt that he was engaged in the murder of the miners in May last, he was hung."[14]

Next morning, September 9,

"At nine o'clock, Colonel Wright convened a board of officers to determine what should be done with the captured horses. They decided that one hundred and thirty should be selected for our use, and the rest shot. It was a disagreeable necessity, but one which could not be avoided. . . . Nothing can more effectually cripple the Indians than to deprive them of their animals."[15]

As in the Southwest, where a man afoot was no man at all and a *reducido* never became a rider for freedom, the Indians in this part of the country had been mounted for so long that they knew no other way of life.

"We learned subsequently that nothing we had done so much prostrated the Indians as this destruction of their horses."[16]

With the Indians' will to resist broken, all that remained to be done now was to meet with the humbled chiefs and proclaim the surrender terms.

"You shall have peace on the following conditions," Colonel Wright told first the Coeur d'Alenes and then the Spokanes. "You must deliver to me, to take to the General, the men who struck the first blow in the affair with Colonel Steptoe. You must deliver to me to take to Walla Walla, one chief and four warriors with their families. You must deliver to me all property taken in the affair with Colonel Steptoe. You must allow all troops and other white men to pass unmolested through your country. You must not allow any hostile Indians to come into your country, and not engage in any hostilities against any white man. . . . I also require that the hatchet shall be buried between you and our friends, the Nez Perces."[17]

Though word was sent to Kamiakin that he would not be harmed if he surrendered, he refused to trust the white man's promises. Another Yakima chief, Ow-hi, did come in, and the rude treatment he received fully justified Kamiakin's suspicion.

12. Ibid., pp. 67–68.
13. Ibid., p. 69.
14. Ibid., p. 70.
15. Ibid., p. 71.
16. Ibid., p. 75.
17. Ibid., p. 84.

Convinced of the truth of the stories that Ow-hi's son, Qualchen, had murdered at least nine white men, Colonel Wright told the older Indian that if his son did not surrender within four days, he, Ow-hi, would be hanged.

Though this message was sent, it did not reach the young brave. For some reason Qualchen rode into camp a few days later, not knowing that his father was a prisoner and that he had been condemned to die without a trial. In a report dated September 24, Colonel Wright states laconically:

"Qualchen came to me at 9 o'clock, and at 9:15 A.M. he was hung."[18]

On the homeward-bound trip a detachment under Major Grier was sent to the Steptoe battleground to recover the buried howitzers and the remains of the dead, returning to the main camp September 25. Many Palouses came in that same evening, seeking peace. They got it on Colonel Wright's terms when he arrested fifteen of them, hanged six on the spot, and took the others along in irons. En route, the Yakima prisoner, Ow-hi, was shot and killed "while trying to escape."

Four days later camp was made on the Palouse River, where a chief named Slowiarchy, who had taken no part in the war, tried to help his people get favorable surrender terms. Colonel Wright was not in a forgiving mood. He would not be doing wrong, he told the Palouses, if he should hang them all.

"He refused to make a written treaty with them and threatened with death all who should cross the Snake. . . . Wright then demanded the surrender of the two Palouses who had murdered miners. After a short consultation among the Indians, one of the murderers came forward. The other could not be found. Wright then called for six men who had stolen the army cattle when the expedition was starting from Fort Walla Walla. They were promptly surrendered. While the council proceeded, the murderer and three of the thieves, who were recognized as notorious marauders, were hanged by the guard from a tree several hundred yards distant. The usual quota of hostages was taken from the Palouse tribe — one chief and four men, with their families."[19]

Since the newly built Fort Taylor would not be needed now, Colonel Wright abandoned it, turning it over to Chief Slowiarchy for whatever use he might wish to make of it. Reaching Fort Walla Walla October 5, the command buried the remains of the soldiers killed in the Steptoe fight with full military honors.

"The Walla Wallas were called into council on October 9th. Wright delivered his customary indictment and asked all who had taken part in recent battles to stand up. Thirty-five rose, and Wright selected for execution four whose reputations were pre-eminently evil. Thus was the last general uprising quelled, and though Wright's methods were harsh, they were regarded as just by the Indians."[20]

By the survivors, perhaps. But the doomed men made no comment that has endured.

Thus, the peace Governor Stevens thought he had secured by treaty finally was brought to the region by force. For the two years of war the Territories of Washington and Oregon eventually handed the federal government a six million dollar bill — "for scalping Indians and violating squaws," as Horace Greeley acidly put it.[21]

In September 1858 General William S. Harney was appointed to command a new military department embracing the area. Following his arrival at Fort Vancouver, his first act was to revoke General John Wool's order excluding Americans from lands east of the Cascades, throwing the interior open to settlement. On March 8, 1859, the U.S. Senate confirmed the treaties made with the Nez Perces, Umatillas, Walla Wallas, Cayuses, and Yakimas, and appropriated funds for their implementation.

At about this same time the motley collection of grogshops, stores, and "parlors of entertainment" that had sprung up a mile east of the military reserve recently established along Garrison Creek in the Walla Walla Valley showed signs of growing into a permanent settlement. If the town were ever going to amount to anything, the saloonkeepers, merchants, and proprietors said, it would need a distinctive name.

For a brief while, in honor of the commander of the new post, the settlement had called itself Steptoeville. For obvious reasons the name did not stick. Someone then suggested that the metropolis adopt as a name the Cayuse Indian word meaning "Place of the Rye Grass," which the ill-fated Whitman Mission had used for the eleven years of its existence. Since no one could agree on the pronunciation of the word, let alone whether it

18. Fuller, *History of the Pacific Northwest,* p. 257.
19. Ibid., p. 259.
20. Ibid.
21. Bancroft, *History of Washington, Idaho, and Montana,* vol. 31, p. 175.

should be spelled *Waiilatpu, Wyeletpo,* or *Wyelatpu,* that name was dropped, too.

Why not call the town Walla Walla?

Why not, indeed.

So it was on the very site where the brush arbor had stood when the Nez Perce Treaty had been signed that the town of Walla Walla was built. Because of the lands ceded by the Nez Perces, the former council ground now lay 120 miles west of the heart of the Nez Perce Reservation — upon which it had been promised the Indians that no white man could trespass without their permission.

But it was from this distant settlement that the first white trespasser came — drawn by the magnet of gold.[22]

22. The name Walla Walla usually is translated to mean "Place of Many Waters," for there are something like eleven streams that descend from the western slopes of the Blue Mountains and flow across the valley floor toward the Columbia fifty miles away. But some years ago I was given a different interpretation by Nesmith Ankeny, whose grandfather, a pioneer banker in the valley, got his start as a packer and trader with miners in the Nez Perce country of northern Idaho Territory.

The first explorers to view the Columbia River Basin from the heights of the Blue Mountains were French, Nesmith Ankeny's grandfather told him, undoubtedly guided on their travels by local Indians. From those heights, the view is spectacular — the broad valley, the big river fifty miles away, and, far to the west and visible only toward sunset of an extremely clear day, the snow-capped peaks of the Cascade Range. After crossing a continent and at last viewing the long-sought River of the West, one of those nameless Frenchmen no doubt spread his hands in a typical Gallic gesture and cried:

"Voila! Voila!"

Since Indians were sharp observers and accurate mimics, it is logical to assume — Nesmith Ankeny's grandfather said — that when the next party of white men came through the country they, too, stopped at the spectacular viewpoint on the crest of the Blue Mountains and gazed to the west. Naturally they asked their Indian guide what the valley was called. In reply he spread his hands as the Frenchman had done earlier and grunted, with a local accent:

"Walla! Walla!"

CHAPTER NINETEEN

GOLD AND NEW TREATIES: 1860–1863

*An Injun showed me a nugget he found in the
Salmon. I swear it was worth at least twenty-four
dollars.*
— George Grigsby, June 1861

LEGEND CLAIMS THAT Jesuit priest Pierre Jean
De Smet discovered gold in a stream a few miles
northeast of the Nez Perce country while visiting
the Flatheads in 1840. Because he felt word of its
presence would mean ruination to the Indians, he
kept quiet, we are told, took no precious metal for
himself, and carried the secret to his grave.[1]

Legend also relates that a member of the Isaac
Stevens railroad route survey party found gold in
the same area in 1853 but was ordered to suppress
his discovery for the same reason — and did. Historians doubt both tales, pointing out that, even
though gold later was discovered in Alder Gulch
and the Coeur d'Alene country, the legends post-
date the finds so must be folklore.

As already noted, each group of adventurers
pushing into the Pacific Northwest sought a different prize: beaver, empire, heathen souls to be
saved, free land in Oregon. But whether British,
American, French-Canadian, or Indian, none was
interested in precious metal until the California
rush of '49 dramatically proved the mineral wealth
of the mountains in the Far West.

According to one early-day historian:

"An Indian from the Nez Perce country found his
way into California during the gold excitement in that
State, and, chancing one day into a gulch where some
miners were at work, made himself friendly and useful,
and told them in his broken English where he was from
and the name of his tribe. He soon made friends.

"Among those miners was one named E. D. Pierce,
who was a visionary and susceptible man. . . . To this
man one day the Nez Perce Indian told a strange weird
tale of how he, with two companions, had been
camping at night in a defile among his native mountains,
when suddenly a light like a brilliant star burst forth from
among the cliffs. They thought it was the Great Spirit's

eye, and watched with superstitious awe until dawn,
when, taking courage with the wakening day, they
sought the spot from where the night twinkling had
looked down upon them, and found a glittering ball that
looked like glass embedded in the solid rock. The Indian
believed it was a great medicine, but could not get it
from its resting place, and were forced to leave it there.

"This was just the kind of tale to make a strong impression upon Captain Pierce, who believed the Indian
had found a diamond more valuable than the famed
Kohinoor, and he determined to become its possessor.
With that purpose he left California and became a resident of Walla Walla. He scouted through the mountains
east of Snake River, and finally induced a party of men
to accompany him, they hoping to find gold, he still
searching for the mythical diamond."[2]

Whether Captain Pierce's prospecting trip into
the mountains north of the Clearwater was in
search of a fist-sized diamond or for gold, this land
now was a part of the newly approved Nez Perce
Indian Reservation. He and his men were halted as
trespassers by Agent Andrew J. Cain. They were
refused permission to prospect in the area and
warned they would be arrested if they returned.

"Pierce, however, found a Nez Perce squaw who
said she could pilot them through by a route not fre-
quented by her people, and the party then set out under
her guidance, spent three days cutting a trail through
small cedars over a mountain, and found itself at length
in a mountain meadow, where they determined to rest
for a while and let their horses recruit.

"While there W. F. Bassett went to a stream that ran
through the meadow gulch, and tried the soil for gold,

---

1. Terrell, *Black Robe,* p. 177. Later, Lieutenant John Mullan, who
was with the Stevens party in 1853, is said to have seen "signs of
gold" in the Coeur d'Alene country.
2. Gilbert, *Historic Sketches,* p. 224. The discoverer's full name
was Elias Davidson Pierce.

finding about three cents in this first panful of dirt. This was the first discovery of that metal in these mountains, and the place where it was found became the noted Oro Fino mines, in what is now Idaho."[3]

Local tradition has it that the Nez Perce woman who guided the Pierce party onto reservation land by the back way was Chief Timothy's eighteen-year-old daughter, Jane, who later married a white man named John Silcott. Building a rough sluice from cedar bark, the party of whites soon recovered eighty dollars in gold dust. Then, being short on supplies, Pierce returned to Walla Walla, spread word of the discovery to a few trusted friends, reoutfitted, and, with a party of fifteen men, returned to the area and dug in for the winter.

Building a cluster of five solid log cabins, which they named Pierce City, they continued to pan for gold despite deepening snow. By January they were so sure they had struck a bonanza that they sent two men to the settlements on snowshoes for more supplies. In March another member of the party followed, carrying $800 in dust to Walla Walla to pay off debts to the merchants. Sent downriver to Portland, the gold and news of the strike "set off a blaze of excitement." Within weeks, men by the thousands were moving toward the interior.

This was in the spring of 1861. A continent's breadth away Fort Sumter was under siege, President Lincoln was about to issue a call for 75,000 troops, and the nation soon would be rent asunder by the Civil War. But in the Nez Perce country there was bigger news.

Gold.

Hordes of eager prospectors poured into the region, violating reservation boundaries with a total disregard for Indian rights. Considering the large number of white trespassers, surprisingly little friction arose between them and the Nez Perces. One reason for this was that the stream beds where gold was found lay in high country, which the Nez Perces used only for hunting, summer pasture for their horses, and seasonal harvesting of roots.

A second reason for their choosing peace rather than conflict was that many of them had become "settled" Indians. Not only had they built up their farms and herds so they could feed themselves, they now had a surplus to sell for cash. One early-day newspaper correspondent relates meeting Chief Reuben, a Nez Perce, on the lower Clearwater in June 1861:

Courtesy Penrose Library, Whitman College
Jane Silcott, daughter of Timothy, who is said to have led the E. D. Pierce party into the first gold strike on the reservation.

"He was there urging the other Indians to permit the whites to go to the mines without molestation, telling them that if the white men dug out the gold the Indians could sell horses, cattle, corn and vegetables and get gold in return."[4]

Still a third, and probably the most important, reason for the Nez Perces keeping the peace was that long years of association with the whites had taught them tolerance and caution. Since the time of Lewis and Clark they had seen plenty of rude, pushy, greedy white men and had learned to put up with them; they had also observed how dangerous, ruthless, and deadly white men could

3. Ibid., p. 225.
4. *Lewiston Teller,* March 31, 1877.

be when given the least excuse, so they had learned to be careful.

Following the original strike in the Orofino district north of the Clearwater, other strikes were made at Orogrande, south of the Clearwater, and at Florence, still farther south in the Salmon River country. In each case, prospectors by the thousands stampeded to the new fields, ignoring all efforts of the agent, the military, or the Nez Perces to stop them. Since this was the domain of Eagle-from-the Light and Looking Glass, these two chiefs warned the prospectors time and again not to trespass on their lands, threatening them with death if they did not turn back. Johnny Healy, a brash, reckless, twenty-one-year-old Irishman at the time, later recalled that one of the miners in his party replied to a threat from an Indian: "Look here, for every white man you kill, a thousand will take his place."

The Indian saw the point, he says, and let them pass. But a few days further down the trail, two of the leaders of the whites were confronted by a band of Indians determined to turn them back.

"Looking Glass, chief of the camp, came to meet them. He seized a horse by the bridle, turned it around and motioned that all must go back. The white men tried to pacify him. He shook his head and frowned. They tried to argue. He held his hands over his ears. They begged permission to camp that night. He motioned that he would kill them all if they did not leave at once . . .

"No one wanted to go back, so they agreed to press forward regardless of consequences; most of them felt the Nez Perces were bluffing anyway. The small party continued towards the Salmon as fast as tired animals could travel, each man holding his rifle across his saddle, cocked and ready for instant use. The Indians circled, whooping and yelling. Grigsby who was of a nervous disposition, started to raise his rifle to fire, but was restrained by the others, who felt that was just what the Nez Perces wanted.

"Sometimes the Indians formed in line of battle, and swept down upon the white men with horrible yells, striking the pack animals with their quirts and poking guns almost in the faces of their victims. The miners went on, trying to act indifferent in spite of the din and suspense, but watching carefully to avoid being taken by surprise."[5]

Unable to turn back the party of whites by shouts and threats, the Indians seized their horses by the bridle reins, jerked them around, and whipped them, forcing the tired animals and exhausted men to retreat five miles or so to the previous night's camp. Joined the next day by another group of prospectors who had been driven back by the Nez Perces, they held a council of war.

"Any white man can lick a dozen Indians," one of the men said.

Counting only fifteen men in the party against an estimated one hundred lodges of Indians, it was agreed that reinforcements should be obtained before going into battle. Returning to Orofino, Healy and two of his friends made the rounds of the town's bars that night, enlisting twenty-five "well-armed, mounted men ready to fight the Nez Perces." Due to a misunderstanding, a sudden onset of cold feet, or an acute case of sobering up, only nine of the twenty-five brave recruits showed up at the appointed meeting place next day.

"The party now numbered twenty-four men. . . . They figured themselves a match for any Indians in the country."[6]

Even so, it was decided to parley with the Nez Perces before charging upon their camp. Looking Glass said:

"You must either go back or fight."

"Fight it is then," shouted a miner.

With the ultimatum laid down and accepted, it appeared that the battle was about to begin. But no one wanted to start it. After a great deal of arguing and milling around in both camps, one of the prospectors made a hare-brained suggestion.

" 'Lets's make a break for the Salmon,' said someone.

"It seemed like the best policy. Their horses were fresh and it was only a short distance. With whooping and yelling that out-did the Nez Perces, the miners broke for the river and went through the Indian line before the redskins had time to guess what they were up to. Upon reaching the Salmon, they camped on a bar, threw up a breastwork and prepared to greet their foe. A day and a night passed and the Indians did not come."[7]

Thus, a confrontation that could have set off a

5. John Linton Struble [pseud. for Virginia Burlingame], "Johnny Healy Strikes It Rich," *Idaho Yesterdays*, Fall 1957, p. 24. If this were Chief Looking Glass the Elder he would have been at least seventy-five years old. More likely it was the old chief's son, Looking Glass the Younger. In *Hear Me, My Chiefs!* by L. V. McWhorter (Caxton Printers, 1952), pp. 182–183, he is described as being "almost six feet tall, well-proportioned, with features denoting strength and tenacity of purpose. He was truly a commanding figure." His Indian name was Ip-pak-ness Way-hay-ken (Looking Glass Around the Neck) while his father's was Ap-push-wa-hite. Both habitually wore a small mirror or flint arrowhead around the neck, thus the name. Haines says the elder Looking Glass died in January 1863 (*Red Eagles*, p. 161).
6. Struble, "Johnny Healy," p. 25.
7. Ibid., p. 26.

bloody war ended in comic-opera fashion without a shot being fired. Since the white prospectors were too stupid to know the risks they were taking, all credit for avoiding a battle must be given to the Nez Perces, who found such crazy behavior so far beyond their comprehension that they simply rode away and let these madmen dig where they pleased.

By law, alcohol was strictly forbidden within the boundaries of the Nez Perce Reservation. As settlements such as Pierce City, Florence, and Elk City grew from camps to sizable towns, this prohibition proved to be something of a problem. Well, not much of a problem. As William Purvine wrote:

"Twelve months ago whiskey might not be even carried across the reservation much less exposed for sale; then was the time when 'vinegar' was in such urgent demand in all the mines that you would see whole trains passing through freighted with half barrels of 'vinegar' for the relief of the poor, suffering, maybe honest miners."[8]

Cynical writers of the day suggested that alcohol calmed the hostility of the Nez Perces, just as it soothed the jangled nerves of the prospectors.

"Whereas Christianity had failed to pacify the Indian, liquor had made him peaceable. The miner declared: 'What a miracle rum has wrought. What Christianity and civilization could not accomplish in decades, liquor has accomplished in a few short months.' What the Spirit failed to effect, spirits had accomplished."[9]

If the Nez Perces had been so inclined they could have caused great suffering among the miners wintering in the high country simply by refusing to sell them food. The winter of 1861–62 was so severe that the Columbia River, the main artery of travel, froze over solid, stopping boat traffic, and the trails were so choked with snow that few food shipments came in.

On his way to Pierce City, G. A. Noble, a physician, wrote that while on the Clearwater,

"our camp was near that of Lawyer, Chief of the Nez Perces. His son, Young Lawyer, resides here and owns the canoes which constitute the ferry. He appears to be a shrewd, sensible man, has a wife and four healthy looking children, and is regarded as an industrious and skillful farmer. These Indians have some fine crops here, well fenced and apparently well cultivated. I had not seen either chicken or egg since June last, but here we saw both chickens and eggs. Chickens three dollars apiece, and eggs four dollars a dozen."

Still another letter tells of the peaceful relations between the Indians and miners:

"The Nez Perces are the most intelligent and exemplary Indians on the North Pacific Coast, and they boast of never having murdered a white man."

Certainly the white men could not make that same boast, for this same writer continues by stating that three Indians "had been murdered by drunken miners."

"In return for the continued friendship in time of want, and generous acts of hospitality, always so readily extended towards the whites by these Indians," William Purvine writes, "they now reap an abundant harvest of every species of villainy and insult."

In addition to having learned tolerance toward rowdy behavior by the whites, the Nez Perces, who were widely traveled, no doubt compared them to other peoples they had known. One writer says:

"The miners may have not been very placid guests on the Indian reservation, but they paid for their food and travel with magic gold dust. The Nez Perces were used to even rowdier neighbors — the horse-stealing Snakes, the terrible Blackfeet. The whites did some uncouth things, but after all should not the aborigines be able to understand uncivilized actions?"[10]

During early summer of 1861, the sternwheeler, *Colonel Wright,* ascended the Snake and Clearwater to *Ahsahka,* near the spot at which Lewis and Clark had built and launched their dugout canoes. As the river fell, it became apparent that the forty-mile stretch upstream from the juncture of the Clearwater with the Snake would be too shallow for navigation by a steamboat most of the year; from then on, that juncture became the unloading point for upriver traffic. Admitting the need for a dock and storage sheds, even though it was within the boundaries of the reservation, the Nez Perces permitted these facilities to be built. No formal permission was given to pitch tents, convert them to cabins, build log and then frame houses, construct stores, lay out streets, and implant in a matter of only a few months a population of twelve hundred people in a boomtown called Lewiston. No matter. The town was created anyway.

In an atttempt to impose some kind of order

8. Donald N. Wells, "Farmers Forgotten: Nez Perce Suppliers of the North Idaho Gold Rush Days," *Idaho Yesterdays,* Summer 1958, p. 31.
9. Ibid., p. 32.
10. Ibid.

The Indian agency at Spalding, Idaho about 1867

upon chaos, Agent C. Hutchins wrote General B. Alvord from Lapwai, July 8, 1862:

"It is required, in order to maintain the laws of the United States on this Indian reservation, to protect the Nez Perce Indians from iniquitious outrages on their persons and property by vicious white men . . . that mounted U.S. troops to the number of at least one company be immediately sent here, and that such be permanently stationed."[11]

Back East a war was on, and almost all regular army troops stationed in the West had departed for the greater conflict. Volunteers now manned posts in the Pacific Northwest, the nearest at Fort Walla Walla, 120 miles to the west. In response to Agent Hutchins' request, Major J. B. Rinearson and Company F, Oregon Volunteers, were sent east, arriving at Lapwai early in August.

At first, Hutchins was pleased.

"However, he quickly learned that Major Rinearson had no intention of removing the whiskey peddlers. . . . The major's response was that his instructions clearly stated that he had no authority to interfere with whites who sold liquor only to other whites, whether or not the sale took place on the reservation."[12]

This piece of bureaucratic evasion resulted in a

decision by General Alvord to establish a permanent post and double the garrison by the addition of a company of infantry made up of Washington Territory Volunteers. Personally accompanying this force, General Alvord spoke to an assembly of Nez Perces October 24, 1862:

"I have come to see you in order to assure you that the Government desires to do all in its power to protect you. You will never have a worse enemy than the whiskey sellers and the bad whites who intrude upon you and commit outrages upon you and your families."[13]

In establishing the post, General Alvord stated that its purpose was to protect the Nez Perces from bad whites. But some years later a surgeon stationed there wrote that the reason for the establishment of Fort Lapwai

"was to protect more effectively the employees of the Agency, who in consequence of a murder committed by

11. Erwin N. Thompson, *Fort Lapwai Historic Resource Study* (Denver: National Park Service, 1973), p. 2. In contrast to many frontier posts, as National Park Service historian Thompson wryly notes, the original purpose of Fort Lapwai was to protect Indians from whites, rather than the other way around.
12. Ibid., pp. 3–4.
13. Ibid., p. 5.

an Indian near the Agency, and his subsequent arrest by the military authorities, became alarmed for their own safety, and refused to remain at their posts, unless the troops were moved nearer to them."[14]

Six months later the military post in the heart of Nez Perce country played yet another role, In May 1863 the scattered bands of the tribe were asked to meet in a major council with the whites to negotiate a new treaty that would recognize the realities of the white settlements on Indian lands, as well as sharply reducing the holdings of the Lower Nez Perces and the Salmon River bands.

"The establishment of the military post at Fort Lapwai last October has in a very material sense paved the way for the conclusion of this treaty by evincing to the Indians a determination, so far as practicable, to protect them from aggression," wrote Calvin H. Hale, Superintendent of Indian Affairs for Washington Territory. "The presence of six companies of troops at Fort Lapwai was very salutary."[15]

Indeed it must have been to the Indian Bureau personnel. But the Nez Perces who were being asked to agree to a new treaty giving up the lands reserved to them forever by the treaty ratified only four years ago must have wondered: *Why is forever such a short time in the white man's world?* And: *Who are we being protected from?*

14. Ibid., p. 6.
15. Ibid., p. 7.

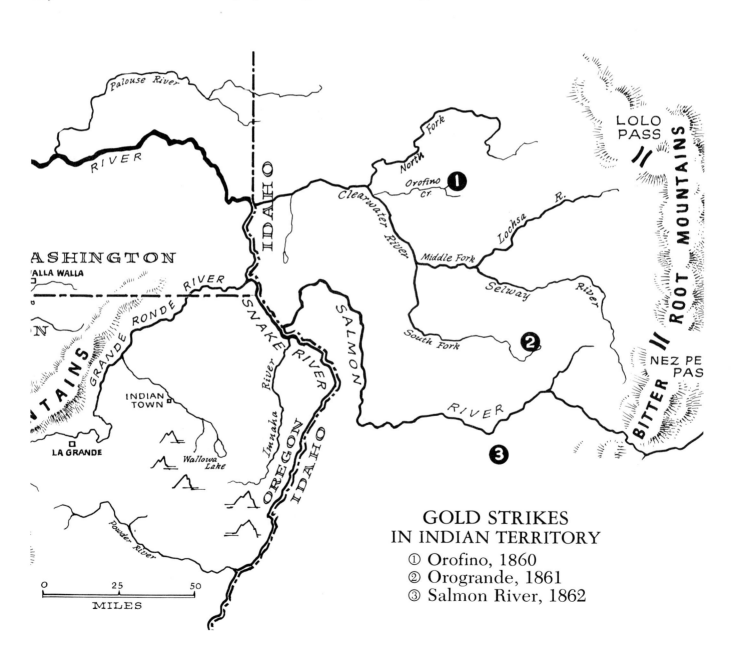

GOLD STRIKES
IN INDIAN TERRITORY
① Orofino, 1860
② Orogrande, 1861
③ Salmon River, 1862

CHAPTER TWENTY

THE "STEAL" TREATY: 1863–1868

When you go into council with the white man,
always remember your country. Do not give it
away. The white man will cheat you out of your
home. I have taken no pay from the United States.
I have never sold our land.

— Tu-eka-kas, Old Joseph, to his
son, Hin-mah-too-yah-lat-kekt,
Young Joseph

THE PAYMENTS AND BENEFITS promised the Nez Perces under the treaty signed in June 1855 and ratified by the U.S. Senate in March 1859 took a long, devious course as they trickled down from the Great White Father to the Indians for whom they were intended. Along the way disproportionate shares stuck to the fingers of contractors, agents, and officials, while schools, sawmills, and gristmills remained unbuilt, tools, clothing, and food undistributed, and salaries promised to tribal leaders unpaid.

The failure of the federal government to live up to its promises gave the leaders of the Lower Nez Perces, who claimed they had not sold their lands, a fine opportunity to say: *"We told you so!"* to Lawyer and his backers. Led by the head of the Wallowa band, Chief Joseph, this faction wanted nothing from the Great White Father but to be left alone.

The third and more militant faction, whose home country lay along the lower Salmon, was led by Eagle-from-the-Light, White Bird, and Looking Glass. They taunted Lawyer and his supporters, challenging the young men to join forces with them and drive the white interlopers out of their country.

Despite these pressures, Chief Lawyer steadfastly supported the 1855 Treaty and remained a firm friend of the whites. In truth, there was no other course open to him. The majority of his supporters were "settled" Indians who had accepted Christianity and developed farms. They no longer had time to go to the buffalo country, let alone get

involved in a war which any sensible Nez Perce knew they could not win.

And Lawyer was a sensible man.

With an innate instinct for survival, he consistently chose the winning side. In the days of Joint Occupancy he had chosen the Americans rather than the British as friends. He had fought on the side of the whites against the Blackfeet in the Battle of Pierre's Hole. He had welcomed the Spaldings, Governor Stevens, and Colonel Wright. When gold was discovered on reservation land and white trespassers poured in by the thousands, he had urged the Nez Perces to let them dig where they chose and build towns where they liked, for he knew that resistance would be useless.

He also knew that important changes were taking place over the United States in general and in the Pacific Northwest in particular. In 1859 Oregon had become a state, placing the Wallowa band of Nez Perces within its borders. In March 1863 Idaho Territory was created out of the eastern portion of Washington Territory. This put the Kamiah, Lapwai, Clearwater, and Salmon River bands within the boundaries of the new territory. West of the Snake, the Palouse Hills domain of Timothy, Red Wolf, and other Lower Nez Perce bands lay within the now-reduced boundaries of Washington Territory.

This meant that the federal reserve set aside for the Nez Perces as a permanent homeland, upon which no white man could trespass without their permission, was split geographically into three polit-

Tamason, also called Timothy, a signer of the treaty of 1868, Washington, D.C., along with Lawyer and Jason

ical units — one state and two territories — with control remaining in the hands of the federal government. Managing such a spread-out reserve obviously was going to be an administrative nightmare.

After a great deal of deploring and hand wringing by the bureaucrats, a typical bureaucratic decision was reached: Instead of attempting to enforce the terms of the 1855 Treaty, which only the Nez Perces were honoring anyway, they would convene a *new* council with the Indians and negotiate a *new* treaty whose adjusted terms would recognize present realities.

Though it had been impossible to obtain funds to meet treaty obligations to the Nez Perces in the form of goods and annuities, a request by the agents for an appropriation of $50,000 for such a council was quickly approved, with the promise that $40,000 of that sum would be in the hands of the agents by November 1862. But

"November came, and the Indians were gathering to the promised council when the commissioners appointed were forced to announce that no funds had come to hand, and to defer the conference until the following May."[1]

While the shortage of funds may have had something to do with delaying the council, it is interesting to note that the two companies of soldiers stationed at Fort Lapwai in November 1862 had been increased to six companies by May 15, 1863, when the council finally convened.

"Much display was made of the power and material of the military branch of the government," Bancroft says, "as well as its munificence in entertaining the whole Nez Perce nation,"[2]

Followers of the chiefs attending the council who opposed drawing up another treaty numbered twelve hundred. The Lawyer faction numbered around two thousand, giving the protreaty faction a two-thirds majority insofar as total numbers were concerned.

Age, infirmity, and death had changed the leadership of the various bands. Tough, indomitable Chief Looking Glass had died in January 1863 at the age of seventy-eight. His son, now in his mid-thirties and just as much a man and a chief as his father had been, was there to take his place, though he let the aggressive, eloquent, older chief, Eagle-from-the-Light, do the talking in council. Spalding's old enemy, Hin-mah-tute-ke-kaikt, "Thunder Strikes" or "Thunder Eyes," was gone.

Photographer and date not recorded thought to be around 1871-1875   *Courtesy Smithsonian Institution*

A son of Tamason, also known as Timothy

His place as head of the Lapwai band had been taken by a chief equally intransigent when it came to dealing with the whites and even more resentful that Lawyer presumed to speak as head chief for the tribe.

Called "Big Thunder" by his people, he claimed that his band owned the land occupied by the agency, plus the Fort Lapwai grounds and the site of the former Spalding Mission. Like his predecessor, he felt that the whites should pay for use of the land. He also believed that since Lawyer received an annual salary, he should too.

With Tu-eka-kas, Chief Joseph the Elder, came his oldest son, Hin-mah-too-yah-lat-kekt, "Thunder Traveling to Distant Mountains," called Young Joseph by the whites. Now twenty-three years old, standing six-feet-two-inches tall in his moccasined feet, and weighing a muscular two hundred pounds, he was a strikingly handsome young man

1. Bancroft, *History of Washington, Idaho, and Montana,* p. 483.
2. Ibid.

to his home in the Willamette Valley and he made the 380-mile trip inland. Having come to the Oregon country at the age of twelve with his uncle, Dr. Marcus Whitman, in 1843 he had grown up with the Nez Perces, knew their language, and was trusted by them.

Late in May the council finally got under way. As the boundaries of the reservation now were drawn, it covered approximately ten thousand square miles. Originally the reason for calling the council had been to give non-Indians the right to mine the streams of the high country, travel where they chose in search of new strikes, and live in established towns. Persuading the Nez Perces to cede the few hundred square miles taken up by mining claims and towns would have been no problem. But that was not what the commissioners suggested. Instead, they made an astounding proposition

"that the Nez Perces should sell all their lands except five or six hundred square miles situated on the south side of the South Fork of the Clearwater, and embracing the Kamiah prairie, to be surveyed into allotments, with the understanding that a patent was to issue to each individual holding land in severalty, with payment for improvements abandoned."[3]

In other words, instead of asking the Nez Perces to cede and be paid for the five or six hundred square miles which the whites now were occupying illegally, the commissioners were asking the Indians to turn over the entire ten-thousand-square-mile reservation to the whites *except* for the five or six hundred square miles into which the whole tribe then would be compressed.

Understandably, the Nez Perces rejected the proposition.

The commissioners then made a second proposal, which they said would be final. The amount of land granted to the Indians would be doubled, $50,000 in agricultural implements would be supplied, $10,000 would be spent on mills, $10,000 to build schools, $6,000 for teachers the first year, and half that amount for the next fourteen years. In addition, all the monies promised in the 1855 Treaty would be paid, plus $4,000 or $5,000 for the horses furnished Governor Stevens and the volunteers during the 1855–56 war. Indians living outside the new reservation would be permitted to sell any houses, barns, or improvements they had

Courtesy Luna House Historical Society
Lewiston, Idaho

Peo-Peo Tholekt — a cousin of Chief Joseph

who had inherited his father's quiet dignity and commanding presence.

Acting as commissioners for the United States were Superintendent Hale, Agents Hutchins and Howell, and ex-mountain man Robert Newell. A substantial number of the Lawyer faction insisted they would accept no interpreter but Perrin Whitman. This delayed opening of the council for two weeks while word requesting his presence was sent

3. Ibid., p. 485.

Courtesy Luna House Historical Society
Lewiston, Idaho

Two Nez Perce braves

domain was in Kamiah, sixty-five miles upriver, while the Lapwai area belonged to Big Thunder, this act of generosity of Lawyer's part was promptly rejected by the local chiefs.

"Again several meetings of the council were held, the non-treaty chiefs being present. They were told by Commissioner Hutchins that . . . although they might persist in refusing their annunities . . . such action would not release them from the obligations of the treaty they had signed in 1855."[5]

Release from treaty obligations, it appeared, was for whites only. Ignoring the admonition, all the chiefs present convened in the most important council the tribe had held since the time of Lewis and Clark. As it continued far into the night, the commissioners became alarmed that a decision might be made by the Nez Perces to end the talks by murdering all the whites present. They dispatched an urgent message to Fort Lapwai saying they were apprehensive for their safety.

4. Ibid., p. 487.
5. Ibid., pp. 487–488.

made on their property to private individuals or to the federal government, providing they did so within a year's time following ratification of the new treaty by the Senate.

When Big Thunder, Three Feathers, Eagle-from-the-Light, and Joseph declared that they never would sell their land, Lawyer at first appeared to agree with them, then suggested to the commissioners that they might consent to letting the miners and settlements stay if a sufficient consideration were made. Some of the chiefs questioned the authority of the commissioners to make a new treaty. This so affronted the dignity of Superintendent Hale that he abruptly terminated the council, saying he had nothing further to offer.

"The withdrawal of the commissioners changed the attitude of Lawyer," Bancroft says, "who intimated that in a few days he would offer a proposition of his own."[4]

In a few days he did. Meeting with the commissioners the evening of June 3, he offered to give up the land upon which the town of Lewiston was built, with twelve miles around it including the Lapwai Agency and military post. Since his own

Courtesy Luna House Historical Society
Lewiston, Idaho

John Spencer and Henry S. Spencer, Jr.

Courtesy Luna House Historical Society
Lewiston, Idaho

Two Indian children

Following the all-night council the Nez Perce leaders opposed to making a new treaty either left the Lapwai campground or attended the talks as mere observers. With the dissenting Indians silent, the commissioners had no difficulty reaching agreement with Lawyer and his supporters, all of whose lands were to be included within the boundaries of the new reservation — one-eighth the size of the one created by the 1855 Treaty.

At the close of the Walla Walla council in 1855 Governor Stevens had recognized fifty-eight Nez Perce leaders as chiefs, had affixed their names to the treaty, and had had each one touch the writing stick as "X" (his mark) was made. Now at Lapwai as the 1863 Treaty was signed, the commissioners found fifty-three "chiefs" to sign the new treaty. Though many of their names were not on the earlier agreement, in number, at least, it appeared that

6. Haines, *Red Eagles*, p. 162; *Oregon Adjutant General's Report*, 1866, p. 18.

In response, Captain George Currey, with a small detachment of cavalry, rode to the Indian camp at one o'clock in the morning to see what was going on. No bloodthirsty deeds were being plotted against the whites, he discovered; instead, the fifty-three chiefs meeting in the big tent were engaged in a serious discussison of the future of the Nez Perce nation.

"He and a comrade were invited into the tent and were given places by the council fire, where they listened to the discussion for several hours," Haines writes. "The chiefs were debating the terms of the proposed treaty in an effort to reach some compromise, but neither group would yield. Finally convinced that there was no hope of agreement, they decided that the proper action was to disband the tribe, each chief becoming an independent leader of his own village."

Outsider though he was, Captain Currey recognized the importance of the scene.

"I withdrew my detachment," he wrote, "having accomplished nothing but that of witnessing the extinguishment of the last council fires of the most powerful Indian nation on the sunset side of the Rocky Mountains."[6]

Courtesy Luna House Historical Society
Lewiston, Idaho

Lizzie McCormick at Lapwai, Idaho

the tribe as a whole assented to the new document.

Actually, every chief except one who signed the new treaty lived within the boundaries of the new reservation. The exception was Timothy, whose village lay west of the Snake on Alpowa Creek; he had been taken care of by a grant of land and the promise of a $600 house. Every nonsigning chief except one lived outside the boundaries of the new reservation. That exception was Big Thunder, who refused to sign because of his antipathy toward Lawyer, even though his band was included within the new reserve and would receive some of the benefits in the way of schools, mills, goods, and annuities.

Among the Indians, there seems to have been no question that they realized the tribe as a whole had been dissolved and that each signing chief spoke only for his own band. But this was not the impression the commissioners gave the federal government in their report. Recognizing a rank piece of chicanery when he saw one, Captain Currey put his disapproval on record.

"Although the treaty goes out to the world as the concurrent agreement of the tribe, it is in reality nothing more than the agreement of Lawyer and his band, numbering in the aggregate not a third part of the Nez Perce tribe."[7]

So one-third of the tribe signed away seven-eighths of the reservation as its boundaries had been laid out in 1855. Traditionally roaming over a region comprising 27,000 square miles, the Nez Perces had seen their homeland cut down to 10,000 square miles, and now to a mere 1,250.

From that day on the dispossessed Nez Perces would call the Treaty of 1863 the "Steal" or "Thief" Treaty. Young Chief Joseph would describe it eloquently:

"Suppose a white man should come to me and say, 'Joseph, I like your horses, and I want to buy them.' I say to him, 'No, my horses suit me, I will not sell them.' Then he goes to my neighbor and says to him: 'Joseph has some good horses. I want to buy them, but he refuses to sell.' My neighbor answers, 'Pay me the money, and I will sell you Joseph's horses.' The white man returns to me, and says, 'Joseph, I have bought your horses and you must let me have them.' If we sold our lands to the Government, this is the way they were bought."[8]

Upon his return to the Wallowa country Old Chief Joseph is said to have torn up his Bible and a copy of the 1863 Treaty. As markers delineating

Courtesy Luna House Historical Society
Lewiston, Idaho

Jane and Pete Types and baby

the western boundary of his territory, he set poles ten inches thick and ten feet long in cairns of rock along the summit of Minam grade, telling a white man through an interpreter that they showed "where his line was to the Wallowa country."

Known as "Old Joseph's Deadline" to early settlers in the area, the markers were maintained by the Nez Perces and seen, if not respected, by the whites for a number of years.[9] As his eyesight and strength failed, Old Joseph came to depend

7. Haines, *Red Eagles*, p. 163; *Oregon Adjutant General's Report*, 1866, p. 18.
8. Helen Addison Howard and Dan L. McGrath, *War Chief Joseph* (Caxton Printers, 1946), p. 74; Chief Joseph, "An Indian's Views of Indian Affairs," *North American Review*, April 1879, pp. 417–418.
9. Grace Bartlett, *The Wallowa Country, 1867–1877* (Enterprise, Oreg., 1976), p. 3. Agent John Monteith, in a letter written August 27, 1872, now in the Lapwai Agency files, claimed that Old Joseph destroyed his Bible and a copy of the treaty. He probably did have a copy of the book of Matthew as translated by Spalding and his assistants, but it is to be doubted that he possessed a copy of the treaty. Other writers of the day put it more symbolically when they say, "He turned back to Egypt," rejecting the white man's religion and never trusting his word again.

Photo by A. Zeno Shindler, Washington, D.C., 1868   *Courtesy Smithsonian Institution*
Kalkalshuatash, also called Jason. A signer of the Treaty of 1868,
Washington, D.C., along with Lawyer and Timothy.

more and more on his son to take responsibility as the leader of his people. Young Joseph later told a writer that his father sent for him just before he died in 1871, took his hand, and admonished him:

"When I am gone, think of your country. You are the chief of these people. They look to you to guide them. Always remember that your father never sold his country. You must stop your ears whenever you are asked to sign a treaty selling your home. A few years more, and white men will be all around you. They have their eyes on this land. My son, never forget my dying words. This country holds your father's body. Never sell the bones of your father and mother."[10]

Meanwhile, the Nez Perces living within the boundaries of the new reservation were being treated no better than the Indians who had refused

to sign the treaty. Torn apart by the Civil War, the federal government took no action on the new treaty, failed to honor most of the terms of the 1855 Treaty, made inadequate appropriations of funds, and paid no heed to the way the money that was appropriated was spent.

"The credit of the Indian Department is utterly destroyed," an investigator reported in 1867, "and the tribe greatly disaffected toward the government, and I think it safe to assert that there is no portion of the United States in which Indian affairs are in so chaotic and disorganized a state as in Idaho Territory."

As a matter of fact, since its creation March 3, 1863, Idaho Territory as a whole had been so chaotic and disorganized that its citizens seldom knew who or where its governor was. Since by law he was also Superintendent of Indian Affairs for the Territory, with the Nez Perce Indian Agent required to channel all correspondence, reports, and requests for funds through him, this doubled the state of chaos. In the summer of 1865, for example, the wildly eccentric Governor Caleb Lyon (who had left Lewiston supposedly headed for Boise but instead went to Portland, San Francisco, New York, and Washington) "has not been heard of in Idaho since early last spring."

When he finally did return to Idaho he bragged that he had been given $50,000 in cash by the federal government with which to "do good" for the Indians. Though he made a trip to Lapwai and promised to build churches and schools for the Nez Perces, nothing of importance was done. Of Governor Lyon, the investigator wrote:

"His absence from his post, however, seems to entail no embarrassment upon the management of Indian affairs. When present, he conducted them with an ignorance unparalleled, and a disregard of the rights and wants of the Indians, and of the laws regulating intercourse with them, deserving the severest rebuke . . .

"I have examined invoices and purchases made by the department or its agents in eastern cities, where the prices charged were from fifty to one hundred percent above the market value of good articles. Upon examination of the goods I have found them, as a general thing, worthless and deficient in quantity. . . . Many articles are purchased which would be utterly useless to the Indians . . . in one case forty dozen pairs of elastic garters were sent out to a tribe in which there was not a single pair of stockings."[11]

10. Howard and McGrath, *War Chief Joseph*, p. 74; *North American Review*, April 1879, p. 419.

11. Haines, *Red Eagles*, pp. 168–169; U.S., Department of the Interior, Records of the Bureau of Indian Affairs, *Special Report, Indian Commission, 1867, pp. 10–12.*

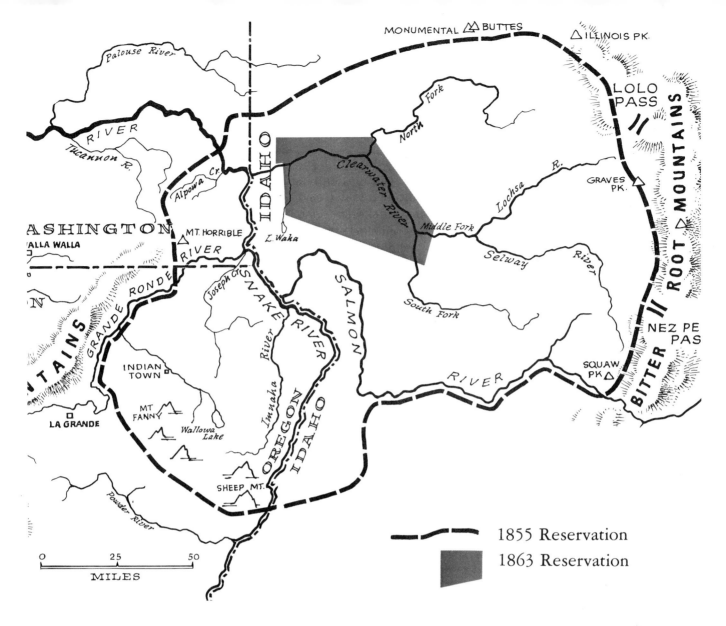

MONUMENTAL BUTTES   ILLINOIS PK.

1855 Reservation

1863 Reservation

Though James O'Neill, agent at Lapwai between 1864 and 1868, was called "one of the better agents" by the federal investigator, he managed to abscond with $10,000 in Nez Perce funds, most of it designated as salaries for teachers, when there were no schools in existence.[12] Compared to Governor Caleb Lyon, who had been summoned East for an accounting of the Indian funds entrusted to him, he was a small-time swindler and a man of little imagination.

Arriving in Washington, D.C., Governor Lyon complained to police that he had been robbed of $47,000 in greenbacks. The cash was being carried on his person, he said, in a money belt secured around his waist under his clothes. It was surreptitiously taken from his belt as he slept on the train, he said, though the belt itself had not been disturbed. When asked if this had been government money, he replied with his usual bold vagueness: "I can account for every dollar I spent in Idaho."[13]

For some obscure reason he was never required to do so, though eventually the monies intended for the Indians were replaced by the government.

In 1867 the treaty reducing the size of the reservation and placing it totally within the borders of Idaho Territory was ratified by the Senate and signed by President Andrew Johnson. The following year, Lawyer, Timothy, Jason, and U-ute-sin-male-cun journeyed to Washington, D.C., where they conferred with federal officials, were feted and photographed, and signed three amendments to the 1863 Treaty having to do with the allotment of lands not needed by the military

12. McWhorter, *Hear Me*, p. 111; U.S., Congress, *House Executive Document No.198*, 42d Cong., 2d sess., 1872, p. 3. McWhorter says that O'Neill acknowledged his fraudulent activities when investigated.

13. *Idaho Statesman*, Dec. 20, 1866.

From a collection of Dennis Williams   *Courtesy Nez Perce National Historic Park*
                                                          National Park Service

The 1868 Treaty delegation to Washington. Left to Right: un-known white man, Timothy, Robert Newell, Lawyer, unknown white man, Jason, unknown white man.

post or agency, the protection of timber on the reservation, and the payment of funds due the schools.[14]

Following the investigation of corruption in the Indian Bureau by Oregon Senator James Nesmith, Congress attempted to correct it by turning administration of the reservation over to the military. This worked a little better, but ere long alcoholic army officers, crooked sutlers, and conniving contractors learned to siphon off funds intended for the Indians just as efficiently as the civilian agents had done. Finally, under the administration of Pres-ident Grant, the federal government gave in to a long-standing plea by humanitarians: Let churches administer the reservations. One by one, reserves across the country were parcelled out to religious groups.

At first the Nez Perces were scheduled to be put under Catholic control — a proposal that brought such an outcry from the Protestants that the plan was hastily changed. The Umatilla Reservation, further west, would be turned over to the Catholics. The Nez Perce Reservation would become the responsibility of the Presbyterians.

Since 1847 Henry Spalding had taught school, preached, farmed, and briefly prospected for gold in the Willamette Valley, the Walla Walla area, and the Clearwater country. Still strong and vigorous, though in his late sixties, and eager to return to the people he loved, he applied for an appointment. He was passed over as agent in favor of a younger man from the Willamette Valley — John B. Monteith.

But much to the delight of Spalding's Nez Perce converts and longtime friends, he was given a government post as superintendent of instruction of the reservation and as Presbyterian minister to the tribe.

14. McWhorter, *Hear Me,* pp. 111–113. McWhorter repeats the story told by some of the Nez Perces that U-ute-sin-male-cun was murdered by the whites because he would not sign the amended treaty in Washington. In a footnote, the editor, Ruth Bordin, says she has found no verification for this story. Other accounts say the chief died of pneumonia.

CHAPTER TWENTY-ONE

HENRY SPALDING COMES HOME: 1869–1874

I have ever desired to return, have never felt at home among the whites. They have sent every year for me to return, have begged to have the mission renewed.

— Henry Spalding, October 1857

EVER SINCE the loyal Nez Perces had escorted the missionary and his family from Lapwai to Fort Walla Walla in December 1847, life had been difficult for the Spaldings. Spiritually willing to bear what must be borne, Eliza had suffered so great a shock that her flesh could no longer respond. Used to the dry, sunny air of Lapwai, she found the gray, rainy weather of the Willamette Valley so depressing and unhealthful that on August 5, 1850, she wrote her sister Lorena:

"I have suffered very much with sickness since we left the Nez Perce country. I think this climate is very unfavorable for diseased lungs & I cannot but feel that I shall not long survive our dear departed ones."[1]

Henry, too, was depressed. Though he organized a church, preached, and taught school, he made only a meager living. During the eleven years he had spent at Lapwai, he had built a comfortable home, raised a substantial garden, built up a herd of cattle, sheep, and swine, constructed a gristmill, and accumulated assets valued at $10,000 — a quite substantial sum for that day.

All that had been left behind. He must start again from scratch — this time without the help of the American Board and the friendly Nez Perces. The recent gold strikes in California had drained the Willamette Valley of cheap labor and abundant food supplies. While his wages for teaching and preaching were only $1 or $2 a day, carpenters, mechanics, and other skilled craftsmen were demanding and getting $5 to $15 a day for their services. In order to obtain a doctor from a distant town to treat his ill wife, Spalding had to pay the exorbitant fee of $100.

"I make my school furnish our bread, meat, sugar," he wrote bleakly, July 20, 1850. "When our present supply of clothing, sent from friends mostly, is expended. I trust the Lord will have a new supply in readiness."[2]

Financially in dire straits and deeply concerned over his wife's failing health, Spalding compounded his personal problems by getting involved in a bitter feud with the Catholics over their role in the Whitman Massacre. As noted earlier, while the hostages were being held by the Cayuses he had written Bishop Blanchet a letter, which included the plea: "By all means keep quiet, and send no war reports; send nothing but proposals for peace."

Learning that the letter had been given to the *Oregon Spectator,* which published it, Spalding's volatile temper flared. In his view this had been a deliberate attempt on the part of the Catholics to humble him and deride the efforts his church had made to Christianize the Nez Perces. On February 8, 1848, he wrote a long, bitter letter to the *Spectator,* explaining his own actions and accusing the Catholics of having deliberately humiliated him.

"The Indians had declared that the Protestants should be murdered, but the Catholics spared. Was it unchristian to ask my life at their hands.?"[3]

The *Spectator* refused to publish the letter, but Spalding had no difficulty finding another publication that would print it. In fact, he was encouraged

1. Drury, *Spalding,* p. 359.
2. Ibid., p. 354.
3. Ibid.

Photographer and date are not recorded but the photo probably was taken during Spalding's trip east in 1871   *Courtesy Smithsonian Institution*

Henry Harmon Spalding

to write a whole series of letters for the *Oregon American and Evangelistic Unionist* excoriating the Catholics. In one of these Spalding accused Bishop Blanchet of boasting:

"Behold, ye inhabitants of Oregon, especially ye adherents of the Catholic church, how speedily and complete is my victory. Arrived but yesterday, today you see a missionary of the heretics, who has been eleven years in the country, at my feet, begging his life . . ."

Pointing out that the priests had not been harmed by the Cayuses, that Father Brouillet had baptized members of the families of the Indian murderers the day after the killings, and that the Catholics had been anxious to take over Waiilatpu — Spalding did not find it in the least illogical to conclude that the priest had incited the Indians to commit the massacre.[4]

What he omitted, of course, was that the Cayuse vengeance had been taken against the local *tewat,* Dr. Whitman, in accordance with a long-standing custom. Nor did he mention the fact that Father Brouillet had supervised burying the victims of the massacre and had done all he could to help the survivors. In all probability his giving final rites to the dying Indian children had contributed toward calming their lust for revenge. As for the Catholics wanting Waiilatpu, it was common knowledge that on several occasions Marcus Whitman had considered selling the mission facilities to the Methodists or some other religious group.

Stung by Spalding's vitrolic accusations, Father J. B. A. Brouillet responded by writing a series of articles defending the actions of the church in general and himself in particular. Published first in papers and later in pamphlets, these widely circulated justifications of Catholic actions soon left the realm of documented fact and became as biased and untruthful as Spalding's own diatribes.

Even as the controversy raged, Eliza Spalding gave up her long fight against physical frailty and died January 9, 1851. She was forty-three years old. Of $42.51 that Spalding spent for her tombstone, $23.70 was for the 948 letters engraved as an epitaph on the marker. Set off in a special sentence was the statement:

She always felt that the Jesuit Missionaries were the leading cause of the massacre.[5]

In an effort to get an objective report on the causes of the Indian wars which followed the

Courtesy Western History Collections,
University of Oklahoma Library

Two Nez Perce Indian girls. One is wearing a blouse decorated with elks teeth.

Whitman Massacre, the Commissioner for Indian Affairs sent a well-qualified journalist, J. Ross Browne, west in 1857 to investigate. Browne noted that one cause was the rivalry between religions.

"As little dependence can be placed upon the statement by one side as by the other," he wrote. "Instead of christianizing the Indians, these sects show a very bad example to them."

As an illustration of his point Browne attached a pamphlet written by Brouillet responding to Spalding's charges. Both the Browne report and the Brouillet pamphlet were published in the *Congressional Record* as an Executive Document.[6] It was several years before Spalding found out

4. Ibid., p. 356.
5. Clifford M. Drury, *First White Women over the Rockies,* vol.1 (Glendale, Calif.: Arthur H. Clark Co., 1963), pp. 232–233.
6. *House Executive Document No. 38.*

Photographer: W. H. Jackson

Courtesy Western History Collections,
University of Oklahoma Library

Indian encampment with skin lodges — also a few war shields. Nez Perce tribe. Locale: Yellowstone River near Shields River, Montana, about 1871.

about it. When he did he was outraged, for he felt such publication gave official government sanction to Brouillet's views. He began a series of lectures and writings aimed at proving his side of the case. Aided by influential members of the church and political figures back East (where the story of his mission to the Nez Perces, conflict with the Catholics, and the Whitman Massacre fascinated large audiences) he traveled to and spoke in Chicago, upstate New York, Boston, and Washington, D.C. During the course of these travels and lectures, the groundwork was laid for the "Marcus Whitman saved Oregon for the United States" legend. It was during this period that Spalding composed what became known as "The Indian Lament" — a speech supposedly made by one of the Nez Perce chiefs who had gone to St. Louis in search of the "Book of Heaven" in 1831.[7]

By December 1870 Henry Spalding had assembled a large collection of documents, testimonials, and letters. With the help of church officials and eastern politicians he was given a hearing with the Senate Committee on Indian Affairs in Washington, D.C., January 25, 1871. He regarded this day as the high point of his life. By then he had remarried, and he wrote his second wife a hasty note just before he left his room to go to the hearing:

"May God help your husband. In five minutes I appear before the Senate, where my case will be heard and this infamous outrage will be corrected."

As at most Senate hearings, the witness was treated courteously and listened to respectfully, and the documentation he had brought along was entered into the record with no judgment made. But Henry Spalding regarded the hearing as total vindication.

"Glory to God!" he wrote his wife. "Bless His Holy Name! Victory complete! The Senate has just ordered by a unanimous vote my manifesto printed and committed to the Committee on Indian Affairs."

Returning to the Pacific Northwest in the spring of 1871, Spalding and his wife went to Lapwai, where he began his duties as superintendent of instruction for the Néz Perces. But instead of a triumphant homecoming and a renewal of warm relationships with the Indians, he found the new agent, John Monteith, standing between him and the students.

Since he and Eliza long ago had translated hymns and the Gospel of St. Matthew into the Nez Perce tongue, Spalding wanted to use them for teaching purposes. Monteith insisted that modern textbooks written in English would be better learning aids. Spalding felt that preaching and religious conversion should be a part of the educational process. Monteith stubbornly maintained that the federal government was paying Spalding's salary as an educator, not a preacher.

For long months the acrimonious dispute between them went on. Finally, in the spring of 1873, a compromise agreeable to all parties was reached: Spalding would resign as superintendent of instruction for the Nez Perces, accept an appointment by the Presbyterian Board as Minister, and move sixty-five miles east to Kamiah, where a church would be built for him and the Indians. Monteith would remain at Lapwai in charge of the agency and the school.

7. See Chapter 6, footnote No. 8, p. 50.

Courtesy Western History Collections,
University of Oklahoma Library

This woman was said to be the first Christian convert among the Umatilla Indians. She was baptized by Henry Spalding.

Each man solemnly pledged not to interfere with the work of the other.[8]

At long last Spalding was free to carry on the work he loved, among the people to whom he had dedicated his life. Secure now with a house, a church, a congregation, and a salary of $1,400 a year, he initiated a religious revival among the Nez Perces more intense and widespread than ever had been known before. His old friend, Chief Lawyer, finally joined the church. An equally old friend, Chief Tack-en-su-a-tis, "Rotten Belly," who for many years had been hostile toward him, mellowed and became a church member, too.

Following each sermon, Nez Perces by the dozens came forward, affirmed their faith, and were baptized. Men with two or more wives "put aside" all their wives but one — or at least pretended to. The probably apocryphal story is told that one old chief, after hearing Spalding say he must put his second wife aside, nodded solemnly and said: "I'll do it — but you tell her."

Invitations to come and hold revivals in their country were sent to Henry Spalding from bands of Indians living outside the Nez Perce Reservation. Invariably he responded, for he loved nothing more than spreading the gospel as an itinerating minister. In his seventieth year he rode fifteen hundred miles during the summer months. Traveling as far afield as the Yakima and Spokane country, he made converts wherever he went, baptizing some twelve hundred Indians during the final years of his life.

Since his eyesight was growing dim and his memory was failing, the criticism made by Agent John Monteith — that Spalding baptized the same convert several times and united in holy wedlock the same couple more than once — no doubt was true. But such nit-picking could not detract from the impressive results of his labors, so far as building church membership among the Indians was concerned.

He remained vigorous to the end. At the age of seventy-one, while chopping firewood, he fell backward off a log drift from a height of eight feet, breaking a rib and injuring himself internally. In May 1874, in bed and ailing, he received a letter from a Cayuse chief named Um-ha-wal-ish, which touched him deeply:

"I write to inform you of our situation and make a request," the chief said. "Many years ago the Martyr Whitman and Father Spalding preached Gospel to us and taught us how to worship God and hope for salvation through our Lord Jesus Christ. We have never forgotten these men nor the doctrine they taught us, though we have had no teacher for many years.

The Catholics have charge of our Reservation, but some of us can never receive their doctrines, nor adopt their practices. Myself with about twenty others are now awaiting for Protestant Baptism, and a respectable minority of our tribe are Protestant in feeling and sentiment.

"We entreat you therefore to send a teacher and minister of the Gospel who may live as near as possible, and visit and preach us. . . . Send him soon for we are hungry and starving for the true bread of life."

When Spalding replied that he was not able to travel but would be pleased to baptize the chief, Um-ha-wal-ish and his wife made the 210-mile ride to Kamiah. Having long since run out of biblical names to give Christianized Indians, Spalding for

8. Drury, *Spalding*, p. 409.

Photo by Waible Patton, Pendleton, Oregon
Molly Minthorne who lived on the Umatilla Reservation. The photographer says that she was blind when the photo was taken and was over 100 years old. Here she displays some of her beadwork made when she could see.

"The baptismal service was held in Spalding's home," an observer wrote. "He was so infirm that he had to be held up in bed so that he could apply the baptismal water to the head of the kneeling chief. As he did so, he said feebly: 'I baptize you Marcus Whitman, in the name of the Father, the Son, and the Holy Ghost.'

"Those present knew that he intended to give the baptismal name of Narcissa Whitman to the wife of the chief. But when she stepped forward, he found himself unable to proceed with the service. So she was baptized by one of Spalding's assistants. Now Marcus and Narcissa Whitman lived once again among the Cayuse."[9]

Hearing that Spalding was gravely ill, ageless Timothy, his first convert, came to see him. According to Mrs. Spalding, before the elderly Nez Perce left he said:

"You are my great interpreter. You was sent by God to me and to this people, to teach us life, the word of God. You are going first. God only is good and great. Jesus alone gives life. Now don't be concerned. I will never turn back, my wife will never turn back, this people will never turn back."[10]

As the end neared Spalding expressed a desire to be taken to Lapwai, even though it was not certain he would survive the trip. Placed on a cot in a farm wagon, which was driven by easy stages the sixty-five miles down the Clearwater, he was given a room in one of the government buildings and was cared for by the army physician assigned to the post.

On August 3, 1874, he died. He was buried close by the mission he had built so long ago. Some years later the remains of Eliza Spalding were transferred from the Willamette Valley to a grave beside him.

The tombstone bearing the anti-Catholic inscription was buried with her.[11]

9. Ibid., p. 415; Spalding-Lowrie Correspondence, May 11, 1874, ed. Clifford M. Drury, *Journal of the Department of History, Presbyterian Church,* vol. 20, May-June-September 1942.

10. Drury, *Spalding,* p. 415.

11. Drury, *First White Women,* p. 233.

the past several years had used names of his own family and friends. Ill as he was, Spalding knew these would be the last two Indians he would *ever* baptize. He had two good Christian names he had long been saving.

CHAPTER TWENTY-TWO

THE RELIGIOUS AGENT, JOHN B. MONTEITH: 1871–1876

*They will teach us to quarrel about God, as the
Catholics and Protestants do on the Nez Perce reservation. We do not want to learn that. We may
quarrel with men sometimes about things on this
earth, but we never quarrel about God.*
— Chief Joseph to the Indian
Commissioners, 1873

PRIOR TO the appointment of John Monteith, February 8, 1871, the Nez Perces had had nine agents in the fifteen years that had passed since the signing of the 1855 Treaty. Of these, only two men — William Craig and Robert Newell — spoke the Nez Perce tongue and understood the Indian way of life. In fact, Craig, though appointed by Governor Stevens to represent the Nez Perces, never was listed as agent by the federal government and received little if any compensation for his services. Suffering a stroke in 1869, Craig died at the age of sixty-two, leaving a son and three daughters — plus a namesakes a town, Craigmont, and a massive height of land overlooking the lower Salmon River, Craig's Mountain.

Once it had been decided to assign the Nez Perce reserve to the Presbyterians, the board of that church nominated John B. Monteith, whose father, William J. Monteith, was a Presbyterian minister in the Willamette Valley. Spalding raised no objection. In fact, he said, the young man was "a good choice."[1]

When Agent Monteith appointed Spalding superintendent of instruction for the Nez Perces at a salary of $1,200 a year and the Presbyterian Board appointed him minister for the tribe at no pay, Spalding was pleased, for his position among the Indians now seemed secure. But after he arrived at Lapwai and took up his duties as teacher and minister, Spalding began to suspect that the agent had become a follower of the Catholic line. As interpreter, for example, he had hired Perrin

Whitman (in Spalding's view a known Catholic sympathizer) who drank. Two of Monteith's relatives had been employed in the Lapwai schools. His brother, Charles E. Monteith, had been appointed as an assistant to the agent.

"Worst of all, Monteith kept complete control of the schools in his own hands," writes Robert Whitner. "Spalding was allowed to visit and speak to the pupils as he wished and he could give religious instruction on Saturdays, but he was allowed to say nothing about how the schools were conducted."[2]

Truth was, Agent Monteith was in no way a Catholic sympathizer; in fact he soon proved himself to be just as firmly opposed to the Catholics as Spalding had been twenty-five years earlier. But he intended to surround himself with people he could trust, and he intended to be boss. If that offended the elderly, old-fashioned zealot who had established a mission among the Nez Perces thirty-five years ago, so be it.

In the summer of 1872 Henry Spalding accepted an appointment as Presbyterian minister and moved upriver to Kamiah. Now Monteith could concentrate on running the temporal affairs of the agency.

The term "settled" Indians was a relative one.

---

1. Robert Lee Whitner, "The Nomination of Nez Perce Agency Personnel by Denominational Groups, 1871–1879," (Master's thesis, Wash. State Coll., 1948), p. 45. Now a professor of history at Whitman College in Walla Walla, Dr. Whitner during his student days cataloged the McWhorter papers, which then were being placed in the Washington State University Library Archives.
2. Ibid., p. 47.

Archie B. Lawyer, Mark Williams and James Reuben with James B. Monteith, agent at the Nez Perce Reservation. The three Nez Perces were appointed as teachers to Chief Joseph's Nez Perces in Indian Territory, arriving there in December, 1878. Presumably this photograph was made before their departure from Idaho in 1878.

The nontreaty Indians living outside the boundaries of the reservation, as set up in 1863, migrated with the seasons, teaching their children the traditional skills they would need to survive. This did not include learning the three Rs in a white man's school.

Inside the boundaries of the reservation a small number of Nez Perces had built houses out of logs or lumber supplied by the sawmill, had fenced fields for gardens and grain, and had obtained domesticated animals that required daily, year-round care. But funds appropriated to build houses trickled down in such inadequate amounts that little progress could be made, and most of the Indians living on the reservation still dwelt in skin tepees. Having seen the advantage of raising a garden and a field of grain, some of them did till the soil. Some raised cattle. And almost all owned horses, which required little care and could be sold for cash to the whites when money was needed.

But skin tepees were light and mobile. Given a good excuse to pack up and go, even reasonably "settled" Nez Perce families frequently packed up and went. Where in time past the journey might have been across Lolo Pass to the buffalo country, now the trips were shorter: when the salmon ran, to fishing grounds at traditional spots on the Clearwater, Snake, and Salmon; when the roots were ready to be gathered, to Weippe, Camas Prairie, or the Palouse Hills; when berries ripened, to the high country.

Not only were these trips for food gathering; they were vacations, social occasions, and great fun. The women worked and gossiped. The men smoked, raced, and gambled. The boys played war games amd went skinny-dipping. At night around the campfires, there were dances, songs, and grandfather tales. What schoolroom could compete with that kind of life?

Granting that John Monteith was honest, well intentioned, and doing his best to carry out the dictates of his government and his church, his "modern" educational methods proved to be far less successful than Spalding's had been. Because the pay was low, the area remote, and living conditions primitive, teachers who came to Lapwai were employed more for their moral character than for their intellectual ability. They seldom stayed more than one school term, and they had as little understanding of the Nez Perce children they were attempting to educate as the children had of them.

Trap a ten-year-old boy who has been running wild outdoors all his life. Tell him he must sit in a stuffy room on a hard bench and get "educated" — whatever that means — instead of growing up to be a hunter-warrior like his father. Make him sit there hour after hour, day after day, listening to a prim, nervous, pasty-faced woman in a long dress saying words in a language he cannot understand. Because he is a well-behaved boy and in school under his parents' orders, after three months of regular attendance he begins to get a glimmer of what the teacher is talking about.

Then one winter afternoon he goes home and finds that, since the supply of firewood is scant near the spot where the family tepee is pitched, his father has decided to move the lodge five miles and pitch it in a sheltered valley fringed by a thick stand of trees. Why carry firewood every day when the tepee can be moved so easily? The move is made. The boy forgets to go to school for a week. Then his mother remembers and insists that he go. He protests. *Me walk ten miles every day? If I've got to go, the least you could do is give me a horse to ride.*

His father, who owns many horses, thinks this is a reasonable request and gives him a spirited, handsome paint pony, with the admonition that he not run it the last mile on a cold day.

Happily the boy sets out for school. On the way he meets a couple of friends, who also have ponies. What are the chances that they will ever reach the school? Probably two — slim and none.

In order to counteract this baneful influence on the youngsters, Monteith and the teachers decided that boarding schools were the only answer. Their writings show that they never considered the enormity of the crime they were committing against these children in attempting to destory every Indian precept they had been taught from birth and replacing them with strict, narrow, white values totally unsuited for Indian nature. In their view,

"The entire social structure of the tribe must be recast, councils and bands must be eliminated, the mild rule of the chiefs must give way to the benevolent despotism of the agent and the ministers of the church."[3]

Photo by William H. Jackson about 1871 in the Yellowstone country   *Courtesy Smithsonian Institution*

Looking Glass mounted on a painted war horse. He was killed in battle in 1877. Yellow Bull and Tom Hill considered him the greatest of all Nez Perce chiefs.

Benevolently despotic though John Monteith's method of educating the Nez Perce children was, it might have succeeded to some degree if it had not been for three disruptive elements:

1. The horse.
2. The Dreamer religion.
3. The nontreaty Nez Perces.

As Spanish priests had learned in the American Southwest two centuries earlier, a mounted Indian was a convert lost, preferring to ride to freedom rather than walk to salvation. More recently, Colonel Wright had proved that the quickest way to subdue an Indian was to set him afoot. Now Mon-

3. Haines, *Red Eagles,* p. 180.

teith was coming to realize that the availability of horses to the Nez Perce children, who literally learned to ride before they learned to walk, was the principal cause of truancy. Not only did the boys play hookey and go galloping around the countryside just for the fun of it; they loved to race their horses against one another. Which attracted a crowd. Which led to betting. Which brought in rowdies from off the reserve. Who brought bottles. Which led to drunkenness and fights . . .

Though he never expressed it in those words, Monteith would have agreed that whether or not the road to Hell was paved with good intentions, it certainly was filled with Nez Perce horses.

The second detriment to educating the Nez Perce children, in Monteith's view, was a new form of paganism called the Dreamer religion. Surfacing a few years after Governor Stevens had made treaties with the Indians east of the Cascades, the basic belief of the Dreamer cult was that, on some not-too-distant day in the future, all the Indians who ever lived would be reborn. When that happened, the Indians would have such overwhelming superiority in numbers that the whites would be forced to go back where they had come from. The country then would be as it had been in olden times. In order to feed such a vast number of Indians, all the wild game that had ever lived would be reborn, too, so that no one would ever go hungry.

Originator of the Dreamer religion was an upper Columbia River medicine man named Smowhala, whose small band, the Wanapums, refused to recognize Kamiakin as their chief and thus held that they were not bound by the 1855 Treaty. Whether Smowhala had been seriously wounded in a fight with Chief Moses, following which he had traveled to far southern lands for five years, or whether he had simply retired to a cave, dreamed the tenets of the new religion, and then come forth and revealed them, is not certain.[4]

But his basic commandment, *"The Earth is our Mother; we must not wound her breast with ploughs and hoes,"* held a great appeal to freedom-loving Indians. Why herd cattle, tend garden patches under a hot sun, or trade horses to the white man for a few pounds of flour and bacon, if olden times were returning? Why get educated, baptized, die, and go to the white man's stuffy Heaven, when on some not-too-distant day all of one's relatives and friends were going to rejoin you

Photo by Jane Gay   *Courtesy Idaho Historical Society*
Billy Williams, an early day Nez Perce Preacher

on earth? Why listen to the white man's talk, when he was about to go away forever?

To Monteith this was heresy of the highest order. Long hair, blankets, avoidance of work, a return to the old ways, and revival of all the myths and legends of the grandfather tales were directly opposed to his strict Presbyterian belief in hard work, faith in a single deity, and a settled way of life. In all probability the Dreamer religion did not play as important a role in the lives of the dissident Nez Perces as he thought. But it and its prophet, Smowhala, were convenient elements to blame.

The third — and sharpest — thorn in Monteith's side, so far as educating reservation Indians was concerned, was the nontreaty Nez Perces. Living along the lower Grande Ronde, Imnaha, and Salmon rivers and, in summer, in the higher Wallowa Valley, they persisted in visiting their relatives and friends on the reserve. Keeping those relatives and friends from going off the reservation and returning their visits was as impossible as damming a stream with a sieve.

4. Click Relander, *Drummers and Dreamers* (Caxton Printers, 1956), p. 35. Variations of the spelling of the prophet's name are as numerous as accounts of his life. Since Click Relander was a respected regional historian and writer, I have used his.

Few places on earth were as beautiful as Wallowa Lake in summertime. Lying at the base of a ten-thousand-foot range of mountains, the four-mile-long, two-mile-wide lake filled a void gouged by a glacier many years earlier. It was crystal clear and extremely deep, and its surface could change from mirrorlike smoothness to choppy roughness in a matter of minutes. According to Nez Perce legend, its depths contained a monster whose favorite morsel was a love-stricken maiden.

Crisscrossing the valley floor, which lay at the forty-five-hundred-foot level, were a number of streams up which salmon and steelhead ran in great numbers. Belly-high grass nourished thousands of beautiful, spirited Nez Perce horses. This was Chief Joseph's country, and he had promised his father, whose bones now lay in a grave near the juncture of the Lostine and Wallowa rivers, that he never would sell it to the white man.

Because of its altitude and short growing season, the Wallowa Valley was not good farming country. There was plenty of grass for cattle or horses six months of the year, but bitter cold and heavy snowfalls required that the animals be fed during the winter or driven to the lower valleys of the Imnaha or Grande Ronde, where the climate was milder. Before 1870 few white men had seen the region, which was well off the emigrant and prospector trails. Now a few ranchers were trickling in, their cattle sharing the grass with the horses of the Nez Perces, with plenty of room for all.

Hospitality was ingrained in the Nez Perces. When a band of reservation Indians visited relatives and friends in the Wallowa Valley, they were feted and fed. When an off-reservation band visited Lapwai or Kamiah, the hospitality was returned. Since the nontreaty Nez Perces had no milk cows, swine herds, garden patches, or grainfields to tie them down, many of them went to the buffalo country each year, turning the homebodies green with envy with tales of the fun they'd had beyond the mountains. Unable to stand such teasing, many of the reservation Indians became temporarily "unsettled" and joined in the travels.

Monteith resented the fact that he had no power over the nontreaty Indians. Even though they were self-sufficient and cost the government nothing, he felt they should be working for a living instead of roaming about the country as they pleased. Sooner or later he feared they would stir up trouble with the Blackfeet, Crow, or Sioux in the buffalo country, which would involve the whole tribe in a war. This became such an obsession with him that he asked the military commandant at Fort Lapwai to put patrols of soldiers on the trails, with orders to turn back all eastward-bound parties. When this request was refused, he declared that any Nez Perce family going to the buffalo country would forfeit its claim to whatever plot of land and improvements it owned on the reservation.

Since the "settled" chiefs no longer wanted to go to the buffalo country, they agreed to this ruling. And since the nontreaty Indians and those living in tepees had no plots of land or improvements, the ruling meant nothing to them.

The gold boom had waned, and white settlers were taking up claims just outside the borders of the reservation, building cabins, barns, and corrals and turning their cattle, sheep, and hogs loose to graze where they pleased. More often than not the herds crossed onto reservation land, where there was far more grass than the horses and cattle of the Indians could eat. Since there were no fences, white and Indian livestock mixed indiscriminately.

Monteith demanded that the boundaries be patrolled by the military to keep white cattle out. The military refused to undertake what obviously would be an unpopular duty. Monteith suggested that trespassing livestock be impounded and their owners fined. The Indian Bureau refused to approve such drastic measures. When he appealed to the whites to keep their stock off the reservation, they replied: "Build a fence." But there was no money for fences.

In an effort to protect their lands, the Indians undertook the tried-and-true remedy of burning off the grass along the boundaries as soon as it turned dry in midsummer, creating a scorched-earth barrier that the livestock of the whites could not cross. This worked, but it made the whites angry and caused them to accuse the Nez Perces of wasting good grass.

To the Indians, the marshy meadows where camas grew belonged to the Nez Perce tribe as a whole, whether on or off the reservation, with each family entitled to digging rights in a certain spot until its food needs were filled. Since the digging process during harvesttime spread the ripened seed pods and assured a good distribution of bulbs for the following year, the Nez Perces never decimated a camas ground. But when white farmers turned their hogs loose to root up young bulbs before the plants could go to seed, the grounds were ruined forever — which angered the Indians.

With no effective way to police the boundaries, white men cut timber on the reservation and hauled it away without fear of prosecution. Inns and stagecoach stations had been built along the main routes of travel, and their owners had been given permission to fence enough land to contain needed facilities. These now expanded far beyond their requirements, to take in hayfields, extensive pasture and farmlands, and water rights that legally belonged to the Indians. Funds appropriated to pay for improvements that were made off the reservation and to pay for the expense of moving nontreaty bands onto the reserve never were received by the Nez Perces for whom the money was meant.

Under the Homestead Act, Indians living off the reservation had the same right as whites to file and prove up on a piece of land. Few attempted to do so, for they did not understand the technicalities of the laws. When they did, their claims often were jumped and their improvements taken over by white men during their absences on trips to gather roots or catch fish. Faced with a choice of going to court, evicting the claim jumper by the use of force, or simply giving up and going elsewhere, the Indian usually gave up and left.

Between the years 1860 and 1877, Haines says, instances of violence between the races were noticeably one-sided; four whites were killed by the Nez Perces and thirty-three Indians by the whites.[5]

According to the federal government, the Wallowa country had been ceded to the United States under the terms of the 1863 Treaty; consequently, a survey party was sent into the region to set up markers and base lines during the late '60s, and the area was declared open for settlement. According to the Wallowa band of Nez Perces, their chiefs had ceded nothing. As soon as markers were set up and base-line stakes driven, the Indians tore them down or pulled them up. Apparently there was no great feeling of hostility between the whites and Indians during these squabbles, though in one instance a surveyor was said to have remained mounted and to have measured distances by counting the strides of his horse so that he might have both hands free to use his rifle if attacked. In another instance a surveyor angered an Indian by locating a reference point and driving a stake within the shelter of the Indian's tepee.[6]

A. C. Smith, the first white outsider to come to the Wallowa country in 1868, spoke the Nez Perce language and got along well with the Indians. When he arrived he found two Frenchmen, Charles LeVar and Louis Yabor, both of whom were married to Nez Perce women and living with the tribe. The men had been trappers, had married sisters, and had adopted the Indian way of life. After looking over the lush grass and abundant water in the Wallowa Valley, Smith decided to bring in a herd of cattle and encourage other white settlers to join him in this beautiful country. In 1871 the first contingent arrived.

"There was some question of how the Indians would receive them," local historian Grace Bartlett writes, "but not much fear, due to the attitude and actions of those with whom they had mingled up to then."[7]

For the last few years of his life Old Joseph was blind, riding with a child on the horse before him to guide it and be his "eyes." It is doubtful that he ever saw this group of white men, though he knew they would come and had warned Young Joseph against them. He certainly could not have realized how rapidly his prophecies would come true.

In August 1871 A. C. Smith filed a land claim. Others soon followed. On September 20 incorporation papers were signed for the Grande Ronde and Wallowa Wagon Road and Bridge Company with Smith, M. B. Rees, and Fred Shoemaker as principals. The new road and bridge company, with capital stock of $10,000,[8] planned to connect the route of the Oregon Trail, the stage road, and the settlements developing in eastern Oregon and Washington Territory. This would bring hundreds of settlers into the Wallowa country, regardless of Indian claims.

In October, Old Joseph died. Soon after his burial ceremony, which several white settlers attended on terms of perfect goodwill with the Indians, the Wallowa Nez Perces left the area, heading for their winter village along the lower Grande Ronde. This moving with the seasons from a high-altitude region of bitter cold and heavy snowfall to a low-altitude region of relative warmth and

5. Haines, *Red Eagles*, p. 199.

6. Bartlett, *Wallowa Country*, p. 5. The author of this well-written, well-researched book has spent a lifetime in the Wallowa region, has talked to many descendants of early settlers, and has had access to Indian as well as white sources. The picture she draws of relationships between the Nez Perces and the white settlers shows much less hostility between them than most accounts. It is, I believe, the true picture.

7. Ibid., p. 7.

8. Ibid., p. 9. *Enterprise* (Oreg.) *Record Chieftan*, April 23, 1914.

an abundance of grass for their livestock was traditional to the Nez Perces.

To white ranchers, such a seasonal move was the height of irresponsibility. When a white man settled on a piece of land, he moved there to stay. He built a well-chinked cabin and solid outbuildings in which his family and livestock would be snug and warm. If the climate were such that feed was needed during the winter for his cattle and horses, he broke land on which to raise grain and cut enough wild hay to carry his stock through the months when the valley floor was covered with snow.

This was the basic difference between the Indian and the white way of life: One adjusted to the seasons by moving and adapting; the other, by staying and preparing. In a country as big as the Wallowa, these differences in life-style need not be irreconcilable — so long as the nomadic Indian and the stay-at-home white man did not lay claim to the same piece of land.

If that should happen, there would be trouble.

by the summer of 1872 around sixty white settlers had ventured into the Wallowa country. When the Nez Perces returned to the high country from their winter village and found the whites there, they protested mildly, saying they did not object to the whites hunting and fishing in the valley, but the whites must not build cabins, bring in herds, or cut hay. In reply the whites pointed out that the Nez Perce tribal leaders had signed a treaty ceding the region to the federal government, which had declared it open for settlement.

For some years it had been the custom of the Indians and whites in the Grande Ronde country and adjacent areas to celebrate the Fourth of July together, Grace Bartlett says, so in true democratic fashion the leaders of both races chose that day, in 1872, to hold a council in which their differences would be discussed.

Speaking for the Nez Perces, Young Joseph said that his father never had signed away his people's rights to the Wallowa country, that it was the home of the band of which he now was chief, and that no white settlements or roads should be built. Speaking for his road and bridge company, A. C. Smith said that he understood the feelings of the Indians and that he would be happy to go to Lapwai and have a talk with the agent and chiefs there. In addition, it was agreed that a letter should be written to the officials in Washington, D.C., re-

questing that some person in authority be sent to Wallowa to "settle differences between Indians and settlers in regard to certain lands."[9]

One incident that could have led to trouble occurred when two white men — Turner and Turgit by name — came into the valley with two barrels of whiskey and attempted to sell it to the Indians. In short order, local white settlers arrested the two men

"and organized a simple court. After some talk, however, we turned them loose with the injunction that the sooner they made themselves scarce around the valley, the better they would fare. They left and were not seen again."[10]

In response to the councils and letters, Agent John Monteith visited the Wallowa country in late August 1872, talked to the Indians and the white settlers, and then wrote his appraisal of the situation to regional and national officials in the Bureau of Indian Affairs. At that time, N. A. Cornoyer was agent for the Umatilla Confederation, near Pendleton, Oregon. Since the Wallowa Valley was in Oregon, Monteith rightly felt that he should tell Cornoyer about the whiskey-selling incident and other Indian-settler squabbles, though the question of whose jurisdiction these occurrences fell under was murky.

In his letter to Cornoyer, Monteith named the whiskey sellers, who lived near the Umatilla Reservation, and the white men who had taken a keg of liquor from them and destroyed it. He offered to send his men and a couple of Indian witnesses if the agent would arrest the whiskey sellers and arrange for their trial, which would have to be held in Portland because this was a federal offense. How such a feat of legal legerdemain could be accomplished, he did not say, though he did express the opinion that the two white men ought to be sent to the penitentiary for their crimes.

Because he was "in a hurry to fix up matters as I had plenty to attend to at home," Monteith spent only two days in the Wallowa Valley. First he talked alone with Chief Joseph, then on August 23 he met with thirty white settlers and eighty Indians. While admitting that the Treaty of 1855 gave the Nez Perces "the right to hunt and fish on their old grounds and herd their stock on unoccupied lands," Monteith pointed out that another treaty

9. Bartlett, *Wallowa Country,* p. 7.
10. Ibid., p. 14.

had been made in 1863 which ceded still more of their lands. To this Joseph replied that his father never had traded off his country, never had received any payments, and repeatedly had said that he would not sell it. Furthermore,

"when he found out the whites were trying to get the Wallowa Valley he tore up the Treaty and his Testament."

In his letter to the Indian commissioner, Monteith made a comment that would have settled the problem once and for all if it had been heeded and acted upon:

"It is a great pity that the valley was ever opened for settlement. It is so high and cold that they can raise nothing but the hardiest kind of vegetables. One man told me that the wheat was frozen after it was in the milk. It is a fine grass country and raising stock is all that can be done to any advantage. It is the only fishery the Nez Perces have and they go there from all directions . . .

"If there is any way by which the Wallowa Valley could be kept for the Indians I would recommend that it be done. There is not one house in the valley as far as I could ascertain but some will be built this fall."[11]

Now there began a paper war of petitions, letters, and newspaper stories written by people who were not living in direct contact with the Wallowa Nez Perces. For example, on January 13, 1873, from La Grande, Oregon, sixty-five miles from Wallowa Lake, a group of eleven men wrote Agent John Monteith:

"We the undersigned and several others have taken claims in the upper or most exposed part of Wallowa Valley. We was ordered off by the Indians and by young Joseph and bro. [ther] who threatened to burn our houses, etc., etc. Now we wish to know if you consider it safe for us to take our families to our places in the spring.

"What protection can you offer? or what assurance can you give us that we will not be molested? Wishing to hear from you at your earliest convenience . . ."[12]

Monteith forwarded the petition to F. F. Walker, Commissioner of Indian Affairs in Washington, D.C., along with a covering letter in which he referred to his visit to the Wallowa country the previous August and expressed the concern he was feeling about the Modoc Indian War:

"Until the recent outbreak in Southern Oregon I had no fears of any difficulty with the 'non-treaty' bands of Nez Perces but under the circumstances I have advised the settlers to keep out of the Wallowa Valley until I have advice from your office. If the Indians in question

are to be kept out of the valley in order to avert difficulties force will have to be used."[13]

This appears to have been the first mention of the use of force by any of the parties involved. It is curious that it should come from an agent appointed by the Presbyterian church and that force be recommended as the only practical way "to avert difficulties."

In February the paper war was escalated when E. S. McComas of La Grande wrote Oregon Governor Leonard F. Grover a letter expressing his alarm at the threatening attitude of the Nez Perces and requesting that the governor ship 200 Springfield rifles to arm the settlers. Since Governor Grover was getting similar requests from other areas which *really* had Indian wars in progress, and since he had no rifles to spare, the 200 Springfields were not supplied.

A sampling of newspaper stories indicates that truth, as usual, was the first casualty of the conflict. On February 22 the La Grande *Mountain Sentinel* remarked: "We fear another Indian scare is about to transpire."

A Wallowa resident named Evans called on the editor of the *Sentinel* and told him that the Nez Perces had evinced hostility toward their former friend, A. C. Smith, who now was working with a crew building a bridge across the Wallowa River, saying that

"Joseph and his Nez Perces had stopped at the Smith bridge and had been very saucy and indicated a desire to cause trouble."[14]

On March 8, A. C. Smith refuted the Evans story, writing of the behavior of Joseph and the Nez Perces:

"Their conduct toward myself and party was not insolent as stated by Mr. Evans, but on the contrary was of the utmost sociable and friendly character; they remained with us about one hour, accepting an invitation to dine"[15]

Hearing that the Modocs had attacked and killed some of the commissioners who were at-

11. Ibid., p. 15.

12. Ibid., p. 20; U.S. Department of the Interior, Records of the Bureau of Indian Affairs, *Idaho Superintendency* (microfilm), 1873.

13. Ibid., p. 20.

14. Ibid., p. 22; *Blue Mountain Sentinel* (LaGrande, Oreg.), Feb. 22, 1873.

15. Bartlett, *Wallowa Country*, p. 23; *Sentinel,* March 8, 1873.

tempting to negotiate peace terms, the *Oregonian* made this scare comment, April 30, 1873:

"If Captain Jack [a Modoc chief] heads for the mountains, plenty of Snakes and Piutes and Joseph's band would join him. Isolated settlers and traders should be wary."[16]

After meeting in Lapwai with Monteith and the nontreaty Nez Perces March 27, 1873, Oregon Superintendent of Indian Affairs T. D. Odeneal made a report to Washington, D.C., that was favorable to Chief Joseph's cause. As a result, the government decided on a reasonable compromise under which a part of the Wallowa country would be set aside as an Indian reservation, with the government to appraise and pay for whatever improvements white settlers had made within its boundaries, and the rest of the country would be opened for settlement. Rumors of this decision reached the area about the time the Modoc War came to its bloody climax.

On April 19 McComas and his friends in the Grande Ronde Valley held a "protest meeting" and again petitioned Governor Grover to send them 200 rifles. Again, the governor had no rifles to spare.

On May 1, the *Oregonian* reported:

"The *Sentinel* learns that if the Nez Perces Chief Joseph's band makes their appearance in the Wallowa Valley, no matter what their bearing may be, the settlers intend to open hostilities with a view of making a quick settlement of the dispute."

Two weeks later the same paper quoted a letter allegedly written by a resident of the Wallowa area:

"Families are coming in every day and there is room for many more that want good homes. We are all going to stay and not leave on account of the Indians, and if the Government sees fit to give this valley to these greasy, dirty and impudent rascals, in less than 12 months there will not be an Indian to occupy it, the settlers will 'go for them.'"[17]

Although militia units were being formed in many eastern Oregon communities as protection against possible Indian uprisings, the leaders of the unit organized in the Wallowa country made it clear that they had no bloodthirsty intentions. On May 17 they requested that the *Sentinel* publish the following notice:

"Whereas, there have been reports circulated to the effect that we, the citizens of Wallowa Valley propose organizing for the purpose of committing criminal onslaught against peaceable Indians

Therefore be it
"Resolved by the Wallowa Volunteers, that we only propose protection to ourselves against the depredations of unfriendly Indians — and then, WAR TO THE KNIFE."[18]

A day later another Wallowa resident wrote:

"As regards the contemplated Indian troubles, I know nothing but hearsay, which is worth less than nothing. . . . I do not think there is much danger of the Indians committing any depredation, notwithstanding all that the Indian agents and superintendents can do to urge the Indians to break out. It is my honest opinion that a majority of the Indian agents steal the goods that the government justly allows red men and then encourages the Indians to murder the settlers."[19]

Though the editor of the *Sentinel* was urging from the safety of his office sixty-five miles away that the citizens of Wallowa drive Joseph and his band from the face of the earth, Superintendent Odeneal, with Monteith's concurrence, calmly recommended to the Secretary of Interior:

"that the band of Indians referred to be permitted to remain in said valley and occupy it during the summer and autumn, or for such times as the weather is suitable, according to their previous custom."

The secretary then ordered:

"that a proper description of said valley be obtained for the purpose of an executive order setting apart this valley for the exclusive use of said Indians, and that white settlers be advised that they are prohibited from entering or settling in said valley."[20]

In response to this sensible solution the editor of the *Sentinel* shrieked in print:

"Those of the people who have not heard the news in some other place giving the Wallowa valley to the Indians, will almost be struck dumb with the intelligence that such was the case. There have been many perfidious officials in Oregon, but the man Odeneal, Superintendent of Indian Affairs, stinks in the nostrils of every decent man east of the Cascades, for the dirty part he has acted in robbing the settlers of the Wallowa of their homes . . .
"We now propose that the whites be put on a reservation and closely guarded so that they may inflict no damage on the noble red men!"[21]

16. Bartlett, *Wallowa Country*, p. 25; *Oregonian* (Portland), April 30, 1873.
17. Bartlett, *Wallowa Country*, p. 26; *Oregonian*, May 15, 1873.
18. Bartlett, *Wallowa Country*, p. 27; *Sentinel*, May 31, 1873.
19. Bartlett, *Wallowa Country*, p. 27; *Sentinel*, May 31, 1873.
20. Bartlett, *Wallowa Country*, p. 29.
21. Ibid., p. 30.

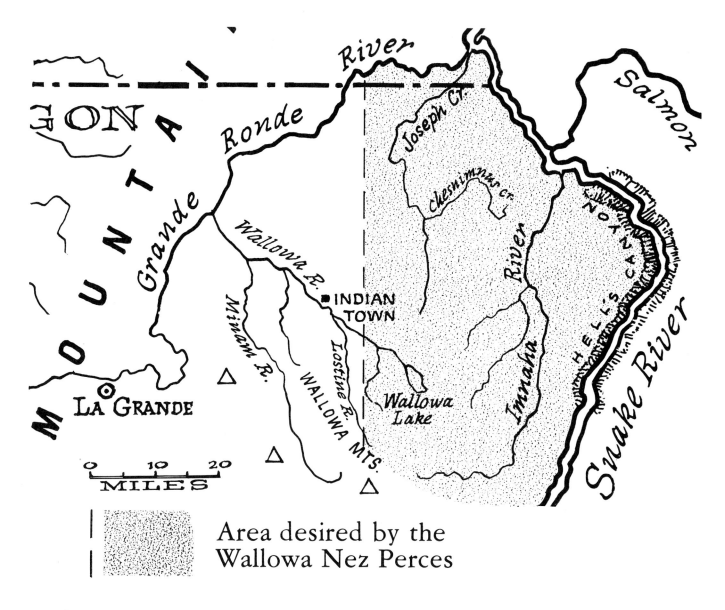

Area desired by the
Wallowa Nez Perces

Despite such biased newspaper ravings, peace prevailed between the white settlers and the Indians in the Wallowa country. In mid-June 1873 an appraising commission composed of Jasper Matheny, W. P. Berry, and Thomas H. Cox arrived from Salem, Oregon, and spent several weeks in the region guided by A. C. Smith.

"They found eighty-seven settlers," Grace Bartlett says. "They also found two incorporated companies there, the Wallowa Road and Bridge Co. and the Prairie Creek Ditch Co. The total improvements in the Wallowa amounted to $67,860, far more than anyone had expected."[22]

While the value of the improvements may have surprised the commissioners, purchasing them certainly would have been a small price to pay for permanent peace. As matters turned out, it was not the expense of establishing a reservation and extinguishing the citizens' claims that caused the later difficulty; it was the sheer stupidity of bureaucrats far removed from the area, who were not aware

that the terms "upper" and "lower" in the Wallowa country referred to altitude and the direction water flowed, not to the way a map was hung on the wall.

What the Department of Interior intended to do was divide the Wallowa region so the "roaming" Nez Perces would have a place to hunt, pitch their tepees, and graze their horses and cattle six months of the year, while the whites took claims and created permanent settlements in the rest of the area. The country most coveted by the Indians was the high, or upper, country, along the headwaters of the numerous streams flowing down out of the mountains, including Wallowa Lake. What the white settlers wanted were the broad, open, well-grassed valleys which lay along the lower reaches of the rivers.

Apparently the bureaucrats who examined a map of the Wallowa county knew that north was

22. Ibid.

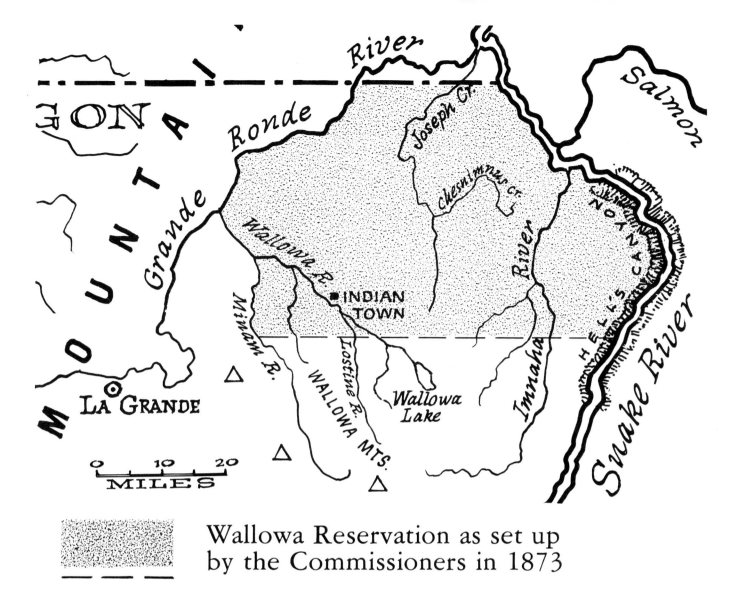

Wallowa Reservation as set up by the Commissioners in 1873

"up," south was "down" — and that was *all* they knew. When the lines were drawn awarding one part of the country to the Indians and the other part to the whites, the lands granted were exactly the reversed of what they should have been.

The decision had been made and the Executive Order signed even before the appraising commission had completed its work, with a warning being sent to Wallowa that no surveys or settlements were to be permitted on lands set aside for the reservation. Correcting a bureaucratic error, once it had been fed into the governmental process, proved to be as impossible as checking an avalanche with a broom. The reaction of the concerned parties was complete bewilderment.

"Why was this done?" Grace Bartlett asks. "Why give the Indians the lower valley with its many established homesteads and its access to the rest of Union County via the wagon road and Mr. Smith's bridge? Why give the settlers the upper valley with its relatively few homesteads, plus Wallowa Lake, which meant so much to the Indians, throwing in as well the mountains and the ancient Indian trails leading to Nez Perce homelands in Idaho and Washington?"[23]

Whatever the reason — and there was none that made sense — the Nez Perces and the settlers might have been able to adapt and make adjustment to the Executive Order if it had been put into effect within a reasonable period of time. It was not. Instead, the rights of the settlers to be reimbursed for improvements made on claims within the newly designated reservation and the rights of the Nez Perces to regard this reserve as their home were left in limbo, with no one knowing where he stood.

Despite the verbal and written ravings being uttered and published outside the area, nothing of importance happened to change the peaceful rela-

23. Ibid., p. 34.

tionship between the Nez Perces and the white in-habitants of the Wallowa country from late 1873 to mid-1876. Since 1874 was an election year, candidates for office made glowing promises to "open the Willowa [sic] Valley for settlement," though they could not even spell its name properly, let alone define its boundaries or delineate which were to be white or Indian lands. Agent Monteith continued to put pressure on Chief Joseph to choose a spot in the Wallowa country as a year-round residence for his people; Joseph continued to resist that pressure, quite sensibly preferring to spend the six colder months in the mild climate of the lower Grande Ronde, the six warmer months in the delightfully cool high country adjacent to Wallowa Lake.

Writing to the Indian Bureau in Washington, D.C., Monteith indicated that his patience with Joseph was wearing thin.

"About one year ago the Wallowa Valley was given back to him and his band. I told him at that time unless he and his people were willing to take their farms in said valley and settle down and go to work I was of the opinion that they would not be allowed to keep the valley. . . . Still, no heed has been given to my advice in this respect. They have spent part of their time in the valley and the balance on the Snake River or roaming over the country.

"The only thing that can be done with these Indians is to compel them to remain in one place or the other and to accomplish this force will be necessary."[24]

Though Monteith and the reservation Nez Perces certainly knew better, it was a common misconception among the whites living in the area that the federal government was supporting the Indians with regular handouts of food, clothing, and money. Such was not the case. What precious few dollars were spent by the government usually went to white contractors to build fences, mills, schools, and other improvements, with now and then a meager issue of blankets and clothes.

"If any of the Indians received disbursements from Monteith, it was done secretly or was not reported," Robert Whitner writes, "for there is no record that any such payments were made at any time during the period concerned in this study. In 1877, for example, 90% of the total subsistence of the tribe was obtained through civilized pursuits (farming and livestock raising), the remainder from such traditional occupations as hunting, fishing, and root-gathering. No issue of rations or payment of cash annuities was reported."[25]

This being the case, the only thing the Wallowa Nez Perces could hope to gain from settling down and living on a designated reservation year-around was the eventual building of a few fences, barns, and houses, and perhaps a church and a school if and when funds were appropriated for these purposes. But since their skin tepees were portable and their livestock could be moved from the high country to the low country with the seasons, why bother with "settling" anywhere? As Sitting Bull is reputed to have said at about this time: "God made me an Indian; but he did not make me a reservation Indian."

With the cattle and horses of Indians and whites grazing at will over this grassy valley, where fences were few and boundaries uncertain, it was inevitable that disputes over livestock should occur now and then. In the summer of 1874 the Oregonian reported that an Indian and a white man had exchanged shots, the only casualty being the white man's horse. Regarding this — or perhaps another — fracas, Monteith wrote:

"My informant says that both Indians and whites had their guns ready to commence firing but through interposition of one white man the settlers were prevented from firing. The Indians would not fire first."[26]

After conferring with the military commander of the district, Monteith requested that contingents of troops be stationed during the summer both at Weippe Prairie, where many Nez Perce families went to dig camas, and in the Wallowa country, where the Umatilla Confederation tribes as well as the Nez Perces went to gather salmon and redfish.[27] Staying from early summer until the Indians left the high country in mid-October, the troops served the dual purpose of reassuring the whites and protecting the Indians from the sale of liquor.

"With the exception of two cases, I found that all the settlers I visited were on friendly terms with the Indians and have had no trouble," wrote Lieutenant Thomas Garvey. "The two cases referred to were Mr. McNull

24. Ibid., p. 37; Monteith to Smith, April 28, 1874.

25. Whitner, "Nomination of Nez Perce Agency Personnel," p. 69.

26. Bartlett, Wallowa Country, p. 31; Oregonian, July 20, 1874; Idaho Superintendency, 1874.

27. Redfish were a member of the salmon family prized for their tastiness — what we call sockeye salmon today. Spawning in the gravel stream beds above Wallowa Lake in late August and early September, their normally silver-colored bodies turned a brilliant orange red during the spawning season, thus their name. Because of the high dam built at the lower end of the lake in about 1890, the sockeye runs ended years ago; however, a variant of the fish called "kokanee" or "yank" still exists in the lake and spawns in the stream beds above it, though it is a much smaller fish.

and Mr. Brown, who complained that the Indians allowed their horses to trespass and graze their land. Mr. McNull caught up some of the Indians' stallions and altered them in retaliation. He claims that he done this to prevent his mares from breeding such inferior stock as the Indian ponies. Neither of these men have their places fenced."[28]

"So far as I could discover, from the most careful attention, there is no cause to apprehend any present difficulty with these Indians," another officer wrote. "The settlers generally appear to wish to deal justly by the Indians, and I have heard a majority of the former express the opinion that while that course is pursued they have no fear of hostile acts on the part of the latter."

However, he warned prophetically:

"Should Government decide against locating an Indian reservation there, and order the Indians to leave or remain away, I respectfully suggest that timely and deliberate preparation should be made to enforce that order, and protect the white inhabitants from the rage which probably might inspire the Indians under disappointment in being deprived of what they highly value and apparently consider as justly theirs."[29]

Meanwhile, back in Washington, D.C., the government was changing its mind again. Unable to carry out the Executive Order issued in 1873 (to establish a modest-sized reserve for the Nez Perces in the Wallowa country, pay a paltry $67,800 for the settlers' claims, and open the rest of the region for settlement) Congress gave in to pressure from Oregon politicians. On June 10, 1875, the earlier order was revoked by President Grant, the plan to establish a reservation was cancelled, and the entire area was opened to settlement.

When Agent Monteith heard about the reopening order he immediately requested that troops be sent into the valley to act in case of conflict between the whites and the Indians, who usually arrived in late July. In response, two companies of cavalry under Captain S. G. Whipple were dispatched from Fort Walla Walla, reaching the Wallowa July 29. Though Chief Joseph and the main band of nontreaty Nez Perces had not yet arrived, Captain Whipple reported that Ollokot, Joseph's younger brother, had visited the valley late in June.

"and that he appeared very friendly. Joseph is reported as saying his people were aware the valley was not to be reserved for the use of the Indians; that the white settlers would remain and others come but that the Indians would resort here as formerly and for the same purpose. This may be taken as an indication of amicable intentions on the part of the Indians."[30]

When Chief Joseph and forty-five lodges of his band arrived in mid-August, Captain Whipple held a council with them, stating that the troops were present as friends of both Indians and whites as long as each tried to do right, that the settlers generally had informed him that they did not object to the Indians coming to the valley if they would observe the laws and do no violence to persons or property.

"Joseph replied at considerable length acknowledging the justice of my requirements and promised observance," Whipple writes. "He and several other leading Indians spoke of the bitter disappointment to them that this Valley was thrown open to settlement after it had been for so long a time understood that it should be reserved to them; but that under the circumstances the Indians desired to share it with the white people and hoped they might do it in peace and harmony."[31]

Taking an informal census of the Wallowa country, Captain Whipple noted that 115 white men, women, and children lived there on a permanent basis, while between five and six hundred Indians were there for a few months each year.

By this time General Oliver Otis Howard, the Civil War hero who had lost his right arm during the battle of Fair Oaks, had become commander of the Department of the Columbia, with headquarters in Portland. Commenting on a report he had received from Captain Whipple, he was quick to take credit for peace and make a judgment that would prove to be as mistaken as most of his later ones.

"The troubles at Lapwai and at Wallowa Valley have not thus far resulted in bloodshed but it has been prevented by great carefulness and prevision on the part of Government agents.

"I think it is a great mistake to take from Joseph and his band of Nez Perce Indians that valley. The white people really do not want it. They wish to be bought out. I think gradually this valley will be abandoned by the white people, and possibly Congress can be induced to let these really peaceable Indians have this valley for their own."[32]

Despite General Howard's optimistic prediction, the white settlers did not abandon the Wallowa country; instead, they began to act as if the

---

28. Bartlett, *Wallowa Country*, p. 39. "McNull" probably should be "McNall," though which of the three members of that family (which will be mentioned later) is not clear.
29. Ibid., p. 39.
30. Ibid., p. 43.
31. Ibid.
32. Ibid., p. 45.

entire region belonged exclusively to them, which officially it did. The federal troops returned to Fort Walla Walla in early September. A month or so later Chief Joseph's band went to its winter village on the lower Grande Ronde. In late December some of the white ranchers decided to follow the example of the Nez Perces and winter their cattle on the dry, naturally cured grass of the low-lying Imnaha River valley rather than feed their livestock hand-cut hay. Banding together to make a drive, A. C. Smith and several other men found themselves in dispute with a group of Nez Perce stock raisers over the same piece of grassland.

After an argument, during which firearms were brandished but never used, Smith made a long, cold ride from the lower Imnaha to Union, Oregon, in the Grande Ronde Valley, where he

"layed the matter before Judge Brainard who at once telegraphed to Governor Grover the full particulars. The Governor telegraphed to General Howard, who immediately replied that he was sending two companies under Whipple to Union and asked if there was a military company in the Grande Ronde Valley."

Howard's office then telegraphed to Fort Walla Walla's commanding officer, saying:

"Brainard, County Judge, telegraphed from Union, Oregon, to Governor 28th instant substantially: 'Indians Wallowa have ordered settlers to take stock off range using weapons to enforce same. 1600 head of cattle and 100 horses now off Imnaha. Indians driven them into mountains — cannot subsist there. Citizens can protect themselves but patiently await military. Delay, destruction to stock. Prompt measures positively necessary. Joseph's band have 80 warriors. Governor urgently requests troops to protect settlers.' "[33]

When the actual facts of the situation are compared with Judge E. C. Brainard's telegraphed description, it must be said that his name bore no resemblance to the quality of his judgment. After several weeks of marching and countermarching by two companies of cavalry, which never got within one hundred miles of the scene of the dispute, it was brought to a peaceful conclusion over a pot of coffee without a shot being fired. Even the Indians had a laugh over the matter. Monteith wrote that Joseph

"and most of his band have been spending Christmas and New Years in the vicinity of the Agency attending feasts and having a good time generally. . . . All this trouble took place about one hundred miles from here."[34]

In late June 1876 real trouble did arise be-

tween whites and Indians following a dispute over strayed horses. The principals in it were a Nez Perce named Wil-lot-yah and two white men, A. B. Findley and Wells McNall. The flimsy pole fences erected by the settlers were no more of a barrier for keeping Indian horses out of grainfields and garden patches than they were for keeping settlers' calves and colts inside corrals, and the wandering of animals into areas where they were not wanted was a common and exasperating occurrence. A son of A. B. Findley, who was a neighbor of Wells McNall, later recalled:

"The temporary fence that my brothers had built did not prove to be very satisfactory, for the two calves, when turned out at night, often crawled under the poles and got into the grain; and some of the Indian ponies that belonged to the Indians that camped in Indian town [a summer Nez Perce village near the juncture of the Lostine with the Wallowa River] got in the habit of reaching over the fence to eat the tender grain inside the field and would often crush the fence down and get into the field. Plowing up the ground and fencing it up was objectionable to the Indians anyway, and they may have occasionally helped their horses to get into the grain fields.

"Wells McNall, who lived near my parents, had a better fence than they did, but the ponies got into his field also. He suspected that the Indians had helped them get into the field; so one morning he rounded them up and put them into his corral. When the Indians found them in the corral, they were very angry about it and accused Wells of trying to steal them. He, of course, had no such intention; he was only making it a little tough for the Indians to get their horses so that they would not repeat the offense. While the incident and the dispute over it did not amount to much, it seemed to leave a feeling of ill will on both sides."[35]

Truth was, the three male members of the McNall family — E. F. McNall, Oren McNall, and Wells McNall — stirred up more trouble in the Wallowa Valley with the Nez Perces than any other group of white settlers during that period. It was one of them who had penned up and castrated stallions owned by the Indians. They were rumored to have sold liquor to the Indians. Wells, in particular, was known to be quick-tempered and to have an intense dislike for Indians.

A. B. Findley, on the other hand, was an honest, conscientious, sensitive man, well liked and re-

33. Ibid., p. 47.
34. Ibid., p. 49; Haines, *Red Eagles*, p. 212.
35. Bartlett, *Wallowa Country*, p. 51; H. R. Findley, "Memoirs of Sarah Jane and A. B. Findley," *Oregon Historical Quarterly*, March 1939.

spected by the Indians who knew him, as well as by his white neighbors. One of those neighbors was Wells McNall.

On June 20, 1876, Findley discovered that some of his horses were missing. McNall, who was helping him with the summer work, rode with him in an attempt to track them down. Since white settlers shod their horses while Indians did not, it was no problem distinguishing hoofprints. The trail led north, over the low height of land separating the drainage of the Wallowa River from that of the Chesnimnus. On June 23 the two men followed that trail into the camp of a small group of Nez Perces who were hunting deer in the Whiskey Creek area.

"While searching for the horses," the *Mountain Sentinel* later reported, "they came onto an Indian camp, while its occupants were absent bringing in a number of deer they had killed. The Indians' arms were in the camp and the settlers not knowing whether the Indians were in a friendly mood or not concluded to take possession of the guns until they had a consultation with the Indians.

"In a short time, four or five Indians came to camp loaded with venison and were of course surprised to find their camp and arms in possession of the whites. A parley ensued and the talk was friendly, the Indians denying any knowledge of the lost horses. While this was taking place, a young warrior came up and, seeing his gun in McNall's possession, made a rush for the camp, seized his gun, and a struggle ensued.

"During the encounter, McNall fired, and, it is thought, shot the Indian through the leg. This seemed to enrage him beyond all reason, and his attempts to secure the gun were increased to a frenzy. McNall, who is a small but wiry man, had his hands full; and, becoming convinced that the Indian would secure his gun and being satisfied that he intended to use it, he called to Findley to shoot.

"Findley, realizing the situation, drew up his needle gun and fired, killing the Indian instantly. The other Indians at once beat a hasty retreat. McNall came to Union and stated the case as above given to Judge Brainard. Considerable excitement exists in the Wallowa among the settlers over the circumstances and at last account they were massing for mutual protection."[36]

Since the main band of Nez Perces had not yet arrived in the valley, "massing of the settlers" consisted only of a few of them spending the night at the McNall cabin, then riding down to the Indian camp next day to see what had happened. The Indians had gone, taking the body of the impetuous young hunter, Wil-lot-yah, with them for burial near their winter village. Ironically, two of the missing horses turned up near the Findley ranch a

couple of days later. Adding to the irony was the fact that A. B. Findley, a deeply religious man, was so stricken by what he had done that he offered to give himself up to the Nez Perces for trial and punishment under their laws. He was not permitted to do so by his white neighbors, who censured him not for the killing itself but for the fact that his act might incite the angry Indians to take revenge upon their households. Greatest irony of all was that the Nez Perces, knowing Findley to be a good man and their friend, never placed any blame on him for the killing, putting the fault where it rightfully belonged — on Wells McNall, who had seized the rifle of the young Nez Perce, grappled with him, cursed him, fired the first shot, and then called for Findley to kill him.

As he had done six months earlier, Judge Brainard acted with something less than decisive authority. In his behalf, it must be said that he was a druggist by trade, a parttime magistrate by appointment, and in a nebulous position insofar as jurisdiction, code of laws, and enforcement powers were concerned. There was not much he *could* do in an emergency except send a telegram, write a letter, or make a statement deploring the situation in the local newspaper.

In this case he chose to write Colonel Elmer Otis, commander at Fort Walla Walla:

"Dear Sir: More trouble in the Willowa [sic]. One Finley and McNall accuse the Indians of stealing horses . . . and have managed to kill one of the Joseph band . . .

"The settlers are sufficiently alarmed to mass in the valley. The killing took place yesterday. The two men are censured here. These are all the facts to the present. Will answer questions if required."[37]

Since contingents of troops had been sent into the Wallowa country during the two previous summers to make sure peace prevailed, it at first glance appears strange that Fort Walla Walla made no response to Judge Brainard's letter or that General Howard in Portland did not immediately react to Agent Monteith's appeal that soldiers be sent into the valley "to protect the Indians while fishing." But if at second glance it is noted that the date on which Wil-lot-yah was killed was June 23, 1876, and that two days later, June 25, 1876, the Custer Massacre took place on the Little Big Horn,

36. Bartlett, *Wallowa Country*, pp. 51–52; *Sentinel*, July 1, 1876.
37. Bartlett, *Wallowa Country*, p. 52; Brainard to Colonel Elmer Otis, June 24, 1876, U.S., National Archives, Old Military Records.

it is not difficult to understand why the death of a single Indian in a remote part of Oregon drew little attention from military leaders stunned over the loss of so many of their comrades. From that time on, the right of Indians to live off the reservation as free men would find few champions in the American military, press, and public.

In the Wallowa country, once Findley and McNall had been censured for acting rashly, apprehension of trouble from the Nez Perces soon wore off. Life went on as usual. In August the first boat ever built for the express purpose of seining redfish in Wallowa Lake was launched by a man named John McCall. It was reported that fish by the thousands were appearing in the lake. Having found a way to deplete in a single season a food resource that had nourished the Indian since time immemorial, John McCall and his friends gleefully boasted that they were using a seine eighteen feet deep and one hundred and fifty feet long and were literally hauling in redfish by the wagonload.

When bands of Nez Perces began to arrive in the valley that summer they were not as friendly as they had been in previous years. Instead of visiting the white settlers as before, they set up targets and did a lot of riding back and forth on their swift ponies, hanging under their necks and shooting at a full run. At night they frequently held war dances.

Toward the end of August, Chief Joseph arrived. By then Findley had become so conscience stricken over what he had done that he swore he would never shoot the needle gun again — and he never did. One of his children later wrote:

"A few days after Chief Joseph arrived in Indian Town he came over to visit my parents one evening. Mother was preparing the evening meal and she chanced to look out the door and saw an Indian with the children who were playing in the yard. . . . Fearing that they were in great danger, she quickly ran out where they were, and, as she drew near, she recognized the Indian as Chief Joseph, and her fears seemed to vanish. His friendly salutation reassured her and she returned to work and left the children with him."

Later, when A. B. Findley came in from the fields, they asked Joseph to eat supper with them.

"He accepted the invitation, but soon began to ask Father questions about the difficulty on Whiskey Creek. Father thought it best to tell him all he could about it. Father did not know at that time that the Indians believed that when McNall cursed him [Wil-lot-yah] that he had called on the Spirit Gods who had compelled him [Findley] to shoot the Indian. So Father, in his explanation of the difficulty to the Chief, probably unintentionally confirmed his belief that McNall was to blame for the Indian being killed."[38]

That Chief Joseph bore no malice toward Findley was made clear by the fact that he visited the family on two other occasions before the first of September. In these visits with Findley and other settlers, the Nez Perce leader seems to have been gathering evidence with a patience and sense of justice that would have done credit to the most learned of white investigators — had one been on the scene.

In only one unrelated instance did he lose his temper. That was when he and some of his braves visited the shores of Wallowa Lake and found John McCall and his friends harvesting redfish with their huge seine. In no uncertain terms the Indians told McCall to cease and desist.

"They ordered him to leave," reported the Sentinel, September 2, "and, on his refusal to comply with their modest demands, they assaulted him with a club, knocked him down and destroyed his fishery and gave him due notice that they would not allow him to fish any more in the Wallowa lake."[39]

Having completed his gathering of facts, Joseph consulted with his tribal leaders and then decided upon a course of action. On September 1 Nez Perce couriers visited the home of every white settler in the valley and politely informed them that they were to attend a council next day at Indian Town. The presence of A. B. Findley and Wells McNall was specifically requested.

Since the number of Nez Perces was far greater than that of the whites, the settlers knew that resistance would be useless. Meeting at the McNall cabin, they decided to send Tom Veasey and Jim Davis — two white men whom the Indians liked and trusted — to parley in advance and test the temper of the Indians. The Nez Perces held the two men hostage, sending word to the settlers at the McNall cabin that they all were to come to the Indian village at once.

Seventeen whites did go to the council, though they left Findley and Wells McNall behind.

The talks lasted all day. At their conclusion Joseph issued an ultimatum: Unless the settlers left the valley at the end of the week, they would be driven out by force. After agreeing to meet next

38. Bartlett, Wallowa Country, p. 53; Findley, "Memoirs."
39. Bartlett, Wallowa Country, p. 54; Sentinel, Sept. 2, 1876.

day at the McNall cabin, the settlers were permitted to leave.

While the other men returned to their families scattered over the valley, the Findley's and McNalls gathered at the McNall cabin. Thrusting as many rifle barrels as they could find through chinks in the cabin walls, they made a pretense of being prepared to fight. But when sixty Nez Perce warriors rode up next morning, the whites wisely decided to talk rather than shoot. In fact, as the Indians approached, E. F. McNall sat out in the yard as if unconcerned for his safety.

"Wil-lot-yah's daughter came straight to the cabin," Grace Bartlett writes, "and demanded to see the man who had killed her father. The settlers would not let her come closer than the door . . .

"Mr. Findley wanted to give himself up to the Indians. He was that kind of man. But the others wouldn't let Findley do so."[40]

After an angry exchange of words, the Indians again warned the whites that they must leave the valley, wheeled their horses around, and rode away. Deciding that help was needed, the elder McNall saddled a horse as soon as darkness fell and set out for Fort Walla Walla, a hundred miles away.

The reception given him by Colonel Otis seems to have been on the cool side. In fact, when Otis wrote Judge Brainard next day seeking more information, he made the caustic comment: "It is known here that McNall is not thoroughly reliable."[41]

In response, Brainard wrote another of his unliterary gems:

"State that the report of trouble in the Wallow [sic] valley correspond with the statement made by McNall. That the 2 citizens accused of killing the Indian are ready to stand trial but cannot be convicted on separate evidence & that it is necessary to keep a small force of troops in the valley."[42]

Feeling that he would get no help from the military, E. F. McNall rode back to the Grande Ronde Valley and appealed for volunteers to assist the Wallowa setters in rounding up their livestock and hauling their goods to safety. Twenty-two men responded. Meanwhile, a pair of young men engaged in carrying messages back and forth in the Wallowa Valley very nearly started a war with their foolish boasts.

Their names were Gerard Cochran and Al King. Meeting a Umatilla Indian on the road one day, Cochran told him that the volunteers coming in from the Grande Ronde were going to kill off all the Indians "if they got too gay." Furthermore, he (or King) bragged,

"if Joseph did not behave, all the Indians would be killed and that he himself would kill Joseph and scalp him and wear his scalp as a bridle."[43]

The Umatilla Indian passed on this threat to the Nez Perces, who already were edgy because they had heard that a force of volunteers was on its way. That evening, seventy angry braves, stripped and painted for war, rode up to the ranch where Cochan and King were staying. Seeing them coming, Cochran hid under a haystack in the barn; King went into the house and crawled under a bed.

Tom Veasey, who had acted as a peacemaker a week earlier, was with the Indians. It was only this fact that made the whites at the ranch hopeful that boodshed could be averted.

"The Indians at once asked why they had sent for the Grande Ronde men and were told that they had called for help because the Wallowa settlers were scared. The Indians repeated that they had no wish to fight but if the Grande Ronders longed for a battle let them come out in open ground and the Indians would fight them . . .

"Then the Indians called for the two men who were hiding. The one in the barn was dragged out by his fellows and one of the women in the house went to get the one who had hidden under the bed. She was very angry with him, as were the other settlers, for bragging when the Indians were so excited. She went to the bedroom door and cried: 'You come out of thar or I'll come in and drag you out. We wouldn't be having all this trouble and scare if you had kept your big mouth shut and not bragged so much.'

"Joseph held a long club over the man who had been dragged from the barn, and, with one of the white men interpreting, wanted to know whether this man had lied about the Grande Ronde men coming over and also wanted to know what was this about scalping him.

"The man denied having said it. But the Indian to whom he had said it was standing close by. He promptly told him he was a liar and slapped him. Then the man's father told Joseph that if he would let his son go, he would take him out of the country at once. Joseph agreed to this and the father did take him away, not to return as long as Joseph remained in the valley."[44]

40. Bartlett, *Wallowa Country*, p. 55; Findley, "Memoirs"; J. H. Horner notes.

41. Bartlett, *Wallowa Country*, p. 55; Findley, "Memoirs."

42. Bartlett, *Wallowa Country*, p. 56; Brainard to Otis, September 7, 1876, U.S., National Archives, Old Military Records.

43. Bartlett, *Wallowa Country*, p. 57; *Oregon Historical Quarterly*, March 1939.

44. Bartlett, *Wallowa Country*, p. 58; Findley, "Memoirs."

Thus, once again the good judgment and goodwill of Joseph and the Nez Perces prevented a violent response under great provocation. At this point a comment must be made on the insistence of Joseph and other Nez Perce leaders in speaking only their own tongue when talking with whites on matters of importance. People who knew the Nez Perces of that day agree that many of them had a far better command of English than they admitted. All of them could communicate in the trade language, Chinook Jargon, if they needed to. But as a matter of pride and fluency, Joseph spoke only in his own tongue when in council with the whites.

In any event, a physical confrontation was avoided, and the Indians moved to their campground on the shore of Wallowa Lake. Convinced that the military was needed to keep the peace, Colonel Otis sent a company of cavalry under Lieutenant A. G. Forse into the valley. It arrived September 10. Shortly thereafter Lieutenant Forse met with Joseph, Ollokot, and other Nez Perces and had a friendly discussion of current problems.

Following Forse's assurance that Findley and McNall would be tried for the killing of Wil-lot-yah, Joseph agreed to send two witnesses to Union, Oregon, to testify when the case came to trial. Forse told him

"he must keep his Indians out of the valley, and so long as he was here to remain where he was at the lake, to keep his young stallions and horses by themselves, that the Indians should not interfere with the settlers, and designated the line beyond which his Indians should not go, except when they wanted to go to the settlement to buy provisions, etc., to all of which he said he would agree, and to show his good faith he said he would throw away the bullets they had put in their guns for the purpose of killing the whites who had come to kill him, which he did by forming his Indians in single rank, and discharging their pieces, after which I left him."[45]

Although Lieutenant Forse had promised Joseph that Findley and McNall would be brought to trial, there is no record that McNall ever went to court. But Findley did. The Union County Court records of September 14, 1876, state: "Deft. A. B. Finley is hereby discharged from custody until the close of the examination upon his going bail to the amount of $250.00."

On September 21 he was discharged on the grounds of insufficient evidence when the two Nez Perces whom Joseph had promised to send as witnesses refused to testify. Whether they were bewildered by the court procedure or simply felt that the wrong man was being put on trial is not clear. Since Chief Joseph himself had absolved Findley of blame, it is probable they were obeying his instructions.

On September 23 Findley made a statement in the presence of Judge Brainard and County Clerk R. J. Cates in which he gave his version of the killing. Though he admitted aiming his gun at the Indian because he feared for his own and McNall's lives, he said at the end of his statement:

"I had not decided to shoot when I heard the report of my gun. I was not conscious of pulling the trigger."[46]

In letters written after his return to Fort Walla Walla, Forse expressed the opinion that if he and his troops had not arrived when they did there would have been bloodshed. He expressed confidence that Chief Joseph would keep his word. He noted that the settlers who had left the Wallowa Valley when the trouble began had returned. He urged that the matter of "right to this valley" be settled soon.

Agent John Monteith, General O. O. Howard, and other white officials long had been urging the same thing. In early November the slow-grinding wheels of government, which had left the fate of the region and the nontreaty Nez Perces in limbo for years, finally took measures to settle the question once and for all.

Meeting in Lapwai, a five-member commission appointed to study, debate, and solve the problem, reached a conclusion and made a recommendation to the Secretary of the Interior.

45. Bartlett, *Wallowa Country*, p. 58; Lieutenant Forse letter, September 11, 1876.
46. Bartlett, *Wallowa Country*, p. 98; statement, September 23, 1876.

CHAPTER TWENTY-THREE

A COMMISSION OF REASONABLE MEN:
November 1876–May 1877

Joseph's band do not desire Wallowa Valley for a reservation and for a home. This small band wish the possession of this large section of Oregon simply for room to gratify a wild, roaming disposition and not for a home.
— Governor Leonard F. Grover, July 21, 1873

I have been talking to the whites for many years about the land in question, and it is strange they cannot understand me. The country they claim belonged to my father, and when he died it was given to me and my people, and I will not leave it until I am compelled to.
— Chief Joseph, February 1877

BECAUSE OF the controversy over the ownership of the Wallowa country, Major Henry Clay Wood, assistant adjutant general of the Military Department of the Columbia, was asked to make a careful study of the Treaties of 1855 and 1863 and amendments modifying them. In July 1876 he turned in his report to General Howard, who passed it on to the Secretary of War with his endorsement. Major Wood's conclusions were:

"The non-treaty Nez Perces cannot in law be regarded as bound by the treaty of 1863; and in so far as it attempts to deprive them of a right to occupancy of any land its provisions are null and void."[1]

Speaking of President Grant's 1875 action revoking the 1873 Executive Order which had established a reserve for Chief Joseph's band in the Wallowa country, Wood wrote bluntly:

"If not a crime, it was a blunder. In intercourse with the Indian it is not wise to speak with a forked tongue."[2]

General Howard first met Chief Joseph at the Umatilla Agency while on a tour of inspection during the summer of 1875. In company with ten Nez Perce warriors, including his brother, Ollokot,

Joseph had asked for an interview with the general in hopes that Howard could explain why President Grant had changed his mind about establishing a reservation in the Wallowa country. General Howard writes of this meeting:

"Joseph put his large black eyes on my face, and maintained a fixed look for some time. It did not appear to me as an audacious stare; but I thought he was trying to open the windows of his heart to me, and at the same time endeavoring to read my disposition and character. . . . I think that Joseph and I became then quite good friends."[3]

The commission appointed by the Secretary of Interior to decide the fate of the Wallowa Nez Perces consisted of two men who knew the Indians and the region and three who did not. D. H.

1. Howard and McGrath, *War Chief Joseph,* p. 91; Major Henry Clay Wood, *Joseph and His Land Claims or Status of Young Joseph and His Band of Nez Perce Indians* (Portland, Oreg., 1876), p. 45; second part of quotation from p. 7.
2. Howard and McGrath, *War Chief Joseph,* p. 95; Wood, *Joseph and His Land Claims,* p. 34.
3. Howard and McGrath, *War Chief Joseph,* p. 96; General Oliver Otis Howard, *Chief Joseph: His Pursuit and Capture* (Boston: Lee and Shepard, 1881), p. 29.

This photo was taken by F. J. Haynes in 1877 probably at Bismark, North Dakota just after the Nez Perce War   *Courtesy Smithsonian Institution*

Chief Joseph

General Oliver Otis Howard

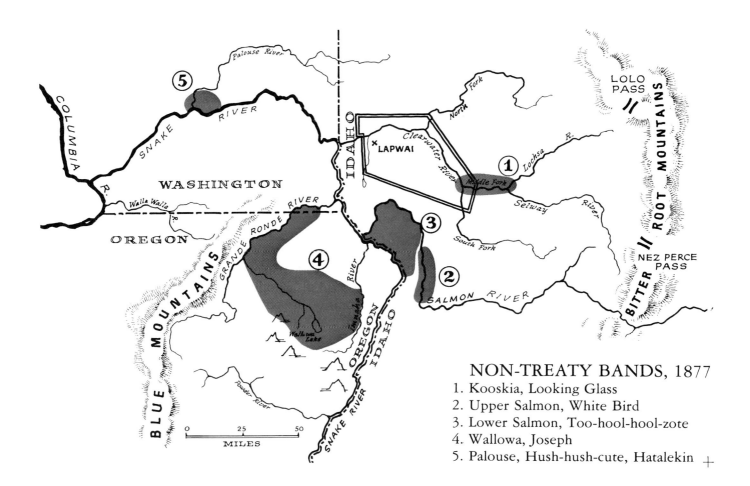

NON-TREATY BANDS, 1877
1. Kooskia, Looking Glass
2. Upper Salmon, White Bird
3. Lower Salmon, Too-hool-hool-zote
4. Wallowa, Joseph
5. Palouse, Hush-hush-cute, Hatalekin +

Jerome, of Saginaw, Michigan, was selected chairman. William Stickney of Washington, D.C., A. C. Barstow of Providence, Rhode Island, Brigadier General O. O. Howard and Major H. C. Wood, both of Portland, completed the commission. Its expressed purpose was:

"to visit these Indians, with a view to secure their permanent settlement on the reservation, their early entrance on a civilized life, and to adjust the difficulties then existing between them and the settlers."[4]

When the commissioners met with Joseph in Lapwai in November 1876 they attempted to convince him that the Wallowa country was not suitable as a permanent home for his band because of a number of reasons:

"The coldness of the climate. . . . It is embraced within the limits of the State of Oregon, which could not be induced to cede jurisdiction. . . . In case of conflict between Joseph and the white settlers, the President might not be able to defend him . . ."

To these not very solid arguments, Joseph replied:

"The earth was his mother. . . . He could not consent to leave the land that bore him. . . . He asked nothing of the President. He was able to take care of himself."[5]

As other councils between whites and Indians had done, this one broke up with no real meeting of minds, for neither side had listened to the other. Convinced that his band still owned the Wallowa, that no government edict could take the country from them, and that the white man's word was not to be depended upon, Chief Joseph left Lapwai

4. Howard and McGrath, War Chief Joseph, p. 101; Helen Hunt Jackson, A Century of Dishonor: The Early Crusade for Indian Reform (New York: Harper Brothers, 1881), p. 125.
5. Howard and McGrath, War Chief Joseph, p. 102; U.S., Department of the Interior, Records of the Bureau of Indian Affairs, Commission Reports, 1875, vol. 1, p. 762, ibid., 1876, vol. 1, p. 449.

and went home. On their part, the commissioners made their decision and filed their report without bothering to let the Wallowa Nez Perces know their conclusions. Their recommendations to the Secretary of Interior were:

1. That the Dreamer medicine men be confined to their agencies, since their influence on the nontreaty Indians was pernicious;
2. That a military post be established in the Wallowa Valley at once;
3. That unless in a reasonable time Joseph consented to be removed, he should be forcibly taken with his people and given lands on the reservation;
4. That if members of his band overran property belonging to the whites, or committed depredations, or disturbed the peace by threats of hostility, then sufficient force should be employed to bring them into subjection.[6]

So once again it was the white authorities, not the Indians, who spoke of the use of force to achieve their ends. To his credit, Major Wood refused to sign the report, making a minority recommendation that "until Joseph commits some overt act of hostility, force should not be used to put him upon any reservation."[7]

Wasting no time, now that a course of action had been outlined, the Department of Interior decided early in January 1877 to remove the Joseph band onto the Lapwai Reservation — by compulsion, if necessary. An order to that effect was issued to Agent Monteith. Given the authority he long had desired, Monteith sent a delegation of reservation Nez Perces to Joseph's winter village in the lower Grande Ronde Valley, asking him to move willingly and soon — or suffer the consequences.

Since Lawyer's death a few years earlier, Reuben had been head chief for the treaty Nez Perces. He was Joseph's brother-in-law. It was he who led the delegation. Going with him was his son, James Reuben; Whisk-tasket, Joseph's father-in-law; and Captain John, a Nez Perce chief long friendly to the whites. Despite these blood ties and the well-reasoned arguments of his relatives, Joseph refused to move to the reservation. The interpreters at the November council must not have translated accurately, he said. The commissioners must have misunderstood him.

But the misunderstandings lay at a far deeper level than inadequate translation. When the delegation returned to Lapwai and reported to Monteith, the agent wrote grimly:

"I think, from Joseph's actions, he will not come on the reserve until compelled to. He has said so [as] much to the Indians who have moved on the reserve, calling them cowards, etc., that he would be lowering himself in his own estimation, as well as in that of his immediate followers, did he not make some show of resistance. By making such resistance, he could say to the other Indians, 'I was overpowered, and did not come of my own choice,' in case he is forced on the reserve."[8]

After making the sensible recommendation that the Joseph band be permitted to spend four to six weeks each summer fishing in the Imnaha country, where there were no roads or settlers, Monteith then threw good sense to the winds, writing J. Q. Smith, Commissioner of Indian Affairs, February 9, 1877:

"I have given Joseph until April 1, 1877, to come on the reserve peaceably. They can come one time just as well as another, having nothing to hinder them in moving."[9]

Though Monteith suggested that the soldiers could force Joseph to make the move, this was a chore they were not prepared to carry out, for their commanding officer had not even been informed of the deadline set by the agent. This is evident in the letter General Howard wrote Monteith March 12, 1877:

"I do not understand that we can take the offensive at all until further instructions from Washington. I am glad, indeed, you did not fix any time for the ultimatum of Joseph's coming."[10]

Monteith's statement that Joseph's band could "come one time just as well as another, having nothing to hinder them in moving" indicates that he knew little and cared less about the life-style of the nontreaty Indians. Most of their wealth was portable, true, but moving took time and could be done only in the proper season. Thousands of their horse and cattle were grazing now over the grassy flats and sheltered draws of the lower country; soon they would drop foals and calves. After a winter on the range and with offspring to nurse, the

6. Howard and McGrath, *War Chief Joseph*, p. 104; *Commission Reports*, 1876.
7. Howard and McGrath, *War Chief Joseph*, p. 105; J. P. Dunn, Jr., *Massacres of the Mountains* (New York: Harper Brothers, 1880), p. 646.
8. Howard and McGrath, *War Chief Joseph*, p. 106; *Commission Reports*, 1876.
9. McWhorter, *Hear Me*, p. 149.
10. Ibid., p. 150.

mares and cows would have neither the strength nor disposition to be rounded up and forced into a rigorous drive, which their young could not possibly survive.

Winter still lay on the land; snowdrifts covered the trails to the high country; no tracts of land had been set aside for the Joseph band on the Lapwai Reservation; no supplies of food, clothing, and fuel awaited them there.

March, April, and May were root-gathering months. June was the month for moving livestock out of the lower valleys toward higher pasture. July and August were months for camas-gathering and fish-catching and curing. September and October were hunting months when the family laid in a supply of deer meat and made pemmican for the winter food supply. By mid-October horses and cattle would be in good condition. Rivers such as the Snake, Salmon, and Clearwater would be at their lowest stage and could be easily crossed. Enough time would have elapsed to have selected

Courtesy Washington State University Library
Duncan McDonald, who wrote the only authentic contemporary Indian story of the Nez Perce War, with Fred Lockley, a writer and historian for the *Oregon Journal.*

homesites on the Lapwai Reservation and to have prepared the nontreaty Nez Perces emotionally for the soul-wrenching process of removing them permanently from their ancestral homeland. If the move had to be made, November 1 would have been a reasonable deadline. April 1 was ridiculous.

On the face of it, the persistent mention of the use of force by the commissioners and Agent Monteith was unnecessary, for by actual count the previous summer the Wallowa band numberd only sixty males. In all confrontations to date, Joseph had made it clear that he would not lead his people into a war against the whites. But once given the authority he long had coveted, Agent John Monteith saw but one goal to be achieved — to put the nontreaty Nez Perces under his personal control.

"Let it always be understood by the Indians that the Agent is their Authority," he wrote, "and that no person can deal with them except through their Agent."[11]

Joseph refused to accept the agent's authority; instead, he literally turned his back on Monteith and the Lapwai Reservation to the east and looked toward his kinsmen on the Umatilla Reservation to the west. There is no recorded statement by him that his band would prefer to go to the Umatilla rather than the Lapwai reserve if it must leave the Wallowa, yet the writings of General Howard, Agent Cornoyer, and others indicate that such a desire must have been in his heart.

"When at Walla Walla in March, I met there Mr. Cornoyer, the Umatilla agent," Howard wrote, "who informed me in substance as follows: Joseph and his people . . . are wishing to cross the Blue Ridge [Blue Mountains] and visit the Umatilla Indians . . . and learn what the government proposes, claiming that the interpreter at Lapwai, in the fall, had not altogether spoken the 'truth.' I replied that he had better encourage these Indians to make their proposed visit. Mr. Cornoyer subsequently visited me in Portland, and told me these Indians were coming, and that he should meet them upon his return to the agency. Therefore I sent my aid-de-camp, Lieut. William H. Boyle, to be present at the Agency interview. This took place April 1.

"Joseph's younger brother, whose name is Ollicut, and Old Too-at or Dreamer, and a few others of Joseph's Indians were there. After the talk Ollicut expressed a desire to see me, and wished me to appoint the time and place. Lieut. Boyle telegraphed me accordingly as soon as he reached Walla Walla. Taking Ollicut for Joseph, I replied that I would meet him at Fort Walla Walla April 19."[12]

11. Ibid., p. 138.
12. Ibid., p. 152.

Mistaking Ollokot for Joseph happened frequently — as Lieutenant Boyle did in person on this occasion and General Howard did by telegraph. But it was clear to Agent Cornoyer and W. C. Painter (both of whom were veterans of the 1855–58 Indian War, friendly toward the non-treaty Nez Perces, and present at the Umatilla Agency council) that it was Ollokot who was speaking for the Wallowa band in place of Chief Joseph, who was ill and remained at home.

Ollokot was as eloquent and forceful a spokesman as Joseph, though not as diplomatic.

"Lieutenant Boyle opened the meeting, with a request that the Indians speak what was on their minds," McWhorter writes. "In the absence of Chief Joseph, Ollokot arose in an unmistakably happy frame of mind. He expressed for himself and his people their warm gratitude to General Howard for his promise that they could come to the Umatilla instead of the Nez Perce reservation, as better suited for their living."[13]

Ollokot's assumption that General Howard had

Photo by Charles Phillips, Walla Walla

Chief Joseph's younger brother, Ollokot, May 1877

endorsed the proposal of the nontreaty Nez Perce to move to the Umatilla rather than the Lapwai Reservation seems to have been but one more of many misunderstandings. Apparently such a change in policy had been discussed by the commissioners. It is possible that Howard sanctioned it, only to be rebuffed by higher authority — in which case, as a good soldier, he would reverse directions without a moment's hesitation. Whatever the case, the delegation of Nez Perces was stunned when Lieutenant Boyle said bluntly:

"You are not coming to the Umatilla Reservation! General Howard orders that you move to the Nez Perce reservation! That you get ready to move at once!"

For some moments the Indians sat in stunned silence. Then Ollokot leaped to his feet and pointed his outstretched arm at the officer, two fingers spread to indicate the forks of a serpent tongue.

"Nesammeiek [liar], who are you? Where is General Howard? He promised to come to this council. I came, a chief to talk to a chief! General Howard sends one of his boys to give orders to the Nez Perces! I did not send one of my young men to talk to a chief! I am a chief and I came! Where is General Howard! General Howard talks with a forked tongue! He has lied to the Nez Perces! Was he ashamed to meet men to whom he talked two ways? Is he — a commander of soldiers — afraid? He has insulted me! Made me ashamed before my people! I am done!"[14]

Though Joseph was still ill and unable to attend the meeting with General Howard at Fort Walla Walla, April 20, 1877, Ollokot, who again spoke for the Wallowa band, had cooled off to the point that he could discuss matters with Howard more calmly.

"There were present Ollicut, Young Chief of the Umatillas, the Dreamer before mentioned, and several other non-treaty Nez Perces," Howard writes. "Besides my aides, several officers of the fort and some citizens were present. The Indian agent Cormoyer and his interpreter, McBain, participated . . .

"The Indians seemed at first to wish to join the Umatillas, then it appears there was a project (probably originating with white men) to combine the reservation Indians of Umatilla with the non-treaty Nez Perces, and ask for them thus joined the Wallowa and Imnaha country, giving up the Umatilla reserve. But I replied that the instructions are definite; that I should send troops very soon to occupy the Wallowa, and proceed to Lapwai as soon as possible in execution of my instructions.

13. Ibid., p. 153.
14. Ibid., p. 154.

"Ollicut, who manifested a good disposition, was evidently afraid to promise anything. . . . I was glad to have him ask to gather the Indians, all the non-treaties, to meet me at Fort Lapwai during my coming visit."[15]

Since the April 1 deadline set by Agent Monteith had been ignored and General Howard had agreed to meet with the nontreaty Nez Perces at Lapwai early in May, the Wallowa band felt no sense of urgency in making a decision to move. In the best tradition of diplomatic bargaining, both Joseph and Ollokot felt that time was on their side; that the longer they kept talking with the whites, the firmer their position to maintain the status quo would be.

During Major Henry Clay Wood's talks with the Indians as he examined the validity of the 1863 Treaty, and later, during the councils at Umatilla and Fort Walla Walla, maps had been drawn by Ollokot and Joseph defining the areas in dispute. In addition, "Young Joseph" (or Ollokot) had made a sketch of men, animals, and guns, depicting the killing of the Indian in the McNall-Findley crime. Several contemporary white and Indian witnesses who viewed these maps and sketches have described them, noting their remarkable accuracy and points of interest. Unfortunately, none of them has survived.[16]

The Lapwai council convened May 3, 1877. Though Salmon, Clearwater, and Snake River bands living outside the boundaries of the reservation had been invited as well as the Wallowa band, only Joseph and fifty of his people were present when the time came for the meeting to begin. When General Howard showed impatience over the absence of the other bands, Joseph said: "You must not be in a hurry to go till all can get in to have a talk."

Reluctantly Howard agreed to wait, but he made no bones of the fact that he intended to waste little time listening to heathen Dreamers talk "earth mother" nonsense. The one-armed Howard, called "Arm-Cut" or "Armless" by the Nez Perces,[17] was known to be an extremely devout man as well as a good soldier. He carried out the precepts of his religion as strictly as he obeyed orders given him by his superiors in the War Department. To him — as to Agent Monteith — the Dreamer faith was not a religion at all; it was paganism in its worst possible form.

Since it was at this council that the future of the Nez Perces living outside the borders of the Lapwai

Courtesy Washington State University
Billy Carter, Ollokot, Middle Bear, about 1876

Reservation was decided once and for all, it is appropriate to note the leaders of those bands and their places of abode. No attempt will be made to reconcile variations in name-spelling, physical description, or character analysis by different writers, for in these areas over the years it seems to have been every historian for him — or her — self. Leaders of the disaffected bands, write Helen Addison Howard and Dan L. McGrath, were (in addition to Joseph) Chiefs Looking Glass, White Bird, Hush-hush-cute, and Tuhulhutsut.

"Looking Glass's people lived on Clear Creek, a tributary of the Middle Fork of the Clearwater River. His band's village was usually located above the town (pres-

15. Ibid., pp. 155–156.
16. Ibid., pp. 157–158.
17. Haruo Aoki, *Nez Perce Texts* (Berkeley and Los Angeles: University of California Press, 1979), p. 115.

ent day) of Kamiah on the eastern side of the Lapwai Reservation. This chief, son of old Chief Looking Glass who signed the Treaty of 1855, was about five feet seven inches in height, ungainly, flat-faced, and nearly forty-five years of age. In the center of his forehead, tied to his scalp lock, hung a round mirror; from this he received his name in English. To the Nez Perces he was known as A-push-wa-hite. Looking Glass had just returned from a buffalo hunt in Montana where his band spent most of the time. Among the whites he was known as a diplomat and a leader of peace.

"White Bird, whose Nez Perce name was Pen-pen-hi-hi (meaning, literally, "White Pelican"), was also known as Joe Hale. He was a heavy-set man of mild countenance, which deceptively masked his shrewd trading ability. Howard describes him as being '. . . a demure-looking Indian, about five feet eight inches tall. His face assumed the condition of impassibility, or rigid fixedness, while in council; and . . . he kept his immense ceremonial hat on, and placed a large eagle's wing in front of his eyes and nose.' This chief's band, when not in Montana hunting buffalo, roamed among the steep mountains along the Salmon River which lay to the south of the reservation. Among the Nez Perces he was the leading warlike spirit, ready and willing to fight the whites any time the other nontreaty bands would rally to his support.

"Hush-hush-cute lived in the Asotin country of southeastern Washington on the west bank of the Snake River. Bright-eyed and oily, he resembled Tuhulhutsut in some respects, but in his manner of extreme cunning inspired distrust in those whites who dealt with him in councils. He was about Joseph's age, close to thirty-six at the time.

"Tuhulhutsut, five feet ten, broad-shouldered, deep-chested, thick of neck, was one of the leading *tewats,* or medicine men, of the Dreamer faith. Although his band on the Snake River was small in numbers, he exerted great influence on the followers of Smohalla's religion, as his oratory was passionate and vindictive. Like the prophet, this old chief could drop his querulous manner and speak smoothly and convincingly.

"Joseph and Alokut presented the finest appearance of the invited chiefs. Alokut, the younger of the two, was even taller than his brother, as graceful and supple as a cougar. Carefree and full of youthful enthusiasm, his happy disposition attracted whites and Indians alike. Clearly he was the idol and leader of the young men."[18]

During the first three days of the council nothing much was accomplished by General Howard and Agent Monteith, though a few of the disaffected Nez Perces did manage to irritate Howard to the point that he threatened to arrest and punish two "Old Dreamers for being saucy and quarrelsome."

"Severity of manner in dealing with savages is believed by many of the Indians' friends to be always uncalled for and decidedly wrong," he wrote later. "It may be so, but the manner of dealing must depend upon the peculiarities of the people with whom you have to deal."[19]

Exactly which tenet of his avowed Christianity allowed him to base his "uncalled for and decidedly wrong" behavior on "the peculiarities" of the people with whom he was dealing, he did not state. But then as a devout Christian and the army general in charge of the Department of the Columbia, he was not required to explain his actions to any lesser beings than God and the Secretary of War.

Knowing how important this council would be, the dissident Nez Perce leaders had met some time before and decided that tough, belligerent, eloquent Too-hool-hool-zote should act as their spokesman, with warlike White Bird backing him up, while more moderate Looking Glass stood by to patch up verbal wounds. Most eloquent Joseph should remain in the background as the voice of wisdom when the ultimate bargain must be made. On the council's fourth day, which began with a prayer by a Christianized Treaty Nez Perce named Alpowa Jim, the growing hostility between General Howard and the Indians' principal spokesman exploded:

"Too-hul-hul-sote, the cross-grained growler, was again designated as the speaker, and he took up his parable," General Howard wrote wearily. "He was, if possible, crosser and more impudent in his abruptness of manner than before. He had the usual long preliminary discussion about the earth being his mother, that she should not be disturbed by hoe or plow, that men should subsist on what grows of itself, etc. He repeated his ideas concerning 'chieftanship,' chieftanship of the earth. Chieftanship cannot be sold, cannot be given away. Mr. Monteith and General Howard, he said, must speak truth about the chieftanship of the earth."

"We do not want to interfere with your religion," Howard answered, "but you must talk about practicable things. Twenty times over you repeat that the earth is your mother, and about chieftanship of the earth. Let us hear it no more, but come to the business at once." Howard then stated that business bluntly. "Do you intend coming on the reservation peacefully?" he demanded, "or shall I put you there with my soldiers?"

Howard already had told the nontreaty Indians that he would give them only thirty days to round up their stock and move all their worldly possessions onto the reserve. When he pointed out that

18. Howard and McGrath, *War Chief Joseph,* pp. 107–108.
19. McWhorter, *Hear Me,* p. 160.

he had brought enough men and guns to enforce that order, Too-hool-hool-zote asked angrily:

"What person pretends to divide the land and put me on it?"

"I am that man," Howard replied.

"You have brought a rifle to a peace council. If you mean but thirty suns for gathering of our stock, yes. We will have to fight."

"Then among the Indians all about me signs of anger began to appear," General Howard later recalled. "Looking Glass dropped his gentle style and made rough answers. White Bird, hiding his face behind the eagle wing, said he had not been brought up to be governed by white men, and Joseph began to finger his tomahawk and his eyes flashed. Too-hool-hool-sote said fiercely:

" 'The Indians may do as they like. I am not going on that land.' "[20]

Though General Howard may have been a deeply religious man and a conscientious army officer, his writings over a period of years give different versions of what he recalled as having happened at a given place and time. In contrast to Howard's statement, the Indians present say that all the Nez Perces were unarmed, and that never at any time did they threaten violence. The whites present claim they saw a gun, knife, or tomahawk under every blanket and that if General Howard had not taken the action he did a massacre would have ensued.

That action was to order To-hool-hool-zote arrested and thrown into the Fort Lapwai guardhouse.

At about the same time it was revealed that on May 3, 1877, the day the council began, Agent Monteith had handed General Howard an official letter which read:

"I would respectfully request that you assist me in the removal of Joseph's and other roving bands of Nez Perce Indians and to locate them upon proper lands within the boundaries of the Nez Perce reservation by the use of such troops as you may deem necessary."[21]

The charade of a friendly discussion between a Commission of Reasonable White Men and the Chiefs of the Nontreaty Nez Perces had been played to its bitter end. To the leaders of the free-roaming bands, there were no options left but to give in or fight. With Chief Too-hool-hool-zote imprisoned and the rifles of the soldiers aimed at their hearts, White Bird, Looking Glass, Hush-hush-cute, and Joseph accepted the inevitable. After making a brief tour of the reserve escorted by General Howard and Agent Monteith, they selected the lands onto which they presently would move their livestock, lodges, and all their earthly possessions. Returning to Fort Lapwai, they respectfully requested that Tool-hool-hool-zote be released. When freed, he, too, accepted the fact that he must move onto the reserve.

The date was May 14, 1877. The nontreaty bands were given exactly thirty days to collect their animals and material possessions and become what God had not made them to be — reservation Indians for the rest of their mortal days on this earth.

20. Ibid., pp. 165–167.
21. Ibid., p. 170.

CHAPTER TWENTY-FOUR

TOWARD THE PROMISED LAND

Our stock is scattered and the Snake River is very high. Let us wait till fall, then the river will be low. We want time to hunt up our stock and gather supplies for the winter.
— Chief Joseph, May 1877

If you let the time run over one day, the soldiers will be there to drive you on the reservation, and cattle outside the reservation at that time will fall into the hands of the white men.
— General O. O. Howard, May 1877

ON THE FACE OF IT, the task confronting the Wallowa Nez Perces — rounding up all their livestock and moving all their people and possessions a hundred miles in a month's time — was impossible. The extent of country over which their horses and cattle ranged comprised a million acres of extremely rugged terrain. Male adult members of the band available to ride in the roundup numbered no more than sixty — barely an adequate crew for a summer-long gathering of the livestock scattered over the area, and certainly not capable of finding and driving thousands of winter-thin, spooky animals from their wilderness range to the Lapwai Reservation in only one month's time.

Since snowmelt in the high country supplied the major portion of the water for the region's rivers, the Wallowa, Imnaha, Grande Ronde, Snake, and Salmon all became raging torrents between mid-May and Mid-June, dangerous even to strong, mature horses and cattle forced to breast the rapid currents, and sure death to the weak and young. Knowing that any Indian livestock left behind would fall into their hands, white settlers in the area certainly were not going to assist the Nez Perces in flushing out strays.

Some writers have claimed that unprincipled white men actually stampeded cattle and horses being bunched together on the west bank of the Snake so they later could catch and claim the animals as their own, but there is no evidence in the form of Nez Perce protests that such a thing ever happened. In any case, the lack of time was working so favorably for the whites that they would have been foolish to have precipitated violence when the Nez Perces were leaving so peaceably.[1]

In order to make sure that the Joseph band complied with his directive to move onto the Lapwai Reservation, General Howard sent Captain S. G. Whipple with a command of five officers, ninety-seven enlisted men, and a Gatling gun into the Wallowa Country early in May. Even as Howard was threatening to use force against the Nez Perces who met with him at Lapwai, Captain Whipple has having trouble marching his troops north from the Wallowa Valley to the Grande Ronde River, taking three days to ride only fifty miles. Though a much smaller river than the Snake, the Grande Ronde in flood frightened the soldiers.

1. Howard and McGrath, *War Chief Joseph,* p. 124; Bureau of American Ethnology, *Fourteenth Annual Report,* pt. 2, pp. 713–714. Grace Bartlett discusses this story and its various versions in Note 8, p. 72, of *Wallowa Country,* concluding with a local-knowledge comment regarding the family of renowned cattle rustlers, the Owsleys: "It was said of them, by the Wallowans, that even if you watched your cattle to the extent of letting them graze over the edge of the canyons, but still hanging on to their tails, an Owsley would come sneaking along, cut off the tail and get away with the animal!"

Wallowa Lake

"Late last night [May 11th] I arrived with the command on the eastern bluff above the crossing," Captain Whipple wrote, "and next morning discovered that Sergeant Hanson had found the river too formidable to attempt and that no detachment was visible on the left bank. The guide [Findley] having crossed here at a low stage of water thought it practicable now, though hazardous, and said he was willing to try it accompanied by another experienced man, who was found in Sergeant Hanson, and who was not averse to the detail. The Sergeant and guide got safely across, by whom I sent the following pencil dispatch."

With the soldiers and the Gatling gun in place on the lower Grande Ronde, prepared to back up Howard's ultimatum, Captain Whipple wrote Howard:

"The pack mules are much jaded. . . . The Grande Ronde here runs through an immense canyon, rendering travel either up or down the river on this side impracticable. The river is wide, deep and swift . . .

"The work of collecting and preparing timber for a raft, to be used in case command should be ordered to cross the river, was well performed under superintendence of 1st Lieutenant A. G. Forse."[2]

Fortunately for the command, it was not re-

quired to cross the Grande Ronde. Howard told Captain Whipple that he need detail only a small "watching force" at the Grande Ronde crossing and could take the rest of his command back to its base in the Wallowa Valley. How dangerous even this smaller river could be was proven the day after Captain Whipple and his troops left. Veterinary-Surgeon S. G. Going and Lieutenant S. M. Rains attempted to cross the Grande Ronde as the others had done. Lieutenant Rains made it, but the veterinary-surgeon was caught by the treacherous current near the far bank, swept under, and drowned.

In none of the Indian accounts of this period did the Nez Perces complain about the weather. But Captain Whipple certainly did. On May 28 he reported:

"During the entire month the weather has been most unpropitious for field operations, there having been long rain storms — with some snow — or frequent hard showers. The ground was made very soft by the excess of moisture which rendered travel very difficult, the horses sinking at nearly every step to the fetlocks, and much of the way to a greater depth; particularly this was the case from the camp to the Lewiston crossing of the Grande Ronde. From the Wallowa Valley to the last named point there is no other road than an Indian trail, upon which no labor has ever been done and over which no wheeled vehicle has been, and as a great por-

2. Bartlett, *Wallowa Country,* p. 61.

Camas Meadows near La Grande, Oregon

tion of the distance is heavily timbered and swampy taking the Gatling gun through proved laborious."[3]

At this same time, in the same weather, and over even more difficult terrain, sixty Nez Perce men were laboriously combing the hills and hollows to round up whatever horses and cattle they could find in the short time allotted them, while back in their village the women, children, and old people packed, pulled down the tepees, and prepared to move. Incredibly, by the end of May the Indians had rounded up an estimated six thousand head of livestock and were loose-herding the animals on the new spring grass of the lower Imnaha Valley.

Running in full early summer flood, the Snake was a monstrous river. Varying in width from several hundred yards to as little as sixty-two feet, it carried a tremendous volume of water through the mile-deep gorge called Hell's Canyon, its current moving with such force that no animal or human pulled into its whirlpools, falls, and rapids could possibly survive. But the river did not frighten the Nez Perces, for they had been crossing it since time immemorial and knew how to overcome its hazards.

Indian tradition and recollections by whites place the principal Nez Perce crossing at Big Eddy, just upriver from present-day Dug Bar Ranch, at River Mile 196 upstream from Lewiston. Gerald J. Tucker, who for thirty-seven years was District Ranger for the U.S. Forest Service in the Wallowa country, has drawn a vivid word picture of the epic scene.

"There were no boats, but the Nez Perce knew how to cross rivers without boats. They made large bundles into a sort of raft which wrapped their goods in almost water-tight bales tied up in the skin coverings of their tepees. These rafts would float and the women and children would either ride the bundles or hold on to the ropes with which they were tied. Then young, athletic men, stripped to their breechclout, pulled the rafts across the river from the backs of swimming horses. This crossing was made without the loss of human life, notwithstanding that the Snake was at extremely high flood stage. . . . However, the crossing of their bands of horses and herds of cattle was not accomplished without a heavy loss.

"In the spring there were many young calves and colts. Those which were plainly too young to swim the raging torrent were left behind with their mothers, but there was a heavy loss in spite of every precaution. . .

"The abandoned cattle and horses were immediately rounded up by renegade whites and furnished

Photo by Bill Gulick

Hell's Canyon

the foundation stock for some of the pioneer ranchers of Wallowa and Asotin counties."[4]

With all his people and a sizable portion of their livestock safely across the Snake, Chief Joseph set up camp with members of four other Nez Perce bands in the lower Salmon River country at a traditional meeting place called *Te-pah-le-wam* ("Split Rocks" or "Deep Cuts") adjoining a small body of water, Tolo Lake. For the next ten days these formerly free, "unsettled" Indians visited with one another, raced horses, gambled, played war games, danced, and talked — mourning a way of life they were being forced to put behind, speculating upon what appeared to be a very bleak future.

Since these were the five bands of Indians soon to become involved in armed conflict with the whites, their numbers and leaders — which have been wildly exaggerated and badly appraised by

3. Ibid., p. 62.
4. Gerald J. Tucker, *The Story of Hells Canyon* (Enterprise, Oreg., 1977), p. 112.

many writers — should be carefully enumerated and described here.

The largest, Chief Joseph's band, numbered fifty-five to sixty adult males. In no sense was Joseph regarded as an overall leader of the nontreaty Nez Perces. As a matter of fact, he was the youngest of the five tribal chiefs, had made only one trip to the buffalo country as an adult, and had never been involved in warfare. Primarily he was a man of peace, determined to avoid bloodshed at any cost. If physical acts of bravery and valor were to be required, his younger brother, Ollokot, was far better equipped to perform them than he. Described as "a striking figure in the prime of life, standing six feet two inches in moccasins, with the trim, erect build of an athlete, with a vivacious, though determined eye, revealing joviality and good will, but holding a glint that betrayed the sleeping tiger within," Ollokot ("Frog") certainly was the chief warrior of the Wallowa band, as well as Joseph's principal advisor. But Joseph himself was not a war leader.[5]

Second in size was the White Bird band of Nez Perces, which numbered around fifty men of warrior age. Called Peopeo Hihih by the Indians, Chief White Bird was in his seventies, the oldest of the nontreaty chiefs.

"Standing just short of six feet, well proportioned, with a splendid physique and stately bearing, he commanded attention wherever seen. A medicine man, and

Photo by Bill Gulick
Wild Sheep Rapids in Hell's Canyon

boasting a long line of noted warrior ancestry, his status and influence with his following was pronounced. As a buffalo hunter and experienced in tribal warfare, he held an honored place in all councils. He was mild in temper and in speech. The charge that he was an advocate of war had no foundations in fact."[6]

Because of his age, White Bird did no fighting. He stayed with the camp contingent of old men, women, and children, as did Joseph, his close friend and ally. For this last meeting before traveling the short distance north to the Lapwai Reservation, the Nez Perces were camped in his band's home territory; his village was located on White Bird Creek at the mouth of White Bird Canyon.

The third band of nontreaty Indians was headed by Chief Looking Glass. Numbering no more than forty men, his group's village was located on the South Fork of the Clearwater, part of the band's domain lying within the boundaries of the 1863 reservation, part of it extending eastward toward the crest of the Bitter Root Mountains. As his father long had done, the younger Chief Looking Glass journeyed to the buffalo country every year to "make meat." While there he had become quite friendly with the Crows, who five years earlier had appealed to the Nez Perces for aid against the Sioux. When help was granted in the form of two hundred fighting men, it was Looking Glass who led his people in a victorious battle against the Sioux, thus his reputation as a war chief was great.

Leading the fourth band, which numbered around thirty men, was the "cross-grained growler," Chief Too-hool-hool-zote. He was described by Mrs. Frances Montieth as "old, fat, ugly, and quarrelsome looking" but was called "a fighter from hell!" by an old pioneer who had known him. He probably was more accurately described by the interpreter, Camille Williams, as

"a tall, heavy man, but not fat or big-bellied, nor was he ugly looking. He was supposed to be the strongest man in the tribe. He was known to carry two grown blacktailed bucks to his lodge, from where he killed them, traveling afoot over the roughest of steep mountain country. No other man was ever known to accomplish such a feat. I was once told, by an old man, that Toohoolhoolzote went on a drunk, and became bothersome, and some of the Indians thought to quiet him by tying him up. Eight men got hold of him but could not get him down, and were obliged to let him go."[7]

5. McWhorter, *Hear Me*, p. 180.
6. Ibid., p. 181.
7. Ibid., p. 184.

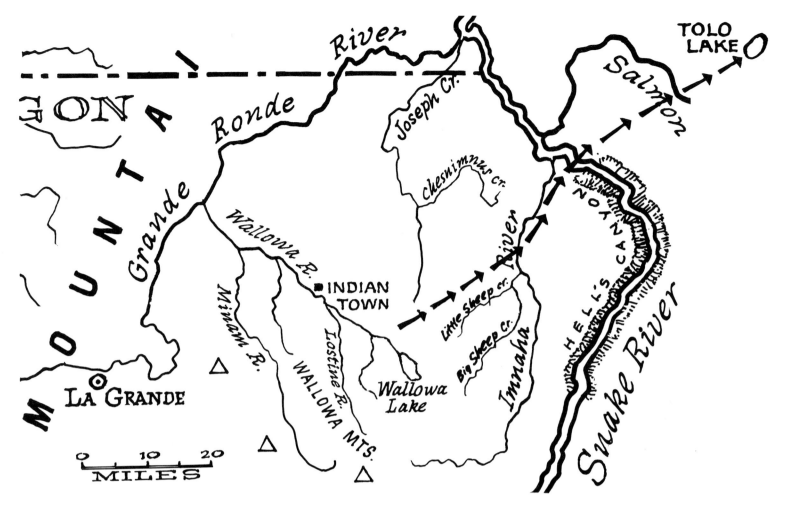

→ → → Route taken by the
Wallowa Nez Perces, June 1877

As a strong proponent of the Dreamer faith, an eloquent speaker, and a man of prodigous physical strength, this elderly chief always was listened to in council. But as he had shown at Lapwai, when he had submitted to the indignity of being arrested and thrown in the guardhouse rather than involve his people in bloodshed, he did not want to start a war.

Last of the five nontreaty bands assembled near Tolo Lake was the once-proud, now-fragmented remnant of the Palouse contingent, a mere sixteen warriors, led by Chief Hah-tal-e-kin, who lived with one group of the band near Palouse Falls, and by Husis-husis Kute ("Naked Head"), who lived with another, known as the *Wawawai* band, fifty miles up the Snake River. Like Too-hool-hool-zote, Huis-huis Kute was a proponent of the Dreamer faith — thus a target for General Howard's dislike and contempt.

In all, the Nez Perces camped in White Bird's

territory on June 12, 1877 — two days before the deadline for their moving onto the Lapwai Reservation — numbered about six hundred souls. Of these, most were women and children. Even counting men too old to do much fighting, the adult males numbered only 191. A later check by both Indian and white historians lists the names of just 155 men who actually took part in the fighting.

Yellow Wolf, a Nez Perce warrior who participated in every battle of the war, later told McWhorter that the Indian participants in the Battle of White Bird Canyon numbered "less than fifty" and that he could "give the names of them all." In contrast, General Howard declared:

"They probably had at that point as many as five hundred Indians bearing arms; many young Indians from other tribes had joined them, delighted to take a hand in the war that Joseph was going to conduct."

Reduce the "five hundred" hostiles to fifty, the "many" Indians from other tribes to two, point out that Joseph had nothing to do with the conduct of the war until its very end, *then* General Howard's statement would bear some resemblance to the truth. As it stands, it is totally false.

As a final salute to a way of life they would lead no more, the Nez Perces camping at *Te-pah-le-wam* staged a parade June 13, the day before they were to move onto the plots of land selected for them within the boundaries of the Lapwai Reservation.

Riding double at the rear of the column on a single horse were two young men of the White Bird band, Wahlitits and Sarpsis Ilppilp. Known to be fine, upstanding young men of good family and character, they were first cousins — or, in Indian parlance, "brothers."

"Wahlitits was mounted in front and when passing through the village his horse stepped on a spread canvas covered with *kouse* roots drying in the sun," McWhorter writes. "Seeing this, Heyoom Moxmox (Yellow Grizzly Bear) spoke in angry derision: 'See what you do! Playing brave you ride over my woman's hard-worked food! If you so brave, why you not go kill the white man who killed your father?' "[8]

A few years earlier Wahlitits' father, Eagle Robe, had owned and farmed a piece of land near the mouth of White Bird Creek. With his permission a white man named Larry Ott settled nearby. Though at first promising not to trespass on Eagle Robe's garden spot, Ott gradually took more and more land, until finally one day he built a fence that excluded the Nez Perce from his own property. Eagle Robe protested, an argument ensued, and suddenly without provocation Larry Ott grabbed a gun and shot the Indian.

Not wanting to start a war, Eagle Robe, as he lay dying, told his son, who at that time was still a boy: "Do nothing to the white man for what he has done to me. Let him live his life!"[9]

Growing to manhood, Wahlitits had respected his father's command. But now, stung by the taunt and burning with resentment at being forced by the whites to give up his freedom and leave his home, he said to Yellow Grizzly Bear, "You will be sorry for your words."

When the parade was over Wahlitits went home and cried, according to Camille Williams. Then he sought his "brother," Sarpsis Ilppilp, and told him he had decided to avenge his father's death and show that he was a man by killing Larry Ott. Would his brother join him? Sarpsis Ilppilp said that he would. The revenge-seeking Indians

left the village early the next morning, heading for Larry Ott's cabin. Accompanying them was a seventeen-year-old nephew, Swan Necklace, whom Wahlitits ordered to come along as a "horse holder," without divulging the purpose of the mission.

Whether the white man had taken alarm and fled or just happened not to be at home is not clear. One Indian account has it that he was so frightened at the presence of the large encampment of Nez Perces in the neighborhood that he disguised himself as a Chinese, joined a group of Orientals mining near Forence, and thus escaped discovery and death. In any event he was not home when the aroused Young Nez Perces reached his cabin. But they had no trouble finding other men who, in their minds, deserved to die.

The first was a white settler named Richard Devine.

A crotchety, elderly man living alone on the Salmon River eight miles above the mouth of Slate Creek, Devine was known to have killed a crippled Nez Perce woman, Dakoopin, in the Imnaha country a few years earlier — for an offense no greater than her removing one of his horses that had strayed into her garden. More recently at his place on Slate Creek, he had set his vicious dogs on Indians passing by and had threatened them with his rifle.

But this time neither his dogs nor his rifle protected him. Invading his cabin without warning, Wahlitits and Sarpsis Ilppilp took the gun away from Devine before he could use it, killed him with it, helped themselves to a supply of cartridges and a horse, then rode in search of other victims.

The second man killed was a rancher named Henry Elfers, whose place was a few miles downriver. He, too, had a reputation for abusing Indians.

Returning to the vicinity of the *Te-pah-le-wam* camp, the two warrior Indians stopped some distance away, sending young Swan Necklace into the camp to tell the people what they had done. Apparently they did this for two reasons: first, to show that theirs had been an act of personal vengeance, for which the White Bird band as a whole was not responsible; second, to invite individual warriors who felt as they did to join them in further acts of retribution against the whites — again,

8. Ibid., p. 190.
9. Ibid., p. 122.

without involving the entire White Bird band. Next morning they were joined by sixteen young Nez Perces, "burning with a spirit of revenge."[10]

When the first attacks took place, Joseph and Ollokot were some miles away, killing beef cattle south of the Salmon River. Ollokot's wife, Wetatonmi, later told how news of the outbreak reached them.

"We stayed on the Salmon a few days, and then came back. We had about twelve horses packed with beef. Nearing the home camp, we saw a rider coming, running his horse. The men said to each other, 'He must have news to tell us.'

"It was Two Moons coming to meet us. He said, 'War has broke out. Three white men killed yesterday!'

"All the men followed Two Moons back to camp, leaving us women to follow with the pack horses. When we reached camp we saw the tepees all down . . . Chief Joseph and Ollocut rode among the people trying to stop them from moving. They called out to them, 'Let us stay here until the army comes! We will make some kind of peace with them.'

"But the peoople would not stay. After some confused shifting, all moved but two tepees. These tepees were Chief Joseph's and his brother's. They were watched closely by the warriors. They suspicioned that we would move to Kamiah or Lapwai."[11]

Chief Looking Glass and his band headed for their village on the South Fork of the Clearwater; Hah-tal-e-kin and his Palouses went along. With Chief Joseph and the Wallowa band unwilling to fight, this left only a small minority of the nontreaty Nez Perces involved in the violence. But as word of the killings was carried first to the nearby white settlements of Mount Idaho and Grangeville, then to Fort Lapwai, and thence to Fort Walla Walla and the country at large, the uprising was magnified into a full-scale war even before a single soldier became involved.

In all, during the three days of bloodletting the number of white victims killed by the Nez Perces in the Salmon River and Mount Idaho area numbered from fourteen to twenty-two, accordingly to whose accounting is accepted as accurate. General Howard gives the lower figure; a local resident named Arthur Chapman the higher.

"Chapman was a low-principled scoundrel," McWhorter writes, "wedded after the tribal ritual to a Umatilla woman. Speaking the Nez Perce language fluently, he became General Howard's interpreter throughout the Nez Perce campaign and later accompanied the Nez Perce group into exile as interpreter."[12]

In a more objective appraisal of Arthur I. Chapman, historian John McDermott says that as a boy, during the Rogue River Indian Wars of 1855–56, he carried dispatches for the army from The Dalles to Fort Walla Walla, then:

"in 1861 he settled on White Bird Creek near the mouth of the rivulet that now bears his name, and the following year he began raising cattle and horses. For several years he operated a ferry across the Salmon River near the mouth of White Bird Creek, and tradition has it that because of the experience he earned the nickname 'Ad,' an abbreviation for Admiral. He later moved his ranching headquarters to the mouth of White Bird Creek. In 1874 he sold his land and buildings to J. J. Manuel and settled on Cottonwood Creek, about eight miles from Mount Idaho, where he continued to raise horses. At the time of the outbreak, he claimed to own 400 head."[13]

McDermott describes Chapman as "apparently rough and ready — easy to anger and quick to strike out." McWhorter claims that he brutally assaulted two Indian boys he had caught stealing watermelons, helped hang an Indian named Wolf Head, and unjustly accused Chief Joseph of murdering a white woman during the Salmon River raids, a slander that would stain Joseph's reputation for the rest of his life.

"There are reports that Chapman was on the tribal blacklist for selling Nez Perce beef to the Chinese miners," McDermott writes, "but he apparently maintained good relations with some of the Indians despite his shortcomings. Looking Glass was his friend, and there were others."[14]

Indicative of his friendship for Chapman is the fact that Looking Glass gave the white rancher his first word of the Salmon River raids.

"In the afternoon of June 14, 1877, two friendly Indians, Looking Glass and Yellow Bear, rode up to my place and told me that Joseph's band were on the war path, were very near to my place," Chapman wrote, "and I should go at once; that they had already killed seven white men. I then started to go to my house. They then called me back and told me to go immediately. I then told my two hired men what I had heard, and told them to take my three stallions from the stable and go to town. I got on my horse and started to town ahead of the two men, and as I started I could see the Indians coming."[15]

10. Ibid., p. 207.
11. Ibid., pp. 195–196.
12. Ibid., p. 215n.
13. John D. McDermott, *Forlorn Hope: The Battle of White Bird Canyon and the Beginning of the Nez Perce War* (Idaho Historical Society, Caxton Printers, 1978), p. 73.
14. Ibid., p. 74.
15. Ibid., p. 35.

Reaching the small settlement of Mount Idaho, Chapman dispatched an Indian messenger to Fort Lapwai, sixty-five miles to the northwest. He then conferred with the white townspeople as to how they should defend themselves until help from the soldiers arrived. Organizing a company of volunteers and electing Chapman its captain, the townspeople and ranchers gathered in Mount Idaho and began throwing up breastworks, casting bullets, and preparing defenses.

Next morning Chapman again met near his ranch with Looking Glass and his brother, Tucallasasena, who gave him the latest news of the continuing killings on the Salmon River. He managed to persuade Tucallasasena to ride back to Mount Idaho with him and to carry another message to Captain Perry at Fort Lapwai. In essence, the message said that an Indian war had started and only a quick, overpowering attack by federal troops would save the lives and property of the whites in the area.

Since General Howard had just arrived at Fort Lapwai to make sure the nontreaty Nez Perces were moving onto the reservation by June 14, there was no need for the post's commandant, Captain David Perry, to waste any time requesting orders from his superior. At the moment, only two companies of cavalry were available at Fort Lapwai. In hopes that Captain Perry and his one hundred men could keep the estimated five hundred hostiles occupied until reinforcements arrived, Howard ordered Perry to outfit and march as quickly as he could. Perry packed rations for five days and issued forty rounds of ammunition per man, preparing for what he and Howard both felt would be a brief campaign. According to Howard, as the column started to leave at 8 P.M., June 15, Perry said:

> "Good-by, general!"
> "Good-by, colonel. You must not get whipped."
> "There is no danger of that, sir."[16]

After the soldiers had disappeared into the growing darkness, General Howard retired to his quarters, where for the next several nights and days he paced the floor in deep concern for his officers and men. But he was confident enough to write in one of his official dispatches: "Think they will make short work of it."

Custer had thought that, too.

16. Ibid., p. 54; Oliver Otis Howard, *Nez Perce Joseph* (Boston: Lee and Shepard, 1881), p. 99.

CHAPTER TWENTY-FIVE

THE BATTLE OF WHITE BIRD CANYON

*The citizens informed Perry that they knew the
Nez Perces well, that the Indians were cowardly
scoundrels, and that they could whip them easily if
they only had enough rifles.*
— Citizens of Mount Idaho, June 16, 1877

ALTHOUGH General Howard's brilliant, outspoken adjutant, Lieutenant Charles Erskine Scott Wood, later would write: "I am afraid it would not do to make history from the diaries of soldiers," there is no better way to gain an understanding of the first encounter between the Nez Perces and the federal troops than to read the account written by Sergeant John P. Schorr, Company F, Twenty-first Cavalry, who was there.

"We left Fort Lapwai about 8 P.M. on the 15th, and rode all that night with a short rest to get a bite to eat for man and horse. We then again took up the march and on 16th June, we saw the many depredations committed by the Indians such as killing of horses, and robbing prairie schooners and burning down ranches and I guess the Red Devils were pretty well filled up with fire water.

"Noon on the 16th found us at Cottonwood or Norton's ranch. . . . Here we had another short rest, then off again for Mount Idaho, arrived there about 10 P.M., and with about four hours rest found us in the saddle again.

"At 2 A.M. we were rousted out of what little sleep we could catch in the saddle when a halt without dismounting had been ordered. We were near entering the White Bird Canyon to make a surprise attack on the Indians at daybreak. But let me state right here, we were to have the surprise of our lives."[1]

In just thirty hours the command had traveled more than seventy miles over steep, muddy, timbered terrain. Now with both man and beast bone-weary, the unseasoned troops, untrained mounts, and a handful of undisciplined volunteers sat waiting for dawn to come so they could go charging down the steep, rocky slope of a deep canyon in a surprise attack against a foe on his home grounds whose position and strength were mostly unknown.

If ever there were a formula for military disaster, it had been perfectly mixed here.

In justice to Captain Perry, pressures had been put upon him that were hard to resist. Late the previous afternoon a group of citizens led by Ad Chapman had ridden out from Mount Idaho to meet the soldiers. Already the Nez Perces were on the run, Chapman said. Unless caught and attacked immediately, they would be out of reach shortly after daylight tomorrow. It was this group of citizens that told Perry what "cowardly scoundrels" the Nez Perces were.

"Perry knew that if he allowed the Nez Perce to escape without making any effort to overtake them, he would be loudly criticized by the settlers," McDermott writes. "He finally decided to lay the matter before his officers and summoned Trimble, Parnell, and Theller for a conference. After explaining the situation, Perry asked for their opinion and found them in agreement. They believed the attempt should be made."[2]

Being unacquainted with the terrain over which the attack must be made, Perry asked Chapman to come along as guide and to supply him with as many citizen volunteers as he could muster. Chapman promised "twenty-five or thirty" men, but when the group showed up it numbered only eleven.

This was the force now waiting to make a "surprise" attack on the Indians camped on the floor of White Bird Canyon — ninety-nine officers and men of the United States Army, most of whom had fired only a few shots in practice and none in bat-

1. McWhorter, *Hear Me*, pp. 234–235.
2. McDermott, *Forlorn Hope*, p. 72.

Published in Harper's Weekly   Courtesy Penrose Library, Whitman College

Sketches of the Nez Perce War

tle, and eleven citizen volunteers with no training or discipline whatsoever.

Shortly after the column crested the divide, the blood-curdling cry of a coyote split the darkness, Sergeant Schorr reported, a cry which he knew was made by no animal.

"At that sudden nerve-shivering howl I felt my hair standing up, well knowing its import. There was no repitition, no answering echo. Just that one eerie, prophetic, death-laden cry that could not be misinterpreted."[3]

As the cry died away, one of the most expert horsemen among the Nez Perces, an ex-slave named Itskimze Kin ("Feet and Hands Cut Off" or "No Feet") mounted and rode into the encampment with news of the approach of the soldiers.[4] The Indians still hoped for peace.

Photo by Bill Gulick

Whitebird Hill looking south

*Courtesy Western History Collections,
University of Oklahoma Library*

One of the guns and gun cases identified as Nez Perce, the other as Sioux, having belonged to Sitting Bull.

"Ollokot urged the warriors to comply with the ruling of the chiefs and older warriors, not to fire the first shot. The young chief wanted first to learn the intention of the soldiers . . .

"The Nez Perces sent a commission of six, carrying a white flag, to meet the troop commander on a mission of peace. The leader of this party, Wettiwetti Howlis ("Vicious Weasel") was a man of splendid repute, known to the whites as John Boyd. This peace mission had strict instructions not to fire unless fired upon."[5]

Daylight came around 4 A.M. that Sunday morning, June 17, 1877. As the light grew and he saw the ruggedness of the terrain, Captain Perry grew apprehensive. But Ad Chapman assured him

3. McWhorter, *Hear Me,* p. 238.

4. Ibid., p. 239; McDermott, *Forlorn Hope,* p. 81n. "No Feet had been a slave to the Yakima chief Kamiakin," McDermott says. "The chief had purchased him from some tribe further west, and his tribal origin has never been determined. No Feet had lost both feet and one of his hands when Kamiakin left him outdoors, shackled with traps, one sub-zero night to punish him for stealing. Later Kamiakin gave the Indian his freedom, and he settled among the Nez Perce. Because of his condition, he spent a great deal of time on horseback and became an excellent rider."

5. McWhorter, *Hear Me,* 244.

that after a mile or so the canyon opened out into a comparatively smooth valley, where the cavalry could fight well.

Perry was cautious. He detailed Lieutenant Theller and eight men to move out ahead as an advance guard. With them was a trumpeter, Private John M. Jones, who five weeks earlier had gone on a drunk and got himself arrested and thrown in the Fort Lapwai guardhouse. While sobering up there, he had been joined by the "cross-grained growler," Chief Too-hool-hool-zote. Despite their differences in age, race, and language, the two men had become such good friends that upon his release Trumpeter Jones had boasted that if war came he was sure the Indians never would shoot at *him*.

A Nez Perce hide tepee and two Nez Perce men. Chokeberries are spread on the hide in front.

Also sent out as scouts were several unarmed Lapwai Nez Perces who had accompanied the command, along with Chapman and the citizen volunteers. Moving ahead of the column at a distance of one hundred yards, the advance detail was under strict instructions to halt the moment the enemy was sighted, to deploy in defensive position, and to immediately send word back to Captain Perry that a confrontation was imminent. As was customary, each of the two companies had a bugler, whose trumpeted calls were extremely important in carrying the orders of the officers to the men through the dust and din of battle over wide distances.

"Abraham Brooks and Frank Husush, two of the Nez Perce scouts, rode ahead of the detachment," McDermott writes. "Signs told them they were nearing the Indian camp, and they reported their discovery to Theller. Ad Chapman immediately spurred his horse forward to see for himself. Reaching the place where the ground sloped downward before rising to form the crest of the ridge, he looked to his right and saw the peace party coming toward him. Apparently the Indians had ridden around the west end of the ridge and were angling east to intercept the soldiers before they rode over the divide. Without a moment's hesitation Chapman opened fire."[6]

As noted earlier, the six Nez Perces peace envoys were under strict orders not to fire unless fired upon. After Chapman had shot twice in their direction, they turned back and sought cover. From the Indian camp below them, groups, of warriors began riding up the slope to fight the soldiers. Seeing this movement, Lieutenant Theller deployed his men and ordered trumpeter Jones to blow the call to battle that would bring the main force forward. Still mounted, trumpeter Jones put the mouthpiece of the bugle to his lips.

Two Moons gives the Indian account of the way the battle began:

"I join with the others, among them Yellow Wolf and my partner, Otstotpoo ('Fire Body'), an old-like man. There was a gun report to the north and soon, right away, we saw a man wearing a broad, whitish hat and riding a white horse coming fast from the north. He was on high flat land along a rock-topped ridge lying just west of us. That rider was Chapman, a known bad man. When he saw us he fired across at us but his shot was lost.

"Several, maybe twenty, soldiers followed close after Chapman. There was a bugler and when the party all stopped, this bugler rode a little ahead of them. He

6. McDermott, *Forlorn Hope,* p. 84.

began calling orders on his trumpet. Otstotpoo said to me, 'You now watch! I will make a good shot and kill that bugler!''

"He did make the long-distance shot, and dead dropped the bugler from his horse. Chapman and his soldiers whirled and rode rapidly away from there."[7]

Since the Battle of White Bird Canyon has been related by historians and analyzed by military experts in far greater detail than space allows here, we will touch only on its high points and its effect on the Nez Perces who took part in it. Contrary to statements made by General Howard, less than fifty Indians were active in the battle. Fighting on their own ground, they did not require any grand strategy devised by a "Red Napoleon." The Nez Perces simply fought in the Indian way — exposing themselves as little as possible, making every shot count, inflicting as much damage on the enemy as

Courtesy Luna House Historical Society
Lewiston, Idaho

Peo-peo Tholekt

Photo courtesy of Robert R. Beale,
Pomeroy, Washington

Albert Moore, one of the Nez Perce warrior survivors of the Chief Joseph War. He was 37 years old when this picture was taken, in the 1890s. His dress and hairstyle are pure old-time Nez Perce, with none of the feathers and other trappings borrowed from plains tribes.

they could, while receiving very little damage themselves.

For generations they had been horse Indians. They rode only their best-trained horses when they made meat in the buffalo country, and they rode these same horses when they went into battle. The mounts of the cavalrymen never had heard shots fired from their backs, let alone heard bullets whistling toward them. It was inevitable that they

7. McWhorter, *Hear Me*, p. 246.

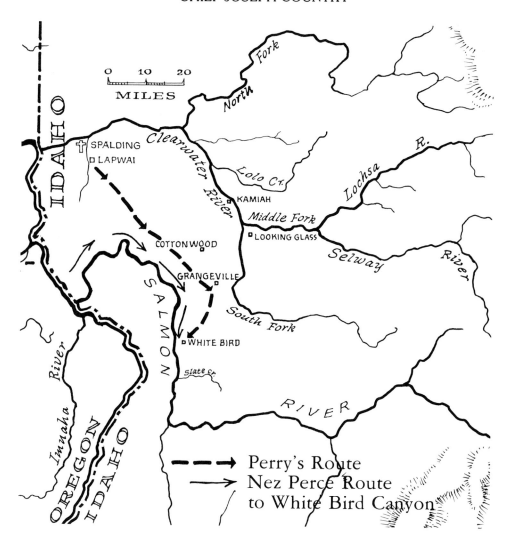

Perry's Route
Nez Perce Route
to White Bird Canyon

should go wild with fear, pitching and bolting. When white cavalrymen went into action, the standard tactic was to dismount and fight on foot, with one man holding his own and three other mounts in some sheltered spot. With his hands full controlling four terror-stricken animals, he could do no fighting — which reduced the firepower of his troop by one-fourth.

The Nez Perces, on the other hand, had so accustomed their horses to the sound of gunfire that "an Indian pony would stand and eat grass while its owner fought."[8] Though one company of cavalrymen did dismount and fight on foot, the other for some obscure reason was permitted to shoot from the backs of their horses, with the result that their fire was wildly inaccurate. The often-repeated story that the Nez Perces stampeded a band of wild horses toward the soldiers in order to frighten the cavalry horses is not true, the Indians say. Aboard every one of those apparently riderless animals was

a daring, athletic Indian, clinging like a burr to the far side, holding on with a moccasined toe hooked across the horse's back and a hand grasping a hunk of mane, guiding the animal with a length of braided rawhide looped around its lower jaw.

Hollywood to the contrary, no Indian in his right mind ever attempted to shoot a rifle at an enemy while performing this stunt. With ammunition scarce and expensive, the Nez Perce fighting man wanted every shot to count. Sergeant Michael McCarthy, a participant in the battle, describes one technique used by the Indians:

"When a warrior wanted to fire, he rolled off the pony to the ground, took deliberate aim, and crawled on again — the pony remaining quiet and patient during the firing, lying by the roadside."[9]

Despite Captain Perry's efforts to rally his

8. McDermott, *Forlorn Hope,* p. 153.
9. Ibid., pp. 153–154.

Courtesy Luna House Historical Society
Lewiston, Idaho

Nez Perce woman with children

slowly, with half of your men moving in deliberate fashion while the other half covers for them" were read to mean "Every man for himself" or "We've lost the fight — run like hell." By all credible accounts Ad Chapman time and again prevented a regrouping in a defensible position by shouting to the officer trying to set up such a stand that there was a better place further on, leaving the disorganized, strung-out, stunned, exhausted soldiers behind to be shot or clubbed to death by the Indians.

It was not until he had reached the Henry Johnson ranch, four miles beyond the head of White Bird Canyon, that Captain Perry was able to halt his fleeing men and take a defensive position on a high point of land. By then he was so deep in shock that he had completely lost track of time,

10. Ibid., p. 198.

Photo from Agnes Moses, Kamiah, Idaho   *Courtesy Idaho Historical Society*
Tolo's daughter taken about 1890

Tolo — a Nez Perce woman. She rode form Slate Creek to the Florence mining camps during the Indian troubles on the Salmon River in 1877 to warn the whites of their danger and to get help.

troops and make a stand, he could not organize a defensive line that would hold. Following the first charge by the Indians, the citizen volunteers jumped on their horses and headed for home — with Ad Chapman and his broad-brimmed white hat leading the way. Since they and Lieutenant Theller's detail were being counted upon by Captain Perry to hold the high ground to the left, that flank was now exposed. From the vacated height the Indians poured a murderous fire into the rest of the command.

Nobody had thought to retrieve trumpeter Jones's bugle. Desperately needing a means of communicating orders to his officers and men, Captain Perry managed to locate Captain Trimble's trumpeter. Unfortunately he had lost his bugle. There was a spare around someplace, but no one could find it.

"A Cavalry command on a battlefield without a trumpeter," Captain Perry would later say wryly, "is like a ship at sea without a helm."[10]

In the din of battle, Perry's voice could carry no more than a few yards. Hand signals which he intended to mean "Hold up and make a stand on that ridge a hundred yards to the rear" or "Retreat

remarking to Lieutenant Parnell that since it now was seven o'clock, he was sure that they could defend this position until dark.

"Astonished, Parnell informed his commander that it was about 7 o'clock in the morning, not evening, and that each of his men had only ten rounds of ammunition left."[11]

In contrast to Ad Chapman, who had initiated the battle by firing at the peace envoys, then turned tail and fled, the two young warriors who had started the uprising by killing the white settlers on Salmon River showed a bravery long remembered by their people.

"I, Two Moons, saw Sarpsis Ilppilp, Wahlitits, and Tipyahlahnah Kapskaps, all wearing full length red blanket coats and two of them on fine-looking grey horses, come riding side by side at the head of the charge. These three warriors came through that wild charge and mixing up the soldiers, untouched by the hail of enemy bullets. . . . After this battle, these three men were known as the 'Three Red Coats.' "[12]

Incredibly, the only casualties suffered by the Nez Perces in the battle were three men slightly wounded. Troop losses were thirty-four men killed, two wounded. As Captain Perry wrote in his report to General Howard, in proportion to the number of soldiers involved, the disaster was equal in magnitude to the Custer Massacre just a year earlier.

Like that disaster, news of it stunned the army and the nation.

11. Ibid., p. 94.
12. McWhorter, *Hear Me,* p. 247.

CHAPTER TWENTY-SIX

HIDE AND SEEK

Seven days after the first battle, General Howard arrived in the Nez Perces country, bringing seven hundred more soldiers. It was now war in earnest. We crossed over Salmon River, hoping General Howard would follow. We were not disappointed.

— Chief Joseph, April 1879

IN HIS REPORT to General Howard, Captain Perry estimated the number of hostiles encountered during the Battle of White Bird Canyon at 125, but he warned that it would take "at least 500 men to whip them." General Howard immediately upped his subordinate's appraisal of the forces arrayed against the army to "at least five hundred Indians bearing arms."

Even before the battle, Howard had ordered all available troops stationed at posts throughout Washington and Oregon to come to Fort Lapwai; now he extended the summons to military stations as distant as Sitka, Alaska, San Francisco, and Atlanta, Georgia. This time he would lead the troops. Within a week he had assembled a force of four hundred fighting men and a hundred or so scouts and packers. Equipped for a lengthy campaign, he led the command out of Fort Lapwai on June 22, leaving Captain Perry and the remnants of two companies behind to stand guard at the post.

Reaching the White Bird Canyon battleground, Howard detailed squads to the grisly tasks of burying the dead, then moved on to the site of the Nez Perce camp near the juncture of White Bird Creek with the Salmon River. There his worst fear was confirmed. The Indians were gone, leaving behind clear signs that they had crossed the turbulent Salmon and now were on the loose in the wild, rugged country to the south and west. Much as he and his troops dreaded the swift, deep, rapids-filled river, it must be crossed if the Nez Perces were to be caught and forced into battle. Preparations for the crossing were begun.

Meanwhile, the victorious White Bird and Joseph bands had been joined the day after the battle by two renowned and experienced warriors, Rainbow and Five Wounds, who had just returned from the buffalo country. In a council of tribal leaders it was decided to cross the Salmon, move down it a short distance, and there await the coming of the soldiers. As Joseph's band had done three weeks earlier in crossing the far more dangerous Snake, this crossing was made with no fuss or bother and no loss of goods or lives.

But behind them, the soldiers were having problems. One of these was the lack of information about the Indians. The main question troubling Howard was whether the entire band of hostiles was camped on the far side of the river or had left just a small group behind while the main body went elsewhere. If the Joseph band, for example, decided to return to the Wallowa country, that could mean serious trouble for the settlers, for Captain Whipple and his troops were no longer there to protect them.

Finally Howard decided to cross the entire command. Lieut. Harry L. Bailey, Company B, Twenty-first Infantry, wrote on June 30:

"Have just crossed the swift and dangerous Salmon River in a skiff with four men and four oarsmen. The stream at this point is about 200 yards wide, with a plunging current. By a good deal of labor and loss of time, a large rope had been stretched across. . . . This morning a number of horses and mules were made to swim the river and a famous swim they made of it.

Some of them were turned over and over, and others carried away down the stream, but I think all got over."[1]

Crossing the five hundred men, two Gatling guns, a small piece of field artillery, all their horses, arms, and supplies took the whole of one day. Meanwhile, the main body of Nez Perces, which was camped not far away, loaded up and moved some twenty miles down the Salmon to what was called Craig's Ferry. Next morning they recrossed the river here, leaving the soldiers with nothing to combat but the country and the elements.

It took Howard and his troops forty-eight hours to travel the same distance the Indians had traversed in half a day.

"The 5th of July brought us to Craig's Ferry," Howard writes, "where it became evident that all the Indians had passed back and taken the trail toward the Cottonwood, 16 miles distant. At first I hoped by a prompt crossing to join Perry . . . but having no boats, a raft had

Dead Mule Trail

been constructed from the timber of a cabin near the ferry."

The cabin belonged to a Nez Perce Indian named Luke Billy, who had gone to work for the army as a scout. What his feelings were as he watched the soldiers tear down his house and use its timbers to make a clumsy, unwieldy raft can only be guessed. He must have wondered why the white men were going to all that trouble when a buffalo hide stretched over a frame of willows would have served the purpose just as well.

"Our first attempt on the morning of the 6th to cross the river, here a perfect torrent, lost us our raft," Howard writes mournfully, "which tumbled down the rapids at a swift rate, with all on board, for three or four miles."

The home Luke Billy now watched vanish downriver had been a substantial one. Colonel W. P. Parnell (then a Lieutenant serving with Howard) later testified that its timbers were a foot thick and thirty or forty feet long. Twenty-three years after the war, Luke Billy was still trying to collect from the government for its loss.[2]

Unable to cross the Salmon at this point, Howard ordered a retrograde march upriver, made the crossing near the mouth of White Bird Creek, and then retraced his route to Grangeville, which he reached July 8. In the two weeks since his force had left Fort Lapwai he had accomplished exactly nothing.

Meanwhile, acting under Howard's orders, one of his subordinate officers precipitated a confrontation that turned a band of peaceful Nez Perces into deadly foes. As noted earlier, Chief Looking Glass and his people wanted nothing to do the the war. After giving news of the outbreak to Ad Chapman, Looking Glass and his band returned to their village on the South Fork of the Clearwater, fifty miles northeast of the White Bird Canyon area.

While preparing to cross the Salmon the first time, General Howard had received a disturbing dispatch. His official report says:

"The evening of the 29th [June] positive information is obtained that Looking Glass, who, with his people, had stood aloof from the hostiles, had been furnishing reinforcements to them of at least twenty warriors, and that he proposed to join them in person, on the first favorable opportunity. . . . With a view of preventing the

1. McWhorter, *Hear Me*, p. 276.
2. Ibid., p. 281.

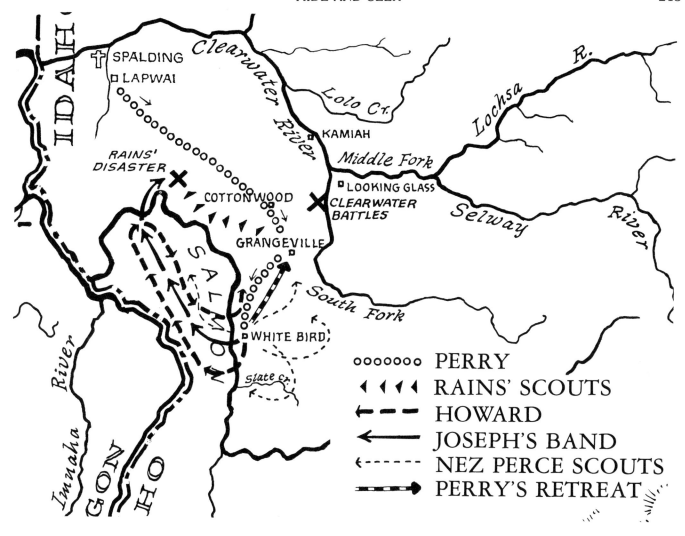

PERRY

RAINS' SCOUTS

HOWARD

JOSEPH'S BAND

NEZ PERCE SCOUTS

PERRY'S RETREAT

completion of this treachery, I sent Captain Whipple . . . to surprise and capture this chief and all that belonged to him."[3]

Howard told Captain Whipple that as soon as Chief Looking Glass and the Indians camped with him had been captured, the prisoners were to be turned over "for safe keeping" to the Mount Idaho Volunteers. How safe they would have been in the hands of Ad Chapman and his brave followers may well be questioned. At any rate, Captain Whipple and his command reached the village early Sunday morning, July 1. According to Peopeo Tholekt, who was in the chief's tepee at the time, Looking Glass told him to go out and meet the soldiers.

"Say to them, 'Leave us alone. We are living here peacefully and want no trouble.' "

Peopeo Tholekt mounted his horse and rode out to talk to the soldiers.

"One man greeted me friendly in Nez Perce," he later told McWhorter, "and I gave him my Chief's message that we want no trouble and therefore had I come from my people.

"But those soldiers would not listen. They seemed drinking. They came near killing me. I understood little English. One said to me, 'You Looking Glass?' He jabbed me in the ribs with his gun muzzle. He did not hit easy! The first man told him, 'Hold on! This not Looking Glass! Only one of his boys.' "[4]

Ordered by the soldiers to go back to the village and tell Looking Glass that he must come and talk with them, Peopeo Tholekt did so. But having seen the whites mistreat his messenger, the chief was suspicious and refused to go. After more confused parleying and threats by the whites, someone fired a shot. And the battle — if that is what it should be called — began.

3. Ibid., p. 262; *Annual Report of the Secretary of War* (Washington, D.C., 1877), 1:120.
4. McWhorter, *Hear Me*, pp. 264–266.

"An opportunity was given Looking Glass to surrender," Captain Whipple reported, "which he at first promised to accept, but afterwards defiantly refused, and the result was that several Indians were killed, the camp, with a large amount of supplies, destroyed, and seven hundred and twenty-five ponies captured and driven to Mount Idaho."

If by "several Indians killed" Whipple means the Nez Perce wife of Peter Pliater and the baby strapped to her back, then his fatality list is accurate, for they were the only Nez Perces who lost their lives during the encounter. They drowned when the mother's horse was pulled under as she was crossing the Clearwater in an attempt to escape the hail of bullets ripping through the tepees. The outcome of the attack was negative.

"Of course this stirred up a new hornet's nest," General Howard lamented, "and did not get Looking Glass and his treacherous companions into custody."[5]

With his village looted and burned and his peaceful intentions scorned, Chief Looking Glass and his band wasted no time joining forces with the hostiles. Meeting Joseph, White Bird, Too-hool-hool-zote, and Hah-tal-e-kin near Cottonwood on Camas Prairie, Looking Glass expressed his changed feelings in a bitter speech:

"Two days ago my camp was attacked by the soldiers. I tried to surrender in every way I could. My horses, lodges, and everything I had was taken away from me by the soldiers we had done so much for. Now, my people, as long as I live I will never make peace with the treacherous Americans. I am ready for war."[6]

Following the attack on the Looking Glass village, Captain Whipple and his men moved to Cottonwood, some thirteen miles northwest of Grangeville. The captain was unaware of the fact that by now, July 5, General Howard and his troops had crossed to the south side of the Salmon and were converting a cabin into a raft at Craig's Ferry. Nor did he know that the main body of Nez Perces had recrossed the river at the same point and were now heading in his direction. He therefore sent a pair of white scouts out looking for hostiles. The two citizen volunteers, William Foster and Charles Blewett, found some Indians, all right. In fact, they blundered directly into the path of the main band of angry Nez Perce warriors.

Before he could turn his horse around, Blewett was shot out of the saddle by an Indian named Red Spy. Foster managed to escape, returning to Captain Whipple's command on a horse nearly killed by hard riding. Wanting more information about the number and identity of the hostiles, Whipple detailed Lieutenant S. M. Rains and ten soldiers to go to the place of the encounter, with William Foster as their guide. Unfortunately for these twelve men, they met the Indians just as the Nez Perce warriors were preparing to mount a surprise attack on the entire Whipple command. Yellow Wolf, who as one of the warriors, tells what happened.

"In the draw I saw my friends gathered together. When I got where I could see them better, they made a left swerve. I looked in this new direction, and saw a blanket waving, a signal of war. I ran my horse that way

5. Ibid., p. 263; Howard, *Nez Perce Joseph,* p. 149.

6. Duncan MacDonald, "The Nez Perces, the History of Their Troubles and the Campaign of 1877," *New North-West,* April 26–December 20, 1878. Reprinted with an introduction and notes by Merle W. Wells, *Idaho Yesterdays,* Spring 1977 and Winter 1978. As Dr. Wells points out, Indian accounts of the Nez Perce War received little attention until Chief Joseph published his story in the *North American Review* in 1879. However, in Deer Lodge, Montana, in 1878, the editor of the *New North-West* asked Duncan MacDonald to go to Canada, interview the Nez Perce survivors who had fled there — which included White Bird — and obtain their side of the story.

"This arrangement for an early venture into oral history had great merit," Dr. Wells writes. "A son of Angus MacDonald (October 15, 1816 — February 1, 1889), who came from the highlands of Scotland to become a prominent administrator for the Hudson's Bay Company in the Pacific Northwest, Duncan also was a nephew of Eagle of the Light, who led a major Nez Perce band during the Idaho gold rush. (Angus MacDonald had married Eagle of the Light's sister sometime around 1840 and had a large and talented family who could appreciate both white and Nez Perce culture.) A few years before the war, Eagle of the Light had retired to Montana from the Salmon country after failing to exclude miners from his land, and White Bird had succeeded him as leader of the band which had the misfortune to begin the Nez Perce War. The war immediately embroiled Joseph's Wallowa band as well, and several others could not avoid belligerence either. But the incidents which precipitated hostilities occurred in White Bird's lands and involved his people."

At the beginning of the newspaper series, MacDonald explained the terms agreed to with the publisher:

"The writer, a relative of Looking Glass and White Bird, has entered into arrangements with the *New North-West* to prepare a series of papers giving the Nez Perces version of their troubles and their remarkable campaign. It is a condition of the publication that the views shall be related from their standpoint, and as full particulars as possible will be given of the tribe and their great expedition. The author has been for some time collecting data from the prominent actors in the great drama, and the time required to elicit incidents of the campaign will be occupied in preliminary narrative."

Since he had a good command of both Nez Perce and English, MacDonald was the ideal man for relating the Indian side of the story. Even so, he felt he must point out how eloquent an Indian could be in his own tongue. He wrote:

"Be it known, however, that my command of the English language is by no means adequate to give a fair idea of the capacity of even a moderate Indian speaker, There are, I believe, few white men who, in variety of expression, vividness of description, intonation, or even grace of action, surpass the first-class orators of the Red Men."

and, reaching a small hump, I saw about twelve soldiers . . .

"There was shooting, and one soldier fell from his horse. Then another went down a little way from us. Soon a third fell; and another and another, not far apart, went to the ground. Some distance on, a man — maybe wounded — got down from his horse and was killed. I will not hide anything. That part of the fight was not long. Those six soldiers did not get up.

"The remaining six soldiers ran their horses up a hill, maybe one half mile. Then they jumped off and lay among the rocks, and began shooting.

"Those soldiers were trapped. They had no show. When they began shooting, it was just like their calling, 'Come on! Come on!' A calling to death."[7]

Surrounded by an overwhelming force of nontreaty Nez Perces — whose supply of arms had been augmented by sixty-three excellent Springfield rifles lost by the troopers during the Battle of White Bird Canyon — Lieutenant Rains and his detail were wiped out to the last man. As yet, the only damage the soldiers had been able to inflict on the Indians was the destruction of one of their villages, the capture of some of their horses, and the accidental drowning of a mother and child.

Twenty miles to the southeast, in Mount Idaho, Captain D. B. Randall organized a company of sixteen armed citizens and led them toward Cottonwood, where he planned to join forces with the soldiers. This was on the morning of July 5, the day the two scouts, Lieutenant Rains, and his detail were killed. It was also the day Luke Billy saw his cabin vanish down the Salmon.

Meanwhile, on July 4, Captain Perry had left Fort Lapwai with a packtrain of ammunition and supplies, lightly escorted, bound for Cottonwood, where he expected to meet Howard's command, Instead, he was surprised to run into Captain Whipple, who told him what had happened. As senior officer, Perry took command.

Made cautious by the recent defeats, he put the soldiers to work digging entrenchments at Cottonwood so they could better defend themselves in case of an attack by a large number of hostiles. While engaged in this task, he and his men saw a group of whites a mile or two away being attacked by Indians. This was Captain's Randall's group of Mount Idaho Volunteers. Again, Yellow Wolf relates the encounter:

"Coming to the wagon road, we looked in the direction of the ferry [Craig's Ferry]. We saw them — about twenty armed horsemen. Not uniformed soldiers, but more like citizens . . .

"Then those men made for us. We were lined across their path. As they charged we gave way — let them go through. We then struck after them, racing to flank both sides. The shooting became faster, and soon those whites stopped and dismounted. The fighting was from about half-past ten o'clock to middle of afternoon. We did not know why the soldiers in their dugout rifle pits did not come to the fighting. We could see them where they were on higher ground. They seemed a little afraid."[8]

Indeed, a charge of cowardice later was made against Captain Perry by his junior officer, Captain Whipple, who said:

"Noting that there was some commotion at the brow of the hill, where a few citizens had gathered, and that Captain Perry was walking toward me, I turned and met him, asking, at the same time, the cause of the excitement. He replied, 'Some citizens, a couple of miles away, on the Mount Idaho Road, are surrounded by Indians, and being all cut to pieces, and nothing can be done to help them!'
" 'Why not?' "
" 'It is too late.' "[9]

Later Perry would claim that he at first regarded the disturbance as a ruse to get the soldiers away from their entrenchments but that as soon as he understood the situation he rushed a detachment to the scene.[10] Since the fight lasted several hours, according to Yellow Wolf, and Perry appears to have been shamed into sending troops to the rescue by the courageous action of twenty-five volunteers led by George Shearer, Perry certainly was being cautious about committing his troops to action. But then, he had good reason to be cautious.

In any event, as Yellow Wolf tells it:

"The sun was halfway down the afternoon sky when, looking back, we saw soldiers coming, their big gun in the lead.

"The chiefs now called out, 'Let us quit for a while.'

"Hearing that order, we left the fighting, taking Weesculatat with us. Three times wounded at beginning of fight, he lived until about dark. With two bad wounds, he could not hold his life. Not old, about middle-aged, he was first warrior killed. We lost a good fighter."[11]

7. Lucullus Virgil McWhorter, *Yellow Wolf: His Own Story* (Caxton Printers, 1940), pp. 71–72.
8. Ibid., p. 76.
9. McWhorter, *Hear Me,* p. 292; Howard, *Nez Perce Joseph,* p. 153.
10. McWhorter, *Hear Me,* p. 293; Cyrus T. Brady, ed., *Northwestern Fights and Fighters* (New York: Doubleday, Page & Co., 1909), p. 125.
11. McWhorter, *Yellow Wolf,* p. 125.

Ironically, the white volunteer who shot the Indian was a young man named Charley Crooks, who had been raised among the Nez Perces and whose father was considered to be such a good friend that the Indians in an earlier fight had yelled at him that if he would take his father's horse and go home they would not harm him.

Casualties in the fight for the volunteers were three men wounded and two killed, the mortalities being Captain D. B. Randall and Ben Evans.

At this point in the war only one Nez Perce warrior had died in battle. Up to July 6, 1877, the whites had lost forty-six fighting men and twenty-two noncombatants.

CHAPTER TWENTY-SEVEN

BATTLE OF THE CLEARWATER: JULY 11–12, 1877

I do not know how many men Howard had in
these great battles, but as near as I can ascertain he
must have had two or three men to each Indian.
— Duncan MacDonald, *New North-West*, 1878

AFTER LURING Howard's command across the Salmon and traveling twenty-five miles west to Craig's Ferry, the Wallowa band was well on its way toward its home country, if it wished to return there. But Joseph knew that a return to the Valley of Winding Waters was impossible now, so he went along with White Bird and Too-hool-hool-zote in the decision to recross the Salmon and head northeast across Camas Prairie.

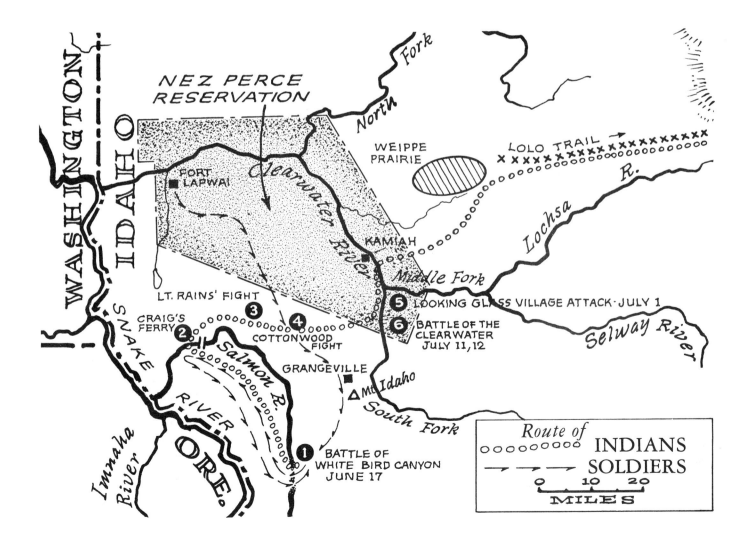

der, a symbol of embarrassment to the American Army, and a man whose presence worried Canadian officials.

Following the annihilation of Lieutenant Rains and his men and the skirmish with Captain Randall's volunteers near Cottonwood, the non-treaty Nez Perces moved at a leisurely pace across Camas Prairie to the South Fork of the Clearwater, setting up camp a few miles upstream from its junction with the Middle Fork of the Clearwater.

On July 9 General Howard reported:

"If Joseph will remain one day longer burning houses and bragging of his victories, I will be able to strike him a blow."[2]

Never mind that Joseph was neither burning nor bragging, the publicity process had begun that would turn Howard into a bloody-handed villain or a bright-shining hero in the minds of the newspaper-reading American public. As a victorious Civil War commander, head of the Freedmen Bureau in the South during the Reconstruction

1. Duncan MacDonald, "The Nez Perces," *Idaho Yesterdays,* Spring 1977, p. 15.
2. McWhorter, *Hear Me,* p. 295.

Courtesy Montana Historical Society
Chief Joseph

"All this time they were councilling to determine what was best to do," MacDonald writes, "whether they should leave the region of country which they were in and move toward the Snake country, or go to the Buffalo Plains and join Sitting Bull in the British Possessions. Some wanted to surrender to Howard, but they feared they would be shot or hung."[1]

The great Sioux leader, Sitting Bull, had fled to Canada with a number of his followers following their stunning victory over General George Armstrong Custer a year earlier. Safe for the time being because Canadian authorities refused to send him back to the United States against his will, he was a great hero to Indians north and south of the bor-

Harper's Weekly   *Courtesy Penrose Library, Whitman College*
Chief Joseph, a not very accurate likeness

Period, and the sixth-ranking general in the U.S. Army, he made news with every statement he issued. If he chose to simplify the Nez Perce War into a contest of strategies between himself and a "Red Napoleon" named Chief Joseph, where was the reporter who would object? This was front-page copy.

Under the guidance of Ad Chapman, Howard led a mixed force of cavalry, infantry, and artillery toward the spot where Chapman thought the hostiles would be camped. Thanks to Chapman's bad judgment, Howard and his troops missed the village of the hostiles by several miles, had to backtrack, and then found themselves in a poor position to attack. They attacked anyway — and the conflict was on.

For the better part of two days the Battle of the Clearwater continued in sporadic fashion, with neither side inclined to mount a serious attack. All the Indians wanted to do was protect their village. Lying prone behind the rocks strewn over the bare slope across which the soldiers must charge, the Nez Perces could fight from excellent cover. On higher ground, cut off from water, with little natural cover, and on terrain where they could not use their howitzer and Gatling guns to good effect, the soldiers had to be content with long-range fire aimed in the general direction of mostly unseen targets. Even when the target was seen, the marksmenship of the troopers was extremely poor.

"At this era of our army we had had almost no target practice," Lieutenant Harry L. Bailey writes. "A number of us saw a poor old horse, probably wounded, standing for some hours out in my front, and I suppose several hundreds of bullets were fired at him without apparent effect. That was one of the lessons I had about our shooting when we had in our army three shots per man per month for target practice."[3]

Most of the casualties were suffered early in the fight. Strung out in a line over two miles long and stumbling onto the village by accident, Howard's command never was in a position to mount a concerted attack in force. Fewer than one hundred Nez Perces were able to turn back four times their number, with tough old Too-hool-hool-zote and twenty-four of his warriors acting as dismounted sharpshooters, first in one position, then in another, all along the defensive front.

One tragic aspect of the war that has never been fully understood by non-Indians was the way it split Nez Perce families asunder. Since only one-fifth of the tribe belonged to the nontreaty bands, the warring Indians were a distinct minority. It was natural that the peaceful, reservation-dwelling majority should resent the trouble the uprising was causing them. At the same time, among many whites and Indians both on and off the reservation, a great sympathy existed for the minority group and its struggle to live free. Torn by conflicting feelings, individual Indians now and then changed sides.

One of these was a Christian Nez Perce, Joe Albert, whose Indian name was Elaskolatat. Enlisting as a scout for the army at the beginning of the campaign, he had served with Captain Perry during the White Bird Canyon Battle and now was with the white soldiers during the Clearwater conflict.

"Evidently at the Clearwater there was some friendly communication between General Howard's Christian Nez Perce scouts and the Dreamer patriots, for Elaskolatat learned of the death of his father, Weesculatat, who fell in the Captain Randall fight near Cottonwood. The son immediately resolved to abrogate his allegiance to the government and return to his own people. He did not await the dark covering of night, but under the glaring blaze of the July sun, he dashed across the shot-ripped field for the Nez Perce quarters, gaining them safely despite the firing of troops and warriors; the

3. Ibid., pp. 307–308; McWhorter, *Yellow Wolf*, p. 103.

Artist Concept, Harper's Weekly   Courtesy Penrose Library, Whitman College
October 27, 1877

Joseph and his brethern

former because of his appparent intent, the latter because of his uniform."[4]

Ridding himself of that uniform and putting on Indian clothes, the ex-scout threw himself into the battle on the side of his people. That evening he was shot through the thigh. But he kept on fighting through the rest of the Battle of the Clearwater — and in all the battles to come.

On the other hand,

"there also seem to have been desertions from the Nez Perce side during the Clearwater fighting. Alikkees ("Hair Cut Short," known as Alec Hays), a creditable fighter, stuck no longer than this two-days' battle. Allahkoliken ("Buck Antler's") became scared and ran away the first day and joined the Christians."[5]

Judging from the reluctance of both General Howard and the Indian leaders to commit their forces to a decisive battle, the line between being prudent and becoming scared and running away was hard to define. Since the soldiers would not attack, the Indians saw no point in pressing the fight. One by one, warriors left their defensive positions, returned to the village, packed up, and prepared to leave. The evacuation began in the morning and continued until midafternoon in full view of the soldiers, but nothing was done to halt it. Not until the village was empty of Indians did General Howard at last order a charge. Of this pointless attack, he bragged: "For a few minutes there was a stubborn resistance at Joseph's barricades; then his whole line gave way."[6]

Whether any Indian line remained to give way

Photo by Jane Gay   Courtesy Idaho Historical Society
Joe Kentuck called "a typical Nez Perce"

is questionable, for the main body of nontreaty Nez Perces was permitted to move downriver to the vicinity of Kamiah without molestation, while the soldiers occupied the site of the village and appropriated whatever goods and valuables had been left behind.

"It was a wonder to see the tons and tons of flour and other foods, and fine Indian goods, mostly burned. There was gold dust, jewelry, and fine silver tableware, some of which I judged dated from an early Hudson's Bay period. All this being brought to light, the packers and citizens helped themselves, while I tried to get a few souvenirs, but as fast as I got a little bundle, someone took it from me as I was looking after the troops."[7]

Historians call the Battle of the Clearwater a draw, which seems fair enough, for certainly neither side won a clear-cut victory or suffered a decisive defeat. General Howard's casualties were fifteen killed and twenty-seven wounded. By their own count the Nez Perces had four killed and five

From a painting by John Mix Stanley   Courtesy Penrose Library, Whitman College
Fort Owen — Flathead village

4. McWhorter, *Hear Me*, p. 309.
5. Ibid., p. 310.
6. Ibid., p. 321.
7. Ibid., p. 322.

Courtesy Montana Historical Society

Yellow Wolf. He was a nephew of Chief Joseph and fought all during the Nez Perce War later surviving to recount his experiences to L. V. McWhorter who has written the most comprehensive story of the Nez Perce War from the Indian point of view. In 1936 he was the last living Nez Perce Indian who took part in the Battle of the Big Hole.

wounded, though Howard set their losses much higher.

Badly in need of a piece of good news after the setbacks he had suffered, Howard raised no objections when Captain Keeler, who had been with the supply train, dispatched a wire:

"Have been with General Howard in the battle today, which he reports in detail. I consider this a most important success. Joseph is in full flight westward. Nothing can surpass the vigor of General Howard's movements and action."[8]

"The Indians fought as well as any troops I ever saw," Howard reported to his superior, General Irwin McDowell, "and so did ours, not one man failing in duty."[9]

Though the public may admire a general who praises his enemy and his troops, it does not like a loser. At that moment Howard needed a win, as was noted in a return telegram from General McDowell:

"These dispatches came most opportunely, for your enemies had raised a great clamor against you, which, the press reported, had not been without its effect in Washington. They have been silenced, but I think they (like Joseph's band) have been scotched — not killed — and will rise again if they have a chance."[10]

How prophetic those words were would soon be seen.

8. Ibid., p. 324.
9. Ibid.
10. Ibid., p. 325.

CHAPTER TWENTY-EIGHT

FLIGHT ACROSS LOLO TRAIL: JULY 16–27, 1877

*Listen to me, my chiefs! The Crows are the
same as my brothers! If you go there with me you
will be safe!*
— Chief Looking Glass, July 15, 1877

IN THE KAMIAH AREA, the Middle Fork of the Clearwater flows in a northwesterly direction, so Captain Keeler's dispatch stating that the Indians were "in full flight westward" was partially correct. But it was not the intention of the nontreaty bands, which now numbered two hundred and fifty fighting men plus four hundred or so women, children, and old people, to go downriver to Lapwai and the heart of the reservation. There, they knew, they would face the hostility of four-fifths of the tribe, bondage, trial for their crimes, and possibly death. Their only hope for freedom lay in the mountain wilderness north and east of the Clearwater. Again they prepared for the crossing of a swift, turbulent river, with a practiced skill that made it look easy.

"You have asked me how we crossed the Salmon and other deep, swift streams with our families and goods," Yellow Wolf responded to a question from McWhorter. "I will tell you all, how done. Owning that country, the Nez Perces knew all such streams. Crossed them often without difficulty . . .

"We had plenty of buffalo robes. With them we made hide boats. In making such a boat, the hide, hair side up, was spread on the ground. Across the hide were laid green willow or other limber poles about the thickness of your thumb. The hide and poles were bent up and lashed to other bent poles forming a long circled rim. The rim was on outside. That was all. Such boats carried big loads, and children and old people rode on top of the packs. . . . No paddles used. Boats were hauled by ponies guided by men. Two, maybe three or four, ponies to a boat. Two men swam at the sides to steady it."[1]

Not being pressed by the soldiers, the Indians made camp for the night on the left bank of the river. The next morning they put together boats and began ferrying their people and goods to the far shore.

"While this was doing, we saw the soldiers riding down the distant hill toward us. We found hiding and waited for soldiers. When they reached the riverbank, we fired across at them. We thought we killed one."[2]

If the soldiers did not know by now that the Nez Perces were excellent marksmen, they were slow learners. But General Howard certainly was exercising caution. Instead of attempting to cross the river here in the face of deadly hostile fire, he decided to go down the Clearwater half a day's march to Dunwell's Ferry, where the crossing could be made in peace and safety. Describing the march downriver as an attempt at strategy, Howard writes:

"There was a junction of trails beyond him [Joseph], fifteen or twenty miles off. Could I but get there! Perhaps I could by going back a little, then down the river and across; quick, indeed, if at all, and secret! But their eyes were too sharp for the success of this manuever, for I had not proceeded more than six miles before the Indians began to break camp, and to retreat, in good earnest, along the Lolo Trail toward Montana and the east."[3]

Chief Joseph is given credit by some writers for having delayed pursuit and fooled Howard by conducting a lengthy "wa-wa" across the river with the general, in which he proposed surrendering if proper terms were offered. With all action by the military suspended until the Indians had gotten out of danger, Joseph then is supposed to have laughed at Howard, turned his bare bottom toward

---

1. McWhorter *Yellow Wolf*, p. 62; McWhorter, *Hear Me*, p. 326.
2. McWhorter *Yellow Wolf*, p. 103.
3. Ibid., p. 103n; Howard, *Nez Perce Joseph*, pp. 168–169.

him, and slapped a buttock in derision as a farewell gesture.

It did not happen quite that way. Apparently Howard was given the impression that some of the Indians might surrender, which did cause him to delay in giving marching orders (though he hardly needed a reason for doing that). But it was not Joseph who gave Howard the reverse salute. It was a young warrior named Zya Timenna, a relative of Yellow Wolf. In response, a soldier fired a shot, which missed as usual, and the warrior hopped on his horse and rode away laughing.[4]

By July 15 the nontreaty bands had traveled thirty miles in a northeasterly direction to the ancient tribal camas-gathering grounds and camping place, Weippe Prairie. There they met Chief Temme Ilppilp ("Red Heart") and his band, just returned from the buffalo country after a year's absence. Hearing about the conflict, Chief Red Heart, his seventeen warriors, and the twenty-eight women and children in the band decided to have nothing to do with the war. Instead, they headed toward the reservation and what they thought would be a life of peace. But when the Red Heart band met General Howard and the soldiers their reception was not at all what they expected. Instead of being treated kindly for having chosen the path of peace, they were treated as hostiles who had surrendered after being defeated in battle.

"These peaceable, innocent people were seized and conducted to Kamiah, where their horses, saddles, and other equipment were confiscated, and under a guard of cavalry were marched sixty miles on foot through the stifling dust and blistering July heat, to Fort Lapwai."[5]

At last General Howard could report that he had taken a substantial number of Indian prisoners — never mind how. And prisoners they remained for the next nine months. Twenty-three adult men, nine adult women, and one three-year-old boy were held under military guard at Fort Lapwai, then moved by wagon to Lewiston and by boat downriver to Fort Vancouver. Watched over by members of the post's band, they were finally released and sent home April 22, 1878.

Participating in the council at Weippe were Chiefs Joseph, White Bird, Looking Glass, Too-hool-hool-zote, and Hah-tal-e-kin. Also present were the renowned warriors, Rainbow and Five Wounds, who, having recently returned from the buffalo country, could give the council reliable in-

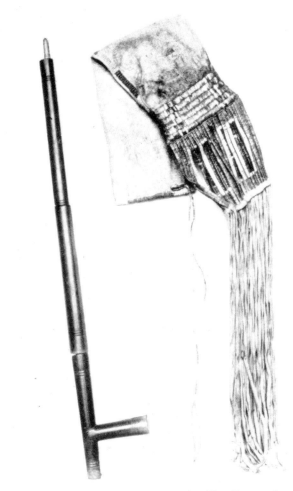

Peace pipe and pouch, given to the Nez Perces by the Crows in 1872, as a token of eternal friendship. On display at the Luna House Historical Museum, Lewiston, Idaho.

formation regarding enemies and allies there. A number of possibilities were discussed. They could cross the Bitter Root Mountains by the Lolo Trail, go north through the land of the Flatheads to Canada, or they could turn south into the land of the Shoshones, from whence they could double back into the Salmon and Snake River country. For a time, White Bird amd Joseph favored the latter alternative.

But the Flatheads, and their nearby neighbors, the Blackfeet, might not be friendly. The safer course might be to go south up the Bitter Root Valley to the headwaters of the North Fork of the Salmon, swing east through the Big Hole Country, Camas Meadows, and Yellowstone Park, then fol-

4. McWhorter, *Hear Me*, p. 329.
5. McWhorter, *Yellow Wolf*, pp. 310–312; McWhorter, *Hear Me*, p. 332.

low Stinking Water or Clark's Fork east into the country of the Crows.

Joseph expressed strong objections to flight of any kind. After asking the chiefs what they were fighting for and saying that he did not want to die in a strange land, he challenged them boldly:

"Some of you tried to say, once, that I was afraid of the whites. Stay here with me now, and you shall have plenty of fighting. We will put our women behind us in these mountains, and die in our own land fighting for them. I would rather do that than run I know not where."[6]

Rainbow and Five Wounds claimed that the Crows were talking about going on the warpath against the whites. Looking Glass insisted that the Crows were his friends, bound to the Nez Perces as blood brothers by the alliance made with them against the Sioux in 1874 and symbolized by their gift of the peace pipe, which, until returned, meant that the two tribes were sworn friends.

Not trusting the Crows, Wottolen and Two Moons opposed going to their country. On the other hand, a returning group of buffalo-hunting Nez Perces had left a lot of good horses with their Flathead "cousins" in the lower Bitter Root Valley. Why not go there and count on the Flatheads for help?

The final decision of the council was to cross Lolo Trail to the buffalo country, under the leadership of Looking Glass. On the morning of July 16 camp was broken and the exodus of six hundred and fifty nontreaty Nez Perces from their ancestral homelands began. Since their tepee poles had been left behind in the village deserted on the South Fork of the Clearwater — and would have been an extra burden for their horses to drag along

6. Howard and McGrath, *War Chief Joseph,* p. 187; Charles Erskine Scott Wood, "Chief Joseph, the Nez Perce," *Century Magazine,* May 1884, p. 138.

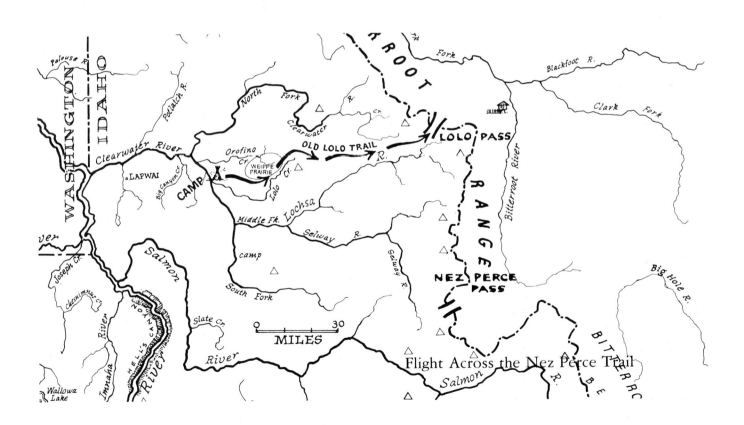

Flight Across the Nez Perce Trail

on that steep, narrow, rugged trail — shelter for the next few weeks would be only what they could improvise each night. The fanciful tale told by some writers that the Nez Perces drove a herd of beef cattle with them, is just that — a fanciful tale — for they took no cattle along. They did take horses, though — lots of them — one for every man, women, and child old enough to ride, plus from two to three thousand spare animals. They used them unmercifully, as they always had, for in their traditional way of life only the strongest animals survived.

As rear guard, five young warrior volunteers were left behind at Weippe Prairie,

"to remain at the camping ground for three suns, watching for enemy scouts and troops. If none were seen during that time, they were to come on and overtake the camp. But should enemies be sighted, two were to ride ahead with news of the danger, so that the warriors could prepare to hold the troops back on the trail until the families could escape to a place of safety."[7]

The Lolo Trail could easily be blocked by a few warriors. It was narrow and steep and wound through a heavy growth of trees, forcing the pursuing soldiers to move up the rocky path in single-file. This gave rise to an imaginative tale that the retreating Nez Perces sawed through the bases of tall trees, greased the saw marks so they would not show, and left the trees standing on their stumps, to be pushed over once the troops had moved into the trap. This would form a log corral within which the soldiers could then be butchered by the Indians.

This is another tale that did not happen. In the first place, the Nez Perces had no saws, only axes. In the second place, they did not know — as, indeed, no one ever has known — how to pull off such a gravity-defying feat. In the third place, they discouraged pursuit in a far easier, more conventional way — with rifle shots fired from ambush.

General Howard sent a dozen or so Christian Nez Perce scouts, led by Captain John and James Reuben, ahead of the main body of troops with orders to pursue the hostiles for "two marches" and find out what direction they were headed. The scouts managed to make contact with the rear guard of the fleeing Nez Perces in only half a day. They were then ordered to ride still further ahead to investigate the increasingly fresh sign.

Shortly after the scouts disappeared into the timber, the sound of gunfire was heard. Major Mason, far to the rear with the regulars, responded

Photo probably by C. A. Zimmerman, 1866-67   *Courtesy Smithsonian Institution*

Tzi-Kal-Tza — son of Captain William Clark of the Lewis and Clark Expedition of the years 1804-5-6. The date of this man's birth was either about June, 1806, or March, 1807. Probably he was born about the latter date, for the reason that the Lewis and Clark Expedition camped for a few days only with the Chopunnish or Nez Perce tribe of Indians in the latter part of September, 1805, while on its return in 1806 it made camp with those Indians from May 14 to June 10, enjoying a comfortable period of rest and refreshment. He was engaged in the Nez Perce Indian War in Idaho and Montana, and was made prisoner with Chief Joseph at the Battle of Bear Paw Mountains, and was sent with Joseph and other prisoners to Indian territory, where he died in 1878 or 1879, aged about 72 years.

by ordering the mule-packed howitzer unloaded and prepared for action. What he intended to shoot at is not known — but his troops found a target. When a detachment of volunteers came galloping back to inform the regulars that hostilities were under way, the soldiers got so excited they

7. McWhorter, *Hear Me,* p. 335.

started shooting — at the volunteers. As usual, they missed.

Missing, too, when Captain John, James Reuben and the scouts came riding back, was a Nez Perce known as John Levi, or Sheared Wolf. He was found a while later, lying in the grass with forty-five bullet holes in his body.[8] According to Nez Perce accounts he got what he deserved, for the nontreaty Indians had on several occasions captured Indians who were scouting for Howard, warned them to cease and desist, and then let them go.

"We knew you had taken up arms against us, but for relations sake we let you go. You promised us before that you would remain at your homes and not help Howard destroy us. Every word you promised us has proved a lie. . . . We will let you go again [but] I want you to understand that the next Nez Perce scouts we capture acting under Howard, we will kill at once."

Aware of this threat, Captain John had exclaimed: "Here are some fresh tracks. Let us go back. There is danger around here."

As the scouts turned to retreat, the hostiles opened fire. All the scouts except Sheared Wolf managed to get away. Dangerously wounded, he fell to the ground and was lying there when the hostiles found him. According to Watz-am-yas, a member of the Nez Perce rear guard, the Christian Nez Perce begged:

"Spare my life; I am badly wounded and have news to tell you."

"Yes," replied Watz-am-yas, "we have spared your lives too often. You can tell us your news after you get to the happy hunting grounds."

With that, he put a bullet through the scout's head.[9]

Rugged though the trail was, the Nez Perces were so accustomed to traveling it that Yellow Wolf passed over its difficulties with a mere four words placed as a minor phrase in the middle of a sentence: "For about six days, coming through the mountains, we saw no more fighting."[10]

Compare that with the description of the Lolo Trail by General Howard:

"The trail ahead being obstructed by fallen trees of all sizes and descriptions, uprooted by the winds and matted together in every possible troublesome way, a company of forty 'pioneers' with axes, was organized and sent to open the trail, wherever possible. It is true that the Indians had gone over this trail ahead of the troops but they had jammed their ponies through, over

Courtesy Montana Historical Society

Lucy Clark, the great-granddaughter of Capt. Clark, with her father and mother.

and under the rocks, around, over and under logs and fallen trees and through the densest undergrowth, and left blood to mark their path, with abandoned animals with broken legs or stretched dead on the trail."

Over this kind of terrain, Howard considered sixteen miles a day excellent progress for his troops. When asked why the soldiers had so much trouble traversing country that the Nez Perces considered ordinary, Howard repeated the comment of his guide, Ad Chapman, who said ungrammatically: "No man living can get so much out of a horse, like an Indian can."

Furthermore, Howard added:

"Had we, for three days, along the Lolo Trail, followed closely the hostiles' unmerciful example, we would not have had ten mules left on their feet fit to carry our sugar, coffee, and hard-bread."[11]

Leaving General Howard and his troops struggling up the trail far behind them, the Nez Perces topped Lolo Pass, paused to camp and rest for a time near a marshy meadow on the eastern slope of the Bitter Root Mountains, then moved on at a leisurely pace toward the broad, peaceful valley occupied by their "cousins," the Flatheads, and by the white merchants and ranchers with whom they long had traded for goods and horses on

8. Ibid., p. 337.
9. Duncan MacDonald, "The Nez Perces," *Idaho Yesterdays,* Spring 1977.
10. McWhorter, *Yellow Wolf,* p. 168.
11. Howard, *Nez Perce Joseph,* pp. 179–180.

friendly terms during their trips to and from the buffalo country.

In the view of the tribal leaders, remaining behind in the Nez Perce country would have meant a long and bloody war. Leaving their homeland meant choosing the path of peace, for they could not imagine that the soldiers would follow them very far.

But the soldiers *were* following them, though very slowly. Furthermore, having received word that "hostiles" were about to "invade" the Bitter Root Valley, a thin, blue line of thirty regulars was preparing to block the way — backed by two hundred brave volunteers, and a number of Flathead Indians who might be persuaded to turn traitor to their own kind if the prospect of loot in the form of goods and horses was great enough.

To show how much in earnest they were, the soldiers were doing a thing unknown to the Nez Perces in their style of warfare. They were felling trees to barricade the mouth of Lolo Canyon. Did they actually think that a few downed trees would stop the Indian? Curious to find out, Looking Glass, Joseph, and the other tribal leaders raised a white flag and rode down to the barricade to have a talk with the bluecoat in charge of its defense.

CHAPTER TWENTY-NINE

FORT FIZZLE

*If the officer wishes to build corrals for the Nez
Perces he may, but they will not hold us back. We
are not horses.*
— Chief Looking Glass, July 27, 1877

THOUGH THE defensive forces available to Captain Charles C. Rawn were equal in number to those of the "invading" Nez Perces, they lacked two vital motives that welded the hostiles into a forminable fighting unit: first, a cause for which they were prepared to fight to the death; second, the desperation of battle-hardened exiles with nothing to lose but their freedom. In command of Company L, Seventh Infantry, and just recently posted to the newly built Fort Missoula a few miles to the north, Captain Rawn had assembled his forces as hastily as he could after receiving orders to intercept and delay the hostiles by all possible means. What was possible was not known, since

the disparate elements of his command never had been tested as individual units under fire, let alone as a force working together.

Since erecting a stockade would serve to protect their own bodies, the thirty regulars could be depended upon to work like beaver and fight like demons, for they knew they would stand no chance if they tried to run. The fifty Flatheads were something else. To insure their support, vague promises had been made that they would not be confirmed to a reduced reservation; that the soldiers would regard their assistance as a most friendly act, for which they would reap a rich reward in goodwill; and that, if the hostiles surrendered, no one would strenuously object if the Flatheads helped themselves to Nez Perces horses and goods.

In order to make sure no friendly Indian got shot, Captain Rawn ordered each Flathead warrior to tie a white cloth around his forehead. But he seems to have had strong doubts that the "whitehead" Flatheads would remain loyal if bullets started to fly.

As for the two hundred volunteers, their motives ranged from whiskey courage through the attitude that "an Indian fight ought to be a lot of fun" to the more serious-minded mood of ranchers and merchants ready and willing to fight to protect their homes and businesses — if a fight could not be avoided.

As he conferred with the hostile chiefs on neutral ground outside the fort, Captain Rawn put up the best front he could. *"Lay down your arms,"* he told them sternly. *"The only terms I can offer you are unconditional surrender."*

Patiently Looking Glass explained that he did

*Photo by K. D. Swan, 1935,
U.S. Forest Service*

Courtesy Washington State University Library

Fort Fizzle

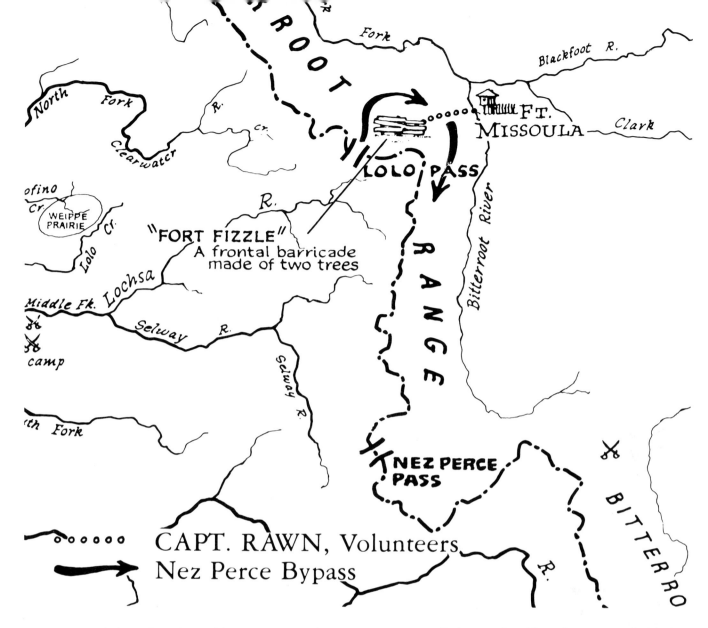

North Fork

Clearwater

ofino Cr.

WEIPPE PRAIRIE

Lolo Cr.

Middle Fk. Lochsa

camp

th Fork

Selway R.

Selway R.

Fork

Blackfoot R.

FT. MISSOULA

Clark

LOLO PASS

RANGE

Bitterroot River

"FORT FIZZLE"
A frontal barricade
made of two trees

NEZ PERCE
PASS

BITTER RO

R.

o o o o o o CAPT. RAWN, Volunteers
⟶ Nez Perce Bypass

not want to fight either the soldiers or the civilians on this side of the mountains; that the nontreaty Nez Perces had left the war behind in Idaho.

"The idea of the Indians, uneducated as they were, was that the people of Montana had no identity with the people of Idaho," Duncan MacDonald writes, "and that they were entirely separate and distinct, having nothing to do with each other."[1]

In a masterful combination of diplomacy and the threat of force, Looking Glass managed to convince the volunteers that they would not be harmed or their property stolen if they permitted the Nez Perces to cross the upper Bitter Root Valley in peace; to impress upon the Flatheads that the Nez Perces wished peace but would fight even their own relatives if they had to; and, finally, to make it crystal clear to Captain Rawn that he was dealing with a foe he had better respect.

"If you want my arms so bad, you can start taking them," Looking Glass told the army officer through the interpreter, Delaware Jim. "I made up my mind before leaving Idaho that we would talk with the white man only through our guns."[2]

Deserted by the Flatheads and the volunteers, Captain Rawn had no choice but to let the Nez Perces pass. In later reports he made it sound as though he had done everything an officer in his position could have done under the circumstances. The truth is, he did exactly what he should have done — nothing. If his soldiers had been so foolish as to open fire on the Indian, they would have been killed to the last man.

Protected by a dozen warriors who stayed between the main body of Nez Perces and the breastworks below, the long column of women, children, old people, loose horses, and packhorses

1. Duncan MacDonald, "The Nez Perces," *Idaho Yesterdays,* Winter 1978, p. 2.
2. Ibid., p. 5.

Courtesy University of Montana

A survivor of the Big Hole Battle. She was killed shortly after the battle in an unrelated incident.

Photo courtesy of John Pinkham   Courtesy Nez Perce National Historic Park
National Park Service

Wetyetmas Wahyakt (Swan Necklace). Although he was implicated in precipitating the Nez Perce War, his identity was never revealed by his fellow warriors. Under the name of John Minthorn he lived for years on the Nez Perce Reservation, where he died in the early thirties.

carrying camp supplies moved along the sides of the steep, tree-covered hills flanking the fort, beginning the movement with the first light of dawn, and continuing well into the morning. The voice of Looking Glass could be heard addressing his warriors:

"Don't shoot, don't shoot. Let the white man shoot first."

Fortunately for them, the soldiers did not shoot. What they did not know was that, hidden behind rocks and fallen trees on the slope above them, Indian sharpshooters were in perfect position to pick them off — despite the barricade, whose wall on that side was too low to protect them.

As the caravan moved out across the relatively flat, open floor of the valley, a group of volunteers who had swallowed a bit of liquid courage decided to demonstrate how brave they were by mounting a charge at the column of women and children. At once, Looking Glass signaled a band of warriors forward into a position between the whites and the head of the column. Seeing the warriors coming toward them soured whiskey courage into well-watered vinegar in the veins of the volunteers. Admitting that he had turned tail and ridden as fast as he could go in the opposite direction, one of the volunteers later recalled sheepishly:

"I don't know what I did with my gun. Somehow I

lost it. I remember using my hat to whip my horse to a swifter pace. Although he was a fast runner, I thought that I never was on a slower mount. The Indians did not fire on us, nor did they appear to hasten in their gait. Perhaps they thought we were staging a free riding exhibition for their amusement."[3]

With Fort Fizzle behind them and a verbal peace treaty made with the white settlers, the leaders of the nontreaty bands held another council regarding the route to be taken. White Bird, Too-hool-hool-zote, Red Owl, Two Moons, and Wootolen favored turning north, traveling down the Bitter Root Valley through the country of the Flatheads, and then on to Canada. Looking Glass, Five Wounds, and Rainbow wanted to go south, up the Bitter Root Valley, then east through the Big Hole country, Camas Meadows, and Yellowstone Park to the land of their Crow allies. Chief Joseph took no part in the council, declaring: "I have no words! You know the country, I do not!"[4]

Since Looking Glass had succeeded so well as a leader up to this point, his route was chosen.

At about this time the fleeing Indians were joined by six lodges of Nez Perces who had taken up more or less permanent residence in the Bitter Root Valley. They were also joined by the Yakima, Owhi; by a half-blood Delaware named Tom Hill; and by a small-statured, shrewd, part-blood Nez Perce known variously as Kiniknik, Squalsac, Lean Elk, or Poker Joe.

With a fondness and talent for cards and fast horses, Poker Joe had spent a good deal of time in the buffalo country. On his way back to Idaho with his family, he had been within six miles of Kamiah when

"he learned of hostilities, and not wishing to become entangled in a broil, turned back. In some manner, while high in the mountains, he gashed his leg with a knife, and landed back in the valley with a limp. He was accused by the whites of having been wounded in battle, and unable to convince them otherwise, he joined up with the buffalo hunters."[5]

At Stevensville, a small settlement on their route, the Nez Perces went into the stores of the white merchants and purchased whatever supplies they needed, paying the high prices asked in gold dust, coin, or horses. For this "trafficking with the enemy," the white merchants later were criticized by some citizens. They responded that if they had not sold the supplies, the Indians easily could have taken what they wanted without making payment of any kind. And business *was* business . . .

This photo was taken about 1920   *Courtesy Nez Perce National Historic Park
National Park Service*

Blanket of the Sun. As a young man he fought in the Nez Perce War, survived, later assumed the white name Jackson Sundown. He became a well known professional rodeo rider.

Only on two occasions during the movement of the Indians up the valley were there instances of misbehavior on the part of the Nez Perces — and these Looking Glass was quick to discipline. The first occurred when a young brave got inebriated on whiskey foolishly given him by a white blacksmith. Looking Glass ordered the young man put under guard and escorted back to camp.

In the second occurrence, several unruly members of Chief Too-hool-hool-zote's band raided the deserted home of a rancher named Myron Lockwood, packing off several hundred pounds of flour, bacon, and other supplies.

"When the pillagers reached camp and it became known what they had done, Chief Looking Glass grew angry and told them that they must pay Lockwood for the grub, which they did by leaving three good horses in his field, first branding them with his own iron."[6]

3. McWhorter, *Yellow Wolf*, p. 108n.
4. McWhorter, *Hear Me*, p. 357.
5. Ibid., p. 360.
6. Ibid., p. 361.

Albert Moore — Charlie Wilson

The pace set by Looking Glass was an easy one, twelve to fifteen miles a day. Why hurry? Peace had been made with the white settlers; General Howard and his bluecoats were far behind in Idaho. Ahead lay a pleasant country with plenty of water, grass, and trees, where they would go into camp soon and cut tepee poles for their lodges before moving on toward the land of his brothers, the Crows. Why hurry?

But a few of the Nez Perces were having uneasy premonitions. One morning Wahlitits, one of the Red Coat warriors who had started the war, rode through camp calling loudly to the people:

"My brothers, my sisters, I am telling you! In a dream last night I saw myself killed. I will be killed soon! I do not care. I am willing to die. But first, I will kill some soldiers."[7]

Lone Bird, who was known to be a brave fighter, also urged that they speed up the pace of their flight.

"My shaking heart tells me trouble and death will overtake us if we make no hurry through this land!" he proclaimed to the people in the camp. "I can not smother, I can not hide that which I see. I must speak what is revealed to me. Let us be gone to the buffalo country!"[8]

Looking Glass still refused to move any faster. Reaching their traditional camping ground on the Big Hole River, the Nez Perces settled in for a stay of several days. The first night, Wottolen, who had strong medicine powers, dreamed of soldiers. His dream so impressed a group of young Nez Perce warriors that they decided ten or twelve of them should select the fastest horses they could find, ride back down the Bitter Root Valley on a scout, and see if a force of soldiers was on their trail. Going to a elderly Indian named Burning Coals, who owned a number of good horses, two of the young Nez Perce warriors said: "Loan us your horses."

"No," said Burning Coals, who liked his horses very much and did not want to see them ridden hard by a bunch of reckless young men, "I will not loan you my horses."

According to Yellow Wolf, Chief Looking Glass and White Bull also opposed scouting their back trail. Looking Glass was against everything not first thought of by himself, Yellow Wolf said, while White Bull always sided with Looking Glass.

"No more fighting!" they both said. "War is quit."[9]

They were mistaken. War was suspended, not quit. Alerted by messages from General Howard and Captain Rawn, Colonel John Gibbon, with 15 officers, 146 men, and all the soldiers that Rawn could spare from his command had left Fort Missoula August 4 on the trail of the dawdling non-treaty Nez Perces. Transporting the foot soldiers by wagon much of the way, the command made from twenty-five to thirty miles a day, traveling twice as fast as the Indians.

At Stevensville, a day's march south of Missoula, the Gibbon command was joined by thirty-five citizen volunteers — the very same white settlers who had been only too glad to agree to a verbal peace treaty a few days ago when they had been outnumbered and thought themselves threatened by the Nez Perces.

Now, offered loot in the form of Nez Perce horses and goods if they helped the military, the good citizens had no compunctions against unilaterally abrogating that treaty.

Peace was quit now. At the first opportunity, war would be resumed against Nez Perce men, women, and children — hopefully by a surprise dawn attack when the possibility of resistance by the Indians would be negligible.

7. McWhorter, Yellow Wolf, p. 108.
8. Ibid., p. 109.
9. Ibid., pp. 101, 110.

CHAPTER THIRTY

BATTLE OF THE BIG HOLE: AUGUST 9, 1877

Why are we retreating? Since the world was made, brave men fight for their women and children. Are we going to run to the mountains and let the whites kill our women and children before our eyes?

— Chief White Bird

Bronze by Dave Manuel

Battle of Big Hole. Wounded Head, a young Nez Perce brave, was injured when Colonel John Gibbon and the U.S. Army caught up with Chief Joseph's band at Big Hole. He bears not only the hurt of losing his land, but also a pain in his heart for his wounded wife and child. His child died four days later, victim of a cavalry bullet. About thirty dead warriors and fifty dead women and children were left in the wake of the battle. The bronze, ''Battle of Big Hole,'' was created to honor the courageous and proud people of the Nez Perce Nation, the artist says, who fought and lost their lives in a losing battle to keep the land they lived on and loved. The artist based this sculpture on a story told him by a Nez Perce in recent years.

LYING JUST A few miles east of the Continental Divide at an elevation of 6,800 feet, the Big Hole area where the Nez Perces traditionally camped on their way to and from the buffalo country was called *Izh-kum-ziz-la-kik* by its aboriginal owners, the Flatheads, because its extensive meadows were honeycombed with the burrows of small picket-pin ground squirrels. Here in late summer, days were warm and nights cool, grass was abundant for the horses, camas was available in the marshy areas, the clear mountain stream teemed with fish, firewood was readily at hand, and the slopes to the west were covered with lodgepole pine. After their long, tiring weeks of flight, a few days of rest in this pleasant spot was a welcome prospect.

In all, eighty-nine lodges were pitched on the open flat in a V-shaped alignment, after tepee poles had been cut, peeled, and set up. Still a rich tribe so far as possessions went, the Nez Perces used treated hides as lodge covers, rather than canvas as did many of the poorer reservation Indians. Camped in the area were some eight hundred nontreaty Nez Perces, of which one hundred and twenty-five were warriors.[1]

Reaching the campsite the afternoon of August 7, refusing to scout the back trail because they were sure war was quit, Looking Glass and the

1. The Bighole National Battlefield, under the jurisdiction of the National Park Service, has a Visitor Center, with pamphlets which give details of the battle. A network of well-marked trails provides a vivid recreation of the conflict. The difference in figures shown for the military forces appears to stem from whether volunteers are included in the count and whether the reserve and escort for the howitzer and wagons are counted or excluded from the total attacking force.

other leaders relaxed. Hunting parties rode out in search of game. Some of the women dug and cooked camas, while others cut tepee poles. The boys fished, swam, and played games.

Behind them, Colonel Gibbon's command, which had been covering twice as much ground as the Nez Perces each day, reached the head of the Bitter Root Valley in late afternoon August 7. A scouting party sent ahead located the Indian camp the morning of August 8, dispatched word back to Gibbon, then withdrew four or five miles, awaiting the arrival of the main force. Wanting to move quickly and quietly, Colonel Gibbon ordered that only two days rations and one hundred rounds of ammunition be issued to each man. The wagons, the mountain howitzer, and extra supplies were left behind to be brought up later. He then moved out at 10 P.M. in a silent march through the night. Long before dawn, August 9, the command reached the Big Hole Basin. Here it halted on the

timbered hills overlooking the sleeping village and waited for the coming of day. The force numbered 191 men.[2]

The Nez Perces knew that white men were in the area. In their leisurely trip up the valley and across the divide they frequently had seen whites on the trail. This gave them no concern, for they had made peace with these local people. It was only General Howard who wanted to make war on them, they thought, and in all probability he was still far behind in Idaho.

The nephew of Chief White Bird, who was nine or ten years old at the time, later remembered the Big Hole encampment:

"We came to that place in the afternoon, toward evening. We stayed that night and next day. Evening came on again, and it was after sundown, not too late, lots of us children were playing. It was below the camp,

2. McWhorter, *Hear Me,* p. 366. *Big Hole Pamphlet* says 182.

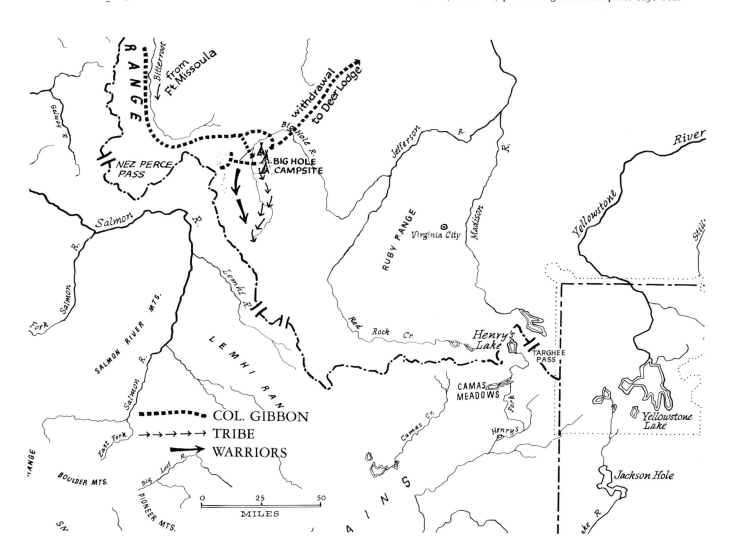

Photo Courtesy of Big Hole National Battlefield   Courtesy Idaho Historical Society

Colonel John Gibbon, commanded the 7th Infantry at Fort Shaw, Montana, which attacked the Nez Perce at Big Hole in 1877.

"I started and she told me to go up the creek to some bushes out in the stream. I noticed one woman digging in the bank so she could hide. We reached the bushes, and mother sat down, her head only out of the water. I stood up, the water to my neck. . . . Five of us were there, and two more came. One little girl was shot through the under part of her upper arm. She held the arm up from the cold water, it hurt so. It was a big bullet hole. I could see through it.

"It was not full light when we ran to the creek, but it grew light and the sun came up. An Indian, who had been shooting fast at the soldiers, was killed. The woman I saw digging was shot in the left breast. She pitched into the water and I saw her struggling. She floated by us and mother caught and drew the body to her. She placed the dying woman's head on a sandbar just out of the water. She was soon dead. A fine-looking woman, and I remember the blood coloring the water."[3]

Given the advantage of position, firepower, and surprise, the failure of Colonel Gibbon's force to overwhelm the Indian camp in short order is dif-

3. McWhorter, Hear Me, pp. 375–377.

toward the creek that we boys played the stick or bone game. . . . It finally grew dark and we had a fire for light and warmth.

"Two men came there wrapped in gray blankets. They stood close, and we saw they were white men. Foolishly we said nothing to the older people about it. We ran away and came back to our playing . . .

"Just about this time I became tired. I went to bed and to sleep, resting until morning. Of course I was in the same tepee with my father and mother.

"Father got up early to go look after the horses. Another man was perhaps forty steps ahead of him, going for his horses; the soldiers shot him down. They did not try to capture him, but killed him first thing. Father saw the gun flash, heard the report and turned back to camp.

"Right away the troops began shooting. Bullets were like hail on the camp; on the tepees. The noise was like Gatling guns, as I have since heard them. The sound awoke me. I heard bullets ripping the tepee walls, pattering like raindrops.

"I did as my mother told me. Horses hitched overnight, ready to go for other horses, were all killed. I ran only a little ways when I came to a low place in the ground. I stopped and lay down. Several women were there, and mother came fast after me.

"Mother picked me up, saying, 'Come, son, let us get away somewhere.' She took my right hand in her left and we ran. A bullet took off her middle finger, the end of her thumb, and shot off my thumb, as you see. The same bullet did it all, Mother pointed to the creek and said, 'Get down to the water! Then we may escape away!'

This was taken around 1930.   Courtesy Washington State University Library
Forest Service photograph

Bullet holes in lodgepole pine tree, Big Hole Battleground

Photo courtesy of Big Hole National Battlefield   *Courtesy Idaho Historical Society*
Chief Joseph's coat

Signal for the attack was to be the firing of three volleys, followed by a concerted, three-pronged charge. As in earlier battles, the presence of untrained men ruined the plan. In command of a mixed company of volunteers and regulars stationed opposite the northern end of the village, Lieutenant James H. Bradley had not yet gotten his men into position when the killing of Na-tal-le-kin by the citizen soldiers aroused the Indian camp. Though still back in the trees, Lieutenant Bradley ordered the three volleys fired, then led the charge down the slope, across the stream, and toward the hostile camp.

Only three men followed him. The rest of the company remained behind in the timber. Caught in the open by quick-reacting Nez Perce warriors, Lieutenant Bradley and a volunteer named Morrow were shot and killed. This left the company leaderless, freed the northern end of the village of pressure against it, and permitted its warriors to go to the aid of the rest of the camp.

At first it appeared that the battle would be a short one, for in less than twenty minutes the

ficult to understand. Certainly no fault can be found in the way he planned the attack. Three units of his command were to charge down the hill, across the stream, and into the sleeping village simultaneously. A fourth unit was held back as a reserve force. It seems to have been understood by the soldiers and the citizen volunteers that they were to shoot at everything that moved and that no prisoners were to be taken, though specific orders of that nature cannot be documented.

In execution of the well-laid plan, several things went wrong. In the predawn darkness an elderly Nez Perce with failing eyesight was one of the five Indians leaving the village and going out to the horse herd to select mounts for the coming day. Four of the men were afoot. They sensed that enemies lay hidden in the timber ahead, turned around, and hurried back to the village. But Na-tal-le-kin, the old man, was riding a horse, because he knew its eyesight was better than his own. As the animal approached the hiding place of the soldiers, three citizen volunteers opened fire, killing the old man instantly.

Thus, at the cost of his own life, Na-tal-le-kin alerted the village to its danger.

Photo by Lavalleur   *Courtesy Washington State University Library*
"The Invocation" Peo-Peo Tholekt, about 1911

center and right flank forces overran the camp and were riddling the tepees with rifle shots. Following Colonel Gibbon's orders, the soldiers began setting fire to anything that would burn. Children were crying, women were screaming, warriors were seizing whatever weapons they could find and running out to fight the foe. Over the din, the strong voices of Looking Glass and White Bird could be heard as the chiefs tried to rally their people.

Unbelievably, the tide of battle bagan to turn in favor of the Indians. As daylight grew and more warriors found and began to use weapons, the attackers began to suffer serious casualties. Receiving a thigh wound himself, Colonel Gibbon ordered the command to withdraw from the village and take a defensive position along the timbered slope on the far side of the Big Hole River.

The marksmanship of the Nez Perce amazed him.

"Almost every time one of their rifles went off," he reported later, "one of our party was sure to fall."[4]

In hand-to-hand combat, the Indians fought with the ferocious courage of people defending their families, their freedom, and all their earthly possessions. Grizzly Bear Youth, a Nez Perce warrior, related his personal experiences in the battle:

"When I was following the soldiers, trying to kill as many a possible, a big, ugly volunteer turned around swearing and made for me. I suppose he had no time to load his needle gun, so he swung it over his head by the barrel and rushed at me to strike me over the head with the butt end. I did the same thing. We both struck and each received a blow on the head. The volunteer's gun put a brand on my forehead that will be seen as long as I live. My blow on his head made him fall on his back. I jumped on him and tried to hold him down. The volunteer was a powerful man. He turned me over and got on top. He got his hand on my throat and commenced choking me. I was almost gone and had just strength left to make signs to a warrior, who was coming up, to shoot him. This was Red Owl's son, who ran up, put his needle gun to the volunteer's side and fired. The ball passed through him and killed him. But I had my arm around the waist of the man when the shot was fired and the ball after going through the man broke my arm."[5]

After the Indian camp had rallied and driven the soldiers back into the timber, Two Moons heard that his friend, the noted warrior Rainbow, had been killed early in the battle. Going to where the body lay, he recalled what Rainbow had told him regarding his protective medicine:

"I have the promise given that in any battle I engage

Photo courtesy of Big Hole National Battlefield   Courtesy Idaho Historical Society
Rock rifle pits constructed by the Nez Perce at their first evening campsite following the Battle of Big Hole.

in after sunrise, I shall not be killed. I can there walk among my enemies. I can face the point of the gun. My body no thicker than a hair, the enemies can never hit me, but if I have any battle or fighting before the sunrise, I shall be killed."

Since the whites had attacked before dawn, Two Moons noted sadly, the protective medicine of Rainbow was not in effect. Five Wounds, Rainbow's close friend, wept when he saw the body.

"My brother has passed away," he lamented. "I too will now go, as did his father and my father die in the war. They lay side by side where the battle was strongest; and now I shall lie down beside my brother warmate. He is no more, and I shall see that I follow him."[6]

Shortly thereafter, Five Wounds made a lone suicidal charge against the entrenched soldiers, falling only a few steps away from where they were dug in.

"Another great warrior was gone," Two Moons said. "His mind no longer on the battle, his *Wyakin* power

4. Mark H. Brown, *Flight of the Nez Perce* (New York: G. P. Putnam's Sons, 1967), p. 255.
5. Duncan MacDonald, "The Nez Perces," *Idaho Yesterdays*, Winter 1978, p. 10.
6. McWhorter, *Hear Me*, p. 386.

Chief Joseph's rifle and ceremonial robe at Fort Benton Museum

Left to Right: John Miller, Many Moons (who was possibly a Shoshoni Bannock) on Madison Junction, Yellowstone National Park, August 12, 1935.

had left him. There was nothing to protect him from enemy bullets."[7]

The idea that friends close in life should be equally close in death was part of Nez Perce warrior philosophy. Wahlitits, one of the young men who had started the war by avenging his father's murder, was asleep in his tepee when the soldiers attacked the village. Seizing his gun he ran outside, dropped behind a log, and began firing at the

troopers in Captain's Logan's company. Beside him, Wahlitits's wife was wounded. After killing at least one soldier, Wahlitits was shot — and killed — probably by Captain Logan himself. The Indian warrior's wife picked up her dead husband's rifle and killed Captain Logan. Moments later, she herself was killed by the soldiers.

Hearing about the death of his brother, Sarpsis Ilppilp, who also had participated in the Salmon River killing of the whites, made a rash charge at the troop entrenchments and was killed.[8]

As in earlier battles, Chief Joseph took no active part in the fighting. Two Moons recalled meeting him shortly after the battle began. Carrying a

Remains of rifle pits at Big Hole

7. Ibid., p. 388.
8. Ibid., p. 389. Before going to war a Nez Perce brave composed his personal death song, which he then sang for one or more trusted friends who memorized it. In the event the warrior was killed without having an opportunity to sing his death song, it was the sacred duty of his surviving friend to sing it for him the next time that friend visited the place of his death. Marcus Ware, Lewiston attorney and historian, tells of hearing an elderly Nez Perce do just that during a visit to the Big Hole Battlefield in the early 1930s. Not sure that his comrade had had time to sing his death song before he was killed in 1877, the old Nez Perce sang it for him more than fifty years later.

Courtesy Washington State University Library
Yellow Wolf's mother

Courtesy Washington State University Library
Two Moons and his wife, Lets-Koho-kates-Wenien: "Hat on the Side of the Head."

baby in his arms, Joseph said: "Remember I have no gun for defending myself."

"Skip for your life," Two Moons replied, "Without the gun you can do nothing. Save the child!"[9]

While Indian testimony such as that given by Two Moons, Peopeo Tholekt, and others destroys the image of Chief Joseph as a war leader and master strategist — which was largely created by General Howard and poorly informed newspaper reporters — it in no way diminishes his stature as a man. For the Nez Perces there were no noncombatants in this war. There were women, children, and old people to be looked after. Tepees must be struck, belongings packed, and the wounded cared for. If the two thousand horses owned by the five bands had been scattered or lost, the Indians would have had no recourse but to remain camped in the Big Hole Basin until more soldiers arrived, when they must surrender or die. Without horses they could not travel.

While Looking Glass, Too-hool-hool-zote, and Ollokot commanded a company of sixty sharpshooters which kept the dug-in soldiers pinned down, Joseph and White Bird oversaw the breaking of camp. Indians too severely wounded to ride were strapped to travoises. By noon, lodges were struck, the horses were packed, and the main body of Nez Perces was on the move again, traveling now in a southeasterly direction along the base of the spur of mountains which formed the Continental Divide.

Meanwhile, Colonel Gibbon and the embattled soldiers were wondering what had happened to the twelve-pound mountain howitzer, the two thousand rounds of rifle ammunition, and the twenty-man escort which was supposed to join them in midmorning. Here, too, well-laid plans had gone awry. According to Peopeo Tholekt:

9. McWhorter, *Hear Me*, p. 385.

Photo courtesy of Big Hole National Battlefield   Courtesy Idaho Historical Society

Mountain howitzer on prairie carriage. Property of National Park Service.

General Howard

Photo courtesy of Big Hole National Battlefield   Courtesy Idaho Historical Society

Camas Meadows Battlefield arms (rifles, knives, etc.)

"Passing the battle on the upper side, I rode up the creek. Hearing cannon shots, I whipped my horse and galloped along the hillside till I came in sight of the cannon, standing fast to six mules. Kettalkpoosmin [Flathead name], rushing forward shot and killed the soldier loading the cannon, while Temettiki, shooting, dropped the off-lead mules. The man taking care of the ammunition escaped, skipping for his life to shelter of brush. Kettalkpoosmin and Temettiki both hurried to the mules and I took the cannon. I said to them, 'We will take it down near to the trenches and use it against the soldiers.' "

But Peo's companions refused to let him use the mules. Unharnessing the animals, they took them away, along with the two thousand rounds of rifle ammunition. Left alone, Peo hitched his lone horse to the cannon, which was mounted on a two-wheeled carriage, and tried to drag it into position over the rough, timbered terrain. But it

"soon got stuck on a rock. I then unscrewed the wheels, taking them off the spindles. I took the gun from its resting [place], rolled it down a steep bluff, where I buried it."[10]

10. Ibid., pp. 391–392.

For the rest of that day, that night, and until just after dark the next day, the force of sixty Nez Perce sharpshooters kept the soldiers pinned down. Then, having given their people plenty of time to move out, and knowing that General Howard and the troops under his command would be reaching the scene shortly, the Indian warriors began to withdraw.

The Battle of Big Hole was over.

Losses for Colonel Gibbon's command had been heavy. Of its seventeen officers, fourteen had been killed or wounded. In all, the soldiers had lost thirty-one men killed and thirty-eight wounded — a higher percentage of casualties than was suffered by the Light Brigade at Balaklava during the Crimean War.

On their part, the Nez Perces had lost between sixty and ninety Indians killed, with a number more wounded. Some of their greatest warriors were dead.

Faith in Chief Looking Glass as a leader had been badly shaken, for it was he who had assured them the war was over. As they fled southeast in confusion, mourning their dead, they now looked to Lean Elk for leadership, and for a time he seemed uncertain as to what their future course should be.

Of one thing they could be sure: All white men were their enemies now. From this day on the whites they encountered would be neither trusted nor shown mercy.

Photo by Bill Keller
The Big Hole National Battlefield visitor center dedication September 14, 1968. Left to Right: Mrs. Viola Morris, Nez Perce, Josiah Red Wolf, last known survivor of Big Hole Battle, Mrs. Nazie Ramsey, daughter of Josiah Red Wolf.

CHAPTER THIRTY-ONE

LEAN ELK TAKES OVER

From the Big Hole, Chief Hototo (Lean Elk) was the guide and leader of the Nez Perces. He had been all over that country, east and north, and he knew the land and the trails. . . . The people covered many miles each sun. They were outdistancing the soldiers, gaining on them all the time. Everybody was glad.
— Wottolen, Tribal Historian[1]

WHITE SOLDIERS and civilian volunteers were not the only enemies arrayed against the fleeing Nez Perces. Following the Big Hole Battle, a group of Bannock scouts led by Buffalo Horn ghoulishly dug up, scalped, and mutilated the corpses of Nez Perce men, women, and children which had been hastily buried in shallow graves. Coming upon ill, weary, old men and women too feeble to travel, whom the Nez Perces had left alongside the trail, the Bannocks quickly killed and scalped them. The army officers were unable — or unwilling — to stop them.

Understandably, publicity engendered by the flight of the Nez Perces and their victories over the army caused reservation Indians all over the West to evince signs of discontent. In the opinion of some of the agents and chiefs, a bit of action was the medicine needed to soothe their troubled spirits. From the Fort Hall Agency, where both Bannocks and Western Shoshonis were confined, Agent W. H. Danielson wired Commissioner Smith August 13, 1877, saying he could enlist two hundred warriors to fight the Nez Perces. "They would do good service," he said. "It would be good for the Agency to have them thus employed."[2]

General Sheridan liked the idea and authorized Danielson to enlist fifty scouts for thirty days and have them report to General Howard.

Not to be outdone in patriotism — if that is what it should be called — Agent James J. Patten, in behalf of the Eastern Shoshonis located on the Wind River Reservation in Wyoming, wired Commission Smith, August 31:

"Chief Washakie says if they [officers] will give him a chance to mount his warriors when they [Nez Perces] come he can whip them in less than a day."[3]

Even among the Nez Perce tribe itself there were Indians eager to work as scouts for the army. One of these was Captain John (Jokais), whose loyalty to the whites went back twenty-two years to service with Governor Stevens and Colonel Wright. Another was Old George (Meopkowit), who, General Howard said, "had an Indian look, but kept his hair short and always was good-natured."[4]

Out of justice to these two Nez Perce scouts it should be noted that both men had daughters with the nontreaty bands, that they acted as guides rather than as combatants, and that on several occasions they went as peace emissaries from the military to the hostile camp.

Capable though Lean Elk proved to be in putting distance between his people and the pursuing troops, he indicated his distrust of Looking Glass and his plan to seek refuge in the land of the Crows, directly to the east, by maintaining a south-

1. McWhorter, *Hear Me*, p. 406n.
2. Merrill D. Beal, *I Will Fight No More Forever* (Seattle: University of Washington Press, 1963), p. 151.
3. Ibid.
4. Howard, *Nez Perce Joseph*, p. 211.

Big Hole batt'efield site

erly course along the base of the Bitter Root Mountains toward the land of the Shoshones. In marked contrast to their behavior while traveling up the Bitter Root Valley, where they took no goods without payment, the Nez Perces now stripped the country of every usable horse. Their justification for doing so was twofold: first, to rest the horses in their own herd; second, to deprive the pursuing soldiers of fresh mounts.

At Horse Prairie, August 13, a scouting party led by Yellow Wolf approached the Montague-Winters ranch, where seven white men were living. Because of the danger from Indians, the women and children had been sent to nearby Bannack City for safety.

An impetuous man named William Flynn had loaded his shotgun and declared he would "settle with the damned Indians" if they appeared. He at-

Sam Tilden, nephew of Chief Joseph. His mother was a sister to Chief Joseph. Sam was 8 years old at the outbreak of the war and he night-herded the horses on the retreat across the Lolo Trail. At the Surrender of Bear Paw he escaped to Sitting Bull's camp in Canada. Later he returned to the United States and attended Carlisle College. Coming back to the Lapwai Reservation he did native police work. He was transferred to the Flat Head Reservation in Montana to continue police work until 1935, when he retired. He died in February, 1965.

tempted to do so, discharged his shotgun, and was shot dead on the kitchen floor of the ranch house. Two more men were killed in a nearby field where they were loading hay. Five miles up the valley another man was killed, while his companion escaped. At both places all the horses capable of traveling were taken.

Photo by Bill Gulick

The Lemhi River, Idaho

At Bannock Pass the Nez Perces turned west, passing over the low ridge of mountains into the land of the Lemhis, a small band of Shoshones led by a chief named Tendoy.

Though a Shoshone, Chief Tendoy always had been a man of peace and was respected by the white settlers who lived in the Lemhi Valley. Lean Elk hoped he could be persuaded to intercede with the military on behalf of the nontreaty Nez Perces and bring this hopeless conflict to an end. But Chief Tendoy's reception to the fleeing Nez Perces was cold. Making it clear that he did not want the Nez Perces in his part of the country and that he would give them no aid, comfort, or assistance in returning to their homeland, he urged them in the strongest possible terms to keep moving east.

Reluctantly, they did so.

The Continental Divide in that part of the country takes many confused twists and turns. Even though the Nez Perces now were traveling in a southeasterly direction up the Lemhi Valley, they remained on the Pacific side of the divide. Though there is no difference in appearance, the range called the Bitter Roots becomes the Beaverhead Mountains south of Lemhi Pass, then, turning east, the Centennial Mountains, where the divide runs in an east-west rather than a north-south direction.

In fact, so convoluted does the Continental Divide become in the Henry's Lake area, just west of Yellowstone Park, that an east-west crossing of a

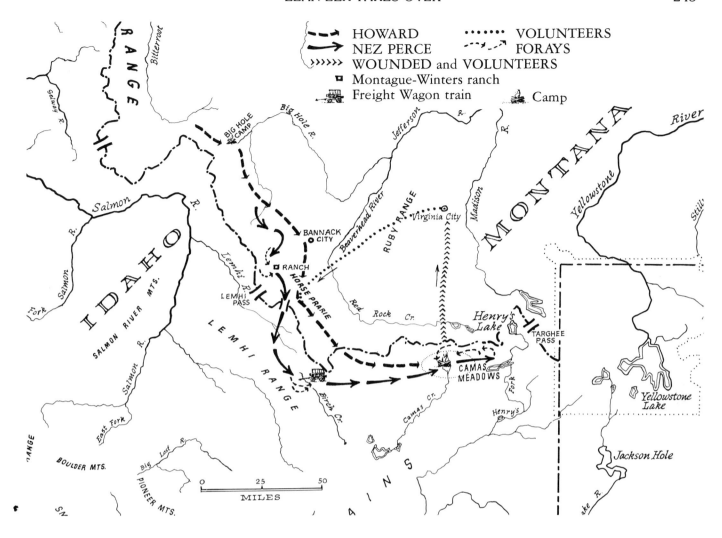

low ridge takes the traveler from the Pacific to the Atlantic slope, rather than the other way round as logic would indicate.

So far as the Nez Perces were concerned, it was of no importance which ocean a stream flowed toward, as long as the terrain was passable, the grass good, and food and firewood readily at hand. But in traveling south, then east, then finally northeast toward Henry's Lake and Targhee Pass at the west entrance to Yellowstone Park, they were taking the long arc of a semicircle. The distance could be greatly shortened by the soldiers if they cut across the upper chord.

Once it had been determined that the fleeing bands were turning east, General Howard felt he had a golden opportunity to head off the hostiles and force them into a decisive battle. All he need do was march his command directly east, beat the Nez Perces to Targhee Pass, dig in there, and force them to fight or surrender. As with so many mili-

tary plans during the campaign, this one shattered on the rocks of Indian unpredictability, civilian panic, and the inability of a company commander to carry out a simple order.

By accident, a party of Nez Perce braves met a freight-wagon train bound for Salmon, Idaho, in the Birch Creek area. Containing four wagons and a trailer, the train carried a load of merchandise that included whiskey. At first the meeting was friendly enough, though the Indians indicated that they wanted the eight horses with the train. One word led to another, and then the impatient Indians started shooting. One white man escaped; two Chinese with the wagon train were released after being forced to entertain the Nez Perces by cavorting around on their hands and knees like horses; the whiskey barrels were opened, and, during the ensuing drunken melee, Kettalkpoosmim, the warrior who had participated in the capture of the cannon at Big Hole, was mortally wounded by a blood brother.[5]

Disgusted with the behavior of the young men, the chiefs poured out what was left of the whiskey, set the wagons and merchandise afire, and moved on. Shortly thereafter, word of the theft of two hundred horses and the killing of ranchhands on Horse Prairie, plus the looting of the freight wagons and the murders on Birch Creek, reached General Howard — and forced him to alter his plans.

Positive though he was that the Nez Perces were heading for Targhee Pass, General Howard could not ignore the pleas for protection being sent him from settlements such as Salmon, Idaho, Bannack City and Virginia City, Montana. Time and again groups of citizen volunteers rode out to meet Howard, offered to help him fight Indians (so long as he made short work of it and let them fight in their own way), demanded that he send troops to protect their property (though no hostiles were anywhere near it), and insisted that he do both at the same time without further delay (even though that meant dispatching his troops in several directions at once).

Courtesy Idaho Historical Society

Josiah Red Wolf. Last survivor of the Nez Perce War

Photo by Bill Gulick

Upper Mesa Falls, Henry's Fork

Being as much a politician as he was a general, Howard compromised. Turning back from Bannack City, where he actually was between the Nez Perces and Targhee Pass, he marched his command west toward the Lemhi Valley, into which the hostiles had detoured. That night word reached him that the Indians were on the move again, this time traveling in a southeasterly direction that eventually would take them where he had figured they were going in the first place. He ordered his

5. McWhorter, *Hear Me*, pp. 409–410; McWhorter, *Yellow Wolf*, p. 165. Yellow Wolf told McWhorter: "The Indians were getting bad. Ketalkpoosmin called out: 'If soldiers come they will kill us all!'

"He and all the sober warriors were appointed by the chiefs to spill the whiskey on the ground. Peopeo Tholekt was one who helped, and I, Yellow Wolf, helped.

"Two drunk Indians shot at each other, one getting head grazed by bullet. Itsiyiyi Opseen (Coyote with Flints) stabbed Heyoom Pishkish, an oversized man later known by whites as Lame John, under right arm. Heyoom did not grunt, did not lie down. He had a strong Power and became well.

"Ketalkpoosmin was shot by Pahka Alyanakt (Five Snows) who was mad drunk. Of course, drinking Indians did not want the whiskey spilled. Ketalkpoosmin after two, maybe three, suns' travel, was left at camp to die. He asked to be left. He could not hold to life. A good warrior, he had much in capturing the cannon-gun at Big Hole fight. Pahka Alyanakt was killed at last battle."

Photo taken at Lewiston, Idaho in September, 1961   *Courtesy Idaho Historical Society*

Nez Perce Indians — Left to Right: Sam Tilden, Philleo Nash, Josiah Red Wolf, Albert Moore

command to reverse direction, going east, then south. On the other side of the Centennial Mountains the Nez Perces were riding southeast then east.

The Indians were traveling much faster. When Howard at last passed through a gap in the range and intercepted their trail, he was exasperated to learn they now were a day's march ahead of him. In desperation he dispatched Lieutenant George Bacon with forty well-mounted cavalrymen directly overland to Targhee Pass, with orders to block the passage of the hostiles when they showed up and "hold them" there.

How such a small force could "hold" a much larger band of deadly, desperate warriors, General Howard did not say. Fortunately no confrontation between the two forces occurred, Lieutenant

Bacon reached Targhee Pass well ahead of the Indians, waited two days, and decided the hostiles already had gone by that point. Without waiting for further orders he returned to rejoin the main command, leaving the vital pass unguarded.

Later, General Howard would accuse Lieutenant Bacon of lacking courage and running away from a fight. In view of the odds against him, Bacon should have been complimented for his good sense.

Meanwhile, the afternoon of August 19, the fleeing Nez Perces and General Howard's command made camp only a few miles apart, the soldiers in a marshy, well-watered area known as Camas Meadows, the Indians just beyond a rocky ridge southwest of Henry's Lake. Each had scouted the other's position well. When Buffalo Horn urged Howard to attack the Nez Perces at once, Howard declined. Men and horses were exhausted, he said; Lieutenant Bacon and his company were in position to halt and hold the hostiles at Targhee Pass; what the troops needed most now was a good night's rest.

In the camp of the Nez Perces, some of the war leaders were making audacious plans to disturb that rest. Wottolen, who was there, tells what happened:

"It was the night before that to Black Hair, who was wounded and could not sleep, there came a good vision. He saw the warriors go back over the trail in the darkness to where we were then camped and bring away the soldiers' horses. So, when one of our scouts brought word that General Howard had stopped at Camas Meadows, our old camp, Black Hair's vision was considered. We knew all that country, and in council it was determined to make an attack and try capturing all the horses and pack mules of the enemies just as Black Hair had seen and foretold.

"It was about the middle of the forenight that we started, riding slowly back over the trail. Towards morning, drawing near the soldiers camp, we halt to form plan of attack. We older men must decide in council how the approach is to be made.

"We divide into three companies. Looking Glass and White Bull speak to attack on horseback; while Two Moons and I argue to go on foot. . . . I said, 'We will go among the soldiers afoot. Securing many of their guns, we will kill General Howard and his leading men. We can then whip back the soldiers and in the meantime drive off with all their horses and pack mules.'

"But some objected. They wanted their horses. An Indian does not like to be far from his horse in any fighting. Chief Looking Glass, who generally opposed plans not his own, spoke, 'No, we must have our horses. . . . It will spoil everything to go afoot.'

"While thus talking, Ollocot rode up and said, 'Breaking morning is coming, Let us go!' Young Chief Ollocot was a brave leader of the young men and delivering his short speech, he turned his horse and rode away. Teeweeyownah, myself, and others followed. Our company halts before drawing too near the enemy. The horses' feet must not be heard against the rocks. Active young men dismount and go forward among the enemies' horses, cutting them loose and removing bells from pack animals.

"With Left Hand and Five Lightnings I am set to guard a point not far from the nearest soldiers' tents. In this, we must lay close to the ground.

"Too soon the alarm is sprung! Not many cavalry horses are yet cut loose when a gun gives off a report. It is back of the front riders, back toward the rear.

" 'Who in hell do shooting?'

"Our plans are now spoiled. The signal shot was not to come from that direction. When the gun sounded, fired by Otskai, as we learned later, the Indians gallop close, and shooting into the soldiers' camp. Yelling loudly, the horses are quickly stampeded out from there. Back over the trail they go, headed in right direction by Indians stationed for that business.

"The stampeded horses gone, we do not stay to fight soldiers. We leave them firing like crazy people in the darkness. Nothing they can hit. We try driving the herd fast; but the speed is slow. Daylight soon coming, we have only mules! Just a few horses in the herd. Then we know why the slow traveling."[6]

Taking part in this daring raid on the soldier camp were some twenty-eight Nez Perce warriors. Otskai, the man who fired the shot that set off the alarm prematurely, was Yellow Wolf's cousin and noted for his odd behavior.

"Always Otskai was doing something like that," Wottolen told McWhorter. "Crazy actions. Nervous, he broke our plans for getting all the horses."[7]

"A brave warrior, a good fighter, but at times his head did not act right," Yellow Wolf said. "Would do things at the wrong time. But nobody could say Otsaki was afraid, that he ever hid from the fighting!"[8]

When Wottolen was asked if Otskai had been punished for his action, the tribal historian replied: "He was laughed at, made fun of. I did not hear him make excuse for the careless shooting."[9]

Whatever excuse he might have made could not have equalled the imaginative account of the raid told by General Howard and given broad credence by the press. According to Howard, security measures taken to protect the Camas Meadows camp that night had been so tight that only a military genius of Chief Joseph's stature could have gotten to the horse herd. This is the way he did it, Howard said:

"Joseph had so organized a few of his Indians, and marched them toward camp, as to make the picket think it was Bacon's party coming back. They, the Indians, came on by fours, steadily, and very like our troopers, till challenged. Not being able to reply correctly, the picket fired upon them. This was doubtless the first sound. Then came the big firing and yelling, and then, quickly enough, the reply from our camp."[10]

Never mind that the Nez Perces knew nothing about Lieutenant Bacon's party, that Joseph was not even in the raiding group, and that it was Ots-

6. McWhorter, *Hear Me*, pp. 417–419.
7. Ibid., p. 419n.
8. McWhorter, *Yellow Wolf*, p. 131.
9. McWhorter, *Hear Me*, p. 419n.
10. Howard, *Nez Perce Joseph*, pp. 226–227.

Courtesy Idaho Historical Society

Albert Moore, at the age of 98. This picture was taken at Lapwai in 1960. In an earlier chapter note the picture of Albert Moore taken at age 37.

kai who fired the premature shot. General Howard's story made a very clever fellow out of that red rascal, Joseph, but not quite clever enough to learn the secret password and fool an alert picket.

When daylight came, General Howard ordered three companies of cavalry to pursue the Indians, bring them to bay, do battle with them, and recover the stolen animals. Acting with traditional stubbornness, twenty of the mules proved too contrary to drive, so the raiders — who disliked mules anyway — left them behind for the soldiers to recapture. So far as bringing the Indians to bay was concerned, that was no problem, for in the rock-strewn, broken country five miles northeast of the soldiers' camp a dozen or so Nez Perce warriors dismounted, hid their horses, and lay in ambush waiting for their pursuers.

When the shooting began, one company of cavalry attempted a frontal assault but got such a hot reception that it withdrew and sought shelter behind rocks, of which there were plenty in the area. The other two companies spread right and left in an attempt to flank the entrenched sharpshooters. Before they could complete the maneuver, Indian reinforcements arrived, and *they* spread right and left, outflanking the flankers and pouring such a withering fire into the soldiers that the battalion commander, Major Sanford, who was with one of the flanking companies, ordered all three companies to withdraw. His own and the other flanking company did so at once, but Captain Norwood, whose company had taken refuge in the rocks, felt that ordering his men to leave their sheltered position would be suicidal, so he kept them where they were.

Having finished breakfast at last, General Howard and the rest of his command rode forward to see how the battle was going. When Howard learned that Major Sanford had withdrawn and left Captain Norwood's company surrounded by an overwhelming force of hostiles, he ordered a charge by the entire command. Then, with Norwood's company rescued and the Nez Perces withdrawing, General Howard led all his troops back to the camp in Camas Meadows, where they rested the remainder of that day and night.

In the skirmish, the Nez Perces had not lost a man. The military losses were three men killed, five wounded, and one hundred and eighty pack mules stolen. With his men exhausted from the long campaign, their shoes worn out, their clothing threadbare and insufficiently warm for this high mountain country, General Howard knew that his command was in no condition to go on until it had been re-outfitted.

His only consolation was that Captain Bacon and his forty men were awaiting the Nez Perces in Targhee Pass — or so he thought.

Disappointed though the Nez Perces were in stealing mules instead of horses, their brilliantly conceived, boldly executed venture had crippled General Howard's command so badly that it never again would get close enough to the fleeing Indians to see their dust, let alone engage them in battle. Which probably was just as well.

CHAPTER THIRTY-TWO

THROUGH YELLOWSTONE NATIONAL PARK:
August 23–September 6, 1877

> *It was, I think, twelve suns from the Big Hole*
> *that we camped on the southwest side of a fine*
> *lake. Camped for about one sun. Then we went*
> *through a gap into the Yellowstone Park. We did*
> *not follow the usual Nez Perce trail. We traveled*
> *over a hunting trail instead.*
>
> *We were troubled about direction for a short*
> *half-sun, but soon found the right way. No help*
> *from Crow Indians! No help from anybody but one*
> *white man. It was like this.*
>
> — Yellow Wolf[1]

THE MOST BRUTAL aspect of the Nez Perce War was the way the military commanders enlisted the aid of other Indian tribes against the homeless exiles. Shortly after the Camas Meadows skirmish, fifty Bannocks from the Fort Hall Reservation, led by Captain S. G. Fisher, joined General Howard's command, which was camped near Henry's Lake. To celebrate, Buffalo Horn asked if the Indians might have a dance.

"Oh, yes, let them dance," Howard said.

What with drumming, chanting, neighing of horses and braying of mules the din kept everybody awake until midnight. When it was finally over, Chief Buffalo Horn and a half blood called Rainé came to General Howard's tent and asked an additional favor — authority to kill Captain John, Old George, and another Nez Perce scout traveling with the command.

"Rainé said George and the other Indians were traitors," Howard writes, "that they had rejoiced openly at Joseph's success in surprising our mule herd . . .

"We had George brought forward, to face his accusers. He was so frank and evidently so honest, that the story against him was not for a moment believed, and Buffalo Horn was denied the small favor of killing the three. He was very angry in consequence, and never quite forgave me for this refusal."[2]

This was the beginning of Howard's disen-

chantment with the Bannocks as scouts and allies. Despite the fact that their white commander, Captain Fisher, had no trouble leading them forward from the main command and making contact with the Nez Perce rear guard, with whom a few long-range shots were exchanged, the Bannocks showed a marked reluctance to fight at close quarters with their traditional enemy, even for the tempting reward of many good horses. It was much easier to run off army mounts, they decided, defecting with forty animals belonging to Spurgin's trail-building crew. Demonstrating that he could act decisively when he had to, General Howard found an excellent way to get the horses back.

First, he arrested ten of the scouts and placed them under armed guard. When an old Bannock chief assured him they had not stolen any horses, Howard said:

"What you say may be true, but Indians are good to hunt horses. They follow blind trails better than white men. Send out some of your young men and look up my lost horses. I will never set the prisoners free till the horses are brought back."

In a few hours a group of young Indians drove

1. McWhorter, *Yellow Wolf*, p. 170.
2. Howard, *Nez Perce Joseph*, pp. 232–233.

twenty of the missing horses into camp. That was all the lost horses they had been able to find, the old chief told Howard.

"All right," he replied, "I shall never let the prisoners go till I see the other twenty horses."

That night the rest of the lost horses found their way back to camp, Howard says. Thus ended his use of Bannocks as scouts and allies. The only damage they had done the Nez Perces during their campaign with Howard had been the killing of several old people left behind because they were too weak to travel.[3]

Established in 1872, Yellowstone National Park at the time of the Nez Perce visit was more wilderness than park. Almost no improvements in the way of roads, bridges, or shelters had been undertaken, and Congress had appropriated no money for its development. Even so, five hundred hardy tourists had come to see its wonders during each of the first few years of its existence; this year, the number of visitors would double.[4]

Just five days before the fleeing Nez Perces entered the park, its most famous visitor to date left it. He was none other than General of the Army William T. Sherman. Well aware of the fact that the hostiles were being chased in the park's direction, Sherman was positive they would not dare to enter it because the area was "to their superstitious minds associated with hell by reason of its geysers and hot springs."[5]

Returning to Fort Ellis, northwest of Yellowstone Park (near present-day Bozeman, Montana) on August 18, after a fifteen-day tour of the park, General Sherman soon would learn how badly the war with the Nez Perces was going and would take measures to improve matters by ordering new military units to join the pursuit.

Meanwhile, the Nez Perces, not in the least awed by the geysers and hot springs, were entering the park and acquiring a tour guide in a rather unique way. With his cousin, Otskai, Yellow Wolf rode out ahead of the main band at noon one day. Then:

"We heard chopping. Maybe it was soldiers? We went there where we heard the chopping. It was a white man doing cooking. We went to him, one on each side, in back of him. We grabbed him! He was armed but did not offer fight. Otskai understood a little English and talked with him."[6]

Described by Yellow Wolf as "an oldlike man,"

John Shively was a prospector who had been on his way from the Black Hills to Montana when his horses strayed away from camp. Taken to Lean Elk, he was asked if he knew this country well; when he said that he did, he was told that if he would guide the Nez Perces back to trails with which they were familiar, he would be rewarded with the gift of a horse and would not be harmed. Within half a day he led the Indians back to a trail they knew. He stayed with them for several days, helping with the pack animals, making himself generally useful, and gaining their respect with his friendliness and amiability. Then, taking advantage of their laxness in guarding him, he slipped away without waiting for his promised reward, which Yellow Wolf later swore would have been given to him, along with his freedom, if he had been in less of a hurry to leave.

Not as fortunate as John Shively was a party of tourists encountered by the Nez Perces a day after his capture. Consisting of seven men and two women, the group had been camping in the park for a week. Suddenly confronted by Yellow Wolf and four of his friends, the leader of the group — a man named William Dingee — had enough presence of mind to give them a friendly greeting, shaking hands with all of them.

"Because I shook hands with him put me in mind not to kill him," Yellow Wolf said. "While we were there, the leading white man gave us sugar, flour, and two good pieces of bacon. The food made our hearts friendly."

But a moment later, another man — George Cowan — came out of the tent and spoke angrily to Dingee, and the gifts of food to the hungry Indians stopped. Demanding in a blunt, overbearing manner to be escorted to Chief Joseph, he was warned by Yellow Wolf that the Nez Perces were "double-minded"; that is, the more moderate older leaders might not harm them, while some of the rash, hot-headed young men might kill them on sight. Cowan would not be put off; he insisted on being escorted to Chief Joseph.

"Whatever now happened to their lives, I could not

3. Ibid., p. 244.
4. Aubrey L. Haines, *The Yellowstone Story* (Boulder: Colorado Associated University Press; Yellowstone National Park, Wyo.: Yellowstone Library and Museum Assoc., 1977), vol. 2, p. 498. From its opening in 1872 through 1877, an estimated 3,300 tourists visited the park.
5. Ibid., vol. 1, p. 218.
6. McWhorter, *Yellow Wolf*, p. 171.

help," Yellow Wolf says. "It was their own mind — their own work . . .

"At last, after we traveled part of that sun, I heard a great noise ahead of us. The other Indians had seen us. . . . Mad, those warriors took the white people from us."[7]

After a confused day and night of being stripped of most of their food and weapons, of accepting worn-out Indian ponies in exchange for their own mounts, of being released and then recaptured, two of the men were shot while trying to escape — mortally, it appeared at the time, though eventually both of the wounded men got back to civilization and recovered from their injuries.

As the Nez Perce made their way through the thick timber and deep canyons in a northeasterly direction across the park, small scouting parties sent out in advance engaged in several skirmishes with white sportsmen and tourists. Though dispatches filed with regional newspapers and telegraphed to the eastern press claimed eight or ten whites were killed in each engagement, only two fatalities can be definitely verified — the deaths of Charles Kenck and Richard Dietrich.

Among the survivors who would tell stories of their narrow escapes for the rest of their lives, one was a black man, Ben Stone, who was employed as a cook with one of the tourist parties. Hearing how tenaciously a Nez Perce brave had pursued Stone, Duncan MacDonald, when he went to Canada asked White Bird if that particular Indian had survived the war. He had.

"A young warrior responded that he was the one who had been after the colored individual," Mac Donald wrote. "Stone managed to make his escape by climbing a tree. The Indian being interrogated as to why he wanted him so badly said: 'I just wanted his scalp. Colored men's hair is good medicine for sore ears.' "[8]

Though it had no bearing upon the fate of the Nez Perces, the survival saga of George Cowan is so incredible that it must be told here. First he was knocked off his horse by a shot in the thigh. When his wife rushed over to protect him by throwing her body upon his, a Nez Perce pulled her away, thrust a pistol against Cowan's head, and fired. Left for dead, he came to a few hours later. When he started to get up he was seen by an Indian and shot again — this time in the left side.

Some hours after dark he regained consciousness again and started crawling toward Lower Geyser Basin, nine miles away. It took him three days to reach it. There, in a former camp, he found matches, gathered up spilled coffee grains and an empty can, and made coffee. Next day he crawled over to the road, where he was found by two of Howard's scouts, Captain S. G. Fisher and J. W. Redington.

They patched him up as best they could, fixed him some food, and left him by a roaring fire with the assurance that the main force would gather him up within two days. But more misfortunes were to come.

"Cowan ate enough to keep himself alive and lay down in silent joy to sleep the night through. Towards morning he was awakened by awful heat, and found to his dismay that the vegetable mold he was lying on had taken fire and encircled him with flames. He rose on hands and knees and, suffering terribly, crawled across the charred area to safety. His hands and legs were badly burned."[9]

And still more . . .

Picked up by Howard's column, Cowan underwent crude candlelight surgery for removal of the bullet from his skull. When he requested that he be sent back by wagon along the relatively easy trail to Henry's Lake, General Howard refused, taking the wounded man north with the troops for an extremely rough ride over terrain so steep that a road had to be built as they went along.

Nearing Fort Ellis at long last, the wagon overturned, spilling Cowan down the hill. When finally put to bed in a Bozeman hotel, the bedstead collapsed, rolling him out onto the floor.

"At this final indignity," Aubrey Haines writes, "he suggested that they try artillery if they couldn't kill him any other way!"[10]

Reaching home at last on October 5, he eventually recovered from his wounds, had the bullet that had been removed from his skull made into a watch fob, and several times over the ensuing years returned to the park to relate his experiences to curious listeners.

For the fleeing Nez Perces there was a choice of three routes through the mountain wilderness of Yellowstone Park to the open plains beyond:

1. North down the Yellowstone River.

7. Ibid., p. 175.

8. MacDonald, "The Nez Perces," *Idaho Yesterdays,* Winter 1978, p. 23.

9. Beal, *I Will Fight No More,* p. 175; S. G. Fisher, "A Scout for General Howard," *Ogden Daily Pilot,* October 18, 1891.

10. Haines, *Yellowstone Story,* vol. 1, p. 326.

2. East down the Shoshone River (then called the Stinking Water).

3. Northeast down Clark's Fork, which eventually flowed into the Yellowstone.

Why Lean Elk, who appears to have been doing the decision making at this time, chose the route he did has long been a matter of debate among white and Indian historians. The Nez Perces had an excellent corps of scouts, knew the country well, and had proved time and again that even with all their old people and baggage they could travel twice as far in a day's time as their pursuers. Thus, the suggestion that their avoidance of the trap being set for them was pure accident is simply not acceptable. They knew exactly what they intended to do — and did it very well.

Some distance to the rear, General Howard's command was making its slow way north along the Yellowstone River toward Baronett's Bridge, where it would swing right up the East Fork of the Yellowstone. Directly behind and in closer contact with the Nez Perces was Captain Fisher and what was left of his increasingly disgruntled Bannock scouts, who were as weary of living on half-rations as he was "becoming tired of trying to get the soldiers and the hostiles together; 'Uncle Sam's' boys are too slow for this business."[11]

To the northeast, Colonel Samuel Sturgis with 360 men was getting into position to block a descent of the Clark's Fork, if the hostiles chose that route, or, if given a day or so advance warning, to ride southeast forty miles to block their flight down the Shoshone. Because of the ruggedness of the country and the alertness of the Nez Perce advance scouts, who managed either to kill or scare off couriers carrying messages from Howard to Sturgis and vice versa, there was little or no communica-

11. Beal, *I Will Fight No More*, p. 179; Fisher, "Scout for General Howard."

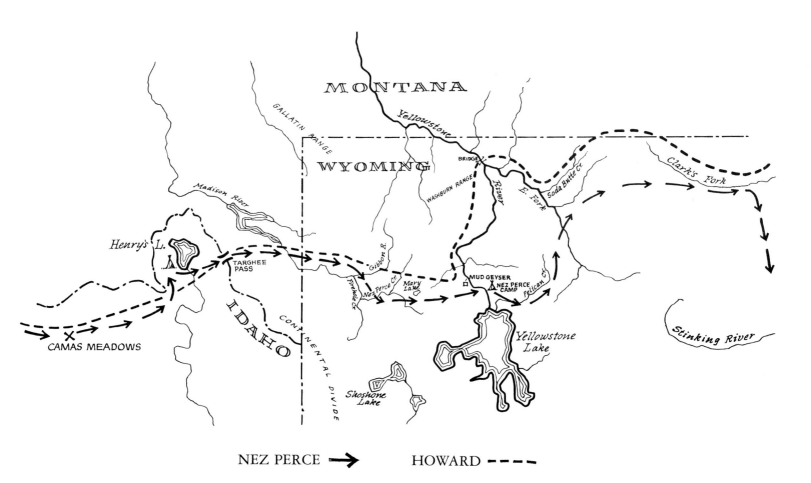

NEZ PERCE ➔   HOWARD ----

tion between the various military units that were attempting to trap the hostiles.

Reaching the Clark's Fork several days before the Nez Perces were due to arrive, Colonel Sturgis sent scouting details into the high country looking for unfriendly Indians. They found none. Deciding that the Nez Perces had chosen to go down the Shoshone River, Colonel Sturgis moved his command into position there, a long day's ride away. He had every reason to believe that the hostiles had chosen that route, for the most reliable scout in the area, Captain Fisher reported:

"To the east, from the top of the divide, the enemy's trail bore off toward the south-east, which direction my Indians told me would take them onto the Stinkingwater. . . . After leaving the summit the enemy followed the trail toward the Stinkingwater about two miles, and then attempted to elude pursuit by concealing their trail. To do this, the hostiles 'milled,' drove their ponies around in every direction, when, instead of going out of the basin in the direction they had been traveling and across an open plain, they turned short off to the north, passing along the steep side of the mountain through the timber for several miles. When we reached the point where the enemy had endeavored to cache their trail, we scattered out in every direction looking for it. At first the scouts were at a loss to know which way they had gone but after spending some time in the search I was so fortunate as to stumble onto the trail. I then went back to appraise the command of this new change of direction, leaving the other scouts, to follow after the Indians. Returning, we followed through a very narrow and rocky canyon down to Clark's Fork, at a point about two miles below where it comes out of a canyon."[12]

Chagrined though the military leaders were at having the fleeing hostiles elude them, the officers expressed unstinted admiration for the deception of the move and the Indians' skill as horsemen in taking their entire band and baggage over a trail that appeared to be impassable.

"The baffling Nez Perce route across the Absarokas

was probably this," Merrill Beal writes. "From Cache Creek they crossed Sunlight Pass and descended the Sunlight River for a dozen miles. Then, they quartered northward to Trail Creek, which they ascended to Lodgepole Divide. They descended Lodgepole Creek to its point of confluence with Crandall Creek, which they then followed to the Clark Fork. It was a rough hunter's trail, wholly unsuited for the passage of nearly seven hundred people with all their possessions and herds of horses."[13]

Lieutenant Wood said the canyon through which the Indians filed was like a gigantic railroad tunnel. Howard described it as "a strange canyon, where rocks on each side were so near together that two horses abreast could hardly pass."

But pass through the canyon to the lower section of Clark's Fork the fleeing Nez Perces did. By the time Howard reached the same point, the exiles were a full day's ride ahead of him. By the time Sturgis got there, they were two days ahead. In open country now, with a fifty-mile advantage and no serious obstacles between them and the Canadian border, it appeared that the Nez Perces had won their race to freedom.

Still, General Howard's duty was clear: he must continue the chase. After conferring with Sturgis, he sent messengers to Colonel Nelson A. Miles, whose command was stationed at Fort Keogh in eastern Montana, urging him to take all necessary measures to intercept the hostiles. Since Colonel Sturgis's troops were fresher, Howard let him press on in pursuit of the Nez Perces, while his own command followed at a more leisurely pace.

Meanwhile, ahead of the soldiers, Chief Looking Glass again recalled the promises made him by his blood brothers, the Crows.

12. Beal, *I Will Fight No More*, p. 188.
13. Ibid., p. 189.

CHAPTER THIRTY-THREE

CANYON CREEK TO COW ISLAND LANDING:
September 13–23, 1877

I rode closer. Eeh! Crows! A new tribe fighting
Chief Joseph. Many snows the Crows had been
our friends. But now, like the Bitterroot Salish,
turned enemies.
My heart was just like fire . . ."

— Yellow Wolf[1]

EVEN THOUGH he deeply resented the intrusion of whites into his homeland and the restrictions placed on his traditional way of life, Looking Glass had refused to join the other nontreaty bands in a war against the whites until his own peaceful village was attacked by soldiers. Then it was only natural that he should remember the promises made him by his buffalo-country brothers, the Crows.

Following the Nez Perce escape from the wilds of Yellowstone Park by the Clark's Fork route, Chief Looking Glass held a conference with the Crows, some historians say, though their evidence is scant.

"He succeeded in contacting leaders of both segments of the Crow nation, the Mountain and the River clans," Merrill Beal writes. "Neither clan could be persuaded to join the hostiles. The Crows evidently considered Nez Perce resistance a lost cause. The Mountain chiefs declared strict neutrality, but the more sedentary River Crows were definitely partial to the whites. Governed by expediency and cupidity, they were ready to despoil the Nez Perces as opportunity afforded."[2]

"One of the romantic myths that has developed around the Nez Perce war is that Chief Looking Glass, about the time the tribe was approaching the Yellowstone, made a trip northwest to the Crow reservation to ask these traditional friends to aid his people," McWhorter writes. "Here he met an unfriendly council, one of his warriors was killed, and Looking Glass left, disappointed, to rejoin his tribe."[3]

While it is impossible to present evidence that the visit *did not* happen, McWhorter adds weight to the negative side of the story when he states:

"No Nez Perce warrior whose story was recorded indicated that Looking Glass went to the Crows for help and was rebuffed. Instead, the Nez Perces apparently met a few Crow warriors while en route from Yellowstone to Canyon Creek. These proved friendly, gave them ammunition, and possibly promised, in case of a fight, to fire their guns in the air, which a few may actually have done."[4]

In any event the Crows soon showed their true feelings with deeds that left no doubt regarding their professed eternal friendship.

Meanwhile, Yellow Wolf met a *hohots* (grizzly bear) . . .

Weary from doing double duty scouting and night-guarding, he sat down on a creek bank while letting his horses drink, and fell asleep. Presently he dreamed he heard a voice saying urgently: "Look out for *hohots!* Look out for *hohots!*"

Still he kept sleeping. Then the voice said again: "Look out for *hohots! Hohots* coming close to you!"

"I was partly awake now," he said, in relating the story to McWhorter. "I turned my head where was a noise, *Eeh!* I saw it — a big *hohots*. My rifle was in my hands. I sprang up as I threw back the hammer. The *hohots* made for me, a bad sound coming from his mouth. As he stood up, I held my rifle ready. The bear came stepping to the muzzle of my gun. Just touched it

1. McWhorter, *Yellow Wolf*, pp. 187, 194.
2. Beal, *I Will Fight No More*, p. 190.
3. McWhorter, *Hear Me*, p. 459.
4. Ibid., p. 460.

when I pulled the trigger. He fell, and I finished him with my war club. Struck him on the ear.

"You ask if I was afraid? No, I was not scared. The bear had no gun."⁵

While the Nez Perces moved north at a leisurely pace, Colonel Sturgis pushed his troops to their limit in an effort to catch up. Shortly after both forces crossed the Yellowstone River, near the mouth of a summer-dry wash called Canyon Creek, about ten miles west of present-day Billings, Montana, his advance scouts caught up with the Nez Perce rear guard. Sure that a decisive battle was imminent, Colonel Sturgis gave a curious order.

He dismounted his troops and had them advance as skirmishers on foot.

Since for several miles the valley of Canyon Creek was broad, flat, and open, the mounted Indians had no difficulty keeping well out of rifle range of their infantry pursuers, who, after slogging along on foot for three or four miles, were too exhausted to move very fast. By then Canyon Creek had narrowed and its sides had become too steep for a flanking move by mounted men or for the use of artillery, which the Sturgis command had available in the form of two light cannons. Quick to see the strategic advantage of the terrain, the Nez Perce leaders hurried the pack animals, women, children, and old people into the ever-narrowing canyon, while a few sharpshooters took cover in sheltered positions and blocked the advance of the troopers with a withering fire.

"A single Indian, Teeto Hoonnod, manned the mouth of the canyon toward the close of the skirmishing, and held back the whole line of troopers," McWhorter writes. "The warriors were satisfied with delaying the troops, as the bulk of the tribe gained safety, and made no attempt to encourage a general engagement. They saw no advantage to be gained from a battle."⁶

Well aware of how fiercely the Nez Perces had fought at White Bird Canyon and at Big Hole, Colonel Sturgis seems to have assumed that the moment the first shot was fired, they would turn on his troops and charge as they had done before. Thus, he made a defensive move by dismounting his troops in a situation where a swift mounted charge would have been much more effective. It has been suggested by some historians that recent Indian battles other than Big Hole and White Bird Canyon inclined Sturgis toward caution. He had lost a son on the Little Big Horn.

Whatever the reason for his prudence, the end

result was that the army had blundered again. Exhausted and running so low on rations that some of the soldiers began killing and eating their worn-out horses, the Sturgis command gave up the pursuit and went into camp, where it was presently joined by General Howard and his troops, which were in no better shape.

Disappointed with the feeble effort made by the white soldiers, a hundred or so Crows began harassing the Nez Perces, shooting at stragglers and attempting to run off horses. Yellow Wolf emphatically denied General Howard's story that the Crows only pretended to attack the Nez Perces, while actually helping them by being their guides.

"Not true! The Crows fought us. They killed one warrior and two old, unarmed men. They did not act as guides for us. We had men who knew the country, who scouted far ahead all the time. They found each day the way to go . . .

"Some Crows told Chief Looking Glass not to travel too fast. Said they would join and help us. But Looking Glass paid no attention. He now knew they were against us. He knew the Crows were lying, that they wanted the soldiers to catch up with us. Although they had been helped in battle, we all knew not to trust the Crows."⁷

After a couple of days of ineffectual skirmishing with the Nez Perce rear guard, the Crows abandoned the chase and went home, having taken no more than the thirty or forty sound horses that Yellow Wolf admitted were "lost."

For the next six days the Nez Perces moved north without molestation by red or white attackers, reaching the south bank of the Missouri River at a place called Cow Island Landing. It was now September 23 and the river was at its lowest stage of the year. Even for shallow-craft steamboats, this was as far upriver as a loaded craft could go. Consequently, a large supply of food, utensils, and other items needed by government survey crews and the military was stored in a depot on the north bank, protected by tents and guarded by a dozen soldiers and two civilians.

To the seven hundred tired, hungry, poorly clad hostiles, who had lost, mislaid, or worn out a great deal of their camping gear during their three-month trek through the wilderness, the well-

5. McWhorter, *Yellow Wolf*, p. 184.
6. McWhorter, *Hear Me*, p. 462.
7. McWhorter, *Yellow Wolf*, pp. 188–189. The help in battle alluded to by Yellow Wolf was that given by the Nez Perces to the Crows in a decisive fight with the Sioux in July 1874. The engagement was fought on Pryor Creek, where it joins the Yellowstone, in south-central Montana.

Scenes of the Nez Perce War as seen by *Harper's Weekly* artist

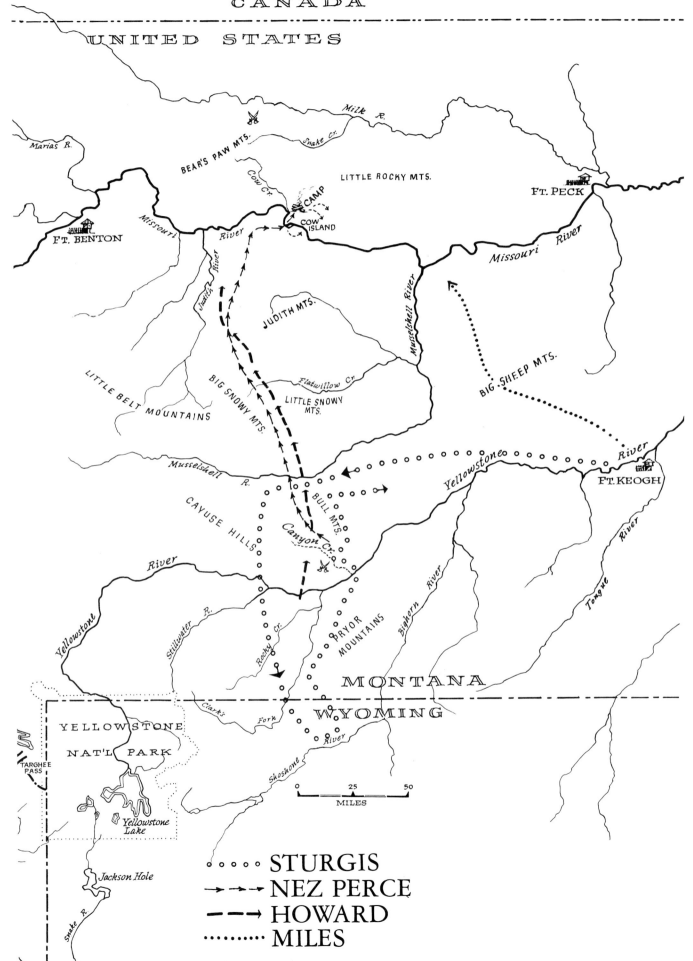

CANADA

UNITED STATES

Marias R.

Milk R.

BEAR'S PAW MTS.

Snake Cr.

LITTLE ROCKY MTS.

FT. PECK

Cow Cr.

CAMP

COW ISLAND

FT. BENTON

Missouri

River

Missouri River

Judith River

JUDITH MTS.

Musselshell River

BIG SHEEP MTS.

LITTLE BELT MOUNTAINS

BIG SNOWY MTS.

Flatwillow Cr.

LITTLE SNOWY MTS.

Musselshell

R.

Yellowstone

River

FT. KEOGH

CAYUSE HILLS

BULL MTS.

Canyon Cr.

Bighorn River

Tongue River

Stillwater R.

Rocky Cr.

PRYOR MOUNTAINS

Yellowstone

River

MONTANA

Clark's

Fork

WYOMING

TARGHEE PASS

YELLOWSTONE NAT'L PARK

Shoshone

River

25   50

MILES

Yellowstone Lake

Jackson Hole

Snake R.

· · · · · STURGIS
→ → → NEZ PERCE
– – – HOWARD
· · · · · · MILES

stocked supply depot was almost too good to be true. In a council of chiefs it was decided to send twenty warriors across the river as guards, swim the pack animals and people to the north bank, then set up camp two miles or so from the depot.

"If the soldiers do not fire on us," the chiefs said, "we will do no shooting."[8]

Faced with such overwhelming odds, the soldiers forted up and waited to see what the Nez Perces would do. When the band of warriors rode toward the depot, a civilian employed by the agent in charge of Cow Island came out to greet them. They refused to talk to him, asking to speak to the leader of the soldiers. Sergeant William Moelchert came out then and asked what they wanted.

Politely, the warriors asked him to give them supplies from his ample store. Politely, he refused. They offered to buy what they needed. He still refused. Would he give them something to eat? Grudgingly, he gave them a side of bacon and half a sack of hardtack. Sending that meager present back to camp, the Indians decided that if the needed supplies would not be given or could not be bought, they must be taken. Shortly thereafter, the shooting began.

Having the good sense to fort up behind wagons and river bank bluffs well removed from the supply depot, the defenders did not force the hostiles to dispose of them before getting to the supplies — which the Nez Perces could have done

easily enough. For most of the night and part of the next day token shots were exchanged in a token attack and resistance, with a token Indian and two token whites receiving minor wounds. Meanwhile, Peopeo Tholekt said:

"we took whatever we needed, flour, sugar, coffee, bacon, and beans. Anything whoever wanted it. Some took pans and pots for the cooking. We figured it was soldier supplies, so set fire to what we did not take. We had the privilege to do this. It was in the war."[9]

Ironically, getting supplies to troops in the field had been a major problem for the army quartermaster, for it was difficult to predict where deposits of rations, ammunition, and clothing should be made along a rugged, mostly roadless route extending more than a thousand miles through several military districts. As far as the Nez Perces were concerned, the service was great.

Next morning the Indians moved on, well fed and well supplied. In this northern land the late September nights were becoming cold, the days were getting shorter, and the older people were growing weary of the never-ending traveling. Now that the Missouri River had been crossed, nothing lay between the exiles and their goal but the rolling grassland of the high plains.

Canada and freedom were less than one hundred miles away.

8. Ibid., p. 198.
9. McWhorter, *Hear Me,* p. 471.

CHAPTER THIRTY-FOUR

BATTLE OF BEAR'S PAW MOUNTAINS:
September 30–October 5, 1877

Looking Glass upbraided Poker Joe [Lean Elk] for his hurrying; for causing the old people weariness; told him that he was no chief, that he himself was a chief and that he would be the leader. Poker Joe replied, "All right, Looking Glass, you can lead. I am trying to save the people, doing my best to cross into Canada before the soldiers find us. You can take command, but I think we will be caught and killed."

— Many Wounds[1]

TOWARD NOON, some ten miles north of Cow Island Landing, the Nez Perces were given another opportunity for looting when they encountered a slow-moving wagon train drawn by oxen and loaded with supplies. Killing three of the teamsters while the rest escaped into the hills, the Indians took what they wanted, in the process of which they discovered that part of the cargo was whiskey. At that crucial moment, soldiers were sighted riding over a ridge to the south. Forgetting the firewater, the hostiles put torch to the wagons, mounted their horses and rode back to do battle with the newcomers.

This was a contingent of thirty-six mounted volunteers, commanded by Major Guido Ilges, from Fort Benton. Knowing that the Indians were in the area, Major Ilges was leading his company on a cautious scout, seeking information he could pass on to Howard or Miles. Reaching Cow Island Landing that morning, he had observed the damage done there, then set out on the trail of the Indians. He caught up with them just in time to watch them overwhelm the freight-wagon train.

With his small force there was nothing he could do about it. After a brief exchange of shots, in which one of the volunteers was killed, he broke off the skirmish and rode back to Cow Island Landing, from which he dispatched couriers to Howard and Miles.

Shortly after the attack on the wagon train, Looking Glass replaced Lean Elk as leader of the Nez Perces. After their trek everybody was tired. The horses were footsore and jaded. There was good grass in this part of the country and many buffalo. So far as the Indians knew, the only army troops in the area were those with General Howard, who was far behind. Why not take their time? By starting late each morning, traveling slowly during the day, and making camp early each afternoon, the horses would be given a chance to regain their strength and the young men time to hunt and bring in meat they would need for the winter.

No doubt Lean Elk was as disgusted with having constantly to urge laggards to move along as they were sick of the sound of his scolding voice. No doubt the series of victories won over the whites since Big Hole had made many of the Indians forget that disaster and had restored their faith in Looking Glass. No doubt a glaze of fatigue dulled minds and clouded judgments after one hundred days and thirteen hundred miles of flight.

In any case, Lean Elk was out as leader now, and Looking Glass was in. Confidently, he took the people north in easy stages, following a route across rolling grassland turned brown by early autumn frost, passing between broken hills called the

---

1. McWhorter, *Hear Me*, pp. 473–474.

Snowy Mountains and the Judith Mountains, the Little Rockies and the Bear's Paw Mountains. Hunters ranging ahead killed a number of buffalo the morning of September 29. At noon Looking Glass ordered a halt so that camp could be made, fires built, and a good meal cooked.

In this land of great distances and far horizons, the site selected for the camp was not very attractive. There were no trees, the creek which ran through the low swale was sluggish and small, and the view was cut off by surrounding ridges. But buffalo chips could be gathered in quantity for the cooking fires, the ridges blocked out the cold night breeze, and the water in Snake Creek would fill their needs.

The Canadian border lay just forty-five miles to the north. An easy two days' travel. Before undertaking the final segment of their journey, they would rest a while here.

Realizing after the Canyon Creek skirmish that the chances of his weary troops catching the Indians were very small, General Howard sent a message to Colonel Nelson A. Miles at Fort Keogh, urging him to assemble whatever troops he had at hand, then angle northwest across the country in a final desperate effort to intercept the hostiles before they reached the Canadian border.

An ambitious, energetic commander who knew a golden opportunity for a brigadier-generalship when he saw one, Colonel Miles wasted no time. The message from Howard reached him September 17. He spent the entire night ferrying his troops across the Yellowstone River, where he put together a wagon train filled with rations for thirty days. By the time marching orders were given next morning, he had assembled a force of six hundred men, consisting of a mixed bag of infantrymen mounted on captured Sioux ponies, two battalions of cavalry on army horses, a Hotchkiss gun, and thirty Cheyenne and Sioux auxiliaries.

Not only was Miles an energetic commander; he was a lucky one. Moving his command at a forced-march rate for twelve days and two hundred miles, he still needed a couple of fortunate happenings to put his troops in the right place at the right time. Despite the fact that he sent scouts five to twenty miles in advance and to the flanks, his information regarding the whereabouts and route of the hostiles was so outdated that he almost missed them entirely.

Nearing the Missouri River some sixty miles

From a painting by John Mix Stanley   *Courtesy Penrose Library, Whitman College*

Milk River — Bear's Paw Mountain in the distance

downstream from Cow Island Landing the evening of September 23 and needing the assistance of a river steamer to cross part of his command to the north bank, he ordered Lieutenant Biddle to mount a detail and ride up or downriver, whichever he thought best, looking for a handy steamboat to help them.

"I do not think that Lieutenant Biddle drew rein until he stood on the bank of the Missouri just in time to hail the last regular steamer going down the river that season," Colonel Miles writes, ". . . and when we reached the Missouri the next morning we found the steamer tied up at the bank awaiting us."[2]

2. General Nelson A. Miles, *Personal Recollections* (Chicago and New York: Werner and Co., 1896), p. 264.

From a painting by John Mix Stanley   *Courtesy Penrose Library, Whitman College*

Bear's Paw

Thinking that the Nez Perces were still fifty or seventy-five miles south of the river, Colonel Miles had a battalion of the Second Cavalry under Captain Tyler transferred to the north bank by the steamer. The duty of this battalion would be "to prevent the Nez Perces from crossing at any of the ferries above," Miles writes, which shows how little he knew about Nez Perce river-crossing ability.

The rest of the command, with the wagon train, would march upriver along the south bank, with the scouts ranging ahead to make contact with the hostiles somewhere south of the river. Since there appeared to be no further need for the steamer, Colonel Miles thanked its accommodating master, Captain Baldwin, and bade him a pleasant farewell.

There then occurred another lucky break for the army. Miles writes:

"As our command was being prepared to march to the west, and while the steamer was but a short distance away, three men came down the river in a boat and announced the fact that the Nez Perces had crossed the Missouri some sixty miles to the west of us, at a point known as Cow Island . . .

"The steamer was then beyond hailing distance, but quick as thought, Sergeant McHugh, whose piece of artillery was resting on the bank of the river, was ordered to charge his gun and train it down the river and commence throwing shot and shell as rapidly as possible. The reverberation of the cannon down between the high bluffs of the river, and the bursting of shells in the air on the left bank could be heard for several miles down the Missouri, and I knew that if these sounds reached the ears of that thorough soldier, Baldwin, he would turn back to the sound of the guns.

"I was not mistaken in the man; in the course of twenty or thirty minutes the soldiers sung out: 'Here she comes.' And a most welcome sight it was, to see the black column of smoke as the steamer rounded the bend far below and came puffing up against the strong current."[3]

With the help of the steamer, the entire command was quickly transferred to the north side of the river. Thanks to information supplied by Major Ilges, Miles now knew where the hostiles were headed and the route they would take to get there. His present position and the nature of the terrain to the northwest gave him an excellent opportunity to approach the Indians without being detected.

"The Little Rocky Mountains is a range some fifty miles in extent, running northwest and southeast," he writes. "Beyond the northern point about ten miles is a range known as the Bear's Paw Mountains, with a low divide connecting the two. My information was that the Nez Perces had taken the course that would bring them through this pass between the two ranges. Instead of going to the west of the Little Rocky Mountains, though I knew the Nez Perces to be in that direction, I marched along the base of the mountains on the east side, thereby concealing the command from the observation of the Indians, while my scouts were kept well on the crests of the mountains and to the west whenever possible."[4]

Transferring the supplies to pack animals, marching from dawn to dark for four straight days, disturbing the buffalo herds as little as possible by prohibiting the firing of rifles, the command camped on the northeast side of the Little Rockies the night of September 29, with its presence still undetected by the Nez Perces. Early the next morning it prepared for battle and resumed its march toward the low swale at the base of the Bear's Paw Mountains, eight miles away. As was their custom, several Cheyenne and Sioux warriors rode with the advance scouts, wearing their most ragged clothes and mounted upon their poorest horses.

"Suddenly one of these advance scouts, a young warrior, was seen galloping at full speed back over the prairie," Miles writes. "He said something in Sioux or Cheyenne to the Indians as he passed them, and it was evident that he brought information of the discovery of the Nez Perce camp. . . . They appeared to be perfectly wild with delight, and as unlike what they had seemed twenty minutes before as two scenes of a drama."[5]

Because of the lack of wood and the abundance of buffalo chips here, the Nez Perce called the camp on Snake Creek *Tsanim Alikos Pah* ("Place of Manure Fire"), Yellow Wolf told McWhorter, and he quickly dispelled the myth that the Indians thought they had reached Canada.

"We knew distance to Canadian line. Knew how long it would take to travel there. But there was no hurrying by Chief Looking Glass, leader since crossing the big river."[6]

Yellow Wolf also made it clear that the attack by the soldiers was not a complete surprise, even though it came from an unexpected direction.

"Next morning [September 30], not too early, while some were still eating breakfast, two scouts came galloping from the south, from the direction we had come. As

3. Ibid., pp. 265–266.
4. Ibid., p. 266.
5. Ibid., pp. 276, 268.
6. McWhorter, *Yellow Wolf,* p. 204.

INDIAN STRONGHOLD IN THE RAVINES

BOMB-PROOF EXCAVATIONS.

GEORGE A. HUSTON, GUIDE

SOUNDING THE BUGLE FOR THE TRUCE

SENDING FLAG OF TRUCE TO THE INDIAN CAMP.

THE BATTLE — ADVANCE OF THE SKIRMISH LINE.

Scenes of the Nez Perce War by *Harper's Weekly* artists

they drew near, they called loudly, 'Stampeding buffalo! Soldiers! Soldiers!

"Some families had packs partly ready and horses caught. But Chief Looking Glass, now head of camp, mounted his horse and rode around ordering, 'Do not hurry! Go slow! Plenty, plenty time. Let children eat all wanted!'

"This slowed people down . . .

"Because of Chief Looking Glass, we were caught.

"It was about one hour later when a scout was seen coming from the same direction. He was running his horse to its best. On the highest bluff he circled about, and waved the blanket signal: 'Enemies right on us! Soon the attack!'

"A wild stir hit the people. Great hurrying everywhere. I was still in my uncle's camp, my home. I saw this uncle, Chief Joseph, leap to the open. His voice was above all the noise as he called 'Horses! Horses! Save the horses!'

"I grabbed my rifle and cartridge belts and ran with others for our horses. Warriors were hurrying to the bluffs to meet the soldiers. Soon, from the south came a noise — a rumble like stampeding buffaloes. Reaching higher ground north of our camp I looked back. Hundreds of soldiers charging in two wide, circling wings. They were surrounding our camp. I saw Sioux or Cheyenne Indians taking lead ahead of soldiers. I ran a short distance, then heard the rifle reports. I stopped. Turning, I saw soldiers firing at everybody. I could get none of the horses. All running from guns."[7]

Thus, the final battle began. Once again, mounted soldiers had charged a camp containing women, children, and old people, as well as warriors, in a surprise attack with what seemed to be overwhelming superiority in numbers and firepower.

Once again, incredibly, the Indians struck back with a stunningly fierce resistance.

During that first charge, Colonel Miles's command managed to capture one-third of the Nez Perce horse herd, amounting to six or seven hundred animals, to cut off several families from the camp, and to inflict most of the casualties suffered by the Indians during the battle. But the soldiers paid a bitter price.

"Captain Hale, Lieutenant Biddle, and twenty-two soldiers had been killed, four officers and thirty-eight enlisted men wounded," McWhorter writes. "Further cavalry charges could be attempted only with great losses; the alternative was to lay siege to the village."[8]

On their part, the Nez Perces had lost twenty-two people killed and an unknown number wounded. Yellow Wolf tells how Heyoom Iklakit, a Nez Perce warrior, exchanged sign-talk with a Cheyenne chief, asking him why the Cheyenne

and Sioux were making war on their red brothers. He was assured by the Cheyenne: "I will never shoot you. I will shoot in the air."

"The Cheyenne chief lied to Heyoom," Yellow Wolf said bitterly. "He rode south about forty steps from where he talked, and met a Nez Perce woman mounted. He caught her bridle and with his six-shooter shot and killed the woman. I saw her fall to the ground."[9]

Unfortunately for the Nez Perces, their fatalities included many of their leading chiefs and bravest warriors. Ollokot, Joseph's younger brother, was killed early in the fighting, as was Too-hool-hool-zote, the "cross-grained growler." In the confusion of the first encircling attack from two directions at once, with Cheyenne and Sioux warriors riding in the lead,

"a bad mistake was made by Husishusis Kute," Yellow Wolf said sadly. "Three brave warriors, Koyehkown, Kowwaspo, and Peopeo Ipsewahk were in a washout southeast of camp. They were too far toward the enemy line. Husishusis thought them enemy Indians and killed them all. He had a magazine rifle and was a good shot. With every shot he would say, 'I got one!' or 'I got him!'

"Lean Elk was also killed by mistake. A Nez Perce saw him across a small canyon, mistook him for one of the enemies, and shot him."[10]

Holding the higher ground and encircling the Indian camp so that none of its occupants could escape, Colonel Miles ordered the Hotchkiss gun brought up and the encampment shelled. That proved ineffectual because the muzzle of the piece could not be depressed sufficiently to bear on the valley below, where the Indians were digging shelters in the soft, moist earth. Miles then tried to cut the Nez Perces off from water by sending two troops of cavalry down the hill to take and hold the creek, but heavy gunfire from the hostiles forced tha soldiers back. As darkness fell, turning a chilly, rainy day into a cold, snowy night, the troops kept watch on the heights; Nez Perce warriors dug rifle pits on the middle slopes; and down in the bottom of the valley old men, women, and children excavated a protective network of caves, tunnels, and living quarters that in the next few days and nights became amazing in extent.

"We digged the trenches with camas hooks and

7. Ibid., pp. 205–206
8. McWhorter, *Hear Me*, p. 484.
9. McWhorter, *Yellow Wolf*, p. 207. In a footnote, p. 208, McWhorter says ten different tribes were drawn on for scout services against the Nez Perces.
10. Ibid., p. 209.

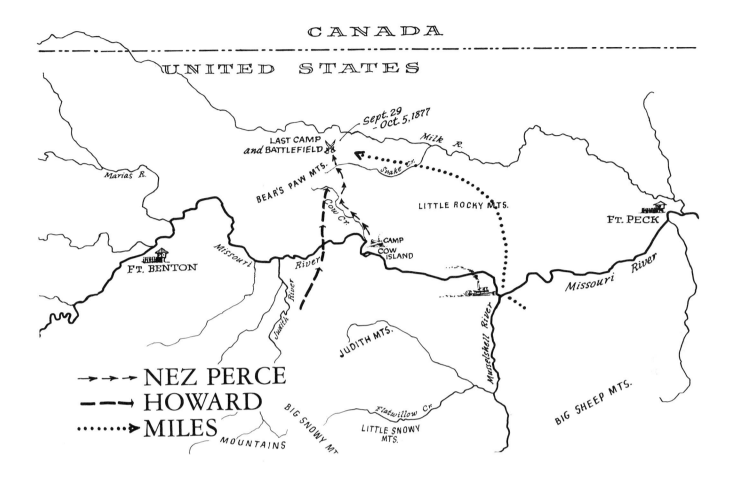

NEZ PERCE
HOWARD
MILES

butcher knives," an unnamed woman survivor told McWhorter. "With pans we threw out the dirt. We could not do much cooking. Dried meat and some other grub would be handed around. If not enough for all, it would be given to the children first. I was three days without food. Children cried with hunger and cold. Old people suffering in silence. Misery everywhere. Cold and dampness all around. In the small creek there was water, but we could get it only at night. In traveling, we had buffalo horns for purpose of water. With strings we could let them down while crossing streams horseback. We carried them with us all the time. They came handy here."[11]

"We slept only by naps," Wetatonmi, Ollokot's widow said, "sitting in our pits; leaning forward or back against the dirt wall. Many of the warriors stayed in ther rifle pits all the time."[12]

The tribal historian, Wottolen, gives an interesting account of how each day's casualties were recorded:

"Alahoos, an oldlike man who was still strong, made

announcements of all incidents and events each day. All knew him and reported to him who had been wounded or killed in battle, who was missing or had disappeared. The names of all were known throughout the land."[13]

By morning, October 1, five inches of snow covered the ground, and the weather was very cold. In a way the soldiers suffered more than the Indians. Until their wagon train arrived with tents and supplies, they had no shelter or fuel — they did not know about the ample store of buffalo chips underfoot. The Indians, on the other hand, knew the chips were there, could feel them with their feet through the blanket of snow, and could use them to make small fires in their trenches.

During the morning Colonel Miles raised a white flag and had a man call out in Chinook Jar-

11. McWhorter, *Hear Me*, pp. 485–486.
12. Ibid., p. 486.
13. Ibid., p. 486n.

Courtesy Montana Historical Society

The volunteer hostage, 2nd Lieutenant Lovell Jerome. He was held by the Nez Perces while Chief Joseph was being held by General Miles. Eventually they were exchanged, the truce was cancelled, and the battle went on.

gon that he wanted to talk with Chief Joseph. He assumed from General Howard's statements to newspaper reporters that Joseph was the tribal leader. Neither White Bird nor Looking Glass objected to letting him be their spokesman, for they deeply mistrusted the soldiers and still hoped either to escape to Canada or be aided on this side of the border by Sitting Bull and the two thousand warriors reputed to be under his command.

This is the way Yellow Wolf described that first meeting between Chief Joseph and General Miles:

"The chiefs held council and Chief Joseph said, 'Yes, I would like to see General Miles.'

"Tom Hill, interpreter, went to see what General Miles wanted, to tell General Miles, 'Yes, Joseph would like to see you.' After some time, we saw Tom Hill with General Miles and a few men come halfway. They stopped and Tom Hill called to Chief Joseph. Chief Joseph with two or three warriors went to meet them.

"I did not go where they met. I looked around. There was a hollow place off a distance in the ground. I went there and lay down. I could see General Miles

where Chief Joseph met him. I could see plainly where they stood. I was saying to myself, 'Whenever they shoot Chief Joseph, *I* will shoot from here!'

"There was talk for a while, and Chief Joseph and General Miles made peace. Some guns were given up. Then there was a trick. I saw Chief Joseph taken to the soldier camp a prisoner!

"The white flag was pulled down!

"The white flag was a lie!

"The warriors came back, and right away a soldier officer [Lieutenant Lovell H. Jerome] rode into our camp. Chief Yellow Bull yelled a warning and grabbed him. I could see him take the officer to the main shelter pit. When I saw all this — Chief Joseph taken away — I ran to where the captured soldier was being held. Held that Chief Joseph might not be hurt. He had on a yellow-colored outside coat to keep off the wet. A strong-looking young man, he did not say much. Looked around, but seemed not much afraid. I do not think he was bad scared.

"The chiefs instructed the warriors to guard him. Ordered: 'Treat him right! He is one of the commanders!'"[14]

14. McWhorter, *Yellow Wolf*, pp. 214–215.

Photo by David F. Barry, date not recorded thought to be about 1880s   *Courtesy Smithsonian Institution*

Steps, a brother of Chief Joseph who lived with the Sioux at Standing Rock Agency.

Photo by Charles M. Bell, Washington, D.C., probably around 1897   *Courtesy Smithsonian Institution*

Chief Joseph with his nephew Ahlakat, Ben Beveridge, and Amos F. Wilkinson

Apparently during the surrender conference Colonel Miles had asked the Nez Perces to give up all their rifles. Chief Joseph requested that they be permitted to keep half their weapons in order to kill game, and somewhere during the discussion the meeting of minds broke down. When Joseph started to return to the Nez Perce camp, Colonel Miles, frustrated because he had been unable to end the fighting on his terms, detained Joseph on some pretext after letting the other Indians leave.

Earlier (later, by Indian accounts) he asked Lieutenant Jerome to "go see what the Indians are doing." Misunderstanding, Lieutenant Jerome rode into the midst of the Nez Perces and was seized as a counterhostage. Colonel Miles was thus put in the uncomfortable position of risking a subordinate's life in a questionable cause.

While the Indians say that Joseph was treated very badly, Lieutenant Jerome was treated very well. In fact, the lieutenant wrote a letter to his commander next morning which said:

"I had good supper, good bed. I had plenty of blankets. This morning I had a good breakfast. I am treated like I was at home. I hope you officers are treating Joseph as I am treated."

But Chief Joseph was not treated right. Yellow Wolf says:

"Chief Joseph was bound hands and feet. They took a double blanket. Soldiers rolled him in it like you roll a papoose on cradle board. Chief Joseph could not use arms, could not walk about. He was put where there were mules, not in soldier tent. That was how Chief Joseph was treated all night."[15]

Curiously enough, in future interviews with white reporters Chief Joseph made no complaint regarding his treatment that night. Understandably enough, Colonel Miles mentioned the incident only in an oblique way. According to him, it was the Nez Perces who asked for the truce, pretended to

15. Ibid., p. 217.

surrender their arms, then reneged on their agreement.

"While this was going on I directed Lieutenant Jerome to ascertain what the Indians were doing in their village, supposing that he would go to the edge of the bluff and look down into the camp," Miles writes. "Misunderstanding my instructions, he went down into the ravine, whereupon he was seized and held until he was exchanged for Chief Joseph."[16]

Whatever the sequence of events, Chief Joseph was not held until the hostiles surrendered, as Colonel Miles desired, nor was Lieutenant Jerome killed in an act of revenge, as a rash young Nez Perce warrior named Chuslum Hihhih wanted. Instead, they were taken to the "halfway ground," were exchanged, shook hands, and returned to their people.

The white flag was lowered.

And the fighting began again.

"Some warriors talked to charge the soldiers and fight it out," Yellow Wolf says. "If we whipped them, we would be free. If we could not whip, we would all be killed and no more trouble. But others said, 'No! The solders are too strong. There are the big guns, the cannon guns. If we are killed, we leave women and children, old people and many wounded. We cannot charge the soldiers.' "[17]

On the morning of the fifth day of the siege, the soldiers finally scored a hit with the cannon, when they at last managed to bring it to bear on the floor of the grassy swale.

"It was towards noon that a bursting shell struck and broke in a shelter pit," Yellow Wolf says sadly, "burying four women, a little boy, and a girl of about twelve snows. This girl, Atsipeeten, her grandmother, Intetah, were both killed. The other three women and the boy were rescued. The two dead were left in the cave-in pit."[18]

Colonel Miles was concerned that some of the Nez Perces who had escaped the surprise attack early in the battle might make it to Canada and bring help from Sitting Bull. He sent Lieutenant Maus and a detachment of scouts in pursuit, with orders to capture or kill them. Several were captured and brought back during the next few days. Others had the misfortune of encountering a band of Assiniboines, who, instead of giving them aid, killed them.

On the night of October 4 General Howard and a dozen of his men arrived at the Bear's Paw siege site. At first Colonel Miles gave the general a cool reception. Then, upon being assured by

Photo taken by DeLancey Gill around 1900   *Courtesy Smithsonian Institution*
Peopeo-Takakt, cousin of Chief Joseph. He was born in 1861.

Howard that "I had no desire to assume immediate command of the field but would be glad to have him finish the work he had so well begun,"[19] Miles greeted his old comrade in arms in a much more friendly manner.

Still with Howard were the Nez Perce scouts, Captain John and Old George. At the general's suggestion they went into the hostile camp under a white flag. Pleased to hear that both their daughters were still alive, the two scouts urged the Nez Perces to surrender. Howard's main command was only a day's march away, they said, and when it arrived further resistance would be useless. Surrender would involve no trials or executions; those who surrendered would be given food, clothing, medical care, and honorable treatment as prisoners of war. Furthermore, it was the clearly expressed

16. Miles, *Recollections*, p. 274.
17. McWhorter, *Yellow Wolf*, pp. 218–219.
18. Ibid., p. 220.
19. McWhorter, *Hear Me*, p. 491.

intention of the military that when the Indians were captured they were to be returned to the Nez Perce Reservation in Idaho.

Even on those terms, Chief White Bird would not surrender. Though in his seventies now, he made it clear he would rather die in a desperate attempt to reach freedom in Canada than go back to Lapwai as a prisoner of the white man. Looking Glass felt the same way.

"I am older than you," he said to Chief Joseph. "I have my experiences with a man of two faces and two tongues. If you surrender, you will be sorry; and in your sorrow you will feel rather to be dead, than suffer that deception."

"Many of our people are out on the hills, naked and freezing," Joseph replied. "The women are suffering with cold, the children crying with the chilly dampness of the shelter pits. For myself I do not care. It is for them I am going to surrender."

"I will never surrender to a deceitful white chief," Looking Glass said.[20]

This was the last conversation between the two men. A short while later, as Looking Glass lay smoking and talking with other warriors in one of the exposed rifle pits, his attention was called to the approach of a mounted Indian.

"Believing that the Sioux had at last arrived to rescue them from their besiegers, the chief sprang up out of the pit, looking at the Indian in the distance. He turned to call out the news to his comrades, when a bullet struck his forehead, and he fell dead instead at their feet. This was the last Nez Perce casualty of the Bear Paw battle, and the only man to be killed after the first day's fighting. The only other casualties after the initial attack were the woman and child smothered in the cave-in shelter pit."[21]

Except for White Bird, who had made up his mind to leave camp under cover of darkness and flee toward Canada with as many Indians as cared to go with him, Joseph was the only Nez Perce leader left now. Too-hool-hool-zote, Hal-tal-e-kin, Looking Glass, Lean Elk, Ollokot — all were dead. Of the more than seven hundred Nez Perces who had begun the epic flight 106 days before and 1,300 miles away, 96 had been killed during the campaign, 36 of them women and children.

White Bird would take with him an estimated 233 people, 140 men and boys and 93 women and girls. These figures include those who fled the morning of the first attck and the handful who crept out during the siege.

Photo by Bill Gulick

Bear's Paw Battlefield

Joseph would surrender 87 men, 184 women, and 147 children. [22]

Like all such dramatic events, there later would be many accounts by many witnesses of what happened and what was said, the accuracy of which we will make no attempt to evaluate here. Certainly the most vivid, best-written account is that set down by General Howard's adjutant, Lieutenant Charles Erskine Scott Wood, who watched Joseph ride up the hill on that cold, gray afternoon, October 5, 1877:

"Three or four men hung around Joseph clinging to his knees and saddle blanket. All were bare-headed. Joseph's hair hung in two braids on either side of his face. He wore a blanket — I do not remember the color — I would say gray with a black stripe. . . . He wore moccasin leggings. His rifle was across the pommel in front of him. When he dismounted he picked up the rifle, pulled his blanket closer around him, and walked to General Howard and offered him the rifle. Howard waved him to Miles. He then walked to Miles and

20. McWhorter, *Hear Me*, 495; Duncan MacDonald to McWhorter, Dec. 15, 1929.
21. McWhorter, *Hear Me*, p. 495.
22. Ibid., p. 499.

handed him the rifle. Then he stepped back, adjusted his blanket to leave his right arm free, and began his speech.

" 'Tell General Howard I know his heart. What he told me before I have in my heart. I am tired of fighting. Our chiefs are killed. Looking Glass is dead. The old men are all killed. It is the young men who say yes or no. He who led the young men is dead. It is cold and we have no blankets. The little children are freezing to death. My people, some of them, have run away into the hills, and have no blankets, no food; no one knows where they are, perhaps freezing to death. I want time to look for my children and see how many of them I can find. Maybe I shall find them among the dead. Hear me, my chiefs. I am tired; my heart is sick and sad. From where the sun now stands, I will fight no more.' "[23]

For Joseph and his people, the long, cruel war was over. But for White Bird and his band, a bitter ordeal by cold and hunger still lay between them and freedom.

23. Ibid., pp. 497–498; *Annual Report of the Secretary of War* (Washington, D.C., 1877), 1:630, "Howard's Official Report, December 27, 1877," from a transcription made by C. E. S. Wood as the interpreter translated Joseph's remarks. The interpreter was Arthur Chapman. For an interesting discussion of the nine different versions of the message that are in existence, see Haruo Aoki, *Nez Perce Texts,* pp. 120–123.

CHAPTER THIRTY-FIVE

FLIGHT TO CANADA: OCTOBER 1877

*It was in the night when I escaped with Chief
White Bird and his band all afoot. . . . It was lone-
some, the leaving.*
— Wetatonmi, widow of Ollokot[1]

MOST OF THE Nez Perces who attempted to escape to Canada following the Bear's Paw Mountain Battle were members of the Looking Glass or
White Bird bands. There were a few exceptions,
individuals or groups cut off from the Snake Creek
camp by the first attack, widows whose husbands
had been members of bands choosing to surrender
while their sisters still had living husbands belonging to a band choosing flight, or simply persons to
whom freedom at any cost appealed more than
surrender.

Typical of a group whose flight north had been
more accident than design was that of Wounded
Head's wife, who, with ten women, a few children,
and some men, had been able to flee moments
after the first cavalry charge.

"We mounted horses and left. Only one blanket, I
rode bareback as did the rest. Going quite a distance,
we stopped. . . . There we stayed till the evening drew
on. Not only ourselves, but Chief Joseph's older wife
and daughter are with us. But people are scattered
everywhere, hungry, freezing. Almost naked, they had
escaped from the camp when the soldiers came charging and shooting."[2]

Somehow evading notice by the detachment of
Cheyenne and Sioux scouts sent out by Colonel
Miles, the group traveled north through the bitter
cold and the falling snow, with nothing to eat for
four days. On the fifth day they found and killed a
buffalo; the next day they met a band of Chippewa
Indians who were friendly, giving them moccasins,
food and shelter.

Black Eagle, then a boy in his teens, related a
similar experience:

"I do not remember how long we were in reaching
Sitting Bull's camp. It was two or three days before we
reached some Crees who gave me moccasins and other
clothing. Barefooted, I had no coat, no hat, no blanket.
It was cold and stormy as we traveled. It was about all I
could do to keep from death by freezing. . . . On Milk
River, Crees gave us buffalo meat and moccasins."[3]

Not so fortunate were other groups of refugees.
On October 6 General Howard wrote:

"Miles received information, at 2 P.M., from the Red
River half-breeds, of thirty Indians, twenty of them
wounded in Miles' fight, who had escaped across the
boundary. Also, from scouts, of six killed by the Assiniboines, of two or three killed by the Gros Ventres."[4]

Probably the last Nez Perce to flee the Bear's
Paw camp and head for Canada was Yellow Wolf,
Chief Joseph's nephew. Following the surrender,
he says:

"Near morning came, and Chief Joseph said to me:
'You better go find your mother and my daughter. Bring
them here!'

"That would be good, I thought, seeing my mother.
The first sun of the fighting, my mother and my uncle's
[Chief Joseph's] daughter made escape. Yes, I would go
find them.

"I stood with blanket about me, with rifle inside my
legging. Not a long rifle, this that I fought with. I had
both cartridge belts under my shirt. I would not stay! I
would not go with the people, wherever the soldiers
took them. Nor would I hide myself about that battlefield.

"During the night soldier guards were all about us.
Only the guards; all other soldiers sleeping. I waited until

1. McWhorter, *Hear Me*, pp. 510–511.
2. Ibid., p. 508.
3. Ibid., p. 510.
4. Howard, *Nez Perce Joseph*, pp. 269–270.

Photo courtesy of Big Hole National Battlefield   *Courtesy Idaho Historical Society*
Identified at White Bird, this Nez Perce man is probably a son of
the Chief White Bird who escaped to Canada.

just breaking morning. My mind was made up what to do. I would not hide myself. I would walk out past those guards. They would see me, and if they tried stopping me, that would be good. I would kill them both."[5]

Slipping past the guards without being challenged, Yellow Wolf walked through several inches of snow in his badly worn moccasins to a canyon where he knew a horse was hidden. Finding it, he mounted and rode north all day through a blinding snowstorm that completely obscured all trails. Toward evening he stumbled upon an Indian camp that he was sure must be hostile, but with his magazine rifle and two well-filled carridge belts, he thought, "I am the same as ten men!"

Riding boldly into the camp, he found that these were Nez Perces, the very people he sought.

"We all then went. I would not take my mother and Chief's Joseph's daugher back to the soldiers."[6]

A few days later, they met the Sioux . . .

The possibility that Chief Sitting Bull and the two thousand Sioux exiles living in Canada might get together with Chief Joseph and his seven hundred Nez Perces and do battle against American troops deeply worried General Howard and Colonel Miles and greatly intrigued the newspaper-reading public, which was following the campaign as if it were some kind of game — with many of the readers pulling for the Indians. If such a thing had happened, the results would have been interesting, to say the least. According to Indian accounts, their dream almost came true.

The first group of Nez Perces to reach the Sioux were some of the older men, who could communicate only through sign language. In attempting to tell the Sioux that their people were being attacked south of the border on a stream called Snake Creek, the Nez Perces made the sign meaning "water" or "stream." Thinking they meant the Missouri River, which was too far away for a rescue effort to be practical, the Sioux felt unable to help.

When a larger group arrived, a better means of communication was established. With the proximity of the battlefield now understood, the Sioux organized a war party led by Sitting Bull and containing several hundred braves, which started south next morning. Before it had gone far it met some of White Bird's refugees, who told about Joseph's surrender. Realizing it was too late to help, most of the war party turned back, escorting the refugees to the Sioux camp.

"But a small company of the Sioux and ten Nez Perces went on to see where the fighting took place," Peopeo Tholekt told McWhorter. "Everything was still. Nothing living was seen anywhere on that field. But we found some of our dead who were unburied, and buried them as best we could. There was nothing to be done, and we returned to Chief Sitting Bull's village. The Sioux talking about the location said, 'This would have been no distance for us to ride. It was just from head to pillow.' "[7]

5. McWhorter, *Yellow Wolf,* pp. 229–230.
6. Ibid., p. 232.
7. McWhorter, *Hear Me,* pp. 513–514.

Which was to say, if the Sioux had known such a great battle was taking place only a day's ride away, they would have picked up their arms and gone to the aid of their blood brothers.

All Indian accounts agree that the hospitality shown the Nez Perces by the Sioux exiles was warm, friendly, and generous.

"The meeting of the two chiefs for the first time had been one of vivid contrasts," McWhorter writes. "Sitting Bull with his proud and undefeated warriors, his six race horses beside him; White Bird afoot with his motley band of frozen, hungry refugees; the war paint and feather and splendid horses of the Sioux alongside the Nez Perce women and children who had only pieces of blanket wrapped around their feet. But Sitting Bull dismounted from his fine pony and led his warriors in wailing and crying when told what had happened to the Nez Perce resistance."[8]

For a time after their arrival in Canada the indigent Nez Perces were divided and housed with Sioux families in a winter camp located in a canyon about a day's ride north of the border. As time passed, the newcomers formed a village of their own, though the men of the two tribes continued to hunt together on the friendliest of terms. With so many Indians in the area, buffalo grew so scarce that occasional hunting parties violated their promise not to cross the border or to infringe on the territory of the Gros Ventres and the Assiniboines, which made for bad feelings with those tribes.

"I was always cold and hungry and not enough to eat," recalled White Hawk, who was a child at the time. "But the Sioux were also hungry. Their grub was scarce."[9]

Sam Tilden, another nephew of Chief Joseph, who was nine years old at the time his family fled to Canada with the White Bird band, later recalled the great kindness with which Chief Sitting Bull greeted the refugees.

"He came up to each and every one of us, man, woman, and child, and shook our hand. With even the youngest children, he did that — came up and shook our hand."[10]

For a time, at least, the 233 people in Chief White Bird's band had found freedom, friends, and a home in which they felt reasonably comfortable.

For the 418 people in Chief Joseph's band, their search for these same things was just beginning.

8. Ibid., p. 514; Duncan MacDonald to McWhorter, May 30, 1930.
9. McWhorter, *Hear Me,* p. 516.
10. Statement by Sam Tilden to Marcus Ware, Lewiston, in 1930s.

CHAPTER THIRTY-SIX

EEIKISH PAH — THE HOT COUNTRY: 1878–1885

*The white people have too many chiefs. They
do not understand each other.*
— Chief Joseph, April 1879

SINCE WINTER was at hand and the mountain passes to the west soon would be choked with snow, General Howard decided it would not be practical to return the Indian prisoners to the Lapwai Reservation just now. He issued an order to Colonel Miles:

"On account of the cost of transportation of the Nez Perces to the Pacific coast, I deem it best to retain them all at some place within your district, where they can be kept under military control until spring. Then unless you receive instructions from higher authority, you are hereby directed to have them sent under proper guard to my department, where I will take charge of them and carry out the instructions I have already received."[1]

Those instructions, which had come from General McDowell in San Francisco, stated unequivocally that the nontreaty Nez Perces, when finally subdued, were to be returned to the Idaho reservation. Despite this commitment Howard seems to have sensed that the original plan might be changed. In his report of the campaign, he wrote:

"But as I had made arrangements with Colonel Miles respecting the Indians, which he and I deemed most important, and as we feared, without a full and proper explanation to General Sheridan, that we might be overruled, we though it best for the public interests that I should go through to Chicago and see General Sheridan."[2]

So while Colonel Miles and his troops escorted the prisoners overland to Fort Keogh, General Howard hurried east to Chicago. Traveling with the overland party were eleven hundred or so captured Nez Perce horses. As a reward for the loyal service of the Cheyenne and Sioux scouts, Colonel Miles kept his promise to them.

"I directed the officer in charge of the Nez Perce herd to give each of them five ponies as a reward for their gallant service."[3]

But Miles did not keep an implied promise made to General Howard, who generously had let him stay in command of the Bear's Paw operation and accept Joseph's surrender. Although one version of his report — which he showed Howard — mentioned the one-armed general's presence, this was not the version that reached General Sheridan and the press. That message, dated October 5, totally ignored Howard's presence at Bear's Paw, reading:

"We have had our usual success. We made a very difficult and rapid march across country, and after a severe engagement and being kept under fire for three days, the hostile camp under Chief Joseph surrendered at two o'clock today."[4]

Learning of the slight when he reached Fort Lincoln a week later, General Howard was so incensed that he authorized Lieutenant Wood to write and release to the newspapers the *true* version of the surrender. Before it appeared in the Chicago papers, Colonel Miles sent in an amended report, in which he did mention Howard's presence.

When Howard arrived in Chicago he found Sheridan very angry over the fact that Lieutenant Wood's report had been released without his permission, for it made it appear that his officers were

1. McWhorter, *Hear Me*, p. 525; *Report of Secretary of War*, 1877, 1:631, "Howard to Miles, Oct. 7, 1877."
2. McWhorter, *Hear Me*, p. 526; *Report of Secretary of War*, 1877, 1:633, "Howard's Official Report."
3. Miles, *Recollections*, p. 277.
4. Beal, *I Will Fight No More*, p. 232; Miles to Terry, Oct. 5, 1877, U.S., National Archives Document No. 6260, p. 77, Adjutant General's Office 3464, p. 77n.

bickering and headline hunting. Indignant words were exchanged, and Howard walked out before a full discussion of the real problem — what to do with Joseph and his people — could be held.

Actually, to General Philip Sheridan the problem was not people, it was supply. Subsisting the Nez Perces at Fort Keogh would be too expensive, he felt, so in November he ordered them sent downriver, first to Fort Lincoln, near Bismarck, North Dakota, then to Fort Leavenworth, in eastern Kansas, where the four hundred weary exiles arrived November 27, 1877. Here they were to be held as prisoners of war until the following spring.

"The camping place selected by the commandant for these Indians . . . was in the Missouri River bottom, about two miles above the fort, between a lagoon and the river, the worst possible place that could have been selected; and the sanitary conditions of the Indians proved it. The physician in charge said that one-half could be said to be sick, and all were affected by the poisonous malaria of the camp."[5]

During the first six months that the exiles were held in the Fort Leavenworth pesthole camp, twenty-one deaths occurred. Obviously, the Indians could not be held as prisoners of war forever. Neither could they be sent back to their homeland, for every community through which they had passed had drawn up indictments against them. The simplest solution appeared to be to send them to Indian Territory, which since the 1830s had been a dumping ground for tribes uprooted by relocation or war.

"This will be no hardship to them," one commissioner wrote with abysmal ignorance, "as the difference in temperature between that latitude and their old home is inconsiderable."[6]

Chief Joseph did not agree. Comparing the miserable, humid, malaria-infested lands assigned to the Nez Perces on the Quapaw Reservation in the northeastern part of what is now Oklahoma to the high, cool, healthful Wallowa Valley from which he and his people had been driven, he said:

"I think very little of this country. It is like a poor man; it amounts to nothing."[7]

By October 1878 forty-seven more captives had died. Ironically, the white man who had precipitated the war by firing the first shot at White Bird Canyon, Arthur Chapman, had gone to work for the government as an official interpreter for the Nez Perces. In exile with them, he found the climate so bad that during a full day's delay in a swel-

Harper's Magazine Sketch   *Courtesy Penrose Library, Whitman College*
Nez Perces in Kansas

tering railway station while making a transfer to the new reservation home, he was prostrated with the heat. So were Chief Joseph's wife and three Nez Perce children — the latter of whom died during the journey.

It was Chapman, strangely enough, who accompanied Chief Joseph and Yellow Bull to Washington, D.C., acting as interpreter in the hearings and interviews that did much to create sympathy for the Nez Perce plight and give Joseph his reputation as an eloquent spokesman for his people. Since the account published in the April 1879 issue of the *North American Review,* comes as close to being a personal statement of Joseph's thoughts and feelings on the war as he ever made, we quote it at length here, beginning with the surrender:

"General Miles had promised that we might return to our own country with what stock we had left. . . . I believed General Miles, or I never would have surrendered. I have heard that he has been censured for making the promise to return us to Lapwai. He could not have made any other terms with me at that time. I could have held him in check until my friends came to my assistance, and then neither of the generals nor their soldiers would have ever left Bear Paw Mountain alive.

"I was told we could go with General Miles to

5. McWhorter, *Hear Me*, p. 529; Bureau of Indian Affairs, *Commission Reports,* 1878, p. xxxiii.
6. McWhorter, *Hear Me*, p. 530.
7. Ibid., p. 532; U.S., Congress, *Senate Miscellaneous Document No. 53,* 45th Cong., 3d sess., 1878, 2:77, Joseph testifying before a joint congressional committee, October 1878.

Tongue River and stay there until spring, when we would be sent back to our country. . . . After our arrival at Tongue River, General Miles received orders to take us to Bismarck. The reason given was that subsistence would be cheaper there.

"General Miles was opposed to this order. He said, 'You must not blame me. I have endeavored to keep my word, but the chief who is over me has given the order, and I must obey it or resign. That would do you no good. Some other officer would carry out the order.'

"General Miles turned my people over to another soldier, and we were taken to Bismarck. Captain Johnson, who now had charge of us, received an order to take us to Fort Leavenworth. At Leavenworth we were placed on a low river bottom, with no water except river water to drink and cook with. We had always lived in a healthy country, where the mountains were high and the water was cold and clear. Many of my people sickened and died, and we buried them in this strange land. I can not tell you how much my heart suffered for my people while at Leavenworth . . .

"During the hot days [July 1878] we received notice that we were to be moved farther away from our country. . . . We were ordered to get into the railroad cars. Three of my people died on the way to Baxter Springs. It is worse to die there than to die fighting in the mountains.

"We were moved from Baxter Springs [Kansas] to the Indian Territory, and set down without our lodges. We had but little medicine, and we were nearly all sick. Seventy of my people have died since we moved there.

"We have had a great many visitors who have talked many ways. Some of the chiefs [General Fish and Colonel Stickney] from Washington came to see us, and selected lands for us to live upon. We have not moved to that land, for it is not a good place to live.

"The Commissioner Chief [E. A. Hayt] came to see us. I told him, as I told everyone, that I expected General Miles' word would be carried out. He said it 'could not be done; that white men now lived in my country and all the land was taken up; that if I returned to Wallowa, I could not live in peace; that law-papers were out against my young men who began the war, and that the Government could not protect my people.'

"The Commissioner Chief [Mr. Hayt] invited me to go with him and hunt for a better home than we have now. I like the land we found [west of the Osage reservation] better than any place I have seen in that country; but it is not a healthy land. There are no mountains and rivers. The water is warm. It is not a good country for stock. I do not believe my people can live there. I am afraid they will all die . . .

"Then the Inspector Chief [General McNiel] came to my camp and we had a long talk. He said I ought to have a home in the mountain country north, and that he would write a letter to the Great Chief in Washington. Again the hope of seeing the mountains of Idaho and Oregon grew up in my heart.

"At last I was granted permission to come to Washington and bring my friend Yellow Bull and our interpreter with me. I am glad we came. I have shaken

Photographer and date not recorded;   *Courtesy Smithsonian Institution*
probably about 1878

Yellow Bull

hands with a great many friends, but there are some things I want to know which no one seems able to explain. I can not understand why so many chiefs are allowed to talk so many different ways, and promise so many different things. I have been to the Great Father Chief [the President], the next Great Chief [Secretary of the Interior], the Commissioner Chief [Hayt], the Law Chief [General Butler], and many other law chiefs [Congressman], and they all say they are my friends, and that I shall have justice, but while their mouths all talk right I do not understand why nothing is done. Good words do not last long unless they amount to something.

"Words do not pay for dead people. They do not pay for my country, now overrun by white men. They do not protect my father's grave. They do not pay for all my horses and cattle. Good words will not give me back my children. Good words will not make good the promise of your War Chief General Miles. Good words will not give my people good health and stop them from dying. Good words will not get my people a home where they can live in peace and take care of themselves.

"I am tired of talk that comes to nothing. It makes my heart sick when I remember all the good words and all the broken promises. There has been too much talking by men who had no right to talk . . .

"If the white man wants to live in peace with the

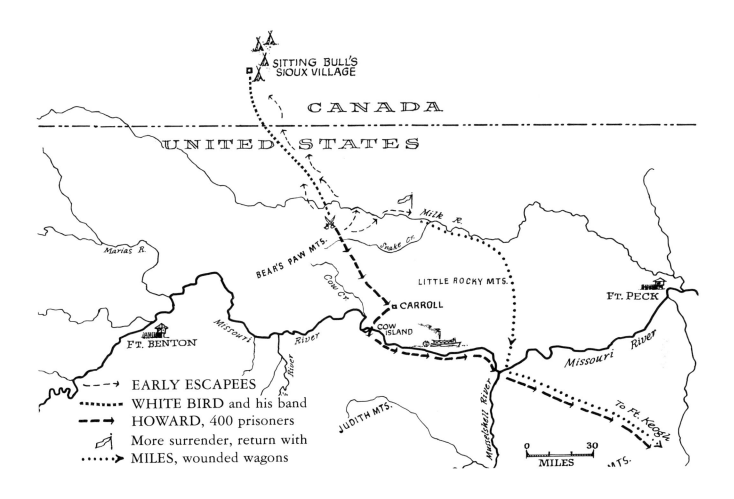

EARLY ESCAPEES

WHITE BIRD and his band

HOWARD, 400 prisoners

More surrender, return with

MILES, wounded wagons

Indians he can live in peace. There need be no trouble. Treat all men alike. Give them all the same law. Give them an even chance to live and grow. All men were made by the same Great Spirit Chief. They are all brothers. The earth is the mother of all people, and all people should have equal rights upon it. You might as well expect the rivers to run backward as that any man who was born a free man should be contented when penned up and denied liberty to go where he pleases.

"If you tie a horse to a stake, do you expect he will grow fat? If you pen an Indian up on a small spot of earth, and compel him to stay there, he will not be contented, nor will he grow and prosper. I have asked some of the great white chiefs where they get their authority to say to the Indian that he shall stay in one place, while he sees white men going where they please. They cannot tell me.

"I only ask the Government to be treated as all other men are treated. If I cannot go to my own home, let me have a home in some country where my people will not die so fast. I would like to go to Bitter Root Valley. There my people would be healthy; where they are now they are dying. Three have died since I left my camp to come to Washington.

"When I think of our condition my heart is heavy. I see men of my race treated as outlaws and driven from country to country, or shot down like animals.

"I know my race must change. We cannot hold our own with the white men as we are. We only ask an even chance to live as other men live. We ask to be recognized as men. We ask that the same law shall work alike on all men. If the Indian breaks the law, punish him by the law. If the white man breaks the law, punish him also.

"Let me be a free man — free to travel, free to stop, free to work, free to trade where I choose, free to choose my own teachers, free to follow the religion of my fathers, free to think and talk and act for myself — and I will obey every law, or submit to the penalty.

"Whenever the white man treats the Indian as they treat each other, then we will have no more wars. We shall all be alike — brothers of one father and one mother, with one sky above us and one country around us, and one government for all. Then the Great Spirit Chief who rules above will smile upon this land, and send rain to wash out the bloody spots made by my brothers' hands from the face of the earth. For this time the Indian race are waiting and praying. I hope that no more groans of wounded men and women will ever go to the ear of the Great Spirit Chief above, and that all people may be one people.

"In-mut-too-yah-lat-lat has spoken for his people."[8]

How accurate the translation of Chief Joseph's words was and how much those words may have been altered by the editor of the magazine are questions still debated by historians. But the basic appeal for justice and a return of the exiles to their homeland reached many sympathetic people. In growing numbers they and their organizations bombarded Congress and the Indian Bureau with petitions demanding that the Nez Perces be permitted to return to their homes. Joining them were representatives of states surrounding Indian Territory, who resented the policy of bringing defeated, impoverished "hostiles" into the region, alloting them land, and subsisting them at public expense. Opposed were Idaho white residents and politicians, who insisited that crimes committed by the nontreaty bands could never be forgotten or forgiven.

In the summer of 1879 the exiles did move 180 miles west to the Ponca Reservation, which they found to be a better location for raising cattle and gardens. A school was started by three Lapwai Nez Perces, James Reuben, Mark Williams, and Archie Lawyer, who acted as both teachers and preachers. Disliking the climate, Williams and Lawyer soon went back to Idaho. Reuben, a devout Presbyterian, stayed on, doing his best with inadequate facilities and funds.

Finally moved by the plea that many of the older women were longing to return to relatives at home, the school was closed in 1883, and James Reuben took twenty-nine members of the band back to Lapwai — two of them old men, the rest widows and orphans. Since Congress had appropriated no funds for the expenses of the trip, the Indians raised the money themselves by selling their handicrafts.

Now it was only a matter of time before the rest of the exiles would be permitted to return to the Pacific Northwest.

"Congress was literally bombarded with pleas for action. In May, of 1884, fourteen petitions were received from groups of citizens from Kansas to Connecticut, ranging from mass meetings to private individuals, all demanding the return of Joseph's Nez Perces to Idaho."[9]

In its next Indian Appropriation Bill, the Senate stipulated that the Secretary of Interior could remove the Nez Perces from the Indian Territory if he so desired. He did. On April 29, 1885, the Indian Commission issued an order that would permit the 268 survivors to leave Indian Territory and go to Arkansas City, Kansas, where they would board a train bound for the Pacific Northwest.

At long last the exiles were going home.

8. "An Indian's View of Indian Affairs," *North American Review*, April 1879, pp. 429–433.
9. McWhorter, *Hear Me*, p. 538.

CHAPTER THIRTY-SEVEN

RETURN OF THE EXILES: MAY 21–28, 1885

*When we reached Wallula, the interpreter
asked us, "Where you want to go? Lapwai and be
Christian, or Colville and just be yourself?"*
— Yellow Wolf

IN JUNE 1878, homesickness and the mistaken belief that they would not be punished made a group
of thirty-four Nez Perce refugees who had fled to
Canada leave Sitting Bull's camp and head for
home. After a long, gruelling trek, during which
they were attacked by soldiers and civilians a
number of times but suffered no casualties, they
reached the reservation, crossing the Bitter Root
Mountains from east to west by way of the Old Nez
Perce Trail. Knowing that their arrival had been
spotted by the Indian police and reported to Agent
John Monteith, the women, children, and older
men turned themselves in.

Though orders had been given by the military
that all such returning exiles were to be arrested
immediately and sent to Indian Territory, these
people were left free and permitted to live with relatives.

A few of the younger men, who had taken an
active part in the fighting, returned to their old
camp in the lower Salmon River country to dig up
valuables cached there, and for a time wandered
like homeless wolves, ready to defend themselves
against attack by white man or red. One of these
was Yellow Wolf, who was now a seasoned warrior.

By his own account, he had no illusions regarding his fate if he turned himself in. He was sure he
would be hanged. Not by order of the soldier chief,
whose men he had fought honorably in the war,
but by order of Agent John Monteith, who hated
him for being a "heathen" Dreamer. Even so, Yellow Wolf decided that since the war was over and
Chief Joseph had surrendered, he must surrender
too. He put aside his rifle, rode into Lapwai, and
gave himself up.

Courtesy Penrose Library, Whitman College
Chief Joseph, one of the last pictures taken of him by Dr. Edwin
Latham on the Colville Reservation, Nespelem.

Chief Joseph's Camp, Nespelem, Colville Reservation

"If the old Agent makes up his mind to hang me, I will take it," he told the Indians who gathered around him. "It is all right. He will get fat off me when he hangs me."[1]

Whether John Monteith would have hanged the young warrior is doubtful, for punishment was not his to administer. Before the interrogation by the agent could go very far, soldiers arrived, arrested Yellow Wolf, and escorted him to the Fort Lapwai guardhouse. There, a sympathetic officer, Captain William Falck, questioned him and then said,

"The white men are mad about you Indians, and if they found you on the Reservation, they would kill you. The Agent can do nothing. He would do nothing. The white men will not bother you, so long as you are in here. Our soldiers will protect you. But do not think you are a prisoner. We put you here just to be away from the whites."[2]

Once again Fort Lapwai was fulfilling the role for which it had been built — protecting the Indians from the whites.

After being held under loose arrest for several days, Yellow Wolf and nine other men were sent to Indian Territory, where they joined Chief Joseph and his people in exile.

"We were not badly treated in captivity," Yellow Wolf says stoically. "We were free so long as we did not come this way, towards Idaho and Wallowa."[3]

In justice to those white people who treated the exiles kindly when given an opportunity to do so, the action taken by Agency Clerk G. D. Fleming should be noted as typical:

"I was head clerk at the Nez Perce Indian Agency in the early eighties, when Charles D. Warner was agent. He was supposed to handle cases touching Reservation governmental affairs, but practically all the petty offenses, real or fancied, came before me for settlement. We held regular court, ofttimes empaneling a jury of six to twelve men. At such times I have heard pleadings by blanketed Indians, long-haired and uneducated — acting in the capacity of attorney — truly remarkable for logic, deep thought, and eloquence of oratorical deliverance.

"During my incumbency, many of the Nez Perce war band who had escaped from General Miles at the last battle and made their homes with the Sioux, Blackfeet, and other tribes, drifted back to the Nez Perce Reservation. These 'hostiles,' as so termed, were all known to the Indian police, who arrested them and brought them to the Agency as soon as discovered. Coming before me, I was supposed to turn them over to the Agent, whose duty was to deliver them to the military post commander, to be transported to the Indian Territory.

"I have always been glad that in no instance did I ever do this. I would talk to the prisoner who never failed to show anxiety to be accorded a chance to prove a sincerity of intentions to be law-abiding and peace-

---

1. McWhorter, *Yellow Wolf,* p. 280.

2. Ibid., p. 284.

3. Ibid., p. 289.

able. I would then turn to the Indian police, pointing to the fact that the refugee had suffered enough; that there was nothing to be gained by holding him (or her) prisoner, to be sent so far from their old home and people; that they were full willing to abide by the laws of the Reservation as prescribed by the Government; and I requested that the brother or sister be turned loose, which was invariably done.

"Not once did any of these forlorn outcasts prove recreant to the trust placed in their promises. They had fought and lost! Returning broken in spirit and in purse, they stoically accepted the inevitable, burying the dead past.

"I had gone to the Agency holding an adverse opinion of the Indian in general. But I soon changed my notion as to his worth and possibilities under proper treatment and environment. That he has been woefully wronged goes unchallenged, to the lasting shame of the Caucasian race."[4]

Once the decision had been made to return the exiles from Indian Territory to the Pacific Northwest, the question arose: How will the whites who lost relatives, friends, and property during the war react to having the Indian "murderers" as neighbors again? Since Joseph had been given so much publicity, he was regarded as the worst criminal, with indictments issued against him in many communities. On May 1, 1885, the Indian Bureau wired Ponca Agent John W. Scott, asking him to consult with the Nez Perces to see if they would consider going to the Colville Reservation in Washington State instead of to the Lapwai reserve. Backing up the request was a personal invitation to Joseph from Chief Moses, a prominent Colville leader and a longtime friend, to come and live in his country.[5]

4. Ibid., pp. 291–292.

5. Robert H. Ruby, "Return of the Nez Perces," *Idaho Yesterdays* 12, no. 1 (Spring 1968), pp. 12–15. Dr. Ruby's article is based on research in the National Archives, which he details, and on interviews with Indian survivors. In collaboration with John A. Brown he has written a number of excellent books on various Indian tribes of the Pacific Northwest, including the Cayuse, Chinook, Spokane, and Colville.

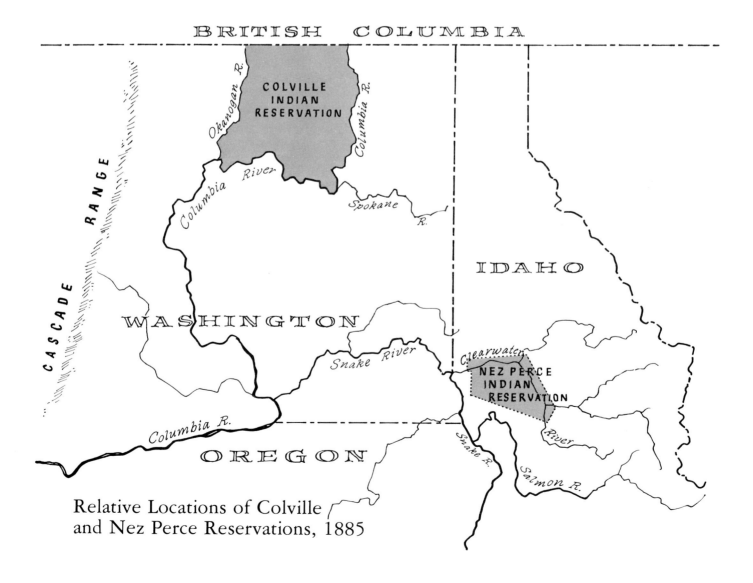

Relative Locations of Colville and Nez Perce Reservations, 1885

Nez Perce Riders during the celebration at Nespelem in late 1880s or '90s.

Tom Hill, Sr. (Wis-Tah-Mal-We-Yat or "Trail Boss"). There are variations in spelling of the Indian name. Three of his fingers were shot off in 1877 war or in the Cheyenne-Nez Perce War of 1870.

Still hoping to go back to the Wallowa area and sure that if he went to Lapwai he would lose all chances of returning to his ancestral homeland, Chief Joseph accepted the invitation from his friend. He and the other warriors against whom feeling ran high in Idaho would go to the Colville Reservation, while the Indians with relatives and friends on the Lapwai reserve would go there, hoping that their family ties would protect them from white vengeance.

Dr. W. H. Faulkner, a physician and special agent for the U.S Indian Office, was put in charge of the transfer. Though he was sympathetic toward the Indians, he proved to be just as impatient as General Howard had been eight years earlier in setting a deadline for their move.

"Faulkner arrived at the Agency May 5 to find the Indians not yet ready to depart," Robert H. Ruby writes. "Agent Scott judged it would take two weeks before they could possibly dispose of all their stock. In spite of this, the doctor told Joseph he expected his people to leave Friday May 21, ready or not, and made preparations accordingly. The Nez Perces were thus forced to dispose of their animals quickly and cheaply."[6]

A few days before departure, Dr. Faulkner did permit the Nez Perces to take time off from their preparations to visit the graves of relatives who had died during the stay of the exiles in this unhealthy land. One of Chief Joseph's daughters was among those who had succumbed to the diseases that had reduced the tribe's numbers by more than one-half while in exile.

"Before daybreak on May 21 the Indians were awakened and put to tearing down the tipis before starting over the prairie for Arkansas City, where they would

board a train. A fine mist began falling. Then came rain, which drizzled steadily through the day. There was not room enough in the wagons for everyone . . . so the men plodded in the mud. Women walked with their men, all twenty-five miles made that day."[7]

Reaching Arkansas City, Kansas, at midnight the second day, the sodden, weary refugees and their baggage were loaded onto the "emigrant sleeping cars" of the Atchinson, Topeka and Santa Fe Railroad the next morning. Joining them were a number of bewildered children who had been attending the Chilloco Indian School, some of whom had been so frightened at the prospect of riding on a train that they had tried to hide under their beds at the boarding school. Yellow Bull, who had not expected the children to be released, was so overjoyed that he rushed up with tears in his eyes to thank Dr. Faulkner.

The journey took five days. Reaching McPherson, Kansas, at 9 P.M. the first night, the 35,000

6. Ibid., p. 13.
7. Ibid.

Photo by Major Lee Moorhouse around 1900   Courtesy Smithsonian Institution
Stephen Reuben

the former site of the long-vanished trading post named after their tribe, Fort Nez Perces, now called Wallula, A Nez Perce word meaning "mouth of the waters."

Dr. Faulkner refused to let the railroad crew divide the train, saying that his orders were to take the entire band through to Wallula Junction before separating it. Going into the telegraph office and wiring the Indian Bureau for further instructions at 7 P.M. that evening, he was joined by Captain Frank D. Baldwin, Fifth Infantry, who was serving as judge advocate on General Miles staff.

"Many were out for Joseph's scalp, Baldwin warned the doctor, and he urged him to move on in any way possible. Faulkner decided to follow this advice. Feeling was mounting steadily against the chief and his people. Already indictments were issued for the arrest of Joseph — twelve of them at least, accusing the chief of murder. One United States marshal would be in Pocatello in the morning to attempt to get Joseph behind bars. Faulkner explained the imminent danger to Joseph. A crowd of curious began to gather around the train. Faulkner was more fearful than Joseph. Railroad agent Morse agreed to take all the Indians together as far as Wallula Junc-

8. Ibid., p. 14.

pounds of baggage and the nearly three hundred Indians were transferred to a Union Pacific train.

"The doctor was aware of what seemed to be a thousand curious folks crowding around for a glimpse of Joseph and his Indians. By midnight, they were ready to roll out on the Union Pacific through Denver, Colorado, and Cheyenne, Wyoming, to Pocatello, Idaho."[8]

The trip was not an easy one. For rations the Indians carried 2,000 pounds of hard bread, 160 pounds of sugar, 2,498 pounds of precooked beef, and 140 pounds of coffee, prepared during various stops when the travelers could get out, build a fire, and brew it.

At Pocatello railroad officials started making preparations to divide the train, sending the Indians bound for the Colville Reservation north to Butte, then west to Spokane over the Utah Northern and Northern Pacific lines. Those headed for Lapwai would take the Union Pacific northwest to Wallula Junction. While the route to be taken mattered little to most of the returning exiles, Chief Joseph must have known that the first ran through the country of their bitter enemies, the Bannocks, crossing their retreat trail just a few miles west of the Camas Meadows site, while the second led to

Photo by Major Lee Moorhouse around 1900   Courtesy Smithsonian Institution
The Reuben Brothers

tion. Without waiting for Office instructions, the doctor ordered the train to roll early the next morning."⁹

Crossing the flat, sage-covered plains of southern Idaho Territory at the breathtaking speed of forty miles an hour, picking up a company of Third Infantry, commanded by Captain Dempsey, as protection en route (probably from Fort Boise), making the long, twisting climb over northeastern Oregon's Blue Mountains within sight of the south slope of Chief Joseph's beloved Wallowa Mountains, winding down the western side of the Blues through the Umatilla Indian Reservation, then turning north to the Columbia and Washington Territory, the well-traveled Indians reached Wallula Junction May 27, 1885.

By now Yellow Wolf's old enemy, John Monteith, was dead. His place had been taken by his brother, Charles E. Monteith. Charles was waiting at Wallula, ready to make the final division of the tribe and escort his portion back to the Lapwai Reservation. While no written instructions, rules, or standards have been found by historians as to

Photo taken about 1897 by Wells M. Sawyer   *Courtesy Smithsonian Institution*
of the Bureau of American Ethnology
Ahlakat, son of the Ahlakat who served with Chief Joseph and was Chief Joseph's brother.

which was a good and which a bad Indian, Yellow Wolf seems to have told it about right. Those Indians who would agree to cut their hair and become Christians could go to Lapwai. Those who kept their hair and their belief in the old ways must go to the Colville Reservation.

In bidding good-bye to ninety-two adults, twelve youngsters, and fourteen infants, Chief Joseph spoke briefly to them as a group. Many years later Josiah Red Wolf, who was seven years old at the time, told Robert Ruby what he remembered of Joseph's words:

"I'm not going back to my country. My own people [whites] will fight me. I'm going where Chuckatas [Chief Moses] is."¹⁰

From Wallula Junction the Lapwai group went by train to Riparia, fifty miles up the Snake River, then to Lewiston by boat, thence overland twelve miles to the reservation and what from now on would be their home. Their eight-year oddessey was over.

9. Ibid., p. 15.
10. Ibid.

Courtesy Luna House Historical Society
Lewiston, Idaho

Corbett Lawyer

The Colville band continued on by train to Spokane Falls, then by wagons sixty-five miles west to Fort Spokane, which was adjacent to the Colville Reservation. In the group were 120 adults, including Chief Joseph and Yellow Bull, who was second in command, 16 children, and 14 infants. Fearing a loss of business because of his presence in the area, merchants in the town of Colville, just outside the reservation, called Joseph a "large, fat-faced, scheming, cruel-looking cuss" and members of his band "thieves, murderers, and demons," subscribing to the theory that "the very best Indians are those planted beneath the roses."

From his behavior under extremely trying circumstances during the past month, it is doubtful that Dr. Faulkner would have agreed with that indictment of his wards. Officially, his responsibility had ended when the exiles reached Spokane Falls.

"However, so concerned was he for many who were ill," writes Robert H. Ruby, who is himself a practicing surgeon in Moses Lakes, Washington, as well as a historian, "that he traveled along with them to Fort Spokane, and personally delivered the sick to the care of the Post Surgeon."[11]

Chief Joseph's band had come home, too.

Courtesy Idaho Historical Society

Nez Perce riders, Nespelem, late '80s or '90s

11. Ibid.

CHAPTER THIRTY-EIGHT

LAND ALLOTMENT: 1889–1892

In our reading we followed the children of Israel through their temptations and discouragements of the wilderness way. My pupils were reading their own souls' history, and they knew it. The sinning and repenting, wandering and returning, was, and is, theirs, as well as ours, the difference being that among these people, the wanderer is made known by his return to the blanket and long hair worn by his heathen friends. Only one of our Kamiah church-members wears these emblems now.

— Kate McBeth, Missionary

Courtesy Idaho Historical Society

Chief Joseph and Kate McBeth, a teacher missionary

HORSES, DRIVERS, AND WAGONS were sent to Lewiston to meet the Snake River stern-wheeler carrying the Christian refugees and bring them home. The reservation Nez Perces gathered at Lapwai, Monday, June 1, to greet them. The scene is graphically described by George Deffenbaugh, a white Presbyterian missionary, who was there:

"It was expected that the company would reach here about 4 P.M., but long before noon the people began to assemble by scores. About 3 o'clock there was a stir among the groups sitting in the shade of the cottonwood trees. In twenty minutes a large semi-circle formed; men and women standing eight and ten deep, to the number of five hundred. Presently the wagons containing women and children came on the grounds, followed by the men and boys on horseback. After alighting they took a position along the diameter of a half circle, 116 in all. Everything in readiness, hats were lifted and Elder Solomon [Whitman] stepped forward and offered devout thanksgiving and prayer. This was followed by a short address of welcome on the part of the Church by Rev. Silas Whitman. Following him, James Lawyer made a similar speech, as representative of the civil authorities. Then an earnest response was made by Tom Hill.

"At the close of his speech, hand-shaking began, which lasted for over an hour. . . . Friend met with friend, fathers and mothers with their long-lost sons and daughters . . .

"Near the end of the line a different scene. Some having taken the hands of all present, and missing the

Photo by Jane Gay   Courtesy Idaho Historical Society
Survey Party

Courtesy Nez Perce National Historic Park
Washington State University Library

The Indian Agency Staff: (1) The carpenter (2) missionary; at his right, the farmer; at his left, the doctor (3) clerk (4) blacksmith (5) Agent Warren.

faces of those they had hoped to see, gave vent to their sorrow in uncontrollable weeping."[1]

Though most of the reservation Nez Perces were Christians, years of strenuous missionary effort had failed to kill their love of July Fourth celebrations and horse racing. Kate McBeth claimed that Hudson's Bay Company employees had taught the Indians "that it was good to have a gay time" on the Fourth of July, which seems an odd thing for a Britisher to teach. More likely the Nez Perces had observed Americans celebrating the holiday at fur rendezvous, thought it great fun, and brought the custom home with them. Then they improved on it.

"During the time Mr. Spalding was away, from 1847 to 1871, they gathered to celebrate the Fourth, not for one day, but for two weeks, by drinking, gambling, horse-racing and getting new wives."[2]

Even in the name of patriotism that was too much of a gay time for the missionaries. From 1871 through 1886 the Fourth of July was observed with a religious camp meeting near the Lapwai church, where there was no room for a race track and no drinking, gambling, horse racing, or wife swapping were allowed. But two years after the exiles came home, the new agent, George Norris, whom Miss Mcbeth describes as "a Boston lawyer," decided he would like to sponsor an old-

1. Allen Conrad Morrill and Eleanor Dunlop Morrill, *Out of the Blanket* (Moscow: University of Idaho Press, 1978), p. 229; *Foreign Missionary*, July 1885.
2. Kate C. McBeth, *The Nez Perces Since Lewis and Clark* (New York: Fleming H. Revell Co., 1908), p. 163.

Photo by Jane Gay   Courtesy Idaho Historical Society
Camp Sunday — Edson Briggs and Alice Fletcher

Photo by Jane Gay   Courtesy Idaho Historical Society
Alloting land to Nez Perces. Alice Fletcher at left standing with Wiliam Caldwell and Abraham Brooks (with cane) known as Blind Abraham who was one of Howard's scouts. He was wounded pursuing hostiles on Lolo Trail. Edson Briggs holding surveying rod.

Nez Perce land allotment. Trail lots case at Ed Conner's fish camp. Alice Fletcher at left and James Stewart.

Kate McBeth and group of Nez Perce women at first church at Lapwai.

fashioned, two-week Fourth of July celebration, holding the camp meeting on the Fort Lapwai grounds from Wednesday, June 29, through Sunday, July 3, then commemorating the return of the exiles by having Chief Joseph and his warriors put on a mock battle Monday afternoon, July 4, and holding horse races at the nearby racetrack all the rest of the week.

The idea horrified Kate McBeth, who flatly refused to attend either the services or the races. Her missionary cohort, Mr. Deffenbaugh, also deplored the plan but was called away from Lapwai on business without making his feelings clear to the Nez Perce trainee who was working with him. In good faith,

"the native minister who was assisting Mr. Deffenbaugh announced from the pulpit that the people would pitch their tents up at the fort on Wednesday. There would be religious services each day and communion on Sabbath."[3]

With a mock battle to follow on Monday afternoon, and horse races each day for the rest of the week.

"Mr. Deffenbaugh came home . . . and found the people preparing to go into camp," Kate McBeth writes. "What could he do at this time? I told him what I would do. That I should not appear on the ground for any, not even a religious service. Mr. Deffenbaugh felt that he must go and assist in the sacrament."[4]

Which he did, presumably staying for the rest of the program, which Miss McBeth describes, presumably from hearsay:

"Such a Fourth they had not had since their heathenism. The agent rode at the head of the procession, which was spectacular enough to please him and the more than two hundred whites from Lewiston and the region round about, who stood watching the display from the verandas of the fort buildings, enjoying the

Rev. Archie Lawyer and family

3. Ibid., pp. 164–165.
4. Ibid., p. 165.

Black Eagle

Walla Walla Presbytery: (1) Elder Thomas Moore, Lapwai; (2) Elder Bartholomew Moody, Meadow Creek; (3) the Reverend James Hines, North Fork; (4) the Reverend Sample; (5) the Reverend A. Adair; (6) Elder _____, Waitsburg; (7) Dr. Gunn, synodical missionary; (8) Elder _____; (9) the Reverend Archie Lawyer; (10) the Reverend Peter Lindsley; (11) Elder Jason Conditt; (12) Student Harry Hays; (13) K. C. McBeth; (14) Mrs. Allen, Kendrick; (15) the Reverend Allen; (16) the Reverend Belden, Kansas City (NM); (17) the Reverend Woods; (18) Peter Wallace; (19) (Elder Samuel) North Fork Joe Peterson; (20) Licentate McAtee (Kenneth); (21) the Reverend Robert Parsons, Meadow Creek; (22) the Reverend Silas Whitman; (23) the Reverend Robert Williams.

sight, even to the naked men who helped to make up the procession."[5]

Wherever she got her information it appears to have been accurate, for a correspondent for the *Lewiston Teller,* who was on the scene, wrote:

"The leader [Joseph] or chief, was dressed in undress uniform, in fact about all he had on was a head dress of feathers and a piece of cloth about his loins; his body was decorated in the most hideous manner with different colored paints; the rest of the band were attired in a similar manner, the only difference being in the color of the paint which they used; the horses they rode, many on them very beautiful animals, were also covered with paint. The Indians were fully armed, some with spears, others with rifles, pistols, bow and arrows, tomahawks, clubs, etc. During the drill they kept up a most horrible yelling, then they would stop and begin their war song, which sounded like a dirge. Take them altogether, they were a diabolical crowd. We were informed by several of the old members of the tribe that it was a very correct representation."[6]

By this time, with the war ten years in the past, feelings against Joseph had cooled down to the point that he felt safe paying brief visits to Lapwai. In fact, when tracts of land were allotted in sever-

Lapwai Nez Perce — Felix Corbett and wife

alty a few years later he was offered one but refused it, for he still hoped to return to Wallowa.

Federal policy toward the nation's native population had undergone many changes since 1776.

5. Ibid.

6. Ibid., p. 166.

Photo by Jane Gay   Courtesy Idaho Historical Society
Mrs. Lawyer Winnowing Grain, Kamiah

Courtesy Nez Perce National Historic Park
National Park Service

Corbett Lawyer

First, each Indian tribe had been treated as a sovereign country, with treaties made between it and the United States. In 1871 that policy was abandoned, with agreements taking the place of treaties. For a time the Indians were charges of the military, then of church groups, and finally government wards. On February 8, 1887, still another policy change was made when Congress passed the General Land in Severalty Act, commonly called The Dawes Bill or the Allotment Act.

Its altruistic purpose was to make individual Indians secure in their title to certain pieces of land;

Photo by Jane Gay   Courtesy Idaho Historical Society
Nine Pipes' widow and sisters, Kamiah, September 1887. (1) Unidentified; (2) Annie, M. [1] Nine Pipes, M. [2] John Red Wolf, half brother of Josiah Red Wolf. These are children of Nine Pipes; (3) Ellen; (4) Maria Moffett, mother of Eddie Hayes.

Photo by Jane Gay   Courtesy Idaho Historical Society
Kamiah, Idaho. First council to discuss allotment, at First Presbyterian Church. Alice Fletcher at left.

Lapwai, Idaho, school children

Kamiah, Idaho, dwellings — The Sue McBeth cabin, Alice
Fletcher, Joe Briggs, James Stewart.

its not-so-generous result was to declare unallotted lands "surplus," selling them to the highest bidders and distributing the proceeds to members of the affected tribes.

In the spring of 1889 the allotment process began very quietly for the Nez Perces on the Lap-

wai Reservation with the arrival at the Hotel de France in Lewiston of a remarkable pair of New England spinsters, Miss Alice Fletcher and Miss Jane Gay. A qualified anthropologist and an expert on Indians, Miss Fletcher was fifty-one years old, had worked as an assistant in the Peabody Museum at Harvard University, and had recently completed allotting lands to the Winnebago tribe further east. Miss Gay was fifty-nine years old, well educated and well traveled. She worked as Miss Fletcher's secretary during the day and recorded their adventures after hours in blunt, colorful prose.

To say that the local people were surprised by the arrival of the two ladies would be too mild. They were stunned.

"Why in thunder did the Government send a woman to do this work?" Jane Gay quotes a local citizen as demanding. "We could have got a holt of a man."

Nez Perce children

Camp Corbett. House at mouth of Lawyer's Canyon

Courtesy Nez Perce National Historic Park, National Park Service

Signers of Treaty of 1893. *Standing:* (1) Nobe Henry (Squaw Man), (2) Eddie Conner, (3) Jim Reubens, (4) James Hines, (5) Jona Hayes, (6) Peopeo Moxmox, (7) James Grant, son of U.S. Grant, (8) Tom Hill, (9) Harrison Kipp, (10) Archie Lawyer, chairman, (11) U-chin-mel-lik-kin, (12) James Lawyer, (13) William Wheeler, (14) Bob Stanton, (15) Sam Frank, (16) I-her-chits-ker-neen (Bkartholomew), (17) Charles Gordon, (18) Edward Smith, (19) Jim Stuart, (20) Felix corbett. *Seated:* (1) Perrin Whitman, interpreter, (2) Cyrus Beede, (3) James F. Allen, (4) Bob Schliecher, (5) Warren Robinson, agent.

Like a pack of hounds circling a couple of porcupines, the white ranchers could find no way to get "a holt" on this self-sufficient pair of ladies.

"There is nothing romantic about these cattlemen," Miss Gay writes. "For the greater part, they are farmers in the neighborhood who raise crops on their own land

Courtesy Nez Perce National Historic Park, National Park Service

Photo taken in 1895 at the opening of Nez Perce Reservation. First payment to Nez Perce for allotments sold. Left to Right: Fred Bremmer (Kendrick Bank representative) Three Feathers (Mee-Taht Waaph-Tess) Samuel Martin (Clerk, Indian agency) Red Horn (Taa-Wis Ill-Blip), Eddie Conner (half-breed interpreter), J. Howard Howe. Lewiston National Bank handled the cashing of the warrants. 1895, Spalding, Idaho.

and turn out their cattle to overrun the Reservation. We are told that there are 10,000 head now eating the grass of the Indians, who are also cattlemen in their own right, and have none too much pasturage for their own herds."

When the ranchers suggested to Alice Fletcher that she allot the Nez Perces pieces of land "down in the canyons where they belong," she told them she meant to carry out the intent of the law. To this outrageous statement, Jane Gay says, one citizen responded:

"What do we want with law? We don't want no law. Never had no law; we've got along so far taking care of ourselves; we done what we wanted to and ain't got no use for the law in this country."[7]

Since the first part of her task was to measure and inventory reservation lands, Miss Fletcher went looking for a qualified surveyor. She found one in Edson Briggs, a Vermont-raised man who had been in the area long enough to know his way around, a big, broad-shouldered, muscular man weighing a hefty 260 pounds. Assembling a crew, the party went to Lapwai, where they were scrutinized carefully by the guardian of Nez Perce minds and morals, Kate McBeth. Once the missionary-teacher learned that the purpose of the Allotment Act was to "settle" the Indians, she approved and gave Miss Fletcher all the assistance she could.

Under the terms of the act, the head of each household would be allotted 160 acres of land. Each single person over eighteen years of age would be allotted eighty acres; each single person under eighteen would be allotted forty acres. So far as possible, each Indian would be allotted land in or near his traditional home.

At first the work went slowly, for the very idea of individual ownership of land was new to the Nez Perces. But with patience, tact, and New England persistance Miss Fletcher kept at her task through four consecutive summers, covering every square mile of the reservation and registering every qualified member of the tribe. Though land was offered Joseph and other Nez Perces who had settled on the Colville reserve, only a few of them came to Lapwai. One of these was Yellow Bull, who insisted on being given an allotment that included Red Rock Springs. When Miss Fletcher objected to

7. Morrill, *Out of the Blanket,* p. 295; Jane Gay, "Choup-Nit-Ki," Washington, D.C., 1895, vol. 1, p. 13. Manuscript in the Women's Archives, Radcliffe College, Cambridge, Mass.; Microfilm, Idaho Historical Society, Boise.

Photo by Jane Gay   Courtesy Idaho Historical Society

Nez Perce Indians and sick children. Women are: (1) Fanny Samuels, mother of Milton George; (2) Mrs. Moos Moos John(athan) half-sister to Mrs. Felix Corbett.

his settling there, saying that the land was poor and would not be good for farming, Yellow Bull still insisted on having it, saying:

"I drank of that spring when I was a boy, and when sick and tossing in fever in Indian Territory I drank of it in my dreams. Give me the Red Rock Spring or I want nothing."[8]

He got the spring — but Miss Fletcher also allotted him a good piece of farmland.

The "Measuring Woman" and her party gradually won the confidence of the Indians, as tribal members were enumerated with painstaking thoroughness. It required an estimated forty miles of travel to make an allotment for one family. The party discovered in surveying 800,000 acres of reservation land that the original rough survey had not conformed to the terms of the 1855 treaty — and that each new boundary drawn under succeeding treaties and agreements had cheated the Nez Perces out of more land.

Miss Gay was not impressed by the capacity of the Nez Perces for hard work.

"They can ride ponies all day but walking is a new sensation. Their leg muscles are flabby and sharp stones cut moccasined feet. . . . The poor fellows succumb crossing a canyon of only half pitch and they faint on the mountains when the thermometer is only 110 in the shade."

If General Howard had had a few officers like Miss Gay, the war would have ended much sooner. As a general indictment of the Nez Perces and those altruistic white people who were trying to help them, she wrote:

"Work is the only salvation for anybody and I for one do not see the use of trying to keep alive a race that will not work. You see I am not a missionary spirit."[9]

Yet she seems to have had some romance left in her independent soul, for when Chief Joseph came to the Lapwai Reservation to consult with Alice Fletcher, Miss Gay admired him greatly writing:

"It was good to see an unsubjugated Indian. . . . He cannot be persuaded to take his land upon the Reservation. He will have none but the Wallowa valley, from which he was driven; he will remain landless and homeless if he cannot have his own again. . . . One could not help respecting the man who still stood firmly for his rights, after having fought and suffered and been defeated in the struggle for their maintenance."[10]

Miss Fletcher's work was finally completed after twenty-two months in the field, spread over a period of four years. As she prepared to leave for the last time in 1892, Kate McBeth asked if she planned to return.

"No, I cannot come back to visit you," she said. "The people would want all their allotments changed at the sight of my face."[11]

Though allotments had been made and lands declared surplus had been sold to the government in 1892, cash payments to the Nez Perces did not arrive until the fall of 1895. Fearing that unscrupulous white men would quickly separate the Indians from their money, the authorities sent a company of soldiers from Fort Walla Walla to keep order. The precaution proved unnecessary. Shrewd traders that they were, the Indians did not spend their windfall foolishly.

"Many of them had debts," Kate McBeth writes. "I think, with few exceptions, they hunted up their creditors and paid them. Two Nez Perces came as straight to my house as they could, with the money in their pockets. One of them had owed me — perhaps for ten years. The other one had years before been sick, and of my own will I sent a physician to him. He now wished to pay for this. Of course, his money was not received. Honesty is a well-known trait among the Nez Perce tribe — so well known, that when anything is missing around a white man's ranch, he will say, 'It was no Indian that took it.' "[12]

8. McBeth, "Nez Perce Since Lewis and Clark, pp. 186–187.
9. Morrill, Out of the Blanket, p. 304.
10. Ibid., p. 311.
11. Ibid., p. 336.
12. McBeth, Nez Perce Since Lewis and Clark, pp. 188–189.

Like the expansion and contraction of the shoreline of an immense inland lake, the living space of the Nez Perces had been dramatically altered during the past one hundred and fifty years. Before he obtained the horse, the man of the family called a longhouse set on a canyon sandbar home; yet he was free to travel by foot or canoe over a region 27,000 square miles in extent. Once he got the horse this home became portable, and he was free to roam over ten times as much territory. Beginning in 1855, and with each treaty or agreement made thereafter, his freedom of movement had been restricted, and the amount of land he could call his roaming room had become ever smaller. Now his territory had been reduced again — this time to one hundred and sixty acres, one-quarter square mile.

For better or for worse, he was "settled."

CHAPTER THIRTY-NINE

TWILIGHT YEARS AT COLVILLE: 1885–1904

*On the Colville we found wild game aplenty.
Fish, berries, and all kinds of roots. Everything so
fine many wanted to remain there, after learning
Wallowa was not to be returned to us.*

— Yellow Wolf

SOME TEN YEARS older than Joseph, Chief Moses was officially recognized as the leader of five Salish tribes, the Wenatchees, Entiats, Chelans, Methows, and Okanogans. He also claimed he was head chief of the San Poils, Nespelems, and Colvilles, though certain leaders among those — such as the badly crippled, outspoken San Poil chief, Skolaskin — violently denied his authority. First established by Executive Order in 1872, with its boundaries modified in 1879, 1880, and again in 1884, the Colville Reservation lay between the Columbia and Okanogan rivers, extending north to the Canadian line. It was a large reserve, with plenty of good water, timber, and grass. Eventually, fragments of seventeen different tribes of Plateau Indians would be placed on the reservation. Chief Moses would be their principal spokesman.

Big, strong, a formidable warrior as a young man, a born leader, and a shrewd politician, Moses long ago had learned that it was more profitable to play on the white man's fears than to fight him. During the Nez Perce War, when the whites feared that a word from him would turn a horde of Plateau Indian tribes into hostiles supporting Joseph, he did a great deal of conferring with other chiefs, then later made much of the fact that he had kept the tribes at peace so must be regarded as a friend of the whites. As a reward he was given a big reservation, an expense-paid trip to Washington, D.C., and the privilege of shaking hands with President Rutherford B. Hayes.

En route home he asked permission to detour south into Indian Territory for a visit with his friend, Chief Joseph. His request was denied as "inap-

propriate," but there is evidence that he was in communication with the Nez Perce leader. Eventually they reached a meeting of minds on a matter of mutual interest — namely, pooling their influence and negotiating skill to get a better deal for their people out of the federal government.

"Apparently unknown to the government officials, Joseph had managed to send three of his men — Otskai, Joe Albert and one other — with a message to Moses, asking permission to live in Colville," Robert Ruby and John Brown write. "They would recognize Moses as chief; and in case Moses should die first, Joseph would succeed him. Moses sent back word that

Courtesy Idaho Historical Society

Nez Perce Indians meeting the steamboat at Lewiston, 1885

Photo by F. F. Avery   *Courtesy Washington State University Library*
Dr. Latham and N. Sutherland about 1910

Photo by L. V. McWhorter   *Courtesy Washington State University Library*
Thomas Lindsey

the exiles would be welcome. . . . Needless to say, Skolaskin was furious."[1]

Though they were good friends, Joseph and Moses had totally different personalities. Joseph was soft-spoken and dignified, drank nothing stronger than sugared coffee, and was content with

only two wives. Moses was loud and talkative, loved his toddy, and usually had at least five wives. When asked how many children he had, he thought for a few moments, then shook his head and admitted he had lost track. When a Catholic priest sent word to him that he must put aside all but one of his wives, Moses asked Agent Gwydir if the priest had a wife. Gwydir told him the priest was not allowed to have a wife. Moses thought that over, then said, "Tell the Blackrobe that I will give him one of my wives if he will keep his mouth shut!"[2]

At first the Nez Perces were placed across the Columbia from Fort Spokane,

"so that they could be protected from the soldiers, who it was feared would ravish their women, and from Moses, whose drinking and gambling propensities would do them no good."[3]

Poorly clad, badly sheltered, and provided with insufficient food, the returned exiles now were con-

Photo by Major Lee Moorhouse, July 4, 1906   *Courtesy Smithsonian Institution*
Mounted Warriors

1. Robert H. Ruby and John A. Brown, *Half-Sun on the Columbia: A Biography of Chief Moses* (Norman: University of Oklahoma Press, 1965), pp. 220–221.
2. Ibid., p. 244.
3. Ibid., p. 222.

Chief Joseph

The home of Chief Joseph, Nespelem, Washington, on the Colville Reservation.

fronted with the hostility of the San Poils, into whose living space they had intruded. Calling Moses's and Joseph's peoples "murderers and horse thieves," Skolaskin launched such a violent attack on the government for placing the Nez Perces in San Poil territory that Joseph asked that they be permitted to move fifty miles west, to the Nespelem Valley. The request was granted.

"Moses was delighted with the decision and prepared his people to receive the Nez Perces royally. . . . The first week of December, Joseph and 132 Nez Perces rode into the Nespelem Valley to the cheers of Moses' people and the jeers of the Nespelems."[4]

Themselves a displaced people, the Nez Perces once again were being imposed upon a band of Indians who did not want to share their living space with strangers. They were wholly dependent upon the federal government for rations because indifferent agents let two years pass before supplying seed grain and farming tools. Some of the improverished exiles desperately tried to replace the horses they had been forced to sell in Indian Territory by betting blankets issued them for warmth against Nespelem ponies in gambling games.

Even if they had wanted to become farmers, which they did not, they would have found it impossible. What little tillable land existed in the area

already was occupied by the Nespelems, who refused to share it. In an effort to keep the Nez Perces at home and force them to farm land they did not have, with tools that had not yet arrived, the agent issued an order requiring all Indians to have permits before leaving the reservation — an order completely ignored by the Nez Perces. Yet so dependent had they become upon the government for food that when several of them went to Lapwai for an extended visit with relatives, Chief Joseph sent his nephew with a message urging them to

4. Ibid., p. 230.

Chief Joseph, seated, with General Gibbon on the shore of Lake Chelan.

Courtesy Umatilla County Museum

Chief Joseph seated with General Howard at Carlisle, about 1901.

Courtesy Smithsonian Institution

Delegation to Washington in 1903. Left to Right: Whitman, Ahlakat, Chief Joseph, and Peopeo-Taklakt.

come back to Nespelem in time to get their share of a beef issue.

As time passed, the friendship between Joseph and Moses cooled somewhat, with Joseph blaming Moses for encouraging the local whiskey trade and Moses blaming Joseph for his people's aversion to work. An invitation to come to Portland and share the limelight at the Exposition of 1891 brought them together again, giving then both national publicity as two of the best-known Indians of the day.

By a curious turn of events, General Howard's aide, Lieutenant Charles Erskine Scott Wood, had become Chief Joseph's best white friend. A brilliant man and a born rebel at heart, Lieutenant Wood had served with Howard through the Bannock War in 1878, had gone east with him when Howard

Courtesy Idaho Historical Society

The Lapwai Agency, around 1900

In 1889 he had brought Chief Joseph to Portland to pose for the New York sculptor, Olin Warner, who was doing a series of large medallions of famous Indian chiefs. Now, in addition to appearing as stars at the 1891 Exposition, the two chiefs were honored guests in Wood's home. When wine was served at dinner one evening, with Joseph not touching his, Moses kept it from going to waste by emptying first his own glass then the one placed in front of his abstemious friend.

Wood's twelve-year-old son, Erskine, who loved hunting, fishing, and horses, was so fascinated by the two Indian chiefs that his father asked Joseph if the boy could visit him the next summer. Joseph graciously invited him to do so. In July 1892 young Erskine went to Nespelem and was taken into Joseph's tepee as a member of the family. He liked it so well, and was so well liked in return, that he did not go home until Christmas. The following year, 1893, he returned for a second visit during the fall, this one shortened to a mere three months.

Though he kept a diary both years, the first one was lost. The one written during his 1893 stay has

Courtesy Yakima Nation Collection

A. C. Smith, an early day Wallowa Valley settler, and Chief Joseph after the Nez Perce War.

was apointed superintendent of West Point, and, having long been interested in law, had studied at nearby Columbia and earned a degree. Although he was a West Point graduate, a decade of military discipline and two Indian wars had given him his fill of the army, so in 1883 he resigned his commission, came west to Portland, and began practicing law.

Following the surrender at Bear's Paw, Lieutenant Wood had been assigned the task of watching over Chief Joseph, seeing to his creature comforts, and protecting him from the curious. It had been Wood who recorded Joseph's surrender speech. Although he respected Howard as a man, he had been sharply critical of the general for his failure to return the Nez Perces to Idaho, as promised, and had done everything he could to persuade the government to return the exiles from Indian Territory to the Pacific Northwest.

Courtesy Oregon Historical Society

Erskine Wood at the age of 14

Erskine Wood, age 98, as he addressed the Oregon Historical Society annual dinner in 1977.

The Chief Joseph medallion commissioned by Charles Erskine Scott Wood.

been preserved and published, along with his comments on Chief Joseph as he remembered him.

"He was the kindest of fathers to me," Erskine Wood writes, "looking after me, providing for me, caring for me, and, it must be said, sometimes gently rebuking me when necessary . . .

"I have been asked whether he was somber. No, he was not. Neither was he merry or boisterous or prone to

loud laughter. But he was not morose, nor overwhelmed by his misfortune(s). He bore them like the great man he was. Within the limits of the reservation he lived his life quietly with a calm and dignified acceptance of his fate."

Preoccupied with going to high school and college and a three-year battle with tuberculosis, Erskine Wood never saw Chief Joseph again after their parting in December 1893. Many years later he wrote:

"But the regret that has lived with me longest occurred at our saying goodbye. We had ridden from the camp at Nespelem down to the Columbia River, where I was to cross in a dugout canoe to Barry, the trading post on the other side, and there be met by a team to drive me to the railroad. Joseph and I sat on our horses on the bluffs of the Columbia overlooking the river. It was time to part. My father had written me to tell Joseph that if there was anything my father could do for him he was, through me, to let my father know. I gave this message to Joseph, and he said that he would like a good stallion to improve the breed of his pony herd. I looked on Joseph as such as great man, a noble chief driven out of his ancestral home, I revered him so, that I thought his request for a stallion was too puny — was beneath him. I thought he ought to ask if my father could do anything to repair the great wrong done him, perhaps get him back a portion of his Wallowa Valley or something like that, so that when Joseph asked for a mere stallion, I shook my head and said, 'No, that was not what my father meant! Joseph accepted this calmly and we said no more. But I always regretted my utter stupidity. A fine stallion which would have upbred Joseph's herd of

Chief Joseph's home, Nespelem, Washington, 1902

Yellow Bull

ponies would have been a wonderful thing for him. Just the kind of a thing in his Indian life that he needed, and of course well within the ability of my father to get for him. But just because I exalted him so high I deprived him of it, and it is something I shall always regret."[5]

Refusing to take an allotment of land on the Lapwai Reservation because he hoped to return to the Wallowa or to the Umatilla Reservation, Chief Joseph made a trip to Washington, D.C., during the summer of 1897 and presented his request to the authorities. Though his appeal was strongly supported by General Howard and General Miles, it was denied. During the trip he visited New York City, where he rode beside General Howard in a parade celebrating the dedication of President Grant's tomb. While there he was offered a starring role in Buffalo Bill's Wild West Show, which he declined.

In 1899 his friend, Chief Moses, died at the age of seventy-one. Following the funeral, a great potlatch was held, during which a buckskin suit and war bonnet given Moses by Sitting Bull was passed on to Chief Joseph "with a moving speech amid chanting and weeping."[6]

Pressured by Joseph's friends in high places, U.S. Indian Inspector James McLaughlin came to Nespelem in June 1900 and made a tour of the Wallowa country with Joseph to investigate the feasibility of purchasing tracts of land there for

Joseph and those of his people who wished to return to their ancestral home. His conclusion, in which the Nespelem agent, the Indian Bureau, and the whites living in northeastern Oregon concurred, was that it would not be practical to return Joseph to the Wallowa.

In the winter of 1903 Joseph made yet another trip to Washington, D.C., repeating the request he had made many times before:

5. Erskine Wood, *Days with Chief Joseph: Diary and Recollections* (Portland: Oregon Historical Society, 1970). I had the pleasure of interviewing Erskine Wood in Portland April 19, 1979, when he was just five months away from his one-hundredth birthday. He had walked nine blocks to the downtown building where he still maintained a law office and was "a little tired," he said, but his memory was still sharp and clear, failing him only once when he got a bit irritated because he could not remember whether a certain event during his stay with Chief Joseph occurred in 1892 or 1893.

6. Ruby and Brown, *Half-Sun*, p. 348. A potlatch is a combination feast and extended celebration honoring the deceased person, during which most of his possessions are given away to relatives and close friends.

Chief Joseph with two of his wives, far right and far left, and three of his eight children, about 1890 at Nespelem.

"My home is in the Wallowa Valley, and I want to go back there to live. My father and mother are buried there. If the government would only give me a small piece of land for my people in the Wallowa Valley, with a teacher, that is all I would ask."[7]

On this trip he visited the Carlisle Indian School in Pennsylvania, saw his old friends Howard and Miles, and met the railroad magnate, James J. Hill, and President Theodore Roosevelt. All of them treated him with respect and sympathy but could do nothing for him.

On September 21, 1904, at the age of sixty-four, Joseph died in his lodge at Nespelem, still a exile from the land of the winding waters. Dr. Edwin Latham, the agency physician who had become Chief Joseph's friend, probably gave an accurate if not very scientific cause of death when he said: "He died of a broken heart."

7. Beal, *I Will Fight No More*, p. 300.

CHAPTER FORTY

THE NEZ PERCES TODAY: 1905–1980

*It must be borne in mind that the Indian was
the original owner of the United States. With the
Treaty concept, as we came westward, the gov-
ernment dealt with Indian tribes as nations.*
— Clifford Allen, Nez Perce
August 18, 1979[1]

WITH THE INDIAN question apparently settled
once and for all by placing them on reservations,
federal policy toward the Nez Perces during the
first half of this century was to give them a bare
minimum in the way of assistance, education, and
health care. Both the Colville and Lapwai reserves
were in regions lightly populated by white people,
so even though individual Indians owned very little
land, the nearby National Forests and federally
controlled rangelands gave them plenty of room to
hunt, camp, dig roots, and roam as they had done
in olden times. Even more important as a food
source, salmon, steelhead, and sturgeon still ran in
great numbers up the Columbia, Snake, Clearwater, and Salmon rivers.

Then in the 1930s the dam-building era began.
The first, Bonneville, was built primarily to elimi-
nate a navigation bottleneck of white water called
the Lower, Middle, and Upper Cascades, fifty miles
upriver from Portland. The dam was only one
hundred feet high, so it was not difficult to install an
ascending series of pools up which anadromous
fish could climb with no great difficulty. The second, Grand Coulee, just adjacent to Nespelem on
the upper Columbia, was built to provide jobs,
supply cheap electrical power, and irrigate a million
acres of desert land. Since it was 550 feet high,
fish-passage facilities were not feasible so were not
included. This did not seem to matter at the time,
for the only fish-spawning streams being eliminated

1. Clifford Allen, Nez Perce representative, "Talks with the Nez
Perce," Symposium sponsored by the Wallowa County Historical
Society and the Oregon Humanities Commission, Joseph, Oreg.,
August 17–18, 1979.

Courtesy Umatilla County Historical Society
Major Lee Moorhouse

Photo by Major Lee Moorhouse, 1898   *Courtesy Smithsonian Institution*
Cayuse twin girls — A-Low-Pum and Tox-E-Lox

Bowman photo taken on the Umatilla Reservation   Courtesy Waible Patton Collection
Green Fly, Nez Perce

Courtesy Waible Patton Collection
Mother of the Cayuse twins — this photo was taken by W. S. Bowman in 1899 a year after Lee Moorhouse took his famous twins picture. Bowman felt that the mother of the Cayuse twins should have some publicity. Among the Cayuse, as with other Indian tribes, the survival of twins was extremely rare, for twins were considered bad luck and one of them was usually killed.

were a thousand upriver miles running through sparsely populated country, most of which was in Canada and need not be considered. There would always be plenty of fish, the experts said.

Trouble was, these were experts on dam-building, power generation, navigation, and irrigation — not fish preservation. In the short space of forty years they have been proven dead wrong, with the once-abundant fish runs in the Nez Perce country now apparently lost forever.

Prior to the dam-building era, the various forks of the Clearwater, Salmon, and Snake rivers comprised the finest natural anadromous fish hatchery in the Pacific Northwest. Now, migrating fish must find their way up the ladders and through the still-water pools of Bonneville, The Dalles, John Day, and McNary dams on the Columbia, then negotiate the hazards of Ice Harbor, Lower Monmental, Little Goose, and Lower Granite on the Snake before reaching the streams of their birth. One of these, the entire fifty-five miles of the North Fork of the Clearwater, has been wiped out as a spawning area by Dworshak Dam, which is 717 feet high. Road building, logging, and pollution in environmentally fragile areas have added to the survival problem, as have nitrogen poisoning in the still pools behind the dams and the butchery by turbine blades of young fish headed downriver when they are sucked into the hydroelectric power generators.

Add the fact that 15 percent of the upstream-migrating fish reaching the foot of a given dam will fail to negotiate the ladders and will never get to spawning grounds. With all this, chances of the runs being maintained become extremely low, despite frantic efforts of the fish experts to save them. These efforts have included the building of multimillion dollar upstream hatcheries, the carrying of young fish by barge and tanker truck downstream around the turbines and nitrogen hazards, and, fi-

Photo taken by DeLancey in Washington, D.C., 1908   *Courtesy Smithsonian Institution*

Blanket of the Sun, also called Jackson Sundown

After surviving the Nez Perce War at the age of eleven, Blanket of the Sun adopted the name Jackson Sundown and became one of the best bronc riders in the country. The Pendleton, Oregon, Round-Up began in 1910 and soon became the finest event of its kind. Despite the fact that bronc riding was a young man's sport, Jackson Sundown competed in 1916 at the age of fifty. Though he was a favorite of the spectators and had the respect of his white fellow competitors, the judges insisted that he make several re-rides, bringing accusations that they were averse to giving first prize to an Indian.

Having heard this story for years, I wrote Waible Patton, a pioneer Pendleton photographer, asking if it were true. This was his reply:

> Yes, that story about Jackson Sundown is a true one. Father took me when I was just a kid, and I was there. They made Sundown do several re-rides. The reason was he was wearing the old-fashioned angora wool chaps, which had wool about six inches long. Just before he made his last ride, one of the other cowboys came up to him and said: "Jackson, those chaps of yours make it look like you're loosening up in the saddle. Take them off and put on mine, which are plain, slick leather."
>
> Jackson did that and made his last ride. It was getting late in the day, and the sun was going down in the west. It seemed like everybody in the crowd was yelling: "Sundown! Sundown! Sundown!"
>
> When he finished the ride the judges gave him the title. Whether there would have been trouble if they hadn't, I don't know, but Jackson was a good rider and he really deserved to win. I witnessed the event and it is a true story.

In addition to being awarded the World Champion Bronc Rider prize, Jackson Sundown was given a Golden Belt Buckle by the *Police Gazette* for being the outstanding Rodeo Performer of the Year. He was in good company. Hoot Gibson, the western movie star, won this award in 1912, and Yakima Canutt, the famous Hollywood stuntman and action-movie director, won it in 1917 and again in 1919.

Photo by Lee Moorhouse   *Courtesy Waible Patton*

Jackson Sundown, 1916, just after he won the bucking contest

Photo by DeLancey Gill   *Courtesy Smithsonian Institution*

Delegation to Washington in 1912. Left to Right: Pile of Clouds; Yellow Bull, sitting; Aleck Morse; Tom Hill.

Photo by Bill Lilley, Walla Walla

On the 100th anniversary of the signing of the Stevens Treaty in the Walla Walla Valley, members of the Umatilla Confederation and the Yakima and Nez Perce tribes re-enacted negotiations and the signing of the treaty in Walla Walla in an outdoor production authored by Bill Gulick. Several hundred Indians and whites took part, along with leaders of the various tribes. The Indians pictured here are members of the Walla Walla, Cayuse, and Umatilla tribes, which are now joined together as the Umatilla Confederation on the reservation near Pendleton, Oregon. Also pictured are members of the Yakima nation and the Nez Perce tribe.

nally, the closure of rivers in the Nez Perce country to *all* fishing — including that of the Indians.

It is here that the most heated controversy has arisen between Indians and whites. Stated as briefly as possible, authorities in Idaho, Washington, and Oregon say they have the right to pass and enforce laws designed to preserve the fish runs. The Nez Perces say that, since their fishing rights were given to them by treaties made with the federal government, the state had no jurisdiction.

So far the Nez Perces have been upheld in *every* case that has been carried to the U.S Supreme Court.

"Congress has the plenary right to amend those treaties, and is under some pressure to do so," Alvin Josephy says. "But since the Indians then could sue the federal government for substantial damages, which very likely would be awarded, there is little likelihood that Congress will amend the treaties in the forseeable future."[2]

So, ironically, the treaties which took away so much Nez Perce land and so drastically reduced their freedom as a people now have become documents to be treasured by them. After vainly protesting a policy of termination of the reservation system in the 1950s, Indian tribes all over the Northwest began organizing, hiring lawyers, and going to court to enforce their treaty rights. When The Dalles Dam was built just downriver from Celilo Falls, flooding that traditional fishing place out of existence forever, tribes that had fished there for generations were awarded substantial sums for the losses they had suffered.

Later, in a decision that is still having repercussions, Federal Judge George Boldt ruled that when the treaty gave the Indians "the right to take fish at the usual and accustomed places in common with citizens of the territory," this meant that the Indians were entitled to 50 percent of the fish, if they chose to take that many, with no regard to proportionate numbers in the Indian-white population. The Boldt decision has been upheld by the Supreme Court.

Despite the anguished outcries of whites, who feel that the ruling is unfair, the Indians of the Pacific Northwest so far have taken less than 10 percent, rather than 50 pecent, of the fish. During a recent year, for example, lower Columbia River and Pacific Ocean fishermen took a total of twelve million salmon and steelhead. Of this number, the

2. Ibid., statement by Alvin M. Josephy, Jr., historian.

Photo by Bill Lilley

During the 1955 re-enactment, Norma Blackeagle, a descendant of the original Chief Blackeagle who made the trip to St. Louis in 1831 in search of the white man's Book of Heaven, was flown from Walla Walla to St. Louis and back by Dr. Don C. Platner over much of the same route that her ancestor followed. As noted earlier in the book, the original Chief Blackeagle died and was buried in St. Louis.

Photo by Bill Lilley, Walla Walla

A re-enactment of the Stevens Treaty in 1955. Left to Right: Caleb Carter, Nez Perce historian, Lapwai, Idaho; Bill Gulick, author, Walla Walla; Joesph Garry, Spokane Indian, grandson of Spokane Garry, president of National Council of American Indians; Charles Luce, attorney for the Umatilla Confederation, and Clarence Burke, Chief of the Umatilla Confederation. July 11, 1955.

commercial fishermen caught ten million; sports fishermen, one million; and Indians, one million.[3]

In the streams of the Nez Perce country, no fish at all were caught by white sportsmen — the runs had been so depleted that the states of Washington, Oregon, and Idaho had closed down anadromous fishing totally.

Except for the Nez Perces, that is. A few of them still fished "at the usual and accustomed places" whenever they wanted to and by whatever means they chose to use. Some of them have been arrested by state fish and game wardens, but so far none of them has been convicted of any crime.

"Since November 4, 1963 to January, 1976, there have been 29 related cases filed or decisions made on the Indian fishing rights here in the Northwest," Allen Slickpoo says. "The decisions have consistently upheld the Indians."[4]

3. Gary Young, Director, Yakima Nation Museum and Library Center, "Indians and the Rival Fishermen," Symposium sponsored by Whitman College and the Washington Humanities Commission, Walla Walla, April 13, 1976.
4. Ibid., statement by Allen Slickpoo, Nez Perce, director of History and Culture Projects.

Photo by Billy Lilley, Walla Walla

Stevens Treaty re-enactment 1955. Participants identified, Left to Right, *Standing:* Unidentified; Cy Wilkinson, Nez Perce; _____ Speedis, Yakima; Sam Slickpoo, Nez Perce; Chuck (?) Speedis, Yakima. *Seated:* Alex Saluskin, Yakima; Bill Gulick, author; Charles Luce, attorney; Caleb Carter, Nez Perce. Unjust though the treaty may have been, it has remained a document upon which the Indians base much of their sovereignty, land, fish, and water rights today, and it has stood up under a number of court tests.

This insistence on fishing where and when he pleases in no way makes the Nez Perces a game hog indifferent to preserving an endangered species. The point he is trying to make is that, since he is reserved this right by federal treaty as a vital matter of subsistence, it cannot be taken from him by a law made and enforced by the state. As a matter of personal observance, I have never known an Indian to catch more fish than he could eat — though I have known a number of white men who do just that. When conservation measures are needed and the white man is willing to sit down with the Indian and discuss those measures without insisting that the Indian submit to an authority that has no jurisdiction over him, then the preservation problem can be settled. The Nez Perce will forego his fish. He will not forego his legal rights.

If the 1855 treaties gave the Nez Perce fishing rights that turned out to be more valuable than they appeared at the time, then the 1872 Executive Order creating the Colville Reservation was a monumental underestimation of the worth of that piece of land. Recently discovered on the reservation, Colville Confederated Tribes have announced, are raw metal deposits of molybdenum and copper estimated to be worth in the neighborhood of one billion dollars.

"A huge open pit mine planned about 10 miles east of Grand Coulee Dam could turn hundreds of outdoor-oriented Colville Indians into industrial-age miners, an impact study notes," says a recent newspaper story. "The Mount Tolman copper-molybdenum mine proposed by AMAX Inc. would provide an estimated 760 jobs for Indians by 1990, raising the average tribal income to $31,400 a year, 40% higher than might be expected without the mine, according to a preliminary draft environmental impact statement . . .

"Mine revenues, if paid out in per capita dividends, could give each member of the tribe $4,220 a year. The

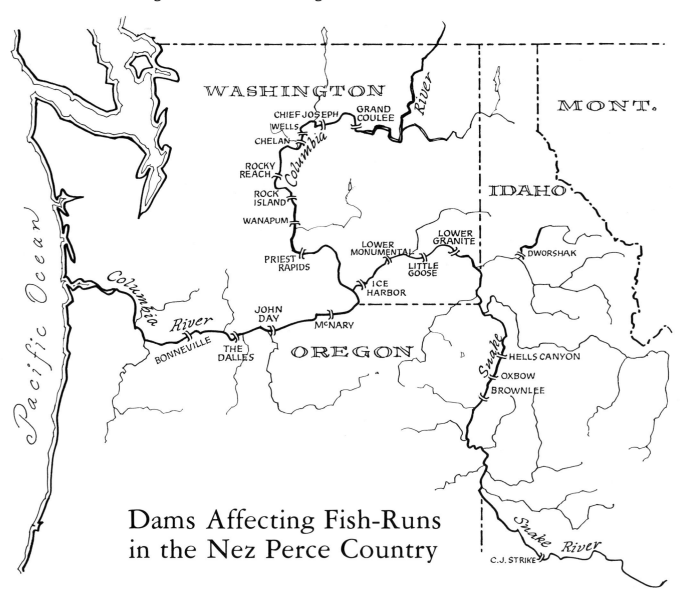

Dams Affecting Fish-Runs
in the Nez Perce Country

Courtesy Oregon Historical Society

Anna Kash Kash

Courtesy U.S. Army Corps of Engineers, LeRoy Allen

Relocating Indian graves in the Alpowa Creek area before the backwaters from Lower Granite Dam flooded the site. May 1973.

Photo courtesy Dick Torrey, Walla Walla

Celilo Falls on the Columbia River just before this important fishery was obliterated by the building of The Dalles Dam in 1956.

tribal government must plan for the day in about 43 years when the mine shuts down, the report says."[5]

Like all of us, the Nez Perces today live in a far more complicated world than did their ancestors. Perhaps with that comment we should leave them — an interesting people with a dramatic history, a people of great integrity and honor, a people to be remembered for all time to come.

5. *Spokesman-Review.* p. A22, Aug. 10, 1980.

BIBLIOGRAPHY

Authors

Agenbroad, L. D. "The Five Fingers Buffalo Jump." Paper delivered at the Thirty-Third Annual Meeting of the Society of American Archaeology, Santa Fe, N. Mex., May 1968.

————. "The 'Y' Buffalo Jump, Owyhee County, Idaho." Paper Delivered at the Annual Meeting of the Society of American Archaeology, Mexico City, May 1970.

Allen, Miss A. J. *Ten Years in Oregon: Being the Record of Dr. Elijah White.* Ithaca, N.Y., 1848.

Aoki, Haruo. *Nez Perce Grammar.* Berkeley and Los Angeles: University of California Press, 1973.

————. *Nez Perce Texts.* Berkeley and Los Angeles: University of California Press, 1979.

Applegate, Jesse. *A Day with the Cow Column.* Chicago: Caxton Club, 1934.

Bailey, Robert G. *River of No Return.* Lewiston, Idaho: R. G. Bailey Printing, Co., 1935. Rev. Ed. 1947.

Ball, John, *Autobiography.* Compiled by his daughters, Kate Ball Powers, Flora Ball Hopkins, and Lucy Ball. Grand Rapids: Dean-Hicks Co., 1925.

Bancroft, Hubert Howe. *History of the Northwest Coast. Works,* vol. 28. San Francisco, 1884.

————. *History of Oregon. Works,* vol. 29. San Francisco, 1886.

————. *History of Washington, Idaho, and Montana. Works,* vol. 31. San Francisco, 1890.

Bartlett, Grace. *The Wallowa Country, 1867–1877.* Enterprise, Oreg., 1976.

Beal, Merrill D. *I Will Fight No More Forever.* Seattle: University of Washington Press, 1963.

Binns, Archie. *Peter Skene Ogden.* Portland, Oreg.: Binfords & Mort, 1968.

Brady, Cyrus T., ed. *Northwestern Fights and Fighters.* New York: Doubleday, Page & Co., 1909.

Brouillet, J. B. A. "Authentic Account of the Murder of Dr. Whitman." U.S., Congress, *House Executive Document No. 38,* 35th Cong., 1st sess., 1858.

Brown, Jennie Broughton. *Fort Hall on the Oregon Trail.* Caxton Printers, 1932.

Brown, Mark H. *Flight of the Nez Perce.* New York: G. P. Putnam's Sons, 1967.

Butler, B. Robert. "Contributions to the Prehistory of the Columbia Plateau." *Occasional Papers,* no. 9. Idaho State College Museum, 1962.

Cannon, Miles. *Toward the Setting Sun.* Portland, Oreg.: Columbian Press, 1953.

Case, Robert Ormond. "Once to Every Warrior." In *The Empire Builders.* New York: Doubleday & Co., 1947.

Chief Joseph. "An Indian's View of Indian Affairs." *North American Review* 128 (April 1879).

Chittenden, Hiram Martin. *American Fur Trade of the Far West.* 2 vols. 1902. Reprint. Stanford, Calif.: Academic Reprints, 1954.

Chuinard, E. G. *Only One Man Died: The Medical Aspects of the Lewis and Clark Expedition.* Glendale, Calif.: Arthur H. Clark Co., 1979.

Cox, Ross. *The Columbia River.* Edited and with an introduction by Edgar I. Stewart and Jane R. Stewart. 1831. Reprint. Norman: University of Oklahoma Press, 1957.

Curtis, Edward S. *Indian Days of Long Ago.* New York: World Books, 1914.

————. *Portraits from North American Indian Life.* Introductions by A. D. Coleman and T. C. McLuhan. New York: Promontory Press, 1972.

Daugherty, Richard D., and Kirk, Ruth. *Exploring Washington Archaeology.* Seattle: University of Washington Press, 1978.

Delaney, Matilda Sager. *The Whitman Massacre.* Spokane, 1920.

Denhardt, Robert Moorman. *The Horse of the Americas.* Norman: University of Oklahoma Press, 1947.

De Smet, Pierre Jean. *Oregon Missions and Travels over the Rocky Mountains in 1845–46.* New York, 1847.

DeVoto, Bernard, ed. *The Journals of Lewis and Clark.* Boston: Houghton Mifflin Co., 1953.

Dobie, J. Frank. *The Mustangs.* Boston: Little, Brown & Co., Bantam Books, 1954.

Drury, Clifford M. *Chief Lawyer of the Nez Perces.* Glendale, Calif.: Arthur H. Clark Co., 1979.

————, ed. *The Diaries and Letters of Henry H. Spalding.* Glendale, Calif.: Arthur H. Clark Co., 1958.

————. *First White Women over the Rockies,* vol. 1. Glendale, Calif.: Arthur H. Clark Co., 1963.

————. *Henry Harmon Spalding.* Caxton Printers, 1936.

————. *Marcus and Narcissa Whitman and the Opening of Old Oregon.* Glendale, Calif.: Arthur H. Clark., 1973.

————, ed. "Spalding-Lowrie Correspondence, May 11, 1874." *Journal of the Department of History, Presbyterian Church* 20 (May-June-September 1942).

Dunn, J. P., Jr. *Massacres of the Mountains.* New York: Harper Brothers, 1880.

Evans, Elwood. "Annual Address." Fifth Annual Reunion. *Transactions of the Oregon Association 1877.*

Feathers, Joseph J. S., ed., and guest authors. *These Are the Nez Perce Nation.* Lewiston, Idaho: Lewis-Clark Normal Press, 1970.

Fuller, George W. *A History of the Pacific Northwest.* 2d ed., rev. New York: Alfred A. Knopf, 1938.

Gay, Jane. "Choup-Nit-Ki," vol. 1. Washington, D.C., 1895. Manuscript in the Women's Archives, Radcliffe College, Cambridge, Mass.; Microfilm, Idaho Historical Society, Boise.

Gidley, M. *With One Sky Above Us.* New York: G. P. Putnam's Sons, 1979.

Gilbert, Frank T. *Historic Sketches of Walla Walla, Whitman, Columbia, and Garfield Counties, Washington Territory, 1882.* Portland, Oreg., 1882.

Gould, Marshall Alan. "Nez Perce Social Groups: An Ecological Interpretation." Ph.D. dissertation, Washington State University, 1977.

Gray, William H. *History of Oregon, 1792–1849*. Portland, Oreg.: Harris & Holman; New York: American News Company; San Francisco: H. H. Bancroft Co., 1870.

Gulick, Bill. *Snake River Country*. Caxton Printers, 1971. Rev. ed. 1978.

Hafen, LeRoy R., ed. *The Mountain Men and the Fur Trade of the Far West*, vol. 2. Glendale, Calif.: Arthur H. Clark Co., 1965.

Haines, Aubrey L. *The Yellowstone Story*. 2 vols. Boulder: Colorado Associated University Press; Yellowstone National Park, Wyo.: Yellowstone Library and Museum Association, 1977.

Haines, Francis. *Appaloosa: The Spotted Horse in Art and History*. Austin, University of Texas Press, 1963. Pulbished for the Amon Carter Museum of Western Art, Fort Worth.

———. *Red Eagles of the Northwest: The Story of Chief Joseph and His People*. Portland, Oreg.: Scholastic Press, 1939.

Harbinger, Lucy Jane. "The Importance of Food Plants in the Maintenance of Nez Perce Cultural Identity." Master's thesis, Washington State University, 1964.

Harris, Burton. *John Colter: His Years in the Rockies*. New York: Charles Scribner's Sons, 1952.

Howard, Helen Addison, and McGrath, Dan L. *War Chief Joseph*. Caxton Printers, 1946.

Howard, Oliver Otis. *Chief Joseph: His Pursuit and Capture*. Boston: Lee and Shepard, 1881.

———. *Nez Perce Joseph*. Boston: Lee and Shepard, 1881.

Irving, Washington. *Astoria*. New York, 1887.

———. *The Adventures of Captain Bonneville, U.S.A., in the Rocky Mountains and the Far West*. 1837. Reprint. Norman: University of Oklahoma Press, 1961. Edited by Edgeley W. Todd.

Jackson, Helen Hunt. *A Century of Dishonor: The Early Crusade for Indian Reform*. New York: Harper Brothers, 1881.

Johnson, C. T. [pseud. for T. C. Elliott]. "The Evolution of a Lament." *Washington Historical Quarterly* 2, no. 2 (April 1908).

Josephy, Alvin M., Jr. *The Nez Perce Indians and the Opening of the Northwest*. New Haven: Yale University Press, 1971.

Jones, Nard. *The Great Command*. Boston: Little, Brown & Co., 1959.

Kip Lawrence. *Army Life on the Pacific: A Journal of the Expedition Against the Northern Indians. . . .* Redfield, N.Y., 1859.

———. *Indian Council at Walla Walla*. 1897. Facsimile reproduction. Seattle: Shorey Publications, 1971.

Kirk, Ruth, and Daugherty, Richard D. *Exploring Washington Archaeology*. Seattle: University of Washington Press, 1978.

Kuykendall, Elgin V. *Historic Glimpes of Asotin County, Washington*. Clarkston Herald Press, 1954.

McBeth, Kate C. *The Nez Perces Since Lewis and Clark*. New York: Fleming H. Revell Co., 1908.

McDermott, John D. *Forlorn Hope: The Battle of White Bird Canyon and the Beginning of the Nez Perce War*. Idaho Historical Society, Caxton Printers, 1978.

MacDonald, Duncan. "The Nez Perces, the History Of Their Troubles and the Campaign of 1877." *New North-West*, April 26–December 20, 1878. Reprinted with an introduction and notes by Merle W. Wells, *Idaho Yesterdays*, Spring 1977 and Winter 1978.

McWhorter, Lucullus Virgil. *Hear Me, My Chiefs!* Edited by Ruth Bordin. Caxton Printers, 1952.

———. *Tragedy of the Wahk-Shum: The Death of Andrew J. Bolon, Indian Agent to the Yakima Nation in mid-September, 1855*. Reprint. Fairfield, Wash.: Ye Galleon Press, 1968.

———. *Yellow Wolf, His Own Story*. Caxton Printers, 1940.

Miles, Nelson A. *Personal Recollections*. Chicago and New York: Werner and Co., 1896.

Morrill, Allen Conrad, and Morrill, Eleanor Dunlop. *Out of the Blanket*. Moscow, University of Idaho Press, 1978.

Pambrun, Andrew Dominique. *Sixty Years on the Frontier in the Pacific Northwest*. Edited by Glen C. Adams. Fairfield, Wash.: Ye Galleon Press, 1978.

Parker, Samuel. *Journal of an Exploring Tour Beyond the Rocky Mountains*. Ithaca, N.Y., 1838.

Relander, Click. *Drummers and Dreamers*. Caxton Printers, 1956.

Rhodenbaugh, Edward F. *Sketches of Idaho Geology*. 2d ed. Caxton Printers, 1961.

Rich, E. E., ed. *Peter Skene Ogden's Snake Country Journals, 1824–25 and 1825–26*, vol. 13. London: Hudson's Bay Record Society, 1950.

———. *Ogden's Journals, 1827–28 and 1828–29*, vol. 14.

Ross, Alexander. *Adventures of the First Settlers on the Oregon or Columbia River, 1810–13*, vol. 7. Edited by Reuben Golden Thwaites. 1840. Reprint. Glendale, Calif.: Arthur H. Clark Co., 1904.

———. *The Fur Hunters of the Far West*. Edited by Kenneth Spaulding. 1855. Reprint. Norman: University of Oklahoma Press, 1956.

Ross, Clyde P., and Forrester, J. Donald. *Outline of the Geology of Idaho*. Moscow: Idaho Bureau of Mines, 1958.

Ruby, Robert H. "Return of the Nez Perces." *Idaho Yesterdays* 12, no. 1 (Spring 1968).

Ruby, Robert H., and Brown, John A. *Half-Sun on the Columbia: A Biography of Chief Moses*. Norman: University of Oklahoma Press, 1965.

Sanderson, William E. *Horses Are for Warriors*. Caxton Printers, 1954.

Sheller, Roscoe. *The Name Was Olney*. Yakima, Wash.: Franklin Press, 1965.

Simpson, George Gaylord. *Horses*. New York: Doubleday Anchor Books, 1961. Published in cooperation with the American Museum of Natural History.

Slickpoo, Allen P., Sr., Project Director, Nez Perce Tribe, and Walker, Deward F., Jr., Technical Advisor. *Noon Nee-me-poo (We The Nez Perces): Culture and History of the Nez Perces*, vol. 1. Boulder: University of Colorado Press, 1973. Published for the Nez Perce Tribal Council, Lapwai, Idaho.

Stegner, Wallace. *The Sound of Mountain Water*. New York: Doubleday & Co., 1969.

Stevens, Hazard. *The Life of Isaac Ingalls Stevens*. 2 vols. Boston: Houghton Mifflin Co., 1901.

Stevens, Isaac Ingalls. Introduction and covering letter. *Transcript of Official Proceedings, Walla Walla Council, May–June 1855*.

Struble, John Linton [pseud. for Virginia Burlingame]. "Johnny Healy Strikes It Rich." *Idaho Yesterdays*, Fall 1957.

Stuart, Granville. *Montana As It Is: Being a General Description of its Resources. . . .* New York, 1865.

Sullivan, Maurice S. *Jedediah Smith, Trader and Trailbreaker*. New York: Press of the Pioneers, 1936.

Terrell, John Upton. *Black Robe: The Life of Pierre-Jean De Smet, Missionary, Explorer, and Pioneer*. New York: Doubleday & Co., 1964.

Thompson, Erwin N. *Fort Lapwai Historic Resource Study*. Denver: National Park Service, 1973.

———. *Shallow Grave at Waiilatpu*. Portland: Oregon Historical Society, 1969.

Thwaites, Reuben Golden, ed. *Original Journals of the Lewis and Clark Expedition*, vols. 3, 4, and 5. New York: Dodd, Mead & Co., 1904.

Tucker, Gerald J. *The Story of Hells Canyon*. Enterprise, Oreg., 1977.

U.S., Department of Agriculture, Forest Service. *Range Plant Handbook*. 1937.

Vestal, Stanley [pseud. for Walter Stanley Campbell]. *Kit Carson, the Happy Warrior of the Old West*. Boston: Houghton Mifflin Co., 1928.

Victor, Frances Fuller. *The River of the West.* Hartford, Conn., 1870.

Wells, Donald N. "Farmers Forgotten: Nez Perce Suppliers of the North Idaho Gold Rush Days." *Idaho Yesterdays,* Summer 1958.

Whitner, Robert Lee. "The Nomination of Nez Perce Agency Personnel by Denominational Groups, 1871–1879." Master's thesis, Washington State College, 1948.

Wood, Charles Erskine Scott. "Chief Joseph, the Nez Perce." *Century Magazine,* May 1884.

Wood, Erskine. *Days with Chief Joseph: Diary and Recollections.* Portland: Oregon Historical Society, 1970.

Wood, Henry Clay. *Joseph and His Land Claims or Status of Young Joseph and His Band of Nez Perce Indians.* Portland, Oreg., 1876.

Periodicals

Blue Mountain Sentinel (LaGrande, Oreg.), Feb. 22, 1873.
Blue Mountain Sentinel, March 8, 1873.
Blue Mountain Sentinel, May 31, 1873.
Blue Mountain Sentinel, July 1, 1876.
Blue Mountain Sentinel, Sept. 2, 1876.
Century Magazine, May 1884.
Enterprise (Oreg.) *Record Chieftan*, April 23, 1914.
Harper's Weekly, Aug. 18, 1877.
Harper's Weekly, Sept. 1, 1877.
Harper's Weekly, Oct. 27, 1877.
Harper's Weekly, Nov. 17, 1877.
Idaho Statesman (Boise), Dec. 20, 1866.
Idaho Yesterdays, Fall 1957.
Idaho Yesterdays, Summer 1958.
Idaho Yesterdays, Spring 1968.
Idaho Yesterdays, Spring 1977.
Idaho Yesterdays, Winter 1978.

Lewiston (Idaho) *Teller*, March 31, 1877.
Lewiston (Idaho) *Tribune*, July 18, 1916.
Lewiston Tribune, March 3, 1918.
New North-West (Deer Lodge, Mont.), April 26-Dec. 20, 1878.
North American Review, April 1879.
Ogden Daily Pilot, Oct. 18, 1891.
Oregonian (Portland), April 30, 1873.
Oregonian, May 15, 1873.
Oregonian, July 20, 1874.
Oregon Historical Quarterly, March 1939.
Spokesman-Review (Spokane), Aug. 10, 1980.
Tebiwa 14, no. 1, Idaho State University Museum.
Union-Bulletin (Walla Walla), Nov. 27, 1978.
Washington Historical Quarterly, April 1908.
Weekly Oregonian, Aug. 25, 1855.

Public Agency Documents

Annual Report of the Secretary of War. Washington D.C., 1877.
Bureau of American Ethnology. *Fourteenth Annual Report*, pt. 2.
U.S., Congress. *House Executive Document No. 38.* 35th Cong., 1st sess., 1858.
———. *House Executive Document No. 198.* 42d Cong., 2d sess., 1872.
———. *Senate Miscellaneous Document No. 53.* 45th Cong., 3d sess., 1878.
U.S., Department of the Interior. Records of the Bureau of Indian Affairs, *Commission Reports*, 1875, vol. 1.

———. *Commission Reports*, 1876, vol. 1.
———. *Commission Reports*, 1878.
———. *Idaho Superintendency*, 1873 Microfilm.
———. *Special Report, Indian Commission*, 1867.
U.S., National Archives. *Document No. 6260, Adjutant General's Office 3464*, 1877.
———. Old Military Records, 1876.

Miscellaneous

Big Hole National Battlefield Pamphlet and Guides. National Park Service.
Idaho Historical Society. Microfilm. "Choup-Nit-Ki" by Jane Gay.
Indian Archives, Oklahoma Historical Society, Microfilm: Quapaw Agency Letterpressbook:
   Ponca Agency, vol. 1, Aug. 5, 1878 to May 25, 1881.
   Ponca Agency, vol. 2, Mar. 2, 1881 to Nov. 2, 1881.
   Ponca Agency, vol. 3, Nov. 12, 1881 to July 9, 1882.
   Ponca Agency, vol. 4, June 12, 1882 to Oct. 31, 1882.
   Ponca Agency, vol. 5, Sept. 1, 1882 to Dec. 31, 1884.
   Ponca Agency, vol. 6, Jan. 28, 1884 to May 25, 1885.
   Quapaw Agency, May 1, 1872 to May 25, 1899.

Journal of the Department of History, Presbyterian Church 20, May-June-September 1942.
Nez Perce Historic Site Pamphlet and Guides. National Park Service.
Occasional Papers, no. 9. Idaho State College Museum, 1962.
Transactions of the Oregon Pioneer Association, 1877.
Transactions of the Oregon Pioneer Association, 1891.
Transcript of Official Proceedings, Walla Walla Council, May–June 1855, with introduction and covering letter by Isaac Ingalls Stevens.

INDEX

— A —

Alcohol, 148, 149, 174, 175
Allen, Clifford, 303
Allotment Act (Dawes Bill), 290, 291, 292
Appushwa-hite, See Looking Glass

— B —

Bacon, Lt. George, 247
Bailey, Lt. Harry L., 211, 212, 219, 220
Baldwin, Captain, 262
Bannock Scouts, 242, 250, 253, 254
Batholith, 3
Battle of Four Lakes, 140, 141
Battle of Pierre's Hole, 53
Bear's Paw Mountains Battle, 260–270
Biddle, Lt., 261, 264
Birch Creek Fight, 245
Black Eagle, 271
Boldt, Judge George, 306
Bolon, Andrew J., 118, 122, 123
Bonneville, Louis Eulalie de, 52, 54–59
Bradley, Lt. James H., 236
Briggs, Edson, 292
Broken Arm, 20, 25, 27, 28, 29
Brooks, Abraham, 206
Brouillet, Father J. B. A., 90, 92
Buffalo Horn, 242, 248, 250
Buffalo Jumps, 5

— C —

Camas Meadows Battle, 247, 248, 249
Canyon Creek Fight, 256
Captain John (Jokais), 119, 129, 130, 189, 225, 226, 242, 268
Catholic Missionaries, 134
Celilo Falls Trail, 3, 4
Chapman, Arthur I. (Ad), 201, 202, 203, 205, 206, 207, 209, 210, 219, 226, 275
Cheyenne Scouts, 261, 262, 264, 271
Chinook Jargon, 4, 11
Clark, William, 22, 24, 25, 26, 28, 29, 34, 47, 49
Clarke, John, 36, 37, 38
Co-mos-pilo, 102, 106

Cornoyer, Captain Narcisse A., 125, 126, 127
Cow Island Landing, 256
Cowan, George, 251, 252
Craig, Isabel, 78
Craig, William, 77, 78, 79, 80, 82, 86, 90, 99, 113, 129, 130, 132, 167
Craig's Ferry, 212
Cumming, Colonel Alfred, 112, 114, 115, 116
Cutnose, 26, 27, 29

— D —

Dams, 303–308
Deffenbaugh, George, 286, 288
Delaware, Jim, 112, 113
DeSmet, Pierre Jean, 9, 77, 145
Dietrich, Richard, 252
Dingee, William, 251
Disosway, G. P., 50
Dreamer Religion, 170, 189, 192

— E —

Eagle-from-the-Light, 104, 109, 113, 131, 151, 153, 155
Education, 168, 169
Ellis, 85, 96, 100

— F —

Falck, Capt. William, 280
Faulkner, Dr. W. H, 282–285
Findley, A. B., 180–184
Fisher, Capt. S. G., 250, 252–254
Five Crows, 82, 86, 102, 106, 118
Five Wounds, 211, 223, 224, 237
Fleming, G. D., 280, 281
Fletcher, Alice, 291, 292, 293
Flynn, William, 243, 244
Fontenelle, Lucien, 62
Food Plants, 8, 9
Fort Benton, 112, 117, 260
Fort Fizzle, 228–232
Fort Keogh, 254, 274, 275
Fort Leavenworth, 275, 276
Fort Lapwai, 149, 150, 280

Fort Lincoln, 274, 275
Fort Nez Perces, 40, 45
Fort Hall Agency, 242

— G —

Gay, Jane, 291, 292, 293
Gibbon, Col. John, 232, 234, 235, 237, 239, 241
Gold Miners and Gold Mining, 145–147
Gray, William H., 70–73, 75
Grizzly Bear Youth, 237

— H —

Hah-ta-le-kin, 199, 201, 223, 269
Hall, Edwin, O., 76
Haller, Major Granville O., 122, 123
Head-flattening, 50
Hill, Tom, 86, 88, 89
Hill, Tom (interpreter), 266
Hin-mah-tute-ke-kaikt, See Old James
Horse:
    Distribution, 16
    Eohippus, 13
    Extinction, 14
    Migration route, 14
    Nez Perce, 17
    Nez Perce aquisition, 16
    Spanish, 14
Horse Prairie Fight, 243
Howard, General Oliver Otis, 179, 180, 184, 185, 191–194, 199, 200, 202, 211–214, 218, 219, 221–223, 226, 245–251, 254, 261, 268, 269, 274, 275, 301, 302
Hunt, Wilson Price Expedition, 34, 35
Husishusis, 264
Husush, Frank, 206

— I —

Ilges, Major Guido, 260
Indian Bows, 9
Indian Lament, 48n, 50n, 164
Indian Reservations, 104, 105, 110, 113, 117, 275, 278, 282–285, 308

Indian Tribes:
  Assiniboines, 268, 271
  Blackfeet, 33, 53, 54, 112, 115, 116
  Cayuse, 88–90, 92, 94, 95, 100, 103
  Chippewa, 271
  Coeur d'Alene, 135, 142
  Cree, 271
  Crows, 224, 255, 256
  Flathead, 46, 49, 50, 53, 77, 228, 229
  Gros Bentres, 271
  Nespelem, 297
  Palouse, 143
  Shoshone (Snake), 44, 45
  Sioux, 261, 262, 264, 271
  Spokane, 120, 136, 142
  Umatilla, 104
  Walla, Walla, 86
  Yakima, 100, 111, 129, 136
Iroquois, 42, 43, 47
Ish-hol-hoats-toats, See Lawyer
Itskimze Kin, 205, 205n

— J —

Jackson, Sundown, 305
Jerome, Lt. Lovell H., 266, 267, 268
Joint Occupancy Treaty, 39, 52, 60, 93, 96
Jones, John M., 206, 207
Joseph (the Elder), 74, 75, 86, 99, 107, 131, 151, 153, 155, 157, 158, 173, 174
Joseph (Young), 153, 157, 174, 179, 182–185, 188–190, 198, 217, 222–224, 231, 238, 239, 264, 266–270, 274–278, 280–285, 289, 293, 295–302
Josephy, Alvin M., 306
Josiah Red Wolf, 284

— K —

Kamiakin, 100, 107, 108, 118, 131, 137
Kelly, Colonel James K., 125, 126, 127
Kenck, Charles, 252
Kettalkpoosmim, 240, 245, 246
Kip, Lawrence, 98, 99, 138–141

— L —

Lapwai Press, 76
Latham, Dr. Edwin, 302
Lawyer, Archie, 278
Lawyer, 47, 52, 53, 74, 98, 99, 100, 102 103, 104, 105, 108, 109, 113, 121 130, 131, 151, 155, 159, 165
Lean Elk (Poker Joe), 231, 241, 242, 244 253, 260, 264, 269
Lee, Jason, 59, 60, 73, 83
Lewis, Joe, 88, 89

Lewis, Merriwether, 25, 26, 27, 28, 31, 33, 34
Lewis and Clark Party, 21, 22, 23, 26, 30, 31
Loess, 3
Lolo Trail, 4, 5, 223–227
Lone Bird, 232
Longhouses, 7, 8
Looking Glass, 107, 108, 113, 120, 147, 151, 153
Looking Glass (younger), 192, 193, 198, 212, 213, 214, 223, 224, 227, 228, 229, 230, 231, 232, 233, 237, 239, 241, 255, 260, 261, 262, 264, 266, 269
Lovejoy, Asa, 83
Lower Nez Perce, 11, 55, 56, 151
Lyon, Caleb, 158, 159

— M —

McBeth, Kate, 286, 287, 288, 292, 293
McCarthy, Sgt. Michael, 208
McDowell, General Irwin, 221, 274
McKenzie, Donald, 36, 37, 38, 39, 40, 41
McLaughlin, James, 301
McNall, Wells, 180, 181, 182, 184
Meek, Joe, 77, 78, 80, 94, 95, 96
Miles, Col. Nelson A., 254, 261, 262, 264, 265, 266, 267, 268, 269, 274, 275, 276, 301, 302
Moelchert, Sgt. William, 259
Mo-sheel, 122, 123
Monteith, Charles E., 284
Monteith, John B., 164, 165, 167, 168, 169, 170, 174, 175, 178, 184, 189, 190, 279, 280, 284
Moses, 170, 281, 295, 296, 297, 298, 299, 301
Mt. Idaho Volunteers, 213, 214, 215, 216

— N —

Non-Treaty (Nez Perce) Bands, 197, 198, 199
Norris, George, 287, 288
Norwood, Capt. Randolph, 249
Na-tal-le-kin, 236
Newell, Robert, 77, 78, 79, 80, 154, 167
Nez-Perce-Flathead Delegation, 46, 47, 48, 49
Nez Perce Laws, 85, 86

— O —

Ogden, Peter Skene, 44, 45, 93, 94
Old George (Meopkowit), 242, 268
Old James, 74, 78, 82, 86, 99, 131
Old Nez Perce Trail, 4

Ollokot, 179, 191, 192, 193, 198, 205, 239, 248, 264, 269
Olney, Nathan, 124, 126, 128
Oregon Volunteers, 125, 126, 127, 128
Otskai, 248, 251, 295
Ots-tot-poo, 206, 207

— P —

Pacific Fur Company, 36, 37, 39
Palmer, Joel, 98, 102, 106, 107, 109
Pambrun, Pierre C., 58
Parker, Samuel, 62, 64, 65, 66, 67, 68
Parnell, Lt. William R., 210
Pearson, W. H., 112, 113, 115, 117, 118, 119
Peo-peo-mox-mox, 86, 100, 102, 104, 106, 107, 118, 123, 124, 125, 126, 127, 128
Peopeo Tholekt, 213, 239, 240, 259, 272
Perry, Capt. David, 202, 203, 205, 206, 208, 209, 210, 211, 215
Pierce, Elias D., 145, 146

— R —

Rainbow, 211, 223, 224, 237
Rains, Lt. Sevier M., 196, 214, 215
Rawn, Capt. Charles C., 228, 229
Redington, J. W., 252
Reuben, James, 189, 225, 226, 278
Rock Shelters, 7
Ross, Alexander, 36, 37, 38, 41, 42, 43
Rotten Belly, See Tack-en-su-a-tis

— S —

Salmon River Uprising, 200, 201
Sanford, Major George B., 249
Sarpsis Ilppilp, 200, 210, 238
Schorr, John P., 203, 205
Sheridan, General Phillip, 129, 242, 274, 275
Sherman, General William T., 251
Shively, John, 251
Simpson, Sir George, 41, 44, 45
Sitting Bull, 268, 272, 273
Skolaskin, 295, 297
Slickpoo, Allen, 307
Smith, A. C., 173, 174, 176, 177, 180
Smith, Asa B., 76
Smith, Jedediah, 43, 46
Snake Creek Camp, 262, 264, 272
Social Conduct, 66
Spalding, Eliza, 68, 69, 70, 72, 90, 92, 161, 163, 166
Spalding, Eliza (daughter), 88, 90, 92, 93, 94
Spalding, Henry Harmon, 68, 69, 70, 71, 72, 73, 74, 75, 76, 77, 80, 82, 83, 84,

86, 87, 88, 89, 90, 92, 93, 94, 160,
    161, 163, 164, 165, 166, 167
Speelyi, 6, 7
Spokane Garry, 47, 120, 142
Spotted Eagle, 132
Steptoe, Colonel E. J., 130, 131, 132, 133,
    134, 135, 136, 137
Steptoe Disaster, 136, 137
Stevens, Isaac Ingalls, 97–117, 119–121,
    129–134
Stickus, 105
Stone, Ben, 252
Sturgis, Col. Samuel, 253, 254

— T —

Tack-en-su-a-tis, 65, 67, 69, 74, 82, 165
Ta-moot-sin, See Timothy
Taylor, Capt. O. H. P., 136, 139
Teeto Hoonnod, 256
Temme Ilppilp, 223
Tendoy, 244
Tetoharsky, 21–25
Theller, Lt. Edward R., 206, 209
Tilden, Sam, 273
Timothy, 47, 74, 75, 82, 86, 87, 92, 94,
    99, 109, 113, 131, 135, 136, 137, 157,
    159, 166
Tin-tin-meet-see, 109

Tool-hool-hool-zote, 193, 194, 198, 199,
    206, 217, 219, 223, 239, 264, 269
Trade Goods, 18
Trappers and Trapping, 33, 41–45
Tun-nach-e-mul-tolt, See Broken Arm
Twisted Hair, 20, 22–27
Two Moons, 206, 210, 237, 238, 239, 248
Tyler, Capt. George, 262

— U —

Upper Nez Perce, 9, 11, 45

— W —

Wahlitits, 200, 210, 232, 238
Wa-lam-mot-ti-nin, See Twisted Hair
Walker, William, 49, 50
Ware, Marcus, J., 4
Washakie, 242
Washington Volunteers, 129, 130, 131,
    149
Wetatonmi, 201, 265, 271
Wet-khoo-weis, 21
Whipple, Capt. Steven G., 179, 195, 196,
    213, 214, 215
White Bird, 151, 193, 198, 217, 223, 233,
    234, 237, 239, 269, 271, 273
White Bird Canyon Battle, 203–210

White, Elijah, 82, 83, 85, 86
Whitman, Marcus, 62, 64, 65, 68, 69, 70,
    82, 83, 84, 88, 89, 166
Whitman, Narcissa, 65, 68, 69, 70, 88, 89,
    94, 166
Whitman, Perrin, 154, 167
Williams, Mark, 278
Wood, Erskine, 299, 300, 301
Wood, Lt. Charles Erskine Scott, 203, 254,
    269, 274, 298, 299
Wool, General John E., 121, 129, 134,
    138
Wottolen, 224, 232, 248
Wright, Colonel George, 129, 130, 133,
    138, 140, 142, 143
Wyeth, Nathaniel J., 21-54, 59-61

— Y —

Yel-lept, 25
Yellow Bull, 266, 276, 292, 293
Yellowstone National Park, 250–254
Yellow Wolf, 199, 214, 215, 222, 226,
    232, 251, 252, 255, 256, 262, 264,
    266, 267, 268, 271, 272, 279, 280,
    295
Young Chief, 100, 106, 107, 118
Young, Gary, 306, 307

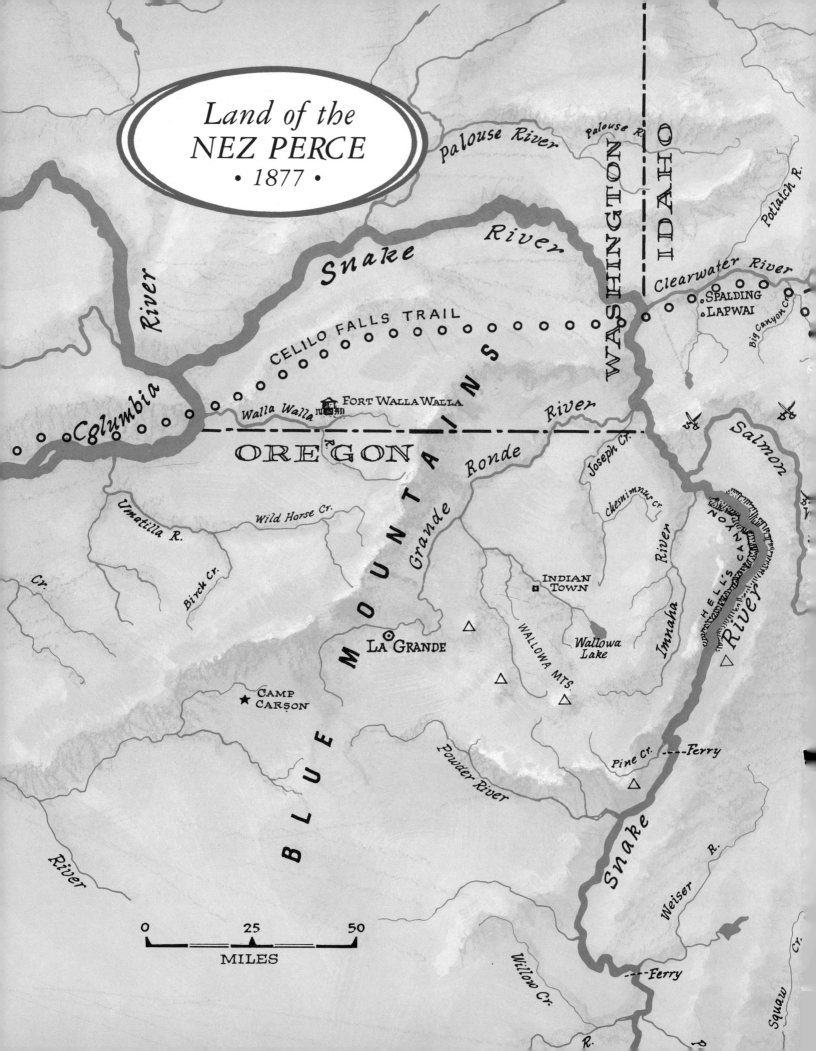

Land of the
NEZ PERCE
· 1877 ·

Palouse River

Palouse R.

WASHINGTON

IDAHO

Snake   River

Clearwater River

Potlatch R.

SPALDING

LAPWAI

CELILO FALLS TRAIL

Big Canyon Cr.

Columbia

River

River

Snake

Walla Walla

FORT WALLA WALLA

River

Salmon

OREGON

Grande

Ronde

Joseph Cr.

Umatilla R.

Wild Horse Cr.

Chesnimnus Cr.

River

HELL'S CANYON

Cr.

Birch Cr.

INDIAN
TOWN

Imnaha

River

BLUE   MOUNTAINS

LA GRANDE

WALLOWA MTS.

Wallowa
Lake

River

CAMP
CARSON

Powder River

Pine Cr.   ----Ferry

River

Snake

Weiser R.

River

Willow Cr.

----Ferry

Squaw Cr.

0   25   50

MILES